Alfonso X, the Learned

Studies in the History of Christian Traditions

General Editor

Robert J. Bast

Knoxville, Tennessee

In cooperation with

Henry Chadwick, Cambridge
Scott H. Hendrix, Princeton, New Jersey
Paul C.H. Lim, Nashville, Tennessee
Eric Saak, Indianapolis, Indiana
Brian Tierney, Ithaca, New York
Arjo Vanderjagt, Groningen
John Van Engen, Notre Dame, Indiana

Founding Editor

Heiko A. Oberman †

VOLUME 146

Alfonso X, the Learned

A Biography

By

H. Salvador Martínez

English translation by
Odile Cisneros

BRILL

LEIDEN • BOSTON
2010

On the cover: The portrait of Alfonso with a book dictating the *Cantigas* to a scribe. Códice Rico, Bibl. Escorial, Ms. T.I.1, fol. 5v (detail), Cantiga 1, Prólogo B.

The translation of this work has been made possible with the financial support of the Dirección General del Libro, Archivos y Bibliotecas del Ministerio de Cultura de España.

This book is printed on acid-free paper.

Library of Congress Cataloging-in-Publication Data

Martínez, H. Salvador.
  [Alfonso X, el Sabio. English]
  Alfonso X, the Learned : a biography / by H. Salvador Martínez ; English translation by Odile Cisneros.
    p. cm. — (Studies in the history of Christian traditions, ISSN 1573-5664 ; v. 146)
  Includes bibliographical references and index.
  ISBN 978-90-04-18147-2
  1. Alfonso X, King of Castile and Leon, 1221–1284. 2. Castile (Spain)—History—Alfonso X, 1252–1284. 3. Castile (Spain)—Kings and rulers—Biography. I. Title.
II. Title: Alfonso 10, the Learned. III. Title: Alfonso the Tenth, the Learned.
IV. Series.

  DP140.3.M36713 2010
  946'.02092—dc22
  [B]

                                                                              2009053996

ISSN 1573-5664
ISBN 978 90 04 18147 2

PRINTED IN THE NETHERLANDS

CONTENTS

ACKNOWLEDGMENTS

The translator would like to acknowledge the help of two graduate students from the Department of Modern Languages and Cultural Studies at the University of Alberta for their invaluable assistance in this project. Thanks to Dennis Kilfoy and Melissa Cameron for their help tracking down the quotations from published translations.

ABBREVIATIONS

A-A	Al-Andalus
AEM	Anuario de Estudios Medievales
AH	Archivo Hispalense
AHDE	Anuario de Historia del Derecho Español
AHLM	Asociación Hispánica de Literatura Medieval
AL	Archivos Leoneses
BAE	Biblioteca de Autores Españoles
BC	The Bulletin of the Cantigueiros de Santa Maria
BH	Bulletin Hispanique
BHS	Bulletin of Hispanic Studies
BIFG	Boletín de la Institución Fernán González
BRAE	Boletín de la Real Academia Española
BRAH	Boletín de la Real Academia de la Historia
CAX	Crónica de Alfonso X
CH	Cuadernos Hispanoamericanos
CHE	Cuadernos de Historia de España
EH	Exemplaria Hispanica
EHR	English Historical Review
ES	España Sagrada
H	Hispania (Madrid)
HID	Historia. Instituciones. Derecho
Hisp.	Hispania (USA)
HR	Hispanic Review
KRQ	Kentucky Romance Quarterly
MGH	Monumenta Germaniae Historica
MHE	Memorial Histórico Español
MLR	The Modern Language Review
NRFH	Nueva Revista de Filología Hispánica
PL	Patrologia Latina
PMLA	Periodicals of the Modern Language Association
R	Romania
RABM	Revista de Archivos Biliotecas y Museos
RCEH	Revista Canadiense de Estudios Hispánicos
RH	Revue Hispanique
RHM	Revista Hispánica Moderna

RFE Revista de Filología Española
RO   Revista de Occidente
RPh Romance Philology
RPH Revista Portuguesa de História
RQ   Romance Quarterly
RR   The Romanic Review
S   Speculum
V   Viator
VR   Vox Romanica

LIST OF ILLUSTRATIONS

Colour plates of illustrations 2–10 can be found in a separate section following page xiv.

COLOUR PLATES

Illustration 2, p. 220

Illustration 3, p. 221

Illustration 4, p. 222

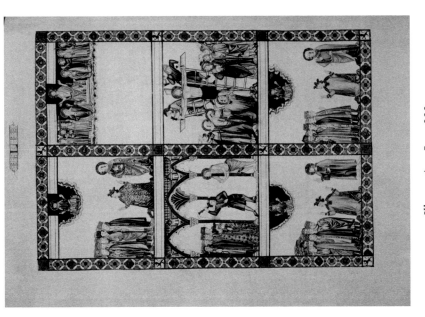

Illustration 6, p. 234

Illustration 5, p. 233

Illustration 8, p. 259

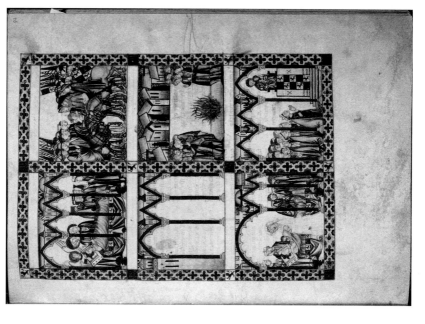

Illustration 7, p. 254

Illustration 10, p. 528

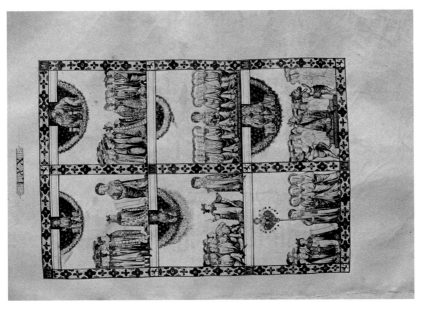

Illustration 9, p. 527

INTRODUCTION

THE "ALFONSINE ERA"

> This is the kingdom of the lord king don Alfonso, who, in his knowledge, good judgment and intelligence, righteousness, kindness, piety, and nobility, surpassed all learned kings. And therefore we deemed it fitting to set as the beginning of the era the year this noble king began to reign so that this era may be known and proclaimed, as were other eras before, so that it may last and the name of the noble king may endure forever. And we determined that the beginning would be the year 1252 and we called it the "Alfonsine era." (*Alfonsine Astronomical Tables*)

The year 2003 when this work appeared in its original version was the 750th anniversary of the proclamation of the "Alfonsine Era." We cannot accuse the authors of the *Alfonsine Astronomical Tables* of mere propaganda or flattery when they surprise us with such a weighty declaration in the prologue to that work. They also tell us that, just as in the past when historical accounts were done according to the various eras, starting in 1252 they will be done according to the "Alfonsine era" so that "it may last and the name of the noble king may endure forever." Composed at the beginning of that long reign, it must be recognized that the scientists who worked on the *Tables* were astonishingly farsighted. Thirty-two years later, the Christian West would have confirmation of this: Alfonso "in his knowledge, good judgment and intelligence, righteousness, kindness, piety, and nobility, surpassed all learned kings," to such an extent that according to the early testimony of his nephew, the great writer don Juan Manuel, "he set out to increase knowledge to the best of his ability, and he did this to such an extent, that it could be said that from king Ptolemy to these days no other king or man did as much as him." *(Book on Hunting)*. Besides being a great ruler, Alfonso was the first humanist king who, consciously integrated knowledge into the duties and obligations of the Crown. Likewise, he was the first professional king of letters who, in addition presenting himself to his subjects as a ruler and legislator, also did so as a teacher and intellectual guide of his people, making knowledge available to all, so everyone could benefit from it. Don Juan Manuel wrote in one of his letters:

No one could say more or even as much as he in the field of letters. And this for many reasons: first because of the great intelligence God granted him; second, because of the great disposition he had to perform noble and profitable tasks; third, because he housed in his court many teachers of the sciences and knowledge, which was a good thing, and all with the purpose of advancing knowledge and ennobling his kingdoms, because we find that in all the sciences he produced many works and all very good. (*Abbreviated Chronicle*)

Alfonso was lucky enough to occupy the throne in a unique period in European cultural history. He could have said with Alexander Neckham, "we are like dwarfs on the shoulders of giants, that's why we can see more and farther." Medieval Christendom had reached an unprecedented level of economic development.[1] In the cultural sphere, the splendor of the "Renaissance of the 12th century" was followed by the progressive and innovative 13th century, termed by J. Le Goff "the Enlightenment century" ("le siècle des lumières").[2] And the collaborators of the Alfonsine works in the prologue to the Learned King's most important scientific work did not hesitate to label his reign "the Alfonsine era." This was no exaggeration given the results and the unmatched cultural patrimony he left behind. Intellectual figures, works, and translations from many places converge and change the world of science and letters with great speed. The three great cultures, Latin, Greek and Muslim, clash and influence each other. And Alfonso is the great beneficiary of it all. At his court gathered scholars representing all three traditions. From this unprecedented cultural crossroads was born in the royal *scriptorium* a new vision of the national past in the *Estoria de España* (*EE*) (*History of Spain*) and of universal history in the *General Estoria* (*GE*) (*General History*), which is reflected in the extraordinary production of scientific, legal, poetic, and even leisure works that would occupy the mind of the Learned King in the next thirty-two years of his reign.

---

[1] This aspect of social progress has been masterfully emphasized by G. Duby in his two great works: *Rural Economy and Country Life in the Medieval West*, trans. C. Postan, Columbia, SC: The University of South Carolina Press, 1976; and *Año 1000–año 2000. La huella de nuestros miedos*, Barcelona, 1995.

[2] J. Le Goff, *Le XIIIᵉ siècle. L'apogée de la Chretienté (v. 1180–v. 1330)*, Paris, 1982, p. 85; see also his work *Los intelectuales en la Edad Media*, Barcelona, 1986; Ch.H. Haskins, *The Renaissance of the Twelfth Century*, Cambridge: Harvard University Press, 1927.

Regarding the reconquest of the peninsular territory, a great worry for Western Christians, it could be said that, when Alfonso reached the throne, the territories that at the end of the 12th century were in the hands of the minor Muslim kings of the South had been almost completely unified under the crown of his father. On his deathbed, Fernando III declared that he bequeathed his heir complete dominion, through conquest or submission, of the entire territory of al-Andalus, but he demanded from his son the commitment to maintain and expand the territory until it reached the confines of the former Visigoth empire: "And he even said more: 'Son, you are rich in lands and have many and good vassals, more than any other king of Christendom; make an effort to do good and be good, because you have the means to do it.' And he added: "Lord, I leave you all the land from the sea to here that the Moors seized from king Rodrigo of Spain; under your lordship is the entire territory, the conquered lands and those subjected to tribute. If you are able to preserve it in this state, you will be a king as good as I; and if you are able to conquer more, you will be a better king than I; and if you fail in this, you will not be as good as I."[3] These words of his father would weigh down on his conscience as a nightmare that pushed him, in certain instances, to political and military adventures with disastrous consequences.

If regarding the question of the reconquest of territory Alfonso practically found everything done, we could also say that his cultural program also did not start with nothing. And he was the first to acknowledge this. Alfonso's debt to his father in all areas was incalculable and permeated all aspects of his personal life as well as all his activities as king and man of letters. Fernando III, as can be clearly gleaned from the eulogy that his son made of him in the *Setenario*, was the model that Alfonso attempted to emulate during his entire life. Throughout that work the various aspects of paternal influence will become obvious in the origins of his work as a writer, an educator, and a statesman.

---

[3] *Estoria de España (EE), o Primera Crónica General de España que mandó Componer Alfonso el Sabio y se continuaba bajo Sancho IV en 1289*, ed. R. Menéndez Pidal, 2 vols., Madrid: Gredos, 1955 (PCG), II, pp. 772–773b–a. See the commentary to this passage by A. Rodríguez López, "'Rico fincas de tierra et de muchos buenos vasallos, más que rey que en la cristiandat ssea'. La herencia regia de Alfonso X," *Cahiers de Linguistique hispanique médiévale*, 23 (2000), pp. 243–261.

Alfonso tells us that his father asked him to write the *Setenario*, a programmatic work that would serve future kings as a handbook, and that the people in general would use to learn the norms of Christian interaction, to be educated in the sciences and letters, and become an educated and respected people. Alfonso took to heart his father's desire and command by carrying out the literary and scientific activity in the vernacular that his father had initiated. Through this activity he aspired to elevate his kingdom to the dignity envisioned by his father. His political program, the unification of the Peninsular territory through the submission of Muslim kings and the acceptance of his hegemony by other Christian kingdoms along with his educational program available to all was what would allow him to raise the kingdom to such a level that it would merit the title of empire and he of emperor, which his father chose never to bear. From Fernando's perspective, the Alfonsine empire should be an empire of culture—his father aspired to nothing less. But at a certain moment, in 1256, Alfonso conceived of other ideals and other imperial ambitions that went beyond the confines of the Peninsula. Naturally, the project was so ambitious that Alfonso, despite Herculean efforts, was unable to complete it. Three centuries would still go by before a Spanish king would bear the title of emperor, and it was not exactly because he was a Spanish king. But this did not keep him from attempting it with all his might.

Fernando III, know as *San Fernando* [Fernando the Saint], was also a model for his son regarding relations with the various ethnic and religious groups that lived in the Peninsula. Although he was a conqueror whose main objective was the submission of Islam in the Peninsula, don Fernando was guided in his relations to people of other faiths by a policy of tolerance and mutual respect. As long as they would obey and pay the tribute agreed, Muslims were free to follow their religious practices, their habits, and customs. Whereas regarding the Jews, since they were not an independent political or military power, they were considered for all practical purposes just like any other subjects of the crown, but with their specific particularities.

When Alfonso acceded to the throne, it could be said that his kingdom was a "crucible of cultures," and during his kingdom he would do everything possible to maintain and fuse those cultures in all areas of knowledge and social interaction. The fine arts were integrated into the miniatures of the *Cantigas*. In the sciences, he employed collaborators from all three religions. In law, he attracted to his court the best European legal scholars and he also legislated over the three cultures. And in history he addressed all beliefs, using all kinds of sources: Biblical, pagan, patristic, and contemporary.

It is difficult to determine if Alfonso reached a tolerant attitude towards both groups because of a genuine philosophical and legal conviction that they were all equal before the law or simply because he realized he needed them for his cultural projects. However, it is undoubted that the historical elements of the two dominant minorities in the Peninsula, Jews and Mudéjares, would be forged decisively during his reign. His attitude towards Islam outside of the Peninsula would prove very different.

Due to the retaliations by Almoravids and Almohads, the mass immigration of Jews from the territories of al-Andalus, where they were persecuted and from which they were eventually expelled, headed towards the Christian cities of the North. Something similar also happened with Mudéjares, who, following the conquests of Fernando III, settled en masse in the Lower Extremadura, the kingdom of Murcia, and in the valley of the Guadalquivir. The Jews who settled from the end of the 12th century and throughout the reigns of Fernando and Alfonso X among the Christians of the North organized themselves as a complete, separate, and, in its own way, self-sufficient society within certain territories occupied by a Christian society unable to assimilate them, often because they did not want to be assimilated due to unbridgeable religious differences. The assimilation of the Mudéjares, who were religiously more fragmented, was relatively easier.

Frequently, when speaking about the *convivencia* or interaction among the various religious groups, Iberian monarchies were considered tripartite societies with different religions, while, as Luis Suárez Fernández writes, "the reality that is borne out by the documents differs considerably. Jews and Muslims were microsocieties linked to the king only by personal dependency, which differs from the legal relations of the normal subjects."[4] Therefore, whoever killed a Jew, paid a "caloña" or fine to the king, as a vassal would. And such "caloñas" in the periods of good relations with the monarchy were quite high. Living together mixed with the Christian population did not alter their legal condition, which to a certain extent was one of privilege: they were part of the treasury of the king, with all the advantages and

---

[4] *Los judíos españoles en la Edad Media*, Madrid: Rialp, 1988, p. 91.

disadvantages that their position entailed, defined by M. Kriegel as "the advantage of serfdom."[5] At first glance, the expression "serfdom" that describes the condition of the Jews in all of Europe and not only in the Spanish crown may seem strong, especially when applied to a minority that was traditionally oppressed. But in reality, it is not so much the case if we consider that, in Alfonso's juridical conception of the king, all subjects were serfs of the crown, even the clergy. Alfonso, therefore, inherited from his father, not only the kingdom but also the model to launch a program of unprecedented institutional reforms in medieval Christian Spain.[6]

On the occasion of the celebration of the seven hundred years of his death, the publications around the life and works of Alfonso X have multiplied exponentially. So much so, that more titles have appeared in the last 18 years than in the seven centuries before. Why then a new biography of Alfonso X? Simply because Alfonso X is still a largely unknown figure, and even after this one, he will continue to be one. But this should surprise no one. The period that goes from his accession to the throne in 1253 until the death of his great-grandchild, Alfonso XI, in 1355 has been one of the most ignored by historical research in the past. Therefore, there is still a long way to go, although it is also true that in the last years the period has been revisited by many studies, perhaps because it is believed that the 13th century is the starting point of many aspects of the modern state.[7] Figures from the same century but inferior to Alfonso in intellectual and political caliber have been the subjects of three times as many monographs as the father of the Castilian language. His name is pronounced with almost religious respect and admiration, but his works, which have still to be published in their entirety, continue to gather dust in libraries and archives, or continue to deteriorate in computer hard drives and CD-ROMs, at least on this side of the Atlantic. The distinguished American historian Robert I. Burns, in the prologue to a collection

---

[5] *Les juifs a la fin du Moyen Age dans l'Europe méditerranéene*, Paris, 1979, p. 13. See also A. Neuman, *The Jews in Spain. Their Social, Political and Cultural Life during the Middle Ages*, I, Philadelphia, 1944, p. 166 and ff.

[6] The problematic issues of *convivencia* are discussed with more detail in H. Salvador Martínez, *La convivencia en la España del siglo XIII. Perspectivas alfonsíes*, Madrid: Ediciones Polifemo, 2007.

[7] Cf. P. Lineham, *History and the Historians of Medieval Spain*, Oxford: Clarendon Press, 1993, p. 413 and notes 1–2.

of essays on Alfonso X and James the Conqueror, writes, "Neither is well known to Americans, imprisoned as we are in nineteenth-century historiography, which centers on remoter lands of medieval northern Europe and which scarcely notices the Mediterranean heartlands."[8] Despite the noble efforts of this distinguished Jesuit and of many other of his fellow Americans, things do not seem to have changed much in the years following the 700th anniversary, judging by the three copies of the volume of the symposium promoted by Father Burns in the three most important university libraries in New York (Columbia, NYU, and Fordham, this last one a Jesuit institution), which remain untouched, much like the day they arrived in the stacks. There is no sign of the proverbial student damage.

Among the recent publications on Alfonso X, those that stand are biographical. Each one of the four or five most important biographies that have been published in the last years have their individual features and merits, but in general, due to new historiographical trends, they all exhibit the tendency to study the subject of the biography more in the context of the institutions of government than of his personality. This approach to the subject is indeed very understandable, especially when personal details do not reveal much. Penetrating Alfonso's inner self is not easy.

The Learned King, who devoted himself to all aspects of intellectual life and showed an unmatched curiosity and interest in all the literary, scientific and philosophical novelties of his day, however did not devote himself to himself, except indirectly: through allusion, metaphor, and poetry.[9] He did not leave behind a personal diary or a book of memoirs such as *Llibre dels feyts* by his father-in-law, Jaime I of Aragón. And the countless documents that remain, eloquent as they may be about his politics or the institutions of the kingdom, are not very helpful to discover how he felt or how he lived in private. All must be deduced from other sources, which, because of their poetic or allegoric nature, have always been considered unreliable, historiographically speaking. However, nowadays we know, to our great satisfaction that the Learned King left an imprint of both his public and

---

[8] *The Worlds of Alfonso the Learned and James the Conqueror. Intellect and Force in the Middle Ages*, Princeton, NJ: Princeton University Press, 1985, Introduction.

[9] The historian J. O'Callaghan employs this approach in his recent monograph *Alfonso X and the Cantigas de Santa María. A Poetic Biography*, The Medieval Mediterranean Series, 16, Leiden–Boston–Cologne: Brill, 1998.

private personality on his works in many of his commentaries and glosses. We thus find his profile unexpectedly in historical works and in the *Cantigas* as well as in his letters and the many prologues he wrote for his scientific translations.

In order to write a relatively adequate biography of Alfonso X it would be necessary, therefore, to take into account not only the abundant documentation in his archive and his rich correspondence, which has been almost completely ignored. As in Dante's case, his life would have to be tracked down in his entire oeuvre. Hence, in the seventeen prologues written personally by him or dictated, in many of his *Cantigas*, and especially in his historiography, we find countless personal observations that no archival document can supply us with. The intellectual and moral profile of the Learned King is revealed, above all, in innumerable autobiographical references scattered throughout his *Estoria de España* and especially in his *General Estoria*. It is there that he identifies his ideals and aspirations with those of the historical and mythological figures he admired: Alfonso is Jupiter and Hermes, powerful and wise, but, at the same time, he is Nimrod, "the first king of the world," creator of marvelous cities and dream empires and promoter of a lay culture apart from the official priestly class. The Learned King makes use of allegory, myth, epic, or hagiographic legend to introduce in the story a personal dimension that reveals to the reader some of the secrets of his personality. Francisco Rico, who has already used this method, writes, "Thanks to this approach, the *General Estoria* often becomes a mirror of 13th-century Spain."[10] These works contain a wealth of detail that make reference to concrete situations in the life of the king, of his family and his collaborators, which suggests that Alfonso intervened directly in their composition, or at least in their revision, as he himself comments regarding the way in which a king is the author of a book "…because he composes the argument, lays out its logic, gathers all the materials, he orders them and corrects them."

The Alfonsine works throw sufficient light in order to reconstruct not only the essential periods of his life, but also his thought and even his personal taste. The following example of his love of freedom of expression is sufficient illustration of this view. Alfonso never made

---

[10] *Alfonso X y la General Estoria*, pp. 94–95; see also P. Linehan, *History and the Historians*, pp. 489–490.

a specific statement about this issue, but it is clear that that's how he felt when, in praising Tiberius Caesar Augustus, he writes in *Estoria de España*: "And when some in the city would speak ill of him, or attributed bad news to him, or composed a satirical song about him or his family, he was not bothered nor did he misbehave against anyone; instead, he said that in a free city, there should be freedom of expression and of the will of men to say what they wanted" (I, p. 111a). This constitutes very high praise of freedom of expression in the 13th century when European monarchies were on their way to absolutism. Statements such as this one, added to the conventional sources scattered throughout thousands of folios and whose exploration has been a hard task, have been very useful in this reconstruction of his personality.

About his passion for history, for instance, we have priceless details in unsuspected documents, such as, for instance, the privilege granted to the citizens of the town of Pampliega on the occasion of the discovery of the tomb of the Visigoth king Wamba. In fact, some of his works, the *Siete Partidas*, for example, contain the best documentation we could expect about Castilian society in the 13th century, covering all aspects of life, from the womb to the tomb. All social classes and all strata are discussed. More than a legal code, they are a manual of human life, in which relations among the various groups and the individuals themselves constitute its primary fabric. The pages devoted to the king and his court are an example of what the Learned King and his court must have been like. Naturally, the two great themes of his personal life, his reign and don Sancho's treason and the rebellion of the nobles are the object of constant comment whenever the occasion lends itself to that, both in the *GE* as in the *Cantigas*. Alfonso reflects above all on all these personal calamities and other public events in such an intimate and personal tone that they could hardly be attributed to his collaborators.

All in all, however, our intention was not to compose a virtual biography of Alfonso on the basis of the numerous personal observations the Learned King made directly and more frequently indirectly and in the third person, in his lyric poetry and his two historical works and in the mentioned prologues in such a way that it would result in an autobiography such as Benvenuto Cellini's *Vita* or Saint Augustine's *Confessions*. What we have tried to do is illustrate, starting from the postulate of the king's direct participation in the composition of a great part of his oeuvre, something that today is beyond all doubt, namely, how this participation makes his biographical allusions valid, regardless of how veiled they may be under a poetic or allegoric guise.

Understandably, introducing sources of this nature in a biography that pretends to be historical has been frowned upon by "purist" historians; but we should not forget that Alfonso was very conscious of all he wrote and there is no personal allusion whether through myth or directly, which had not been meticulously weighed by the Learned King in regards to its content as well as its form. The stylistic criterion he employed in the final drafts of his works is well known to us thanks to the prologue of his *Libro de la ochava esfera* (Book of the Eighth Sphere): "And later this king ordered its composition and removed the arguments he considered superfluous and repeated and that were not in correct Castilian, and he set other arguments that seemed to him to fit better, and regarding the language, he corrected it himself."[11] For this reason, the use of his work, where he left along with his personality the imprint of his style, seems to me one of the most logical paths to reconstructing his life. However, given the size of his literary corpus, it is practically impossible to illustrate all aspects of his biography in this way, hence the need to use his works selectively in reconstructing the various periods of his life.

As any humanist, Alfonso dealt with historiography, and he produced not only the first general history of the nation, the *Estoria de España*, and of the world, the *General Estoria*, but at the same time he created the form of expression of such history, namely, Castilian prose.[12] In that field too, Alfonso is a child of his century on account of his encyclopedic knowledge. His was the century in which all knowledge from the past was gathered in great collections named *summas*. From St. Thomas Aquinas's *Summa theologica* to the *Summa of Trojan History*, everything in all fields must be said with the largest number of sources, in great detail, and with the greatest number of words, everything gathered in massive tomes. Alfonso's two great historiographic compilations, therefore, follow the fashion of his day, although according to don Juan Manuel, his uncle "very carefully ordered the Chronicle of Spain and he put everything down very correctly and with very solid arguments and the least number of words" (*Crónica abreviada*). The great novelty, however, is not so much in the fact that

---

[11] In A. García Solalinde, *Antología de Alfonso X*, Madrid: Espasa-Calpe, 1941, p. 180.
[12] Cf. R. Menéndez Pidal, *PCG*, I, p. LII.

a history of the nation and a world history were being composed—this had been done already by Rodrigo Jiménez de Rada, Luke of Tuy, and many others in Europe—but rather that Alfonso chose the vernacular to write historical compilations of such magnitude and importance.

Alfonso X's *estorias* are exceptional in many ways in the context of medieval Spanish letters. No other genre was more popular or more fertile, and, nevertheless, no other has been less studied by modern criticism. If for the rest of the works, whether in prose or in verse, the manuscripts are unique or very few, there are dozens and even hundreds of manuscripts of the *estorias*, creating a veritable headache for scholars of all periods. The difficulty of unraveling this entangled tradition of historical chronicles has indeed been one of the reasons why this field has been neglected. On the other hand, from the historiographic perspective of today, it is difficult for us to understand the unitary concept of culture medieval people had, hence the effort of modern scholars to separate the field of history from that of fiction, poetry, mythology, etc. But when such fields prove inseparable, as is the case frequently in Alfonsine works, the genre that suffers most is history, which, as a result of our modern criteria and prejudices, must appear always as an objective and smooth narrative devoid of all the obstacles of subjectivity, expository commentary, rhetorical amplification, and, above all, mythology and legend. Alfonso X's historical oeuvre, as in general the work of all medieval historians, which obviously does not fulfill such conditions of "purity," has had to withstand the most severe critiques of the professionals of history starting in the Renaissance and all the way up to our days. However, we must recognize that this too was a legitimate way to write history, regardless of how much it may bother us nowadays.

Therefore, taking into account all these factors we have constructed our biography of the Learned King around six main narrative nuclei. The first one describes Alfonso's apprenticeship in its three aspects, family origins and physical development (Chapter 1); intellectual education as an apprentice of wisdom (Chapter 2); and the upbringing of a prince that should assume the responsibilities of government. This era ended with his proclamation as king of Castile in the spring of 1252 (Chapter 3), when Alfonso was already more than thirty years old and had acquired good diplomatic and military experience as well as extensive intellectual training. The second nucleus is made up of three chapters (4–6) and presents the history of his imperial aspirations and his final failure after his meeting with pope Gregory X in Beaucaire in 1275. The third narrative nucleus covers a topic seldom addressed in biographies of Alfonso: illness and intellectual production (Chapters 7–8). Nowadays we know the Learned King suffered many and very serious illnesses which deformed his physical appearance in very ugly ways and also produced profound psychic changes. However, it was precisely in the decade of political crisis and moral depression (1269–1279), when some of his most important works were produced. The flexible structure of these two chapters on his illnesses allows us, on the one hand, to explore the psyche of the Learned King, and on the other, to analyze the creative process of some of his works and establish the chronological parameters of some of them. The fourth nucleus (Chapters 9–10) deals with one of Alfonso's great tragedies and disappointments: the rebellion and *desnaturación* or defection of the nobility. For Alfonso, who was dedicated to renewing laws and traditional legal codes using the same norms of behavior for all, this was a period of anguish and moral defeat, because in order to save his kingdom from the fearsome Moorish invasions that devastated the South, he practically had to give in to all the demands of that privileged class who, in spite of himself, he could not do without if he wanted to defend the integrity of the kingdom. For a man such as Alfonso, proud of his legal knowledge and his farsightedness as legislator, having to give in to that sort of blackmail was an unprecedented humiliation that set back his program of institutional and legal reform. The fifth nucleus (Chapters 11–12) focuses on the problems of succession following the unexpected death of the heir don Fernando de la Cerda in 1275. Pressured by the nobility, the queen, and the Church, and against what he had laid down in the *Partidas*, he chose as his heir, his eldest son, don Sancho, but without any conviction. Finally, in the sixth nucleus (Chapters 13–15) we offer the narrative of the dramatic history of the most learned of king of the Middle Ages, who was first abandoned by everyone (his wife, children, the nobility, the clergy, and the town councils), and was later deposed and dispossessed of his royal powers and functions. The lack of understanding, ungratefulness and betrayal of don Sancho and of all sectors of the kingdom that supported the rebel in such an ignoble act could not have been greater. Vis-à-vis such political and personal cataclysm which fostered civil war, chaos, and a new wave of Moorish invasions, Alfonso, after having resorted to all Christian kings and the pope and being ignored by all, was ultimately forced, in order to save his personal honor and his crown, to request the protection of his very enemies, the emir of Morocco and his fearsome warriors, against whom he had fought a merciless fight until not long before. It is an absurd and chilling story that seems more like a fable, more inhumane than King Lear's, which Alfonso himself had narrated in the *General Estoria*.

Before closing this introduction, I would like to respond to a couple of objections that were raised during my research. Besides the contribution to the dissemination of culture among his subjects in the Castilian language, which was accessible to all, Alfonso was also interested in the political and social conditions and the spreading of culture to the rest of the Europe of his time. We could not say if the immediate cause that awakened this interest in him was the fact that he was named by the Republic of Pisa candidate to the imperial crown, or whether his "pan-European" plans were prior to that. He had, it is clear, reason enough to do this. Related as he was to all European dynasties, after being elected King of the Romans, Alfonso must have felt himself at the head of Europe. From Sicily to Norway and from Byzantium to Lisbon, passing through Hungary, Germany, England, France, Navarra, and Aragón, he had a relative at every court. When his aunt, Juana of Brienne, empress of Orient, was traveling around the European courts to raise funds to rescue her son who had been imprisoned by the Venetians, Alfonso offered to pay the entire sum, saying he too had great interest in the matter. In all his meetings with the nobility of Europe, such as the one held in 1269 on the occasion of the wedding of his son and heir Fernando, Alfonso must have felt very much at home, as among family.

Outside the confines of Christian Europe, his reputation as a learned man and a patron of intellectual pursuits also spread to the Maghreb and the Islamic world all the way to Egypt and throughout the Middle East. It is not surprising, therefore, that when he was elected King of the Romans and he saw the imperial crown within his reach, he thought about the compilation of a code of laws that would be extended to all people in Europe. Alfonso's concept of Europe was not the same one held nowadays in Brussels, but the goal of his vision of Europe was the same: the unification of laws for living together applying to all peoples gathered under the same imperial crown. It was the premature dream of a farsighted man that was not yet a reality.

But in the same way that we do not see the justification in Padre Mariana's 16th-century traditional reproach that Alfonso lost the earth for looking up to the sky and contemplating the stars,[13] a judgment now rejected by all modern critics, we also do not agree with Américo Castro's opinion that Alfonso's work "remained confined to his land, because it was not written in the international language of contemporary Europe, which Alfonso was uninterested in including in his panorama of culture; it was meaningful and effective for those in Spain who shared his life orientation."[14] Even ignoring the fact that Alfonso had most of his important scientific works translated into Latin precisely so they would be accessible to other Europeans, I do not believe that many scholars today would agree with Castro's opinion and would deny that Alfonso was very active in the international politics of his day. Sufficient proof of this would be the story of his quest for the imperial crown and the establishment of political and commercial relations with the Italian republics, the various German duchies, and the kings of France, England, and Norway. Therefore, we think R.I. Burns' opinion is more accurate when he writes that, "Castro's position here seems extreme," arguing also that Alfonso must be considered the main link in the transfer of knowledge from the Islamic world to the West, not only to his own people but to all the peoples of Europe.[15] Alfonso, who was related to most of the European dynasties, was interested in Europe, and Europe was equally interested in Alfonso and his enlightened court.[16] According to M. González Jiménez, "Alfonso deployed a complex network of diplomatic relations with the European countries which matched the political realities of

---

[13] "Dum coelum considerat observabatque astra, terram amisit" (*Historia de rebus Hispaniae*, Madrid: P. Rodríguez, 1592, p. 649).

[14] *La realidad histórica de España*, 6th ed., Mexico: Editorial Porrúa, 1975, p. 160.

[15] According to this distinguished scholar:

Alfonso is not a freak or a break with European tradition, however idiosyncratic the Castilian model seems on the surface. It is more true to say that we moderns broke with him, when the northern industrial countries of the early nineteenth century invented a nationalistic historiography that moved Europe's medieval center north to jibe with its more modern center and marginalized the heartlands of its Mediterranean-centered self. As we recapture our wider history in our own day, Alfonso the Learned can be seen as a major actor in a widely based transfer of learning and letters from Islam to the West, particularly but by no means exclusively for his own country in that universal transfer.

("*Stupor mundi*: Alfonso X of Castile, the Learned," in R.I. Burns, S.J., ed., *Emperor of Culture. Alfonso X the Learned of Castile and his Thirteenth-Century Renaissance*, Philadelphia: University of Pennsylvania Press, 1990, pp. 12 and 13.)

[16] See the essays gathered in the beautiful volume, *Alfonso X. Aportaciones de un rey castellano a la construcción de Europa*, Coordinación M. Rodríguez Llopis, Murcia: Consejería de Cultura y Educación, 1997.

his day. From 1256 on, his aspiration to the imperial title left its mark on many of Alfonso's actions. In any event, it should remain clear that, during those years, Peninsular and European politics constantly crisscross as in pieces on a chessboard."[17]

As we shall see, it was precisely his political and social activity at all levels, national and international, legal and legislative, linguistic, and even in terms of environmental protection, that would end up costing him not only the imperial crown, but also that of his own kingdom. In the midst of so much controversy, the Learned King was able to keep his calm and impartiality, conscious, in his skepticism, that the opinions of peoples, as the narratives in books and even truth itself, are often doubtful:

> Many things have been written and they tell things in many ways; this is the reason that the truth of things is in doubt; therefore, whoever reads must be careful to chose the best for what he intends to prove, and read such writings with great care.

This has also been the criterion that has guided us in the composition of this biography.

I would like to express my sincere gratitude to all those who on both sides of the Atlantic have given me advice and helped me carry out this task. I would in particular like to thank D. Ramón Alba and Ediciones Polifemo for their interest in the publication of the original of this work and the care they put in preparing the edition. I would also like to express my thanks to Odile Cisneros, who had already worked with the original text, for her extraordinary effort to make this work available to English readers, and to Brill for their interest in publishing it. I am most grateful to Robert J. Bast, Editor-in-chief of Studies in the Histories of Christian Traditions, for accepting this biography of King Alfonso X in his prestigious series and for generously lending his expertise in copyediting to render my translation easier to read. All these have saved this book from many small errors; any that remain are of course my own. Finally, I would like to thank the Ministry of Culture of Spain, which, through their Book Director, D. Rogelio Blanco, sponsored the English translation of this work.

New York, on the 750th anniversary of the "Alfonsine Era"

---

[17] *Alfonso X, el Sabio: 1252–1284*, Corona de España, Reyes de Castilla y León, 1, Palencia: Diputación Provincial, 1993, p. 61.

CHAPTER ONE

THE APPRENTICESHIP OF A GREAT KING

> *Rex, decus Hesperie, thesaurus philosophie*
> *El rey, que es fermosura de Espanna et thesoro de la*
> *filosofia*
>
> (The King, who is the ornament of Spain and trea-
> sure of its philosophy)
>
> (Ms. Escur. *Y-i-2*, fol. 1v)

1. *Birth and Ancestors*

We are the product of our genes and education. If that is true of all human beings, it perhaps applied best to the subject of our biography, Alfonso X, King of Castile and León, justly termed *the Learned* or *the Wise*.[1]

According to the documents available, he was born in the imperial city of Toledo on Tuesday, November 23, 1221, on the Feast of St. Clement.[2] The birth at Toledo was probably accidental, as his mother, accompanying her husband, who was headed south to crush the rebellion of the Lord de Molina, had to take refuge in the imperial city in order to give birth. Beatriz and her husband were also accompanied by her inseparable mother-in-law, Queen Berenguela (1180–1246), who was often present at her son's military campaigns. She was probably the one who suggested the name for the newborn, Alfonso, in memory

---

[1] The bibliography on the life, reign, and culture of the times of Alfonso X is vast. The main biographies and important studies as well as the various collections of documents consulted are gathered in the Bibliography at the end of this volume. In the notes, these works are frequently quoted in abbreviated form.

[2] It is Alfonso himself who declares: "Because we were born in the city of Toledo and we received there the baptism," *Privilegio* dated February 21, 1253 (AHN, *Liber Privilegiorum Toletanae Ecclesiae*, fol. 182 r–v, published in *MHE*, I, pp. 5–8); "I was born the day of Saint Clement," Letter of concession, May 25, 1254 (AHN, Sellos, publ. in *MHE*, I, p. 43); "we prayed to Saint Clement in whose day we were born," Testament of Alfonso X, Seville, November 8, 1283 (*MHE*, II, p. 111). Both details are confirmed in *Anales Toledanos II*: "Tuesday, day of Saint Clement, on the 23rd day of November was born the infant don Alfonso, son of king don Fernando of Castile..."] (ed. *ES*, XXIII, Madrid, 1799, p. 406).

of her father, the great Alfonso VIII, hero of the battle of Las Navas de Tolosa (1212). The newborn was immediately entrusted to the care of a nurse, the noblewoman Urraca Pérez, and her husband, don García Alvarez de Toledo, who were always cherished by Fernando III and Alfonso himself.[3]

At three months, the child was transferred along with his nurse to Burgos. On March 21, 1222, with the court at Burgos, representatives of the city were summoned to acknowledge and vow fidelity to the new heir. The act took place in the cathedral, in the presence of the entire court, noblemen, and the church officials. The four month-old Alfonso was held by his nurse, doña Urraca, while the representatives of the cities, one by one, proceeded to make a vow of fidelity and obedience.[4] The summer of that same year, the child was entrusted to the caretaker García Fernández de Villamayor and his wife, doña Mayor Arias, who would later be granted lands by Alfonso, when he became king, in recognition of their many services, especially for his healthy upbringing in Villaldemiro and Celada del Camino, some twenty kilometers from Burgos, in the Arlanzón lowlands.[5]

There is speculation that the selection of both nurse and caretaker was highly influenced by Queen Berenguela, for don García, besides having repeatedly proven his fidelity to the crown in its struggle against don Álvaro de Lara, happened to be Berenguela's butler; previously he

---

[3] The name of the nurse appears in a grant document by Fernando III quoted by E. Flórez, *Reinas cathólicas*, I, p. 446. Regarding the care that should be taken in the selection of the nurse for the children of kings, there are many details in the *Segunda Partida*:

   [...] wherefore the ancient sages, who discussed these matters in a natural way, declared that the children of kings should have nurses who afforded sufficient milk; that they should be well bred, healthy, handsome, belong to good families, have good habits and especially that they should not be very high-tempered. For where they afford abundance of milk and are well-formed and healthy, they will bring up healthy and vigorous children; and if they are handsome and graceful, the children will love them more, and take greater pleasure in seeing them, and permit them to control them better. (*Partida* II, Tit. VII, Law III, *Las Siete Partidas*, 4 vols., ed. Robert I. Burns, trans. By Samuel Parsons Scott, Philadelphia: University of Pennsylvania Press, 2001. vol. 2, p. 300. All quotations in English from this work come from this edition, unless otherwise noted.)

[4] This act is remembered in a diploma issued by Fernando III to the city of Burgos and granted on the next day, March 22 (in J. González, *Reinado y diplomas de Fernando III*, II, p. 194).

[5] "because don García Fernández and his wife doña Mayor Arias raised me and performed many services and especially because they raised me in Villaldemiro and in Celada..." (in A. Ballesteros, *Alfonso X el Sabio*, p. 50).

had served as butler to her mother, doña Leonor of England, wife of Alfonso VIII of Castile, and would subsequently serve her son, Fernando III. Queen Berenguela had a deep regard for, and trust in, this noble Castilian, whom she entrusted with the knightly upbringing of her grandson and the future king. Don García's selection, aside from his fidelity to the crown, was also probably influenced by an old Castilian custom to raise royal children away from the court, in small villages and in close contact with the countryside. It was believed this would fortify their physical and mental health, protecting them from the disturbances and bustle of the court, which was constantly moving and was for this reason not a healthy environment.[6] According to present day psychiatrists, this type of upbringing, away from contact with the parents, particularly the father, caused serious emotional disturbances in Alfonso's character, which he would never overcome.[7]

Little is known about Alfonso X's childhood, but according to tradition he spent his childhood and adolescence, from ages 2 or 3 to 13, (1223–1231), under the supervision of his caretaker, away from the influence of the court and in direct contact with the people he was to rule. Among his childhood companions were the children of García Fernández, who later had important positions in the court and, and his own siblings who began to arrive little by little.[8] We should also mention his best friend, Nuño González de Lara, nephew of don

---

[6] Both the *Segunda Partida* as well as don Juan Manuel, a trustworthy witness, tell us that this was the custom at the time, which was also followed during his father's upbringing, the prince don Juan, Alfonso X's youngest brother; and therefore we can assume that he too received the same upbringing as Alfonso:

> And because at the time it was not customary to raise the children of kings with such great insanity as today, understanding that great expense should be put at the service of God and for the advancement of the holy faith and of the kingdom, and what could be excused of expenses that they had to save for that, they raised their children maintaining the health of their bodies in the simplest way they could; so that as soon as they could take them away from the place where they were born, they gave them to someone to raise in their home. And in this way he gave the prince don Manuel to don Pero López de Ayala and he raised him in Pampliega and in Villalmunno, which today is a desert, and in Mayamud, and in the region of Can de Munno where he owned property. And when the prince was grown, the king decided he should study at hope, and he studied in the house of the king, his father, for a long time. (*Libro de las armas*, ed. J.M. Blecua, *Obras completas*, 2 vols., Madrid: Gredos, 1981, I, pp. 123–124)

[7] F. Torres González, "Rasgos médico-psicológicos de Alfonso el Sabio" in *Alfonso X y Ciudad Real: Conferencias pronunciadas con motivo del VII centenario de la muerte del Rey Sabio (1284–1984)*, ed. M. Espadas Burgos, Ciudad Real, 1986, pp. 107–140.

[8] Six male children: Fadrique, Fernando, Enrique, Felipe, Sancho, Manuel, and three girls: Leonor, Berenguela, and María. With his second wife, doña Juana de

Alvaro Núñez de Lara, whom we shall discuss later on and who was also raised in the estates owned by the Laras near Villaldemiro and Celada. Nuño, deemed by chroniclers as the wisest mind of the nobility, was always admired by Alfonso. According to Alfonso's modern biographer, Antonio Ballesteros, Alfonso also spent time in Allariz (Orense), where don García Fernández de Villamayor and his wife owned lands.[9]

During these visits to Galicia Alfonso would have had the chance to learn the language, be in touch with the poetry and music of the troubadours of the region, and hear the popular legends and tales of magic and superstition that Galician literature is known for. Likewise, in Burgos he learned the language of Castile, which would then become the official language of his kingdoms and in which he would write all of his work in prose. Don García Fernández, his old caretaker and a trusted man in the court since the days of his great grandfather Alfonso VIII, taught the art of war, courtly habits, and the difficult art of ruling and how to treat his subjects.

Despite lack of documentation on his childhood, Alfonso indeed had a clear memory of certain events that occurred during that period. In his celebrated collection of Marian religious poetry, the *Cantigas de Santa María* (*Songs of Holy Mary*),[10] Alfonso tells of events he witnessed in his childhood and adolescence. The *cantiga* 122 deals with the miraculous resurrection of his sister Berenguela, and 256 with the healing of his mother, Queen Beatriz. The *cantiga* tells how she fell seriously ill in Cuenca, and prominent doctors, who had come from Montpellier, predicted she would not survive. But, thanks to the Virgin's intervention, the queen recovered. Alfonso affirms, "Although I was a little boy, I remember it happened like this, for I was present

---

Ponthieu Don Fernando had five more: four boys, Fernando, Luis, Simón, and Juan, and one girl, doña Leonor.

[9] Cf. *Alfonso X*, pp. 48, 50–51. His father, Fernando III, had also been raised in Galicia, as Alfonso X himself tells us in one of his *Cantigas*, telling of how he was cured by the Virgin Mary of a serious illness as a boy (*Cantiga* 221). In the summer of 1232 Fernando III donated to the caretakers of prince don Alfonso the township of Manzaneda de Limia (today Maceda, three leagues from Orense); it is therefore possible that it was in this township and surroundings that Alfonso spent a good deal of his childhood. Cf. J. González, *Reinado y diplomas de Fernando III*, II, pp. 552–553.

[10] All references to Alfonso's *Cantigas* in English come from the English translation, *Songs of Holy Mary of Alfonso X, The Wise: A Translation of the* Cantigas de Santa Maria, trans. Kathleen Kulp-Hill, Tempe, Arizona: Arizona Center for Medieval and Renaissance Studies, 2000.

and saw and heard everything" (*Cantiga* 256, p. 312). Alfonso was probably five or six when this miracle occurred. The miracle of his sister's resurrection probably took place some years later, but certainly before November 5, 1235, when doña Beatriz died, since she played an important role in praying to the Virgin for her daughter's life. This could have happened when Alfonso was a teenager. In the *cantiga* he composed years later as an adult and well-seasoned in matters of State, he speaks unhesitatingly about his presence at the site of the miracle, as if had just occurred: "I shall tell a miracle I saw which the Virgin performed in Toledo in Her chapel there" (*Cantiga*, 122, p. 150).

The narratives of both miracles reveal how his devotion to Mary began and developed, and the role his mother played in that devotion from his childhood. Because of his childlike mentality and insecurity in later years, always in need of affection and support, Alfonso must have kept in mind the scene of his mother's healing as a constant reference. Hence, years later, when he lost his earthly mother in his adolescence, he held on to the heavenly mother as his sole anchor.

2. *His Grandmother: Berenguela, the Great*

It is not possible to speak of Alfonso X (and of his father Fernando III) without mentioning the exceptional figure of Berenguela, grand-mother of the former and mother of the latter. The daughter of Alfonso VIII and Eleanor (or Leonor) Plantagenet of England, she played a similar role in the Spain of the 13th century to that of Queen Isabella in 15th century Spain. Queen Berenguela, in the words of her grandson, was the one who ordered "all the things and all the deeds of the kingdom."[11] She was also the one who, after his father, exerted the most influence on Alfonso's spiritual makeup, and, while alive, on the kingdom's political direction. Her grandson's words reveal more than what has traditionally been acknowledged, because they probably point towards the very reason for his father's and his own accession to the throne of Castile-León.

Because of her farsighted personality, she could not leave such an important affair as the selection of the wife of her first born, don Fernando, to chance. The daughter of the great Alfonso VIII was the

---

[11] *PCG*, II, p. 718a.

kingdom's sentinel, and, in a warring century dominated by male protagonists, she was the prototype of the "strong woman" the Bible speaks of. She was, in the words of the Learned King: "[...] a very wise lady and a great expert and sharp in political affairs and understood the risks of government."[12] Her steadfast temper and political talent for solving complex conflicts fill the political annals of the Christian kingdoms of the first half of the 13th century. Her grandson has written unforgettable pages about this invincible woman who, using her exquisite tact, placed her eldest son, don Fernando, upon the throne of Castile and then of León, thus anticipating the first great political union of the Peninsula. She also managed to link the heir to the two kingdoms with the European house of Staufen, who held the title of emperors of the West. And we will also never know if it was Berenguela who inspired first her son's and then her grandson's idea of a Roman Germanic Empire headed by a Castilian emperor. Queen Berenguela, of course, managed the affairs of the kingdom on behalf, first of her son and then of her grandson, up until the end of her life, watching over the union of the kingdoms with the same zeal of a lioness protecting her cubs. No one or nothing could stand in the way of her designs, as she was always prepared to defend them with finesse and tact, but, when necessary, to fight for them tooth and nail. Her overprotection of her son, don Fernando, according to her grandson, don Alfonso, also extended to his moral and personal life, and to his physical integrity, which was an extraordinary attitude in a society where war and wounds were a sign of greatness:

> And the noble queen doña Berenguela, mother of king don Fernando, with love and great affection for her son, wanting to prevent him from avenging the ills the Moors had done him, made him dedicate to God, as the story goes, the beginnings of his knighthood, and extending for a longer time the truce he had negotiated with the Arabs, and she did not allow him to move against them.[13]

When Berenguela was still an eight year-old child, she was granted in marriage to Conrad of Hohenstaufen, Duke of Rothenburg, first born son of Frederick I Barbarossa (1152–1190).[14] Historians wonder about

---

[12] *PCG*, II, p. 718a.
[13] *PCG*, II, p. 720a.
[14] Cf. Jiménez de Rada, *De rebus Hispaniae*, VII, 24; and J. González, *El reino de Castilla en la época de Alfonso VIII*, 3 vols., Madrid, 1960, II, nos. 467–471,

how her parents, Alfonso VIII of Castile and Leonor Plantagenet (daughter of Henry II of England), sought such a remote alliance, creating thus countless problems with the papacy because of their association with the Staufen imperial family. There are several hypotheses we will not go into at the moment, but it's important to point out that the reigning houses in Europe had a tendency to establish links with other kingdoms, and the easiest way of doing this was through marriage agreements. What is certain is that prince Conrad, following the marriage treaty signed at Seligenstadt in April 1188, traveled to Spain in June of that year and was knighted by Alfonso VIII, father of the betrothed, in a solemn ceremony held at the church of San Zoilo de Carrión;[15] then, Alfonso VIII: "took the *infanta* lady Berenguela, his first daughter, and betrothed her to don Conrad, son of the emperor."[16] During that ceremony, the Castilian king also knighted his cousin, Alfonso, King Alfonso IX of León (1188–1230). Conrad stayed in Spain until at least 1190, when Alfonso VIII and Leonor had their first male child and the future heir to the throne. It is believed that it was this event that caused Conrad to lose interest in the marriage, since it no longer entailed the crown of Castile, and with no further explanation, he returned to Germany.

Our source, Alfonso X's *Estoria de España*, which in this episode follows closely don Rodrigo Jiménez de Rada, Archbishop of Toledo (*De rebus Hispaniae*, VII, XXIV), provides no explanation for the failure of the marriage. It simply states: "But the said Conrad, once he returned to Germany, was opposed to the betrothal that he had vowed to Lady Berenguela, and they were discharged from the vow of marrying each other by don Gonzalo, primate of Toledo and of Spain, and don Gregorio cardinal-deacon of Saint Angel, delegate of the Apostolic See, that is to say of the Apostolic See of Rome."[17] Some historians claim that it was Berenguela who insisted on ending the marriage vow given

---

pp. 800–808, 857–863 (text of the marriage agreement of Conrad to Berenguela between Alfonso VIII and Frederick I of Germany).

[15] The marriage contract signed at Seligenstadt had been prepared in a *curia* or papal court celebrated at San Esteban de Gormaz in May of 1187. Cf. J.F. O'Callaghan, "The Beginnings of the Cortes of León-Castile," *The American Historical Review*, 74 (1969), pp. 1512–1513.

[16] *PCG*, II, chap. 997, p. 677a.

[17] *PCG*, II, chap. 997, p. 677a.

the "repulsion" she felt towards consummating a marriage she had been forced into against her will.[18]

Freed from the commitment to the German prince, Berenguela, following her mother's will and with the consent of her father, was finally able to marry Alfonso IX of León in 1197. It was a calculated political decision that Alfonso VIII had made nine years earlier (1188) during a visit the young king of León had paid him at Carrión de los Condes on the occasion of Berenguela's marriage engagement to Conrad. At the time, Alfonso VIII had demanded from the young king of León to marry the daughter he would give him as a condition for the peace between the kingdoms. Nobody could have foreseen at the time that it would be Berenguela. Alfonso IX had no choice but to give in to the firm will of his cousin and, as a sign of obedience, he agreed to be knighted by the Castilian king. The king of León, for his part, had to kiss his hand in front of numerous witnesses as a sign of submission. That was a humiliation Alfonso IX would never forgive his cousin and future father-in-law with whom, from that moment on, he always had difficult relations, to the point that he even declared war and allied himself with the Muslims against him. Furthermore, to avenge the humiliation and affirm his old independence, Alfonso IX broke his promise of marrying one of Alfonso VIII's daughters and married instead Teresa, daughter of don Sancho, King of Portugal (February 1191).[19]

The marriage of Alfonso IX and Berenguela, celebrated in October 1197, was vigorously promoted by Queen Leonor, who viewed the union as the only way to reach and maintain the peace between the two kingdoms. That was the opinion of don Rodrigo Jiménez de Rada, Archbishop of Toledo:

> And because his intention [Alfonso VIII's] was to attack the king of León, with greater strength, some, who feared the risk of war, managed with friendly advice to make the king of León ask the king of Castile for his daughter Berenguela in marriage. And although the noble king was reticent about this, because he and the king of León were related by blood, queen Leonor, wife of the noble Alfonso, who was extremely prudent, weighed very carefully the risk of the situation, which could

---

[18] Mondéjar, *Alfonso VIII*, pp. 174–176.
[19] Cf. Jiménez de Rada, *De rebus Hispaniae*, VII, 24; and J. González, *Alfonso IX. Colección Diplomática*, 2 vols. Madrid: Instituto Jerónimo Zurita, CSIC, 1944, I, pp. 309–311.

be solved with such a union. And he granted him in marriage the said daughter to the king of León, who had gone to Valladolid accompanied by nobles, and granted her a dowry fitting of such a maiden, and once the wedding was celebrated with great pomp, he took her to his kingdom.[20]

As expected, the marriage brought peace to the kingdoms but also created a series of serious problems for the couple.

At 17, Berenguela was very aware of the political significance of that marriage agreement. The king of León had already been married to Teresa of Portugal and, although their marriage had been officially annulled three years earlier by pope Celestine III (1191–1198) because of blood ties (they were first cousins), the royal couple continued having children, totaling three, two daughters and one son: Sancha, Fernando, and Dulce. Despite being the second, Fernando, because he was a boy, became the heir to the throne of León up until 1201, when Alfonso IX and Berenguela had their first son, also named Fernando.[21] The marriage of Alfonso and Teresa, contrary to what was customary among the nobility, was based on love, therefore the separation imposed by the pope had left the king very resentful with regard to marriage. The pope, however, was inflexible and took drastic measures to ensure the separation, including the excommunication of the royal couple and the placing of their kingdoms under interdict, should they insist on living together. The marriage of Alfonso IX of León with Teresa of Portugal finally ended in 1194. The worst consequence of this annulment was not the separation of the married couple, but perhaps the fact that since the children became illegitimate, they were excluded from the line of succession to the throne; therefore, only the children of Alfonso IX and Berenguela acquired the right to inherit the kingdom of León. The marriage to Berenguela also had serious difficulties.

Both marriage partners had suffered bitter experiences in marriage: Alfonso IX of León with Teresa, and Berenguela with Conrad. The marriage to Berenguela, who was a second niece of the king, appeared to be destined to end similarly. Indeed, it did happen in this way. But it is worth noting that none of the church officials present at the assembly gathered on the occasion of the wedding expressed any reservations. Not even the Archbishop of Spain, don Rodrigo Jiménez

---

[20] *De rebus Hispaniae*, VII, 31.
[21] Cf. J. González, *Alfonso IX*, I, pp. 309–311.

de Rada, who, in his celebrated history *De rebus Hispaniae*, does not hint at any canonical impediment, for the blood ties were between the father of the bride and the groom and not between the marriage partners.[22] The hierarchy of the Spanish Church and Queen Leonor were not so concerned with blood ties or the violation of a remote canonical impediment as they were with the peace between Christian kings of the Peninsula.

Alfonso X in his *Estoria de España* attributes the arrangement of the marriage between Alfonso IX of León and Berenguela of Castile to her mother, doña Leonor Plantagenet, who through an astounding logic managed to effect the marriage despite the blood ties. According to don Rodrigo Jiménez de Rada, doña Leonor, who "who was extremely prudent, weighed very carefully the risk of the situation, which could be solved with such a union," and thus avoid more bloodshed. For the queen, the wellbeing of both kingdoms was more important than the observation of moral norms that, whenever necessary, could be easily dispensed with, as was customary. In note 23 below, we provide the reference to a passage that displays her quasi-Machiavellian reasoning that the "good men," of the kingdom in a dramatic meeting with doña Leonor, had laid out in order to justify the marriage, as Alfonso X recounts in chapter 1004 of his *Estoria de España*.[23]

It was a curious and remarkably practical way of reasoning: the marriage was more of a favor to the people than a sin; and even if it was a sin, the "good men" told the queen, then there would be a time for fasting and penitence to ask for forgiveness. Meanwhile, there would be peace in the kingdoms and at the same time there would be a successor on the throne. Later, they said, the pope could forgive the impediment, or they would separate.

But the popes in Rome did not agree. Both Celestine III (1191–1198) as well as the new pope, Innocent III (1198–1216), in 1209, following a bitter dispute, declared the marriage null and void for reasons of blood ties, insisting that "our ruling should prevail over this incestuous union." There was a period of intense negotiations with Rome

---

[22] Alfonso IX was the son of Fernando II of León, who, in turn, was the son of Alfonso VII of León; likewise, Berenguela was the daughter of Alfonso VIII, who was the son of Sancho III of Castile, and he, in turn, the son of Alfonso VII. In other words, Alfonso IX of León and Alfonso VIII of Castile were the grandchildren of emperor Alfonso VII, and therefore, cousins. Berenguela was, therefore, the niece of her husband, Alfonso IX.

[23] *EE*, II, p. 683a.

by the Castilian bishops on behalf of the royal couple. But Innocent III, one of the most rigorous popes in medieval times regarding the observance of canonical law, did not give in a bit to the pressures emanating from the courts of Castile and León or the Castilian prelates who insisted on the dispensation of this irregularity for the sake of preserving the peace and harmony between the two kingdoms. They even agreed to offer the pope the immense sum of 20,000 silver marks and to finance 200 soldiers (crusaders) every year in defense of Christianity if the pope would agree to the marriage dispensation. All was in vain; the pope would not budge. In this case too, as in the case of the marriage to Teresa, to effect the separation, the pope had to excommunicate both partners and place the entire city of León under interdict.

The annulment was a veritable family trauma, because the couple loved each other, and they were also well aware of the political need to safeguard their marriage union, hence their refusal to separate. Indeed, it took them six years to comply with the pope's will. Meanwhile, they had three daughters: Leonor, Constanza, and Berenguela.[24] Finally, in 1201, the first boy, Fernando, was born, and a year later, a second male child, don Alfonso de Molina, who was always his brother's firm collaborator. Besides the eight children mentioned, Alfonso IX de León also sired eleven other children by different women, lovers, and concubines, totaling 19 offspring.[25]

According to the historians and chroniclers of the period, besides his philandering habits, Alfonso IX had an unstable temperament and was good friends with gossipmongers and diviners. Jiménez de Rada, who also had a deep admiration for the king and dedicated several chapters to his military campaigns, also affirmed: "He was a pious, courageous, and benevolent man, but he let himself be carried away by the gossip of schemers";[26] Fr. Juan Gil de Zamora, in his biography of Alfonso IX, also affirmed that the king of León often behaved

---

[24] Leonor, the eldest, died in her childhood on November 12, 1202. Constanza became a nun in the Monastery of Las Huelgas in Burgos, founded by her grandfather, Alfonso VIII, and died there in 1242. Berenguela was married in 1224 to John of Brienne, who for some time was king of Jerusalem (1210–1225) (J. de Rada, *De rebus Hispaniae*, VII, 24).

[25] Cf. J. González, *Alfonso IX*, I, pp. 314–321.

[26] *De rebus* VII, 24, p. 293.

under the influence of wizards and quacks;[27] and his grandson, the Wise King, confirmed the opinion of both chroniclers.[28] Alfonso X, as we will see, inherited from his paternal grandfather many of his good qualities, but also some of his moral flaws.

Having had a previous annulment, Alfonso IX, in the eyes of the pope, now seemed a stubborn repeat offender according to canonical law. He also seemed more reluctant to follow the pope's ruling than his wife. For her part, Berenguela seemed devastated, not so much because of the personal drama that ensued the cruel declaration, but rather from its social consequences. The queen, who had always shown deep concern for the wellbeing of her subjects, seemed worried and unable to explain the lack of understanding and obstinacy of the pope. The social consequences of excommunication were disastrous. A city or a kingdom that incurred interdict was the image of death. The churches were closed for worship, dead people remained at home, unable to receive a proper burial, and there was the bitter awareness of knowing that vis-à-vis the church and society, all her children were illegitimate because of the "nefarious copulation," as their marriage was called in a letter from the pope dated May 25, 1199. Four years later, the pope, in a bull from June 5, 1203, went further, explicitly declaring as "illegitimate the offspring born of that incestuous union, which, according to legitimate constitutions is not to have any rights to [inherit] paternal property."[29] To top it all off, in another bull dated June 20, 1204, Innocent III himself decreed that doña Berenguela should not receive any dowry for she did not merit a prize, but rather a punishment.[30]

The papal sanctions left Berenguela thunderstruck: she was a profoundly religious woman who was completely devoted to the moral

---

[27] "...intervenientibus auriculariorum susurriis et maledicis, Aldephonsus, eorum consilio" (ed. F. Fita, *BRAH*, XIII [1888], pp. 291–295, p. 292).

[28] "Mas porque, assí como dixiemos, este rey don Alffonsso de León se demudaua et se traye de unas cosas en otras que se non semeiauan, et esto uinie por los murmuriadores et losenieros quel murmuriauan a las oreias en poridad yl loseniauan..." (*PCG*, II, p. 677a).

According to the modern historian Antonio Ballesteros:

> The spirited monarch of León, full of qualities, educated, bellicose, a repopulator of conquered lands, and highly concerned with the duties of royalty, was undermined by two harmful inclinations: sensuality and the propensity to believe gossipmongers who would pour into his ears words of adulation or poisonous kinds of discord. (*Alfonso X el Sabio*, Barcelona: El Albir, 1963, p. 5)

[29] In D. Mansilla Reoyo, *La documentación pontificia hasta Inocencio III (965–1216)*, Rome, 1955, pp. 305–306.

[30] Cf. *Crónica de los reyes de Castilla*, ed. by L. Charlo Brea, Cádiz, 1984, p. 51.

education of her children (her eldest would attain the sainthood) and
to the wellbeing of her subjects. The interests of the kingdom and the
expectations of the papacy were irreconcilable. Guaranteeing the legitimate succession for her son must have been the first and foremost
preoccupation of Queen Berenguela; but to achieve that she first had
to change the pope's decision.

Besides the papal decisions, there was a treaty that predated the
decrees issued by Rome which could serve as juridical basis to legitimate
don Fernando's succession. This was the Treaty of Cabreros (March
26, 1206) signed by Alfonso VIII of Castile, father of Berenguela, and
Alfonso IX of León through which not only were Berenguela's possessions made legitimate, but also the succession of Fernando III to the
throne of León, upon the death of his father.[31] The treaty was enthu-
siastically ratified by the nobility, the clergy and the representatives
of cities. Facing the new political realities that ensued the death of
Alfonso VIII (1214) and of his successor, Enrique I (a thirteen year-
old who died tragically in 1217), Berenguela, the legitimate heir to the
throne of Castile, once more brought to the pope's attention the issue
of the right of succession of her son Fernando, according to the Treaty
of Cabreros, which was still in effect. Rome had to reverse its position.
In 1218 Honorius III (1216–1227), who had succeeded Innocent III,
approved what was agreed at the Treaty of Cabreros, making doña
Berenguela's son heir to the throne of León; but not by virtue of the
marriage, which had been annulled, but rather by virtue of "having
adopted him solemnly according to the customs of the kingdom."[32]
The Treaty of Cabreros and the papal bull permanently removed all
canonical impediments and gave Fernando III the uncontested right
to succeed his father as king.

According to don Rodrigo Jiménez de Rada, who had contact with
Queen Berenguela for years, the queen "seeking refuge behind the
walls of modesty above all the women in the world" (De rebus, IX,
chap. V), did not want to have anything else to do with men and,
despite her well-known piety, never forgot the suffering that the pope's
stubbornness had caused her. Deep down, I think, doña Berenguela

---

[31] Cf. J. González, *Alfonso VIII*, III, doc. 782.
[32] In D. Mansilla Reoyo, *La documentación pontificia*, pp. 141–142. Nobody knows
what "customs of the kingdom" the pope was referring to; but for 13th-century Castilians, one motive could justify the other, for this was what they had suggested to Queen
Leonor, as noted above.

came to believe that the annulment sentence was based not so much on religious reasons, as on obscure political motives that lacked the foresight to maintain the peace between the two kingdoms, hence her reluctance to accept the sentence. But in the end, with the goal of preserving the peace, the noble queen did comply and separated from her husband and abandoned the court of León.

Following the separation, in May 1204, doña Berenguela returned to the court of her father in Burgos, leaving her son Fernando, who was about 3 years old, with his father in León. She devoted the rest of her life (42 long years) to works of charity and patronage, and above all to the various political affairs of the kingdom of Castile and, after 1230, also to those of León.

3. *Berenguela, Creator of the Castile-León Union*

In October 1214 the great Alfonso VIII died, leaving his thirteen year-old son Enrique I (1214–1217), as successor to the throne of Castile.[33] Immediately the issue of the king's age came up. It was assumed that his mother, Queen Leonor would become the regent, but she was so ill that she died shortly after her husband. Before dying, she named her daughter Queen Berenguela guardian of the young Enrique and the kingdom of Castile. Doña Berenguela, after having entrusted the custody and upbringing of her brother to a gentleman from Palencia by the name of García Lorenzo, immediately created a regency council made up of herself, the Archbishop of Toledo and the Bishop of Palencia. It was not long before the noblemen appeared before the Council to protest the arrangement and demand that it be one of them who should take care of the young king's upbringing and the regency, specifically proposing don Álvaro Núñez de Lara for this role. Berenguela, in order not to cause a rift with those who held military power and could create problems given an attack by Muslims in the south or the neighboring kingdom of León, agreed to a compromise: she would

---

[33] Alfonso VIII and Leonor had five children: Berenguela, the eldest, Fernando, Blanca (who married Louis VIII of France and was the mother of Saint Louis IX of France), Enrique, and Urraca (who married Alfonso II of Portugal). Fernando, the oldest son and heir, died at age 22, on October 14, 1211, in the mountains of San Vicente, returning from a military campaign against the Muslims. The next male in line of succession was Enrique and, as last resort, the eldest daughter, Berenguela, former queen of León. Blanca and Urraca were already married to kings.

hand over the regular government of the kingdom to count Álvaro Núñez de Lara, who would also be the caretaker and regent; but in all matters of greater importance, she would be the one who would have the last word. Don Alvaro kissed Berenguela's hand as a sign of submission and acceptance of the conditions.[34]

One of Alvaro's first initiatives was to manage to get Enrique I to declare war against the noblemen don Lope Díaz de Haro and don Rodrigo Díaz de los Cameros, representatives of the other great family/clan who, together with the Laras, shared political and economic control of Christian Spain. When doña Berenguela found out, she was furious and deemed the action a violation of the regency agreement. The kingdom's peace depended on a balance of power between these two mighty families, the Laras, with their center of power in the north, and the Haros, with extensive dominion in the recently conquered territories in the south. The king could not hold on to the throne without the support of these two families; but at the same time he had to be careful not to offend the one who was in the opposing camp. Don Álvaro de Lara's ambition led to civil war. During the attack on Autillo de Campos, where doña Berenguela and her followers had sought refuge under the protection of a nobleman, Gonzalo Rodríguez, the young don Enrique, who had been brought by don Álvaro to Palencia, was wounded by a tile hurled from above by another young man, Íñigo de Mendoza, while he played with other young men who were following don Álvaro's army. Enrique I, a thirteen year-old boy heir to the throne of Castile, died a few days later.[35]

Don Álvaro tried to conceal don Enrique's death for a while, going to great lengths to hide the body in the Castle of Tariego. Although it is unclear how, Queen Berenguela found out about the death of her brother, possibly through one of the Meneses, and sending secrete emissaries to León under the pretence of wanting desperately to see her son, had the young don Fernando brought from Toro, where he who was in the company of his father, to Autillo, where she was staying with her supporters. Berenguela's envoys, two prominent figures in

---

[34] Cf. Jiménez de Rada, De rebus, IX, 1; PCG, II, chap. 1025; and J. González, Reinado y diplomas de Fernando III, II, p. 428.
[35] Jiménez de Rada, De rebus, IX, 4. Don Enrique died June 6, 1217 in the palace of the bishop of Palencia, don Tello Téllez de Meneses, who had left the city to join the supporters of doña Berenguela in Autillo. For an essentially similar version of the events according to Alfonso X, see the PCG, II, ch. 1028, pp. 712–713.

Castilian politics (don Lope Díaz de Haro, Lord of Vizcaya, and don Gonzalo Ruiz Girón, butler of both Alfonso VIII and later Enrique I), were very careful not to reveal to Alfonso IX the death of don Enrique. According to the *The Latin Chronicle of the Kings of Castile* [henceforth *CLRC*], "Truly indeed was this a useful pretext, for if it had not been done so prudently, perhaps today the Castilians would not have their own king."[36]

The death of the young don Enrique automatically ceded the throne to his sister Berenguela, as sole successor of Alfonso VIII. As was to be expected, the invasion of Castile by the troops of her ex-husband Alfonso IX of León, happened quickly, supported by don Alvaro de Lara's troops. But the Castilians, who had gathered in great numbers at Valladolid, proclaimed Berenguela as queen. She immediately transferred the crown to her son Fernando, who was present there (July 2, 1217). The *CLRC* narrates the event in these terms:

> One of the people, speaking for all, who were all agreed on this, recognized that the kingdom of Castile belonged by right to Queen Lady Berenguela and that everyone recognized her as Lady and Queen of the kingdom of Castile. Nevertheless, they all unanimously begged her to turn over to her oldest son, Lord Fernando, the kingdom which was hers by proprietary right, because she was a woman and could not bear the burden of governing the kingdom. (*CLRC*, p. 76)

The Castilians did not have to insist much because that was exactly what Berenguela had in mind: "Seeing what she had ardently desired," the *Chronicle* goes on to say, "she willingly consented to their request and granted the kingdom to her son. He was acclaimed by all in a great shout: 'Long live the king!'" (ibid.).

The story of the transfer of the crown of Castile from doña Berenguela to her son is told in very similar terms by don Rodrigo Jiménez de Rada, who includes more details because he happened to be present at the event (*De rebus*, IV, 5). Alfonso X, on the contrary, would pay close attention to the historical documentation supporting that transfer of power, seeking to justify the legitimacy of his grandmother's, his father's, and thus his own succession.[37]

---

[36] *The Latin Chronicle of the Kings of Castile,* translated with an Introduction and notes by Joseph F. O'Callaghan, Tempe, Arizona Studies: Arizona Center for Medieval and Renaissance Studies, 2002, chap. 33, p. 74.

[37] (*PCG*, II, chap. 1029, p. 713b).

Years later, after the death of his father, Alfonso IX of León (Villa-nueva de Sarria, Badajoz, September 24, 1230), other historical and family circumstances led Fernando to also acquire the throne of León. As we said, his father, before marrying Berenguela, had been mar-ried to Teresa of Portugal, with whom he had three children, a boy who died young (1214), and two girls, Sancha and Dulce. Following their separation in 1195, Queen Teresa returned to Portugal with her younger children, Fernando and Dulce, while the first-born, doña San-cha, remained in León with her father. Contrary to what was customary in Castile, in León females were not allowed accession to the throne, and despite all of Alfonso IX's efforts to place his daughter Sancha upon the throne, even by attempting to marry her to a crownless king such as John of Brienne, King of Jerusalem (see note 22 above), he did not succeed, being blocked by doña Berenguela's actions.

And so it came to be that in the spring of 1224, when John of Bri-enne was traveling through Castile on a pilgrimage to Santiago de Compostela, he took a detour to Toledo in order to visit the young king of Castile, don Fernando. He then had talks with Queen Beren-guela, who convinced him to marry one of her daughters, who was also named Berenguela. Thus, Berenguela, who always looked after her first-born's interests, was able to ensure that the potential marriage of John of Brienne to Sancha, would not take place and thwart the suc-cession of Fernando to the throne of León after the death of Alfonso IX. On his way back from Santiago, John of Brienne passed through Burgos once more, where he married princess Berenguela. The mother and brother of the bride accompanied the couple to Logroño, where, with many gifts, they bid farewell to them.

As last resort, Alfonso IX of León declared his daughters Sancha and Dulce as heirs; but the people of León who had recognized Fernando in 1206, following the death of Alfonso IX (September 24, 1230), refused to accept them. Besides the rejection of Sancha and Dulce on the part of the people of León, there was a real agreement between the sisters and Fernando, negotiated once more by his mother in a meeting at Valencia de don Juan, a city close to León, together with doña Teresa and her two daughters, who at the time were already 36 and 38 years old, respectively. The agreement at Valencia de don Juan, according to which Sancha and Dulce renounced the throne of León in favor of their half-brother don Fernando, is known as "the pact of the moth-ers." The agreement was signed at Benavente on December 11, 1230, and stipulated that Fernando would pay a yearly stipend of 30,000 maravedís for life to each of his half-sisters, and would grant several castles as compensation for relinquishing their rights to the throne.

Hence, the son of Alfonso IX and Berenguela, thanks to his mother's political skill and diplomatic tact, acceded to the throne of León (October 7, 1230), instead of his half-sisters, uniting forever the crowns of León and Castile, and, as Alfonso X writes in his *Estoria*: "and from then on this king Fernando was called 'king of Castile and León,' the two kingdoms he had legitimately inherited from his father and his mother…thus they were united starting from that moment in this king don Fernando and from his time onward, they were always together."[38]

4. *His Parents: Fernando and Beatriz*

The future conqueror of Seville had been born in the happy times of Alfonso IX and Berenguela, when the specter of separation did not haunt the Castilian court, when the bold Berenguela used to accompany her husband on his military campaigns against the Muslims. In fact, don Fernando was born during a trip, on June 24, 1201, on the feast of St. John, on a mountain (hence his nicknames "Montano" or "Montesino"), where the monastery of Valparaíso was later built, between Salamanca and Zamora.[39] Berenguela did not allow her son to be breastfed by nurses, but rather, as her grandson don Alfonso recounts, she "gave him her milk and nursed him very sweetly" (*PCG*, II, p. 732). But later her duties as queen forced her to leave her son in Galicia, in the hands of nurses and caretakers. The child, nonetheless, was growing up weak and sickly, so that he had to be taken to Burgos, where he lived in the Monastery of Las Huelgas and was looked after by his grandfather, Alfonso VIII, founder of the monastery, and by his mother. This detail is known thanks to his famous son, Alfonso X, who in his *Cantiga* 221, describes how his father was miraculously cured

---

[38] Cf. *PCG*, II, chap. 1039, p. 723b. Cf. J. González, *Reinado y diplomas de Fernando III*, II, doc. 272.

[39] "Hic Fernandus rex *montanus* dictus est, quia in monte quodam inter Zamoram et Salmanticam natus fuit" (Gil de Zamora, "Biografías de San Fernando y de Alfonso el Sabio," ed. F. Fita, *BRAH*, V [1885], pp. 308–328, p. 308). Cf. Ballesteros, *Alfonso X*, p. 12; J. González, *Reinado y diplomas de Fernando III*, I, pp. 62–63; C. Pescador del Hoyo, "Cuándo y dónde nació Fernando III, el Santo," *RABM*, 73 (1966), pp. 499–553; and G. Martínez Díez, *Fernando III, 1217–1252*, Palencia: Editorial La Olmeda, 1993.

from a serious bowel illness by the Virgin of Oña: "For he could not sleep at all nor eat the slightest thing, and many large worms came out of him, for death had already conquered his life without much struggle" (lines 43–47, p. 265). In the same *cantiga*, we are told that after his transfer from Galicia to Burgos, Fernando remained under the care of his grandfather ("who loved him dearly"), and of his grandmother, Queen Leonor, "daughter of the king of England," and of his mother ("who took much delight in him").

We do not know much about Fernando III's childhood nor about the education he received, which is alluded to in primitive sources: "[...] King Fernando ruled his kingdom in peace and tranquility, inspired in all by the noble queen (Berenguela), who raised her son with so much care that [he] held the reins of the kingdom and country with peace and moderation until the twenty-fifth year of his reign, following the example of his grandfather, the noble Alfonso [VIII]," writes D. Rodrigo.[40] Fr. Gil de Zamora only says: "He always had with him very prudent Catholic gentlemen to whom both he and his mother always entrusted all decisions."[41] Obviously, Fr. Gil's observation and many similar ones by other early biographers tend to present don Fernando with the aura of sainthood that surrounded him during his life. But his son left us an image of an ideal king, the perfect Christian knight, and an enlightened prince.[42]

When everything collapsed due to her marriage separation and the death of her father (October 5, 1214), Berenguela renounced the throne of Castile in favor of her son Fernando, still a young 18 year-old. As regent of the Castilian crown, she dedicated herself to piously educating her son in the same way that her sister Blanca was doing with her son Louis IX of France (Saint Louis, 1226–1270). Don Rodrigo, who knew Queen Berenguela well, left us the best testimony of the religious education she gave her son:

> For this noble Queen Berenguela raised her son in such good behavior that the noble queen, without forgetting any virtue or any grace, inculcated in his heart good intentions, like milk and honey sprinkled with

[40] *De rebus*, IX, 10, p. 341.

[41] "Habebat secum prudentissimos catholicos viros quibus tam ipse quam mater totum suum consilium commitebant" ("Biografías," ed. F. Fita, in *BRAH*, V (1885) p. 310).

[42] On his father's upbringing, see Alfonso X in the *PCG*, II, ch. 1047, esp. pp. 734–735; and the impressive praise of his father in the *Setenario*.

grace, and always nursed him with her breast full of virtues, and even when he was a man and had gained the strength of age, his mother never failed to carefully instruct him in the things that are pleasing to God and men, because she never instilled in him women's concerns but, rather, those of greatness. (*De rebus*, IX, 17, pp. 351–352)

This religious education continued while doña Berenguela was alive; but it was not merely spiritual, for after having placed him at the head of two kingdoms, she helped him with all the political and religious campaigns he is known for, zealously protecting him and tirelessly defending the interests of the kingdom. Fernando corresponded to her devotion by granting her queenly honors, putting her name next to his in all important documents issued by his chancellery, as if they were co-rulers. Later, Berenguela would show the same affection and diligence for her beloved grandson Alfonso as she had done for her son.

After placing his son on the throne of Castile, the first major family and political concern of Berenguela was to find him a wife. The future of kingdoms in the Middle Ages often depended on the right or wrong marriage choice. But Berenguela, an obliging mother, also had in mind the spiritual and Christian life of her son, knowing that marriage would sublimate and sanctify the sexual needs of the young prince, who, like his cousin Louis of France, was destined to become a saint: "...because it was improper of such a great prince like don Fernando, king of Castile, to live a disorderly life and without being married to a fine lady, Queen Berenguela, his mother, who always wanted to save him from immoral and inconvenient situations, she thought of how to marry off the said Fernando, her son, and married him to Lady Beatrice...".[43]

Given the painful personal background described above, Berenguela exercised great caution in the selection of the bride. At the time in Spain, the situation regarding the availability of marriageable women was such that practically all Spanish princesses (and many British and French ones too) were related by blood. Berenguela must have thought of her own experience, and decided the best thing to do was to find a

---

[43] *PCG*, II, p. 718a. Eighteen years later, when don Fernando was already thirty-six years old, had six children, and was a widower, his mother still looked after his virtue. According to don Rodrigo, doña Berenguela began to look again for a wife for him for the same reasons: "And so that the virtue of the king would not be undermined with illicit relations, his mother, the noble queen, thought of giving him as a wife a noble maiden of noble stock called Juana, great-granddaughter of the illustrious king of France" (*De rebus*, IX, XVIII, p. 352). Cf. *PCG*, II, p. 735a–b.

bride that could not possibly be related by blood. It is not clear what led her to choose, among the various European dynasties, the house of Swabia, with whom she herself had not had a very positive experience. But given the annulment of her marriage, there is a distinct possibility that the choice was a calculated protest against the pope Innocent III, declared enemy of Ghibelline Hohenstaufens, and who had brought about the end of her marriage.[44]

The bride chosen was Elizabeth (or Eliza) of Swabia, known in Castilian historiography as Beatriz, the fourth daughter of Philip of Swabia, son of Frederick I Barbarossa, and therefore cousin of the last emperor of the Holy Roman Germanic Empire, Frederick II, from the illustrious family of the Hohenstaufens. The mother of Beatriz was the princess Irene, sister of the emperor of Byzantium, Alexis IV (or Isaac Angelos, 1185–1204). Beatriz was thus related to the two most prominent Christian dynasties of East and West.

According to don Rodrigo Jiménez de Rada: "[Beatriz] was a very noble German maiden, very beautiful and honest in her habits" (*De rebus*, IX, 10). She had been born in 1198, thus she was three years younger than Fernando, born in 1201.[45] Historians still wonder how Berenguela found out about Beatriz's virtues, and how she managed to contact the imperial court of Frederick II, ask for her hand and obtain it. But we know today that the firm purpose of the mother of the young king took over such a crucial decision and the choice of wife for her first born.[46]

It is worth stopping here to review the genealogy of princess Beatriz, because it will allow us to understand the motives that led Berenguela to choose her, particularly since it displays the multiple reasons that her grandson, Alfonso X had to aspire to the Roman Germanic Empire. Elizabeth-Beatriz, was the daughter of Philip of Swabia and Irene (Maria) Angelos of Byzantium. Her father, Philip, King of the Romans, was

---

[44] This is the opinion of, among others, C. Segura Graino, "Semblanza humana de Alfonso el Sabio," in *Alfonso X el Sabio, vida, obra y época*, Actas del Congreso Internacional, I, Madrid: Sociedad Española de Estudios Medievales, 1989, pp. 11–29, 12.

[45] Cf. A. Ballesteros, *Alfonso X*, p. 39. C. Socarrás believes, on the contrary, that Beatriz was a year younger than Fernando, having been born in 1202 (*Alfonso X of Castile: A Study on Imperialistic Frustration*, Barcelona: Ediciones Hispam, 1984, p. 102, note 32).

[46] According to J. González, an important role may have been played by doña Berenguela's sister, doña Blanca, queen of France, and perhaps even by the empress Constanza, wife of Frederick II, in whose court the young princess was growing up (*Reinado y diplomas de Fernando III*, I, p. 97).

the son of the German Frederick I Barbarossa, who had obtained the crown fighting the candidacy of Otto I of Brunswick, who belonged to the rival family and was the pope's favorite candidate. Her mother, Irene, was the daughter of Isaac II Angelos, emperor of Byzantium, and Irene Commena, daughter of Andronicus I and Theodora Commena, daughter of John Commenus. Irene was also the sister of Isaac, or Alexis, Angelos IV, who for some time was emperor of Constantinople. Therefore, princess Beatriz was the granddaughter of two emperors, Frederick I, from the West, and Isaac Angelos, from the East. She was also the niece of two emperors: Henry VI of Germany and Alexis Angelos of Constantinople; and also first cousin of the emperor Frederick II of Sicily, in whose court she resided when the Castilian delegation arrived to ask for her hand on behalf of Queen Berenguela (*De rebus*, IX, 10).

In 1218 doña Berenguela sent a delegation to the Empire, headed by the bishop of Burgos don Mauricio, to negotiate with Frederick II the marriage of his cousin Beatriz to the heir of Castile. Queen Berenguela was confident she would obtain the hand of the princess, since she knew that Frederick II, married to the princess Constanza de Aragón, Berenguela's cousin, was very anxious to unite the house of Swabia to the throne of Castile. In fact, at the end of November 1219, the young Princess Beatriz arrived in Burgos to marry the heir to the throne of Castile. For his part, don Fernando was always thankful to his "sweetest" mother for her wise choice.

In light of this genealogical background, we can begin to see why Alfonso X, a professional historian who was located at the historical juncture of the *Great Interregnum*, held on to his maternal lineage in order to obtain the two other imperial crowns of the East and West. The third one, the Hispanic-Visigoth, already belonged to him. If his mother was the umbilical cord that tied him to the origins of royalty and empire, his paternal grandmother had tied the cord that gave natural and political life to him as well as to his father, paternal uncles and brothers, for whom Berenguela found a privileged niche in the various houses of peninsular society at the end of the 13th century.[47]

---

[47] She also took care of the upbringing of her two grandchildren, Sancho and Felipe; those she could not get a crown for, she managed to place in high Church offices: don Sancho was elected bishop of Toledo and don Felipe, of Seville. Both young children were entrusted to one of the most learned men of Spain in the 13th century, the Archbishop of Toledo, don Rodrigo Jiménez de Rada, who prepared them

As Rodrigo Jiménez de Rada writes, she was the only "strong woman" who "is rightly admired by our age, because neither the present one or that of our parents found a similar one" (*De rebus*, IX, XVII, p. 352). Doña Berenguela died on November 8, 1246.[48]

When don Mauricio, Bishop of Burgos, joined Fernando and Beatriz in holy matrimony on November 30, 1219, Beatriz was, according to don Rodrigo Jiménez de Rada who knew her for more than 16 years, a beautiful German blonde, small and very refined, with a good upbringing, wise and honest. The wedding scene, according to many scholars, is recorded in a sculpture in the cloister of the Burgos cathedral where don Fernando is shown giving doña Beatriz the wedding ring, while Beatriz, smiling, delicately lifts her tunic with the right hand.[49] Despite don Rodrigo's praise, modern historians have scrutinized the young princess's background. According to Ballesteros, before her arrival in Spain, Beatriz had already been engaged twice, first to a nephew of pope Innocent III, the great enemy of the Staufens; and then to Count Otto of Wittelsbach, the same nobleman who had been the assassin of her father. When her parents died, Beatriz lived with Otto IV of Brunswick, his father's rival who was married to her older sister, also called Beatriz. Could the wise doña Berenguela have known about these events in the past of her future daughter-in-law?

Sixteen years after the lavish wedding in the Burgos cathedral and after having ten children, this apparently everlasting beauty came to an end. Doña Beatriz of Swabia was 37 years old when death surprised her at Toro, on November 5, 1235.[50] Her body was taken to the Mon-

---

for the high ecclesiastical posts they were destined to hold. Later, Queen Berenguela's two grandsons were sent to the most prestigious European university, the University of Paris, where their teachers included Saint Albert the Great; they were probably schoolmates of Saint Thomas Aquinas's.

[48] The textile gallery at the Monasterio de las Huelgas, where she is buried, preserves the lavish Moorish pillow placed under her head when she was shrouded for burial. The pillow bears an inscription in Arabic Kufic script that reads: "There is no other God but Allah." It is a remarkable epitaph sealing the grave of a deeply Christian queen, the mother of a holy king and the daughter of the vanquisher of the followers of Allah in the battle of Las Navas de Tolosa.

[49] The art historian R. Cómez Ramos believes however that it is Alfonso X and his wife, doña Violante (*Las empresas artísticas de Alfonso X el Sabio*, Sevilla, 1979).

[50] "…en la era de mill e dozientos et setenta et tres annos, et andaua el anno de la Encarnación del Sennor en mill e dozientos et treynta et cinco. Et ese anno morió la reyna donna Beatriz en la uilla de Toro, et adoxiéronla al monesterio de las Huelgas de Burgos a enterrar; et enterráronla realmente et en real onra, çerca del rey don Enrrique" (*PCG*, ch. 1045a). Cf. J. de Rada, *De rebus*, IX, 15.

asterio de las Huelgas and was buried very near to the grave of don Enrique I, Queen Berenguela's brother, who died from a blow to the head with a tile. Forty years later, in 1281, according to the anonymous chronicle of Silos, Alfonso X had the uncorrupted remains of his mother transferred to Seville, to be buried near her husband, don Fernando III.[51]

When doña Beatriz died, the young prince Alfonso was only fourteen years old, and because he had been raised away from the court for the most part, he did not have a great chance to live in touch with his mother. However, the memory of that noble woman, whose blood ran in his veins, would be a constant point of reference throughout his life. The presence of Beatriz, an unassuming woman who spent her entire life dedicated to her husband and children, had great significance for the history of relations between the kingdom of Castile and the Empire, specifically with Germany. Due to her presence at the Castilian court, political leaders in the peninsula became increasingly aware of their dependency on Christian Europe and vice versa.

Beatriz left behind eight children; the eldest, Alfonso, was barely fourteen, and the youngest, don Manuel, only one. Despite don Fernando's dedication to raising his children, the lack of a loving mother must have left them with a profound trauma. Alfonso, of course,

---

A great poet of the court, the Galician Pero da Ponte, wrote a moving "planctus" for doña Beatriz. Cf. Pero da Ponte, *Poesie*, ed. S. Panunzio, *Biblioteca di Filologia Romanza*, X, Bari: Adriatica Editrice, 1967.

[51] Cf. D.W. Lomax, "Una crónica inédita de Silos," in *Homenaje a Fr. Justo Pérez de Urbel*, I, Madrid, 1976, p. 332. *Cantiga* 292 describes the transfer of the remains of Queen Beatriz to Seville at Alfonso's request, and the construction of his parents' mausoleum. In 1948, when the medical/legal examination of Alfonso X's remains was carried out, his mother's remains were also examined. According to the report, the body appeared perfectly preserved, like a mummy. Finger- and toenails were admirably well preserved, "with the fingernails trimmed at an angle…as a notable particularity, we can point to the fact that the teeth were intact and preserved the original shine of the dentine, except for the two front teeth—one lower and one upper—which were found in the casket. The teeth are very small, short and even" (J. Delgado Roig, "Examen médico legal de unos restos históricos: los cadáveres de Alfonso X el Sabio y Doña Beatriz de Suabia," *AH*, 9, 1948, pp. 139–140). According to Dr. Delgado's calculations, doña Beatriz must have been 1.54 meters tall. "The mother of the Learned King was therefore quite short without being overly small." In her casket was found, in perfect skeletal form, the round head of a bird with a curved beak. According to Dr. Delgado, "The remains of this bird belong to a species similar to that of the goldfinch of Spain" (p. 140). Obviously, the queen, following the customs of the period, was buried with her favorite pet, the same as her son Alfonso. These findings reveal that doña Beatriz always had an elegant and delicate figure, resembling her portrayal in the sculpture in the Burgos cathedral mentioned above.

seems to have missed her much, for he remembers her frequently in his writings. Although she was outshined in politics by her mother-in-law, Queen Berenguela, who also outlived her, when it came to personal qualities, Alfonso inherited much from his mother. Besides his good looks, Alfonso inherited his mother's tenacity, or as some say, her Germanic stubbornness; also a passion for culture and the arts, particularly music, as well as an endless intellectual curiosity with no precedent among peninsular rulers. These were the qualities that would allow him to reach cultural horizons never before achieved in any European court. Likewise, he made knowledge the highest goal of any human being. The legacy of Beatriz of Swabia to Castile was indeed the best thing the imperial court could offer: the scientific and cultural renaissance of Frederick II's court, where she had been raised in contact with Muslim and Jewish scientists. These ideals would go on to inspire her son as well. Personally, Alfonso was convinced he had inherited from his mother all that made him into Alfonso X, that is, her imperial royalty, for, through her, he had become a successor to the first king of the world, the mythical Nimrod, from whom, according to genealogies traced in the *General Estoria*, Alfonso believed he was descended.

Besides mythical/biblical genealogies, Alfonso X never forgot the debt he owed to his parents, particularly the one that allowed him to legitimately aspire to the most coveted crown of the world. In the *Setenario*, which, according to the modern editor of the work "is indeed the most personal of all the works attributed to Alfonso the Learned," and the only one explicitly quoted in his last will, when singing the praises of his father, he remembers the favors he received as follows "The first is that he made us a man; because God wanted him to be our father and that through him we would come to this world. The second, that he made us in a noble place and with a woman of great lineage, to whom God granted many graces, for he wanted her to be good in all the good qualities that a woman could have."[52] (As we will see, a very different attitude from that of his son, Sancho!)

Two years after the death of doña Beatriz, in November 1237, Fernando III was married again at Burgos to Juana of Ponthieu, heiress to the County of Ponthieu. As in the first marriage, the matchmaker

---

[52] *Setenario*, ed. K.H. Vanderford, Buenos Aires: Instituto de Filología, 1945, reprint, Barcelona: Editorial Crítica, 1984, p. 10.

and negotiator was his mother, Queen Berenguela, perhaps aided by her sister doña Blanca, queen of France. In the selection of the second wife, doña Berenguela explicitly excluded peninsular princesses for the purpose of, once more, avoiding blood ties; still, the candidate also had a remote relation to Fernando. The two were descended from Alfonso VII, Fernando's great-grandfather and Juana's great-great-grandfather. Fernando was 35 and Juana was a bit younger. He had five children with her: Fernando, Leonor, Luis, Simón, and Juan. When don Fernando was married again, Alfonso was already sixteen years old, and it appears that he had little contact with his stepmother. The few times he mentions her in his *Estoria de España* reveal a bit of distance and detachment, although he always remained duly respectful.[53]

From his childhood, Alfonso had been educated by caretakers and experts in the arts of war and diplomacy. But perhaps the greatest influence was his father, who made him participate in the most important decisions from a tender age. In the same passage of the *Setenario* quoted above, he reminds us how thankful he was to his father for the trust placed in him despite his youth. We know that when Alfonso was 19, don Fernando gave him a house and granted him revenue from several cities (León, Salamanca, Alba de Tormes, and others in Castile, and Écija in Andalucía) that the prince could use to have a certain independence and that allowed him to have his own court, frequented by childhood friends such as Nuño González de Lara and the children of his caretaker, don García Fernández de Villamayor.[54]

There were also other gifts: "The third blessing we received was that he loved us very much and trusted me and welcomed me in his counsel and in his conversations, although our age was not very advanced

---

[53] One of the few known instances of contact between Alfonso and his stepmother reveal much about the strained relationship between them. When Fernando III ceded some land property to doña Juana, Alfonso was opposed to the grant following a juridical principle which would later become important for his concept of the power of the king. According to that principle, a king could not make use of conquered territories as he did of his horse or falcon, since they belonged to the State, and were therefore inalienable. The concessions made to doña Juana could one day be excluded from Alfonso's kingdom, hence his opposition to this transaction. Don Fernando agreed that his son was right. But in his deathbed, Fernando III, as Alfonso himself writes in his *Estoria de España*: "Et rogól [a don Alfonso] por la reyna que la touiese por madre et que la onrrase et la mantouiese siempre en su onra commo a reyna conuiene..." (*PCG*, II, p. 772). Alfonso faithfully respected his father's last will. Cf. A. Pérez Algar, *Alfonso X, El Sabio. Biografía*, Madrid, 1997, pp. 70–78.

[54] Cf. A. Ballesteros, "Burgos y la rebelión del infante don Sancho," *BRAH*, CXIX (1946), 98; and *Alfonso X*, pp. 76–84.

that we would be able to give him the advice that matched his nobility and his deeds."[55] According to some critics,[56] these words, written in hindsight, in a period of maturity and when he was probably already dealing with the devastating consequences of the rebellion of his son don Sancho, seem particularly significant, especially in light of the following passage:

> The fourth blessing was that he honored me in so many ways, more than any king of Spain had ever honored a son. The fifth was that he granted me many favors with which I could serve him, which is the kind of grace a lord bestows on a vassal, so that he may serve him.... The sixth was that he counseled me very ably, showing me how to be good and worthy of his blessings. Likewise, he made me understand things so that I would not fall into error, in such a way that my reputation would be undermined or harmed. The seventh blessing was that he pardoned me when I committed any errors against him or against any other. (*Set.* p. 10)

It is therefore clear that Alfonso admired his father deeply, and his father, for his part, always had a close relationship with him, placing full trust in him, consulting him in the most serious matters of state.

Despite this clear sign of gratitude on the part of the Learned King for the help and care of his father in his apprenticeship in government, some modern scholars argue that Alfonso was introverted and immature throughout his life precisely because of a lack of contact with a father figure, who, for reasons of state and because of the customs followed in the upbringing of princes in Castilian courts, was far from his son during the early childhood years when he most needed his physical presence.[57] Don Fernando, given his occupations, could not always be by his son's side during his childhood. But, of the few records that remain, it cannot be said that he simply saw him every now and then; everything seems to point to the fact that don Fernando took great care in the upbringing of his heir from his early childhood.

---

[55] *Setenario*, p. 10. In the same paragraph, when speaking of the favors received from his father, Alfonso recalls how the holy king had a positive influence on his formative years.

[56] J.R. Craddock, "El *Setenario*: última e inconclusa refundición alfonsina de la primera *Partida*," *AHDE*, 56 (1986), pp. 441–466.

[57] "There was very little contact between these two figures—the prince and the holy king—in the period in which we most need our father to form our personality: more or less, from age 4 to age 10 [...] When Alfonso was able to interact more frequently with his father, it was already too late for that to leave an indelible mark on his temperament." (F. Torres González, "Rasgos médico-psicológicos de Alfonso el Sabio," pp. 119–120)

In 1242 Fernando named Alfonso *alférez real* (royal standardbearer), a position with direct responsibility in the process of reconquering the territories that were still under Muslim control in the peninsula. Thus, in 1243, when during an illness that kept don Fernando in Burgos, he entrusted Alfonso with the conquest of Murcia, the command must not have come as a surprise to the young prince. Alfonso did not only plan with great strategic ability the siege that led to conquest via negotiations instead of war, but he also achieved a peace treaty with the vanquished, whereby the entire structure of the Muslim state was preserved in exchange for submission and obedience to the king of Castile, a condition that matched Fernando's policies during the Reconquest.[58]

The debt that Alfonso had acquired with his father as well as the admiration he professed for him went far beyond what we could call the limits of a prince's upbringing, because they extended to all aspects of his personality and human endeavors. Alfonso speaks of the enlightened environment of Fernando's court, and in particular of his father as the incarnation of the perfect Christian knight, the prudent and discreet courtier, and the humanist prince, supporter of artists and concerned about all of the most refined manifestations of culture of his time, such as sports, board games and music:

> And besides all of this, he was skillful at all the skills a good knight should possess, because he was skilled at throwing the *bohordo* and the lance and taking up arms and being well-armed and handsomely so. He knew well the art of hunting all game, as well as playing board games and chess and other good and varied table games; he liked the singing of men and he himself knew how to sing; likewise, he liked courtly troubadours and singers and jongleurs who could play instruments well; he liked all this very much and he was a discriminating connoisseur in this matter. (*Set.*, p. 13)[59]

Scholars who study the diplomas of Alfonso's chancellery, as well as the forewords to his most important works, indicate that when he mentions "family," in the forewords he is referring to don Fernando

---

[58] Speaking of the conquests of his father in the *Setenario*, Alfonso took pride in his role in the conquest of Murcia: "Por ssu linaie ganó el rregno de Murcia, e sennaladamiente por ssu fijo el mayor don Alfonso" (p. 15).

[59] In his father's praise, Alfonso did not forget to note his religiosity, both in the *PCG* (*Primera Crónica General*, II, chaps. 1132–1133, pp. 722–723, and see below our chap. 3, pp. 97–98) and in the *Cantigas* (Cf. *Cantiga* 292).

and doña Beatriz; while in the diplomas "family," means his wife and children. There are several theories explaining this particularity.[60] In any event, it is clear that when Alfonso traced his genealogy in the frontispiece of the works he deemed everlasting, he associated his parents with the execution of his cultural project, and naming them in such a context was an act of gratitude for the care they took in his education; he also expressed his debt to them for giving him life both physically and spiritually.

---

[60] Cf. A. Cárdenas, "Alfonso's *Scriptorium* and Chancery: the Role of the Prologue in Bonding the *Translatio Studii* to the *Translatio Potestatis*," in *Emperor of Culture*, p. 100.

CHAPTER TWO

A PRINCE'S EDUCATION

1. *Teachers and Books*

The education of the most learned king of the Middle Ages has been a topic that has intrigued all Alfonso X scholars. Where, when, and how he acquired the vast knowledge that allowed him to write and sponsor works that cover all areas of knowledge, from stones to stars, his *Lapidarios* (*Lapidaries,* or *Books About Stones*) and his *Libros del saber de Astronomía* (*Books of the Wisdom of Astronomy*), still surprise us nowadays. Regardless of the help he received from collaborators, there still was a mind that conceived and executed everything, and this exceptional mind must have had, besides a natural gift, a superior education.

Between 1231, when Alfonso turned ten and participated in the "Jerez cavalcade" against the Moors, which we will discuss at the end of this chapter, and the year 1234, when, at the age of only 14 the possibility of marrying him to Blanche of Champagne emerged, we know practically nothing about the young prince. Apparently these were the years when he acquired his solid humanistic education, focusing on the liberal arts, the basis of education in the Middle Ages and the goal set by his parents, tutors and teachers from a young age. According to the early testimony of Fr. Gil de Zamora, who frequented the court of Alfonso X for many years, and perhaps his father's too, "after the delightful years of childhood, as was customary for the children of kings, the young prince began to show from his teenage years a sharp wit, a penchant for studying, and an extraordinary memory".[1]

His education must have speeded up during those obscure four years of his adolescence, when his father, due to ill health, began to increasingly entrust him with more responsibilities in the government of the kingdom. But we know precious little about the teachers who imparted this humanistic education. In hindsight and according to

---

[1] In F. Fita, "Biografías de San Fernando y de Alfonso X por Gil de Zamora," *BRAH*, V (1885), p. 319.

testimonies of prominent literary figures who frequented the court of Fernando III, such as the master Roldán, Pedro Gallego, Fernando Martínez de Zamora, Jofré de Loaísa and the bishop don Remondo de Losana, to quote just a few law specialists, the teachers were indeed great experts in the liberal arts, and one of them must have been in charge of prince Alfonso's education.[2] There's speculation that others must also have been involved in his education, for instance, the famous Italian jurist, Jacobo de la Junta (d. 1294), brought to the court for that purpose. E.N. van Kleffens argues this is the case, but it seems this could not have happened before 1257, when his presence in Spain is first recorded.[3]

In any event, what is certain is that the court of his father was an educated and refined environment. Alfonso and his siblings, and later his own children, grew up in a privileged, cosmopolitan and international environment, under the care of a German mother educated in the court of Frederick II, surrounded by counselors arrived from the Empire and a father who identified with troubadours and intellectuals from all corners of Europe as well as Muslim philosophers and scientists and Jewish doctors. No records of his teachers remain, but there is information about prominent intellectual figures at the court of his father who were present at the court during Alfonso's formative years. Between the years 1210 and 1217 the great Scotsman Michael Scot settled in Toledo. He translated the works of Aristotle from the Arabic. The founding of the *studium generale* at Palencia by his great-grandfather attracted scholars of all branches of knowledge, some eager to learn the sciences and philosophy preserved by Spanish Arab and Jewish scholars. Between 1221 and 1230 the English philosopher and theologian Odo of Cheriton resided in the city as teacher in the *studium*. He had a great impact on Castilian literature.[4] The Palencia *studium* also hosted as teachers many Italian jurists, among whom

---

[2] Brief monographs with a critical bibliography on each can be consulted in R.A. MacDonald, ed., *Espéculo. Texto jurídico atribuido al Rey de Castilla Don Alfonso X, el Sabio*, Madison, 1990, Appendix 5, pp. 481–504. J.M. Nieto Soria, *Iglesia y poder real en Castilla. El episcopado (1250–1350)*, Madrid, 1988, *passim*.

[3] E.N. van Kleffens, *Hispanic Law until the End of the Middle Ages*, Edinburgh: Edinburgh University, 1968, p. 149 and pp. 178–179; Cf. R.A. MacDonald, ed., *Espéculo*, pp. 486–488, no. 63.

[4] Cf. A.C. Friend, "Master Odo of Cheriton," *Speculum*, XXIII, 4 (1948), pp. 641–658; and A. Rucquoi, "La double vie du *studium* de Palencia," in *Homenaje a Antonio García y García, Studia Gratiana*, XXIX (1998), pp. 723–748.

was Geraldo Lombardo, who was named archdeacon of the church of Palencia and *magister* Lanfranco, who also received a church position in the cathedral.[5] But perhaps the most celebrated of the Italians that Alfonso VIII gathered at Palencia, according to D. Rodrigo Jiménez de Rada, was Ugolino da Sasso, a native of Cremona, who had studied at Bologna and later taught at Montpellier. As has been recently shown, some of the juridical texts by Ugolino written towards 1190 clearly reveal that he was one of the teachers at the *studium* at Palencia.[6] The Italian teachers brought to Castile the disciplines they had most expertise in, such as the *trivium* and the study of Roman law. Palencia was also well known for the study of grammar, which included a study of the parts of discourse and of *auctores*, which provided the student with a training in reading and understanding the classics and the Bible.[7]

It is true that, in contrast to his two brothers, don Felipe and don Enrique, who were sent to the University of Paris, Alfonso X's humanistic training seems somewhat paradoxical. The most religious king of medieval Spain and one who achieved sainthood, Fernando III, did not want his first-born to be educated in a monastery nor under the tutelage of a well-known prelate nor even under the great teachers of the school of arts or Parisian scholasticism. Alfonso's education was entrusted to lay figures, more known for their military than literary virtues. In the Middle Ages, however, to raise and educate a future king meant, above all, to train a warrior and a perfect Christian knight. This should be kept in mind when judging the nature of Alfonso's cultural revolution, which was essentially lay.

In a period when the Castilian court was a traveling one, it is difficult to know where exactly Alfonso was educated. A vague testimony by Saint Albert the Great in his treatise *De mineralibus* indicates that he coincided in Paris with the "son of the king of Castile"; but we do not know whether he is referring to Alfonso X or his brother Felipe, who certainly spent time in Paris at the time. At first sight, it seems that Saint Albert's words might refer to Alfonso, but it is somewhat difficult to match Albert's remark with Alfonso's chronology, which

---

[5] Cf. T. Abajo Martín, T.: *Documentación de la catedral de Palencia* (1035–1247), Palencia, 1986, nos. 105 and 151; F.J. Hernández, *Los cartularios de Toledo. Catálogo documental*, Madrid: Fundación Ramón Areces, 1985, nos. 60–61, pp. 63–64.

[6] Cf. D. Maffei, "Fra Cremona, Montpellier e Palencia nel secolo XII: Ricerche su Ugolino da Sesso," *Revista Española de Derecho Canónico*, 47 (1990), 34–41.

[7] Cf. F. Rico, "La Clerecía del Mester," *Hispanic Review*, 53, 1 (1985), pp. 1–23.

is well-known and leaves little room for a lengthy absence from Castile in that decade.[8]

2. Curriculum Artium: *The Liberal Arts*

We are indebted to Alfonso X for what we could call the description of the *curriculum* that all students had to go through in the Middle Ages. Commenting in his *General Estoria* on the didactic content of a famous rhetoric manual entitled *Summa de la Rectorica*, he describes the process of learning in great detail.[9]

According to the popular manual, the training of a man of letters in the Middle Ages began with the study of the seven liberal arts. This course of study, however, was not accessible to all; it was a privilege of the high social classes and of those who aspired to high ecclesiastical office. In another passage of his *General Estoria*, commenting on the Roman Christian philosopher Boethius (480–524), Alfonso writes, "Boethius, who was a very wise gentleman, said that it does not befit any other man better than a king to learn the good knowledge [...] Thus, the king who despises to acquire knowledge despises God from whom all knowledge comes" (*GE*, II, 1, V, 16). For Alfonso, the study of "good knowledge" was a starting point and a goal. In order to do so, whoever wants to devote himself to it must first be free to do so: "And let me tell you that one of the reasons why these seven arts were called 'liberal' is because they require that man be freed from any preocupation and impediment to learn" (*GE*, I, 320b); in another passage of the same work, he specifies even more the concept of freedom: "according to Ramiro, commenting on Donatus and other experts, these seven arts, and no other forms of learning, are called 'liberal' for these two reasons: for these two reasons: first, beacause they should not be learned by any other than free men, who are not slaves, or by any man who lives from his own labor; the second, because all those

---

[8] Albertus Magnus, *De mineralibus* [*Book of Minerals*], ed. D. Wyckoff, Oxford, 1967, p. 128. If Alfonso was in Paris, it had to be before 1243, and more concretely, between 1240 and the end of 1242; but even these years are problematic; he was clearly not absent from the Peninsula from 1243 on, when we know he was helping his father in the conquest of Murcia, first, and then later in that of Andalusia. See A. García Avilés, "Alfonso X, Albumasar y la profecía del nacimiento de Cristo," *Imafronte*, 8–9 (1992–1993), pp. 189–200, esp. p. 198.

[9] *GE*, II, 1, 57b–58a.

who study them must be free from any care or presure that some one may impose on them, because all this is needed in order to learn them" (*GE*, I, 193b).[10]

The terming of these arts or knowledge as liberal, according to Alfonso, was due (as Remigius of Auxerre also explains in his comment on Donatus), in the first place, to the social standing of whomever aspired to become knowledgeable; in other words, he had to be free. He also had to be free from manual work for his sustenance, and, finally, he had to be free from all earthly worries and cares. These conditions automatically excluded the vast majority of medieval men and women, who had to work from dawn to dusk in order to survive.[11]

The goal of the arts, therefore, was knowledge; and the final objective was wisdom and knowledge which lead to God and make us similar to him: "…every man who is full of virtues and knowledge resembles God because though Him all comes; and the more knowledge one has, the more he resembles God and the closer he becomes to His nature" (*GE*, II, 1, 290a). For a man like Alfonso, who had a true passion for didacticism and for placing knowledge at everyone's reach, the prerequisite to be "free" (in the double sense as explained), appears to be surpassed in this last passage by the ultimate goal of knowledge, which, as we will see in the Conclusion, was to render man similar to God.

a. Trivio

A reading of Alfonso X's works, especially his *General Estoria, Setenario* and slightly less so his *Partidas*, reveals a profound knowledge of the liberal arts ("the mercurial servants or handmaids"), not only of their theoretical aspects but also of their practical applications.[12]

---

[10] Although a few lines above Alfonso, explicitly mentions "Donat, e Precian, e Remigio," it is believed that Ramiro is the same as Remigio, identified as Remigius of Auxierre (Remigius Autissiodorensis), one of the most prolific commentators of the Carolingian period, to whom are attributed many commentaries of the classics and of commentators of the classics such as Donatus. The reference to Remigius of Auxierre on the topic of liberal arts could not be more apropos, as he is credited with many changes in their structure and composition. Alfonso and his collaborators were well-informed of the latest literary trends.

[11] Alfonso describes the privileged environment in which the ancient Athenians surrounded those dedicated to study: (*GE*, I, 193a).

[12] The three arts of the *trivium* are grammar, dialectics and rhetoric, and they lead the way to the understanding of "the other four ways called *quadrivium*": arithmetic, music, geometry and astrology (*GE*, I, 193b, 194a, 196b). Furthermore, in another section of the same work dedicated to Mercury, Alfonso states the objective of the

Although some of the execution of the works was left to collaborators, the literary spirit and unity behind them is uniquely Alfonso's.
This spirit is solidly built upon grammar, constructed through dialectics, and decorated with rhetoric. But the so-called trivial arts, which
were the warhorse of cathedral schools and monasteries, were only
propaedeutic, that is, a means to achieve wisdom, the true goal of all
rational beings, a goal that cannot be reached without the arts of the
quadruuio: "And the first three of these seven arts are the *trivium*,
which means three ways or paths that show man how to reach something, and this is how to reason correctly. And the last four are the
quadrivium, which means four ways or paths to know correctly and to
learn how to achieve knowledge with certainty, that is to say to know
the nature of things" (193b47–194a).

According to this tradition transmitted by all wisdom literature, the
education of a prince should begin at age seven, for biological reasons that had to do with the nature of human intellectual development
(based on the state of knowledge in medieval times). Alfonso writes,
"until age seven a man is called boy, beacause he does not have the
required intelligence to know things, but when he reaches the next
seven, which render him fourteen years old, he reaches the age of
understanding and can distinguish between good and evil, and reaches
marriageable age."[13]

In the *Libro de Alexandre* (ca. 1204), which, according to present-
day scholars, was born in the context of the intellectual world of the
first Castilian university (at Palencia), and which according to R.S.
Willis, would be a kind of *speculum principum* dedicated to Fernando
III or Alfonso X, there is a scene that portrays one of the first models
of a prince's education written in the vernacular. The young Alexander
speaks with his teacher, Aristotle, and says:

> Master, you have taught me and thanks to you I learned;
> You have done me great good, I wouldn't know how to thank you;
> My father gave me to you when I was seven years old,
> Because you were the best of teachers (stanza 38)[14]

---

trivium, concluding that since Mercury possessed these three sciences in a great degree,
"las llamaron los sabios ministras mercuriales, que quieren seer tanto cuemo seru-
ientes de Mercurio" [the wise men called them mercurial handmaids, which means
servants of Mercury] (*GE*, II, 57b).

[13] *Espéculo*, ed. G. Martínez Díez, Avila: Fundación Sánchez Albornoz, 1985, p. 306.

[14] *Libro de Alexandre*, ed. J. Cañas, Madrid: Cátedra, 1988; Cf. R.S. Willis, "*Mester
de Clerecía*: a definition of the *Libro de Alexandre*," *Romance Philology*, X (1956–1957),

It is worth noting that the education Alexander is receiving aims at shaping his personality for the purposes of ruling the kingdom and not to become a church leader or a *magister* at a *studium generale*. According to all evidence, this too would have been the education that the young don Alfonso received, hence the *Libro de Alexandre* could be a good model for such an education. The *Libro* states how Alexander received instruction in the seven liberal arts (first in grammar, logic, and rhetoric, the *trivium*; and then in the four arts of the *quadrivium*). He thus was able to penetrate the secrets of all arts:

> I know the seven arts with all their contents;
> I know well the qualities of all elements;
> Of the signs of the sun I know only the foundation
> The value of a single accent does not elude me (stanza 45)

In a stanza that appears to have been written with Alfonso in mind, Aristotle praises his disciple in the following way:

> You are the son of a king, you have a great education,
> In you I see wits I would like for myself,
> From childhood you've shown great warring courage
> You are the best of those alive today (stanza 52)[15]

Aristotle admired in his disciple the three great qualities that he himself would want to possess: royalty, "clerecía" (or culture), and "caballería" (or military value). According to this goal of education throughout the Middle Ages, Alfonso, during the years of his adolescence, was educated in grammar, logic, and rhetoric, disciplines that made him into a "learned" man, a condition that manifested itself in his familiarity with texts and teachers he quotes frequently in his works. These texts, except in rare exceptions, were not studied directly though a single work or author, but rather in the manuals that circulated in the medieval schools, the *summas, florilegia* and *collections* of fragments of the

---

212–224; I. Uría, "El *Libro de Alexandre* y la Universidad de Palencia," in *Actas del I Congreso de Historia de Palencia*, Palencia: Diputación, 1987, IV, pp. 431–442; J. Saugnieux, *Berceo y las culturas del siglo XIII*, Logroño: Servicio de Cultura de la Exma. Diputación Provincial, 1957.

[15] On the influence of the *Libro de Alexandre* in Alfonso's works, especially the *Partidas*, Cf. A.E. Ramadori, "Los consejos de Aristóteles en tres textos hispanos del siglo XIII," in *Actas II Congreso Argentino de Hispanistas*, Mendoza: Universidad Nacional de Cuyo, vol. II, 1989, pp. 65–79. For an overview of the problem of education in the Middle Ages and a bibliography, Cf. N. Zeballos Ortega, "Alfonso X y las artes liberales," in *Arts libéraux et philosophie au Moyen Age: Actes du Quatrième Congrès International de Philosophie Médiévale*, Montréal-Paris, 1968, pp. 627–629.

classics that Alfonso often made use of in his historical works. Among them, he frequently quoted the *Summa de la Rectorica* "in its beautiful and stylish Latin" (*GE*, II, 1, p. 57a).

Thus at a young age Alfonso must have taken his first steps into the disciplines of the *trivium*, beginning with grammar, which he says "…teaches us how to write letters and by joining them, how to compose the words properly so that they make sense; and they called it grammar, which means knowledge of letters, because this art teaches us how to accomplish perfect reasoning by using syllables and words" (*GE*, I, 194a).

Moving from Alfonso's education to his passion for the liberal arts, it becomes clear that this was a topic that fascinated him and to which he returned time and again. In the *Setenario* he portrays the liberal arts as essential instruments for the attainment of wisdom:

> Knowledge, according to what learned men have said, makes man reach all his goals in the things he intends to do and finish. Therefore, learned men organized knowledge into seven branches they called the 'arts', and these are subtle and noble masters they invented in order to know things with certainty and to act accordingly, both regarding heavenly things as well as earthly ones.[16]

For Alfonso, who lived in the spirit of the latest Aristotelian scientific/philosophical trends, the liberal arts were more than an instrument to attain humanistic knowledge; they also had a bearing on the natural and experimental sciences for they were "maestrías ssotiles e nobles" ["subtle and noble masteries"] which lead us to knowledge "ciertamientre e obrar dellas ssegunt conuiniese, tan bien en las [cosas] celestiales commo en las terrenales" [with certainty and to use them as it is convenient both in the celestial as well as in the earthly enterprises"]. The emphasis here is on "to know with certainty," for certainty is the goal of natural sciences, in the field of heavenly bodies as well as earthly realities, according to the new Aristotelian philosophy that began to spread throughout Europe.[17]

---

[16] "Knowledge, according to what learned men have said, makes man reach all his goals in the things he intends to do and finish. Therefore, learned men organized knowledge into the seven branches of knowledge they called the arts, and these are subtle and noble masters they invented in order to know things with certainty and to act accordingly, both regarding heavenly things as well as earthly ones" (p. 29).

[17] H.S. Martínez, "*Paideia* y filantropía. Sentido y alcance del humanismo alfonsí," in *Clarines de pluma. Homenaje a Antonio Regalado*, Madrid: Editorial Síntesis, 2004, pp. 75–96. An excellent collection of essays on the "new Aristotle" is O. Weijers y

A topic such as that of the liberal arts, which had an impact on education, could not be absent from a programmatic work like the *Setenario* which presented itself like a manual for the eduation of future kings, and hence of all subjects, present and future. The *Setenario* is a sort of literary, political, and religious *idearium* that, from the beginnings of Alfonso's reign, contains the cultural program he attempted to carry out throughout his 36-year rule. It is a strange, experimental, miscellaneous, and encyclopedic work, the first of its kind in the vernacular. Rafael Lapesa writes, "The reader gets lost in a tangle of similarities that in many cases are sanctioned by the ecclesiastic tradition, but are frequently unusual or initially appear capricious or absurd."[18] It includes political philosophy, law, sciences, astrology, literature, allegorical interpretation of pagan myths and Christian mysteries, and it is also a manual for the education of princes and a catechism for the subjects of the kingdom.

There are traces of the *Setenario* in practically all the works of the Alfonsine *scriptorium*, which shows how it constituted the master plan he built his entire cultural edifice on. Today, from the perspective of his extant works, it seems like the testing ground upon which Alfonso experimented with the themes and techniques he would later apply to the rest of his works. The close connection with the *Partidas*, especially the first one, is beyond question, but it also influenced the *Second Partida*.[19] A more important and less explored matter is the presence of the *Setenario* in the *General Estoria,* particularly in the use of definition techniques and etymologies first used in the *Setenario*, which shows Alfonso's early interest in vocabulary, content, and etymologies of words, as well as their metaphorical/allegoric content. According to Lapesa, the *Setenario* is also the origin of "the two pillars supporting the *General Estoria*: the symbolism of history and the assumption of Classical Antiquity, through allegory into God's redemption plan."[20]

L. Holtz, eds., *L'enseignement des disciplines à la Faculté des arts (Paris et Oxford, XIIIe–XVe siècles)*. Actes du colloque international. (Studia Artistarum: Études sus la Faculté des Arts dans les Universités Médiévales, 4), Turnhout: Brepols, 1997.

[18] "Símbolos y palabras en el *Setenario* de Alfonso X," in the introduction to the reedition of the *Setenario* by K.H. Vanderford, Barcelona: Editorial Crítica, 1984, pp. VII–VIII.

[19] Cf. J.R. Craddock, "El *Setenario*: última e inconclusa refundición alfonsina de la Primera Partida," *AHDE*, 56 (1986), 441–466; J.A. Arias Bonet, "La Primera Partida y el problema de sus diferentes versiones a la luz del manuscrito del British Museum," in the introduction to his edition of *Primera Partida*, Universidad de Valladolid, 1975.

[20] "Símbolos y palabras en el *Setenario* de Alfonso X," p. XXV.

It is precisely in the *Setenario*, perhaps because it was his first approach to the topic, that Alfonso introduced some fundamental changes in the traditional view of the liberal arts, which would later become the norm of higher education in the *Studium Generale*. One change is regarding the number of the arts. To the traditional seven (grammar, logic, rhetoric, arithmetic, geometry, music and astronomy), Alfonso added: medicine ("ffísica," p. 36) and metaphysics, which for the Learned King was "the most subtle of them all because through this all things are known according their nature, both spiritual as well as earthly" (p. 38, 14). The most significant change, however, had to do with the order of priority or importance of such arts vis-à-vis the education of the wise man and the allegorical interpretation given to them in order to maintain the seven-tier structure of the work. The first three, traditionally known as the disciplines of the *trivium*, for Alfonso are simply propaedeutic disciplines: "Thus, these three arts that for this reason became one, according to the wise men should be counted as one and they placed it at the entrance to the other arts, because reason clarified everything with certainty, each one according to its nature" (p. 31). This was a radical change with respect to the tradition that viewed grammar as " the origin and foundation of the rest of literary arts."[21] Saint Isidore, witnessing the treatment given to the seven arts in Antiquity, dedicated an entire book to grammar (I), another one to rhetoric and dialectics (II), and, in decreasing order, gathers all the other arts (geometry, music, astronomy) into a single book (III). He also deals with medicine (IV), but outside the *curriculum artium*. And, of course, he does not discuss metaphysics because, according to him, it does not belong in the seven liberal arts. Those were the priorities for St. Isidore and subsequent generations of teachers. St. Julian of Toledo, for instance, follows the Isidorian tradition in his *Ars Grammatica*.

In the *Setenario*, however, Alfonso follows a well-established tendency in the thirteenth century, devoting only a few brief remarks to grammar, which nonetheless are quite pertinent to the knowledge displayed in the rest of his written works. He then dedicates a paragraph to logic ("which shows the true way of speaking," p. 30) and another one to rhetoric ("by which is understood to teach the way to speak

---

[21] San Isidoro de Sevilla, *Etimologías*, I, 5, ed. J. Oroz Reta and M.A. Marcos Casquero, 2 vols., Madrid: BAC, 1982, I, p. 284.

beautifully," ib.), but he does not seem particularly interested in the
arts of the *trivium*, especially in grammar. In fact, he concludes the
treatise on the disciplines of the *trivium* with an unexpected turn to
the terrain of allegory, not in the pagan style of the School of Chartres,
but rather by creating a new, original allegorical dimension, which was
typical of this type of Christian pedagogical work. He then goes on
to discuss the arts of the *quadrivium,* which in the *Setenario,* structured around the allegorical value of the number 7, increase until they
reach the same number. The first part is precisely the group of the
three arts of the *trivium*; the rest are: arithmetic, geometry, music,
astrology, physics and metaphysics (pp. 31–40). Naturally, following
the allegorical methods, each of these three is divided and analyzed
into seven parts. In this way, for instance, arithmetic contains these
seven sub-arts (p. 31). As we suggested, Alfonso dedicates much space
to the exposition of the arts, of the *quadrivium,* extracting from each
of them rich Christian allegories. Here he showed a particular interest in the scientific disciplines, especially *medicine,* discussing also its
moral/allegorical meaning.[22]

The last section on the seven arts in the *Setenario* is dedicated to
his favorite discipline, metaphysics, "the most noble and most subtle"
of all. His minitreatise on metaphysics is a brief terminological survey
where he reviews again the four fundamental concepts that make it up:
ens, prima causa, intelligencia, causae secundae, intellectus, substancia,
and *accidentes,* to conclude: "Thus through these seven arts men learn
how to know God and everything he has made, what is the nature of
things and how they work. Furthermore, they learned of the seven
heavens where the seven stars, called planets, are and the names of
each one of them" (pp. 39–40).

Alfonso returns to the topic of the seven liberal arts in the *Partidas,*
where he stresses their divine origin. However, the first impression
one has when reading the different observations in the *Partidas* on the
arts and their role in education seems to point to a regression on the
part of Alfonso to an Isidorian view, with an emphasis on grammar

---

[22] And in all these seven things the name of God is shown, which is the nature that
orders all other natures. Because he knows the illnesses since he is the one who
gives them to those who deserve them, both illnesses of the soul as of the body.
And he knows why they happen or should happen...For this reason he is the
perfect physician who heals both sins as well as illnesses, something no other
physician can do (pp. 37–38).

and rhetoric. Although the *Partidas,* in literary terms is less innovative than the *Setenario,* the first impression remains just that, a first
impression. Speaking in the *Partida* I, law 48, for instance, of what
a bishop needs to know in order to properly run the bishopric (and
this could be said of priests in their parish churches), Alfonso points
out the following three: "first, the law, second, the arts, and third, the
earthly thing." The first is the law that has to do with knowledge and
the teaching of the Sacred Scriptures and theology: "Because he must
be knowledgeble about the law so that he can teach the others how
they can save the souls of those who have been entrusted to them. And
this is the reason why the holy fathers established that each the church
of each archbishopric must have a master who teaches divinity" (fol.
27a).[23] Here *saberes* [knowledge] clearly refers to the liberal arts, whose
knowledge has a specific end: "to understand the holy scriptures" (fol.
27a). In other words, for Alfonso, understanding the sacred scriptures
and its hermeneutics depend on a good knowledge of the humanistic
disciplines of the *trivium,* without which the priest cannot penetrate
their meaning or explain it to the people.

b. *His Teachers*

From his childhood, Alfonso had the gift of an insatiable intellectual
curiosity, but his educational process, given the conditions of his itinerant life as the heir to the throne of Castile in the thirteenth century,
happened not only throughout his childhood and adolescence but
during his entire life. All his early biographers and his collaborators
remind us that he frequently disappeared from public life for long
periods of time in order to gather manuscripts for his works or in
order to seek refuge in a secluded place and quietly work on his cultural projects. His nephew and admirer, don Juan Manuel, a reliable
witness like no other, tells us in this regard:

> [...] we found that for all the sciences he wrote many books and all
> very good because he had plenty of time to study the subjects he wanted
> to write about, because he would live in certain places for one or two
> years, and sometimes more, and according to those who lived under

---

[23] *Primera Partida,* Ms. British Museum, Add. 20, 787, CD-ROM transcription by
the Seminary of Medieval Spanish Studies, University of Wisconsin: Madison, 1998;
Cf. the edition by J.A. Arias-Bonet, *Alfonso el Sabio. Primera Partida,* Valladolid,
1975.

his protection, those who spoke with him what they wanted and when he wanted, in such a way that he had a lot of time available to study what he wanted to on his own and even to see and determine things about knowledge that he entrusted to teachers and the learned men at his court.[24]

This inclination to study must have begun early on, and although the affairs of the kingdom, once he was king, absorbed him completely, he would still find the time, amidst his political obligations, to hone his intellectual education. Learning was a lifelong process and preoccupation for him, and surrounding himself with teachers and manuscripts was part of that process. One of his early works from that period is the *Tablas Alfonsíes* [*The Alfonsine Tables*], and when death surprised him, he was working on a new topic, books on pleasure and pastimes. This shows, on the one hand, his passion for science in general, in particular, astronomy, a science in which he tirelessly sought the solution to personal and political problems, and on the other, his search for spiritual peace in the discovery of new intellectual activities, such as board games.[25]

The information we have available nowadays, allows us to more accurately guess who his teachers of rhetoric were, among which was one of the greatest experts of *artes dictaminis* of his time: Ponce de Provence, the author of an *Epistolarium*, or art of writing letters, written, in Ponce's own words, "at the request of Alfonso, noble man, favorite disciple." The words could not be clearer. Calling Alfonso "noble man," rather than king, and locating the date of composition of the work as 1252, clearly indicate that Ponce was present in the Castilian court when Alfonso was a prince, that is, during his crucial formative years.[26]

---

[24] *Crónica abreviada*, ed. J.M. Blecua, D. Juan Manuel, *Obras completas*, 2 vols., Madrid: Gredos, 1981–1983, II, pp. 504–815, p. 36.

[25] Cf. A. García Solalinde, "Alfonso X, astrólogo," *RFE*, 13 (1926), pp. 350–356. Alfonso's early interest in the sciences, especially astronomy, to which he dedicated 19 treatises, is one of the least known and studied aspects on the part of modern critics who have mostly dealt with his works on law, historiography, poetry, and music. See A. Cárdenas, "A survey of Scholarship on the Scientific Treatises of Alfonso X, el Sabio," *La Corónica*, 11 (1983), p. 231.

[26] Cf. Ch. Faulhaber, *Latin Rhetorical Theory in Thirteenth and Fourteenth Century Castile*, Berkeley, UC Publications in Modern Philology, 103, UC Press, 1972, pp. 98–99. The *Epistolarium* is a practical manual on letter-writing written at Alfonso's request and based on Ponce's own *Summa dictaminis*. Most manuscripts cite the *Epistolarium*'s date of composition as 1259, but, as we said earlier, it is assumed that

As we will discuss later on, Alfonso owes to Ponce de Provence much more than his letter-writing ability. Ponce was one of the itinerant masters of the Middle Ages. Before joining the Court of Castile, he had taught at Toulouse, Montpellier, and Orléans, where he became one of the most prominent figures of the *artes dictaminis*, which were founded according to the guidelines of the Chartres masters of rhetoric.[27] The fact that Ponce of Provence taught on both sides of the Pyrenees could well be the connection between the humanism of the school of Chartres and its numerous traces in Alfonso's oeuvre.

Also present at the court was another great master of rhetoric, the Englishman Geoffrey of Everseley, a close friend of Alfonso's and his ambassador in Rome and at the English court. This celebrated rhetorician also dedicated to Alfonso a treatise on the art of letter-writing entitled *Ars Epistolaris Ornatus,* whose manuscript is found at the Perugia's Biblioteca Comunale Augusta (Ms. F.62). Geoffrey was in Spain at least between 1276 and 1283, the year he died while performing his duties as notary and ambassador between Alfonso and Edward I of England. According to Bertolucci, he would have written the treatise on the art of letter-writing in Spain between 1266 and 1275, and most likely towards 1270.[28] This means that Geoffrey would have arrived in Spain several years earlier than what the documents show, and also that he was fairly familiar with Alfonso, as his correspondence with him indicates.[29]

Alfonso's request would have been before 1252, otherwise he would not have called him "noble man," but rather king of Castile.

[27] L.J. Paetow, *The Arts Course at Medieval Universities with Special Reference to Grammar and Rhetoric,* University of Illinois, The University Studies, III, 7, Urbana-Champaign: University Press, 1910, pp. 36–49; A. Cherval, *Les Écoles de Chartres au Moyen Age,* Paris, 1949, pp. 79–106.

[28] V. Bertolucci Pizzorusso, "Un trattato di *Ars dictandi* dedicato ad Alfonso X," *Studi Mediolatini e Volgari,* 15–16 (1968), pp. 3–88, esp. pp. 7–12. The work is still unpublished, although Bertolucci has promised an edition. Other scholars who have discussed this work are N. Delholm-Young, "The cursus in England," *Oxford Essays in Medieval History Presented to Herbert Edward Salter,* Oxford: At the Clarendon Press, 1934, pp. 68–103; Ch.-V. Langlois, "Formulaires de lettres du XIIᵉ, du XIIIᵉ et du XIVᵉ siècle," *Notices et Estraits des Manuscrits de la Bibliothèque Nationale et Autres Bibliothèques,* 35, ii (1897), pp. 409–434; Ch. Faulhaber, *Latin Rhetorical Theory in Thirteenth and Fouteenth Century Castile,* pp. 99–103.

[29] Ballesteros transcribes several letters between Edward and Alfonso, in which his confidant and ambassador figures prominently (*Alfonso X,* pp. 920–923); and Cf. Rymer (*Foedera,* I, II, pp. 157–158), who transcribes a letter from Edward I to Alfonso dated January 8, 1277 regarding the dispatch of Geoffrey.

Geoffrey responded to the trust Alfonso placed in him by dedicating the work to him and showering him with praise throughout its pages: "The Englishman Geoffrey composed this work in honor of don Alfonso, illustrious king of Castile and also León".[30] He not only praised Alfonso's greatness as a king, but also inserted in his work (which was written in Latin) examples of Alfonso's letters in Castilian in order to illustrate with vernacular models certain epistolary techniques. Regarding the *exordium*, for instance, he reproduces the following examples from Alfonso's letters: "From us, don Alfonso, by the grace of God, King of Castile...to you, don Abenmafón, King of Niebla, health and grace"; the king of Murcia addresses Alfonso in the following manner: "To the most high and noble lord don Alfonso, by the grace of God king of Castile[...], I, don Muhammed King of Murcia, kiss your hands and your feet."[31] It is not clear what purpose is served by these examples in the vernacular, but it seems to go beyond a simple tribute to the Castilian king. When we consider that Alfonso was also writing his literary works in the vernacular, we must conclude that Geoffrey wanted his *summa dictaminis* to become a practical/theoretical basis not ony for his patron, but also for the subjects of the kingdom. Especially since the "studio salmantino" ["the University of Salamanca"] is explicitly mentioned (Bertolucci, p. 20), we should not ignore the possibility that the work could have been written at Alfonso's request as a model of *ars dictaminis* at the University of Salamanca.[32]

A prominent figure in peninsular letters in the thirteenth century was the Franciscan Fr. Juan Gil de Zamora ("Iohannes Egidii Zamorensis"), one of the most prolific writers of the thirteenth century, although all of his extant work is in Latin. He wrote the important historical work *De Preconiis Hispaniae* (ca. 1278–1280) and many minor biographies, among which are those of Fernando III and his son Alfonso X.[33] He seems to have studied law at Salamanca and theology and arts at Paris between 1273 and 1278.[34]

---

[30] In Bertolucci, art. cit., p. 14.

[31] Both examples are quoted by Ch. Faulhaber, *Latin Rhetorical Theory*, p. 101.

[32] Cf. Ch. Faulhaber, op. cit., pp. 102–103.

[33] Besides *De preconiis Hispaniae* (ed. by M. de Castro y Castro, Madrid: Universidad de Madrid, Facultad de Filosofía y Letras, 1955), his historical works are practically all unpublished.

[34] Cf. M. de Castro y Castro, the introduction to the edition: "Gil de Zamora y la provincia franciscana de Santiago," pp. XXXV–CXXVI, for a reconstruction of Fr.

Although he must have been an important figure in the court of Alfonso X (some claim he was his confessor),[35] Fr. Gil de Zamora did not influence the literary education of the young prince, because he was not born before 1241, although it is speculated that he died around 1318. If this chronology is correct, we should reject the opinion of Gil González Dávila, who claimed he was the secretary of Fernando III, who died in 1252, that is when Fr. Gil was only eleven or twelve years old. However it is also true that according to the late testimony by the humanist Alfonso de Madrigal, *el Tostado*, Fr. Gil died at an old age, having lost the memory of the works he had written.[36]

We do not know when he was first in touch with Alfonso, in whose court he acted as "notary." Without indicating the source, Ballesteros claims he accompanied him on a trip to Seville in 1260s,[37] which would mean Fr. Gil frequented the court of Alfonso X before joining the Franciscan Order where, according to his modern biographer, he professed towards 1269 or 1270.[38] The hypothesis of his presence at the court of Alfonso in 1260 seems improbable; on the other hand, it would explain his continued collaboration in Alfonso's cultural project, according to some scholars. Fr. Gil would have maintained continued contact with the Alfonsine *scriptorium*, at least during the last twenty-four years of his reign, which were the most productive in the literary field.[39] This hypothesis should be considered, as Fr. Gil is thought to be one of Alfonso's main collaborators in the compilation of the *Cantigas* (see later on, chap. 8), but also of the historical works. The Franciscan authored many Marian devotional works related to Alfonso's song-books, and as an expert musicologist, he must be considered one of

---

Gil's biography. See also Ch. Faulhaber, *Latin Rhetorical Theory*, pp. 103–121; and his edition of *Dictaminis Epithalamium*, Pisa: Pacini Editore, 1978, pp. 7–9.

[35] Cf. T. y J. Carreras Artau, *Historia de la filosofía española: Filosofía cristiana de los siglos XIII al XV*, 2 vols., Madrid: Real Academia de Ciencias Exactas, Físicas y Naturales, 1939–1943, I, p. 13.

[36] Cf. Castro y Castro, op. cit., p. CXXV. Fr. Gil was a prolific writer in all fields, therefore it is possible the testimony of *el Tostado* may not be exempt of irony when he affirms that he had forgotten the works he had written, precisely because there were too many of them.

[37] *Alfonso X*, p. 302.

[38] Cf. Castro y Castro, *De preconiis Hispaniae*, p. LVI.

[39] There are many arguments in support of this conclusion, for instance the fact that in his *Dictaminis Epithalamium* there is a letter of consolation from the Franciscan to Alfonso on the occasion of the death of his son, who, given the context of the letter (ed. cit., pp. 135–136), could be no other than Fernando, who died in 1275.

the main collaborators in the composition not only of the literary and theological content, but also of the music of the *Cantigas*.

In the vast literary production of Fr. Gil, we must point out here, because they relate directly to Alfonso X's literary education in rhetoric and the liberal arts, the aforementioned letter-writing manual *Dictaminis Epithalamium*, composed by the Francisan before 1282.[40] Although the date is relatively late to assume any literary influence on Alfonso X, who died two years later, we cannot exclude the fact that if Fr. Gil had been at the *scriptorium* since the sixties, this work could have circulated before in manuscript form and even been read by Alfonso himself. This hypothesis would confirm the fact that the *Dictaminis Epithalamium* is dedicated to a colleague of his, Fr. Philip of Perugia, who was named bishop of Fiesole in 1282. Since Fr. Gil does not address his friend as a bishop, it is plausible that the work was written before the dedication and probably between 1277 and 1278,[41] allowing us to conclude that the manuscript could have circulated in Alfonso's courts at least during the last six years the Franciscan spent there. Like Geoffrey of Eversely, Fr. Gil included several samples of letters from Alfonso's chancellery, which is a sign of the close relationship with the king.[42] Fr. Gil's *Epithalamium*, in contrast to Everseley's treatise which frequently gets lost in abstruse theoretical issues, is eminently practical, containing a sampling of letters for all occasions and could easily have been a model for his disciple, prince Sancho, as well as for Alfonso himself.

Although there is no direct proof, there is some indication of influence by Fr. Gil and by Geoffrey de Everseley in Alfonso's intellectual education. According to tradition, Alfonso X entrusted the Franciscan with the education of his son Sancho, for whom Fr. Gil wrote his most important historical work, *De preconiis Hispaniae*, describing himself as "his most humble scribe" in the dedication.[43] *De preconiis* is

---

[40] See the edition by Ch. Faulhaber, *Juan Gil de Zamora, Dictaminis Epithalamium*, ed. intr. and notes, Pisa: Pacini Editore, 1978. Fr. Gil also dealt with the liberal arts in his manual *Ars Musica* and in the *Prosodion seu de accentu et de dubilibus Biblie*.

[41] This is the date when the Father General of the Franciscan Order, Jerome of Ascoli, was in Spain to celebrate the Provincial Chapter of the Franciscan Province of Castile, mentioned in the *Dictaminis Epithalamium* (ed. cit., p. 180, note 8).

[42] Of course Fr. Gil knew Alfonso, the education he had received, and his personality and habits very well. In the praise he wrote he stressed Alfonso's prodigal generosity (in F. Fita, "Biografías," *BRAH*, V, 1885, p. 319).

[43] *Liber de preconiis Hispaniae*, p. 3.

structured around two fundamental ideas: instructing the prince on
the norms of ethical conduct that all who aspire to rule a kingdom
should possess, giving him lessons on the history of Spain and the
Empire and at the same time, presenting the reader with a glorification
of the history of his native city, Zamora. But Fr. Gil, who was up-to-
date on the political ideas and literary fashions of his time, specifically
dedicates three complete treatises (III, IV and X) and the last part of
two more (VI and VII) to the topic of the education of a prince. These
treatises, admittedly not very original since they are a compilation of
prevous texts on a prince's education, are nevertheless a true political
catechism and they form an authentic mirror that could be termed *De
strenuitate regis.*[44]

The date of composition of *De preconiis* (1278) seems too late to
influence Alfonso X's political education; nevertheless, we must think
that the presence of the Franciscan in the court and the *scriptorium*
from the seventies on, when he was probably forging his ideas and
works, could also have influenced the political conception on the origin of royal authority that the king had. There is an entire section
in *De preconiis* in which he repeatedly insists on the double relationship of the king and God (pp. 521–526) and vis-à-vis the people
(pp. 526–541). That is where Fr. Gil, probably influenced by the spiritual movements of Franciscans hailing from Italy, argues that the
prince is the image of God, a sort of vicar, clearly indicating that he is
a demigod, locating royalty on a sort of supernatural order. This conception of the divine origin of the king and his power will dominate
political thinking during the reign of Sancho IV, a diligent student of
the Franciscan, but with nefarious consequences, both publicly and on
his family relations, given his haughty temperament.[45]

As we will see, Alfonso also adopted a very similar concept of the
king and his power, one he could have developed in contact with the

---

[44] On the sources of these treatises, see the introduction to the edition by M. de
Castro, pp. LXXIX–LXXXVIII; see also, M. de Castro "Las ideas políticas y la forma-
ción del príncipe en el *De preconiis Hispaniae* del franciscano Fr. Juan Gil de Zamora
(1278)," *Hispania* (Madrid), XXII (1962), pp. 507–541.

[45] Sancho was the only Castilian king who, due to his belief in the semidivine
nature of royal power, considered also, according to an eyewitness, the theologian
Alvaro Pelayo, that he had thaumaturgic qualities, which he exerted on a woman possessed by the devil by putting his foot on her throat and reading "from a little book"
("in quodam libelo"). See: J.M. Nieto Soria, *Fundamentos ideológicos del poder real en
Castilla (siglos XIII–XVI)*, Madrid, 1988, pp. 68–69.

ideas of his collaborator. Regarding the second issue, relations with the subjects, another key point in *De preconiis*, and one on which Fr. Gil, as a good Franciscan, insists time and again, is that the authority received by the king from God should be put in the service of the needs of the people, reminding him: "You are for the good of the people, and not the people for the good of you." In this process, the king must make use of prudent and honest counselors who will keep him informed of the needs of the people, preventing him from following his ambition or economic interests.

The education of the young prince Sancho in the liberal arts also included music, a field in which Fr. Gil was a renowned master, having written a treatise called *Ars Musica*.[46] Besides the mention in the dedication of *De preconiis Hispaniae*, there is no archival document directly relating Fr. Gil to his disciple, don Sancho, except a letter dated December 26, 1278, where he mentions Fr. Gil among his counselors and eloquently refers to him as "doctor."[47]

Despite the lacunae in the documentation, we can speak with relative certainty regarding the collaboration of Fr. Gil in some of the most culturally typical works of Sancho. Fr. Gil, along with other of Sancho's collaborators such as Maestre Alonso de Paredes, the medical doctor of prince don Fernando (heir of Sancho IV), and Pero Gómez Barroso, a priest and secretary of don Sancho, had an important role in the production of two of the most salient works of the so-called *molinismo* (a political and intellectual movement that developed around the figure of Queen María de Molina, Sancho IV's wife), namely *Lucidario* and *Castigos e documentos,* both the product of Sancho IV's *scriptorium* and traditionally attributed to the son of Alfonso X.[48]

---

[46] According to P.O. Kristeller, it is preserved in the Archivio Capitolare Vaticano (Ms.H.29), Cf. *Iter Italicum,* I, p. 29; II, p. 429.

[47] Text in C. Fernández Duro, *Memorias históricas de la ciudad de Zamora, su provincia y obispado,* 4 vols., Madrid: Rivadeneyra, 1882–1883, I, p. 469; and Castro y Castro, *De preconiis,* pp. LXVII–LXVIII.

[48] Cf. M. Gaibrois de Ballesteros, *Historia del reinado de Sancho IV de Castilla,* 3 vols., Madrid: Tipografía de la *RABM,* 1922, I, pp. LXXIII–LXXV; R.P. Kinkade, *Los "Lucidarios" españoles,* Madrid: Gredos, 1968, pp. 36–37; and "Sancho IV: puente literario entre Alfonso el Sabio y Juan Manuel," *PMLA,* 87 (1972), pp. 1039–1051; M. Zapata y Torres, "Algo sobre el *Libro del consejo e los consejeros* y sus fuentes," in *Smith College Studies in Modern Languages,* 21 (1940), pp. 258–269. *Libro del consejo e de los conjeros,* derived from *Castigos,* is attributed precisely to Pero Gómez Barroso, one of the foremost intellectuals at Sancho's court.

In sum, it was the contact with these and other specialists that allowed Alfonso to acquire the extraordinary artistic sensibility and intellectual maturity manifested in all his cultural endeavors. He had complete command of the *artes dictaminis*, as is evidenced in his correspondence both in Latin and Castilian, a typical example of which is his letter to his son, Fernando, and several others included in the anonymous work, *Crónica de Alfonso X.*[49]

c. Quadruuio: *Continuity and Change*

Knowledge and practice of the arts of the *trivium* were only one part of Alfonso's cultural project. The disciplines that truly fascinated him throughout his life were those that comprised the *quadrivium* (or *quadruuio*). It is clear that because of their complexity and constant progress due to the dissemintion of Aristotle's *libri naturales* and the work of Arab scientists, Alfonso's learning process was not limited to a specific period but was rather continuous, as is demonstrated in many passages in the *General Estoria* and in the prologues to all his scientific works.

Alfonso's apprenticeship in the *quadrivial arts* must have developed in contact with the scholars who frequented the court of his father and his own. Of course, through the prologues, Alfonso appears deeply involved in the subject matter of the book in question, in a position to contribute with innovative ideas, both in the selection of works to be translated, as well as the method, precision, and style of the translation. All of this presupposes an extraordinary training he could not have acquired in his adolescence and youth. If in the *trivium* he dared to innovate secular tradition, in the *quadruuio* Alfonso, from his youth, explored a new world of experimental science and speculative philosophy until then unknown in the West.

Scholars before Alfonso had already undertaken the theoretical task of the division or classification of the sciences before the dissemination of Aristotle's works, but it was due to the propagation of Aristotle's *libri naturales* and *Metaphysics,* thanks to Muslim philosophers and intellectuals, that a true obsession overtook thirteenth-century scholars.[50]

---

[49] The letter to his son Fernando can be seen in the Spanish version of this work (*Alfonso X*, Apéndice VII, pp. 604–608).

[50] Cf. J.-A. Weisheipl, "Classification of the Sciences in Medieval Thought," *Medieval Studies*, XXVII (1965), pp. 54–90; J. Maritain, *Problème de la classification des*

Until the middle of the previous century, the only known classification was by Seneca in his Letter LXXXVIII to his son Lucilius, where the Cordovan philosopher presented the "liberal arts" and the "liberal studies" as the way and goal of men concerned with spiritual education, explaining precisely that the term "liberal" distinguishes them from the "mechanical arts," pointing to the fact that they are worthy of study by all free men. Seneca's letter dividing the arts into "liberal" and "mechanical" is perhaps the oldest classification of the sciences that occupied the minds of medieval and renaissance thinkers. The liberal arts were seven, and their order remained unchanged from the fall of the Roman Empire, throughout the Middle Ages and Renaissance: grammar, rhetoric, dialectics, arithmetic, geometry, music, and astrology. But it was Boethius who at the end of the fifth century called the last four the *quadrivium* (four roads); the name *trivium* as a designation for the first three does not appear until the ninth century.

Alfonso, who practiced them all, seems not to have invested much intellectual energy in their classification and division, perhaps because it was not a major preoccupation among the Muslim thinkers and scientists who collaborated with him. The team of scholars gathered around Alfonso, following the systematizations by Al-farabi and Avicenna and their adoption by Gundisalvus, followed the general scheme that all Europe would follow, with the appropriate changes imposed by the dissemination of Aristotle's *libri naturales* and *Metaphysics*.[51] Alfonso and his collaborators probably found it easy to accommodate the new knowledge to the existing scheme of the seven arts or the ones "above" them.

Following a tradition begun in the previous century by the humanists of the school of Chartres, Alfonso gives precedence to the arts of the *quadruuio*, because "following nature…they speak of things according their quantity" (*GE*, I, 194a), while those in the *triuio* "speak of words and of the names of things" (*GE*, I, 194a) and we are told: "that things existed before words and before their names naturally" (194a). This was a firmly established doctrine with the theoreticians of the School of Chartres, who referred to the branches of the *trivium*

---

sciences d'Aristote à Saint Thomas, Paris, 1901; J.Chatillon, (s.v.), in *La pensée encyclo-pédique au Moyen Age*, pp. 66–72; E. de Bruyne, *Estudios de estética medieval*, 3 vols., Madrid: Gredos, 1959, II, pp. 389–394.

[51] Dominicus Gundisalvus, *De divisione philosophiae*, ed., L. Baur, Münster 1903, pp. 196–202.

as the "artes sermonicales" or verbal disciplines, while the arts of the *quadrivium* were called the "real" arts or arts of "res" (things). The former are used to express wisdom through eloquence; the latter are philosophy proper.[52]

Alfonso, therefore, acknowledged the priority of the arts of the *quadrivium* (in medieval philosophical terms, Alfonso is a "realist," not a "nominalist"), and despite sharing with the Chartres philosophers the notion that things had precedence over their names, his concern with making knowledge more accessible leads him to declare: "But because things can neither be taught nor learned properly except through the names they have, therefore, though according to nature, these four arts of the *quadrivium* should go first and the other three of the *trivium* at the end...the learned men for this reason put the three belonging to the *trivium* first, followed by the four of the *quadrivium*" (*GE*, I, 194a).

Although Alfonso's remark might seem irrelevant, it carries much weight, because behind it lays an entire new philosophic Aristotelian vision that postulates the existence of reality before its name, or the scientific and rational conception of the world before its nomenclature. Alfonso's deep pedagogic and didactic concern is evidenced in his illustration of this concept with a comparison taken from everyday life, comparing the arts of the *trivium* with a key that opens a door lock: "[...] just as locks are opened by keys, the arts of the *trivium* are the keys that open all other arts of knowledge, so that men may understand them better" (*GE*, I, 196b). However, in contrast to the first Chartrian thinkers, in Alfonso's time, Aristotle's scientific works were already being disseminated, as well as the ideas of the schools of the "Victorines" and the last Chartrian philosophers for whom ideal science was, above all, a science of observation, of analysis and of the causal explanation of the data of immediate experience, rather than an allegory of the great book of Nature written by the Creator, as it was believed a generation earlier.

The change of subject matter of the *quadrivium* in the *General Estoria* constitutes a greater innovation with respect to what it was traditionally. Alfonso X, who sponsored the translation of a complete series of scientific works and who, as we will see, was an enthusiastic

---

[52] A. Cherval, *Les écoles de Chartres au Moyen Age, du Ve au XVI siècle*, Paris, 1895.

admirer of Aristotle, tells us that the object is "to know how to learn something with certainty and this is attained by getting at the quantity of things" (*GE*, I, 194a). Under the influence of Aristotle, he went from the study of *qualitas* (quality), typical of the traditional *quadrivium*, to that of *quantitas* (quantity), determined by geometry and astrology (*GE*, I, 196a), which is also a fundamental aspect of Aristotelian metaphysical realism, whose methodological prerequisite is the scientific observation and analysis of reality. Regarding the quadrivial arts, he writes: "And the four are all about understanding and demonstration carried out with proofs, therefore they should go first in the order" (*GE*, I, 194a). In other words, mathematics and experimental science predominate, which should precede the study of the trivium, but for propedeutic reasons, the opposite order should be followed.

d. *Beyond the* Artes. *The Goal of the Wise Man*

Alfonso lived in a period of unprecedented scientific and philosophical effervescence in medieval Christian Spain. Averroes' Aristotelianism permeated in a predominant way the intellectual life of the court, and from there it spread to all of Europe. Francisco Rico writes: "In the days of Alfonso X...the liberal arts had become too narrow."[53] It makes sense, then, that, under the influence of Aristotelian/Muslim philosophy received through figures such as Al-farabi, Avicenna, and Ibn Rush—known to the west as Averroes—, Alfonso would have added to the seven traditional arts of Christian Europe, three more recently established ones: metaphysics, physics, and ethics.

About the first one he writes, "The most noble of all the other arts of knowledge [...] is metaphysics, which means 'above and beyond nature', as well as near God, the angels, and souls" (*GE*, I, 196b). In the *Setenario* he had already described it as "the most noble and subtle of them all, because through this one [art] all things are known according to their nature" (p. 36). Regarding the second, *physics,* understood as "natural knowledge of medicine," he had already written in the *Setenario*; but in the *GE* he extends its scope to the knowledge of all natural things, for it deals with

---

[53] *Alfonso el Sabio y la "General Estoria". Tres lecciones.* Barcelona: Ediciones Ariel, 1972; 2nd ed., 1984, p. 143.

> [N]ature, in order to know all the things that have bodies, such as
> the heavens and the stars and other things under the heavens, and to
> understand their nature, how they are made, are born, and die; and the
> nature of elements must be known and how each of them works in these
> matters. (*GE*, I, 196b)

In the *General Estoria*, Alfonso defined the object of "physics" more
precisely as the science dealing with the study of the cosmos, *latu
sensu*, from stars to atoms, including *medicine* (here for the first time
"physician" means doctor of medicine: *GE*, I, 541) as well as *magic*,
a science in which Alfonso was deeply interested. There are also passages that indicate that both of these sciences (medicine and magic)
were parts of astrology (II, 2, 340b; II, 1, 86a).

Finally, on *ethics*, he writes,"[it is the] science that deals with habits because it teaches man how he should acquire good habits and
through them earn a good name" (*GE*, I, 196b–197a). Among the sciences that go beyond the seven liberal arts, in the *Partidas* Alfonso
adds *law*, a very popular subject introduced into universities in the
thirteenth century.

It is not easy to speculate about Alfonso's ideas on the systematiza-
tion of law in the schema of the ten disciplines, because he does not
make any statement about this. It seems that it could have belonged
partly to ethics and partly to eloquence or rhetoric. The same happens
with *history*. We could imagine he might have taken a stance similar to
current opinions at the time that classifed it under grammar. But given
the goal of his own historical works, he must have also thought it part
of ethics, when it came to content, and eloquence, when it came to
exposition. Alfonso, who dealt extensively with historiography and its
problems, always saw that history was an exemplary discipline for the
education of people, showing them the actions of past people, whether
to imitate them if they were good, or avoid them if they were bad.
For Alfonso, the *curriculum studiorum* could not be complete without
these disciplines "that are above the seven liberal arts" (*GE*, I, 196b).

Finally, Alfonso also includes *philosophy* among the *quadrivial arts*,
using the word in its two meanings. The first, that etymologically indicates what it means: love of wisdom; and the second, as a discipline
dealing with matters of the world as well as those going beyond physical experience, i.e., metaphysics. In the study of the arts and their relation to philosophy as a sumpreme science, Alfonso uses the second
meaning for a concrete purpose:

> And pagans, who strove to say things in a secret way and through simi-
> larities, such as the ones you have heard here, called philosophy, which
> is an art of knowledge that encompasses all other knowledge, a garden,
> and they called the seven arts of the trivium and the quadrivium, trees
> that give branches and apples and fruit and leaves made of gold in that
> garden, such as the arts are in philosophy. (*GE*, II, 1, 284a)

Carried away by the influence of Aristotelian thought when ancient
humanism was crumbling under the pressure of logic and the *libri naturales*, Alfonso conceived of the seven liberal arts as golden branches,
apples, fruit, and leaves growing in the garden of philosophy. Fundamentally, his is the attempt of a humanist to save traditional knowledge, adapting it to the new intellectual exigencies of unprecedented
scientific/philosophic currents.

These last three disciplines would complete the ten sciences that
make up the *curriculum studiorum* according to the Alfonsine concept
of humanistic knowledge. As we will see later on, other disciplines
were left pending, which he himself would institute at educational
centers he founded and which are not mentioned here. Among them,
is *theology*, "which means to talk about what belongs to God" (II, 1,
269a). Considering the definition of metaphysics, it seems that theology would be included in it. Among other disciplines that Alfonso
devoted his scientific endeavors to, *magic* seems to be clearly associated with astronomy.[54] *Medicine*, labeled "physics" (I, 686b), and its
practitioners ["physicians"] (I, 541b13–14), although at times related
to magic,[55] clearly belongs to the natural sciences.[56]

Hence Alfonso, as a humanist king, attributed paramount importance to the seven liberal arts in his own education and that of his
subjects. Their goal is to produce a "wise man." Although Alfonso frequently identified the "wise man" with the "philosopher," the passages
from *General Estoria* we discussed, indicate that a complete education

---

[54] "Because [the wise men and women versed in magic] explain that magic is a
mode and part of the art of astronomy" (*GE*, II, 2, 340b); in another passage he says:
"he who knows the art of magic is a magus, and the science of magic is an art of
knowledge used by those who know about it to guide themselves according to the
movements of the heavenly bodies in order to know earthly matters" (II, 1, 86a).

[55] Among the benefits that men derive from "magic," Alfonso cites medical remedies (*GE*, II, 2, 341b).

[56] Cf. F. Rico, *Alfonso X el Sabio y la GE*, pp. 149–150 and note 6; F. Rubio, O.S.A.,
"Breve estudio de la magia en la *General Estoria* de Alfonso el Sabio," *La Ciudad de
Dios*, CLXXII (1959), pp. 485–498.

leading to true wisdom is one that, based on the *curriculum* of the seven liberal arts, is completed with the other three sciences: "And the three arts of the *trivium*, as we said, teach men to be well-reasoned, and the four of the *quadrivium* make him perfect and complete in kindness and lead him to unparalleled blessings" (*GE*, I, 197a).

Alfonso's intellectual commitment to knowledge extends to aspects most unthinkable to us nowadays, which were, nevertheless, very important to a "wise man" in the thirteenth century. Scientific/philosophic development, as represented in the seven liberal arts, also had an impact on the field of literary hermeneutics. The Chartresian concepts of "res" and "voces" (or "things" and "words") mentioned above are key principles in the exposition and analysis of literary texts, whether sacred or profane. Alfonso learned this method from his contact with Biblical hermeneutics practiced at the time in rabbinical schools and afterwards by Christian exegetes, and he applied it as well to profane literature.[57] According to this theory, before the allegorical meaning of a text comes its "real" sense, that is its historical or literal meaning, and the latter must be understood in order to reach the former.[58]

This may serve as an example for those who think the Middle Ages were essentially a period of symbolism and allegory, when, in reality, from Saint Augustine himself, the father of metaphorical and allegorical language, there had been an insistence on the idea that the essential value of the Bible lies, above all, in the historical and immediate sense, for the truths it reveals or the precepts it imposes. Only secondarily does its value stem from what those historical realities mean spiritually.

We should therefore not discard the possibility that it was the influence of this somewhat historicist interpretation of the sacred texts, along with the influence of Aristotelian scientific realism, that Alfonso incorporated practically the entire Bible and other profane works into

---

[57] For the topic of the senses of the Bible, see H. De Lubac, *Exégèse médiévale. Les quatre sens de l'Ecriture*, 4 vols., Paris, 1959–1964; B. Smalley, *The Study of the Bible in the Middle Ages*, 3d ed., Oxford, 1984; and "La Glossa Ordinaria," *Recherches de Theologie ancienne et médiévale*, 9 (1937), pp. 365–400; H. Hailperin, *Rashi and Christian Scholars*, Pittsburgh, 1963; A. Gabrois, "The *Hebraica Veritas* and Jewish-Christian Intellectual Relations in the Twelfth Century," *Speculum*, L (1975), pp. 613–634.

[58] Hugh of St Victor writes: "Since the perfect understanding of mystical meaning is based on what the letter presents to us, I am amazed by the temerity of those who pretend to be masters of allegorical explanation while ignoring the original meaning of the letter" (*De Script.*, *PL*, vol. 175, p. 13).

his historical works because, like many learned men of the period, he believed that those narratives were, above all, literally historical, although they were frequently covered by the *integumentum* of a fable or literary myth.

But Alfonso was, above all, an educator, and therefore he was aware that wisdom is the product of mental balance and the combination of many other factors. Some can be emphasized, but deep down, all are necessary to maintain the balance of judgment that distinguishes the wise man. Regarding the passage on "the knowledge that Mercury had," Alfonso adds later how all disciplines must be intimately connected in order for man to reach true wisdom for, "reason and wisdom came together in one, and reason is the *trivium* and wisdom the *quadrivium*, and from this union it is said a work emerged which will never be undone or lost, because reason will always need wisdom, and wisdom, reason, just as the *trivium* needs the *quadrivium* and vice versa. And it seems that for the wise man to appear and be wise, he must be well-reasoned, and the well-reasoned, in order to be and appear wise, much use his reason with wisdom in those things that the *trivium* does to reason" (*GE*, II, 1, 57b–58a).[59]

In conclusion, as Francisco Rico has rightly pointed out, "Alfonso, despite obvious concessions to trends at the time, remains in line with Thierry of Chartres, whose *Eptatheucon* invites 'ad cultum humanitatis' precisely thought the classical seven 'artes sermonicales' ("arts of words") and 'real arts' ("arts of things"). He is in line with Juan of Garlandia, who urges the return of liberal disciplines, so badly treated at universities; and with the Oxford masters who dedicate themselves to the *quadruuium*, forgotten in Paris. In the context of the 13th century, Alfonso remains one of the last enclaves where classical humanism thrives being assailed violently by metaphysics and logic. And this is not the lesser aspect of the generosity with which the *General Estoria* makes room for old 'auctores.'"[60]

All of this is true, but we must not forget that for Alfonso, the seven liberal arts have a wider scope than the humanistic/literary one of the

---

[59] Cf. H.S. Martínez, "*Paideia* y filantropía. Sentido y alcance del humanismo alfonsí," in *Clarines de pluma. Homenaje a Antonio Regalado*, Madrid: Editorial Síntesis, 2004, pp. 75–96.

[60] *Alfonso X y la General Estoria*, pp. 155–156. For Thierry of Chartres, Cf. E. Jeauneau, "Le 'Prologus in Eptatheucon' de Thierry de Chartres," *Medieval Studies*, XVI (1954), pp. 171–175; on Garlandia, Cf. E. Gilson, *La filosofía en la Edad Media*, Madrid, II, p. 47; both quoted by Francisco Rico.

classics. They also have a scientific dimension; but not because he wants to confront the sciences with the humanities, but because the latter are part of all knowledge that man needs in order to live like a rational being and reach the knowledge of God. In the *Setenario*, he makes it clear that it is the knowledge of things that leads us to the knowledge of God, who is its cause; but such knowledge implies the study of both metaphysics ("what they are in themselves"), as well as physics or mechanics ("how they work"). Here the study of physics would thus encompass all knowledge of nature, including astronomy.[61]

Knowledge about what "what was to come through what had already happened" (future and past) is what led Alfonso in his exploration of all sciences, whose synthesis he thought he had found in the study of astronomy and its practical application, astrology. In the *Partidas*, Alfonso condemned incompetent astrologists who abused the good faith of simple people, because they profaned the true meaning of a science he deemed extremely useful. However, he himself was a passionate astrologist, and he devoted many translations and original works to this science. For him, it was a serious science, of great public and private use, although he has been chastised by historians for his interest in it. There seems to be a misunderstanding in this critical attitude on the part of his detractors. As the great scholar of Alfonso's work wrote regarding his passionate interest in this science: "Cultivating the art of astrology required considerable knowledge of astronomy and therefore it was possible that there were astronomers who were not astrologists, but there can't be astrologists who are not astronomers... The answer [to the question], without reservations, is that the Learned King frankly accepts the hypothesis of astrology. This is based on three well-known facts: 1) His direct intervention in research or translation works; 2) The way he recruited his collaborators; 3) the

---

[61] *Setenario*, pp. 39–40. Regarding the origin of astronomy and how it was the vehicle to know the other sciences, there's a very interesting passage in the *GE* where the old woman Goghgobon, a descendant of Nimrod and the giants, reveals to Aesculap the secrets of the book of Hermes, which Aesculap had found but could not decipher: "Likewise, she told him that through what is above in the heavens and sheds light down here on us, that they identified and composed those twenty-four signs which are the branches of knowledge through which man can understand and know what is to come and what has already happened" (II, 1, 39b). It's worth noting Goghgobon was the niece of Nimrod, the first king of the world whom Alfonso considered his ancestor.

selection or acceptance of works to be translated."[62] Beyond this explanation, we can say that the profound and essentially philosophical and
scientific reason appears in the prologue of *Libro de las cruzes*, the first
astrological treatise in Castilian:

> And because he read, and all wise men confirm this, the words of Aris-
> totle that say that the bodies down below, which are the earthly ones,
> are sustained and are governed by the movements of the bodies above,
> which are the heavenly ones, it was God's will that it be understood and
> known that the science and knowledge of the meanings of the heavenly
> bodies over the earthly ones was very necessary for man. (p. 1)

3. *Languages*

We cannot close this chapter on the education of Alfonso X without
mentioning one of its fundamental aspects: the learning of languages
which allowed him to carry out his cultural project and make it available to all of his subjects. His intellectual curiosity, stimulated by an
exceptional education, was indeed something that kept him abreast
of the latest trends in all fields throughout his life. Hence the breadth
of his cultural interest in poetry and poetics, rhetoric, history, law,
music, astronomy, astrology, philosophy, archaelogy, the study of
stones, fiction, the fine arts, board games, and leisure. This curiosity
also extended to languages. He certainly possessed good command of
all Peninsular languages, including Galician-Portuguese, Catalan, Arabic, Hebrew, and some foreign ones, such as French, Provencal and
maybe German, which he might have learned from his own mother,
Beatriz of Swabia.[63]

As part of the program that focused the interests of the king on
aesthetic pleasure, devoting his free time to cultivating the beautiful,
Alfonso decided to personally translate from the French *Estoria de
Ultramar* [Overseas History], and he also commissioned a translation
into Galician of *Estoria del Santo Grial* [History of the Holy Grail],

---

[62] "Nota preliminar" in *Libro de las cruzes,* ed. Ll.A. Kasten and L.B. Kiddle,
Madrid – Madison: CSIC, 1961, p. VIII.

[63] Regarding the various peninsular languages he spoke, we have the testimony of
the prologue of Part Six of the *GE* where he writes: "I, don Alfonso, by the grace of
God [...] ordered the composition of this book after gathering all the ancient books
and chronicles and all the histories in Latin, in Hebrew, and in Arabic that had been
lost or had fallen into oblivion, as was said at the beginning of the other ages" (ed.
CD-ROM, Medieval Studies, Wisconsin, p. 2).

creating not only a new field in letters, the chivalric novel, but also a literary topos that will repeat itself until the 17th century: *arms and letters*. Within these same literary interests, one can see his interest in the figure of Alexander the Great, an important hero in history and medieval fiction to whom he also dedicated many pages in his works.[64]

His knowledge of Greek is however more questionable, although there's evidence that in his *scriptorium* this language was used; he himself makes lexical-philological commentaries on a great number of Greek words.[65]

Regarding Latin, it was the Marqués de Santillana who gathered a tradition according to which Alfonso wrote Latin verse: "In this kingdom of Castile, king don Alfonso the Learned wisely spoke in Latin, and I saw those who knew his poems [*cantigas*], and it is even said that he was greatly skilled at versifying in the Latin language."[66] We do not know what verses he is referring to, since the only known ones are on the dedication to the shipyards of Seville, which he probably did not write and which are part of the back cover of *Estoria de España*, quoted at the beginning of Chapter 1.

But Alfonso did understand Latin, as is evidenced by the meticulous reading of Latin manuscripts and books and his use of passages from them in his own historical works, as well as the many phrases and direct quotes from the classics and other medieval writers with their respective translations and commentaries found in those same works or the various prologues to the scientific works. More proof of his knowledge of Latin are the lexical, philological, and semantic commentaries he continuously makes in his works extending to a detailed analysis of the classics (mainly Ovid, Virgil, Stacius, Lucan, Cicero, and Seneca). His passion for these and other "auctores" can be seen in his incomparable praise of some of them (using a technique known as *accessus ad auctores*) and in the textual commentaries.[67] In these

---

[64] P. Sánchez-Prieto Borja, "La técnica de la traducción en la *General Estoria*: La historia de Alejandro Magno en GE4," Actas del IV Congreso de la AHLM, Lisboa: Ediçoes Cosmos, 1993, pp. 221–232.

[65] Cf., for instance, *GE*, I, p. 198b, on the origin of the names of Athens, from *a-thanatos*, without death.

[66] *El Proemio e Carta*, ed. M.Durán, in Marqués de Santillana, *Poesías completas*, 2 vols., Madrid: Castalia, 1980, II, p. 219.

[67] E.A. Quinn, *The Medieval Accessus ad Auctores*, New York: Fordham University Press, 1986. [first published as "The Medieval *Accessus ad Auctores*," *Traditio*, 3 (1945), pp. 215–264.]

commentaries and glosses he frequently expresses a true intellectual pleasure in "espaladinarlos" or explicating them.[68]

Finally, regarding his knowledge of Arabic, probably his most crucial contact with the cultural world of Islam happened as a result of the conquest of Murcia. It was then when, according to the opinion of many scholars, Alfonso realized the hidden potential of those new subjects that Christianity had attempted to eliminate for more than five centuries. That encounter would leave in him an indelible mark. Alfonso's biographers and more recently the historians of Islamic Spain have noted that Alfonso's Islamic education probably took place in the *madrassa* at Murcia, under the care of Ibn Abû Bakr al-Riquti, who would welcome Muslim, Jewish, and Christian students in his school.[69] This knowledge, according to J. Torres Fontes, would have been taught in the vernacular, and, according to this same scholar, Alfonso attended the lessons of this Islamic teacher in the castle of Monteagudo, where he "probably learned Arabic perfectly."[70]

It was precisely his linguistic and scientific/literary knowledge which led him along with the great teachers, to acquire an exceptional humanistic education and above all, to gather around himself a team of literary figures, poets, jurists, musicians, painters, miniature artists, scientists, and historians who had come from all the corners of Europe, from Islam and Judaism who would collaborate with him in a literary and erudite corpus unparalleled in Europe in the thirteenth century.[71]

4. *The "Mirrors of Princes" in Alfonso's Education*

Besides what Alfonso owed to his father in other fields, he also owed him much with regard to his social and political education in his teenage years and early adulthood, as Fernando III took great care in the preparation of his heir.

---

[68] D.A. García Solalinde promised a book on the Latin culture of Alfonso X: (*GE*, I, p. XXI, note), but it is not known if he completed it. It is not part of the list of his works published in *La Corónica*, 17 (1988), p. 114.

[69] Cf. F. de la Granja, "Una polémica religiosa en Murcia en tiempos de Alfonso el Sabio," *Al-Andalus*, 31 (1966), pp. 42–72.

[70] "Los mudéjares murcianos en el siglo XIII," *Murgetana*, 17 (1961), pp. 74–75.

[71] J. O'Callaghan, *The Learned King. The Reign of Alfonso X of Castile*, Philadelphia: University of Pennsylvania Pres, 1993, p. 169; and R.I. Burns, "Stupor mundi: Alfonso X of Castile, the Learned," pp. 1–13.

Aside from the seven liberal arts, geared towards forming the future king's mind according to Greek and Latin classical models, there were in medieval Spain a series of works from the Arabic/Oriental tradition that were also meant for the practical education of a future ruler. These works, known as "mirrors of princes," were collections of didactic/ wisdom literature consisting of fables and apologies in the form of a dialogue between a teacher and a student. They taught many norms of conduct, practical wisdom to help the future king in resolving day-to-day issues of the kingdom. These "political catechisms" would recommend the use of prudence, cunning, practical knowledge, good measure, tact, and wit in order to avoid the traps constantly laid out by political enemies and ambitious and greedy counselors, gossipmongers or traitors.

The popular *Calila e Dimna* belongs to this genre, having been "translated from Arabic into Latin and Castilian as commanded by the prince don Alfonso, son of the very noble King Fernando," in most likelihood in 1251.[72] For M.J. Lacarra: "At least in Alfonso's court, *Calila* was not considered a book of fables, but rather a compendium of wisdom, as is shown by the fact that the method employed in its translation was the same as the one used for scientific works."[73]

According to this didactic/wisdom tradition, Fernando III commissioned for his heir and his other children a manual for the education of princes known as *Libro de los doze sabios* or *Tratado de la nobleza y lealtad*.[74] Unlike *Calila e Dimna* and the other works cited in note 72, this was not a translation from the Arabic but rather an origi-

---

[72] See the ed. by J.M. Cacho Blecua y M.J. Lacarra, *Calila e Dimna*, Madrid: Castalia, 1984, esp. pp. 12–19. The splendid Castilian translation, despite various Latin translations already in circulation, was done directly from Arabic, as has been shown by Alvaro Galmés de Fuentes, "Influencias sintácticas y estilísticas del árabe en la prosa medieval castellana," *BRAE*, XXXV (1955), esp. p. 230. Among the works in the same genre, also translated from the Arabic during the rule of Fernando III, Alfonso X and Sancho IV are: el *Libro de los engaños e de los asayamientos de las mugeres*, a version of *Sendebar*, whose translation was commissioned by the prince don Fadrique, Alfonso X's brother, in 1253; *Poridat de Poridades, Libro de los buenos proverbios, Bonium o Bocados de oro, Flores de Filosofía* and a few other, less important ones. Cf. L. Kasten, "*Poridat de las Poridades*: A Spanish Form of the Western Text of the *Secretum secretorum*," *RPh* 5 (1951–1952), pp. 180–190.

[73] M.J. Lacarra, *Cuentística medieval en España: los orígenes*, Zaragoza: Departamento de Literatura Española, Universidad de Zaragoza, 1984, especially the section entitled: "El *Calila* y los espejos de príncipes," pp. 33–39.

[74] *El Libro de los doze sabios, o Tratado de la nobleza y lealtad (ca. 1237)*, ed. J.K. Walsh, Madrid: Real Academia Española (Anejos del *BRAE*, 29), 1975.

nal composition in Castilian, although it shares with them a narrative structure. The author, a Christian, was probably one of the scholars working in Fernando III's *scriptorium*. He places in the mouths of twelve wise men phrases taken from the Bible, especially from the New Testament, along with fables from Eastern didactic works. The work is one of the first examples of cultural symbiosis of the three cultures of medieval Spain.[75]

As we know it today, this work displays a complex narrative structure, halfway between wisdom literature and fiction, but it is clearly a *speculum principis* (in which the prince can "look into it as into a mirror"). According to the prologue, Fernando III gathered a council of twelve wise men and entrusted them with the composition of a treatise on wisdom that could aid in the education of his children (the king had fifteen children, ten with his first wife, Beatriz of Swabia, and five with the second, Juana de Ponthieu). When the composition was concluded, the wise men recommended that the king give a copy to each of his children (pp. 71–72). We do not know whether Fernando followed their advice or not, but judging from the behavior of most of Alfonso's siblings, they learned very little from the good advice in the book, as the work was not composed according to what is stated in the prologue. Alfonso clearly profited more from it than his siblings, for he incorporated several elements of this manual into his "regiment of princes," i.e. the *Segunda Partida*, and this is also explained by the mystery surrounding the origin of *Libro de los doze sabios*.

Later in his adult life, when he was already king, Alfonso continued to consult other manuals on the education of princes and on advice for kings (known as "mirrors"), such as Vincent of Beauvais's *Speculum historiale* (explicitly quoted in his last will), and from 1277 on, the best-known medieval work on the education of princes, *De regimine principum* by Egidius Romanus, also frequently cited in his works.[76]

---

[75] In the same genre as *Libro de los doce sabios* we also find *Libro de la saviessa*, el *Libro del consejo y de los consejeros* and the better known *Castigos e documentos del rey don Sancho*, a work that Alfonso X's son dedicated to his son don Fernando. Cf. A. Pérez Priego, "Imágenes literarias en torno a la condición del príncipe en el *Libro de los castigos*," in *La literatura en la época de Sancho IV*, 1996, pp. 257–265. See note 48 above.

[76] Regarding the "espejos de príncipes" ["mirrors of princes"], cf. J. Krynen, *L'empire du roi. Idées et croyances politiques en France. XIII–XVᵉ siècle*, Paris, 1993, p. 171 and ff.; and Cf. J. García de Castrojeriz, *Glosa castellana al "Regimiento de príncipes" de Egidio Romano*, ed. J. Beneyto Pérez, 4 vols., Madrid: Instituto de Estudios Políticos, 1947–1948. For a wider perspective on the topic, cf. L. Kruger Born, "The

But the Learned King would return often to the work given to him by his father in his youth. Traces of *Libro de los doze sabios* can be found in several of his works written after 1255, with many references in the Segunda Partida which, according to J.K. Walsh, "…is a "mirror of princes", quite complete and a superb example of this renewed effort to define the role of the monarch."[77]

Perhaps no other document describes to us the future king's appreticeship and the nature of the society he lived in and had to shape better than the *Siete Partidas*, especially the *Segunda*, which, as we have suggested above, could be perfectly considered a veritable manual on the education of princes. We do not know for sure what materials existing in Fernando's *scriptorium* were incorporated into Alfonso's juridical works, therefore we cannot know if the material on princely education in the *Segunda Partida* is a reflection of previous experince or a radical innovation on the part of Alfonso. But given the content and educational goal of *Libro de los doze sabios*, Alfonso probably speaks from experience when saying that kings and queens should teach their descendants what is convenient to their status: "to read and to write, for this is of great benefit to those who understand it, in order to learn more easily what they desire to know and to be better able to keep their secrets."[78] In this same Partida, Alfonso insists on why the king should be a learned man, not only for personal but also state reasons:

> A king should be eager to learn the sciences, for, by means of them, he will understand the affairs of sovereigns and will better know how to act with regard to them. Moreover, by knowing how to read, he will be better able to keep his secrets, and be master of them, which under other circumstances he would not well do. For, by want of familiarity with these things, he would necessarily have to admit someone else into his confidence, in order that he might know them, and there might happen to him what King Solomon said, namely: "He who places his secret in the power of another, becomes his slave; and he who knows how to keep it, is the master of his own heart, which is very becoming to a king. (II, 5.16)[79]

Perfect Prince: A Study in Thirteenth and Fourteenth Century Ideals," *Speculum*, 3 (1928), pp. 470–504.

[77] Op. cit., p. 43.

[78] *Las Siete Partidas*, II, Tit. VII, Law X, trans. Samuel Parsons Scott, Philadelphia: University of Pennsylvania Press, 2001, p. 306.

[79] *Las Siete Partidas*, II, Tit. V, Law XVI, trans. Samuel Parsons Scott, Philadelphia: University of Pennsylvania Press, 2001, p. 294.

The "disciplines" Alfonso mentions are the seven liberal arts, emphasizing too that the king must be able to read to safeguard his secrets.

Many passages in the *Segunda Partida* show the type of education Alfonso must have received before his ascent to the throne. Title 7, laws 2–8 deal with the physical education and social behavior caretakers must impart to the children of kings; Title 5 speaks of the requirements a good king should have to rule properly and serve as example to his subjects.

We cannot be entirely sure if the educational system described in the *Segunda Partida* is what the young Alfonso went through, or if it is an educational model described by him for future heirs to the throne of Castile. But the existence of texts on the "regiment of princes" such as *Poridat de poridades*, used frequently by Alfonso, leads us to believe he received a very similar education to that described in the *Partidas*.[80]

Besides a polished theoretical education in the liberal arts, Alfonso also received a practical education in the execution of his kingly duties, including a certain refinement in manners reflecting royal nobility and dignity, known by preceptors as *curialitas*. This was a behavior and lifestyle that distinguished the king and those around him. The *Partidas*, hence, also instructed the guardian in his educational duties and regarding his role in shaping the character and personality of the future king. Alfonso dedicated much space in the *Segunda Partida* (Title 5, laws 4–8) to this topic, insisting on how students should learn how to eat neatly and drink in moderation, practice personal hygiene and speak correctly, according to their state and condition:

> The faculties of speech and reason are what distinguish men from other animals, and although they are derived from intelligence, they cannot be manifested without words. For this reason, all men should endeavour to be rational, and especially should those be so who occupy high positions, because persons remember their words more than those of others. Wherefore it is eminently proper for tutors who have charge of the sons of kings, to try to teach them to speak well and politely [...] it is called polite when it is not uttered loudly, or in a very low tone, or very

---

[80] Many quotes from Aristotle in the *Partidas* come from *Poridat de poridades*, attributed to Aristotle via Arabic, coming from the Arabic encyclopaedia *Sirr al-asrār*, and known in the West as *Secreta secretorum* [Secret of Secrets]. It was translated from Latin into Hebrew by Judah Al-Harizi, and into Castilian with the title *Poridat de poridades* (cf. Seudo Aristóteles, *Poridat de las Poridades*, ed. Ll.A. Kasten, Madrid: S. Aguirre, 1957).

rapidly, or very slowly, and when it is spoken with the tongue, and not by gesticulation with the limbs, exhibiting boorishness by means of them; as for instance, by moving them very frequently, so that a person seems to men to attempt to explain what he says rather by means of them, than by speech: for this is a great mark of ill-breeding, and weakens the argument. Moreover, the words should be satisfactory, for as it is bad when there are too many, it is not good when there are too few (5, 7)...[81]

Practical education also involved the personal and private life of the heir to the throne, including his sex life. At a time when it was perfectly normal, especially among the male nobility, to have concubines and lovers, the Learned King states in the *Partidas* (II, 5, 3), how the heir to the crown should behave in his sex life, avoiding "vile" and "inconvenient" women when it comes to "creating a lineage":

> This should be avoided for two reasons: first, lest they degrade the nobleness of his line; second, in order that they be not begotten in unsuitable places. For a king degrades his lineage when he makes use of vile women, or of many of them, because if he should have children by them, neither he nor his government will be so honorable: and also because he will not have them legitimately, as the law directs. By being much given to women in this way, he will sustain thereby great injury of body, and will lose his soul also by this means; for these are two things which ill become every man, and especially a king, wherefore King Solomon said that wine and women, when they are much used, cause even wise men to deny God.[82]

In this regard, Alfonso was not very far from his model Aristotle, who recommended to the young Alexander:

> Always behave in a prudent way in what you have to do,
> Speak with your vassals about all your plans,
> They will be more loyal if you do things so;
> Be especially wary of loving women. (stanza 53)

5. *The Art of War*

Alfonso's primitive biographers who knew him personally, Fr. Gil de Zamora or Jofré de Loaysa, ignore his childhood or adolescence. This is understandable for, at the time, childhood was brief. Impoverished

---

[81] *Las Siete Partidas*, II, Tit. VII, law VII, trans. Samuel Parsons Scott, p. 304.
[82] *Las Siete Partidas*, II, Tit. V, law III, trans. Samuel Parsons Scott, p. 287.

children had to work from an early age in order to survive, and the children of the nobility, especially kings, despite Fr. Gil de Zamora's remark that they had a blissful childhood, had to learn the difficult art of war, another way of learning to survive. The use of weapons and military strategy were essential components of a medieval prince's education. Princely education manuals and Alfonso himself in his works insisted on the importance of this matter in a prince's apprenticeship (*Partida* II, 4, 19).

The most important activities of the young Alfonso during his intellectual and military apprenticeship period were indeed accompanying his father on military campaigns against the Moors in the South and hunting parties. During these campaigns, the young prince interacted with the company and participated in their activities in and outside the military camp, all of which were necessary for training himself in the hard life of the medieval warrior and in military arts. This is also the period when he probably began his romantic involvements. Among the most celebrated of his various lovers and concubines was the noblewoman doña María de Guzmán (or Mayor Guillén de Guzmán), with whom he had the longest and most sincere of his relationships from age 19 (1240), and it would have ended in marriage if reasons of state had not interfered.[83] He had a daughter with doña Mayor, whom he named after his mother, Beatriz. She would become one of Alfonso's most beloved children, and the only who accompanied him during a lonely period in Seville when everyone else abandoned him. Beatriz was given in marriage to Alfonso III of Portugal in 1254 as part of the agreements on the Algarve dispute. Dom Dinis, one of the greatest medieval Portuguese kings, was born from this marriage.

As mentioned, in the *Partidas* (II, 5, 3), Alfonso described how the king should behave in his sex life, avoiding "vile" and "inconvenient" women when thinking about "creating a lineage." Doña Mayor was clearly not in this category, thus Alfonso loved and respected her,

---

[83] Doña Mayor Guillén was descended from the illustrious Guzmán family. Alfonso seems to have had a fairly stable relationship with her, at least during the time he was single. We know that in the winter of 1244, during a pause in the conquest of Cartagena, the young prince visited Alcocer (Guadalajara), hometown of doña Mayor, who had already given him a daughter. Alfonso in fact had three children out of wedlock with doña Mayor. The noblewoman was a discreet, reserved person, with many good qualities. On doña Mayor, see A. Pérez Arribas, *Alcocer, historia y arte*, Guadalajara: Ed. OPE, 1974, pp. 64–67; and J. Llampayas, *Alfonso X: el hombre, el rey y el Sabio*, Madrid: Biblioteca Nueva, 1947, p. 53 and ff.

as well as the daugher they had. All seems to indicate that, upon his
ascent to the throne, he followed all the prescriptions of the *Partidas*, at least with respect to "vile" women.[84] In contrast to his paternal
grandfather, Alfonso IX, and his father-in-law, don Jaime of Aragón,
who led sexual lives not in keeping with royal dignity, Alfonso was
much more well-bred and exemplary, although, as it was customary,
he did have several lovers, even after his marriage (doña María, ex-
wife of Alvar Fáñez de Lara, and doña Dalanda, who was probably of
Jewish or Moorish descent); with them he had at least four children
out of wedlock whose names appear in his last will.

Besides what could have been the sexual habits and customs of the
nobility in the thirteenth century, including the fact that having lovers
was a sign of distinction, psychologists in our day attribute the continuous change of lovers to introverted and immature people, which
seems to have been Alfonso's case. This produced unstable feelings in
his love life. In Alfonso's case, there was not a single "blessed" woman,
but rather several. That need to change would indicate the instability
and inconsistency of his feelings, which is typical of immature people.[85]

Regarding his studies and exercise of the art of war, it should not
surprise us that Alfonso, at the young age of ten, was already participating in a military campaign in 1231, having as counselor and
protector one of the most celebrated warriors of the time, don Alvar
Pérez de Castro, known as *el Castellano*.[86] The objective of the military
campaign of 1231 was to maintain control of the conquered areas in
lower Andalusia. One of the main actions took place near Jerez, when
the Christian troops of Pérez de Castro had to confront the army of
Ibn Hud of Murcia. Known as the "Jerez Cavalcade," it was described

---

[84] The *Cantiga* 10 contains a graphic, perhaps autobiographical vision of Afonso's
thought expressed in *Las Partidas*. In the sixth sketch, we see the king who, for the
love of the Virgin, renounced carnal love; with the help of the Virgin, he rejects the
devil and a group of women who, for their seductive aspect, may be the "vile" women
the *Partidas* speak of.

[85] F. Torres González, "Rasgos médico-psicológicos de Alfonso el Sabio" in *Alfonso
X y Ciudad Real*, pp. 107–140. See also chap. 8.

[86] In his *Estoria de España*, Alfonso tells us in the third person how his father "sent
his son, the prince don Alfonso, to go on the expedition to the land of the Moors;
and he sent don Alvar Pérez de Castro, el Castellano, to go with him as his guardian
and as commander of the army, because the prince was still very young and since he
had no strength and Alvar Pérez was a very skillful and courageous man" (*PCG*, II,
chap. 1040, p. 724b).

in great detail by Alfonso in four chapters of his *Estoria de España*.[87]
The impressive and extraordinarily violent clash between the warring
parties must have left a lasting impression on the ten year-old, who
remembered it in highly dramatic passages in his detailed narrative:
"Et las bozes et los alaridos de los moros, et los roydos de los atan-
bores et de los annafiles eran tan grandes que semeiaua que el çielo et
la tierra todo se fondía" ["And the voices and the cries of the Moors
and the noise of the drums and the Moorish trumpets were so great
that it seemed that earth and heaven were caving in"].[88] Alfonso had
to witness, for the first time in his life, the "beheading" of five hundred
Moorish prisoners that don Alvar had entrusted to him in the rear-
guard.[89] He also witnessed how Christians fought at the cry of "Saint
James! And some times, Castile!"; and in his teenage imagination, like
in that of many of the Muslims and Christians present there, he claims
to have seen the traditional image of St. James fighting next to the
heavenly army amid the Christian warriors: "And they say, and the
Moors themselves confirmed it later, that Santiago appeared there on
a white horse and with a white banner in one hand and a sword in
the other, and that with him were a legion of white knights; and they
even affirm they saw angels above them in the air; and that these white
knights appeared to assail them more than anyone else. And also a
great number of Christians saw this vision."[90] That the Moors did not
dare raise their heads in fear of St. James as a result of this episode
is indeed a pious belief (II, chap. 1044, p. 729a). What is certain is
that Alfonso learned much about the art of war participating in military campaigns, although he was "very young and not yet too strong,"
and that the conquest of Jerez was a landmark in the reconquest of
al-Andalus.

In conclusion, when Alfonso reached the throne, he was an intellectually mature man, with extensive political, scientific, historical, literary, military, and practical training, despite the opinions of
his detractors to the contrary. He also learned much from real life
and from his contact with his subjects, as well as in military camps,

---

[87] *PCG*, chaps. 1040–1044.
[88] *PCG*, II, chap. 1043, p. 726b.
[89] The prince was covering the rear, and he held five hundred Moors who had been
captured during the expedition; and don Alvar Pérez, who was at the front, gave
orders to have them decapitated, and they did. (II, chap. 1043, p. 726a–b)
[90] *PGG*, II, p. 727a.

surrounded by soldiers and merry folk, including troubadours, poets, women soldiers, and other protagonists of the merry life. His interest in satirical poetry and burlesque compositions that appear in his *cantigas de escarnio* (*songs of mockery*) are also a result of such contact.[91] His festive poetry and his profane songs, as well as his composition dedicated to the *Dean de Calés*, an obscene piece, were the product of his early years, when he was only a prince and was surrounded by friends his age, and did not have either his grandmother Berenguela nor his father by his side, chiding him, nor did he have government duties to tend to.

6. New Horizons

At age 31, in full physical and intellectual maturity, gifted with a prodigious intelligence primed by an exceptional education in all areas of knowledge, with military and government experience unprecedented for any prince in the Middle Ages, and with a boundless curiosity, Alfonso was perfectly prepared, not only to reign but also to launch the cultural revolution that earned him the label of the "Learned King."

In fact, given these precedents, once invested as king, he would almost immediately begin to execute his most ambitious projects. In his early works, such as the *Partidas*, there are numerous allusions to the usefulness of education and knowledge for future rulers but also for society in general. The *leitmotif* of his vernacular cultural revolution appears clearly laid out in a Latin-Castilian bilingual note that opens his first great historiographic project, *Estoria de España*. This note, placed under a miniature that shows Alfonso on the throne surrounded by courtiers and townspeople, portrays the pedagogical objectives of his entire oeuvre. In his bilingualism, Alfonso clearly indicates the step forward towards a vernacular culture, and he would never look back:

> The noble prince of Spain [...] named Alfonso [...] who by his merits surpasses all praise [...] makes the deeds of Spain known in this book, in such a way that through it, one can know many things that

---

[91] E. Ramos, *Las Cantigas de escarnio y maldecir de Alfonso X*, Lugo: Reprografía Alvarellos, 1973; J. Paredes Núñez, "Las cantigas profanas de Alfonso X el Sabio," in *La lengua y la literatura en tiempos de Alfonso X el Sabio*, Actas del Congreso Internacional, Murcia, 1984–1985, pp. 449–466.

are to come. Therefore, if through past things someone wants to know the future ones, may he not reject this work, but rather keep it in mind. It is useful to read it many times because we can see many things you will profit from and in the difficult things, you will learn lessons [...] through it, you will flee from the worse things and embrace the best. Oh Spain! If you take the gifts that the wisdom of the king offers you, you will shine with fame and grow in beauty. The king, who is the beauty of Spain and the treasure of her philosophy, gives teaching to the Spaniards; may the good embrace the good teachings and give the vain ones to the vain.[92]

In reality, Alfonso, given his inclination towards letters and culture in general, took after his maternal great-grandfather don Alfonso VIII, founder of the first Castilian university at Palencia. He also shared in his father's attitude towards knowledge as tool for the wise ruler, as is clear from the letter on the founding of the University of Salamanca: "Because I understand that it is to benefit my kingdom and my land that I grant and order that schools be instituted in Salamanca."[93] The progressive attitude of his forebears towards education was complemented by the increasing use his father made of the vernacular, Castilian, in his office, according to studies by Julio González: "...it increasingly and with relative integrity appeared in personal documents and began to emerge in royal edicts; during his time, it would end up imposing itself in the last decade."[94]

The young prince thus had good models to imitate, both on his father's side as on his mother's side. Alfonso was, to use a favorite expression of his, what the stars had predicted: what he carried in his genes but also the result of the fine education his parents gave him. The most prominent figure in his intellectual education, besides his father, was his paternal grandmother, Queen Berenguela, who devoted herself to him, as she had to his father. Alfonso, in turn, showered her with admiration and praise in his *Estoria de España*.

However, none of his forebears could have been the model for the most original aspect of his cultural revolution: his opening up to new

---

[92] *Estoria de España*, Ms. Escur. Y-i-2, fol. 1v. The beautiful and richly decorated illustration allows us to classify the manuscript as the "regal Alfonsine codex," composed for Alfonso.

[93] C. Ajo González y Sainz de Zúniga, *Historia de las universidades hispánicas*, 10 vols., Madrid: CSIC, 1957–1975, I, p. 436.

[94] *Reinado y diplomas de Fernando III*, 3 vols., Córdoba: Monte de Piedad y Caja de Ahorros, 1980–1986, I, p. 19.

horizons determined by his deep understanding of the complex social reality of the Iberian Peninsula. We could not close this chapter on Alfonso X's education without mentioning, albeit briefly, one of its most important aspects: his extraordinary knowledge and understanding of Judeo-Muslim culture.[95]

From the discussion up to this point, it becomes clear that Alfonso X, as was expected, received an education steeped in the Western Greek and Latin and Christian traditions, although it was imparted outside of the religious institutions of the period. His education, for the most part lay, must have left a deep mark on his personality, for, despite his respect for Latin Church culture which dominated Christian Peninsular society, he never excessively praised it nor its representatives at the time, which leads us to consider the Judeo-Muslim aspect of his education.

The two geographical poles along which his life developed were Toledo, which had a vibrant Arab-Jewish culture even after the Christian conquest (1085), always reinforced by new Mozarab and Jewish immigrants escaping from the south; and Seville, a city where, following his conquest, Alfonso resided for long periods, because that was the location of his father's court and where he would be buried. Direct contact with a culture and a language that for four centuries had dominated the intellectual life of his native city and Seville, which he called "the most noble of Spain,"[96] must have inspired projects in the young prince which later became the basis of a cultural revolution unprecedented in Christian Europe. In Seville, Alfonso established the capital of the kingdom and the most important cultural center of the peninsula. There he founded the schools of "Latin and Arabic." Seville became his Athens and as a new Creon, he imparted his cultural message to all his subjects.[97]

The influence of Muslim culture on Alfonso's public and private life has already been noted. The music, the art in the illustrations of the *Cantigas*, the games, the refinement and pleasure, and even the decorative objects in the court of Alfonso X displayed his preference for all

---

[95] Cf. H.S. Martínez, *La convivencia en la España del siglo XIII. Perspectivas alfonsíes*, Madrid: Ediciones Polifemo, 2006, which includes an extensive bibliography on the subject.

[96] *Setenario*, p. 16.

[97] On the relations between Seville and Alfonsine culture, cf. F. Rico, *Alfonso X y la GE*, pp. 118, 159 and ff., and p. 206.

things Oriental. We are not saying that Alfonso was a philo-Muslim and therefore an enemy of Christianity, as papal documents insinuate when they associate him with the worse elements of the Sicilian Hohenstaufens, who also sympathized with Muslim culture. Alfonso's political philosophy and religious foundations were firmly anchored in Christian doctrine, as is shown by his unfulfilled dream of becoming emperor of the Christians. But we would like to stress the causes and motives, both personal as well as official as king, that led him to such a change in attitude towards the traditional culture of Christian Spain that happened during his reign. Such a change entailed the abandonment of traditional theological-ecclesiastic culture as well as the incorporation and assimilation of the Peninsular cultures of a great number of his subjects, namely Jewish and Muslim culture. Márquez Villanueva writes: "[T]hat great cultural thaw was a new humanism, which, for the first time, acknowledged non-Christian thought on equal footing and completely independently from religion. This concept straddled East and West, but it was mostly the East that engendered this attitude of an appreciation of knowledge and radically new ways of confronting man and nature."[98]

This change, in a society that was steeped in theological-Christian culture and was essentially as anti-Jewish and anti-Muslim as the rest of Europe at the time, represented in the opinion of many, a very dangerous compromise with the enemy of Christianity. Rome, along with all of Christendom, was clamoring for a crusade that would end with Islam's domination forever, and they must have been horrified at the ease with which this Castilian Ghibelline moved between Jews and Muslims. It is therefore not surprising that the pope denied him the title of emperor, even when Alfonso was as qualified as any candidate to the title.

---

[98] *El concepto*, p. 130.

CHAPTER THREE

ALFONSO KING

1. Alfonso and the Conquest of Murcia and Seville

In a warring society, such as medieval Spain, an important part of a nobleman's education, especially of one who aspired to the throne, was mastering the use of weapons, war strategies, and conquest. Alfonso X had the chance to put his knowledge into practice during the campaigns of the 1230s–40s, when during his father's illness (1243), he headed an army into a new campaign in Andalusia (*PCG*, II, chaps. 1060–1065). At this time, Alfonso practically inherited not so much Fernando III's war strategy as his cultural policy. The policy was based on four main directives geared towards unifying the Peninsular territories still under Islamic domination: Christianizing the lands, repopulating them with Christians brought from the north; unifying them under the crown of Castile, including spreading its language and customs; Romanizing them, that is, uniformly imposing civil law and a central administration; and "mudejarización" or melding the two cultures, Islamic and Christian. These directives also dictated the fundamental attitudes towards reconquered and repopulated lands during Alfonso's reign.[1]

The conquest of Murcia and surroundings did not happen overnight or though a single military campaign. The first military interventions took place towards 1214 with the annexation of Segura de la Sierra, which was finally incorporated into the Crown of Castile between 1220 and 1230. The first land and town grant documents issued by Fernando III to the Order of Santiago as reward for their

---

[1] On the various aspects of Alfonso's cultural policy, cf. R. MacDonald, "Law and Politics: Alfonso's Program of Political Reform," in R.I. Burns, ed., *The Worlds of Alfonso the Learned and James the Conqueror. Intellect and Force in the Middle Ages*, Princeton, NJ: Princeton University Press, 1985. pp. 150–202; F. Márquez Villanueva, *El concepto cultural alfonsí*, Madrid: Editorial Mapfre, 1994; J.F. O'Callaghan, *The Learned King*, pp. 189–195; and "The Ideology of Government in the Reign of Alfonso X of Castile," *EH*, 1 (1991–1992), pp. 1–17.

military aid are dated 1235 and 1239.[2] In 1241 Fernando III asked the
Great Master of Santiago, Rodrigo Yáñez, to create a strategic division
between the kingdoms of Murcia and Granada in order to avoid collaboration between them; in a privilege granted to the Order on July
5, 1243, Fernando III mentioned practically all the towns along the
limits of Segura.[3]

The conquest of the region of Murcia, as was the case with many
others, was achieved thanks to two main factors: the territory's frag-
mentation into small independent emirates and the internal crisis of
these minor kings, which allowed the Christian kings the possibility
to profit from their political and social instability and weakness to
seal mutually favorable agreements among these emirs, independently
from the emir of Murcia, Muhammad ibn Yûsuf ibn Hud. Ibn Hud
acknowledged that many of these leaders were in conflict with him
and that he was unable to control them. This, according to Torres
Fontes, led him to send his son Ahmed towards the end of 1243 to
Toledo in order to interview the prince don Alfonso to explore ways to
subject his own kingdom to the protection of Castile.[4] Alfonso found
himself in Toledo, preparing a new expedition against Andalusia. The
truce his father signed with the King of Granada had expired and
Christians were in danger of losing control of Al-Andalus once more.
Don Fernando entrusted the new expedition to his son, providing a
first-rate army and the support of the royal chamberlain, don Ruy
González Girón. The troops were gathering in Toledo and the final
preparations were being carried out just as the messengers of the King
of Murcia arrived (March 1243). Ibn Hud's messengers proposed to
Alfonso (since his father was still ill at Burgos) the surrender of "the
city of Murcia and all the castles from Alicante all the way to Lorca

---

[2] Cf. D.W. Lomax, *La Orden de Santiago, (MCLXX–MCCXXV)*, Madrid: CSIC,
1965, p. 118; and C. de Ayala Martínez, "La Monarquía y las Ordenes Militares durante
el reinado de Alfonso X," *Hispania*, LI, n. 178 (1991), pp. 409–465; and *La Orden de
Santiago en la evolución política del reinado de Alfonso X (1252–1284)*, Madrid: Universidad Autónoma, 1983.

[3] Cf. M. Rodríguez Llopis, "La evolución del poblamiento en la Sierra de la Segura
(provincias de Albacete y Jaén) durante la Baja Edad Media," *Al-basit*, vol. 19 (Albacete,
1986), pp. 5–32; and "Repercusiones de la política alfonsí en el desarrollo histórico de
la Región de Murcia, in *Alfonso X: aportaciones de un rey castellano a la construcción
de Europa*, Murcia: Región de Murcia, Consejería de Cultura y Educación, 1997, pp.
178–199.

[4] Cf. J. Torres Fontes, *Incorporación del reino de Murcia a la Corona de Castilla*,
Murcia: Academia de Alfonso X, 1973, pp. 36–48.

and Chinchillá," in return for Castile's protection.[5] Alfonso accepted the bargain and called another meeting at Alcaraz to discuss the terms of submission.

The documentation regarding the so-called Treaty or Pact of Alcaraz has been lost, but Professor Torres Fontes, on the basis of other reliable sources and chronicles, has reconstructed a fairly plausible version. Along with the surrender of the cities specified in the treaty, there were also other conditions, some of which should be stressed for the way they reflect what the Castilian policy of reconquest had been at least since Alfonso VI: submission and payment of tribute in exchange for the survival of the emir's and the population's status quo.[6] In the case of the submission of Murcia and its territory, the main conditions were the surrender to the king of Castile of half of all the emirate's revenue, the permission to keep a Castilian garrison and the appointment of a "merino mayor" (leader) for the entire territory. In exchange, the emirate would receive Castile's military protection, would be guaranteed the continuity of its Islamic social and economic system, respect for private property and freedom of religion for all Muslim subjects.[7]

Three important towns were excluded from this pact: Cartagena, Mula, and Lorca. They supported the king of Granada and refused to accept the conditions of submission, but were forced into it. In mid-April of 1244, Alfonso returned to Murcia to launch an attack against the three cities. After the fall of Mula, Lorca resisted but at the end of June, under the pressure of a Castilian military force, the emir was forced to sign a pact similar to that of Alcaraz.[8] Cartagena resisted longer, perhaps thanks to help received from the other side

---

[5] *CAX*, chap. X, pp. 49–51.

[6] Cf. J. Torres Fontes, *op.cit.*; H. Salvador Martínez, *La rebelión de los burgos. Crisis de Estado y coyuntura social*, Madrid: Tecnos, 1992, chap.I: "Una política de alienación," pp. 29–49.

[7] Although *CAX*, chap. X, pp. 49–51, does not explicitly mention a "pact" or "treaty," there must have been some knowledge of it, since the aforementioned conditions of submission are fairly thoroughly laid out. Cf. J. Torres Fontes, "Murcia: la conformación de un reino-frontera," in *La expansión peninsular y mediterránea (1212-1350), Historia de España* ed. by R. Menéndez Pidal, vol.XIII, Madrid: Espasa Calpe, 1990, pp. 431–505. A version of the events as told by one of the protagonists, Alfonso X himself, has also been preserved in his *PCG*, II, chap. 1065, p. 744. For Arab versions of the conquest, see: A. Carmona González, "Textos árabes acerca del reino de Murcia entre 1243 y 1275. Aspectos jurídicos y políticos," *Glossae. Revista de Historia de Derecho Europeo*, vol. 5-6 (1993–1994), esp. pp. 243–244.

[8] On the rebellion and subsequent submission of Lorca, An Arab chronicler writes:

of the Strait. In 1245 Alfonso requested Roy García de Santander, an expert ship-builder, to build the necessary ships for an attack by sea against Cartagena, thus creating the first Castilian fleet.[9] In the spring of 1245, according to Torres Fontes, a land and sea operation forced the emir to capitulate.[10]

The conquest of Granada, one of the many great cities of al-Andalus, carried out by Fernando III and his son Alfonso, was achieved more through diplomacy and political tact than by force of arms. Muhammad I of Granada chose to kiss Fernando III's hand and thus become his vassal, paying a tribute of 150,000 maravedís per year, rather than suffering the horrors of the siege and running the risk of losing everything. Becoming a vassal entailed, besides attending the Cortes whenever they were called, lending military assistant to the king of Castile every time he required it. But the king of Granada also had to surrender the city of Jaén, which had to be vacated of its inhabitants.[11] In exchange, Muhammad ibn al-Ahmer would remain king of Granada as he had been before his surrender, and he would enjoy the protection of Castile, while allowing Christian garrisons to exist in his territories.[12] This highly debated pact made it possible for Granada to survive as a Muslim kingdom for two more centuries instead of having to capitulate in 1248. But it was precisely the continuity of the Muslim kingdom of Granada that produced its period of maximum splendor, including the construction of the Alhambra and other monuments we admire nowadays.

...When the inhabitants surrendered Murcia to the Christians in the month of shawal the year 640 (=1243), [the emir of Lorca] deemed it the wrong decision and expressed his disagreement arguing with them in their language and fighting them with his lance. This brought so much harm to his country that he was forced to beg for peace. And he remained so until his death... (in A. Carmona González, "Textos árabes acerca del reino de Murcia," p. 243).

[9] Years later, in 1273, Alfonso would found, precisely in Cartagena, the Order of Santa María de España as a marine military order that was under the same rule as the Cistercian monks and was devoted to training Christian seamen to fight the infidels by sea. The Order lasted only seven years. Cf. J. Torres Fontes, "La Orden de Santa María de España," in *Miscelánea Medieval Murciana*, 3 (1977), pp. 75–118; C. de Ayala Martínez, *La Orden de Santiago*, p. 44 and ff.

[10] Cf. A. Torres Fontes, "La incorporación de Lorca a la Corona de Castilla," *BRAH*, CLXV (1968), pp. 131–151; and "Del tratado de Alcaraz al de Almizra. De la tenencia al señorío (1243–1244)," in *Miscelánea Medieval Murciana*, XIX–XX (1995–1996), pp. 279–302.

[11] Cf. Bartolomé Ximena Patón, *Historia de la antigua y continuada nobleza de la ciudad de Jaén*, Jaén, 1786.

[12] Cf. F. Pérez Algar, *Alfonso X, El Sabio. Biografía*, Madrid, 1997, pp. 114–117.

It was during this period of conquests in the South that the first known conflict between Fernando III and his son Alfonso occurred. The motive was Alfonso's first venture, the campaign of Portugal, which his father in principle opposed because he did not want to wage war against another Christian king, and even less in this case in which the pope too was involved. Sancho II of Portugal had married a blood relative, doña Mencía López de Haro, the widow of don Alvar Pérez de Castro. Supporters of the future Alfonso III of Portugal, Sancho's brother, feared that their candidate would never reach the throne if Sancho, as was expected, would sire an heir. Practically all Portuguese bishops were behind prince Alfonso of Portugal, and they were at odds with don Sancho because of the excessive taxes he exacted from churches to finance his military conquests of Alentejo and Algarve. The bishops could not find a better reason to depose don Sancho than to request his marriage separation. Pope Innocent IV dictated the separation sentence, but don Sancho refused categorically to leave his wife. In July 1245, the pope had no choice but to depose him and to name his brother Alfonso as *procurador* (representative) of the kingdom.[13]

When prince Alfonso of Castile learned of the deposition, he decided, for an unknown reason, to recruit an army and invade the kingdom of Portugal in order to defend the rights of don Sancho. Don Fernando was radically opposed to the invasion and forbade him to recruit troops, but Alfonso managed to gather a small army at Toro, requesting 300 knights from don Jaime of Aragón, and in December 1246 he marched into Portugal.[14] Aided by supporters of the deposed king, he arrived in Leiría, managed to rescue don Sancho and brought him back with him to Castile. Don Sancho died shortly after and was buried in the cathedral of Toledo next to the graves of Alfonso VII and Sancho III of Castile.[15]

---

[13] Cf. A. Herculano, *História de Portugal*, vol.V, Lisboa: Livraria Bertrand, s.a., pp. 7–10.

[14] On the activities and participation of Jaime I in military campaigns in the 1240s, ending with the conquest of Valencia in 1245 and the border settlement between Castile and Aragón negotiated by a young Alfonso, see *Llibre dels feits*, ed. F. Soldevila, *Les Quatre grans cròniques*, Barcelona: Selecta, 1971, chaps. 127–357.

[15] Noteworthy Spanish sources dealing with this incident include: Fr. Gil de Zamora, "Biografías de Fernando III y Alfonso X," p. 320; *Anales Toledanos III*, quoted ed., *CHE*, p. 177; J. de Loaysa, *Crónica de los reyes de Castilla*, ed. and trans. A. García Martínez, Murcia, 1982, p. 153. Cf. J. Mattoso, *História de Portugal, 2. A monarquia feudal*, Lisboa, 1993, pp. 126–133.

Historians have wondered why Alfonso embarked on an adventure that led him into an open conflict with his father. I believe that considering his political ideology regarding the concept of king and kingdom, which had not yet been formulated in writing but expressed later in all his legal works, we can find a satisfactory explanation for his military action. As is well known, in the *Partidas*, which is the work that best represents his political ideology in a structured way, Alfonso argues for the autonomy of royal power independently from the pope's theocratic universalism.[16] Therefore, excluding other reasons such as possible rights to the Algarve or his nascent Ghibellinism, the main reason to defend the rights of don Sancho was his conviction that the pope had violated the temporary sovereignty of the king of Portugal, lacking a real legal right to depose him, because he was the supreme lord and ruler of his kingdom. Despite his father's reprimand, Alfonso never forgot that political and military adventure. Years later, when his legal works were written, he recalled the story of Sancho's deposition. In the famous *Cantiga* 235, when speaking of the betrayal his own son and noblemen carried out against him, he compared them to what the Portuguese did to their king, affirming that not even don Sancho of Portugal had suffered a similar fate (see below chap. 9).

In 1246, still under the command of prince Alfonso, Castilian troops marched on Triana, at the gates of Seville. However, conquering the largest Muslim city was not as simple as it initially appeared—the city resisted bravely for two years. Capitulation arrived on November 23, 1248, on Alfonso's birthday. The conditions for surrender were very different from those imposed on cities that did not put up military resistance. The basic principle in Fernando's reconquest was that any city or territory that was taken over by force would have to be occupied by Christian dwellers and would have to pay the consequences of total submission, meaning that it would cease being a Muslim city and become a seat of the Christian kingdom to the south.

The conquest of Seville constitutes the most important episode in the Reconquest since Alfonso VI's capture of Toledo in 1085.[17] Both

---

[16] Kings, each one in his kingdom, are the vicars of God, appointed over people to maintain them in justice and in truth in temporal matters, just as an emperor does in his empire...(*Las Siete Partidas*, Partida II, Tit. I, Law V, trans. Samuel Parsons Scott, Philadelphia: University of Pennsylvania Press, 2001, p. 271.; and cf. our Conclusion.)

[17] See the details in Andrés Marcos Burriel, *Memorias para la vida del Santo Rey Don Fernando III*, ed. Miguel de Manuel Rodríguez, Madrid, 1800, repr., Barcelona:

don Fernando and his son Alfonso were captivated by the city's marvels. The prodigious art and culture of the palaces, alcazars, mosques,
gardens, and other public monuments impressed the rough Christian
warriors from the North. Enthralled by the Pearl of the Guadalquivir,
Alfonso wrote moving eulogies of that city in his *Estoria de España*
and even more in the *Setenario,* and he would soon turn the city into
an important Christian-Muslim cultural center.

The Reconquest of the Penisular territories, as we shall see, encoun-
tered many difficulties during Alfonso X's reign, but it could be argued
that it was practically over. The active participation of Alfonso in his
father's campaigns would not have been possible without the mutual
trust and respect they felt for each other.

2. Marriage

During the years prince that Alfonso was learning the art of war and
love, the court of Castile, under the leadership of his father, began the
search for a suitable wife for him. Already in 1234, there had been
an initial attempt at marrying him to Blanche of Champagne. Some
years later, in 1237, during the negotiations that resulted in his father's
marriage to Juana of Ponthieu, there was yet another attempt at marrying him to princess Felipa, the sister of doña Juana. Both endeavors
failed. Now, in 1240, after considering the various candidates, a princess from Aragón was chosen, doña Violante, daughter of don Jaime I
of Aragón and Violante of Hungary. The father of the bride had been
married previously to Leonor of Castile, daughter of Alfonso VIII,
and was thus the sister of Berenguela, the illustrious grandmother of
Alfonso X. The king of Aragón had a son with Leonor, named Alfonso,
but he repudiated his wife after asking the pope to annul his marriage
because he argued that there was a blood ties impediment between
him and Leonor. (They were both indeed grandchildren of Alfonso VII

"El Albir," 1974; D. Ortiz de Zúñiga, *Anales eclasiásticos y seculares de la muy noble
e muy leal ciudad de Sevilla*, 2 vols., Madrid, 1795; P. de Espinosa de los Monteros,
Segunda parte de la Historia y Grandeza de la ciudad de Sevilla, Sevilla, 1630; A. Ball-
esteros Beretta, *Sevilla en el siglo XIII*, Madrid, 1913; M. González Jiménez, M. Borrero
Fernández, I. Montes Romero-Camacho, *Sevilla en tiempos de Alfonso X*, Sevilla, 1987.
A contemporary, Fr. Guillermo de Calzada, abbot of the monastery at Sahagún, a great
friend and admirer of Fernando III, composed a Latin epic panegyric on the victory of
Christians in Seville: Guillelmi Petri de Calciata, *Rithmi de Iulia Romulea seu Ispalensi
Urbe*, ed. D. Catalán and J. Gil, in *AEM*, V (1968), pp. 549–588.

de Castile.) The marriage was annulled, and doña Leonor and her son returned to Castile, where the king married Violante of Hungary, sister of Bela IV of Hungary. Doña Leonor spent the rest of her days locked up in the Monastery of Las Huelgas, founded by her father, while her son Alfonso, notwithstanding the obstacles laid by his stepmother, came to occupy the throne of Aragón upon his father's death.[18]

Prince Alfonso was about twenty and his bride Violante, seven. A seven-year waiting period was therefore imposed before they could marry and consummate the marriage. Meanwhile, Alfonso had several children out of wedlock.[19]

It was precisely during the siege of Seville (1248) that the bishop of Huesca arrived bearing a reminder from Jaime I of Aragón that his daughter had reached the age of fourteen and it was therefore time to carry out the marriage contract. Fernando answered that at the moment he was unable to lift the siege of Seville in order to attend a marriage, and thus requested an extension, assuring the king of Aragón that the marriage would be celebrated as soon as the city fell. Few details are known about this wedding that was celebrated in Valladolid on December 1, 1249, apparently without much display, when Alfonso was already 28 and Violante, 15. King Fernando could not attend, but his wife, Juana of Ponthieu did.[20]

The young queen had a resolute personality and did not compromise in matters relating to her rights and what she wanted to achieve. We will later discuss her tenacity in negotiating agreements with her husband's enemies. Their first child was a girl, Berenguela (1253–1313?), followed one year later by Beatriz (1254–1280), who married

---

[18] The marriage engagement was negotiated by Fernando III and Jaime I towards 1240. Cf. F. Valls-Taberner, "Relacions familiars i politiques entre Jaume el Conqueror i Anfos el Savi," *BH*, XXI (1919), pp. 9–10. F. de Moxó y Montoliu, "El enlace de Alfonso de Castilla con Violante de Aragón: marco político y precisiones cronológicas," *Hispania*, 49 (1989), pp. 69–110.

[19] Among those children, besides doña Beatriz (b. Guadalajara, 1244), Urraca and Martín Alfonso, who became abbot of Valladolid, were also the product of his relationship with doña Mayor Guillén, before his marriage to Violante; while Alfonso (Fernández), also known as *el Niño*, was born to him by doña María Aldonza, after he married Violante. In total, Alfonso had 15 legitimate and illegitimate children whose names are known, the same number of children his father had.

[20] F. de Moxó y Montoliu, "El enlace de Alfonso de Castilla con Violante de Aragón," pp. 69–110. There exists an interesting letter from Alfonso to don Jaime de Aragón, dated at Écija, December 8, 1249, where he explains to his future father-in-law his marriage plans (in M. González Jiménez, *Diplomatario Andaluz de Alfonso X*, Sevilla, 1991, no. 3).

Guillermo VII de Montferrat in 1271. Subsequently and alternating with girls, the coveted male children were born: Fernando, known as de la Cerda (1255–1275), who in 1269 married Blanche, daughter of Louis IX of France. The celebrated Infantes de la Cerda, don Alfonso and don Fernando, were born from this marriage. Other children followed: doña Leonor (1256?–1275); don Sancho (1258–1295), Alfonso's future heir in Castile-León who married doña María de Molina; doña Constanza (1259?–?); don Pedro (1261–1283), who married Marguerite of Narbonne; don Juan (1264–1319), who married Juana de Montferrat; doña Isabel (1265?–?); doña Violante (1266?–?), the wife of the powerful Lord of Vizcaya, Diego López de Haro; and finally don Jaime (1267–1284).

Alfonso X was not happy with doña Violante. She had, as we will see, extraordinary qualities, but, like her mother, according to Ballesteros, "she would inherit the dynastic roughness of the Carpathian mountains, which would inspire a legend about criminal intrigue."[21] When don Fernando, the heir, died prematurely (1275), albeit of a natural death on his way to repress the North African Moorish revolt, the mother queen openly supported the right of succession of Fernando's children, the Infantes de la Cerda, going against the interests of her own son, Sancho. She defended the rights of her grandchildren to such an extent that she even abandoned the court of Castile and her husband in favor of international protectors and alliances that would render her grandchildren successful. Later, she changed her mind and took part in courtly and kingdom plots to claim the rights of her own son, don Sancho, until she succeeded in deposing her own husband from the throne. But Sancho was not grateful to her. In 1295, on his deathbed, don Sancho confessed to his cousin, don Juan Manuel, that also his mother, "who was alive," had cursed him often and that even if she was on her deathbed and wanted to give him her blessing, she would be incapable because she too had not received it from her father. "Likewise I believe, the queen, my mother, did not have the blessing of her father, because he did not love her much because of the suspicion

---

[21] *Alfonso X*, p. 56. On doña Violante, cf. R. Kinkade, "Violante of Aragón (1236–1300): An Historical Overview," *EH*, 2 (1992–1993). On the mother, cf. F.O. Brachfeld, *Doña Violante de Hungría, reina de Aragón*, Madrid, 1842.

he had against her that she was responsible for the death of her sister, princess doña Constanza."[22]

Constanza of Aragón was the first wife of prince don Manuel (d. 1283), Alfonso X's brother. After their marriage, they settled in Castile, where Constanza died suddenly of unknown causes. Don Juan Manuel was born from his father's second marriage to Beatriz of Savoie (Escalona, 1282). In Part II of *Libro de las armas* (Book of Arms), don Juan Manuel cites a popular rumor according to which doña Constanza might have died after eating poisoned cherries given to her by her sister Violante (*quoted ed.*, p. 85). Juan Manuel, who cites the confession of the dying Sancho IV, speculates, albeit with a bit of skepticism, that this was the reason why Jaime I cursed her.

3. Acclamation

Fernando III died in Seville on May 30, 1252.[23] Before his death, according to Alfonso's account, he gathered round his children and wife doña Juana:

> [...] and then, and firstly, he asked his son, don Alfonso, to come near, and he raised his hand towards him, and made the sign of the cross and gave him his blessing, and likewise he did with all the rest of his children...ordering them to answer "Amen." And he said more: 'Son, you will remain rich in lands and in many and noble vassals, more than any other king in Christendom; make an effort to do good and be good, because you have the means to.' And he said more: 'My lord, I leave you all the land from the sea up to here, which the Moors seized from don Rodrigo of Spain; and under your lordship will be all the conquered part and the part paying you tribute. If you know how to keep it in this state in which I leave it to you, you will be as good a king as me, and if you

---

[22] "Razón del rey don Sancho," Tercera parte del *Libro de las armas* de don Juan Manuel, ed. J.M. Blecua, *Obras*, II, pp. 137–138.

[23] Jofré de Loaysa, court historian present at Fernando's death, writes in a letter to a don Jaime de Aragón:
> Lord: I hereby inform you that the king of Castile died on the last day of the month of May, and he was buried the first day of June, in the presence of all of his children, except the Archbishop of Toledo. He was buried in front of the altar of the Church of Santa María in Seville (Archivo de la Corona de Aragón, Cartas Reales, n. 17; quoted by M. González Jiménez, *Alfonso X el Sabio*, pp. 33–34)

For further discussion on whether the death occurred on the 30th or the 31st, as Loaysa argues, see J. González, *Reinado y diplomas de Fernando III*, I, p. 79.

win it on your own, you will be a better king than me, and if you fail in this, you will not be as good as me.[24]

Alfonso would never forget these words uttered by his father. For Alfonso, maintaining the unity of the lands, and perhaps even expanding them, would be a challenge he would face the rest of his life. Upholding the ideal of the unity and indivisibility of the inherited kingdoms, which would be later codified in the *Partidas*, would become an unsolvable dilemma when his critical moment arrived, and he was dispossessed of his crown, with no clear successor, his kingdom torn apart by civil war. The challenge, however, would become greater when he considered what his father had insinuated in mentioning the despicable name of don Rodrigo, saying: "If you know how to keep it in this state in which I leave it to you, you will be as good a king as me, and if you win it on your own, you will be a better king than me, and if you fail in this, you will not be as good as me." Alfonso, who was aware of his father's future conquest plans, knew perfectly well what he was referring to: the project of conquering Northern Africa, an area that had also belonged to the Visigoth Empire until it was lost by don Rodrigo. As Alfonso retells in his *Estoria de España*, his father, Fernando III, eagerly wanted to conquer this North African territory, but he did not succeed.[25] Kneeling at his father's bed, Alfonso must have promised to accomplish the conquest of the lands his father was unable to subdue for lack of time. It was a dream goal, many times attempted, but never achieved. And if, as Alfonso relates in the *Setenario*, his father never wanted to be called emperor until recovering the old territories of the Visigoth Empire,[26] Alfonso himself tried to win both the title of emperor and the North African crusade, without

---

[24] *PCG*, II, chaps. 1132–1133, pp. 772–773b–a. On the impact the message of don Fernando had on his heir and admirer, see Ballesteros, *Alfonso X*, p. 55 and 60; and A. Rodríguez López, "'Rico fincas de tierras et de muchos buenos vasallos, más que rey que en la cristiandat ssea.' La herencia regia de Alfonso X," *Cahiers de Linguistique hispanique médiévale*, 23 (2000), pp. 243–261.

[25] Alfonso devotes practically the entire chapter 1131 of his *Estoria de España* to an exposition of his father's wishes; also, *Crónica de Veinte Reyes*, based on the narrative of the *PCG*, goes to great lengths in its expositions of the crusade plans drafted by Fernando III, who, according to the chronicler, had made major preparations for the venture.

[26] *Setenario*, ed. K. Vanderford, Buenos Aires, 1945. Repr. Barcelona: Crítica, 1984, pp. 9–10. In fact, the same historian who was commissioned by Fernando III to write the history of Spain, Rodrigo Jiménez de Rada, also never gave him the title of emperor.

succeeding at either, however, and even losing his own crown in the process. Reflecting on these two realities and the words of his father, ("and if you win it on your own, you will be a better king than me, and if you fail in this, you will not be as good as me"), while in his Seville retreat at the end of his days, he must have been overcome by a paralyzing anguish.

On June 1, don Fernando's body was transferred from Seville's Alcázar to the Church of Santa María where, as Alfonso writes in his *Estoria de España*, he was buried "On Saturday, the third day after his death." Thirty years later, Alfonso had the remains of his mother, Beatriz of Swabia, removed from the Monastery of Las Huelgas and transferred to the Cathedral of Seville, to be buried next to her husband.[27] In all territories he conquered, Fernando III was venerated as a saint starting in the first half of the fourteenth century, but he was not officially recognized as a saint by Rome until four centuries later, in 1671, while his cousin, Louis IX of France, was proclaimed a saint in his own century (1297), just a few years after his death.

On the same day his father was buried, in the Cathedral of Seville, Alfonso, according to an old Visigoth custom, "was raised as leader" on the freshly sealed grave by the noblemen present at the burial ceremony.[28] The transference of royal power in Castile was always a civil affair, because it was believed power derived from *heredamiento* (an inheritance or succession pact established among the living usually on the occasion of a marriage), and it was transmitted by succession rights from father to son. Hence the dramatic gesture of raising the heir above the grave of the father. Following the acknowledgement on the part of his most powerful subjects, the coronation (if it may be called so) took place, for Alfonso, in a very personal gesture, according to chroniclers and biographers, did not want to be crowned by a Church authority (a bishop or abbot) in a grand religious ceremony.

---

[27] *PCG*, II, chap. 1134, pp. 773–774.

[28] Cf. Jofré de Loaysa, *Crónica*, ed. A. Ubieto Arteta, Valencia: Editorial Anubar, 1971, p. 15; and in the letter to Jaime I de Aragón cited in note 23, he writes: "E tan aína cuemo fue soterrado, estando sobre la fuesa, leuantaron a don Alfonso, et fue cauallero lo primero día de junio. Et el rey enuió por todos los ricos omnes quel uinieren a Seuilla" (Archivo de la Corona de Aragón, Cartas Reales, n. 17). Cf. F. Valls-Taberner, "Relacions familiars," pp. 9–11. See also J. de Zurita, *Anales de la Corona de Aragón*, Zaragoza, 1610 [reprint 1967]; Marqués de Mondéjar, *Memorias históricas del Rey D.Alfonso el Sabio. Observaciones a su Chrónica*, Madrid, Joachin Ibarra, 1777, p. 62.

Instead, he himself took in his own hands the crown his father had worn, which lay on the altar, and placed it on his own head. Such a gesture was a clear sign that the young king was not willing to grant to Church authorities (or any other authority, for that matter) the slightest power (including symbolic) over him and his kingdom. Alfonso's coronation was therefore not accompanied by that quasi sacramental ritual that was part of the ceremony in all other European kingdoms, namely, the unction of hands, the placement of the crown by a bishop, and the delivery of the scepter. This does not mean, however that Alfonso, like the majority of thinkers on the origin of the State and civil power at the time, did not believe in the divine origin of power, but rather that, "in temporal matters," it did not depend on anyone.[29]

The crowning ceremony was usually preceded or followed by the knighting ceremony.[30] In Alfonso X's case, according to the Marqués de Mondéjar, another old Peninsular tradition that excluded the intervention of Church or civil authorities was followed: "And so that it be understood that there will never be any earthly king that may have power over him, he himself will strap the sword, which is a symbol of the cross, around his waist and thus be knighted; and should not be knighted by anyone else."[31] Therefore, according to Mondéjar, Alfonso

---

[29] There are several recent scholarly studies on the sacred or profane character of the Castilian monarchy. The idea of a desacralized Castilian monarchy was put forth by T. Ruiz, "Une royauté sans sacré: La monarchie castillane du Bas Moyen Age," *Annales: Économies, Societés, Civilizations*, 39 (1984), pp. 429–453. In many works, P. Linehan has also argued for the lay character of Castilian kings' crowning ceremonies: "The Accession of Alfonso X (1252) and the Origins of the War of the Spanish Succession," in D.W. Lomax and D. Mackenzie, *God and Man in Medieval Spain*, Warminster, 1989, pp. 59–79; especially in *History and the Historians of Medieval Spain*, Oxford: Clarendon Press, 1993, pp. 426–454. On the other hand, J.M. Nieto Soria has claimed, based on equally valid arguments, that both the Castilian monarchy and crowning ceremonies had a sacred character, "Imágenes religiosas del poder real en Castilla – siglos XIII–XVI," *En la España Medieval*, V/2 (1986), pp. 709–729; in his book *Fundamentos ideológicos del poder real en Castilla (Siglos XIII–XVI)*, Madrid: Eudema, 1988; and more recently in the article: "Origen divino, espíritu laico y poder real en la Castilla del siglo XIII," *AEM*, 27/1 (1997), pp. 43–100.

[30] In a privilege document dated December 6, 1253, Alfonso affirmed: "E por mi que fu[i] hy Rey e reçebí hy cauallería," in A. Ballestros, *El itinerario de Alfonso el Sabio*, I, 1251–1259, Madrid: Tip. de Archivos, 1935, p. 7.

[31] Mondéjar, *Memorias de Alfonso X*, p. 59. This author cites Alonso Núñez de Castro, who tells of a statue of St. James at the Monastery of Las Huelgas in Burgos, which was used in the knighting ceremonies. The image, through a mechanical movement, would give the new king a light blow on the back, thus knighting him without human intervention. This is how Fernando III would have been knighted. The statue was subsequently taken to Seville and was also used to knight Alfonso X (Mondéjar, op. cit., pp. 60–61). This custom was followed until the time of Alfonso XI.

was knighted following the same ritual that had been followed for his father, that is, using the mechanical device of the statue of Santiago; this ceremony most likely took place on Sunday, June 2, 1252.[32] The next day, the people of Seville acclaimed him as king shouting: "Castile, Castile, Castile".[33] The coronation celebrations took place in Seville's Alcázar, the place of choice of Muslim kings, and following the Christian conquest, the preferred residence of Christian monarchs as well.

Mondéjar's account of Alfonso X's knighting ceremony using a mechanical statue, told in his *Memorias de Alfonso el Sabio*, was adopted practically by all of his past and most of his present biographers.[34] Only recently, Peter Linehan, following some critics who had already expressed some doubts, rejected it as having no historical basis, suggesting it instead as a fabrication of the Marquis of Mondéjar in the early years of the eighteenth century and which was then repeated by all subsequent historians.[35] What is known about the statue, of course, contradicts the possibility that it might have been used for such a purpose in the twelfth and thirteenth centuries. Nothing is known before 1332 about its existence or use, when, according to *Crónica de Alfonso XI*, it was used to knight Alfonso XI. This is the first time that primitive chronicles mention the use of a statue for the purpose of knighting a king, but according to this chronicle, it was not in Burgos, but rather in Santiago de Compostela, where the king had gone out on a pilgrimage in order to be knighted.[36]

---

[32] In chap. 1034 of the *PCG* Alfonso X describes his father's knighting ceremony held in 1219 in the Monastery of Las Huelgas, but he does not mention a slap on the neck or a mechanical statue, but rather identifies his grandmother, doña Berenguela, as the one who strapped the sword around him (II, pp. 718–719). Later on and despite his admiration for his grandmother, in the *Partidas*, Alfonso X would ban women, regardless of their status ("por más honra que tubiese, aunque sea enperatriz o reina por herencia," II, 21, 11), from knighting men.

[33] Cf. Mondéjar, *Memorias*, p. 60.

[34] Among others, Ballesteros, *Alfonso X*, p. 54; and R.I. Burns, *The Worlds of Alfonso the Learned and James the Conqueror*, pp. 12–13; J.M. Nieto Soria, "La monarquía bajomedieval castellana," *Homenaje al prof. Juan Torres Fontes*, II, Murcia, 1987, p. 1227; and González Jiménez, *Diplomatario andaluz de Alfonso X*, Sevilla, 1991, p. XXIX, note 3.

[35] *History and Historians*, p. 427 and following, especially p. 593 note 119, where he details the story of the fabrication regarding the statue preserved in the church of Las Huelgas. See also Linehan, "The Accession of Alfonso X (1252)," p. 68 and ff.; and "The Politics of Piety: Aspects of the Castilian Monarchy from Alfonso X to Alfonso XI," *RCEH*, 9 (1985), pp. 385–404, esp. pp. 395 and 396.

[36] Ed. C. Rosell, in *BAE*, 66, *Crónicas de los Reyes de Castilla*, I, Madrid, 1875, pp. 173–392, p. 234a–b. It seems this is not the same statue that is preserved at Las Huelgas.

All of these historiographic traditions regarding the process of the transfer of power clearly show that Alfonso's act of placing the crown in his own head in itself was not groundbreaking in terms of the secularization of political power, but rather that he was following an old tradition. In Peninsular monarchies, except perhaps for the early kings of Asturia-León, such power had always been lay and secular.[37] In contrast to what happened around the same time in France and England, peninsular Christian kings were not invested with the same sacred and almost priestly character that came from the act of the unction of hands and head and the placement of the crown by a bishop of the kingdom (Reims or Canterbury) in a ceremony similar to that of the consecration of priests and bishops.[38]

In Castile, when a new king acceded to the throne, the ritual was a lot simpler, for it consisted only in the acclamation on the part of the people and the oath of fidelity. There was no religious ceremony during the act of coronation. Such was the case of Fernando III in 1217, who was acclaimed king by his subjects on Valladolid's market square, when all those present could not be accommodated in the palace.[39] Apparently, for some time, Alfonso X and his courtiers attempted to incorporate into the *Partidas* an unction ceremony for kings, but the project was not implemented. What Alfonso did make clear repeatedly, both in the *Partidas* as in other writings, especially the *Espéculo*, was that the king is a vicar of God in earthly matters, which supported the idea that his authority derived directly from God ("Dei gratia rex," ["King by the grace of God"]), and that he had no intermediaries, whether they be emperors or popes: "By the grace of God we have no superior over ourselves in temporal matters."[40] On the other hand,

---

[37] This topic was much debated. Alfonso VII's coronation and unction, described in detail in the *Chronica Adefonsi Imperatoris (CAI)* (1148), is defended as legitimate by most Spanish historians, including J.-M. Nieto Soria, *Fundamentos ideológicos del poder real en Castilla*; y *Iglesia y poder real en Castilla. El episcopado, 1250–1350*, Madrid: Universidad Complutense, 1988; but the account of the *CAI* is considered a fabrication by Linehan, *History and the Historians*, pp. 427–31.

[38] Cf. C. Sánchez Albornoz, "La *ordinatio principis* en la España goda y post-visigoda," en *Estudios sobre las instituciones medievales españolas*, p. 705.

[39] *PCG* in chap. 1029, II, pp. 713–714, describe in great detail Fernando III's accession to power in Valladolid's market square in 1217, when he was taken by his mother, Queen Berenguela, and the oath sworn by all his subjects. His knighting ceremony did not occur until November 27, 1219 at the Monastery of Las Huelgas, three days before his marriage to Beatriz.

[40] *Espéculo*, bk. I, law13; cf. J.A. Maravall, "Del régimen feudal al régimen corporativo en el pensamiento de Alfonso X," *BRAH*, 157 (1965), pp. 213–268; pp. 223–225; J.-M. Nieto Soria, *Fundamentos ideológicos*, pp. 112–116. Alfonso X, like most Spanish

Alfonso, in contrast to kings who based the legitimacy of their power on being elected by their own subjects, ruled "by right of *heredamiento* [inheritance]."[41]

Perhaps no other episode in Alfonso's life reveals best this human and demythologized view of the king as well as the secular and lay character of the Castilian monarchy than one narrated in the *Cantigas de Santa María* [*Songs of Holy Mary*], a work that, for many contemporary critics, truly portrays many of the everyday actions of the Learned King and his court. *Cantiga* 321 tells the story of a girl who had a tumor in her throat, which the doctors were unable to cure. Her desperate mother was advised by a "good man" to seek out the help of Alfonso X, convincing her that, "all Christian kings have this power, that as soon as they place their hands on the painful spot, the sick are cured."[42] When the woman, her child, and the "good man" appeared before the king, he told the well-intentioned man: "Friend, to what you tell me I answer you this and say that what you advise me is not worth a miserable fig, although you talk a lot and chatter [...] Because you say I have miraculous power, you speak foolishness."[43] To believe that all Christian kings have healing powers simply because they are kings wasn't worth a trifle for Alfonso X; if someone had said such a thing, "you speak foolishness." Alfonso, naturally was not addressing that simple "good man," but was rather speaking against the neighboring kings of France and England because they pretended to be miraculous healers, healing scrofula (or mumps) by imposing their hands. The Learned King, on the contrary, told the woman to give her child a drink of the water that was used to wash the image of the Virgin, and the girl, the *Cantiga* tells us, recovered her health. God, not kings, through faith in the mediating power of Mary, worked miracles.[44]

---

jurists of his day and subsequent ones, held that the king of Spain was not at all subject to the power of the Emperor of the Holy Roman Empire (according to a proverb, "rex in regno suo imperator est"). Cf. J.A. Maravall, *El concepto de España en la Edad Media*, p. 403 and ff.

[41] *Espéculo*, I, I, 13; cf. Linehan, *History and the Historians*, pp. 431–432 and notes.

[42] *Songs of Holy Mary of Alfonso X, The Wise: A Translation of the* Cantigas de Santa Maria, trans. Kathleen Kulp-Hill, Tempe, Arizona: Arizona Center for Medieval and Renaissance Studies, 2000, p. 389. All quotations in English from this work, unless otherwise indicated, are taken from this edition.

[43] *Songs of Holy Mary*, p. 389.

[44] J. F. O'Callaghan, "The *Cantigas de Santa Maria* as an Historical Source: Two examples (nos. 321 and 386)," in I.J. Katz and J.E. Keller, eds., *Studies on the Cantigas*

4. *Pending Business*

In the final balance that Fernando III, on his deathbed, drew up for
the benefit of his son and heir, it was clear that the conqueror left this
world with the firm conviction that the entire Peninsula had been conquered or subjected to vassalage and tribute payment. The Kingdom of
León-Castile, which in 1252 Alfonso inherited from his father, had the
greatest political and military might of the Peninsula and was one of
the most powerful in Christian Europe. It could also be said that it was
at peace and had good relations with other Peninsular and European
kingdoms. But we cannot forget that everywhere there were also small
political conflicts and family feuds.

Castile was indeed going through a period of peace and prosperity,
following the conquest and subjection of Andalusia. And while great
armies recruited everywhere in Europe were being defeated in the Far
East, in the Western end of Christian Europe, Castilian troops had
taken over practically all territories until then occupied by Peninsular
Muslims. Castile was respected and admired in all of Europe.

Under Fernando III the limits of the Kingdom of Castile-León had
been extended to include the three small Muslim kingdoms of Niebla, Murcia, and Granada. The first two enjoyed a special status, as
protected territories, while Granada was subjected to vassalage and
paid an annual tribute of 250,000 maravedís.[45] Although in the North,
relations with the Kingdom of Navarra were not very amicable, there
was however a truce that allowed the new king of Castile to solve several small pending conflicts. Relations with the Kingdom of Aragón,
on the other hand, were cooler, despite Alfonso and Violante's marriage in 1249. Violante was the daughter of Jaime I, through whom a
pact of friendship had been agreed. The ambitious king of Aragón was
alarmed by Castile's rapid expansion to the South, which made both
kingdoms view each other with suspicion, fearing a sudden outbreak
of old hostilities.

---

de Santa Maria: Art, Music, and Poetry, Madison, WI: Hispanic Seminary, 1987, pp.
387–402.

   [45] *Crónica de Alfonso X,* (from now on *CAX*), Spanish ed. C. Rosell, in *BAE,* LXVI,
Madrid, 1953. chaps. 10 and 58. All quotations in English from this work taken from:
Chronicle of Alfonso X, trans. Shelby Thacker and José Escobar, Lexington, Kentucky:
The University Press of Kentucky, 2002. pp. 49–51, 191–194.

One of Alfonso's first tasks was the renewal of all administrative posts in the kingdom. Analyzing the first diplomas issued by Alfonso X, several important changes are noticeable in the names of those who occupied important positions in Fernando III's court, namely, the *mayordomo* (chamberlain), *alférez* (ensign or standardbearer) and notary of the king. The first position was handed over to Juan García de Villamayor, a childhood friend of Alfonso's; Rodrigo González Girón was appointed to the second position; and he kept, albeit for a short while, Diego López de Haro as royal *alférez*. That is to say, Alfonso chose men of his generation or friends he trusted, or with whom he had an understanding, for the most important positions. He followed the same principle for the high offices in the local administrations of the kingdoms of León and Castile.[46]

But Alfonso's first political crisis was with the neighboring kingdom of Portugal. The conflict derived from the revolt of the aristocrats and the clergy in 1246, which led to the destitution of the Portuguese king, Sancho II and the accession to the throne of his brother, don Alfonso III, count of Bologna and a protégé of the Holy See. As noted above, Sancho II sought the help of Castile in defense of his rights and it was precisely prince Alfonso who, against his father's wishes, lent his assistance to the deposed Portuguese king. Naturally, this action created greater tension with Alfonso III, who launched a military campaign to take over several border towns and extend his rights over the Algarve. Days after his accession to the throne, Alfonso X surveyed the territories around the disputed border, perhaps planning an attack against the Portuguese king. But the attack did not take place because Alfonso III asked for the intervention of Pope Innocent IV, who in a bull dated January 13, 1253 declared that the disputed lands of the Algarve belonged indeed to his protégé, Alfonso III of Portugal.[47] But, to placate the Castilian king, in a meeting convened at Chaves probably in May of that same year, the Portuguese king signed a complicated agreement stating that Castile would enjoy the right to profit from the Algarve until the heir to the Portuguese throne turned seven,

---

[46] Cf. J. González, *Reinado y diplomas de Fernando III*, III, pp. 427–429 (on Fernando III's last diplomas); and I, pp. 95–96 (for Alfonso X's first diplomas). Cf. R. Pérez Bustamante, *El gobierno y la administración territorial de Castilla, 1230–1474*, 2 vols., Madrid, 1976, I, pp. 44–46; and J. Sánchez-Arcilla, "Las reformas de Alfonso X en la organización territorial de la Corona de Castilla," *Revista de la Facultad de Derecho*, 9 (Madrid, Universidad Complutense), pp. 120–125.

[47] In E. Berger, *Les Registres d'Innocent IV*, vol.III, Paris, 1897, no. 6.247, p. 161.

at which point the territories would revert to the Portuguese crown.[48] The pact was sealed, as it often occurred, with an engagement, that of Beatriz, the illegitimate daughter of Alfonso X and his lover doña Mayor Guillén, to Alfonso III of Portugal.[49] The Portuguese king was almost forty, and Beatriz was only ten.

Alfonso X must have been very satisfied with this as his first experience at resolving an international political crisis. He had obtained the use of territories that did not belong to him according to a papal ruling, and perhaps more importantly, he had placed his daughter on the Portuguese throne, becoming a father-in-law to his rival. The Portuguese crisis must have also taught the young Castilian king how carefully one had to proceed when papal diplomacy was involved, because things did not end there.

The Algarve question was the first one to be resolved, but there were still problems to be sorted out with the two other Christian kingdoms, Navarra and Aragón. On October 31, 1234, at scarcely thirteen years of age, Alfonso, heir of Castile, was engaged to Blanca, heir of Navarra, in a marriage pact signed by Alfonso's father and Teobaldo I of Navarra. The pact stated that the child born from that union would one day become the king of both kingdoms. In the pact, the king of Navarra also managed to commit to preserve the crown of Navarra for his daughter Blanca, even if he would one day have a male child from a legitimate wife. In return for such generosity, Fernando III would give Teobaldo life-long tenure of Guipúzcoa and several castles, along with the sum of 2000 maravedís. But, as soon as Teobaldo felt more secure on the throne, he began to show signs of not wanting to hold the agreement. Breaking a marriage agreement such as this one, which entailed the future union of the two kingdoms, was a very serious matter that even justified a declaration of war. But the intervention of pope Gregory IX in 1237 temporarily averted a disaster and managed to get both kings to agree to a truce. Relations were always very tense, in the truce between Navarra and Castile during Fernando III's reign. But armed conflict never exploded, partly too because, as we said, Fernando was opposed to waging war against other Christian monarchs.

---

[48] More details in J. Mattoso, "As relações de Portugal com Castela no reinado de Alfonso X, o Sábio," in *Fragmentos duma composição medieval*, Lisboa, 1987, p. 86.

[49] The narrative of these events, albeit from a different perspective, can also be found in the *CAX*, chap. 7, pp. 41–42.

Things would change with the accession of Alfonso X to the throne. The king of Navarra was a boy at the time, Teobaldo II (his father, Teobaldo I, had died July 8, 1253), and his mother, Marguerite Dampierre, was regent of the kingdom. We will not address the question of Navarra, which was closely connected to that of Gascogne and Leonor of Provence's right to it upon her marriage to Henry III of England. But it's worth mentioning that Alfonso, who was vary aware of the rights Castile claimed over that region, reached an agreement with Henry III whereby he relinquished such rights in exchange for help from the king of England in the Navarra conflict and an African crusade. The treaty was signed at Toledo on March 31, 1254 and sealed with the marriage engagement between prince Edward, heir to the British throne, and Leonor, Alfonso X's half-sister.[50]

In Seville, Alfonso, remembering the affront from almost twenty years earlier, demanded Teobaldo II's submission, a way to obtain the submission of Navarra, and in order to attain it, he threatened to invade not only Navarra, but also the kingdom protecting it, Aragón.[51] According to Pero Marín, the prior of Silos who witnessed many of the events he narrates, the submission of Navarra was agreed upon and sealed as was customary, with a marriage during the Cortes celebrated at Vitoria in January 1256.[52] Alfonso was indeed at Vitoria between December 2, 1255 and January 24, 1256, and although there are no documents supporting the celebration of a Cortes, we know he was accompanied by an extraordinary number of noblemen and clergymen who must have witnessed Teobaldo's act of submission.[53] The act of submission of Navarra raises many questions for scholars, especially if we consider that Teobaldo, at the time, was about to marry a daughter of the king of France. On the other hand, it is difficult to contest an eyewitness's testimony.[54] These same Cortes were also important for another reason: during their celebration, don Fernando, the heir to

---

[50] Cf. Rymer, Foedera..., I, 1, pp. 178–179; and C. de Ayala Martínez, Directrices fundamentales, pp. 53–72; and A. Goodman, "Alfonso X and the English Crown," in Alfonso X el Sabio. Vida, Obra. y Época, Madrid, 1989, pp. 39–54.

[51] Cf. Moret, Annales...bk. XXII, chap. I, p. 258; J. Zurita, Anales de la Corona de Aragón, book III, chap. XLVIII, ed. A.Canellas López, Zaragoza, 1976, p. 571.

[52] Cf. Los "Miráculos romançados" de Pero Marín, Ed., introd. and indexes by Karl-Heinz Anton, Abadía de Silos, 1988, p. 45. Pero Marín's version is confirmed by Carlos de Viana in his Crónica de los reyes de Navarra, ed. C. Orcástegui, Pamplona, 1978, p. 169.

[53] Cf. CAX, chap. 3, pp. 32–34.

[54] Cf. C. de Ayala Martínez, Directrices fundamentales, pp. 137–138.

the throne of Castile born two months earlier, was recognized by the grandees of the kingdom.

After a visit to the monastery at Silos on November 5, 1255, Alfonso set out to Soria accompanied by the abbot, and "While the king was at Soria, with his great army ready to enter Aragón, the king don Jaime, his father-in-law, appeared before him with his sons and daughters, and he subjected himself to the king don Alfonso, that he may do with him and his children and his kingdom as he saw fit; and they immediately married prince don Manuel, the brother of king Alfonso, with princess doña Constanza, daughter of the king of Aragón. Once the kings had made their peace and regained each other's friendship, king don Jaime left for Aragón, and king don Alfonso sent all his people to go to their lands."[55] This act of submission and vassalage on the part of don Jaime to Alfonso is even more difficult to admit than that of the teenage king of Navarra. But the solemn character of the moment, the marriage engagement, and the presence of a reliable eyewitness such as the author of the *Miráculos*, carries considerable weight, especially because the details he provides have been shown to be true when compared to available documents.[56] However, I believe that, more than submission and vassalage, the agreement was more about peace and mutual help. In fact, from that moment on, the relationship between the two most powerful kings of the Peninsula improved considerably. The theory that it was a pact was confirmed by the fact that the meeting was sealed with the marriage between Constanza, daughter of don Jaime, and don Manuel, brother of Alfonso X.[57]

Before closing his chapter on Alfonso's visit in 1255–56 to the Monastery of Silos, Pero Marín writes that when Alfonso told the Abbot of Silos about the three graces he had received from the saint during his last visit, for which he rewarded the Monastery with the city's "martiniega" (tax paid on the day of St. Martin), he said: "And I tell you that Lope Díaz and all his vassals came under my mercy and they

---

[55] *Los "Miráculos romançados" de Pero Marín*, p. 46. We know from Alfonso's *Itinerario* that he was in fact at Soria on February 19, 1256 (Ballesteros, *Itinerario*, p. 153).

[56] The "vistas of Soria" are also narrated by J. Zurita, *Anales...*, bk. III, chap. LII, p. 584; and Moret, *Annales...*, bk.XXII, chap.II, pp. 271–272.

[57] Don Juan Manuel tells us about his parents' marriage: "Et bino el rey de Aragón para Soria et binieron se ý él et el rey de Castilla, et firmaron el casamiento del infante et de la infanta donna Constanza" (*Libro de las armas*, ed. J.M. Blecua, *Obras*, I, p. 130). Cf. F. Valls-Taberner, *Relacions familiars*, p. 283; Ballesteros, *Alfonso X*, p. 152.

delivered Orduna to me, and the king of Navarra became my vassal, and the king of Aragón, my father-in-law, gave me his children and his kingdom to do with them as I saw fit."[58]

Such political ambition on the part of the king of Castile would certainly have in the past alarmed not only the population of Navarra, but also Jaime I of Aragón, who feared that Alfonso would now aspire to dominate the other kingdoms of the Peninsula. If this attitude turned out to be real, it would profoundly alter the balance of political forces in the Peninsula that had previously existed during the reign of Fernando III. It was certainly the fear of a Castilian hegemony that led the king of Aragón before 1256 to establish an alliance with Navarra, when the regent, Queen Marguerite, came to his court in Monteaguado in April 1254 seeking help. Because of this alliance, any attack against Navarra would be considered an attack against Aragón, and vice versa. Some historians believe that, besides fearing the Castilian hegemony, the king of Aragón had other motives to create an alliance between Navarra and Aragón, perhaps rumors that Alfonso was about to repudiate his legitimate wife, Violante, daughter of the king of Aragón, because, after five years of marriage, Violante had only borne him a daughter, Berenguela, and not the desired male heir.[59]

For Alfonso X, who at the time wielded the strongest military power in the Peninsula, subjecting by force the small kingdom of Navarra would not have been difficult. But the alliance with Aragón changed matters. Defeating the combined forces of Navarra and Aragón would have been more difficult, so he gave in and waited for a more favorable occasion. Besides, within Castile, a general discontent among the nobility began to emerge. At the head was the powerful of Lord of Vizcaya, don Diego López de Haro, who had taken hold of Orduna, and a brother of Alfonso's, prince don Enrique. For his part, the king of Aragón also had to crush internal conflicts, such as the revolt of the Valencia region, led by the rebellious Muslim leader al-Azraq, which put the Castile-Aragón conflict on the back burner.[60]

---

[58] *Miráculos romançados*, p. 46.

[59] The text of the Navarra pact is reproduced in A. Huici-Miranda and M.D. Cabanes Pecourt, *Documentación de Jaime I de Aragón*, III (1251–1257), Zaragoza, 1978, no. 646, pp. 130–133. Cf. *CAX*, chap. 2, pp. 30–31.

[60] Cf. P. López Elum, *La conquista y repoblación valenciana durante el reinado de Jaime I*, Valencia, 1995; and J. Hinojosa Montalvo, *Las tierras alicantinas en la Edad Media*, Alicante, 1995.

These precedents, along with internal circumstances in Navarra and Aragón may have granted Alfonso the chance to obtain the submission of the king of Navarra during the Cortes at Vitoria and that of the king of Aragón though the Soria agreement, as well as the handing over of Orduña on the part of don Diego López de Haro, which is also mentioned by Pero Marín. But whatever happened to the mutual help agreement between Navarra and Aragón? After both kingdoms surrendered to Alfonso, it was never mentioned again, although probably as a result of this agreement, the two kingdoms continued as allies. On the other hand, relations between Jaime I (1213–1276) and Alfonso X were very intense from that moment on. Although they experienced ups and downs, in general they were good, especially towards the end of the life of don Jaime, an extraordinary figure, both as a warrior and politician of the thirteenth century, to whom Alfonso turned in his most difficult moments.[61]

We can therefore conclude that the state of Peninsular politics and of the relations between Castile and other kingdoms, as Carlos de Ayala Martínez argues, was one of temporary peace and truce, rather than of friendly relations. According to this scholar, Alfonso X "inherited a political attitude that engendered distrust and a latent hostility, if not an open conflict of the non-Castilian Peninsular group. One could characterize the political attitude inherited from Fernando III, and now clearly defended by Alfonso X, as hegemonic."[62] Obviously, this hegemony, despite Pero Marín's remarks, was never formally recognized by all the other Peninsular kingdoms, especially by Aragón. I am also not very certain that Alfonso attempted to impose it, except in the sense that it supported his aspirations to become the emperor of the Holy Roman Empire, or as a result of the violation of an agreement, such as that with Navarra, when he was acting in sole defense of his legitimate interests. There's no proof that he attempted to dominate Aragón, and if in the early years of his reign he harbored this ambition, beginning with the "Soria vistas," harmony and mutual cooperation prevailed over the political ambitions of both. As we shall

---

[61] On don Jaime, see: R. I. Burns, "The Spirital Life of James de Conqueror, King of Aragón-Catalonia, 1208–1276," *Catholic Historical Review*, 42 (1976), pp. 1–35; and "Castle of Intellect, Castle of Force: The Worlds of Alfonso the Learned and James the Conqueror," in *The Worlds of Alfonso the Learned and James the Conqueror*, pp. 3–22.

[62] C. de Ayala Martínez, *Directrices*, p. 52.; see also his *La monarquía y Burgos durante el reinado de Alfonso X*, Madrid, 1984.

see, on more than one occasion, Alfonso had to request military help and frequently too turned to his father-in-law for advice, since he was much more experienced than him in diplomacy and military matters.

Don Fernando had died without carrying out the "repartimiento," or division of territories that followed the conquest of the cities to the south, among the participating leaders and armies. Seville, the most notable and rich of all cities, still had to be divided up. This was an extremely important matter, for at the time the "repartimiento" was used as a way to compensate the participants and also as a political tactic to maintain and acquire new alliances with powerful noblemen, who were the ones who had real control of military forces. To carry this out in the most calm manner, Alfonso formed a commission of people he trusted: don Remondo, then bishop of Segovia and later of Seville, don Ruy López de Mendoza, and three more members. On May 1, 1253 they presented Alfonso with the impressive final document containing the details of the celebrated *Repartimiento de Sevilla*.[63] The historian of Alfonso's life tells us, in very general terms, that he behaved much better towards the nobility than his father had (chap. 1, pp. 27–29).

Finally, in family, personal, and intimate matters, a delicate question still remained to be solved. Alfonso had always behaved in a courteous and respectful matter towards his stepmother, Juana de Ponthieu, but the same could not be said of his brothers, particularly don Enrique. In the last years before his death, the king don Fernando had been exceedingly generous in his gifts to his wife, doña Juana, and his son, don Enrique, who, rumor had it, was the queen's lover.[64] As future heir, responsible for the possessions of the Crown, Alfonso had had

---

[63] See the edition by J. González, *Repartimiento de Sevilla*, 2 vols., Madrid, 1951.

[64] Fernando III had given doña Juana a vast land patrimony that included among other towns, Carmona, Marchena, Luque, and several other territories and estates in Córdoba, Jaén, and Arjona. Cf. J. González, *Reinado y diplomas de Fernando III*, I, p. 116. He had promised don Enrique dominion of the towns of Arcos, Jerez, Medina Sidonia, and Lebrija, whenever they would be conquered; in the meantime, and as a token of his promise, he had granted him the castles of Morón and Cote. Cf. M. González Jiménez, *Diplomatario Andaluz de Alfonso X*, Sevilla, 1991, n. 15. Don Enrique, a rebellious, adventurous figure inclined to fall in love, was mocked by satirical poetry in the period that paint him as the lover of his stepmother, whose coif he would take with him to battle as a lucky charm. Other poems present queen Juana crying and begging her husband for mercy for the prince. Cf. *Cantigas de amigo dos trovadores galego-portugueses*, ed. J.J. Nunes, Coimbra, 1926–1928, II, p. 132; see also the anthology Lisbon: Centro do Livro Brasileiro, 1973, nos. CXLV, CXLVI. On the rivalry between Alfonso X and his brother Enrique there's a vast literature: cf. M.

several confrontations with his brother Enrique, because of the lack of respect towards his father's wife and his father, rebuking him for his excessive spending. The two beneficiaries, fearing the worst, after the death of the king, handed over the royal diplomas of concession to the Maestre de Calatrava for him to keep in his custody. And indeed, following Fernando's death in 1253, Alfonso presented the issue to the queen, who reached an agreement with the new king, according to which she would only keep the estate of Marchena and other properties, handing the rest over to the crown. Regarding the concessions made to his brother, Alfonso demanded all the privilege documents that had been entrusted to the Maestre de Calatrava, and he personally destroyed them, leaving his younger brother dispossessed of a considerable inheritance. Despite having received extensive benefits during the *Repartimiento de Sevilla*, don Enrique never forgave Alfonso. Doña Juana, for her part, shortly after Fernando's death, returned to her own county of Ponthieu, where she married Juan de Neslé, and died, according to Ballesteros, in 1278.[65]

5. *The First Cortes: Seville 1252–1253*

Alfonso was the first king to plan out his government, especially when it came to monetary and fiscal policy, based on the decisions of the Cortes. The "Cortes generales" were assemblies of the king, his immediate family, the nobility, the clergy (including archbishops, bishops, the masters of the military orders—Santiago, Calatrava, the Templars and Hospitallers), and representatives of the cities.[66] Extant documents indicate that Alfonso summoned the *Cortes generales* on average every two years. "Ayuntamientos," as opposed to "Cortes," were smaller

---

de Riquer, *Obras completas del trovador Cerveri de Girona*, Barcelona, 1947, no. 36, pp. 102–105.

[65] *Alfonso X*, p. 922.

[66] On the topic of the Cortes during the reign of Alfonso X, i.e., number, dates of convocation, composition, and participants, see: *Cortes de los antiguos reinos de León y de Castilla*, Madrid: Real Academia de la Historia, tome I, 1861, on pp. 54–94 we find the notebooks of Alfonso X's Cortes, which were eight, according to the compiler of the volume. Cf. E.S. Procter, *Curia and Cortes in León and Castile 1072–1295*, Cambridge: Cambridge University Press, 1980; J.F. O'Callaghan, *The Cortes of Castile-León, 1188–1350*, Philadelphia: University of Pennsylvania Press, 1989; see also his *Alfonso X, the Cortes, and Government in Medieval Spain*, Aldershot-Brookfield, USA-Singapore-Sidney: Ashgate: Variorum, 1998, p. XIV.

assemblies that gathered only a few of the groups mentioned, and were usually called for a particular purpose in mind or in a specific region. They were summoned much more often than the Cortes.

During the first year of his rule, Alfonso had to deal with an internal crisis that had indeed begun during the last years of the reign of his father and which had then reached and alarming state: the kingdom's economy was practically bankrupt. The *CAX* explains how the prices of all products had risen excessively due to a devaluation of the currency in such a way that, for instance, the king of Granada, who had previously contributed a high percentage to the expenses of the kingdom (250,000 maravedís), now supplied a considerably smaller amount in terms of purchasing power. As a result of this, the chronicler continues, " During this time, because of the changes in the currencies, all things increased in price in the kingdoms of Castile and León and went up a great deal."[67] Hence "In the fourth year of the reign of this King Alfonso (1294 Era, A.D. 1256), many complaints came before him from all over his realms to the effect that prices had increased so much that people could not afford anything."[68] As many scholars have already noted, inflation was the economic scourge of Alfonso's administration.[69]

In order to solve the economic and monetary crisis, Alfonso called the Cortes at Seville (from October 1252 to the first months of 1253), in order to deal with the fact that "prices had increased so much" (*ib.*)[70] The first measure taken immediately was price control: "Because

---

[67] *CAX*, p. 28.

[68] *CAX*, p. 37.

[69] On the economic situation of Castilla-León when Alfonso acceded to the throne and throughout his reign, cf. M. del Carmen Carlé, "El precio de la vida en Castilla del rey Sabio al emplazado," *CHE*, 15 (1951), pp. 132–156; R. Pastor de Togneri, "Ganadería y precios, consideraciones sobre la economía de León y Castilla (siglos XI–XIII)," *CHE*, 35–36 (1962), pp. 37–55; T. Ruiz, "Expansion et changement: la conquête de Castille et la société castillane (1248–1350)," *Annales: ESC*, 34 (1979), pp. 548–565; and J.F. O'Callaghan, "Paths to Ruin: The Economic and Financial Policies of Alfonso the Learned," in R.I.Burns, *The Worlds*, pp. 41–67.

[70] We call "Cortes" the assembly Alfonso had with the three estates (clergy, nobility, and commons) guided by the various notebooks of *posturas* or taxes that were sent to the various city and town councils in Castilla-León. A. Ballesteros published the Nájera notebook ("Las Cortes de 1252," in *Anales de la Junta para la Ampliación de Estudios e Investigaciones Científicas*, III, -Madrid, 1911-, pp. 115–143; and cf. *Alfonso X*, pp. 68–74). Cf. J. F. O'Callaghan, "Catálogo de los Cuadernos," pp. 501–531, included in *Alfonso X, the Cortes, and Government in Medieval Spain*, Appendix IV. Procter doubts that the meeting at Seville in 1252–1253 was a Cortes session (op. cit.); but other scholars accept it. Cf. G. Gross, "Las Cortes de 1252. Ordenamiento otorgado al

of this, the king instituted the *cotos*, which set a price on all things, what amount each one should cost."[71] Hence mandatory fixed prices were established for a list of 61 consumer goods. Other measures complementing this one were adopted in order to lower the price of such products and increase the volume of consumer goods available on the market. Laws and norms were also established to diminish luxury and ostentation in clothing, forbidding the use of certain fabrics and pelts. Even horse accessories were regulated (saddles and bridles, which could not be made from costly materials). The export of economically useful animals such as cows, pigs, horses, mules, and other types of cattle was strictly prohibited in order to increase the amount of meat available in the kingdom. There were even limits set to what each person could eat or the number of guests that could attend a wedding. The activities of resellers or middlemen were also banned, since they too indeed contributed to the increase in prices.

In order to protect the environment and natural resources that agriculture and husbandry depended on, drastic measures were adopted: whoever set a forest on fire was sanctioned with the following punishment: "if they find him, he should be thrown in; and if he can't be caught, all his possessions should be confiscated." In order to avoid water pollution, Alfonso X forbade anyone from "throwing plants, or lime, or any other thing that might poison the fish."[72] Finally, and always looking to reduce prices, the Cortes adopted several fiscal measures regarding the transportation of merchandise, stipulating that cattle would only pay once for *montazgo* (a tribute for the passage of cattle across mountains), and all *portazgos* (the right of passage through city roads bridges or gates) existing before Alfonso's ascent to the throne were frozen. The young king, with the help of the Cortes, was certain that by adopting such drastic measures he would quickly resolve the production and scarcity issues in the kingdom as well as the inflation that had incensed his subjects.[73]

---

consejo de Burgos en las Cortes celebradas en Sevilla el 12 de octubre de 1252 (según el original)," *BRAH*, CLXXXII (1985), pp. 95–114.

[71] *CAX*, p. 37.

[72] Ballesteros, *Alfonso X*, p. 360.

[73] Cf. M.A. Ladero Quesada, "Las reformas fiscales y monetarias de Alfonso X como base del *Estado moderno*," in *Alfonso X. Aportaciones de un rey castellano a la construcción de Europa*, Murcia: Región de Murcia, 1997, pp. 33–54; J.F. O'Callaghan, "Paths to Ruin," in R.I. Burns, *The Worlds*, pp. 41–67; and "The Cortes en Royal Taxa-

But things could not easily be changed from one day to the next in a society where applying controls was not only the king's business. Thus, not much longer after the Cortes of Seville, the price control mechanism stopped working because merchants stopped cooperating:

> If people had trouble affording goods before this, they had it much worse afterward, since the merchants and other people who had things to sell hoarded them and refused to display them for sale. Therefore, everyone was in dire straits; in response, the king had to remove the *cotos* and order that things be sold freely at whatever prices the parties might agree upon.[74]

The author of the chronicle seems to concentrate only on the scarcity of goods due to hoarding, which made it necessary to lift price controls. But many modern scholars have stressed that the crisis was mostly monetary, due precisely to a lack of currency, which was in turn due to a silver shortage, the metal used for coins. Some scholars claim that the currency coined by Alfonso was of very high quality, and this was the very reason why it went out of circulation—it was hoarded by the wealthy, which then increased the prices of all products, since no currency was available to buy them. Regulations known as *posturas* on currency that were approved during the Cortes of Seville were meant as a way to control both hoarding as well as capital drain from the kingdom, seeking also to impose order in terms of prices.[75]

Contrary to popular perception—as demonstrated for example in P. Mariana's oft-quoted phrase, "because of looking up at the stars he lost the land"—these first Cortes demonstrate Alfonso's real interest in the state of the domestic economy and the living conditions of his subjects. All modern scholars of the economic problems during Alfonso's reign affirm that the Cortes of Seville laid down the foundations of the political economy of his kingdom, which Alfonso would successively alter according to various circumstances. In the 1258, 1268, 1272, and

tion," 379–398; J.L. Martín, "Aspectos socioeconómicos del reinado de Alfonso X," in *Estudios Alfonsíes*, Granada, 1985, p. 187.

[74] *CAX*, p. 37.

[75] A good summary of the exchange rates of the various currencies of Alfonso's time is available in M. González Jiménez, *Alfonso X*, pp. 38–39, note 6. Cf. E. Collantes Vidal, "Notas sobre las acuñaciones de Alfonso X," *Acta Numismatica*, VI (1976), pp. 141–166; J. Gautier Dalché, "Remarques sur les premiéres mutations monétaires d'Alphonse X de Castille," in *Melanges en honeur d'Etienne Fournial*, Saint Étienne, 1978, pp. 75–87; Id., "La politique monétaire d'Alphonse X," in *Homenaje al profesor D. Claudio Sánchez Albornoz en sus 90 años*, I, Buenos Aires, 1988.

1281–1282 Cortes, he continued to create norms that implemented measures taken in 1252. This is a clear indication that the causes of the monetary and inflation crisis at the beginning of his reign, which he tried to alleviate with the measures of the Cortes of Seville, should not be sought only in the high costs of territorial expansion and the military effort that Castile had to make during the reign of Fernando III, as one scholar argues.[76] On the contrary, the economic crisis was due to more complex, wide-ranging factors. The solution, however, would remain essentially the same throughout Alfonso's long reign.

Taking stock of Alfonso's first year in power and considering the efforts he made at improving the conditions of his subjects through the measures adopted during the Cortes at Seville, the anonymous author of the chronicle, who did not much sympathize with Alfonso, writes, "In that first year, the king engaged in doing things he thought were of great benefit to his kingdoms, and he stocked and provisioned the towns, villages, and castles that were on the Moorish frontier. He did the same for the towns and villages of the kingdom of Murcia, which were inhabited by Moors, and that he had won as a prince during his father's time."[77] The young king's attitude was thus one of prudence and vigilance, or, as was mentioned in military circles, "si vis pacem, para bellum" ("if you want peace, prepare yourself for war"). Alfonso had inherited a country at peace, but was well aware of the unstable relations with the vanquished that a good part of the economy of the kingdom depended on. Hence, according to the historian, measures were taken to avoid any unexpected situation.

Alfonso's first official contact with the Muslim kingdom of Granada, which had been subjected to Castile from the death of don Fernando, occurred during the 1254 Cortes of Toledo that the Nasrid sultan attended.[78] According to the CAX, on that occasion the king of Castile signed the "treaties and agreements they had formerly held."[79] This

---

[76] Cf. T.F. Ruiz, "Expansión y crisis. La repercusión de la conquista de Sevilla en la sociedad castellana, 1248–1350," in *Sociedad y poder real en Castilla*, Barcelona, 1981, pp. 13–48.

[77] *CAX*, p. 28.

[78] Cf. *CAX*, chap. 3, pp. 32–34. There were two reasons for the summoning of these Cortes: the swearing in of Princess Berenguela, heir to the throne, who was born in the last months of 1253 (doc. in Daumet, *Mémoire sur les relations*, doc. I, pp. 143–146; W. Piskorski, *Las Cortes de Castilla*, Appendix I, p. 196; and Ballesteros, *Alfonso X*, pp. 130–131), and the levying of special taxes (*CAX*, pp. 32–34).

[79] *Chronicle of Alfonso X*, p. 32.

means that in all likelihood, Alfonso ratified the agreements between Castile and Granada signed by his father in 1246, obtaining in return new strategic/military concessions.[80] Alfonso was not expecting major problems because he was convinced everything was firmly agreed upon, and the Nasrid king did not show any signs of discontent.

The political situation on the international front, however, was not as pleasant as on the domestic front. The death of the German emperor Frederick II Hohenstaufen in December 1250, followed closely by that of his son Conrad IV, left a long international political vacuum that lasted over twenty years. This period, known as the "Great Interregnum of the Empire," was an important time in Alfonso's reign, the first twenty years when his initiatives and ambitions reached their zenith in his political career. If on the one hand the lack of a civil head symbolizing the union of Christendom threatened the stability of international politics, from the perspective of Castile, a number of possibilities opened up for Alfonso, among which was the chance to aspire to the imperial crown of his relative Frederick II, given the fact that Alfonso was a descendant of the Staufens.

During the first two years of his reign, Alfonso was also favored by Pope Innocent IV (1243–1254), who viewed with great interest Alfonso's "pious projects" and supported them with exceptional ecclesiastic tax concessions (such as the "tercia") that churches in Castile were supposed to contribute.[81] The "pious projects" the pope refers to in his correspondence with Alfonso evidently had to do with the famous African crusade that Fernando had planned but did not accomplish. According to C. de Ayala, "Alfonso X devised an intervention plan for Northern Africa within the first six months of his government";[82] and that must have excited the pope, as can be gleaned from the papal correspondence from the period. Alfonso and his counselors expected that the pope's favorable attitude regarding the crusade would turn into concrete support when the moment to choose a candidate for the imperial crown arrived. In 1252, in his grandiose Seville palace and surrounded by poets, scientists, and jurists arrived from all parts of

---

[80] According to M.A. Ladero Quesada, don Fernando's pacts constituted the "birth certificate of the emirate of Granada" (*Granada. Historia de un país islámico (1232–1571)*, Madrid. 1979, pp. 101–103).

[81] Cf. E. Berger, *Les Registres d'Innocent IV*, Paris, 1884–1921, III, no. 6.497, p. 213.

[82] *Directrices fundamentales*, p. 81.

Europe, Alfonso must have thought more than once about the possibility of obtaining it. The most immediate concern, however, was the wellbeing of his subjects and the peace of the kingdom.

Beginning in 1254, Alfonso left Seville to tour the northern territories for the first time after having assumed the throne. He was warmly welcomed wherever he went. We know in detail, for instance, about the welcome he received at Sahagún thanks to a thorough report by an anonymous monastery chronicler who witnessed it first hand. In November, he was in Burgos celebrating the Cortes, during which he knighted prince Edward of England and granted him his half-sister Leonor in marriage.[83] During the celebration of the Cortes, the abbot of the Sahagún monastery, Nicolás, invited him to visit his monastery and entreated him to confirm the letters stating the privileges and liberties of the monastery in order to end the unrest the town suffered as a result of the continuous revolts of the burghers. Alfonso replied that as soon as he took care of some urgent business he had pending, he would visit the monastery and the town. In fact, the chronicler, a monk accompanying the abbot to the Burgos Cortes, reports that on Holy Thursday, March 25, 1255, Alfonso entered triumphantly in Sahagún, staying there as a guest for more than a month, until April 27, "and with the property of the aforementioned monastery, through the diligence and solicitude of abbot Nicolás, he was warmly and generously welcomed along with his entire court " (*Anónimo II*, p. 191). The town, well known for its anti-lord revolts, gave the king a lavish reception, which is described in great detail by the author of the chronicle (*Anónimo II*, pp. 185–186). He goes on to say, with great enthusiasm, how that same day Alfonso visited many poor people and handed them large amounts of money and washed their feet. The next day, Good Friday, "humbly dressed in his mourning clothes and barefoot, he visited all the churches of the town, and in each one of them he left two pieces of gold, and that day he did not eat anything but bread and water; and in the following two days, that is, Holy Saturday and the very Holy Day of Easter, he did not want to do anything else

---

[83] "[...] because at that time, that is, in the year twelve hundred ninety-two [1254 AD], around the feast of Saint Martin, he celebrated very grand Cortes with the princes and the noblemen of his kingdoms; he knighted the firstborn and heir to the throne of England, named Edward, and once he was knighted, he married him to the sister of the lord king..." (*Anónimo de Sahagún II*, p. 184).

except spend those holy days in devout services and prayer, secluded in his chamber in great contemplation" (*ib.*, p. 186).

The great historian of the monastery, Romualdo Escalona, cannot resist providing a personal commentary on the anonymous report that reveals an aspect of Alfonso's personality that has been frequently overlooked by historians. He writes, "I have cited these details provided by the anonymous chronicler, who was an eyewitness, in order to reveal the piety and devotion of this king who has been misjudged by others."[84] Easter Monday, Alfonso asked the abbot and monks to bring all the monastery's documents and letters as well as the old and new "fueros" (privilege documents). After studying all the documents, Alfonso approved the concession of a new privilege issued on April 25, 1255. Besides the presence of Alfonso, the documents confirm the attendance of an impressive number of people at the Burgos Cortes, who, like the king, were also lodged at the monastery, as the anonymous author of the chronicle and Escalona proudly point out.[85]

Alfonso received many honors during his tour of the kingdom, but he also took the opportunity to find out about the state of public order and the administration of justice. For instance, in Sahagún, a place with a long history of popular rebellions against the abbot's power, he granted a public hearing to both parties. The rebels were headed by Ruy Fernández, who had been sentenced to death by don Fernando III but at the request of the abbot had already been pardoned. At that point, Ruy also acknowledged to Alfonso that, along with Fernán Pérez and Nicolás Bartolomé, he had continued to plot against the monastery in order to liberate the town from its grip. During the trial held in the presence of the city council, Alfonso and his advisors sentenced the men to death, as the anonymous chronicler reports. When

---

[84] R. Escalona, *Historia del Real Monasterio de Sahagún sacada de la que dexo escrita el padre Maestro Fr. Joseph Pérez*, Madrid, 1782, pp. 150–151.

[85] At the head we find doña Yolanda (Violante), followed by the two princesses, doña Berenguela and doña Beatriz, Alfonso's uncle, don Alfonso de Molina, and from the brothers: don Fadrique, don Enrique, don Manuel, don Fernando, don Felipe, bishop elect of Seville, and don Sancho, bishop elect of Toledo. Other foreign personalities and the kings of Granada confirming the *fuero* were "the king's vassal," don Aboabdille Abenazar, the king of Murcia, don Mahomat Aben Mahomat Abenhut, "the king's vassal," and from Niebla, don Abent Mahafot, "the king's vassal" (text of the fuero in R. Escalona, *Historia del Real monasterio de Sahagún*, Apéndice III, pp. 601–606. Cf. the study by A.M. Barrero García, "Los fueros de Sahagún," *AHDE*, (1972), pp. 385–597; and the essay by J. Puyol, *El abadengo de Sahagún. Contibución al estudio del feudalismo en España*, Madrid, 1915.

the abbot found out about the sentence, he went to see Alfonso and begged on his knees for mercy for the sentenced men. According to the anonymous chronicle, Alfonso replied, "Go to the cloister and stay in peace with your monks. In the meantime, I will think of the answer I should give you. But before the abbot entered the cloister, the king sent his sheriff and other men he had in charge of these things, that, under death penalty, immediately, without wasting time, Ruy Fernández and Fernán Pérez, his nephew and Nicolás Bartolomé, his relative and eleven other men, very quickly, in their homes, should be hanged, a command they fulfilled with no delay" (p. 188).[86]

Many cities and towns in Castile and León also staged extraordinary welcome ceremonies for Alfonso. Everyone had great expectations regarding the young king who was already touted as a very learned man. Echoing the monastery's documents, Escalona writes, "he was a man of great courage, and his spirit was much loftier than was customary in these semi-barbaric times in Spain" (op. cit., p. 148). Following his stay in Sahagún, Alfonso continued his tour of the kingdom: "Finally, the lord king, bidding farewell to the lord abbot and the monks, and asking them to remember him in their prayers, left the said monastery in the year of twelve hundred ninety-three, April 25, 1255; he then marched happily on to Palencia, after having been hosted at the said monastery for more than twenty-five days" (*Anónimo*, p. 191).

---

[86] On the burgher rebellions at Sahagún and the punishments they received during doña Urraca of Castille's reign, see H. Salvador Martínez, *La rebelión de los burgos. Crisis de Estado y coyuntura social*, Madrid: Tecnos, 1991.

CHAPTER FOUR

THE QUEST FOR THE IMPERIAL CROWN

1. *Background on the "Claim to the Empire"*

We are not concerned so much here with analyzing the reasons why
the Learned King so eagerly sought the imperial crown.[1] But I do
believe it is useful to make a few preliminary observations that relate
more directly to the main topic of this book. This imperial aspiration was Alfonso's life obsession at least until 1275 and contributed
much to his demise as a king and as a politician and statesman, as
well as to the economic disintegration of his kingdom. It also made
the most learned king of the Middle Ages into a laughable figure, the
proverbial maniacal monarch who aspired to the impossible ("because
of looking at the stars, he lost the earth"), thus casting shadows on
the most illustrious and impressive cultural project of medieval vernacular humanism. Scholars who have studied Alfonso X's cultural
issues frequently omit or gloss over this topic, possibly because of the
embarrassment it entails in a man so learned. But I believe it is worth
examining for the sake of probing into his psyche and showing some
aspects of his "poorly adapted" personality, while also determining to
what extent his aspirations to the imperial crown were real and objec-
tively legitimate.

The validity of such claims derived not only from genealogy and
dynasty, but also from an ideological conception of the monarchy as
an integrating and absolutist institution, a notion that was relatively
common in 13th-century Europe and the Iberian Peninsula before
that. Such conception involved a view of the monarch's rule over a
number of territories closely resembling the concept of empire. Hence
many kings who preceded Alfonso bore the title "king and emperor"

---

[1] The topic of *fecho d'imperio* (claim to the empire) has been discussed by Alfonso's
biographers and scholars, including Ch. Fraker in several articles gathered in *The Scope
of the History: Studies in the Historiography of Alfonso el Sabio*, Ann Arbor, MI: University of Michigan Press, 1996; C.J. Socarrás, *Alfonso X of Castile: A Study on Imperialistic Frustration*, Barcelona: Ediciones Hispam, 1984; and C. Estepa, "Alfonso X
y el fecho del imperio," *RO*, 43 (1984), pp. 43–53.

and according to the *Setenario*, Alfonso's father Fernando III, facing
the new realities of the reconquest of the Peninsular lands and the
submission of several Muslim kings, aspired "that his dominion be
called Empire and not kingdom, and that he be crowned Emperor,
as were others of his lineage."[2] Seen from this historical/theoretical
perspective, Alfonso's imperial aspirations were not at all obsessive,
abnormal, or fantastic. C. de Ayala argues that "[t]his was the most
original characteristic of the monarchic model Alfonso X set up for
Castile...Hence, Alfonso can be considered the originator of this
unique concept of monarchy which did not necessarily aspire to the
territorial unification of the Peninsula, something unthinkable at the
time from a moderately realist perspective, but he instead ambitioned
an unchallenged primacy over the Peninsular lands in which Castile
would have a leading role, on the basis of its historical legitimacy and
its unmatched political, economic, and military might."[3] This concept
of "empire" as primacy amongst all kings (a status of *primus inter
pares*), which Alfonso knew well, was probably his initial and only
aspiration during the long quest for the crown of the Holy Roman-
Germanic Empire.

However, from 1257 and up until 1275, practically all matters and
needs of the Peninsular kingdoms were made subordinate to the
"claim to the empire." This remains an inexplicable issue in Alfonso
X's personal and political life. Why did Alfonso decide to invest so
much if the expected return was so small? In other words, how can a
man of his intellectual prowess not have perceived that, considering
the Church's animosity towards his relative Frederick II, Alfonso had
practically no chance of obtaining the imperial crown? If his lineage
and Ghibelline politics clearly legitimized his aspirations to the imperial crown, those were the very reasons that rendered him undesirable
in the eyes of the popes. Therefore, it is worth asking whether Alfonso
effectively wanted to become Emperor of the Holy Roman-Germanic
Empire, or if his desire for the title, as some in our days have argued,
was a mainly a matter for internal consumption? That is, did he seek
the title for the prestige it could garner him amongst the kings of the
Iberian Peninsula? Ultimately, the question becomes why he would

---

[2] Ed. Vanderford, Buenos Aires, 1945, p. 13. Cf. H.J. Huffer, *La idea imperial española*, Madrid, 1933.
[3] *Directrices fundamentales*, pp. 153–155.

invest money and energy so heavily in order to purchase international support?[4]

Socarrás argues that the quest for the imperial title must be linked to an old imperial tradition that existed in the Visigoth kingdom and was carried on by the rulers of León, particularly Alfonso VI and VII, who gave themselves the title of emperor.[5] I'm not certain that Alfonso X was thinking about the Peninsular tradition in his own pursuit of the title, especially, and in the first place, because, as some have argued, it had little or no political value—it had been borne by many other noblemen and other individuals with a lower social standing.[6] Furthermore, Alfonso X also defended his prerogative to the title through the line of succession from his mother, Beatriz of Swabia, whose family had borne the title, rather than arguing for it based on Peninsular Visigoth descent. Alfonso aspired to be the emperor of the Holy Roman Empire, and not, as in Alfonso VI's case, "emperor of Christians and pagans"; or "emperor of Castile," as Alfonso I of Aragón, *el Batallador* (the Fighter) called himself; or "emperor of all of Spain" ("imperator totius Hispaniae"), the title that Alfonso VII was honored with as the only Peninsular king whose coronation ceremony, similar to those in other European monarchies, is recorded in detail.[7] According to the *CAI*, calling him an "emperor" was based on the fact that a Christian king (García Ramírez of Pamplona) and a Muslim one (Ibn Hud al Mustansir Sayf al-Dawla, "Zafadola," the last Muslim king of Zaragoza) as well as many Christian lords on both sides of the Pyrenees respected his authority and offered him vassalage. This was obviously an imitation of what happened in the Holy Roman-Germanic Empire, but

---

[4] C. de Ayala maintains that "Alfonso never thought of becoming the Emperor of the Holy Empire. His desire was to control his patrimonial kingdoms and to exercise royal primacy in the Peninsula. The political prestige of the Empire was crucial for that purpose" (p. 155). W.F. Schoen argues something similar in *Alfonso X de Castilla*, Madrid, 1966, p. 101. According to A. Steiger, Alfonso intended to create "a new Roman Empire with a Spanish nationality" ("Alfonso X y la idea imperial," *Arbor*, 18, 1946, p. 395).

[5] C.J. Socarrás, *Alfonso X of Castile*, chaps. I and II, pp. 15–63.

[6] A. García Gallo, "El imperio medieval español," *Arbor*, Sept.-Oct. (1945), pp. 199–228. The Cid, for instance, was called "emperor." Thus the term should not be limited to the technical sense in which "emperor" was understood as a figure of supreme and ecumenical power amongst Christendom.

[7] The ceremony was held at the church of Santa María en León in May 1135, as told in the *Crónica Adefonsi Imperatoris* (hereafter *CAI*), ed. L. Sánchez Belda, Madrid: CSIC, Escuela de Estudios Medievales, 1950, pp. 55–56.

neither the use of the title nor the sacredness of the ceremony lived beyond Alfonso VII's reign.

It may be that for some time Alfonso may have thought about the title of emperor in the same terms it had been used by some Peninsular kings, that is, *primus inter pares*, believing it would grant him hegemony among them, but there is no evidence he sought it, and the iconography proves otherwise. *Lapidario*, translated in 1243 and revised in 1250, does not show any images of presentation, as in all other works after this one (see note 34 below). On the contrary, it was after the official approval by the republics of Pisa and Marseille that Alfonso realized his imperial potential went beyond the confines of the Peninsula, and hence his zeal in obtaining it, though not for the sake of Peninsular hegemony. But I believe that is was from this moment on when his thoughts were filled with the world of international political ambition that could give him greater personal prestige, could improve the economic situation of his subjects, and, above all, could help disseminate his cultural revolution.

In his *Estoria de España*, Alfonso X provides an informative account of Alfonso VII's coronation ceremony, and how as "king of Spain," he had to be approved by the bishops, kings and lords when he assumed the title of Emperor ("And from then on, he always called himself, don Alfonso, emperor of Spain; and, according to the histories, he was the first emperor of Spain.") Such a title, as the chronicler goes on to tell, was confirmed by Pope Innocent II at Alfonso's request, "and thus from then the coronation and the empire were confirmed."[8] It is worth noting that Alfonso, who was eagerly seeking the crown of the Holy Roman Empire when these words were written, did not take advantage of the opportunity alleged in the passage to establish a direct connection to the title borne by his direct ancestor.

A detailed description of Alfonso VII's coronation in the *PCG*, including all sacred elements and the title of emperor he chose for himself on the basis of his feats in Aragón,[9] is what has led many of his modern interpreters to believe that Alfonso's goal in including

---

[8] *PCG*, II, chap. 974, pp. 654a–b. The papal document confirming the title is lost and even if "Rome did not call Alfonso VII 'emperor,' this title was applied to him often by all kinds of writers" (R. Menéndez Pidal *El imperio hispánico y los cinco reinos*, pp. 157–158, and cf. p. 172).

[9] "And since he told them at the court what he had accomplished in Aragón…, he asked them if they agreed that the 'king of Spain,' which is what they called him, should change his name and be called 'emperor'" (*PCG*, II, cap. 974, p. 654a).

such a story was to convey in an political/allegorical fashion the ideal of his coronation and the empire he aspired to as Alfonso VII's successor. But not all scholars agree. Peter Linehan, who has extensively written on the subject, holds that the narrative of the ceremony and of Alfonso VII's anointment in the *CAI*, the strongest historical argument in favor of the crowning and anointment ceremony of Spanish kings, subsequently established by Alfonso X, is dubiously legitimate, for it gave the Archbishop of Toledo a major role that in the original text of the *CAI* he did not have. The text by Alfonso seems to contain that inconsistency when he explicitly writes: "And it was that [i.e., Alfonso VII's coronation] in the Cathedral Church of Santa María de Regla in León which is the capital city of the entire kingdom of León." The doubts are increased by the fact that the great historian and Archbishop of Toledo, Jiménez de Rada, does not mention a single word about the crowning ceremony except for a laconic: "Imposuit sibi imperii diadema" ("Upon his return to León after this [the Aragón campaign], *he put the imperial crown on his own head* and from then on he was called emperor").[10]

It is worth asking then, why Alfonso was so interested in the description of the ceremony in the *CAI*. According to Linehan, the narrative in *Estoria de España* is not by Alfonso X, but rather it was inserted after his death by Sancho IV's chancellor and the Archbishop of Toledo, don Gonzalo Pérez Gudiel, with the king's consent and collaboration. Don Gonzalo probably did this for various reasons: firstly, to legitimize the always doubtful succession of his own king and protector, don Sancho, and the equally questionable succession of his son Fernando IV, about which Sancho himself was doubtful (as he said before dying to his nephew, don Juan Manuel "no one can give what he does not possess," see below); secondly, to exalt the prestige and glory of his archbishopric. Thus, according to Linehan, it was don Gonzalo Pérez who not only inserted the narrative of Alfonso VII crowning in 1135 in the *EE* but who also, to hide his deed, would have retouched the original text in the passages detailing the coronations of Enrique I and Fernando III.[11]

---

[10] *De rebus Hispaniae*, VII, 7. However, it was precisely thanks to the narrative of Alfonso VII's crowning in the *EE* that gave rise to the late historiographic myth (disseminated mostly by Pedro de Alcocer and Francisco de Pisa) of Toledo as the seat of the crowning of the kings of Castile in the Middle Ages. See Linehan, *History and the Historians*, pp. 464–465 and notes.

[11] Cf. *History and the Historians*, p. 479.

Sancho IV's coronation, which was publicly celebrated with great pomp in the Toledo cathedral, was carried out with the sole purpose of mitigating the terrible paternal curse. It was a religious-political ceremony crafted by the Church hierarchy to legitimize the succession of the rebel prince who had been supported by the clergy and the nobility.[12] But this stratagem used by don Gonzalo, who was a representative of "Toledo's mythmaking mafia"[13] looking to make Toledo the new Rome where future emperor-kings would be crowned, did not work. Following Sancho IV's death 1295 and his succession by his son Fernando IV, the inauguration ceremony of the new king did take place in Toledo's Cathedral, but there was no anointment or crowning. Don Gonzalo, the Archbishop, had to content himself with being a mere spectator, for the ceremony was an entirely lay matter, as it had always been. According to Jofré de Loaysa, it was the "barons" who, immediately following the burial of his father, elevated him to the status of king.[14] In other words, it was very similar to what happened in Seville upon Fernando III's death.

It is well known, as we shall see later on, that after Alfonso X's death, his cultural project met with negative reactions due to the influence of doña María de Molina, Sancho IV's wife, and some high-ranking clergy. This produced a radical turn to more traditional positions in politics and theology, including the abandonment of the secular concept of government and the monarchy. It is also true that a great part of the version of *EE* published by Ramón Menéndez Pidal was completed under Sancho IV's reign, so it must be acknowledged that there was ample opportunity to introduce new versions of past facts. But I'm not convinced that such changes, as Linehan argues, were so profound and extensive that they included the revision of historiographic texts in the sense of adjusting them to the new directives of "molinismo."

---

[12] Cf. Linehan, ib., pp. 446–447.

[13] Linehan, op. cit., p. 484.

[14] *Chronica*, chaps. 57–58; *Crónica de Fernando IV*, describes the king's inauguration as follows:

Wednesday, April the twenty-sixth, after having buried the king don Sancho, they then took prince don Fernando and, removing the mourning garments he was wearing on account of his father, they dressed him in noble *tartan* garments, and they placed him on the main altar in the main church of Toledo, and they received him as king and lord, and he vowed to keep the codes of law of the *hidalgos* and of all others in the kingdom…and all those present cried, Castile! Royal! Royal, for the king don Fernando. (chap. I, p. 93a)

Perhaps this and other issues will be resolved when the complete critical edition of Alfonso's *Estoria de España* is published.

If, following Linehan's hypothesis, we must accept that Alfonso X did not pen those pages of *EE*, which according to many scholars contain his strategy for achieving Peninsular hegemony, the basis of his imperial ambition, we must conclude that all that was said about his quest for the imperial crown based on the allegorical and political key of Alfonso VII's crowning is entirely discredited.[15]

Regardless of the explanation for the presence of the narrative of the *CAI* in *EE*, as we noted above, the fact of the matter is that Alfonso did not show any interest in connecting his aspiration to the imperial crown with his own position in the line of succession to the throne of kings or "emperors" of Castile-León. This shows that he either did not believe in the legitimacy of the imperial title of Castile-León, or he remained unconvinced that that was the basis of the genealogical line whereby he believed he could further his claim to the Roman-Germanic imperial title. We do not know why Alfonso distanced himself from the Peninsular line of succession which might have helped him in his quest, but, besides Linehan's hypothesis, it probably had to do with the fact that Alfonso VII divided his kingdom/empire between his two sons, Sancho and Fernando, an action that led to the loss of national unity that was intimately connected to the idea of empire. In fact, when he once more revisits the topic of national unity when singing the praises of his father Fernando, Alfonso says openly about him:

> ...[He] wanted to render his deeds noble and honor them even more, returning his dominion to that state in which it was before and had been maintained in the past by the emperors and kings from whom he was descended...With regard to the idea of the Empire, he wanted his dominion to be called empire, rather than 'kingdom,' and to be crowned Emperor, as others in his lineage had been...All of these things were the counsel that the king don Fernando insistently received from his vassals and all those who agreed with them. But since he was very prudent and very wise, and was always engrossed in great matters, he reflected and understood that even if it was in his own benefit and honor and that of

---

[15] According to Ch. Fraker, Alfonso wrote not only the *EE* but also the *GE* and the *Partidas* and the historical-juridical basis to legitimize his aspirations to hegemony over the Peninsular kingdoms and the crown of the Holy Roman Empire (*The Scope of the History*). C. de Ayala Martínez discusses the consequences of both views in *Directrices fundamentales*, especially in II, pp. 143 and ff.

his subjects to do what they advised him to do, the moment to do it had not yet arrived, explaining with many and good arguments that it could not be done at that time: first, because the land on this side of the ocean had not yet been completely conquered, since the Moors continued to dwell there; and secondly, because men were not yet prepared the way they should be, but instead were far away and there was still much to be done which was beneficial to them, as those from whom they were descended had done.[16]

If we temporarily ignore the second reason, which we will revisit later on, the text seems to imply that, according to don Fernando, there could not be an empire so long as there were areas of the Peninsula that did not accept the authority of a single king. Only Muslim kingdoms were mentioned in this category, while nothing is said of other Christian kingdoms that also existed and were independent. This omission of the Christian kingdoms as an obstacle to the political unity of the country was probably due to the fact that, upon Fernando III's death, all did accept *de facto* (albeit not *de jure*) the hegemony of Castile-León.[17] I believe that Alfonso did not want to rely on his prerogative to the title based on succession rights because he respected the will of his father, who did not want to use it before two conditions were met: the conquest of all territories of the old Visigoth kingdom beyond the Strait of Gibraltar, and the cultural advancement of all his subjects. This was the unfinished project Alfonso would attempt to complete.

In any event, for Alfonso X, who never conquered any more land than his father had, the moment had arrived to aspire to the title of emperor of a larger empire created on a very different basis. Alfonso fantasized about this possibility, and given the circumstances of the *Interregnum* and the fact that in his early years Alfonso had enjoyed the favor and perhaps a certain familiarity with the popes, everything seem to be on his side.[18] He must have felt encouraged by these circumstances to present his candidacy, convinced that he had papal support but not suspecting that Rome's attitude probably had more

---

[16] *Setenario*, pp. 22–23.

[17] The most powerful of all Christian kingdoms in the Peninsula and the most sensitive to Castile's search for hegemony was indeed Jaime I's Aragón. In the *Llibre dels Feyts* Jaime stated that the king of Castile was "one of the most high-ranking and powerful men in the World" (chap. XXXII); cf. A. Rodríguez López, "El reino de Castilla y el Imperio Germánico en la primera mitad del siglo XIII. Fernando III y Federico II," *Homenaje al profesor Abilio Barbero*, Madrid, 1997, pp. 529–549.

[18] See the letters he received from Innocent IV (1243–1254) in *Les Registres d'Innocent IV*, nos. 5.740, 6.691, 6.727, 6.498.

to do with the desire to find a successor to the throne who would fit the interests of the papacy, like the last one had. This does not mean that the pope was willing to grant him the crown even if he appeared sufficiently docile and submissive, but instead that the Holy See was interested in seeing the powerful king of Castile fill the void left by Frederick II in other areas of activity, especially international, as was for example, the African crusade, a matter of great concern for the pope. During the first years of his reign, Alfonso drafted an intervention plan for North Africa, and in a letter dated at Perugia October 4, 1253, the pope assured him he would confirm all agreements Alfonso signed with North African Saracens.[19]

2. The "Holy Roman-Germanic Empire." The Idea of Europe

The Western Roman Empire fell in 476 when the barbarians entered Rome. The idea of empire, however, survived for four more centuries in the West, until, finally, Christmas eve of the year 800, Pope Leo III decided to crown the most famous of Christian kings as emperor, namely, Charlemagne. The crowning was followed by the acclamation: "Carolo Augusto a Deo coronato, magno et pacifico imperatori romanorum, vita et victoria" ["To Charles Augustus, crowned by God, great and peaceful emperor of the Romans, life and victory"]. All those present at St. Peter's Basilica, including the pope, acknowledged him and paid homage to him by lowering their heads as a sign of submission. The West thus acquired its own emperor; the Eastern Empire did not lose its emperor until much later. In fact, Charlemagne and his successors believed themselves to be emperors in the same way Caesar, Augustus, or Tiberius. There are even historians who think that, from the legal point of view, that night in 800 might have been the birth of the idea of Europe, when a geographical concept was transformed into a cultural concept through the adoption of Roman Law,[20] a unifying and agglutinating concept that would forever join the countries that had been subjected to the Empire.

---

[19] Cf. *Les Registres d'Innocent IV*, III, no. 6.014, p. 117. On January 9, 1253 the pope granted the Castilian king the ecclesiastic *tercias* (a special tax) and he ordered the bishops and archbishops of Castile-León to collect 700 marks in their individual parishes (corresponding to that tax) and deliver the amount to the bishop-elect of Seville, the prince Felipe, Alfonso's brother. Cf. *Les Registres*, III, no. 6.497.

[20] Cf. R. Folz, *L'idée d'Empire en Occident du VIe au XIVe siècle*, Paris, 1953.

The new institution of the title and role of Roman Emperor by the pope had long and complex consequences. Firstly, it set an inflexible precedent: the pope would be the supreme arbiter deciding who would be emperor, having the right to grant or deny the crown at will. His judgment could not be appealed because the empire was conceived as an institution at the service of the Church, whose interests had to be defended at all costs. The second precedent was the origin of the candidate to the title of emperor. In principle, any Christian king could aspire to the imperial crown; in practice, nonetheless, only Germanic kings had been crowned, so that the institution became the "Holy Roman-Germanic Empire." In Charlemagne's court, practically all the norms of the Roman Empire were reinstated, including the renewal of Latin, which gave rise to what we could call the first renaissance of arts and letters, and, as mentioned above, law.[21]

Starting with the reinstatement of the empire by Leo III, the emperor was chosen by an election process. This differed from European monarchies where succession was the dominant principle. Before becoming an emperor, the candidate had to be elected as "King of the Romans" before being appointed and crowned by the pope. Being elected "King of the Romans" was a matter that had been resolved by the most prominent German noblemen following several centuries of experiments and at times bloody conflicts. In the bull *Venerabilem* from 1202, Pope Innocent III recognized the right of German princes to elect the "king who would be raised to the status of emperor," but he also reserved for himself the right to examine the elected king, to anoint, consecrate, and crown him as emperor. Following the election, the candidate would be named *Rex Romanorum et semper augustus*; and after his coronation he would carry the title *Imperator Romanorum*. But conflicts did not end because of this. Closer to the times of Alfonso X, the double election of Philip of Swabia and Otto IV of Braunschweig in 1198 produced a bitter conflict between the Staufens, supporters of Philip, and the Guelfs, of Otto. In 1218, after Otto's death, Pope Honorius III recognized and crowned Frederick II of Staufen as emperor in 1220.[22] The papal declaration about the right

---

[21] There's a vast bibliography on the topic, a sample of which can be seen in P. Rich, *Education and Culture in the Barbarian West. From the Sixth through the Eighth Century*, trans. by J.J. Contreni, Columbia, SC, University of South Carolina Press, 1976.

[22] For a history of the emperor's election process and the political and social conflicts that accompanied it see H. Mitteis, *Die deutsche Königswahl*, 2a ed., Brünn-

of a German prince to the title of Roman-Germanic emperor led the imperial chancellor Reginald of Dasel in the mid-12th century to claim for his lord, Frederick I, the *dominium mundi* [world dominion]. Some however, like the great humanist and bishop of Chartres, John of Salisbury (d. 1180), protested against this by saying, "Who has established the Germans as the judges of nations?"[23] Obviously, protests did not go beyond this.

During the *Interregnum* that followed the death of Frederick II's heir, Conrad IV (d. 1254), it was agreed, although not without strong political struggles, that it would be a group of seven German electors who would elect the new King of the Romans from among members of the German nobility.[24] It was therefore very difficult, if not impossible, for any other Christian king to be elected if he did not control vast territories in Germany and had a large number of the electors on his side. The majority could be obtained in many ways: through pacts, agreements of all sorts, and it could also be bought with large sums of money. During the German Diets of June 28 and September 8, 1256, the seven great electors were chosen who would appoint the successor of Frederick II: the Archbishop of Trier, the Archbishop of Cologne, the Archbishop of Mainz, the Palatine Count of the Rhine, the Duke of Saxony, the Marquis of Brandenburg, and the King of Bohemia.[25] The only matter left was to decide on the candidates for the imperial crown.

As mentioned, Frederick II died in December 1250 in a state of excommunication. His death freed the Church from a nightmare that had led the Fathers of the First Council of Lyon (1247) to depose the rebellious emperor. But in the last years of his life, Frederick continued to be in conflict with the popes, which led them to denounce the lineage of the Staufens as a "stock of vipers." Hence, as soon as the opportunity arose, Innocent IV favored as candidate a nobleman who

---

Munich-Viena, 1944, esp. p. 113 and ff; F. Krieger, *König, Reich und Reichsreform im Spätmittelalter*, Munich, 1992, esp. p. 64 and ff; E. Kantorowicz, *Frederick the Second, 1194–1250*, trans. E.O. Lorimer, London: Contable & Co., 1931.

[23] In G. Barraclough, "Federico Barbarroja y el siglo XII," in *Historia desde el mundo actual*, Madrid, 1959, p. 113.

[24] Cf. A. Burson, *Alfons X von Castilien. Ein Beitrag zur Geschichte des grossen Interrägnus mit bisher ungedruckten Briefen*, Münster, 1866.

[25] Cf. W. Giese, "Der Reichstag vom 8. September 1256 und die Entstehung des Alleinstimmrechts der Kurfürsten," *Deutsches Archiv für Erforschung des Mittelalters*, 40 (1984), pp. 562–590, 572–580.

had no connection whatsoever with the Staufens, William of Holland. Conrad I of Hohenstaufen, the son and heir of Frederick II, did not accept the pope's decision and launched a military campaign against William. Conrad too was excommunicated and died shortly after, in 1254, some say from poisoning. That same year, a new pope assumed the papacy, Alexander IV (1254–1261), and he too supported William, who nonetheless died prematurely on January 28, 1256, leaving the position open to other candidates.

Among the direct heirs of the Hohenstaufen only two possibilities were left: Manfred, Frederick II's illegitimate son who was in Sicily, determined to maintain control of that kingdom, and Conradin, son of the late Conrad, who was still a child. None had much of a chance, for obvious reasons, neither with the pope or the electors. Alexander IV chose Edmund, son of Henry III of England, as King of Sicily, with the obvious intention of forever driving the Hohenstaufens out of Italy. As last resort there was still a secondary branch of that "cursed stock" who would perhaps be more moderate and agreeable to the pope's ideals, and, because it had not been in contact with the Ghibelline ideology, could be more acceptable to the German electors and especially to the pope. Alfonso of Castile was a very legitimate candidate in this category.

In order for Alfonso to become a real candidate, he needed a territorial base and an extraordinary political and military force in Germany. Up until 1254, nobody at the Castilian court ever dreamt of creating such a power base, although all were aware of the King's German ancestry. Now, faced with the real possibility of obtaining the highest title available in Christendom, Alfonso and his aides began to lay down the legal and genealogical groundwork to achieve it, while also launching a campaign to seek wider political alliances. Among these was the meeting that the king of Castile had on October 18 of that same year, 1254, with Edward of England in Burgos. One year before, Alfonso had granted Edward the rights to Gascony. At Burgos, Alfonso behaved generously with his guest, granted him, among other gifts, the hand of his half-sister, Leonor, and knighted him.[26] Alfonso

---

[26] In a diploma issued to the Monastery at Las Huelgas, Alfonso writes:
    May all who see this document know that I, don Alfonso..., the first time I came to Burgos after I acceded to the throne, also came here don Eduardo, the first son and heir of king Henry of England, and was knighted by me in the monastery of Santa María la Real of Burgos, and married my sister, the princess doña Leonor,

must have been so impressed with the young prince that, for more than a year, he dated all documents issued by his chancellery with the phrase "The year that Edward, first son and heir of King Henry of England, was knighted at Burgos by the King Alfonso mentioned above."[27] Alfonso had expectations regarding the future king of England. Evidently he had begun a political campaign to rally support for his cause. If his friendship with Edward proved long-lasting, the concrete help he received from him, even at times of great need in the matter of the empire and others, was however insignificant.

Alfonso's connection with the Roman-Germanic Empire and his claim to the imperial crown came via his mother's lineage, for she was the heiress to the Duchy of Swabia, where future emperors had stemmed from. Hence, her descendants had acquired such a right. It is not possible to know whether this matter was discussed at the Toledo Cortes in 1254, for no document remains, but we know the Cortes themselves were celebrated.[28] What we do know is that, beginning with these Cortes, the idea of "going to the Empire" begins to appear more frequently as Alfonso takes the first steps to seek the appropriate political support.

The Duchy of Swabia was part of the inheritance received by Beatriz from Philip of Swabia. Holding the Duchy meant being at the head of the most important fief in Germany in terms of territory and prestige. This position had always been held by the Hohenstaufens, and it was a *sine qua non* condition, first for being elected King of the Romans, and later, crowned as emperor. With the pope's support came the certainty that in a not too distant future Beatriz's successor too would become the emperor of the Holy Roman-Germanic Empire.

But it seems that Fernando III and his wife decided to assign the Duchy to their second-born, don Fadrique, whose name was associated with that of the Roman-Germanic emperor, Frederick I Barbarossa, Beatriz's paternal grandfather. The Marquis of Mondéjar writes that, for the purpose of claiming this right, Beatriz and Fernando sent their son Frederick (Friedrich or Fadrique) to Italy, where he spent four

---

and received the blessing there with her. (in J.M. Lizoaín Garrido, *Documentación del monasterio de Las Huelgas de Burgos 1231–1262*, Burgos, 1985, n. 480)

[27] *Fuero de Sahagún*, in R. Escalona, *Historia del Real monasterio de Sahagún*, Apéndice III, p. 605.

[28] In a privilege dated March 2, 1254 on behalf of the Church of Toledo, Alfonso states: "when I came to Toledo to hold my Cortes there" in Ballesteros, *Alfonso X*, p. 90.

years (1240–1245) at the imperial court of Frederick II in an attempt to have his mother's rights acknowledged and asking for the patrimonial lands due him, including the Duchy of Swabia.[29] It is unclear if the emperor approved or not the request of Beatriz's successors. In any event, at the death of Frederick II, the pope declared the Duchy of Swabia vacant, and assigned it to his favorite candidate, William of Holland. The Swabians, however, categorically refused to accept the authority of William, because he was not a Hohenstaufen. This led Pope Alexander IV to write a letter on February 4, 1255 to the bishops and lords of Swabia asking them not only to recognize Alfonso of Castile as Duke of Swabia, but also to do everything in their power to help him obtain the Duchy.[30]

The pope's concession of the Duchy of Swabia to Alfonso changed all plans at the Castilian court. But for Alfonso this was a great and unexpected step towards the imperial crown.[31] Some believe this is why don Fadrique eventually rebelled against his brother, who, for unclear reasons, ordered his execution. We ignore the real motives the pope had to support Alfonso, since he probably knew about the resistance of the Peninsular kings and the possibility that the Duchy would be granted to don Fadrique following the death of Frederick II. In any event, besides the Swabian disapproval of William of Holland, the pope's support of Alfonso over Fadrique was probably due to the fact that Alfonso was the monarch of a very important kingdom and, as such, would hold more sway among the German electors than his brother, who was neither a king nor would ever be one. Furthermore, Fadrique also had against him the papal resentment against the Hohenstaufens, for he had spent some time in the court of Frederick

---

[29] Mondéjar, *Memorias históricas*, p. 343–346. See also E. Flórez, *Reinas católicas*, I. pp. 461–462. For Ballesteros, Fadrique did not make it to Germany, as some think, but instead, following his father's and grandmother's letters to Gregory IX in support of his cause, don Fadrique, aged 17, went to Italy (1240), to meet Frederick II at Foggia (*Memorias*, pp. 270–271). More about the claims to the Duchy of Swabia by Beatriz and her successors in A. Rodríguez López, "El reino de Castilla y el Imperio Germánico en la primera mitad del siglo XIII. Fernando III y Federico II," in *Homenaje al profesor Abilio Barbero*, Madrid: Ed. del Orto, 1997, pp. 613–630.

[30] The complete text of the letter is available in I. Rodríguez de Lama, *La documentación pontificia de Alejandro IV (1254–1261)*, Rome, 1976, no. 23, pp. 50–51. See also *Les Registres de Alexandre IV*, Paris, 1902, IV, letter dated February 4, 1255; Ballesteros, *Alfonso X*, p. 135.

[31] Cf. Giese, "Der Reichstag…," p. 573.

II and also carried his name. The pope feared that the lengthy contact Fadrique had with the "cursed" emperor might have contaminated him with his ideas. Also, around that time, Alfonso took advantage of the political turning point of the *Interregnum* in order to revive his plans for a crusade in Africa, which generated a positive response on the part of the pope for the new Castilian king and his projects.

The concession of the Duchy of Swabia was the pope's first concrete step towards fulfilling an old request that apparently Prince Alfonso had made in 1246, based on his succession rights as descendant of Beatriz and Frederick I Barbarossa. These two people would be key in Alfonso's creation of a mythical royal-imperial lineage that traced him back to the first king of the world, the biblical king Nimrod, a genealogy Alfonso firmly believed in.[32] The pope's favorable position and his many privileges and concessions may have initially led Alfonso to believe he was the favored candidate to the imperial crown, and, as Ayala Martínez states, such gestures "were interpreted in the Castilian court as indisputable papal support for Alfonso's policies. There is no doubt these were palpable proof of the Holy See's favorable position towards Castile in these very delicate months for Alfonso X."[33]

Papal support granted Alfonso indeed an extraordinary power vis-à-vis the peninsular kingdoms, making him expect their submission. But in the past, popes had also supported other peninsular kings, and this had never led to their hegemony. In Alfonso's case, given his lineage, papal support was connected with his projection on the international scene. Alfonso understood this, and this encouraged him further to seek the imperial crown. As Duke of Swabia and monarch of one of the most powerful kingdoms of Europe, Alfonso had a real chance at obtaining it.

---

[32] Perhaps here it is possible to speak of a connection with the city of Seville as the ancient seat of an empire of which Alfonso believed himself to be the successor. These ideas about an ancient (perhaps mythical) Spanish empire appeared in Alfonso's writing for the first time in the *Setenario*, where he praised Seville as the seat of his father's throne: "Because it [Seville] was in ancient times the house and dwelling of emperors, and there they crowned themselves and celebrated their meetings and decided the things they had to do. And it was also the beginning of the Spanish people; because from it [Seville] and from king Espán, who was its ruler, the entire country takes its name" (ed. K.H. Vanderford, X, p. 19).

[33] *Directrices fundamentales*, p. 84.

3. Pisan Support

In sum, before 1256, it was only or mainly the popes who supported Alfonso's aspirations to the imperial crown. He must have indeed been pleased by the pope's intercession for his acceptance as Duke of Swabia by the Swabians. But there's no evidence Alfonso thought about the imperial crown, and much less that he sought it before January 1256, when William II of Holland died, having been elected King of Romans in 1247.[34] However, the event that encouraged him more, only two months after William's death, was the unexpected arrival of representatives from the city of Pisa. On March 17, 1256, while Alfonso was at Soria meeting with his father-in-law, don Jaime I, a Pisan delegation arrived led by Bandino di Guido Lancia, who invested him as "King of the Romans" in a solemn ceremony, and presented him to the congregation as:

> [...] [T]he highest of all Kings who are or ever were in times worthy of remembrance, especially thanks to the grace of the Holy Spirit, which inspired you divinely and granted you multiple gifts; and may they know too that you, more than others, love peace, truth, mercy and justice, and that you are the most Christian and most Faithful of all; and may they know also that you aspire with all your heart to expanding the honor of our Holy Mother Church, and its peaceful state, as well as that of the Roman Empire; and that the Empire has been vacant for a long time, and has been destroyed by its enemies; and knowing that you were born from the blood of the Dukes of Swabia, to whose house by privilege of Princes and concession of the Pontiffs of the Roman Church the Empire justly and rightly belongs; and that by succession in you the empires divided by abuse can be united, for you are descended from Manuel, who was Emperor of the Romans; and they may be joined again in you as they were in the times of Caesar and of the most Christian Constantine; and the aforementioned encouragement, the attention of the saints, the discretion of men, Princes, Barons, Lords and Communities, and of all the peoples of Italy; and also the Germans and other members of

---

[34] This attitude of indifference towards the imperial crown seems to be confirmed in the iconography of works composed up until this time, such as the *Lapidario* (Escorial, Ms.n.I. 15) that does not contain a single image of presentation of Alfonso as patron. This contrasts with works composed later, when he was already seeking the crown, where he appears with all royal insignia, represented as a "new Charlemagne." Cf. A. Domínguez Rodríguez, "Imágenes de Presentación de la miniatura alfonsí," *Goya*, 131 (1976), pp. 287–291, note 1; see also "Imágenes de un rey trovador de Santa María (Alfonso X en las *Cantigas de Santa María*)," in *Il Medio Oriente e l'Occidente nell'Arte del XIII secolo*, Bologna: Hans Belting, 1982, pp. 229–239.

the empire, have decided to find you worthy of being the King of the Romans and Emperor [...][35]

Bandino gave Alfonso a copy of the Old and New Testaments, a cross, and a sword, and kneeling in front of him, kissed his foot as sign of fidelity. Moved and excited, Alfonso accepted the investiture, and he greeted the Pisans' gesture with an agreement in which he calls himself for the first time "...Alfonso, by the grace of God elected King and Emperor of the Romans [...]" In that document he promised the Pisans protection against their enemies and profitable business contracts in Sicily and on the shores of North Africa, as soon as they were conquered.[36]

Two significant and not entirely explained details must be noted in the Pisan proclamation. The first is the fact that the Pisans based the investiture of Alfonso as "King of the Romans and Emperor" on his descent from the Dukes of Swabia ("...to whose house by privilege of Princes and concession of the Pontiffs of the Roman Church the Empire justly and rightly belongs"), which was true, and on him being a successor of the Byzantine emperor, Manuel I Comnenus (1143–1180), which was only half-true.[37] Alfonso was not descended from the emperors of Byzantium, except in the sense explained in the note, but his wife Violante was, for she was the great-granddaughter of Manuel I. It is quite possible that the skillful Pisans, in their bold action, attempted to suggest to the pope that Alfonso had all the family and political connections necessary to achieve (himself or through a successor) the unification of the Eastern and Western empires ("as they were in the times of Caesar and of the most Christian Constantine") and that, with the Empire, so would the Church be unified. The second detail concerns the boldness of the Pisans in proclaiming Alfonso of Castile as emperor on their own and without possessing any title

---

[35] The proclamation document was dated 15 of the April *Calendas* (March 18), 1256. It was translated into Castilian by the Marquis of Mondéjar, *Memorias*, pp. 132–134 and 139–141, from which this English translation has been made. Cf. A. Steiger, "Alfonso X el Sabio y la idea imperial," *Arbor*, 18 (1946), pp. 275–302; E.F. von Schoen, *Alfonso X de Castilla*, Madrid, 1966.

[36] This document can be found in Socarrás, *op.cit.*, pp. 262–265; and cf. Ballesteros, *Alfonso X*, pp. 159–160; C.C. Bayley, "The Diplomatic Preliminaries of the Double Election of 1257 in Germany," *EHR*, 62 (1947), pp. 474–475.

[37] Alfonso, as mentioned, was the son of Beatriz of Swabia, daughter of Philip of Swabia, and Princess Irene, sister of the emperor of Byzantium, Alexis IV (or Isaac Angelos, 1185–1204). Alfonso's mother was thus a cousin of Frederick II by blood and a niece of the emperor of Byzantium.

or right to do so, knowing also that Frederick II had left legitimate successors, namely his illegitimate son, Manfred, and his grandson, Prince Conradin. Only the German electors were entitled to choose the new emperor.

Scholars have sought a legal explanation for the action of the Pisans in an obscure legal institution of private Roman law known as "negotiorum gestio," according to which a private citizen could take charge of defending the interests of any other without any mandate and without any awareness of the person on whose behalf he acted. In this case, the Pisans were acting without Alfonso's mandate or knowledge, nor the electors' awareness, and took charge of the nomination in secrecy, hiding it from the candidate and the German electors and the pope, who were the ones who were to legitimately nominate him. The goal of their action was to put an end to the ills and material damage to the Empire and their Republic in particular, which had been brought about by the long period of the *Interregnum*.[38]

This may well be the case. However, as Socarrás, following Arnold Busson, has noted, both documents quoted reveal that what really led them to invest Alfonso X as emperor were political and commercial interests. Among these were the lifting of sanctions imposed by the pope through the emperor's intervention and the defense and protection of the republics of Genoa, Florence, and Lucca against their enemies, for which Alfonso promised five hundred armed knights, a captain, and a good contingent of soldiers.[39] Alfonso promised to carry all of this out as soon as the document was signed, regardless of whether he was elected emperor or not. Another document, signed the same day, widely confirms the reasons for the election by the Pisans mentioned above, particularly commercial ones and Alfonso's promise to uphold all imperial privileges from the past.[40] Rereading the documents, it is obvious this was an uneven agreement. "Alfonso," writes a modern biographer, "promised everything—including giving away an army—in exchange for nothing. Pisa, as we know, had no business

---

[38] This theory was put forth by Julius Ficker, in the foreword to J.F. Boehmer, *Regesta Imperii: Die Regesten des Keiserreichts unter Philipp, Otto IV, Friederich II, Heinrich (VII), Conrad IV, Heinrich Raspe, Wilhelm und Richard, 1198–1272*, pp. 16 and 23, and was followed by A. Ballesteros, *Alfonso X*, p. 160.

[39] Socarrás, *Alfonso X*, pp. 150–152; A.Busson, *Die Doppelwahl des Jahres 1257 und das römische Königthum Alfons X von Castilien*, Münster, 1886.

[40] There is a summary of these agreements in C. de Ayala, *Las directrices fundamentales*, pp. 170–171, note 32.

offering imperial crowns: it had as much of a right to offer up the Empire as it did to offer up India."[41]

On September 12 of that same year, three representatives of the General Council of Marseille arrived in order to ratify the friendship and mutual aid agreement that García Pérez, Alfonso's representative in Marseille, had negotiated ahead of time. The ambassadors declared in the name of Marseille that, following Pisa's example, they also acknowledged Alfonso as emperor and promised their obedience and support during the election. Alfonso accepted the nomination and took the city under his wing and the inhabitants as subjects of the empire. The next day, as with the Pisans, he also signed a defense and mutual aid agreement against common enemies, Christian and Muslim.[42]

Ignoring the interests behind the support of Pisa and Marseille for Alfonso's candidacy, it is evident that for Alfonso, whose imperial ambitions had been spurred (he had received the submission of the kings of Aragón and Navarra, and the Byzantine nobility that acknowledged him as lord were present at his court), such support was psychologically the launching pad he needed to plunge headlong into the politics of imperial election. Following this double international recognition, it could be said that the question of the Empire became a true obsession. However, against what many have said, Alfonso was very aware that legally speaking the nomination by Pisa and Marseille meant nothing or very little. Therefore, following the meetings at Soria and Segovia, he sent a delegate to France, seeking the support of Louis IX, and to Germany to do the same with the true electors.[43]

---

[41] F. Pérez Algar, *Alfonso X, el Sabio. Biografía*, Madrid: Studium Generalis, S.L, 1994, p. 184.

[42] Among other promises, Marseille promised ten well-equipped galleon ships that would service him from Sicily to Seville three months a year (from Easter to St. Michael's) against Christians and Saracens. Cf. Ballesteros, *Alfonso X*, pp. 169–170; Bayley, "Diplomatic Preliminaries," p. 476. The texts of the agreements with Marseille are available in V.L. Bourrilly, *Essai sur l'Histoire Politique de la Commune de Marseille des origines à la victoire de Charles d'Anjou (1264)*, Aix-en-Provence, 1926, esp. p. 217.

[43] From Sigüenza, on May 5, 1256 Alfonso sent a letter to his plenipotentiary deputy García Pérez ("Garciam Petri, archidiaconum Marrochitarum"—archdean of Morocco) asking him to defend his interests in Germany before the nobility and clergy. Cf. W. Giese, "Der Reichstag," p. 572; A. Ballesteros, "Alfonso X de Castilla y la Corona de Alemania," *RABM*, five articles in the issues for the years 1916, 1918, and 1919; and *Alfonso X*, p. 166; G. Daumet, *Mémoire sur les relations de la France et de la Castille de 1255 à 1320*, Paris: Bibliothèque de l'École des Hautes Études, 1913, pp. 147–149 (doc. 2, May 2, 1256).

The support of Pisa and Marseille indeed spurred ambitions and desires that Alfonso until then had deemed impossible dreams, and which would soon become for him and his subjects a distressing economic, political, and even religious nightmare. But dreams also keep one alive, and Alfonso was in many ways a childlike dreamer. As is the case with many brilliant men, he began to dream of the Empire and how to get it without properly weighing the consequences of that dream.

If Alfonso truly knew that Pisa's and Marseille's nomination had no legal weight, one may ask why he accepted it. There could be many reasons, but I believe they were basically two: the Pisan nomination and eulogies meant the acquisition of prestige and personal satisfaction (personal flattery) knowing he was recognized as an exceptional figure in European politics and a major player in the political resolution of the *Interregnum*, and, secondly, because, as a king of Castile, a kingdom emerging on the international scene after many centuries of isolation due to the internal strife against Islam, he hoped to extend his sphere of political and cultural influence to Northern Italy, one of the most important commercial areas of Europe at the time, and participate in profitable business contracts with Pisa, Genoa, and Marseille. There also could have been the desire to justify his advantage among Peninsular kings, something more honorific than real, for his political thinking on this matter was clear: "the king is emperor in his own kingdom" (*Partidas*, II. Tit. I, Law I), an axiom in which he excluded himself from exercising power over other kingdoms.

Some scholars, such as Ballesteros, see the Pisan intervention as a manipulation of the pope to "eliminate the offspring of the Staufen dynasty."[44] Others still deem it an absolutely Machiavellian move (*sit venia verbo*) by the pope who attempted to substitute the radical Ghibelline politics of the legitimate successor of Frederick II, Manfred, for Alfonso's "watered-down Ghibellinism." For C. de Ayala Martínez, Alfonso's Ghibellinism "confronting Manfred could encourage the support of many Italian cities who sympathized with Alfonso's distant position as much as they feared Manfred's authoritarianism."[45]

---

[44] *Alfonso X*, p. 135.
[45] *Directrices fundamentales*, p. 174. M. González Jiménez writes, "We are thus faced with a plausible explanation that perhaps would need stronger arguments, but, in any event, it leaves the papacy in a difficult position, for the pope, after having achieved the division of the Ghibelline band, and having used to his advantage Alfonso's naiveté

All this may be possible; and, of course, during this period one can note a certain proximity of the pope towards Pisa, to counter Genoa's crucial move in favor of Manfred. But I believe that, apart from the lucrative contracts, what the Pisans—traditional Ghibelline supporters of Frederick II—really sought was to substitute the late emperor with his distant relative, Alfonso X, the most prestigious Christian king at the time.

Alfonso's meeting with the Pisans at Soria was advantageous for Castile in many respects. New cultural interests emerged as a result of the new relations with the Pisans and the Lombards, for it is believed that at this time the first Italian "notaries" arrived at Alfonso's court. They were to become his faithful collaborators in the work of the chancellery and in many important translation projects.[46] For a humanist like Alfonso, contact with the most advanced scholarly figures and environments of his time, such as the experts in *artes dictandi*, which he so needed for his cultural ventures, must have been a great incentive to maintain such relations, although they carried little economic benefit to the majority of his subjects.[47]

Alfonso was in Soria in 1256, when the Pisans arrived, in order to celebrate the new Cortes, which were to deal mainly with the economic state of the kingdom.[48] Despite measures adopted during the 1252 Seville Cortes, economic conditions had not improved at all. Products were still scarce, and the few that circulated were extremely expensive.

---

or ambition, began, much to Alfonso's despair, to abandon the matter. This would confirm Kantorowicz's thesis of the anathema launched by the pope against the entire cursed lineage of the Staufens, the Spanish branch included" (*Alfonso X*, pp. 79–80). For E. Kantorowicz's view, see his *Frederick II*, New York, 1967, pp. 273–274.

[46] Cf. E. Procter, "The Scientific Works of the Court of Alfonso X of Castile: the King and His Collaborators," *MLR*, XL (1945), pp. 12–29, p. 25.

[47] On the sorry state of the *artes dictandi* in Castile before Alfonso X, see V. Bertolucci Pizzorusso, "Un trattato di *Ars dictandi* dedicato ad Alfonso X," *Studi Mediolatini e Volgari*, 15–16 (1968), pp. 9–88; and the works by Ch. Faulhaber, "Retóricas clásicas y medievales en bibliotecas castellanas," *Abaco* 4 (1973), pp. 151–300; "Las retóricas hispanolatinas medievales (s. XIII–XV)," *Repertorio de Historia de las Ciencias Eclesiásticas de España*, VII (1979), pp. 11–65; see also his book *Latin Rhetorical Theory in Thirteenth and Fourteenth Century Castile*, Berkeley, UC Publications in Modern Philology, 103, UC Press, 1972.

[48] Ballesteros accepts the existence of these Cortes based on the *Historia de Segovia* by Colmenares and the chronology in the king's *Itinerario* (*Alfonso X*, pp. 165–169). No other modern scholar mentions them. However, if we think that Alfonso celebrated his Cortes on average every two years, and we know they were celebrated in 1254 and 1258, then we must conclude that he probably also held them in 1256, or at least had a high-level meeting with representatives of the nobility and the towns.

The norms on price control instituted in order to counter scarcity and the high costs of living were not working. On the contrary, merchants and hoarders, abusing the price control measures, bought things cheap and resold them clandestinely at exorbitant prices.[49] Faced with pressure from the city representatives, "[...] the king had to remove the *cotos* and order that things be sold freely at whatever prices the parties might agree upon."[50] But the swift transition from an economy of absolute control to a completely free market was equally detrimental to the population.

Despite the truly desperate situation of many of his subjects, Alfonso made a radiantly joyous appearance at the Soria Cortes, informing all he had just been elected "King of the Romans" by the city of Pisa, and that such nomination was the definitive step toward being elected emperor of all Christendom. I do not believe many of those present understood what he was talking about. Some among the nobility, especially the cultured clergymen, must have remembered that one of Alfonso's ancestors had himself named "Emperor of Christians and pagans," that is, of all kings in the Peninsula, Christian and Muslim. But now Alfonso spoke of an empire in Italy and Germany, something indeed hard to comprehend for a society that had been practically isolated from the rest of Europe.

The surprise at the announcement of the election must have been followed by panic among the nobility when Alfonso spoke of the need to compile a new legal code founded on Roman law, perhaps suggesting it would be the legal foundation for the new empire. In fact, he explained that work had already begun on June 23 of that year. Alfonso was speaking of the greatest project of his rule in the legal domain, the compilation of the *Siete Partidas*, that, as the Prologue states, "... was begun on the eve of Saint John the Baptist, four years and twenty-three days after the beginning of our reign." One of the most notable results of the Pisan nomination was indeed the definitive turn Alfonso had to give to his entire legislative and political project. The legislation promulgated in the *Espéculo* (on May 5, 1255), followed closely by its practical application in the *Fuero real* (25 August 25, 1255), had become too narrow and insufficient to cover the political perspectives

---

[49] The economic state of the kingdom is described in detail in the *CAX*, chap. 5. p. 37, whose author does not fail to mention all negative things related to Alfonso's rule.

[50] *CAX*, p. 37.

raised by the Pisan embassy. This is how, according to García Gallo, the *Partidas* were born: begun on June 23, 1256, they were concluded according to many scholars on June 23, 1265.[51]

Given the experience of the *Fuero real*, which, as we will see, also led to the rebellion of the nobility, any announcement of legal projects set off alarm bells for those who feared for their privilege. On the other hand, Alfonso continued speaking to the congregation of the need to convince the dignitaries charged with electing him as emperor that he was the best candidate, and the most convincing argument was money, a great deal of money.

The representatives of the cities present at the Cortes could not understand how, in such a state of economic crisis, the king would be thinking about purchasing a title that in their eyes carried no economic benefit. On the contrary, the pact with Pisa turned the cities of Florence, Lucca, and, above all, Genoa, into enemies, and the Genovese were the main commercial suppliers of the Peninsular markets. Alfonso must have realized that the idea of empire did not at all excite his subjects, who where instead worried mainly about their daily bread.

4. *Christina of Norway*

One of the most important international events following Alfonso's nomination as "King of the Romans" was the marriage of Princess Christina, daughter of Haakon IV of Norway (1217–1263), to a brother of the king of Castile, Prince Felipe.[52] Alfonso had repeatedly tried to

---

[51] These are the endpoint dates given in the *Ms. Add. 20787* of the *Primera Partida* in the British Library (see the edition by J.A. Arias Bonet, Valladolid: Universidad, 1975, p. 3). Cf. A. García Gallo, "El *Libro de las Leyes* de Alfonso el Sabio: del *Espéculo* a las *Partidas*," *AHDE*, XXI–XXII (1951–1952), pp. 345–528; and the works by J.R. Craddock, "La cronología de las obras legislativas de Alfonso X el Sabio," *AHDE*, 51 (1981), pp. 365–418; and his bibliographic essay *The Legislative Works of Alfonso X, El Sabio. A Critical Bibliography*, London: Grant and Cutler, 1986.

[52] As is well known, the version of the facts in the *CAX* is quite different:
> Likewise, before his father's death this King Alfonso married doña Violante, daughter of King Jaime of Aragón and sister of King Pedro. He had no son by her; and he became unhappy; seeing that this was due to a lack on her part, he therefore sent his envoys to the King of Norway to entreat the king to send his daughter in marriage. (*CAX*, p. 30)

The *Crónica* dates these events in 1252, clearly suggesting Alfonso intended to repudiate Violante. Early in 1253, according to the *CAX*'s chronology, Christina of Norway

establish relations with the Kingdom of Norway, expecting to obtain
military support in case he had to defend his imperial ambitions, and
material assistance, ships in particular, for his African project. The
Norwegians were also interested in that contact, mostly for commercial reasons, for they needed wheat that was grown abundantly in Castile. They also sought Alfonso's support as "emperor elect" in gaining
control of Lübeck.

When the Pisan delegation arrived in Soria to name Alfonso
emperor, Norwegian ambassadors were also there negotiating commercial agreements with Alfonso. Was this a coincidence? Haakon had
also been proposed as a candidate for the imperial crown in 1247, and
it is probable that Alfonso would seek his help. When the Norwegians
returned home that fall, they were accompanied by an ambassador of
Alfonso's who conveyed a proposal for a friendship and collaboration
treaty between the two kingdoms, and the desire to seal it with a marriage, asking for Princess Christina's hand for one of Alfonso's brothers. Haakon must have pondered this greatly, but the recent support
of the Pisans for Alfonso must have sufficiently convinced him of the
advantages such a marriage could bring, because he gave his consent a
mere month later.[53] Christina left Norway the summer of 1257 and after
going through Yarmouth, England, she arrived in Normandy, where
Louis IX of France awaited her. From there, she went to Spain, where
she was generously welcomed by Jaime I of Aragón, who, according
to an Icelandic saga, was charmed by her beauty and expressed his

---

arrived in Castile, and soon after, Violante had her first child (Berenguela), followed
by Beatriz, Fernando, etc. "On that account, the king was very ashamed that he had
sent for doña Cristina" (*CAX*, p. 32). So he gave her as a wife to his brother don Felipe,
who was bishop elect of Seville but nonetheless had no religious vocation (*ibidem*)."
This version, considered pure fabrication by a chronicler hostile to Alfonso X, as Mondéjar has proved (*Memorias*, p. 584 and ff.), was written for the consumption of the
courtiers of the chronicler's time (circa 1340).

[53] Cf. B. Gelsinger, "A Thirteenth-Century Norwegian-Castilian Alliance," *Medievalia et Humanistica*, New Series, 10 (1981), pp. 55–80, esp. pp. 55–60. The main source
of this episode is Sturla Thordarson, *Hakonar saga Hakonarsonar*, chaps. 289–295, in
C.R. Unger, ed., *Codex Frisianus. En Samling af norske Konge-Sagaer*, pp. 548–553.
The relevant passages of Haakon IV's Saga (*Historia Haquini IV, regis Norvegiae*) were
published by P.A. Munch, "La princesa Cristina de Noruega y el infante don Felipe,
hermano de don Alfonso el Sabio," *BRAH*, 84 (1919), pp. 45–61; V. Almazán, "El
viaje de la Princesa Cristina a Valladolid (1257–1258) según la Saga islandesa del Rey
Hakón," *AL*, 37 (1983), pp. 101–110; A. Hernández Parrales, "El Infante Don Felipe
primer arzobispo electo de Sevilla, después de la reconquista," *AH*, 31 (1959), pp.
195–204. See also J. Valdeón, *Feudalismo y consolidación*, p. 60, 144 and ff.

desire to marry her. But his proposal was rejected by the Norwegians when they discovered the King of Aragón was an elderly man.[54] From Catalonia, the princess went to Castile. She was welcomed in Soria on December 22 by the bishop of the city, don Pedro Fernández de Astorga, and by the prince don Luis; from Soria she headed to Burgos where she celebrated Christmas at the Monastery of Las Huelgas.

Alfonso X, who was already in Valladolid celebrating the new Cortes, went to meet her at Palencia and on January 4, 1258 accompanied her to Valladolid, where she was warmly welcomed by all the townspeople, the nobility, and the clergy who were gathered there for the Cortes.[55] During her stay in the city, great celebrations were held. The Cortes were customarily attended by the royal family (wife, children and siblings of the king), so Alfonso had the opportunity to introduce all of his brothers to the young princess (Fadrique, a brave warrior and fine hunter; Sancho, the archbishop-elect of Toledo; and Felipe, also archbishop-elect of Seville, with no religious vocation, but an accomplished hunter of bears and wild boars. Enrique was in self-imposed exiled on account of his failed rebellion against his brother). Christina chose don Felipe as her husband.

Felipe was the fifth child of Saint Fernando, born at the end of 1231. He had been steered into a Church career under the influence of his paternal grandmother, doña Berenguela. His education was entrusted first to don Rodrigo Jiménez de Rada, archbishop of Toledo, and later to don Juan, bishop of Osma and chancellor of Castile. From his childhood, he received numerous benefices, canonships, and abbotships. In 1246, he was elected bishop by the chapter of Osma, but the pope did not approve the election because he was underage—he was merely 15. In 1248 he was named abbot of Covarrubias, and in February 1249, *procurador* or guardian of the Church of Seville because he was not old enough to be archbishop.[56] He was perhaps the most European

---

[54] In *BRAH*, 84, 1919, p. 47.

[55] *Cortes de los antiguos reinos de León y Castilla*, Madrid: Real Academia de la Historia, 1861–1903, vol.I, pp. 54–63, p. 55. The main issue at these Cortes seems to have been, once more, the state of the kingdom's economy, the stability of the prices of products, and the interest that could be charged on credit, establishing it could not go above 33.33% yearly. Cf. E. Procter, *Curia and Cortes*, pp. 128–129; and Ballesteros, *Alfonso X*, pp. 199–207.

[56] According to J.A. de Morgado, in his *Historia de Sevilla* (1587), it was don Fernando III himself who, following the conquest of the city, named his son don Felipe the first archbishop of Seville, but he never assumed office because subsequently

of Alfonso's brothers. In 1244 he went to study at the University of
Paris, where for a short time he was the student of Saint Albertus Magnus and a classmate of Saint Thomas Aquinas and Saint Bonaventure.
Despite being groomed for an ecclesiastical career, following the death
of his father, he relinquished his benefices and returned to a secular
state, much to his brother Alfonso's chagrin.[57] Faced with the marriage
proposal to a beautiful Nordic princess, he had no problems accepting
the hand of Christina of Norway.

The engagement was celebrated February 6, Ash Wednesday, and
the marriage March 31, the Sunday following Easter. As far as we
know, it was a happy albeit brief marriage. Christina died childless
four years later in Seville, according to some, out to nostalgia for her
beloved Norway. She was buried in a simple sarcophagus in the cloister of the Colegiata of Covarrubias, where don Felipe had been chief
abbot during his time in the Church and where she is still venerated by
Norwegian faithful.[58] Thus the first political-dynastic contact between
two very distant countries, both geographically and culturally, was
sealed.[59]

---

his brother don Alfonso married him off to princess Christina of Norway (book IV,
fol. 100v).

[57] Many years later, in a famous letter to don Felipe, where he reminds him of all
this and the many benefices he had granted him (among them the dominion of Valde-
corneja along with the towns of El Barco de Ávila, Horcajada, and El Mirón), Alfonso
chided him for his ungratefulness at a moment (1268) when the prince had already
joined the rebels who aimed at dethroning Alfonso. Cf. *CAX*, pp. 109–111 and ff.

[58] Cf. *CAX*, pp. 109–111.

[59] After Christina's death, Felipe was married again in 1265, to a mysterious doña
Inés, about whom there is no information; and again in 1269, for the third time, to
Leonor Ruiz de Castro, sister of Ferrán Ruiz de Castro, one of the most active noblemen in the conspiracy against Alfonso X. Prince Felipe also died young, on November
28, 1274, as is stated on the inscription of his lavish grave in the Church of the Templar Knights of Santa María of Villasirga (today Villalcázar de Sirga, 7 km SE from
Carrión de los Condes and not too far from Frómista, in the province of Palencia)
copied by F. de Rades y Andrada, *Chronica de las tres ordenes de Sanctiago, Calatrava
y Alcántara*, Toledo, 1572, fol. 35v. The impressive Church of Santa María la Blanca
of Villalcázar de Sirga, on the Pilgrimage Road to Santiago, preserves (from 1926 in
the Chapel of Santiago) the magnificent Gothic graves in polychromed stone belonging to Prince Felipe and his last wife, doña Leonor. Recently it was speculated that
the woman buried in Leonor's grave could actually be Christina of Norway, but this
hypothesis was disproved when the remains of the princess were inspected on occasion of the renovation of the Cloister of Covarrubias, which proved that the remains
in the sarcophagus at that cloister belong to Christina. Villasirga was a site of great
popular devotion during the Middle Ages for the pilgrims on the Road to Santiago.
Alfonso X was a great devotee of the miraculous image of the Virgen Blanca of Villasirga, which he considered as powerful as St. James himself and in whose honor he

composed twelve *cantigas* singing her miracles. It was probably Alfonso himself who chose that church as his brother's grave. On the church and the pilgrimage, see: R. Inclán Inclán, "Sepulcro del Infante D. Felipe, hijo del rey Fernando III el Santo," *BRAH*, 75 (1919), p. 143 and ff.; J.E. Keller, "King Alfonso's Virgen of Villa-Sirga," in *Middle Ages-Reformation-Volkskunde: Festschrift for J.G. Kunstmann*, Chapel Hill, NC, 1959, p. 79 and ff; and "More on the rivalry between S. María and Santiago de Compostela," *Crítica Hispánica*, I (1979), p. 37 and ff; S. Andrés Ordax, "Villalcázar de Sirga: Santa María la Blanca," in *Castilla y León*, I, *La España Gótica*, IX, Madrid: Ediciones Encuentro, 1989, pp. 274–279; J.E. Antolín Fernández, *Villasirga*, Palencia: Publicaciones de la Institución Tello Téllez de Meneses, no. 30, 1971, pp. 157–223; M.F. Solano y Pereda-Vivanco, "Papeletas sobre escultura funeraria castellana. Los sepulcros de Villalcázar de Sirga," *BSAA*, Fasc.II, p. 97.

CHAPTER FIVE

ALFONSO, KING OF THE ROMANS

1. *The Election*

The support of Pisa and Marseille, of the king of Norway, and in particular the good news coming from Rome made Alfonso optimistic about the possibility of obtaining the imperial crown. But an unexpected obstacle to his aspirations emerged: Richard of Cornwall's candidacy. Richard was the brother of Henry III of England, who, at least at the time, was the ally of Alfonso X. Richard's family ties with the Staufens were tenuous and remote (he was Frederick II's brother-in-law), but he had great personal prestige and was a very wealthy man. Both Richard and Alfonso sent their representatives to Germany in order to obtain votes in exchange for a great deal of money and other promises. Richard's representative was Johann van Avesnes and Alfonso's, the aforementioned archdeacon García Pérez, very active and skillful in public relations, whom Alfonso rewarded with much gold.[1]

The election that was to take place on January 13, 1257 in Frankfurt was truly chaotic. Alfonso's supporters, the Archbishop of Trier, Arnold of Ysenburg, and Duke Albert of Saxony, did not allow the supporter of Richard, Conrad, Bishop of Cologne, to enter into the city. But Conrad was not intimidated, and he met outside the city with Archbishop Gerhard of Mainz and the count of the Palatinate, Ludwig of Bavaria, to elect Richard of Cornwall as King of the Romans.[2] As expected, Alfonso's main supporter, Arnold of Trier, refused to accept the validity of the election, and meeting with the representatives of Saxony and Brandenburg on April 1, 1257, Palm Sunday, he secured their votes for Alfonso X at the price of 20,000 marks each.[3]

---

[1] Cf. A. Ballesteros, "Alfonso X de Castilla y la Corona de Alemania," *RABM*, (1919); and *Alfonso X*, pp. 175–212.

[2] Cf. *MGH, Constitutiones*, vol.II, pp. 484–485; Ballesteros, *Alfonso X*, pp. 280–282; Bayley, "Diplomatic Preliminaries," pp. 467–470.

[3] That is at least what Thomas Wikes claims. Indignantly, Mondéjar denies that Alfonso would have resorted to the "indecent means of a bribe." Jofré de Loaysa says

They each thus had three votes, but were still missing the vote of the King Ottokar of Bohemia, nephew of Alfonso's mother Beatriz of Swabia, and hence Alfonso's first cousin. It appears that Ottokar at first voted for both candidates. Finally, after hesitating, the Bohemian king favored Alfonso, making his election as King of the Romans official. This double election makes obvious the profound divisions in European Christendom at the time.[4]

Alfonso's chronicler narrates these events in a concise fashion, only to emphasize that Alfonso's election garnered him great prestige but at a high cost to his subjects. Another 15 years would have to go by, as well as incalculable expenses that bankrupted Castile, before the problem of the *Interregnum* was solved.[5]

Alfonso was officially informed of the election on August 15, 1257, when a German delegation headed by Eberhard of Waldburg, Bishop of Konstanz, arrived in Burgos.[6] Following the protocol, Alfonso requested three days to deliberate on the acceptance. On the third day, in a solemn ceremony before the German delegates and the entire court, he formally accepted the result of the election, declaring he did so following the advice of the illustrious monarchs of France, Hungary, Aragón, Portugal, and Navarra. He also claimed he did so, not out of the ambition to govern more lands or obtain greater power or riches, but out of the desire to maintain peace, justice, and freedom in the Empire and to serve the greater glory of God and the people's benefit.[7] He then proceeded to set up his imperial court, naming as *senescal* or main caretaker Albert, Lord of Vienne; as chancellor, Enrique, bishop-elect of Spira; and his cousin, Enrique, Duke of Brabant and the son of his

---

in his *Crónica* (chap. 219, 6–7, p. 68) that Alfonso was elected by four votes, while Richard obtained only three. Cf. Ballesteros, *Alfonso X*, p. 177–183 and 454–459; Bayley, "Diplomatic Preliminaries," pp. 473–481.

[4] Cf. W. Giese, "Der Reichstag…," p. 568. See also, A. Burson, *Die Doppelwahl des Jaheres 1275 und das Romische Königtum Alfons X von Castilien. Ein Beitrag zur Geschichte des grossen Interregnums*, Münster, 1866.

[5] *CAX*, chap. 17, pp. 65–67. On Alfonso's squandering of money that would bankrupt his kingdom, see J.F. O'Callaghan, "Paths to Ruin," pp. 41–67; E. S. Procter, *Curia and Cortes in León and Castile 1072–1295*, Cambridge: Cambridge University Press, 1980, pp. 214–216; Ballesteros, *Alfonso X*, pp. 435–445.

[6] The *CAX* mistakenly locates these events in 1268, but their description is quite precise (chap. 18, pp. 68–70).

[7] See the text of the declaration in E. Winkelmann, *Acta imperii inedita saeculi XIII et XIV. Urkunden und Briefe zur Geschichte des Kaiserreichs und des Konigreichs in Sizilien in den Jahren 1198 bis 1400*, 2 vol., Innsbruck: Wagner, 1880, I, p. 463, no. 578.

mother's sister, Mary of Swabia, as his vicar in the Empire, promising him an annual salary of 10,000 *livre tournois* or Tours pounds until he could travel to Germany. Finally, he appointed as protonotary of the Holy Roman Empire Bandino di Lancia, someone who had put great zeal into launching the pro-Alfonso movement.[8]

While Alfonso was busy making plans to govern the Empire, things in Germany had taken a different course. Richard of Cornwall believed the three votes he had obtained gave him the right to the crown, and thus he presented himself in Germany in order to obtain it. Before a large group of ecclesiastics, nobles, knights, and townspeople gathered at Aachen on May 17, 1257, Conrad, Archbishop of Cologne, placed the crown on his head that identified him as the King of the Romans. Faced with this situation and to counter the step taken by his rival, Alfonso had no choice but to travel to Germany, for the German electors would not approve a candidate, despite his lineage, if they were not personally acquainted with him. Alfonso was thus faced with a serious dilemma: either show up in Germany with a large army that would impress his supporters and gain more followers for his cause, or buy the electors with a great deal of money, a method as effective and convincing as military might. The internal problems of the kingdom did not allow him to travel to Germany at that time, so he chose the diplomatic and monetary route, despite the disastrous economic situation of the kingdom.[9]

But Alfonso's alliances and the choice of diplomats who were to represent him before his future subjects were not very fortunate. As his most powerful representative in Germany he nominated his cousin Enrique, Duke of Brabant; for Northern Italy he chose the "Lord of the Mark of Treviso," the despot Ezzelino da Romano, a former collaborator of Frederick II and one of the figures most hated by his subjects on account of his violent and ferocious dictatorship. The Church deemed him a heretic and even preached a crusade against him in order to drive him out of power. How Alfonso managed to associate himself with such a monster, knowing he automatically became an ally of a declared enemy of the pope, is inexplicable. If he truly wanted to be

---

[8] The diplomas containing these appointments can be seen in J. Ficker and E. Winkelmann, eds., *Regesten des Kaiserreichs, 1198–1272*, 3 vols., II, p. 354; and cf. Mondéjar, *Memorias*, p. 158; Ballesteros, *Alfonso X*, p. 189.

[9] Around this time Hugh of Burgundy, Guy, Count of Flanders, and Henri, Duke of Lorraine declared themselves vassals of Alfonso.

crowned by the pope, his alliance with Ezzelino constituted diplomatic and political suicide.

Between the Valladolid 1258 Cortes and the Toledo ones a year later, Alfonso spent most of his time looking for allies and supporters of his cause, especially after the defection of Pisa and Marseille in 1257. The first, defeated by Genoa, had to accept as a condition for peace that it would not acknowledge any emperor except one named by the pope; the second lost its independence after a popular rebellion led by Charles of Anjou, who demanded he break all relations with Alfonso's empire. The search for supporters entailed alliances, pacts, and other political and moral agreements, and especially large sums of money that Alfonso liberally handed out. To obtain these funds, the Learned King, starting with the Valladolid Cortes in 1258, obtained the approval for a double tax ("moneda doblada"), that is, on top of the regular one that was paid every seven years, an extra one that was supposed to help him with his "claim to the empire."[10] The Valladolid Cortes also established other special restrictions regarding luxury clothing and other consumer goods, and even determined what delicacies could be eaten, when, and how much.[11]

At the 1259 Toledo Cortes, which were summoned to deal exclusively with the "claim to the empire,"[12] Alfonso, who had already been recognized as the King of the Romans by foreign princes and subjects, attempted to also proclaim himself supreme lord of all peninsular kingdoms, which, as C. de Ayala notes, were already de facto "in a formal state of vassalage."[13] As in other occasions, the Cortes were not only attended by representatives of other Christian kingdoms (among them, his imperial vassals, Henri of Lorraine, Hugh of Burgundy, and Guy of Flanders) but also by his Muslim subjects, such as the kings of Granada, Murcia, and Niebla.[14]

---

[10] J. F. O'Callaghan, "The Cortes and Royal Taxation during the Reign of Alfonso X of Castile," *Traditio*, 27 (1971), pp. 379–398, 383; Ballesteros, *Alfonso X*, pp. 217; 225–228; 230–234.

[11] Cf. Ballesteros, *Alfonso X*, pp. 199–207; J.F. O'Callahan, "Paths to Ruin," p. 44 and ff.

[12] Document dated February 2, 1260, in Ballesteros, *Alfonso X*, p. 226, and "Itinerario," *BRAH*, 108 (1936), 17, note 1; cf. J.F. O'Callaghan, *The Cortes of Castile-León*, p. 99. Cf. *CAX*, chap. 18, pp. 68–70.

[13] *Directrices fundamentales*, p. 264.

[14] A list of the dignitaries appears in *MHE*, I, *Documentos*, no. 70 (October 2, 1259), pp. 152–154; cf. Ballesteros, *Alfonso X*, pp. 224–229; and J. O'Callaghan, *The Cortes of Castile-León*, pp. 99–100, note 13.

This unifying attitude provoked a negative reaction in some peninsular kings, such as his father-in-law, Jaime I of Aragón. Don Jaime was
hypersensitive to any threat to his territorial hegemony, and, although
he maintained good relations with his son-in-law, he remained suspicious when he became aware of Alfonso's ambitions and expansionist
views. In fact, despite having recognized the supremacy of Castile in
the 1256 Soria pact following the Toledo Cortes, he formally appointed
a proctor (*procurador*) to express opposition to Alfonso's direct or
hegemonic claims over the kingdom of Aragón based on the title of
emperor.[15] It is believed that this was also the reason why don Jaime
offered his son and heir, don Pedro, in marriage to Constance, daughter of Manfred, Frederick II's illegitimate son, who at the time also
aspired to his father's imperial crown. Don Jaime probably thought
that by marrying his son off to an heir of the last emperor of the Holy
Roman Empire, and recognizing Manfred's rule over Italy, or at least
Sicily, he would discourage his son-in-law, sabotaging his chances of
being recognized as emperor in Italy and as lord of the Iberian Peninsula. This was, according to C. de Ayala, "an obvious Sicily-Aragón
treaty sealed with a marriage."[16]

The King of Aragón's stratagem did not go by unnoticed by Alfonso,
who, in a letter dated at Córdoba on September 20, 1260, openly
reacted to his father-in-law's hostile political moves: "in no other affair
could you have been so badly misadvised nor could you have caused
more damage to yourself."[17] Alfonso condemned both the marriage
as well as the crusade plans drafted by his father-in-law, but he was
particularly alarmed by his possible support of Manfred: "in terms of
what concerns us, we consider that no other man in the world received
a greater insult that the one we received from you" (*ibidem*). The marriage was also strongly opposed by the pope and especially the French

---

[15] To this effect, Ballesteros quotes a document by Jaime I he took from Villanueva, dated at Mora, September 27, 1259 (J. Villanueva, *Viaje literario a las iglesias de
España*, Madrid, 12 vols., 1803–1852, I, p. 176); and cf. C. Socarrás, *Alfonso X of Castile*, pp. 172–173; and C. de Ayala Martínez, *Directrices fundamentales*, pp. 176–178
and 207–256.

[16] *Directrices fundamentales*, p. 298. The marriage agreement was formalized in
Barcelona on July 28, 1260. Cf. D. Girona Llagostera, *Mullerament de l'infant En Pere
de Cathalunya ab Madona Constança de Sicilia*, in *CHCA*, I (1909).

[17] *MHE*, I, p. 165.

king, but all to no avail. The wedding took place June 13, 1262 in Montpellier, and the bride received a lavish dowry.[18]

Don Jaime was not on the wrong track. Manfred was gradually acquiring greater power in Italy, while some of Alfonso's most rabid Ghibelline supporters were losing ground, as was the case of the furious anti-papist Margrave of Treviso, Ezzelino da Romano, leader of Padova, who had strongly opposed Manfred's territorial ambitions. In the early months of 1259, Ezzelino was defeated by the Guelf League of Lombardy not far from Milan. Suddenly, Manfred was in control of large areas in Northern Italy that had previously been controlled by Alfonso's allies. Following pressure from the Guelfs, who supported Manfred, Florence too feared for its independence, which indeed it lost the following year at the Battle of Montaperti (September 1260), when Manfred's supporters defeated the Florentines, while Alfonso was unable to help them.[19] With this new victory, Manfred expanded his territories to central Italy.

Despite the King of Aragón's opposition to his son-in-law's possible supremacy in the Peninsula, it should be noted that immediately following his election and despite his good prospects, Alfonso missed the opportunity to be crowned emperor. Following his electoral victory and with most of the European nobility, especially the Germans, behind him, it would have been relatively easy to convince the pope, who was also not opposed to crowning him. Why then, did he not appear in Rome to receive the crown? The answer may be sought in a papal envoy that arrived during the Toledo Cortes in 1259. Cardinal Godfred of Saint George appeared before Alfonso requesting that he abstain from a trip to Rome to be crowned emperor, but he did not reveal the motives for the papal request.[20] Alfonso, who at the time enjoyed great popularity among his supporters, did not suspect what the pope was really planning. He answered the pope's missive by sending to Rome a diplomatic mission headed by his brother, Prince Manuel. Soon thereafter the motive of the pope's request was revealed: the pope favored Richard of Cornwall, whom he had already summoned

---

[18] The marriage certificate can be seen in D. Girona Llagostera, *Mullerament de l'infant Pere*, Appendix XIV.

[19] Cf. S. Runciman, *The Sicilian Vespers*, Cambridge, 1958, p. 40.

[20] Text in I. Rodríguez Lama, *La documentación pontificia de Urbano IV (1261–1264)*, Rome, 1981. no. 413, pp. 374–375.

to Rome to be crowned emperor in a secret letter on April 30 of that same year.[21]

Following the sudden death of Richard of Cornwall, other internal political issues, such as the military campaigns he had to lead to maintain control of lands conquered, may partly explain why Alfonso did not take the definitive steps to be crowned emperor. There is no definitive explanation to this incongruent course of action, but we cannot rule out the possibility that Alfonso wanted to carry out his father's last will, namely, to conquer all lands of the ancient Visigoth empire across the Gibraltar Strait before being crowned emperor. But the Fernandian African crusade project, begun with the unlucky Salé campaign (1260) and the easy conquest of the kingdoms of Niebla and Cádiz (1262), faced serious difficulties. First it was hindered by a Moorish revolt instigated by the opportunistic King of Granada, which put the life of Alfonso and his family at risk; later by the uprisings of Andalusia and Murcia, the losses of Jerez, Arcos, Véjer, and Medina Sidonia; and finally, the nobility's rebellion. There's no doubt that part of the explanation lies in these events that tied down Alfonso to peninsular politics for many years, making him unable to deal with his "quest for the Empire" until late in the seventies. But if his real priority had been to become emperor, he should have found the time for a temporary leave from the affairs of his kingdom, as he did for his cultural projects, or to go to see the pope in 1275. Thus, if he did not do so, it was probably due to the fact that he assumed the crown to be his, and that he could claim it whenever he wanted, or that being crowned emperor was less important than the peace and unity of his kingdoms. When he did attempt to appear in Rome, it was too late, and the pope himself, absurd as it may seem, admonished him for not having done so sooner.

2. Alfonso's Return to Seville: Culture and Diplomacy

On September 22, 1260, Alfonso returned to Seville, where he would reside uninterruptedly until May 15, 1265, and in Andalusia until 1269.[22] Alfonso, like his father, enjoyed the warm South, which, in

---

[21] Cf. W.F. von Schoen, *Alfonso X*, p. 133; C. de Ayala, *Directrices fundamentales*, p. 283, note 271.

[22] Ballesteros, in Chapter VIII of his biography of Alfonso quoted above, on the basis of a number of documents, reconstructs life in the palace during Alfonso's period in Seville.

contrast with the cold and austere Castile, offered him a better climate and sumptuous palaces and gardens unknown in the North. For a king who loved the arts and courtly luxury, the climate of Seville must have been irresistible. He thus decided at the time to transfer his court to that city he called the "most noble [...] of all others in the world."[23] In Seville too, he would found an important cultural center, starting with the study of Latin and Arabic on December 28, 1254, a project successively protected by Alexander IV's pontifical brief (issued at Anagni on June 30, 1260), and later transferring to Toledo the study of astronomy, projects directed by a Cathedral church official, Guillén Arremón Daspa and the Jewish scholar from Toledo, Rabiçag, author of *Astrolabio redondo* (Round Astrolabe), where he demonstrated how to determine the elevation and hours in the city of Seville.

Under Alfonso's protection, Seville became the most important cultural and commercial city of the kingdom. Merchants and grocers from all over Europe and the Middle East, such Maestre Symón and Maestre Bartolomé, set up shop there as well as famous doctors such as Maestre Pedro Catalán, to whom Alfonso granted many favors. Genovese merchants signed very favorable commercial agreements, and it is precisely in these agreements where Alfonso first signs himself as emperor and calls his Seville palace "regia imperatoris," or " the imperial residence."[24]

As the seat of the court, diplomats, scientists, and poets from all parts of Europe and the Middle East met in Seville's palaces and squares. Alfonso welcomed the ambassadors of Al-Malek, the sultan of Egypt, who gifted him with previously unknown presents such as a giraffe and a zebra.[25] Historians disagree on the original date of this visit and its motives. It may have taken place at any point during Alfonso's residence in Seville (between September 22, 1260 and May 15, 1265). The motive, according to scholars, was probably to request Alfonso's

---

[23] *Setenario*, Law X—"De las bondades del rregno de Seuilla" (or the praise of Seville) (*quoted ed.*, pp. 19–20).

[24] See some of these documents in Ballesteros, *Alfonso X*, p. 334 and ff. 25

[25] While King Alfonso was in Seville and all the men with him during this honor that they did for his father, messengers came to him from Alvandexáver, King of Egypt. They brought presents to King Alfonso of many precious cloths of different kinds and of many rare and beautiful jewels. The also brought an animal called an *azorafa* [giraffe], and an ass that was striped with one band white and the other black, and many other kinds of beasts and animals. The king welcomed warmly these messengers and did them great honor and sent them very well pleased from there. (*CAX*, p. 47).

assistance in confronting the threat of Hulagu's Mongols.[26] When the ambassadors returned to Cairo, Al-Malek had been deposed by a coup and supplanted by Baibars I (1260–1277), who defeated the Mongols at the battle of Ain Yalut.

The date and concrete motives of the embassy seem of secondary importance when we ponder the significance of such an event: representatives of the Egyptian Mameluk sultan appear in Seville attracted by Alfonso's reputation not only as the most learned man of his time, but also as the most powerful of all Christian kings. These two ideologically opposed figures met in order to get to know each other and exchange gifts whose cultural significance went beyond the strange animals sent by the "sultan of Babylon" and the typical ones Alfonso may have sent in return. It is also possible, as some suggest, that with the delegation too came several Egyptian astronomers and astrologists with whom Alfonso may have exchanged the latest developments in the fields that his own scholars were working on.[27] It was precisely around this time when he was hard at work on *Libros del saber de astrología*, and that the scholar Azarquiel was carrying out astronomical experiments that led to the *Libro de las tablas alfonsíes*.[28]

During his residence in Seville, Alfonso worked intensely not only on his cultural projects, but also on matters of international politics, especially his relations with the Italian republics which were now being attacked politically and militarily by Frederick's heir, Manfred. Manfred's political activism also placed at risk Alfonso's imperial aspirations, for if the Italian republics were to fall into his grip, Alfonso would lose his strongest support in the eyes of the pope.

To curb Manfred, Florence sent to Castile the famous citizen Brunetto Latini seeking Alfonso's help in exchange for support from the

---

[26] C. de Ayala Martínez, *Directrices fundamentales,* pp. 291–294; P. Martínez Montávez, "Relaciones de Alfonso X de Castilla con el sultán mameluco Baybars y sus sucesores," *Al-Andalus,* 27 (1962), pp. 343–376.

[27] This is what can be gleaned from a period document where Alfonso asks his friend, the Archbishop of Seville, for a mosque that may "house the physicians who came from abroad and to have them close by." (D. Ortiz de Zúñiga, *Anales,* año 1261, n. 3, p. 202). Cf. J. Guichot, *Historia de la ciudad de Sevilla y pueblos importantes de su provincia,* Sevilla, 1882, III, p. 173.

[28] This is the title given to the *Tablas* in the prologue to the edition published by Rico y Sinobas, *Libros del saber de astronomía del Rey D. Alfonso X de Castilla,* Madrid: Eusebio Aguado, 1863–1867, 5 vols., I, XX, n. 1. Cf. J. M. Millás Vallicrosa, "La obra astronómica de Azarquiel y las *Tablas toledanas,*" in his *Estudios sobre historia de la ciencia española,* pp. 126–176.

Florentine Guelfs. Although no documents remain from this visit, we have Brunetto's direct testimony mentioned in his *Tesoretto* (lines 123–134) when speaking of his diplomatic meeting with the "re Nanfosse" (King Alfonso).[29] At the end of the summer of 1260, Alfonso lavishly welcomed the distinguished ambassador in the old palace of the sultans. This illustrious Florentine, accustomed to a Latin-Christian cultural environment, must have been amazed at the court of a Christian king who aspired to become emperor of all Christendom, a place permeated by Oriental culture in which the majority of the king's aides and men of letters were Jews and Muslims.

Brunetto must have taken advantage of the few days he spent in Seville to gather the materials and ideas he wanted to take with him. His official mission, however, was a political and diplomatic one, as he had to convince Alfonso of granting help against Manfred in exchange for Florence's support in the imperial election. The illustrious ambassador unconditionally favored Alfonso's candidacy to the imperial crown, for he found "no one under the moon who on account of his noble lineage and prestige is as worthy as King Alfonso." Having spent time with Alfonso and his advisors, he was convinced that "the high King of Spain, who is now the King of Germany" (that is "King of the Romans"), would obtain the imperial crown and no one would take it away "if God [did] not allow it." The certainty of Alfonso's imminent coronation was what the ambassador and his republic brought to Seville.

But it was already too late. While Latini was in Spain, the political crisis in Florence quickly turned against the Guelfs. Manfred's supporters defeated the Florentine Guelf league at Montaperti in September, and Manfred was elected senator of Rome shortly after.[30] This victory practically wiped out Alfonso's possibilities of dominating Italy, at least for the time being. On his return trip, when passing through Roncesvalles (*Tesoretto*, lines 143–47 and 152–62), Brunetto Latini met a Spanish student returning from Florence and learned from him of the defeat of his fellow citizens. He then decided not to return to Florence and remained in exile in France for the next six years, where he wrote

---

[29] On Brunetto Latini's visit to Seville, see J. Burton Holloway, "The Road through Roncesvalles: Alfonsine Formation of Brunetto Latini and Dante—Diplomacy and Literature," in I. Burns, ed., *Emperor of Culture*, pp. 109–123.

[30] G. Villani, *Cronica*, 8 vols., vol. II, bk. 6, chap. 73, pp. 99–100. R. Davidsohn, *Storia di Firenze*, trans. G.B. Klein, 8 vols., Florence: Sansoni, 1957.

practically all of his work in French, dedicating it to an unknown protector, "biaus dous amis."[31] In 1267 Latini was finally able to return to Italy, probably as part of Charles of Anjou's entourage. Starting in 1269, he held important positions in the Republic of Florence as a protonotary for Anjou, where he died in 1294.

Even if Brunetto Latini's trip to Alfonso's court did not yield the expected diplomatic results, its consequences in the field of letters and culture in general must be considered of paramount importance, for it is believed that thanks to his contacts with Alfonso's *scriptorium*, he was responsible for bringing Muslim Arabic culture to Dante's Florence.[32]

Brunetto Latini was not the only distinguished foreigner to visit Alfonso in Seville. Between the end of 1262 and the beginning of 1263, the empress of Constantinople, Mary of Brienne, arrived in Seville (and not in Burgos as the *CAX* states). She was touring the European courts and the Holy See, raising funds to rescue her son, Philip of Courtenay, who was being held hostage in Venice as a guarantee against a loan taken on by her husband, Baldwin II, the dethroned Latin emperor of Constantinople.[33] The *CAX* erroneously states that it was Baldwin II himself who had fallen into the hands of the Sultan of Egypt.[34] Mary was the daughter of John of Brienne and Princess Berenguela of León, the daughter of Alfonso IX of León and Berenguela the Great, Alfonso

---

[31] Cf. *La rettorica*, I. 10; *Tresor* I. 1.4 and III. 73.1. For Carmody (*Li Livres dou Tresor de Brunetto Latini,* Berkeley: University of California Press, 1948, p.XVIII) this person must have been Davizzo Tosinghi, the illustrious descendant of a family of Florentine bankers; for Holloway (*Twice-Told Tales: Brunetto Latini and Dante Alighieri,* New York: Peter Lang, 1993), the addressee would have been none other than Charles of Anjou.

[32] Cf. F. López Estrada, "Sobre la difusión del *Tesoro* de Brunetto Latini en España," *Gesammelte Aufsitze zur Kulturgeschichte Spaniens,* Serie I, vol.XVI, in *Spanische Forschungen der Gorresgesellschaft,* München, 1960, pp. 137–152; J. Bolton Holloway, "Alfonso el Sabio, Brunetto Latini and Dante Alighieri," *Thought,* 60 (1985), pp. 468–483; the above-cited *Twice-Told Tales: Brunetto Latini and Dante Alighieri,* New York: Peter Lang, 1993.

[33] E. Benito Ruano, "Huéspedes del Imperio de Oriente en la Corte de Alfonso X el Sabio," *Estudios dedicados a don Ramón Menéndez Pidal,* vol.VI, Madrid, 1956, pp. 632–645; R.L. Wolff, "Mortgage and Redemption of an Emperor's Son: Castile and the Latin Empire of Constantinople," *Speculum,* 29 (1954), pp. 45–84. J.F. O'Callaghan thinks the visit took place during the Toledo Cortes in 1259 (*The Cortes of Castile-León,* p. 99).

[34] Cf. *CAX,* chap. 17, pp. 65–67; and Ballesteros, *Alfonso X,* p. 350 and ff. ; C.A. Segura Graíño and A. Torreblanca, "Personajes bizantinos en la corte de Alfonso X," *Anuario de Estudios Medievales,* 15 (1985), pp. 179–188.

X's grandmother. Mary was thus Fernando III's niece, and therefore, Alfonso's aunt by blood. She had come to Spain to ask her nephew to help pay one third of the ransom of fifty silver *quintales* she had to give the Venetians to obtain her son's freedom. Apparently she had already obtained two thirds, one from the pope and the other from the King of France, and expected her nephew to help with the other third. With his customary generosity, Alfonso offered to pay the entire amount, demanding she return the other two parts to the pope and the King of France.

Alfonso's chronicler took the opportunity to praise Alfonso's generosity, "And everyone who heard him appreciated this king of Castile very much. And this [son of the] emperor was released from captivity and he preached the kindness and nobility and great sincerity of king don Alfonso, which was known throughout all lands [...]". On the other hand, the chronicler also criticized the king's liberality, which had plunged Castile into poverty: "And although this deed brought great fame to the king don Alfonso in other lands, however through this and other things king don Alfonso brought great impoverishment to the kingdoms of Castile and León."[35] The author of the *CAX* could not ignore the extreme generosity and prestige of the Learned King of Castile, acknowledged in all corners of the Mediterranean and disseminated by the most varied people who had received his favors or had known him personally or through diplomatic contacts. But he also pointed out how Alfonso's openhandedness towards foreigners during his quest for the imperial crown had left the kingdom bankrupt.

3. *The Overseas Crusade: From Salé to Niebla*

In the midst of all this cultural and diplomatic activity to obtain the imperial crown, Alfonso decided to launch the project to which his father had aspired, and that the papacy had urged him to undertake: an African crusade. The goal of the venture would be to earn him visibility as candidate to emperor of Christendom and to reconquer for Castile lands formerly belonging to the Visigoth Empire and which,

---

[35] Both texts quoted by F. Gómez Redondo, using a different manuscript than that used by the editor of the *CAX* (*Historia de la prosa medieval castellana*, Madrid: Cátedra, 1998, p. 974).

despite his desire, his father had not conquered due to lack of time.[36] The project also provided his subjects, oppressed as they were by a bankrupt economy, with the opportunity to emerge from poverty through the acquisition of a rich booty. The reconquest of ancient and new territories in North Africa carried the prestige of the victory over the enemies of Christendom and gave the pope a clear sign of Alfonso's vocation as a crusader and thus more confidence in his imperial candidacy. Besides these immediate goals, there was also the distant objective of conquering Jerusalem itself.

There's no doubt that the conquest of Salé must be identified with the much-touted crusade. This is supported by many documents, for instance a diploma dated July 27, 1260, where he names his childhood friend, don Juan García de Villamayor, *adelantado mayor de la mar*, or commander of the fleet, accompanied by an expert seaman, don Pedro Martínez de Fe, to carry out the campaign: "for the great desire we have to carry out the overseas Crusade in the service of God and for the greatness of Christianity."[37] There is also Alfonso's request for military help to Jaime of Aragón to participate in a crusade "against the Saracens".[38] But I also believe that the most likely objective of the crusade was not Salé, but the cities in North Africa that were under Visigoth control in the 8th century, as can be gleaned from another diploma where among the Castilian bishops a certain "Lorente, bishop of Çepta [modern Ceuta]" is also mentioned.[39] We can thus conclude that if the city of Salé was chosen as the main objective of the crusade this had to do with its status as a commercial emporium that could yield greater economic benefits in the form of booty.

On September 2, 1260 the small commercial port of Salé, on the Atlantic coast of Morocco, fell to the Christians.[40] When the Moroc-

---

[36] In his deathbed, Fernando III had reminded his son of that incomplete project (*EE*, II, p. 770b27–37). Cf. *Crónica de Veinte Reyes*, ed. Ruiz Asencio, p. 347; and Ch.-E. Dufourcq, "Un project castillant du XIII siècle: la croisade d'Afrique," *Revue d'histoire et de civilisation du Maghreb*, 3 (1966), pp. 26–51.

[37] Cf. *MHE*, I, p. 164; and in M. González Jiménez, *Diplomatario*, n. 231.

[38] Don Jaime's letter authorizing his subjects to participate in the crusade is dated at Lérida, April 3, 1260, but it stated the condition that the sultan of Tunis not be attacked (in *MHE*, I, p. 155), since he had agreements and business deals with him. Furthermore, Alfonso's rebellious brother, don Enrique, was residing at the Hafsid court, and don Jaime wanted to protect him.

[39] Cf. M. González Jiménez, *Diplomatario*, n. 254.

[40] The documents are included in *MHE*, I, no. 72–75, pp. 155–160, 164–166; *CAX*, chap. 19, pp. 71–75. Troops from Aragón also participated in the expedition. Cf.

cans saw such an imposing fleet, they thought that perhaps they were merchant ships, which was also the confirmation they received from the captain, García de Villamayor. It was the last day of Ramadan, and the city was in celebrations. The Christians, according to Muslim sources, took advantage of such circumstances to attack a defenseless city and commit all kinds of atrocities, stealing and pillaging all, killing the men, and raping the women.[41] The emir of Fez, Ibn Yûsuf, soon heard about this, and he arrived in the city with a great army ready to expel the invaders. Such use of force was unnecessary, for the mighty crusaders quickly abandoned the place taking with them a great booty and more than 3000 prisoners who they later sold at a high price.[42]

This was Alfonso's only overseas military adventure launched in preparation for his great crusade to the Holy Land, which the popes expected. But this nebulous adventure was short-lived, for after only 24 days, Alfonso's fleet had to hastily return to the Peninsula. The Christian crusaders behaved like veritable heartless criminals obsessed by the booty and a devastating fury. Neither as a crusade nor as a conquest, the capture (or rather the pillage) of Salé gave Alfonso the prestige he expected. Such an undignified and shameful action made him look like a fool in the eyes of his supporters. Salé is an obscure episode, a dark stain in the biography of the Learned King. It was ignored, for obvious reasons, by the primitive Christian chroniclers with the exception of the author of the *CAX*, and it was widely discussed by the most distinguished Muslim historians.[43]

Alfonso, who was somewhat proud, realized the shameful disaster of Salé and, in order to salvage his reputation vis-à-vis Christendom, during the Seville Cortes in 1261, he spoke of "The project of Africa

---

Ballesteros, *Alfonso X*, pp. 274–284; and his article: "La toma de Salé en tiempos de Alfonso X el Sabio," *Al-Andalus*, VIII (1943), pp. 89–128; A. Huici Miranda, "La toma de Salé por la escuadra de Alfonso X," *Hesperis*, XXXIX (1952), pp. 41–52.

[41] Ibn Jaldun tells of this in his *Histoire des Berbères et des dynasties musulmanes de l'Afrique septentrionale*, IV, Paris, 1978, p. 47; and also Ibn Abi Zar, *Rawd al-Qirtas*, ed. Huici-Miranda, II, Valencia, 1964, p. 571.

[42] The episode was described in a lot of detail also in the *CAX*, chap. 19, pp. 71–75, which should not surprise us because, deep down, it was an undignified adventure of Alfonso's, something the astute chronicler did not forget to criticize.

[43] Alfonso himself, who was not present, remembered the episode in one of his *Cantigas* (328, estr. 30–35) in which he surprisingly corroborates to a great extent the version of Muslim historians. Cf. L. Torres Balbás, "La mezquita de Al-Qanatir y el Santuario de Alfonso el Sabio en el Puerto de Santa María," *Al-Andalus*, 7 (1942), pp. 417–436.

we have begun," proposing the conquest of another Muslim kingdom, the submissive Niebla, which paid tribute to Castile from the times of Fernando III. The kingdom of Niebla, which in the first half of the 13th century also comprised the Algarve before it was conquered by the Portuguese, had been reduced to a limited area east of the Guadiana River. In 1252, following the Algarve pact between Alfonso X and Alfonso III of Portugal, where he ceded the benefits of the Algarve to Castile, the king of Niebla, Ibn Mahfud, fearing for his independence once more renewed his vassalage to Alfonso X, in order to maintain his past independence and autonomy in exchange for tribute.[44]

Alfonso thus had no reason to launch such a campaign against the small kingdom of Niebla, but he did have a historical justification: the reconquest of former Visigoth territories his father had been unable to regain. There was also a strategic reason: Niebla, which was mostly populated by Muslims, blocked access to the African coasts. His conquest was thus part of his ambitious plan of reconquest that began with the Salé adventure, identified as "the African affair we began," or "the affair of the crusade."[45]

The summer of 1261 Alfonso's troops launched their attack on Niebla. Due to a plague of flies that decimated the Christian army, the siege lasted nine and a half months (February 1262), without much resistance from the attacked. According to the *CAX* (which erroneously dates the conquest in 1257), the surrender happened thus:

> [...] King Aben Mafot sent to beseech King Alfonso to let him and those who were with him leave safely with all their belongings and to grant him level farmlands from which he could support himself for the rest of his life. In exchange, he would surrender the town of Niebla and the lands of Algarbe. King Alfonso considered this request satisfactory, and the town of Niebla was handed over to him in this fashion. Alfonso gave to King Aben Mafot land on which to live for the rest of his life, and this property was in the part of the Algarbe that is near Seville. With it came all the rights that the king had there and tithe of the olive oil from the region. Alfonso also gave Aben Mafot the farmland of Seville and assured quantities of *maravedís* from the Jewish quarter of the city of

---

[44] Cf. *CAX*, cap. 6, pp. 38–40; and M. González Jiménez, *En torno a los orígenes de Andalucía*, Sevilla, 1980, pp. 34–35.

[45] Cf. J.F. O'Callaghan, *The Cortes of Castile-León*, pp. 102–104. Cf. M. Rodríguez García, "Idea and Reality of Crusade in Alfonso X's Reign Castile and León, 1252–1284," in Michel Balard, ed., *Autour de la Première Croisade*, Paris, 1996, pp. 379–380.

Seville and other things from which this King Aben Mafot maintained himself honorably for the rest of his life. Some of the places that King Alfonso won at that time he left inhabited by Moors.[46]

The textual transmission of *CAX* is not necessarily the most fortunate, and here it is evident that Alfonso was unable to give Ibn Mahfud "the part of the Algarbe that is near Seville," but that he is speaking, as Manuel González Jiménez has rightly pointed out, about a place called *La Algaba*, located two leagues from Seville, where the king and Muslims from Niebla settled and "the location of one of the most important Moorish communities in Andalusia until the beginning of the 16th century."[47] The conquest of Niebla took place February 12, 1262.[48]

The Niebla conquest and the hosting of the king and many of his subjects in la Huerta del Rey in Sevilla served Alfonso as the pretext to conquer the Algarve, practically annulling the 1252 agreement. But as a sign of gratitude to the King of Portugal for his help in crushing the Mudejar revolt, in 1264 he renounced his rights over the Algarve and was satisfied with simply the right to request a military army of fifty lances whenever he deemed it necessary. Thus Alfonso gave the Algarve back to Portugal,[49] although oddly he continued to use the title "King of the Algarve" at least until 1267, when, at the request of his nephew, Dom Dinis, he finally renounced the military force "tribute."

Spurred on by their success, the Christians occupied other territories beyond those controlled by the King of Niebla, according to the *CAX*: "After King Alfonso had taken Niebla, he won with it all of the Algarbe, which is the town of Niebla with its outlying districts of Gibraleón and Huelva, Serpia, and Mora, Alcatín and Castro Marín, Tavira and Faro, and Loulé."[50] He also directly subjected to the

---

[46] *CAX*, p. 39.

[47] *Alfonso X*, p. 97 note 11; and *La repoblación de la zona de Sevilla en el siglo XIV*, Seville, 1993, 2nd ed., p. 26, note 2; and "El trabajo mudéjar en Andalucía: El caso de Sevilla (siglo XV)," in *VI Simposio Internacional de Mudejarismo*, Teruel, September 16–18, 1993, Teruel, 1995, pp. 35–56.

[48] See the document quoted by Ballesteros, *Alfonso X*, p. 316; and M. González Jiménez, *En torno a los orígenes de Andalucía*, pp. 34–35.

[49] The document can be seen in M. González Jiménez, *Diplomatario*, núm. 290; and the commentary in his *Alfonso X*, pp. 97–98. Cf. F. Pérez-Embid, *La frontera entre el reino de Sevilla y Portugal*, Sevilla, 1975; and J. Verissimo Serrao, *História de Portugal*, p. 140.

[50] *CAX*, p. 39.

Christians the city of Cádiz, and with it, for the first time, the entire southwestern end of the Peninsula.[51]

4. *General Uprising in the South*

Following the conquest of Niebla, and as part of his policy to recover the African coasts for the purpose of an African crusade, Alfonso requested his tributary, the King of Granada, to deliver to him the cities of Algeciras and Tarifa, which allowed direct access to the Strait. From there, Alfonso attempted to launch a campaign against Ceuta and other coastal towns, whose proximity to peninsular ports made him think success would be easier, unlike the disaster of Salé. Mohamed Ibn Yûsuf Ibn Nasr, King of Granada, also known as Ibn el-Ahmer (*the son of the Red*), readily complied with Alfonso's request.[52] But time wore on, and always availing himself of different excuses, he did not surrender the cities. The astute king of Granada was perfectly aware of the strategic value of the cities that Alfonso requested from him and that by delivering them, he would be cutting off direct communication with his Muslim allies. As we shall see, the king's delay had to do with biding his time in order to secretly plot with the King of Murcia and other Muslim kingdoms to the south subjected to Castile, a large, sudden rebellion that took place in 1263 known as the *Mudéjar* revolt in which a large contingent of Moroccan cavalry participated.[53]

We know of this betrayal by the Nasrim king thanks to what is recorded in the *CAX*, and thanks to two letters Alfonso sent in 1264 to the bishops of Cuenca, don Pedro Laurencio (dated in Seville June 20), and of Sigüenza, don Andrés (June 25). Both letters are practically identical in content and their personal tone, as of one who writes to friends and confidantes, reveals the king's intervention in their drafting. In these letters written when the conspiracy had already been discovered and the revolt was in full swing, Alfonso reveals to

---

[51] Cf. Ballesteros, *Alfonso X*, chap.VIII, pp. 297–361; and the works of H. Sancho Sopranis, "La incorporación de Cádiz a la corona de Castilla bajo Alfonso X," in *Hispania*, IX (1949); and "La repoblación y repartimiento de Cádiz por Alfonso X," *Hispania,* XV (1955) pp. 483–539.

[52] Letter of Alfonso X to Pedro Laurencio, bishop of Cuenca, Seville, June 20, 1264, in Ballesteros, *Alfonso X, emperador (electo) de Alemania*, Madrid. 1918, p. 72. Cf. M.A. Ladero Quesada, *Granada, historia de un país islámico (1232–1571)*, p. 103.

[53] Cf. *CAX*, chap. 13, pp. 56–57.

what extent he was aware of the secret plans of the King of Granada, expressing surprise also at the betrayal that the unfaithful vassal had been secretly planning under the pretence of false promises.[54] But the letters reveal that the rebellion was not entirely a surprise; Alfonso did not believe it could happen until it finally did, although the unexpected things were the date and size of the rebellion as well as the number of supporters on both sides of the Strait.

Alfonso's imperial ambitions and the desire to reestablish the prestige lost in the disastrous campaign of Salé now clashed with an obstacle within the kingdom. But Alfonso, despite being 43 and one of the wisest men in all of Europe, naïvely continued believing in the flattering promises of the astute Ibn el-Ahmer. In a letter to the Bishop of Cuenca, he writes:

> We would like to let you know that when we held our Cortes in Toledo (1259–1260) regarding the question of Empire, we sought the advice of the king of Granada on this matter, as a vassal and friend we trusted, and he told us in a letter that if we were not granted the Empire in such a way that it would result in our honor and benefit, that we should not go there, but rather, that we should come to this land and that he would help us and would show us how we could obtain an even greater and better empire than that one.[55]

What Christian king could believe that a Muslim subject who reluctantly paid him tribute would do anything to help him obtain an African Empire greater and better than the Holy Roman Empire? Furthermore, what Christian king would ask the opinion of a Muslim King regarding his aspirations to the imperial crown that represented the supreme authority of Christendom against Islam? If he had not handed over the two cities he requested, how would he help him obtain a larger and better empire on the other side of the Strait?

Given the relations between Fernando III (and later Alfonso) and the King of Granada, we may understand how Alfonso initially did not believe in the secret betrayal. But the King of Granada's alliance with Murcia was now a fact, and had the intention not only to shake the yoke of submission, but something more serious that Alfonso in

---

[54] Both letters are transcribed with full commentary in Ballesteros, *Alfonso X*, pp. 362 and ff.

[55] In Ballesteros, pp. 362–363; and M. González Jiménez, *Diplomatario*, 313–314.

his naïveté could not fathom: his assassination and that of his entire family in the very palace of Seville.[56]

In 1264, when he wrote the letters, Alfonso was so clear about the revolt that on the day he wrote to Pedro Laurencio, he also sent a request to Fr. Martín, Bishop of Segovia, asking him to preach a crusade to raise Castilian troops against the Moorish rebels. In it, he inserted two papal bulls by Innocent IV (1246) and Alexander IV (1259) in which, Alfonso said, the pope "granted to all those who would assist us, or those who we would send, the same pardons that are granted to all those who go to *Outremer*."[57] Alfonso thus saw this struggle not only in political terms as the uprising of a rebellious subject against his lord, but also in religious terms as a crusade against the enemies of Christianity. Alfonso was so upset about the rebellion of this faithful ally, as he says in *Cantiga* 365, that it made him ill.

Alfonso should have suspected that the subjected kings were unhappy. But under pressure from his collaborators in the Reconquest of the South, particularly the military Orders, who requested their due, Alfonso began a land distribution process that often violated the agreements with his tributaries. This land distribution at first involved only the regions conquered as a result of non-compliance with the Alcaraz Treaty, but eventually it extended elsewhere including Murcia, which had accepted the treaty and was under its protection. This land distribution clearly violated the treaty and entirely changed the tenor of the reconquest established by Fernando III regarding the Muslim communities, which were often dispossessed of their lands and farms, and quickly began to decline.

The violation of the Alcaraz Treaty was indeed one of the main reasons for the *Mudéjar* rebellion organized by al-Watiq, Emir of Murcia, deposed in 1238 but back in politics thanks to the support of rural communities and el-Ahmer's connivance, who at Alfonso's request for Algeciras and Tarifa, planned a simultaneous rebellion in all of Andalusia and Murcia with support from North African allies.[58]

The element of surprise and simultaneity of the rebellions in various parts of the South and the kingdom of Murcia is what, according to

---

[56] This is at least what don Jaime affirms in his *Llibre dels Feyts*, edition quoted, chap. 378; and cf. Ballesteros, *Alfonso X*, pp. 369–370.

[57] In Ballesteros, *Alfonso X*, p. 371.

[58] See details and sources in J. Torres Fontes, *La reconquista de Murcia en 1266 por Jaime I de Aragón*, Murcia: Academia de Alfonso X, 1987, p. 208.

the *CAX*, caused real panic in the Castilian court, for the simple reason that such a rebellion meant a well-planned, general conspiracy from the outside.[59] Alfonso specifically accused Muhammad I of Granada as the main perpetrator in his denial to hand over the cities, rendering vassalage to the Sultan of Tunis and finally, conspiring with the Muslims from Andalusia and Murcia to speak "covertly with the Moors that lived in our towns and in our castles and tell them to join together with him on a mutually-agreed on day."[60] Murcia and Cartagena along with the greater part of the villages and castles of bordering areas came under the control of the rebels who devastated the entire area, killing the population and destroying the crops the summer of 1264.[61]

The *Mudéjar* revolt unleashed a serious crisis in the Castilian court. Always attentive to matters of state, Queen Violante did not hesitate to send a messenger to her father requesting help.[62] Meanwhile, the king of Granada arrived with a large army in Seville, believing that by capturing the kingdom's capital things would return to the same state as before Fernando III. But Alfonso and his army reacted vigorously. The battle was violent and with many losses on both sides. In the end, Alfonso emerged victorious.[63]

Following an initial moment of panic, Alfonso could now reorganize his army in order to launch the reconquest of the rebellious lands. In October 1264 he subdued Jerez de la Frontera, Medina Sidonia, Arcos, and other cities and castles. According to the norms of the reconquest, the Muslim population was expelled from all these territories, but the two main centers of the rebellion, Granada and Murcia, still remained to be conquered.

---

[59] *CAX*, chap. 10, pp. 49–51. The two main figures of the rebellion were Ibn el-Ahmer from Granada and Alboaquez (Abu Bakr b. Hud al-Watiq) from Murcia. The latter had recently dethroned his brother Muhammad b. Abu Yafar, who had inherited the throne in 1260 at the death of his father, Muhammad ibn Hud. Cf. E. Molina, "Murcia en el marco histórico del segundo tercio del siglo XIII," in *Historia de la región murciana*, III, Murcia, 1980, pp. 188–262.

[60] Cf. M. González Jiménez, *Diplomatario*, n. 286.

[61] Cf. *CAX*, pp. 49–51.

[62] Cf. C. de Ayala Martínez, "Jaime I y la sublevación mudéjar-granadina de 1264," *Homenaje al profesor Juan Torres Fontes*, vol. I, Murcia: Universidad de Murcia, 1987, pp. 93–108.

[63] Alfonso's and the crusaders' victory is told by Oderico Raynaldo, monk of Saint John of Padua, who concluded his chronicle in 1270 (Ballesteros, *Alfonso X*, p. 374). The strategy and victory are also discussed in the *CAX*, chap. 10, pp. 49–51.

Following the first surprise, the Christians also learned some new war techniques used by the Muslims, devastating in turn lands, villages, and towns, burning crops, cutting the trees in the lowlands of Granada and making Muslim leaders rebel against their king. Among these, we can note the leaders or *arraeces* (from *râ'is*= chief) of Guadix, Málaga, and Comares, from the Banu Ashqilula family, all of whom acquired an important role from this point on.

Muhammed I of Granada realized that he had failed in his project of extending the border all the way to Sierra Morena, where it lay before Fernando III's conquests. Not only had he failed, but after his betrayal, if he wanted to remain a tributary and keep his head on his shoulders, he would have to reach a new agreement with Alfonso. The agreement however would be more difficult to obtain after the one signed between Alfonso and the two *arraeces* from Málaga and Guadix, who had their own power and for the sake of protection had become tributaries of Castile after being tributaries of Granada.[64]

The Castilian army arrived in Granada in June 1265. The King of Granada needed to gain time and avoid an attack from the Castilians. If they conquered the city, a likely thing after the alliance with two very powerful *arraeces*, the King of Granada would lose his kingdom forever, for his status as tributary would surely end. Faced with this, Ibn el-Ahmer sent a messenger to Alfonso requesting a truce that would allow him to comply; during this truce the astute King of Granada was awaiting clandestine military reinforcements from Morocco. In exchange for the truce, Mohammed would pay Alfonso 250,000 maravedís, that is 100,000 more than what his father had agreed to pay. He also promised to break his pact with the rebellious kingdom of Murcia and help the Castilians recover that kingdom.[65]

Alfonso agreed to meet the King of Granada in Alcalá de Benzayde (today Alcalá la Real -Jaén-), near the Granadan border. The King and his eldest son showed up to sign the truce. During the meeting, el-Ahmer managed to save the life of the King of Murcia, Alboaquez, once the city was conquered. Alfonso accepted this condition very much in spite of himself.[66] For his part, Alfonso, had to end his agreement with the *arraeces* because it conflicted with his agreement with

---

[64] The *CAX* details the terms of Alfonso's agreement with the *arraeces* (chap. 15, pp. 60–62).

[65] Cf. *CAX*, chap. 15, pp. 60–62.

[66] *CAX*, chap. 15, pp. 60–62.

Granada. But after much negotiation, Alfonso agreed on a truce with the King of Granada, who insistently demanded a break of the truce and the return of both *arraeces* to his command.[67]

This truce, known as Alcalá de Benzayde agreement, was only a time-gaining maneuver on both ends, and it became highly problematic for Alfonso in a matter of weeks. As the military victor, Alfonso committed a tactical mistake when he allowed Granada to enjoy the same conditions as before the conflict, for he could have demanded the complete elimination of its independence as a Muslim country.

The other rebellious kingdom, Murcia, still remained to be conquered. When Jaime I received his daughter's message through his faithful subject, Beltrán de Vilanova, in June 1264, he records the following commentary in his *Libre dels Feyts*: "In this matter it's the same as when a man tastes a wine: those who want to water it down try first to see if it's strong or weak. This is what the King of Castile has done, using our daughter, for, because of the many faults committed against us, he has not dared to ask for help, and has had our daughter do so. If he sees her letters may not be enough, he will try other means of entreaty." The "faults" the King of Aragón referred to were surely Alfonso's hegemonic ambitions, in general, and his aspirations to the kingdom of Navarra, in particular.

But faced with recent and unexpected news on the international scene, both leaders must have thought it was time to put their differences aside and agree so that they might not lose everything at home and abroad. From mid-1263 on, a certain "thawing" of relations between Alfonso and Jaime can be noticed. It is quite likely that this change that led to a rapprochement and collaboration until Jaime's death was due to the treaty signed by Pope Urbanus IV and Charles, Count of Anjou and Provence, whereby the pope granted Saint Louis's brother the kingdom of Sicily, Manfred's inalienable inheritance. This agreement represented a loss for Jaime and Alfonso because its objective was the elimination of Ghibellism in Italy.

---

[67] *CAX*, chap. 15, p. pp. 60–62. Ballesteros grants much importance to the mediation of the Portuguese female soldier María Peres, known to other troubadours as *la Balteira* (*Alfonso X*, p. 381). Historically, it is not very clear whether Maria Peres had relations on both sides, but see R. Menéndez Pidal, *Poesía juglaresca y juglares. Aspectos de la historia literaria y cultural de España*, Madrid, 1924, p. 224.

But despite his recognition that "the king of Castile is one of the highest and most powerful men in the world," Jaime decided to help his son-in-law, ignoring all his previous actions against him.[68]

Don Jaime's motives for helping in the fight against the Muslim rebellion in the south, and in general against the city of Murcia, were also self-interested.[69] Jaime I's lands bordered the kingdom of Murcia; the simple idea that this kingdom could become independent once more meant that Valencia, then controlled by the King of Aragón, could rise up in arms at any moment. In September 1265, following the approval and financial support of the Catalan courts (although not of Aragón, then dominated by a rebellious nobility) Jaime began marching with his army towards Murcia. Along the way, he subjected all the cities that offered resistance. On December 8, accompanied by his sons don Pedro and don Jaime and his inseparable lover, doña Berenguela Alfonso, Jaime I met his son-in-law Alfonso X and his beloved daughter Violante in Alcaraz.[70] On January 5, 1266, don Jaime's troops raided the rebellious cities, which fell in early February. Don Jaime entered the city February 2, 1266, generously granting it to Alfonso shortly after. After this Christian conquest, Murcia ceased to exist as an independent kingdom, and became part of the territories that were directly dependent on the Castilian crown. Contrary to what was agreed at the time of surrender, the main mosque was taken over by Christian soldiers and was consecrated as a cathedral. The assets were promptly divided, as was customary when a territory was conquered by force; however, there was no general expulsion of the Muslims, as had happened in Jerez and Niebla, where practically no Muslim remained. But King Alboaquez, the accomplice responsible for the rebellion, was deposed by Alfonso, and instead the appoint-

---

[68] C. de Ayala Martínez has dealt with the coalition of these two kings in the cited article "Jaime I y la sublevación mudéjar-granadina de 1264," pp. 93–108; and in his work *Directrices fundamentales*. See also the essays in the collective volume, *The Worlds of Alfonso the Learned and James the Conqueror. Intellect and Force in the Middle Ages*, ed. R.I. Burns, Princeton, NJ: Princeton University Press, 1985.

[69] *Llibre dels Feyts*, chap. XXXII. Inexplicably, the *CAX* completely ignores the intervention by the King of Aragón in the Reconquest of Murcia.

[70] *Llibre dels Feyts*, chap. XXXII and following. See R.I. Burns, "The Spiritual Life of James the Conqueror, King of Aragón-Catalonia, 1208–1276: Portrait and Self-Portrait," *Catholic Historical Review*, 62 (1976), pp. 1–35. Cf. F. Soldevila, *Vida de Jaume I el Conqueridor*, 2 vols., 2nd ed., Barcelona, 1969.

ment fell on a prince from the Ibn Hud family, who was also granted part of the taxes paid by Muslim citizens to their previous king.[71]

The fall of Murcia was also followed by that of many castles and villages on the road to Lorca. Although the conquest was military, armed conflict was negligible. So much so, that as don Jaime's *Llibre dels feyts* states, such conquest happened mainly though negotiation and capitulation. This meant that Muslim communities and populations were guaranteed to the right to continue their normal life as owners of territories, being also free to practice their customs and religion. But the reality was quite different, although Christian chronicles hide these facts. Following the city's partition, Murcia's Muslims were confined to the suburb of Arrixaca, from where many departed in self-imposed exile to Granada under the protection of the King of Granada, who guaranteed them safety until they arrived at the border of his kingdom. However, many Murcia Muslims did not enjoy such protection. One Arab chronicler states that in fact, "all were betrayed on the way there. This happened in a place called Huércal. There they captured the women and children and killed all the men". Among those killed was Abul-Hasan Ali ben Yûsuf, a famous preacher from Murcia, who according to another chronicle "was killed in a treacherous trap the Christians lay in the vicinity of the rural fort of Huércal".[72]

The massive flight of Murcian Muslims south left entire areas uninhabited and had disastrous consequences for agricultural production and water infrastructure, which would take another two centuries to regularize. In religious terms, living together only became possible under subjection to the Christian community, and never on equal terms.[73] Already in 1250, when the general Dominican Chapter held at Toledo decided to send friars to the rescue of captives and for the conversion of Muslims, Muslim culture in the conquered cities, and in particular in Islamic institutions, had almost become extinct. Following the conquest of Murcia, Jaime I's stubbornness in converting the main mosque into the Christian Church of Santa María, and the

---

[71] J. Torres Fontes, *La reconquista de Murcia en 1266 por Jaime I de Aragón*, Murcia 1967.

[72] In A. Carmona González, "Textos árabes acerca del reino de Murcia entre 1243 y 1275. Aspectos jurídicos y políticos," *Glossae. Revista de Historia de Derecho Europeo*, 5–6 (1993–1994), p. 245 and 247.

[73] See H. Salvador Martínez, *Convivencia en la España del siglo XIII. Perspectivas alfonsíes*, Madrid: Ediciones Polifemo, 2006, passim.

arrival of religious institutions that imposed their culture, made the
Muslim community aware that its days were numbered. A Murcian
Muslim's outlook after the arrival of Christianity clearly was very dif-
ferent from what the scholars of the experience of *convivencia* present.
For the clergy, *convivencia* or "living together" meant assimilation, as
the young law scholar Ibn Raship states:

> I used to live in the city of Murcia–May it be recovered by God's will!—
> when its inhabitants suffered the test of subjugation, whose trials God
> spare us and whose snares may he free us from. Sent by the king of the
> Christians, a group of priests and nuns arrived in the city, whose mission
> was—according to their declarations—to dedicate themselves entirely
> to worship and devotion, as well as the study of science (although in
> reality) they were spies who studied the sciences of the Muslims and
> translated them into their language in order to criticize them. May God
> hinder their efforts! They were particularly interested in debating with
> the Muslims and had the reproachable intention of capturing the weak-
> est. The money they spent on this came from their king. This was a great
> honor for them among those sharing their faith. May God eliminate
> them all.[74]

Ignoring the religious zeal of a neophyte mentality that Ibn Raship's
words may entail, the fact is that many other Muslim scholars and
learned men from Murcia, such as the celebrated al-Ricotí, had to
leave the capital to flee the pressure of conversion to Christianity and
instead sought refuge with the King of Granada. He was also right
in his remark that the Christian clergy "studied the sciences of the
Muslims and translated them into their language in order to criticize
them," for that was precisely the strategy of the first Christian polemi-
cists such as the Franciscan, Fr. Pedro Gallego (1197–1267), the first
Bishop of Cartagena after the Reconquest (1250–1267), who translated
from Arabic into Latin for Alfonso X, texts from the Koran and several
Aristotelian works that were preserved in summary in Arabic, such as
the *Liber de animalibus* and the *Regitiva domus* by pseudo-Galen.

The conquest of Murcia by Jaime I of Aragón was also a great lesson in political strategy for Alfonso. The fall of this great city and
the agreements with the *arraeces* of Málaga and Guadix, practically
rendered Alfonso the lord of the South, but from that moment on, he

---

[74] In F. Carmona, "Textos árabes," p. 249. Cf. M. Rodríguez Llopis, "Repercusiones
de la política alfonsí en el desarrollo histórico de la Región de Murcia," in *Alfonso
X: aportaciones de un rey castellano a la construcción de Europa*, Murcia: Región de
Murcia, Consejería de Cultura y Educación, 1997, p. 194.

must have realized the mistake he committed in the Alcalá de Benza-yde agreement, which allowed Granada's independence, along with all the security issues this entailed in the South. According to Pérez Algar, this was "the crucial mistake, the fundamental mistake that would condition the rest of his reign".[75] A Muslim Granada remained the great impediment to an African crusade, and without such crusade, Alfonso's prestige as candidate to the imperial crown was seriously compromised.

We also should not forget that when Alfonso signed the agreement of Alcalá, he was in deep financial trouble and weighed down by enormous money issues, precisely as a result of his imperial quest. The Crown was bankrupt and the people were hungry. Under these circumstances, the 250,000 offered by the King of Granada were a welcome sum to help the economy and keep his imperial project alive. But such funds would disappear the moment Granada ceased to be an independent tax-paying entity. The survival of Granada as a tributary was more profitable than its incorporation to the Castilian crown and the very costly process of repopulating the conquered lands with Christians brought from Castile. Even if politically and strategically the pact was a mistake, from the economic point of view, it had its advantages.

The Muslim revolt was also a good lesson for Alfonso from the perspective of his defense in the South. From 1264 on, defense would be planned differently. Around that time, it becomes noticeable that in the division of conquered lands, Alfonso favored the military religious orders, but demanded that they transfer their Main Convents (or main barracks) to the areas where they had been granted lands. The military religious orders, the best prepared and organized institutions when it came to war, from that point on provided the leaders in the defense of the Christian borders.[76]

The first signs of Alfonso's strategic mistake we alluded to above became evident when a year later the truce with the king of Granada regarding the business with the *arraeces* expired. Muhammad asked Alfonso for the return of his tributaries, as the Alcalá de Benzayde treaty stipulated. In a stormy meeting, Alfonso said he would not comply but

---

[75] *Alfonso X,* p. 228.
[76] Cf. J. Torres Fontes, *Documentos de Alfonso X el Sabio,* Murcia, 1963; y *Fueros y privilegios de Alfonso X al reino de Murcia,* Murcia, 1973.

rather would defend their independence, so they "so they could rule themselves and not obey the King of Granada or any other."[77] The King of Granada, however, was unwilling to lose a considerable part of his kingdom due to a whim of the king of Castile who in his view was also violating the agreement. In reality, Alfonso was not violating any agreement, for what had been agreed on was a truce and not a permanent peace. Hence, once the truce was over, he had the right to go back to a state of war, as it indeed happened. But Ibn el-Ahmer did not see it that way, and he did not waste a lot of time to make Alfonso pay dearly for the violation of the pact, making alliances with the Christian enemies of Alfonso, such as Nuño González de Lara.[78]

5. *Waiting Period in the Imperial Election.*
New Directives in Papal Politics

On May 25, 1261 Alexander IV died. He was someone who, in spite of all, had always been favorable to Alfonso's imperial aspirations. Things, however, would change radically with his successors. Urban IV (1261–1264) was the first in a series of popes who, under France's influence, would put a tragic end to the dynasty of the Staufens. The son of a shoemaker from Troyes, Urban IV was a very intelligent, self-made man. When he was elected pope, he was the Pontiff's Delegate in the Holy Land and was coincidentally in Italy. Chosen by a small college of 8 cardinals, he had never set foot in Rome.

For the new pope, none of the candidates could legitimately aspire to imperial succession for the simple reason that there already was a legitimate successor in Manfred (aside from Prince Conradin, Frederick II's last child). This rendered any election that did not consider Manfred irregular, if not illegitimate. Despite this background, and the fact that the last of the Staufens offered 300,000 gold ounces for his recognition as king of the Two Sicilies, Urban categorically declined the offer, because he did not want to see a single Hohenstaufen in Italy, and much less in Sicily. On the other hand, the double election in 1257 created a precedent that the new pope could not ignore.

---

[77] *CAX*, p. 63.

[78] Cf. *CAX*, chap. 16, pp. 63–64; Ballesteros, *Alfonso X*, p. 405. For the alliance agreement between Muhammad I el-Ahmer and Nuño González de Lara, see below, pp. 312–313.

Given all these complications, Urban decided to consult with the only Christian king who had given sincere signs of placing the interests of Christendom and of the Holy See above personal ambition and political partialities: Louis IX of France.

We do not know what St. Louis' recommendation was, but the fact of the matter is that the new pope, who was intent on changing the course of politics in Italy, offered the crown of Sicily to none other than the king of France's brother, Charles of Anjou, count of Provence. Urban IV urged him to accept the kingdom and become a defender of the pope's cause. Charles accepted. Obviously mistrusting both elected candidates, the pope surely wanted to introduce in the Italian political scene a new figure whose lineage would have all the virtues and faithfulness to the Roman Church of his distinguished brother. The pope's hopes, however, were soon frustrated, for Charles, while not as antipapal as Frederick II, became a true despot who created a wave of wars and social unrest in Italy and became not the liberator but the oppressor of the popes.[79]

Urban IV was a pious, upright and balanced man, even regarding the practice of political nepotism. He was a witness to and partially responsible for the disappearance of the Hohenstaufen dynasty in Italy when during his pontificate the last direct descendant of the great Frederick II, Conradin, was eliminated. But it took him a long time to realize that the successor of the Staufens in Sicily, Charles of Anjou, was behaving as badly or worse than Conradin's grandfather, proceeding in an arbitrary, capricious and cruel manner that alienated rich and poor, lay and religious people alike.[80] As is known, the abuses of Charles of Anjou and his supporters ended tragically with the beheading of all French people in Sicily during the events of the so-called "Sicilian Vespers," from March 30 to April 21, 1282.

The issue of imperial succession was thus shelved for the time being, for the pope decreed it should be resolved though a legal process in 1264, to which all candidates had to send their representatives and

---

[79] See the important work by E. Jordan, *Les origines de la domination angevine en Italie*, Paris, 1909, esp. p. 291 and ff.; and recent studies on the controversial activity of the Count of Provence in Italy: Herde, *Taschenbuch. Karl I. Von Anjou*, Stuttgart, 1979; L. Catalioto, *Terre, baroni e città in Sicilia nell'età di Carlo I d'Angiò*, Messina, 1995; and J. Dunbabin, *Charles I of Anjou: Power, Kingship and State Making in Thirteenth-Century Europe*, (The Medieval World), London and New York: Longman, 1998.

[80] These abuses were denounced by Urban IV himself in one of his letters (Rinaldi, *Annales*, y. 1268, n. 36).

lawyers to publicly prove their right to the crown.[81] In other words, the resolution was delayed. Meanwhile, in his correspondence, Urban IV would address both candidates using the title "rex electus Romanorum."[82]

Urban IV died on October 2, 1264, leaving the matter of the empire unresolved. His successor, Clement IV (1265–1268) was also a Frenchman (Guy Foulquois), had been married, and had been a distinguished jurist at the court of Saint Louis. When his wife died, he dedicated himself fully to a religious life, and became known for his wisdom and holiness. Like Urban, Clement IV sided with the interests of the Capets in Itay, and therefore, from the very first moment, trusted Charles of Anjou as King of Sicily against Manfred, the legitimate successor. He soon realized, however, that Charles was not the desired defender of the Church, but rather its oppressor, demanding constantly large sums of money and soldiers. He also had the nerve to take as his residence the Lateran palace, while the French soldiers committed brutalities and sacrileges in Rome and surroundings.[83] In view of such abuse, the pope refused to crown him king of Sicily, but this was done in his name by five cardinals, on January 6, 1266. On January 20, Charles left Rome to fight Manfred at Benevento. It was a brutal fight. Betrayed by many of his counts, Manfred hurled himself personally onto the battlefield and was killed in the struggle. Dante described him as "Blonde was he, beautiful, and of noble aspect" (*Purgatorio* III, trans. H. W. Longfellow); and although he was as vicious as his father, the author of the *Divina Commedia* believed God forgave him.

[81] On February 1, 1263, Alfonso authorized his representatives at the Holy See, Martín Fernández, bishop of León, García, bishop of Silves, Juan Alfonso, archdeacon of Santiago, and the king's notary in León, and Rodolfo Poggibonsi, representative of Alfonso in the pope's curia, to present his cause to the pope. Cf. Ballesteros, *Alfonso X*, pp. 341–342.

[82] In a letter from Orvieto on July 26, 1263 the pope addressed Alfonso: "regi Castelle ac Legionis illustri, in Romanorum regem electo" ["to the illustrious king of Castille and León, elected King of the Romans"]. Cf. Potthast, *Regesta pontificum romanorum*, II [1511], n. 18633–35; I. Rodríguez de Lama, *La documentación pontificia de Urbano IV (1261–1264)*, Roma, 1981, no. 29, pp. 70–71.

[83] In one of his letters, Clement IV tells Charles: "We inform you that we have not summoned you so that you take over the rights of the Church...We cannot satisfy your desires, for we do not have golden mountains or rivers of gold," in Rinaldi, *Annales ecclesiastici*, y. 1266, n. 6 and 9. Cf. Potthast, *Regesta*, II, 1577, n. 19515. For the atrocities committed by Charles in Sicily, see the terrifying chronicle by Saba Malaspina, *Rerum Sicularum historia*, in Muratori, *Rerum Italicarum scriptores*, 8, pp. 828–829; and cf. L. Catalioto, *Terre, baroni e città*, 1995.

The first obstacle in the process of selection of the imperial candidate was thus eliminated. Manfred's death dealt a blow to all the Ghibellines because the new king of Sicily, who now enjoyed the pope's unconditional support, would institute the Angevin hegemony in Italy, and a new French politics contrary to the Staufens would now dominate the Holy See. For Alfonso, in particular, Manfred's death was a half-victory because now his rival in Italy was no less formidable and had the pope's unconditional support, while he, as a distant Hohenstaufen, had been entirely rejected. The pope's preference must have irritated a Ghibelline Alfonso considerably, since it was difficult to accept that the Holy See would give the Sicilian throne, traditionally linked to the Staufens, to a French prince who had no connection with that kingdom. In the mind of Pope Clement, as that of his predecessors, there was a persistent fear of seeing a Staufen—whether Manfred, Conradin, or the distant Alfonso—as emperor of the Holy Roman Empire.

This and other nationalist reasons led Clement IV to favor even less than his predecessor Alfonso's candidacy. In fact, in a letter to don Remondo, archbishop of Seville, in the spring of 1265, he entreated him to find the right moment to convince the king of Castile to withdraw his candidacy.[84] Deeply involved in the war against the king of Granada, Alfonso ignored the reasoning of his good friend don Remondo, and sent an envoy to Rome asking the pope to decide between him and Richard, as his predecessor had decreed. Alfonso's emissaries stressed the importance of the king of Castile as a defender of Christendom. If the king of Granada and of Murcia were to win, the entire Christendom was jeopardized for the gates of Europe were open to North African Islam. The pope did all he could to help Alfonso, granting him material and spiritual aid in his struggle against Granada, and even requested military help on his behalf from the republics of Genoa and Pisa, but he did not budge regarding the matters of empire. The pope's candidate, although this was not public, was Richard of Cornwall, who, after his liberation from prison, received a letter from the pope instructing him to swiftly assume his imperial responsibilities.[85]

---

[84] In Ballesteros, *Alfonso X*, p. 411.

[85] It's possible that the pope was attempting to speak out of both sides of his face, for while he suggested one thing to don Remondo, in a confidential letter to the pope's envoy in England, Ottobono, he suggested a different one, urging him to insist that Count Richard (to whom he referred as "carissimi in Christi filii nostri Ricardi in Regem Romanorum electi"[Richard, dearest son in Christ, king of the Romans elect]) would end the imperial conflict as soon as possible ("Nam expedit modis omnibus

We do not know how Alfonso reacted to the pope's decision, but we can assume his delegates impressed on the pope that his predecessor had already established a procedure to decide on the question of empire through a trial, that this had not been held, and that Alfonso had not had his hearing. In January 1267, Clement IV, an expert jurist, acknowledged Alfonso's legal argument and set a new deadline for the presenting of evidence for the rights of both parties. These proofs were presented in Alfonso's name most probably by the expert *magister* Rodolfo Poggibonsi, a jurist who was very familiar with papal legal procedures.[86] In June 1267, the pope sent Alfonso a letter and several documents where he argued that Richard had more right to the imperial crown than him, and insisted that he withdraw his candidacy. From this point on, the "question of the empire" entered what we could call a diplomatic phase, with Alfonso disengaging himself personally from the issue and leaving matters in the hands of his representatives.[87]

6. *The 1268 Jerez Cortes*

With the *Mudéjar* rebellion crushed and the kingdoms of Granada and Murcia reconquered, a period of relative peace in the southern territories ensued. Alfonso settled from late 1267 to late 1268 in Jerez and was busy with internal matters of the kingdom, particularly economic problems related to the high cost of living and every day necessities. For this purpose, he called a Cortes in Jerez in 1268, inviting the traditional groups (nobility, clergy, and representatives of the town councils) and the "merchants and other good men of Castile, León, Extremadura" who were most involved in the issues of market supply and goods distribution.[88]

---

imperii negotium terminari" ["it is urgent to end the matter of the empire by all possible means"]). Cf. Ballesteros, *Alfonso X*, p. 413.

[86] The text of this "fundamental instrument of Alfonso's lawsuit" was studied by Ballesteros in his "Discurso de entrada en la Academia de la Historia." Cf. *Alfonso X*, pp. 454–459.

[87] The legal arguments carried on endlessly, and the trial was in danger of coming to a dead end. There were also countless obstacles and setbacks. In 1268, the bishop of Silves, Alfonso's representative, on his way to Rome to present evidence to the pope, passed through Toscana, where a war was being waged between the supporters of Conradin and those of Charles of Anjou (the pope's). There he was robbed and killed, and the documentation was lost. The pope had then to grant a new deadline until June 1, 1269. Cf. Ballesteros, *Alfonso X*, p. 470.

[88] The legal documents are preserved in the *Cuaderno de Sevilla* published in *Cortes de los antiguos reinos de León y Castilla*, Madrid: Real Academia de la Historia, vol. I,

The Jerez Cortes are considered the most important and relevant ones for issues of political economy during Alfonso's reign. All aspects of individual and social life were meticulously legislated in what is perhaps one of the most famous cases of State interventionism in the economy. Very detailed legislation on the circulation of consumer products was prepared, which regulated exports and increased the number of previously legally controlled products. Prices of products, salaries, the value of currency, weights and measures were also set, and the resale of goods was outlawed. Social conduct that could affect the economy was also regulated, for instance, "associations" were prohibited, except those whose purpose was "to feed the poor or provide lighting or bury the dead." Begging and loitering was forbidden, as was gambling and the employment of Christian maids by Jews. Jewish moneylending, wedding expenses, and the clothing of Jews and Muslims were regulated. Christians were also forbidden to wear "long beards unless they were prisoners," or to carry knives longer than the span of a hand.[89] With these norms Alfonso intended to eliminate or prevent the creation of monopolies allowing merchants, farmers, and warehouse owners to fix prices, as well as to economically and socially regulate and standardize the life of his subjects.[90]

During his stay in Andalusia, Alfonso also found the time to vigorously engage in his cultural interests, supporting scientific, historiographical and legal projects.

7. Unexpected Family Complications

During the years needed to pacify the *Mudéjar* revolt, Alfonso was forced to abandon his international activities on behalf of the imperial crown. As a result, many things had happened among his supporters, especially in Italy, where, due to family and political matters, Alfonso was deeply compromised. The situation was changing daily, at least when it came to family matters. In early 1267, Alfonso learned that his brother Enrique, who until then had been distant from European

---

1861, pp. 64–85. Cf. Ballesteros, *Alfonso X*, pp. 435–445; J. O'Callaghan, *The Learned King*, p. 166; M. González Jiménez, *Alfonso X, el Sabio*, p. 83.

[89] Cf. *Cortes de los antiguos reinos de León y Castilla*, pp. 64–85.

[90] Sánchez Albornoz has called this desire to control everything a "directed economy" ("Alfonso el Sabio y la economía dirigida" in *Ensayos sobre historia de España*, Madrid, 1873, pp. 75–82).

politics at the service of the Emir of Tunis, had traveled to Italy and had allied himself with Charles of Anjou, making available to him great sums of money and an army of more than 800 soldiers.[91] It is unclear why Enrique did this, but aside from his conflict with the Sultan of Tunis, he may have done so at the invitation of Charles and the pope, as is stated in the *Anales Toledanos IV*.[92] Both the French king and the pope needed a strong hand to solve the many problems that arose daily in Italy, and the best candidate was a Castilian mercenary who controlled one of the best armies at the time, had considerable money he had accumulated during his years as a mercenary in Tunis, and enjoyed a legendary reputation.[93]

Enrique, Alfonso knew, was not someone who could be trusted: he had an ambitious and adventurous temperament, and outrageous ideas. First, he approached Charles of Anjou with a plan to marry none other than Manfred's widow, Helen, daughter of Epirus, whom Charles held prisoner in Nocera, where she would die five years later. Apparently, the goal of this marriage proposal, which was probably thought up by the pope and not the Castilian prince, was to acquire the kingdom of Constantinople and thus end the schism between the two churches.[94] Charles of Anjou, who feared that Enrique's real goal in the marriage was to take over the Ghibelline leadership of Manfred's supporters, did not want to have any dealings with him. It was then that the unruly prince expected the pope to grant him the island of Sardinia, which, at that time, was partly in the hands of Pisa. The pope had also realized that it was dangerous to associate with such an adventurer (he compares him to lightning, "ut fulgur," in one of his letters), and denied him the crown of Sardinia also sought by the king of Aragón. But to get rid of his obligations to the ambitious prince, he offered him the kingdom of Etruria and named him *Senator* in Rome, promising also he would do his best to get him the hand of one of Jaime I of Aragón's

---

[91] According to Villani, Enrique lent Charles 40,000 gold *doblas* (*Cronaca di Giovanni Villani,* vol.I, Firenze, 1845, pp. 126–127); for Mondéjar the amount was 60,000 (*Memorias,* lib. VIII, chap. V, p. 494); and cf. F. Gregorovius, *Geschichte der Stadt Rom im Mittelalter,* vol. II, Dresden, 1926, p. 28.

[92] Quoted by Ballesteros, *Alfonso X,* p. 461.

[93] Bernat Desclot describes Enrique's adventures in his *Crónica,* ed. M. Coll i Alentorn, 5 vols., chap. 54, II, pp. 163–164; CAX, chap. 8, pp. 43–45.

[94] E. Jordan, ed., *Registres de Clément IV,* p. 414. (There are letters from the pope to Enrique on pp. 409, no. 1232, p. 413, no. 1257; p. 416, no. 1275, that point in that direction.)

daughters.[95] The pope also begged him to join Louis IX of France and help him in his crusade for the Holy Land. Despite these concessions, the pope's double denial of his marriage to Helen and of his control of Sardinia (and with no hope of recovering the money lent to Charles of Anjou, who refused to repay it), Enrique realized that he had nothing to gain from that alliance. Villani states the prince was so indignant at Charles's nerve that he reportedly said, "per lo cor Dio, o il mi matrà, o io il matrò" ("By the body of God! Either he will kill me or I will kill him!"). The threat was nearly carried out.

Still, on July 24, 1268, at the arrival of Conradin in Rome, where Enrique had been named governor or *senador* the previous year, he decided to join his side, proclaiming him as the true heir of the Hohenstaufens. Enrique lavishly fêted the young heir of Frederick II, who was only 14 years old. There were many joyful popular celebrations in Rome. But such show of support placed Enrique in an open conflict with the pope, Charles of Anjou's unconditional supporter, and with his brother Alfonso, for Conradin's triumph as a legitimate candidate to the imperial crown, meant the definitive exclusion of all other contenders. In fact, a few months before his triumphal entry in Rome on May 5, 1268, given the progress of Conradin's supporters in Italy, Clement IV decided to excommunicate the feared grandson of Frederick II, depriving him of the title of king of Jerusalem at the same time as he issued an anathema against Enrique.[96]

Around the same time, another brother of Alfonso, don Fadrique, exiled from Castile and who had also temporarily served the emir of Tunis with Enrique, resurfaced in Sicily and backed the uprising of Conradin's supporters. In the summer of 1268 an armed conflict between Conradin's Ghibellines and Charles of Anjou took place in Tagliacozzo (August 23). Don Enrique was also there to defend his distant relative. The Ghibellines were defeated. Conradin and his friend Frederick of Baden managed to escape to Rome from where he intended to make his way to Sicily by sea, to join the majority of his supporters. But they were betrayed by one of the Frangipanis, and he

---

[95] The pope, in fact, wrote to Jaime I from Viterbo on July 23, 1267 requesting the hand of one of his daughters for don Enrique; but the King of Aragón, who knew the prince well, did not want to have anything to do with this matter.

[96] *Registres de Clement IV*, p. 416, no. 1275. In a letter to the Florentines on April 10, 1267, the pope called Conradin: "a small king coming from the root of the poisonous snake (referring to Frederick II) that infects Tuscany with its breath" (Rinaldi, *Annales*, y. 1268, n. 4–16).

was captured by Charles of Anjou along with Enrique. Conradin was put on trial by Charles, and despite the fact that all jurists consulted except one were favorable to his pardon given his age and the fact he had fought in good faith for his rights, Charles ordered his public beheading in the del Carmine marketplace in Naples, on October 29, 1268. Enrique escaped the beheading because the monks at the Monte Cassino monastery, where he was hiding, turned him in on condition that he be pardoned. Enrique was sent to Charles of Anjou's dungeons, where he remained for 24 years, until he managed to escape in 1294 and returned to Castile.[97] During all of Enrique's years in prison, Alfonso did not intercede with Charles on behalf of his brother. As Ballesteros argues, it was an easy way to eliminate an enemy who had never recognized his legitimacy as the successor of Fernando III.[98] In 1296, following the death of his nephew, Sancho IV, don Enrique, already an old man, became the tutor and caretaker of Fernando IV and shared the regency with María de Molina; he was also named *mayordomo mayor del reino* and *adelantado de la frontera*, positions that suited him well as a past celebrated warrior. He died in Roa in 1303 and was buried in the Church of San Francisco in Valladolid. His brother and war companion, don Fadrique, upon seeing the turn of events in Italy and the end of Conradin and Enrique, decided to return to Tunis.[99] We will discuss his sad end later.

The uprising of Conradin, new heir of the "cursed" Hohenstaufens, and his alliance with two main figures given their background and tested ability to instigate rebellions and wars alarmed the pope. Suddenly, in his correspondence with Alfonso X, Clement IV stops alluding to Richard's imperial rights over his, and treats him with extreme affection. What could have been the reason for this change? The pope was worried that his plans to stabilize Italy and especially Sicily were falling apart, partly because of the political activities of the two Castilians. So he begged Alfonso to make peace with his brother Enrique and return him the lands and property confiscated as a result of his rebel-

---

[97] Enrique was in several prisons, first in Canosa, and then in Santa Maria del Monte in Apulia. Cf. Ballesteros, *Alfonso X*, pp. 460–475. For Enrique's later adventures and subversive activities see G. del Giudice, *Don Arrigo, Infante di Castiglia*, Napoli, 1875. Recently, Enrique's adventurous life has been the subject of Margarita Torres's novel *Enrique Infante de Castilla*, Barcelona: Plaza Janés, 2003.

[98] Ballesteros, *Alfonso X*, pp. 108–109.

[99] G.Villani, *Cronica*, II, pp. 177–192; Desclot, *Crònica*, II, pp. 174–176; other sources in Ballesteros, *Alfonso X*, pp. 463–465.

lion. To prove to Alfonso to what extent he was willing to renegotiate the imperial title, he easily set a new deadline giving him another year (until June 1, 1269) to present the evidence lost due to the robbery and assassination Alfonso's envoy to Rome. Things, however, settled on their own, when Conradin was executed, his supporters died, were scattered or imprisoned, and the pope's favorite, Charles of Anjou, triumphed.

Clement IV died November 28, 1268, and the Church had to endure three long years of political ambitions and internal wars before a new pope was elected. The state of imperial succession at the death of Clement IV was such that the pope, in his extreme diplomatic tact, had conceived of the division of civilian power and the defense of Europe as follows: Alfonso would be in charge of controlling Muslim invasions across the Strait, Charles would deal with the problem of the kingdom of Sicily, and Richard of Cornwall would deal with the matters of the empire. But Richard had not been crowned, and for the reasons stated above, in late years the pope had become closer to Alfonso, hinting that his candidacy had not entirely been thrown out.

This was perhaps the reason why Alfonso, during the period the papal seat was vacant, began to speak of *ida al Imperio* (going to the empire), an expression that appears in Castilian sources between 1270 and 1271, and which does not always mean the same thing. We will see how at times it means going to Italy in support of his supporters, and at others to meet personally with the pope to claim his rights to the imperial crown. Confirming the first sense, Alfonso, during these years, signed various agreements with several Italian cities in which he stipulated protection or military help. Also, given the political climate in Italy, the war between Guelfs and Ghibellines, between 1270 and 1270 the expression seems to mean his desire to go to Italy, especially Lombardy, to defend his supporters, claim the crown and head the Ghibelline party against Charles of Anjou's followers, a project for which he indeed expected the support of his son-in-law, the Marquis Guillermo of Monferrato.[100] It is quite possible that the Castilian court

---

[100] Alfonso's northern Italian supporters kept pushing him to arrive with an army in order to help their struggle against Charles. This is the reason for the visit that Count Ventimiglia and other Lombard supporters paid Alfonso at Requena requesting him to bring to Lombardy an army of 500 to support "those who had elected him as emperor," (*CAX*, p. 188), a phrase that obviously refers to the "election" by his Italian allies, and not by the official German Electors in 1267.

wanted to profit from the circumstance of the papal vacancy to present the new pope with a *fait accompli*. But Clement IV's plans for empire would be radically changed in a way he could not have imagined. In any event, after 1273, *ida al Imperio* indicates mainly Alfonso's visit to the pope to claim the imperial crown.

8. *New International Perspectives*

1269 was an eventful year for Alfonso X, and not in a positive way. It marks the beginning of his most unfortunate period as king. At the beginning of November, Alfonso left his beloved Seville for Castile, where he had to face a new set of political and social problems, perhaps as serious or more than those caused by the *Mudéjar* revolt. Perhaps the only happy event was the wedding of his first born. Everything else seems a chain of unfortunate events described in *Cantiga* 235, as we will see in the next chapter, and will end approximately 12 years later, with all his ideals and ambitions shattered: family betrayal, rebellion of the nobility, and constant and ever so serious illnesses, but particularly, the shame of seeing the candidacy to the imperial crown he had obsessively sought from his youth rejected. Added to this would be the death of his favorite son and successor, of his daughter Leonor, and the sudden and violent death of his brother-in-law, don Sancho, archbishop of Toledo.

The latest developments in Italy, the disappearance from the political scene of his two rivals, Manfred (1266) and Conradin (1268), however, lent him new hope. In his last years the late Clement IV (1268) had also appeared favorable to his candidacy. But due to internal politics, Alfonso had been unable to respond more adequately to the pope's requests. Now, with the Church still lacking a head, Alfonso could devote more efforts to seeking new alliances and support so that when the new pope ascended to the throne, his candidacy might enjoy the greatest favor among the German Electors.

In this context and with the specific goal of gaining the support of the king of France, Alfonso arranged the marriage of his son and heir don Fernando to the princess Blanche (or *Blanca*) daughter of the king of France. An attempt to unite both kingdoms had already taken place in 1255, when by mutual consent with Louis IX, the project of marrying Berenguela, Alfonso's eldest daughter and at the time the heir to the Castilian throne, to Louis, the first-born of the French king. The project did not take place because precisely that year a boy was born to Alfonso, don Fernando, aka "de la Cerda,"[101] and the French king prematurely lost his heir.

But now circumstances had changed, and the desired union of the Castilian heir, Fernando, to Blanche of France, daughter of the most esteemed king of Christendom, was entirely possible. In the marriage agreement reached three years earlier at Saint Germain on September 28, 1266, Alfonso promised to grant Blanche a yearly income of 24,000 maravedís.[102] The marriage agreement also stipulated that the offspring of this marriage would inherit the throne of Castile. This clause introduced a novelty in the traditional succession system of Castile, that is, the *derecho de representación* (right to representation), rather than the traditional *heredamiento* (inheritance). The agreement also provided for the settlement of the dispute with the French king who had argued that his mother, doña Blanca, being older than her sister doña Berenguela, Alfonso X's grandmother, had more right to the throne than her. But the controversy would return many years later.

The groom was fourteen and the bride seventeen. In Agreda, on the road to Castile, Alfonso, having left Seville in early November, met his father-in-law, the king of Aragón, and his impressive entourage who were also headed to the wedding.[103] They both arrived in Burgos on the 27th of November. The following day the bride arrived with a great entourage that included the cream of France's nobility. The wedding, celebrated in Burgos November 20, 1269, was attended by the most distinguished nobles of Spain and the reigning houses of Europe, among them Philip, *el Hermoso* (the Handsome), heir to the throne of France and brother of the bride; Edward I of England, who fifteen years earlier had married Leonor of Castile, Alfonso's half-sister; the aforementioned Jaime I of Aragón, attending the wedding of his first grandchild, and all the nobility of Castile and León, led by Nuño de Lara and don Lope Díaz de Haro. In attendance too was Guillermo,

---

[101] The origin of the moniker "de la Cerda" is unknown, but it seems to have been due to a birthmark the prince had on his chest.

[102] Cf. G. Daumet, *Mémoire sur les relations de la France et de la Castille de 1255 à 1320*; Spanish translation, "Memoria sobre las relaciones entre Francia y Castilla de 1255 a 1320," in *Revista de la Facultad de Derecho. Universidad Complutense*, 9 (1985), pp. 241–242.

[103] Cf. *Llibre del Feyts*, chap. 494.

Marquis of Monferrato, who two years later would marry Alfonso's daughter.[104]

This was a perfect chance for Alfonso to launch his public relations campaign, behaving with all hosts with his proverbial generosity. Attempting to show his prestige to the nobles assembled there, Alfonso, on the day before the wedding, personally knighted his son Fernando as well as several princes and noblemen who had come for the wedding, including prince Edward of England: "Before the wedding, Alfonso knighted his nephew Edward, who was later King of England. Also, Edward knighted counts, dukes, and other high-born men who had come with him from the kingdom of England and the Duchy of Guienne."[105] In turn, don Fernando knighted his brothers don Juan and don Pedro and many nobles, including don Lope Díaz de Haro, but not his younger brother, don Sancho, who categorically refused to be knighted by him.

On the occasion of his son's wedding, Alfonso summoned a Cortes in Burgos, where the topic of the economy was discussed again and the prices of many produces were fixed anew, but mainly the royal finances were addressed. The kingdom's treasury was empty as a result of the war against the rebels in the south, whose debts now had to be paid "in order to carry out the affair of the border and to pay the nobles in cash for the lands they have from us."[106] Also under scrutiny came Alfonso's inordinate expenses to support his cultural projects and especially to buy support for his imperial quest. A good token of Alfonso's money squandering was the wedding for which Alfonso threw away money and gifts as if he were rolling in *maravedís*.

The economic pressures of the past (devaluation of the currency through the reduction of silver content, taxes of all sorts, etc.) had reached the limit of fiscal pressure, and not much more could be obtained from such impoverished subjects. During the Cortes, Alfonso or one of his economists suggested excising one more kind of tax known as *servicio* (service) which could be applied one-off at the king's request and only with the approval of representatives of the kingdom

---

[104] *Chronicón de Cardeña*, ed. E. Flórez, *ES*, XXIII, Madrid, 1767, pp. 370–380, p. 375.

[105] *Chronicle of Alfonso X*, p. 68.

[106] The document is in Ballesteros, "Burgos y la rebelión del infante don Sancho," *BRAH*, CXIX (1946), 113.

gathered at the Cortes. The procedure of how to impose this new tax was constitutionally revolutionary because, for the first time in Castile, it was not the king's free will but the decision of his subjects. In other words, those who footed the kingdom's or empire's bills would also have a say in authorizing the expenditures. In any event, Alfonso obtained the *servicio* he requested.

As don Jaime in his *Llibre* states, it was this set of circumstances, the king's senseless spending and the disproportionate increase in taxes, which led the nobility to show its discontent with Alfonso's government. Envy and the fear to see the international triumph of a man who had bankrupted his kingdom and still imposed taxes on his subjects to pursue the chimera of empire must have so irritated his enemies, that they soon began to take measures against such wasteful lack of control. Don Jaime reports in his autobiography that on the occasion of his presence in the wedding, don Nuño approached him to offer him vassalage. The *CAX* also relates an equally desperate and illegal action on the part of the nobles, one that borders on kidnapping. According to the chronicle, the nobles appeared suddenly in the monastery of San Andrés de Arroyo, a village where doña Juana, Alfonso de Molina's daughter and Alfonso's X cousin, lived, pulled her out of the monastery against her and her father's will, and without the knowledge of Alfonso X, whose authorization for marriage was requisite, married her off to don Lope Díaz de Haro.[107]

Despite this defiance of royal authority (doña Juana, as a prince's daughter, was under royal protection), Alfonso did nothing to punish that shameless action. The *CAX* states clearly the reasons why Alfonso did not act against the rebellious noblemen:

> Although Alfonso found out about it, he did not see the disservice that came to him later, nor did he make them think they should be wary of him, since he had need of them in the war with the Moors and for the matter of the empire.[108]

After the wedding celebrations and the Cortes, Alfonso left Burgos following his father-in-law as far as Tarazona. They spent Christmas there, holding talks for seven days. Don Jaime in his *Llibre* gives us a summary of the content of these conversations, which will be discussed

---

[107] *CAX*, chap. 18, pp. 68–70.
[108] *CAX*, p. 70.

later on.[109] It was a very useful meeting that helped the two most powerful kings of the Peninsula to get to know each other better and to establish a friendship and mutual trust that, with fewer downs than ups, they would maintain until the end of their lives. Alfonso stayed in Castile after his illness at Fitero, until December 1270, when he left for Murcia, arriving in early February 1271.

---

[109] Cf. *Libre dels Feyts*, chaps. 497–498. See later on (chap. 9, p. 316) the advice of don Jaime to Alfonso; and cf. M. González Jiménez, *Alfonso X*, pp. 115–116.

CHAPTER SIX

GREGORY X AND THE END OF IMPERIAL AMBITIONS

1. *Alfonso X and Gregory X*

On September 1, 1271, almost three years after Clement IV's death, a new pope, Gregory X (1272–1276), was finally elected. Teobaldo Visconti was an Italian from Piacenza, and at the time of his election he was in Tolemaida (Saint John of Acre) with Prince Edward of England's crusade. He was not a priest, but he traveled immediately to Italy to be ordained in Rome on March 19, and crowned pope on the 27th of the same month, 1272. When he ascended to the throne of St. Peter, this simple man, a friend of concord, order, and charity, decided to launch his ideals for Christendom: the liberation of Jerusalem, the union of the Greek and Latin churches, and the reconciliation of Guelfs and Ghibellines in Italy.[1]

The new pope quickly realized that he still faced another problem left pending by his predecessor, and a great part of the cause of the divisions among Christians: the succession crisis, or *Interregnum*, in the Holy Roman-Germanic Empire that had been vacant for 20 years and still did not have a solution. From the decisions he would soon make, it was obvious that for Gregory, neither Alfonso X nor Richard, elected "King of the Romans," deserved pontifical support. The selection suddenly became easier when Richard died April 2, 1272. When he learned of his rival's death in the midst of the crisis provoked by the rebellion of the nobles, Alfonso thought it would not be long before his imperial coronation because he was the only elected candidate left. Flattered by the new prospects, Alfonso sent a very affectionate letter to the pope that year in which he described himself as a model king, ready to defend the interests of the Holy See.[2] The letter was followed

---

[1] On the brief but fruitful papacy of Gregory X, cf. Rinaldi, *Annales*, y.1273, n. 28; and Leonardo Bruni d'Arezzo, *Historiarum florentinarum lib.12*, especially, book 3. Cf. L. Gatto, *Il pontificato di Gregorio X, 1271–1276*, Rome, 1959.

[2] Alfonso writes to the pope saying every king will "do whatever he can" to help the new pontiff in devotion to the Holy See, but that he, following the steps of his ancestors on the Castilian throne, will go much further than any other. Letter in Archive of

by an envoy headed by the Dominican friar Ademaro. Alfonso's representatives requested the pope to acknowledge the rights of the king of Castile, and following instructions, they even requested a coronation date. Among other demands, Alfonso asked the pope to prohibit the German elector princes from holding another election that would only jeopardize his rights. This request was the response to a rumor that the pope himself supported a new election by the German princes.

Alfonso could not imagine what Gregory had in store for him. From Orvieto, on September 16, 1272, the pope sent a rejection of all of Alfonso's requests, insisting they had no legal basis, because he still needed to prove he had been legitimately elected. So he had no more right to the crown after the death of his rival, than the day they were both elected. The pope also accused him of having delayed assuming the imperial crown too long after his election as "King of the Romans," which had happened many years earlier.[3]

The new pope must have thought it was not timely but rather rash to impose a foreign monarch on the German people, who, even if a Hohenstaufen, had hardly set foot in Germany. So for the time being he ignored the request of the king of Castile, and around the same time also ignored the entreaties of his favorite, Charles of Anjou, who also requested the crown for his nephew, Philip III, known as *the Bold*.

At the same time as he rejected Alfonso's candidacy, Gregory X sent a letter to his wife, Violante, asking her to convince her husband to accept the pope's decision.[4] Gregory, a pious man and a true crusader, apparently had no esteem or admiration for the king of Castile, whom he considered a kind of magician, in the tradition of his uncle Frederick II. Alfonso, for his part, as a result of the 1275 final decision,

---

the Toledo Cathedral, published by P. Linehan, *Histories and the Historians of Medieval Spain*, p. 509, note 11.

[3] The pope's extremely harsh letter can be seen in J. Guiraud and L. Cardier, *Les Registres de Grégoire X (1271–1276)*, Paris: Bibliothèque des Écoles Françaises d'Athènes et de Rome, 1892–1906, I, pp. 65–67, no. 192 (September 16, 1272); and in S. Domínguez Sánchez, *Documentos de Gregorio X (1272–1276) referentes a España*, León, 1997, pp. 140–144. Cf. *CAX*, chaps. 18–21, pp. 68–84. Ballesteros, *Alfonso X*, pp. 674–677; and W.F. Schoen, *Alfonso X de Castilla*, pp. 168–179.

[4] For Ballesteros, the letter to Violante must have been written much later, for the name of the famous "magister Fredulum, capellanum nostrum," who was not named until much later, is mentioned there. Cf. *Alfonso X*, p. 676.

radically changed his attitude towards the pope, parodying him in a famous poem.[5]

The pope's letter was indeed a great obstacle to Alfonso's aspirations, as he saw his right to the crown dismissed. To have the pope question his right at this point after a thousand envoys and delegations throughout fifteen years must have seemed to him a cavalier action on the part of a biased pope and a hostile clergy. Gregory's remark regarding his negligence to make his rights valid as a result of the election was an insult to his zeal and dedication to the Christian crusade to contain Islam in the Peninsula, as the previous popes had requested and charged him to do. The accusation of negligence when Alfonso had his mind on a more noble cause, such as the defense of Christendom, must have hurt his pride greatly, to the point that he decided to deal with the matter personally from that point on. The pope did not suspect how far the king of Castile would go in the defense of his rights. Alfonso, an expert jurist and legislator, would become a true nightmare for the pope.

But in order to devote himself fully to the imperial quest, Alfonso had to first settle matters in his kingdom. He could not run the risk of losing the throne when he was so near to the empire, so he managed to reach an agreement with the rebellious nobles, at the time the greatest threat, granting them practically all they requested and even compromising his personal safety. Many of the rebels returned to Alfonso's submission, and the king of Granada himself, after much negotiation, accepted the Alcalá de Benzayde pact, which rendered him a vassal and involved an annual tribute of 300,000 *maravedís*, as well as a special contribution of 250,000 *maravedís* in advance for the yearly tribute "to come for the matter of the empire."[6]

---

[5] Among the Alfonso X's satirical compositions is a poem mocking the pope, which begins: "Se me graça ffezesse este papa de Roma" ["If this pope from Rome would grant me the grace…"], which is believed to target precisely Gregory X (in M. Rodrigues Lapa, *Cantigas d'escarhno e de mal dizer dos concioneiros medievais galego-portugueses*, Coimbra: Editorial Galaxia, 1970, no. 33, pp. 62–63). Cf. G. Tavani, "La cantiga d'escarnho e de mal dizer galego-portughese," in *Grundriss der romanische Literatures des Mittelalters*, VI, 1, Heidelberg: Carl Winter, 1968, pp. 309–313.

[6] *CAX*, chap. 48, pp. 154–155 and chap. 58, pp. 191–192. Cf. Ballesteros, *Alfonso X*, p. 676.

2. A New Candidate

Meanwhile, the German electors, with the pope's approval or perhaps under his command (since he had threatened to name the emperor himself if his candidate was not elected), celebrated an election on October 1, 1273 in which Count Rudolf of Habsburg was elected.[7] The election was immediately approved by the pope, who feared that none of the other candidates—Alfonso X of Castile, Philip III of France, Ludwig of Bavaria, and Ottokar of Bohemia—were true defenders of the Holy See's interests or were interested in a crusade to rescue the Holy Lands, as he expected. Rudolf of Habsburg, on the contrary, despite being a vassal to the Hohenstaufens, embodied all the ideals of the Christian prince according to the thought and directives of the pope and the expectations of the German people, as Friedrich Schiller (1759–1805) would later sing in his famous ballad, *Der Graf von Habsburg*. Rudolf was officially crowned King of the Romans at Aquisgran on June 6 of that year. His political program was to renounce imperial dreams over Italy, which suited the interests of Gregory, and to concentrate his attention on the formation of a strong, effective monarchy in Germany. This pious and brave German king was the originator of the Habsburg dynasty, which would bring so much glory to the Church.

The pope recognized his title ("Te Regem Romanorum nominamus") the following year (September 26, 1274), during the Council of Lyon, however not during a public session but in a private meeting of the College of Cardinals, which made the recognition less official, and therefore the verdict easier to overturn, if things did not turn out as the pope expected.[8] When Alfonso's representatives found out about the confirmation, they indignantly got up from their seats and abandoned the Council in protest. A year later, after the pope had already met with Alfonso in Beaucaire, in a meeting held in Lausanne, the pope and Rudolf agreed that he would go to Rome to be crowned emperor during the feast of the Virgin's Purification. The crowning never took

---

[7] Cf. A. Zisterer, *Gregor X und Rudolf von Habsburg*, Freiburg 1891; Ballesteros, *Alfonso X*, pp. 712–732; C.J. Socarrás, *Alfonso X of Castile*, pp. 209–244.

[8] For the documents of this important council, in which, albeit briefly, the union of the Eastern and Western Churches was achieved, see: Rinaldi, *Annales*, a.1273, nn. 6–18; Mansi, *Concil.*, vol. 24, pp. 109–132; and the brief summary in Hefele-Leclercq, *Histoire des Conciles*, vol. VI, pp. 164–167.

place because of the pope's premature death, which happened at Arezzo on January 10, 1276, as he returned from the Council.

Alfonso had been officially invited by the pope (in a letter dated April 13, 1273) to participate in the Council of Lyon (1274). In the letter the pope explained that the question of the empire would be discussed and a definitive solution would be found.[9] Oddly enough, Alfonso did not attend, missing an opportunity to still change the pope's mind. The causes of Alfonso's absence are not known, but given the internal political activities and initiatives he undertook in the period, it may have been due to the signing of agreements with the king of Granada and the rebellion of the nobility. Lack of funds and poor health may have been other important reasons not to undertake the journey.[10] The only Peninsular king in attendance was Jaime of Aragón, along with Alfonso's representatives, the bishop of Astorga, the royal notary don Fernando, and twenty bishops from Castile-León.[11] The king of Aragón returned with very clear notions of what the pope thought regarding the empire and promptly informed Alfonso X of this.

The pope, despite being the enemy of a Ghibelline Alfonso, could not ignore his demands or his legitimate right to the title. Plus, it was the case that Alfonso's Italian policy was being favorably received by his supporters, and indeed produced negative results for the pope. Under Alfonso's influence, in March 1274, Genoa became part of the Ghibelline League of Northern Italy, establishing an alliance with the Marquis of Monferrato, Alfonso's son-in-law, against Charles of Anjou, the pope's ally. Soon afterwards, the famous cities of Pavia and Asti joined in. The pope must have been alarmed, especially when he found out that Genovese vessels were carrying military reinforcements from the king of Castile to Italy. First 300 knights arrived in Genoa, and soon after, in November 1274, a second expedition of 900 men joined the army of the Marquis of Monferrato. Fearing for the stability of his lands and the defeat of a possible ally, Gregory X did not hesitate to use the available weapons: moral censure and excommunication of the Genovese, Pavians, Veronese, Lombards, and particularly against

---

[9] The basic content of the letter can be seen in Ballesteros, *Alfonso X*, p. 709.

[10] According to R. Kinkade, Alfonso's poor health was the main motive for his absence, "Alfonso X, *Cantiga* 235, and the Events of 1269–1278," *Speculum*, 67 (1992), pp. 284–323, pp. 299–300. For Alfonso's illness at Requena in August 1273, cf. Chapter 7, pp. 244–247.

[11] In his *Llibre del feyts* don Jaime tells of the journey to the Council and his excellent reception by the pope and cardinals (May 1, 1274); but he had a disagreement with the pope, and on July 14, 1274 he was back in Barcelona.

Monferrato and the Spanish who were arriving in Italy bearing arms.[12] Alfonso's goal was indeed to contain Charles of Anjou's influence in Italy, but above all he intended to change the result of the election of Rudolf of Habsburg, using Northern Italy as his base.[13]

On November 3, 1274, the pope, already on his way to Lyon, wrote to Alfonso from Chambery a much more moderate letter, personally inviting him to participate in the Council and asking him to collaborate in the crusade to recover the Holy Land.

3. *The 1274 Cortes*

In early March 1274, Alfonso X summoned a new Cortes in Burgos.[14] The main topic was: "the matter of sending knights to the Roman Empire", that is, getting the approval of a contingent of knights to accompany the king on his journey to Italy. Up until now "going to the Empire" meant to travel to Northern Italy to militarily assist his supporters and persuade the pope (not as a military threat) of Alfonso's ability to operate in different parts of the kingdom. With this, he hoped to be recognized as a *de facto* emperor. This renewed interest in Italian matters and his own coronation was indeed only possible after he had made peace with the noble rebels and the king of Granada a few months before. It was also a sign that Alfonso was thinking not just of sending troops but also of traveling to Italy to meet the pope and to personally argue his case.[15]

The approval of the necessary funds to finance traveling to the Empire was the topic that Alfonso had been debating with his advisors since the visit of Count de Ventimiglia in Requena one year before. Now, during the Cortes, the *Crónica* states, he finally got what he needed: "[a]fterward, he consulted with those closest to him concerning

---

[12] In Ballesteros, *Alfonso X*, p. 716.

[13] This is what *Anales Placentinos* clearly indicate (in Ballesteros, *Alfonso X*, p. 711).

[14] The only direct reference to these Cortes appears in a privilege in favor of the town of Pampliega, signed by Alfonso in Palencia April 13, 1274 (in P. Fernández del Pulgar, *Historia secular y eclesiástica de Palencia*, 3 vols., Madrid, 1679–1680, II, pp. 344–345). Cf. Ballesteros, *Alfonso X, Emperador (Electo) de Alemania*, Madrid, 1918, pp. 72–73; E. Procter, *Curia and Cortes*, pp. 135–136; J. O'Callaghan, *Cortes of Castile-León*, p. 101.

[15] The *CAX*, which does not mention the 1274 Cortes, erroneously locates all the preparations in Toledo in 1275, where Alfonso gathered all the nobility to discuss the expenses of the trip (chap. 59, pp. 195–196).

how he would go to the empire. To remedy this difficulty, the king requested from those of his land, until the matter of the empire could be concluded, that they grant him each year two sums of money in addition to the tributes and taxes they had to give. All the great lords and nobles, knights and councils of the cities and towns of the realm approved this." (chap. 18, p. 69)[16] These concessions, along with the financial arrangements obtained from the king of Granada, allowed him to make the preparations for such an expensive trip, as the *CAX* narrates in detail.[17]

Other items on the agenda of these Cortes were the appointment of don Fernando de la Cerda as regent of the kingdom during his father's absence, and the election of an *adelantado mayor* (commander-in-chief) for the Granada border, a position assigned to Nuño González de Lara. During these Cortes too, the cities of León, Castile, and Extremadura, together with several monasteries, promised the king a special tribute for two years, on condition that, due to their extreme poverty, neither Alfonso nor his successor would request it again.[18] Alfonso thus left all matters regarding the kingdom's administration settled, deciding who, when, and how his seal should be used and assigning royal authority to represent him, even considering the possibility he might not return, in which case: "[…] if something happened to him on this journey, he ordered them to hold and preserve for don Fernando the treaty and homage they did him" (*CAX*, chap. 59, p. 196).

Some time after these Cortes, Alfonso decided to personally defend his cause before the pope prior to "going to the Empire" (that is, going to help his supporters in Italy). The fact is that, at the end of 1274, when he arrived with his wife and a numerous entourage at Barcelona, "going to the Empire" meant mainly (if not exclusively) his meeting

---

[16] The *Crónica*, as noted, seems to have the date and concession of these "two services" wrong, but it clearly states that he had general support to cover the expenses for his "journey to the Empire." Cf. J. O'Callaghan, "Cortes and Royal Taxation," pp. 386–388 and documentation cited there.

[17] Chaps. 57–59, pp. 187–197 also discuss where the money would come from and who would be in charge of it as well as all the victuals Alfonso ordered for the long journey (chap. 59, pp. 195–197).

[18] We know about these concessions through the diploma issued in Madrid, March 20, 1274, where Alfonso thanks the councils of Castile and Extremadura for the concessions made during the Burgos Cortes that year. Cf. T.D. Palacio, *Documentos del Archivo General de la Villa de Madrid*, 6 vols., Madrid, 1888–1943, I, pp. 119–122; J. O'Callaghan, "Cortes and Royal Taxation," 4, pp. 115–116, 120, 158–160; and *Cortes of Castile-León*, p. 101.

with the pope who was in Lyon at the time attending the ecumeni-
cal Council; the idea of going to militarily assist his supporters in
Italy does not appear again anywhere in the documentation, though
Alfonso would maintain epistolary and diplomatic relations with the
Italian cities that supported him.

4. *Cultural Interlude: Excavation of King Wamba's Tomb*

Following the Burgos Cortes, Alfonso headed south, arriving in Alicante on October 16, touring first the main cities of Castile. Along the
way, he granted many privileges and letters to churches, monasteries,
and towns to thank them for their sacrifices that had helped him in
his "trip to the Empire."[19] Among the most famous ones is the letter
given on April 13, 1274 to the town of Pampliega (Burgos), where he
stopped to disinter the remains of the Visigoth king Wamba that had
been known to be there since 1254, but that he had not had time to
personally pay homage to. His visit to Pampliega must have reminded
him of the places where he spent his childhood: Celada del Camino
and Villaldemiro, this last one five kilometers from Pampliega.

Alfonso had already been to Pampliaga as king in 1254, on a trip
from Valladolid to Burgos, but that time, as a result of don Diego
Díaz de Haro's rebellion, he did not manage to stay long. But he did
hear from the local townspeople that, according to tradition, at the
entrance of the Church of San Vicente was the grave of king Wamba,
who "before his death took on the religion of the black monks of San
Vicente de Pampliega." In his passion for ancient lore and the historical past, and as a connoisseur of local tradition and the work of don
Rodrigo Jiménez de Rada (*De rebus Hispaniae*, III, 12), which had
also interested his father, he wrote in the diploma to that illustrious
town how after celebrating the cortes at Burgos, he passed through
Pampliega and had King Wamba's tomb excavated, ordering that his
remains be taken to Toledo.[20]

---

[19] In most of these documents the standard phrase "because it was something we
much needed for the matter of the Empire" is repeated with slight variations, which
proves he was intent on carrying out this plan.

[20] The diploma is lost except for a copy of the confirmation by Pedro I and Enrique
II in 1351 (Toledo, Archivo Municipal, I.I.43), published by D. Catalán, "El *Toledano
romanzado* e las *Estorias de los fechos de los godos* del siglo XV," in *Estudios dedicados
a Homer Herriott*, Madison, Wis., 1966, pp. 54–55, 54. Cf. P. Fernández del Pulgar in

Besides satisfying his intellectual curiosity and zeal for ancient things, with this excavation Alfonso intended to honor the memory of that great Visigoth king, a model of good government, secular and religious (he divided the parishes) and of virtues (Alfonso had praised him in his *Estoria de España*, caps. 513–538).[21] He also intended to carry out his father's unfinished project: transferring the remains, Alfonso wanted to honor the city of Toledo, which "in Visigoth times was the head of Spain and where in the past emperors were crowned." These words in a document that is more an account of events than a diploma on the eve of his quest for the imperial crown hints at the possible aspiration to be recognized as the supreme ruler among Peninsular kings.

From Pampliega, Alfonso headed to Valladolid, arriving in late April, and from there to Toro, arriving in mid-May. In early June he was in Zamora to celebrate the assembly of the kingdom, or Cortes, discussing general juridical-administrative matters, establishing new legal procedures for the administration of justice by the *alcaldes de corte* (court mayors). It is probable that Alfonso, soon after the concessions made to the nobles, would deal in the Cortes with the formulations and juridical matters proposed in the *Fuero real*, thus ruling over some of the most clamorous cases, but also granting to the nobles that each appointed *alcalde de corte* would be a knight when a *fijodalgo* went on trial.[22]

It is not known how long Alfonso stayed in Zamora before heading south. But he is believed to have been in Medina del Campo at

---

his *Historia secular y eclesiástica de la ciudad de Palencia*, Madrid, 1679, I, pp. 344–345; R. Izquierdo Benito, *Privilegios reales otorgados a Toledo durante la Edad Media. 1101–1494*, Toledo, 1990, no. 33; and the study by J. Amador de los Ríos, "La leyenda de las sepulturas de Recesvinto y Wamba en Toledo, sus vicisitudes y consecuencias," *RABM*, 17 (1907), 327–365.

[21] The *EE* does not mention the disinterment and transfer of the remains to Toeldo, perhaps, as Diego Catalán suggests, because this part of the work had already been completed ("El Toledano romanzado," pp. 53–54).

[22] The preamble of the so-called *Ordenamiento de Zamora* gives us the details. Cf.: *Cortes de los antiguos reinos de León y Castilla*, I, pp. 87–94. On the nature of this assembly, see E. Procter, *Curia and Cortes*, p. 137; J. O'Callaghan, *Cortes of Castile-León*, p. 120; C. de Ayala and F.J. Villalba, "Las Cortes bajo el reinado de Alfonso X," pp. 239–270. The common opinion of scholars is however that this was a local assembly of the "alcaldes" (mayors) of Castilla-León. Cf. A. Iglesia Ferreirós, "Las Cortes de Zamora de 1274 y los casos de corte," *AHDE*, 41 (1971), pp. 945–972; M.A. Pérez de la Canal, "La justicia de la corte de Castilla durante los siglos XIII al XV," *HID*, 2 (1975), pp. 383–481.

the end of July when he received news of the death of Enrique I of
Navarra. In the beginning, the news must have alarmed him, because
of the political problems that could have derived from the succession
of the throne of Navarra. His trip to the Empire was threatened if the
traditional contender to the Pamplona throne, Aragón, would launch
a political or military adventure. Alfonso, who had recently delegated
many powers to his son and successor, don Fernando, did not want to
deal with complications ensuing from Enrique's death, and his father-
in-law, the prudent and sensible don Jaime, did not do anything that
could change the agreements with his son-in-law. On the contrary,
it was don Fernando, due to his youth and recklessness who, during
Alfonso's absence, might have created a new conflict between Castile
and Navarra by launching an attack against Pamplona. But his military
adventure fortunately did not go past Logroño.[23]

From Medina del Campo Alfonso went on to Cuéllar (August 3)
and Alcalá de Henares (August 28), where according to some scholars
he would celebrate a new Cortes.[24]

Meanwhile in Lyon, the Council had begun on May 7, 1274 with
the presence of many senior clergy coming from many places, as well
as the representatives of Rudolf of Habsburg and Alfonso, and several Spanish bishops. At the end of September, Alfonso was in Santo
Domingo de Silos when he learned that the pope had officially confirmed Rudolf of Habsburg as King of the Romans.[25] Alfonso then
resolved that it was time to meet with the pope to find a solution to
the question of the empire and other pending business, so he quickly
went on to prepare the trip on which he pinned his highest hopes.

At the end of the Council, in a bull dated July 24 and sent to the
king of Castile through his emissaries and accompanied by a special
envoy from the pope, *Magister Fredulus*, prior of Lunello (Maguelone),
Gregory X attempted to alleviate the blow of the declaration in favor of
Rudolf, meeting Alfonso's aspirations with other gifts, but not giving
in regarding the title. After condemning the Castilian noble rebels, in

---

[23] Cf. Ballesteros, *Alfonso X*, pp. 697–705. See the articles in the volume *VII Centenario del Infante Don Fernando de la Cerda*, Ciudad Real: Centro de Estudios Manchegos, 1976.

[24] This is at least what a letter sent from Alcalá December 22, 1275 to the city of
Burgos seems to indicate. Cf. E. González Díez, *Colección diplomática del concejo de
Burgos (884–1369)*, Burgos, 1984, pp. 129–130.

[25] *CAX*, chap. 59, pp. 195–197; Ballesteros, *Alfonso X*, p. 715; R. Kinkade, "Alfonso X,
Cantiga 235," p. 301.

the document the pope argued that for the sake of Christendom he should give up his quest for the imperial crown. In the instructions accompanying the papal document, he urged his envoy, a great Bolognese jurist and skillful diplomat seasoned in imperial negotiations, to achieve by all means Alfonso's resignation in exchange for which the pope would grant him one tenth of all ecclesiastical income from his estates for six years.[26] He also proposed to him, that as a true defender of the faith, he should deal with the Holy Land crusade, rather than seek the imperial crown. Alfonso understood what was going on, and decided at that point, more vigorously than ever, to solve the matter personally, not by sending military aid to Italy, but rather by attending the Council and meeting in person with the pope.

In his trip to the South, after the assembly of the kingdom or Cortes, celebrated in Zamora, Alfonso continued his tour of important Castilian towns where he could receive moral or material support for his imperial project. Toward the end of September we know he was at Santo Domingo de Silos ("And on the Eve of St. Michael's, the King don Alfonso arrived here"), where he witnessed the Saint's miracle in the monastery's church, which was full of people on the day of St. Michael (September 29). The beneficiary of the miracle was a deaf-mute (Juan de Bermeo) whom Alfonso would take with him on his trip to Beaucaire.[27]

5. The Journey to the Empire: Beaucaire

In early October 1274 Alfonso was in Alicante preparing his trip to Lyon to meet the pope. A few days later he had a small fleet prepared with all necessary supplies to travel to Marseille, continuing on along the Rhine until Lyon, where the king would await his arrival. He then continued touring the South and was received triumphantly everywhere. On November 20, he was in Valencia, granting privileges to Murcia and sending various letters to institutions and individuals. His secretary, Bonamic Favila, a figure also mentioned in the *Cantigas*,

---

[26] J. Guiraud, *Les Registres de Grégoire X (1271–1276)*, Paris 1892–1906, no. 649 (Oct. 1275); J. Ríus Serra, *Rationes decimarum Hispaniae (1279–1280)*, 2 vols., Barcelona, 1946–1947, II, pp. 309–312; Cf. P. Linehan, *The Spanish Church and Papacy*, pp. 212–221; Ballesteros, *Alfonso X*, pp. 709–714.

[27] Pero Marín narrates this in lavish detail in his *Miráculos romançados*, pp. 48–49.

appears in all these documents and we know he accompanied him to Beaucaire.[28] Next, according to the famous Catalan chronicler Ramón Muntaner (1265–1336), who narrates in great detail Alfonso's trip to meet with the pope, Alfonso asked permission from his father-in-law, don Jaime, to travel across his territories, according to the chronicler "…for two reasons: the first that he, the queen, and their children wanted very much to see him and the princes; and second because he wanted his fatherly advice before his trip to the Council where he would debate very serious matters".[29]

The Catalan chronicler details the many celebrations held by the king of Aragón in honor of the king of Castile and his large entourage, headed by his daughter and grandchildren, so that "from the day he arrived in his lands until the day he reached Montpellier, the king of Castile or anyone with him, would not have to spend any of their money" (chap. 22, p. 56).

From Alicante, Alfonso and his entourage went to Valencia where they were lavishly fêted with popular celebrations, jousts, wrestling matches by wild men, regattas, and simulated naval battles. Muntaner meticulously details Alfonso's itinerary from Valencia to Barcelona. At the end of November, the royal delegation was in Tortosa. Jaime I met his son-in-law and family and accompanied them to Tarragona, arriving in Barcelona on Saint Clement's day. "And about Barcelona," Muntaner writes, "I need not write, for you can already imagine how they were received and it would be too long a story; but since Barcelona is the most noble and best town that the king of Aragón holds, the festivities and celebrations surpassed those of all other towns" (chap. 23).

In Barcelona Alfonso's father-in-law behaved very generously towards him. He remained there almost a month, until January 22, 1275. During his stay in the city, don Jaime attempted to dissuade Alfonso from visiting the pope, an action he thought was a waste of time, since Gregory would never change his mind. Jaime had already met with the pope and knew this perfectly well. The king of Aragón was up to date on the affairs that had happened during the Council

---

[28] Some of these letters and documents can be seen in Valls & Taberner, *Privilegios*, p. 70 and ff.

[29] *Crònica de Ramon Muntaner*, ed. F. Soldevila, in *Les quatre grans cròniques*, Biblioteca Perenne, 26, Barcelona, 1971. Muntaner devotes chapters 21–23 to Alfonso's journey from Valencia to Montpellier.

and the feelings of the pope regarding the Empire, and repeatedly urged him not to go. But Alfonso did not heed the wise advice of this man who was so experienced in international politics.[30]

While Alfonso and his court were in Barcelona, Raimundo de Penyafort, a famous jurist from his father's court, died. His solemn funeral was attended by the king of Castile and his wife, doña Violante, accompanied by the king of Aragón, many princes, the nobles and bishops of Barcelona, Huesca, and Cuenca, this last one, the notary of Alfonso X, who accompanied him on his trip to Beaucaire.[31] That fall, possibly on November 28, don Felipe, Alfonso's dear brother who had however turned against him during the nobility's revolt, had also died.[32] We do not know how Alfonso learned of his death, but it was most probably during his travels in the south, and certainly before his arrival in Barcelona, where he arrived shortly before Christmas. There is no record that he attended the funeral. Muntaner, who is our guide here, was not aware of don Felipe's death. If politically, this meant one less reason to worry during his absence from the kingdom, the loss of his brother cast a pallor over the festivities in Barcelona.

Meanwhile, the pope continued sending letters to anyone who could dissuade Alfonso from meeting with him.[33] But nothing or no one could achieve that, so accompanied by don Jaime, his wife, a few of his children, and a large group of nobles and advisors, at the end of January he left for France. Ramón Muntaner, our only direct source to reconstruct this part of the itinerary, writes that on March 7, the entourage was in Perpignan ("And don't ask me about the celebration there that lasted eight days"). Alfonso left his wife, Violante, and the children in the town and continued on to Montpellier with a smaller following that probably included his brother Manuel and other Castilian nobles and clergymen.[34] After passing through Narbonne, Béziers,

---

[30] In his *Llibre dels feyts* don Jaime has left us a testimony of the talks he held with Alfonso regarding his *journey to the Empire*.

[31] Cf. F. Valls y Taberner, *San Ramón de Penyafort*, in *Obras selectas*, I,ii, Madrid–Barcelona, 1953.

[32] On the date of don Felipe's death and his lavish tomb in the Templar church of Villalcázar de Sirga, see above chap. 4, pp. 146–147, note 59.

[33] The letters to don Jaime de Aragón and to don Manuel, brother of the king and his close advisor, can be seen in Ballesteros, *Alfonso X*, pp. 722–724.

[34] *Crònica de Ramon Muntaner*, chaps. 22–23. The chronicler remembers how, when he was a child, Alfonso and his wife, Queen Violante stayed at the house of his father on their way to Beaucaire (chap. 23). Some aspects of Muntaner's narrative are also confirmed by another great Catalan chronicler, B. Desclot, in his *Llibre del rei*

and other smaller towns, he arrived in Montpellier at the beginning of April 1275.[35] In Montpellier, according Muntaner, Alfonso stayed two weeks, being lavishly welcomed by the people with great festivities.[36]

While he was in this city, under the king of Aragón's lordship, a letter from the pope arrived suggesting the small town of Beaucaire ("Bellicadrum") as meeting place and the date as the eighth day after Easter, April 21.[37] Beaucaire, on the other bank of the Rhine and facing the famous town of Tarascon, was closer to Montpellier than Lyon, where the pope was attending the Council.[38] We do not know why the pope proposed the change of location, which implied traveling a considerable distance. Possible motives may have been Alfonso's ill health or perhaps that he did not want to meet in a city that was under Jaime I of Aragón, while Beaucaire was under the Count of Provence, Charles of Anjou, an ally of the pope. The pope obviously did not want to run any personal risks when discussing a matter that was already decided beforehand.[39] Alfonso, on the other hand, was a powerful king with many allies and sympathizers everywhere, whom he maintained contact with, even during his stay in Beaucaire.[40] He was also accompanied by his father-in-law, the king of Aragón, who dominated large territories in Provence, and with whom the pope had recently had some differences. Hence the pope's reasons for security concerns.[41] Political circumstances in those turbulent days between the

---

En Pere (in F.Soldevila, *Les quatre grans cròniques*, chap. 66, p. 454). The *Llibre dels feyts* confirms that Violante did really stay in Perpignan and did not go all the way to Montpellier (p. 186).

[35] Muntaner, *Crònica*, chap. 23, pp. 59–60; cf. Ballesteros, *Alfonso X*, pp. 727–728.

[36] *Crònica*, chap. 23, p. 60. Beginning with this part of the itinerary, Muntaner is no longer interested in the trip of the king of Castile, arguing that it goes beyond the limits of his *Crònica*.

[37] Cf. Guiraud and Cardier, *Les registres de Grégoire X et de Jean XXI*, I, pp. 301–302; and Ballesteros, *Alfonso X*, p. 729.

[38] In another letter dated May 3 in Orange, the pope informed Alfonso that he would lodge at Tarascon, and that Alfonso and his followers should do so in Beaucaire (text in Ballesteros, *Alfonso X*, p. 729).

[39] We know that before his meeting with Alfonso, during the Council, the pope, from Lyon, wrote a letter to Rudolf of Habsburg (February 15, 1275) where he called him King of the Romans and even fixed a date and place for his crowning as emperor: November 1 in Rome. Cf. Ballesteros, *Alfonso X*, p. 728.

[40] See, for instance, the letter he sent his supporters May 21 from Pavia, cf. *Annales Placentini Gibellini*, in *MGH*, XVIII, p. 561.

[41] Cf. *Llibre del feyts*, chaps. 524–542; A.R. Lewis, "James de Conqueror: Montpellier and Southern France," in *The Worlds of Alfonso the Learned and James the Conqueror*, ed. R.I. Burns, Princeton, 1985, pp. 130–149.

pope and the Ghibellines demanded prudence and precaution on his end when it came to personal security.

6. The Great Meeting

The pope arrived in Beaucaire on May 10 and so did Alfonso or shortly before.[42] There are no known descriptions or chronicles of the period that describe Alfonso's arrival in Beaucaire, although it is mentioned in a fictionalized history of the Crusades, the popular *Conqueste d'Outremer*.[43] We know the meetings with the pope lasted approximately three months. The supplies the king of Castile had with him and the generosity of the Beaucaire magistrates allowed both courts to spend that time in abundance and plenty. Alfonso's last document from Beaucaire is dated July 20, 1275.[44]

There is no direct information of the meeting with the pope. The *CAX* entirely ignores what happened during the trip, and Muntaner is also unable to give any details on the content of the talks.[45] These can only be reconstructed via the papal correspondence of those days, as well as through Alfonso's letters to his Italian supporters.[46] Based on the data given by this correspondence, we can say the negotiations with the pope dealt with and solved numerous questions, some

---

[42] *CAX*, chap. 66, p. 214; Jofré de Loaysa, *Crónica*, chap. 219.11, p. 76; Ballesteros, *Alfonso X*, pp. 728–731; C. de Ayala Martínez, "Alfonso X: Beaucaire y el fin de la pretensión imperial," *Historia*, 47 (1987), pp. 5–31.

[43] In Dom E. Martene & U. Durand in *Veterum Scriptorum amplissima collectio*, volume V, where chapters XXI–XXVI were inserted under the title: *Guillelmi Archiepiscopi Tyronis continuata belli sacri Historia, Gallico idiomate ab antiquo auctore ante annos CCCC. Conscripta* (cols. 628–752; chap. XXIV col. 747). Even if this text appears in an essentially fictional narrative, it could not reflect the historical reality more accurately: the anonymous chronicler knew that Alfonso had squandered a great deal of money on the imperial project and had obtained nothing in the end.

[44] Cf. Ortiz de Zúñiga, *Anales*, I, p. 288; Ballesteros, *Alfonso X*, p. 731.

[45] "Regarding the king of Castile, I can tell you he went there because he wanted to be emperor of Spain, which he was unable to achieve, and he had to return to his kingdom" (cap. 24, p. 61). I am not certain if the Catalan chronicler committed a linguistic mistake, but I believe that where he says "Spain" he should have said "Rome," unless he meant that he went to see the pope because he wanted to be emperor of Spain, that is, to obtain hegemony over other Peninsular kingdoms, as some scholars claim, something the pope obviously could not grant.

[46] Cf. *Les Registres de Gregoire X (1271–1276)*, ed. J. Guiraud, Paris, 1892–1906, doc. no. 649; and no. 718–721, 838, pp. 308, 345; and, for instance, Alfonso X's letter to the Podestá of Pavia, Lanfranco Pignataro (cf. *Annales Placentini Gibellini*, in *MGH*, XVIII, p. 561).

in favor of Alfonso X. Among the most significant was an economic one. The pope granted one tenth of the Church's revenue in the Peninsula during six years to finance defense actions against the Muslims.[47] Regarding the other requests, in the end Alfonso lost it all.[48]

There was also the matter of the struggle for succession in Navarra, where Enrique, the king who had died in July 1274, had left a 2-year old daughter, Juana, whom Alfonso and Philip of France wanted to marry to one of their family members. Regarding this, the pope informed the Castilian king that he had already obtained the marriage dispensation so she could marry Philip *le Bel* [the Handsome], a nephew of the King of France.

Then, Alfonso requested the pope's intercession before Rudolf to obtain recognition for his rights to the Duchy of Swabia. The request seems superfluous, for they had already been recognized by Innocent IV twenty years earlier, but perhaps at that particular moment in his reign, the approval had a deeper meaning than is often acknowledged. According to widely accepted political theory on royal power, election was not a particularly admired method of selecting who was to rule society, but instead it was inheritance (*heredamiento*) that was considered the natural channel for the transmission of power. This theory was also adopted by Alfonso X in the *Partidas*,[49] whereby it can be concluded that the king has a lot more power in his kingdom than the emperor in the empire (because the latter was elected, while the king inherited it). This does not prevent Alfonso from using the expression "the king is like an emperor in his kingdom" to express the absolute power of the king in his kingdom. Now as is well known, the heirs of the Duchy of Swabia had been *de facto*, if not *de jure*, also traditionally the heirs of the imperial crown. The question at this point then, in order to understand Alfonso's obsession which put him at odds

---

[47] Letter from the pope dated at Lausanne, Ocober 14, 1275. (*Registre*, fasc. 3, no. 649, p. 281). Cf. J. Ríus Serra, *Rationes decimarum Hispaniae (1279–1280)*, 2 vols., Barcelona, 1946–1947, II, pp. 309–312; S. Domínguez Sánchez, *Documentos de Gregorio X (1272–1276) referentes a España*, León, 1997, pp. 193–194; cf. P. Linehan, *Spanish Church and the Papacy*, pp. 213–214; Ballesteros, *Alfonso X*, p. 728.

[48] Ballesteros reminds us that, according to Zurita y Garibay, Alfonso asked the pope, as the king of Aragón had done before, to intercede in the liberation of his brother, prince Enrique, who was still in the jails of Charles of Anjou (*Alfonso X*, p. 770). It is quite probable that it was so, but it is not confirmed by the documents. Of course, it would be years before Enrique would enjoy his freedom again, which means that if the pope truly interceded on his behalf, this had no effect.

[49] *Second Partida*, Tit. I, Law VIII.

with the pope, is, did Alfonso believe that his inalienable rights to the Duchy of Swabia (because they were inherited) also gave him the right to wear the imperial crown of the Holy Roman-Germanic Empire, just as he had inherited the throne of Castile? The electors could choose and the pope could designate, but beyond the election and designation, Alfonso must have thought, there was *heredamiento*, a higher title only he could claim. Faced with Alfonso's claim, the pope promised to write to Rudolf of Habsburg to ask him to recognize and respect the rights of the king of Castile, something Gregory X effectively did. The problem was that Rudolf had already made other arrangements with Ludwig of Bavaria, so Alfonso's request had no effect.[50]

Thus Alfonso had to settle for the *décima* concession since, given the circumstances in the Peninsula, it would come in handy. News had begun to arrive since mid-May about the invasion of the North African Moors and the great devastation they were causing in the South was alarming.

In exchange for this concession, Alfonso apparently had to verbally renounce the imperial crown in the presence of the pope and several witnesses. There's no evidence of a written renunciation, as Ballesteros writes, because the pope "as judge in the conflict, could not in any way demand his renunciation, but only submission to his ruling" (*Alfonso X*, p. 732); but it should also not surprise us that he would have done so as a pure formality and to deal with the commitment. Alfonso's mind was distant, occupied with the serious news arriving from Spain. Hence in terms of substance and motive of the meeting, we can say the result was not what was expected by either of the two parties. The pope expected Alfonso to renounce the crown and participate in the crusade to liberate Palestine. There's no evidence Alfonso did either. Although he showed interest in the overseas crusade, he must have told the pope that he had to solve a more urgent one at home, which at the time worried him more than the imperial crown. And as regards this last item, Alfonso must have told the pope that he was unwilling to give in even a bit in his acquired rights, for which he had been fighting for twenty years. Gregory X, for whom the problem of the imperial crown was almost solved, did not budge—he did not grant him the

---

[50] Cf. *Les Registres de Gregoire X (1271–1276)*, ed. J. Guiraud, Paris, 1892–1906, doc. no. 649; and nos. 718–721, 838, pp. 308, 345; S. Domínguez, *Decumentos de Gregorio X*, pp. 343–345; C. de Ayala Martínez, "Alfonso X: Beaucaire," pp. 15–20.

crown and formally asked him to renounce his rights once and for all. And though the *Annales Ianuenses* seem to indicate Alfonso did it, the facts do not confirm it, for he continued to call himself King of the Romans,[51] and there's no lack of evidence he went on believing in his imperial rights until the end of his life[52] and even in death.[53] But at the end of the meeting, the pope was convinced Alfonso had renounced, and on October 15, two months after the meeting, he wrote to the German princes announcing the Castilian king's definitive renunciation of the imperial crown.[54] This news had disastrous results among Alfonso's supporters in Italy.

As we shall soon see, other more serious and urgent problems required his presence in Spain and perhaps occupied his mind during his last days in Beaucaire, so it may have been he did not much worry about the pope's decision, when the crown of his own kingdom was at stake. Very discouraged and physically ill, he must have thought only of returning to his beloved Seville to save it from the North African

---

[51] In a letter by Gregory X to don Remondo, archbishop of Seville, dated at Valencia September 13, 1275, a few days after the meeting, the pope complained that Alfonso continued to use the title King of the Romans in his correspondence with the German nobility and the Italian communities. He urged him to encourage the king "to give up this and other similar pretensions." The letter seems to indicate that Alfonso's use of the title violated an oath given in front of witnesses who knew perfectly well what he had sworn. That is, a few days after the meeting, Alfonso continued to behave as if nothing had happened. Cf. *Annales Ianuenses*, in *MGH, Sriptores*, XVIII, p. 282. In a letter to the city of Pavia dated at Beaucaire May 2, Alfonso continues to call himself, "Romanorum rex semper augustus," while he denounced the pope for his lack of justice and fairness. Cf. *Annales Placentini Gibellini*, in *MGH, Scriptores*, XVIII, p. 661; and Ballesteros, *Alfonso X*, pp. 772, 778. For the use of imperial insignia after Beaucaire, cf. *Regestum Gregorii X*, 650 (sept. 1275); and *Acta Sanctorum*, maii VII, 363.

[52] In a letter sent from Burgos and dated as late as February 27, 1281 and addressed to the captains and the people of Genoa, he continues to call himself "Alphonsus dei gratia Romanorum Rex, semper Augustus, Castelle et Algarbie Rex…" (in Ballesteros, *Alfonso X*, p. 933). A few days after the privilege granted to Santo Domingo de Silos (March 3, 1281) that had nothing to do with international politics, Alfonso signs himself in Latin, "Nos Alfonsus Dei gratia Rex Romanorum semper Augustus" (ib., p. 936), a truly exceptional case, for internal documents were usually issued in Castilian. Before his death, Alfonso returned briefly to the question of the empire. Cf. J. O'Callaghan, *The Learned King*, pp. 252–53.

[53] When the bodies of Alfonso X and his father were exhumed in 1579, it was discovered that Alfonso had been buried with all the imperial insignias: "It seemed he had his sword, his scepter, and the crown and staff of the Emperor" (D. Ortiz de Zúñiga, *Anales eclesiásticos de la muy noble y muy leal ciudad de Sevilla*, Madrid, 1677, p. 555).

[54] *Les Registres*, fasc. 3, p. 182.

Moorish devastation. The *CAX*, which says nothing about Alfonso's talks with the pope in Beaucaire because it tells us that no documents on the subject could be found, contains, however, a paragraph that is extraordinarily revealing of Alfonso's psychological state at the end of his meeting with the pope:

> Of the things that befell King Alfonso while he went to the empire, the *History* has avoided relating, for it has never found how they happened, although it was found that King Alfonso, being in the Beaucaire, a place near the Ruédano River, learned how Aben Yuzaf with great forces of men crossed from overseas and killed Archbishop Sancho and don Nuño. He also learned that Prince Fernando was dead, and he thought it true that the land at the frontier was in such condition that it could all be lost–or at least a great portion of it—for he did not think that his son Prince Sancho would make an effort to defend it nor that he had there anyone to help him in it. For this reason, and also because he had learned that concerning the matter of the empire they were mocking him, and that he had wasted a very large fortune on this journey, he departed from Belcaire and set out for Castile. (*CAX*, chap. 66, p. 214)

It seems implausible that Alfonso, who arrived at Beaucaire with secretaries and scribes and never missed a chance to record information, did not bring any documentation for his chamber on his conversations with the pope. Knowing what we do about the praxis of Alfonso's chancellery, something radical and drastic must have occurred with the meeting's documentation, which must have been abundant, regarding such an important matter and for which Alfonso had prepared for twenty years.

There are also no known contemporary images of the meeting, except the one on the stained glass windows of the León cathedral where Alfonso is wearing the imperial insignia (crown, orb, and scepter), standing in between the pope and the bishop of León, Martín Fernández (1254–1289).

The chronicler apologizes for not being able to supply details on the meeting of Alfonso and the pope for lack of information, yet he accumulates information on events that took place all along 1275, correctly grouping them under two main headings, and on various minor ones happening in the Peninsula during Alfonso's stay in Beaucaire. Under the first heading is the North African Moorish invasion; under the second, the deaths of family and figures from Alfonso's military politics. These events would certainly influence the negotiations with the pope and Alfonso's imperial aspirations. The first invasion on May 13, 1275, supported by the rebellious nobles, was closely followed by another one on August 16, a more numerous and dreadful wave at the command of the emir of Morocco, Ibn Yûsuf. Under the second heading, the deaths of the *Adelantado de la frontera* (Commander of the Border), don Nuño González de Lara (September 8, 1275), of his brother-in-law, don Sancho, archbishop of Toledo and Primate of Spain (October 20), and of his own son and heir, don Fernando de la Cerda (in November), which he learned about probably when he was already in Spain, all had an even more devastating personal impact.[55]

The first of these events was something Alfonso always feared and almost expected, especially when he refused to return the *arraeces* to the king of Granada's obedience, once the year of the truce was over, as stated in the Seville pact. The second event was unexpected and had unforeseen consequences for the kingdom's succession and stability.

The North African Moorish invasion that Alfonso learned about through don Remondo's letters when he was in meetings with the pope was an ill omen that would hover over his kingdom after Beaucaire. As if his adversity had not been enough (even before the trip the sudden death of his dear brother Felipe had occurred),[56] now an entire series of deaths and calamities in the family would deeply affect him. Returning from Beaucaire to Montpellier he also learned of the death of his daughter Leonor and that of his nephew don Alfonso Manuel, son of his dear brother don Manuel, who had died that same month.[57] The sadness and depression caused by these deaths and others that were the result of the North African Moorish invasions produced the mood he was in at his arrival from Beaucaire.

7. *The Return*

Following the most probable chronology, Alfonso left Beaucaire between the end of July and the beginning of September (or end of

---

[55] For the date of these deaths and their documentation, confronting various sources, see R. Kinkade, "Alfonso X, *Cantiga* 235," pp. 304–305, note 79. See also our chap. 10, pp. 357–365 and notes.

[56] The date of this death, as discussed above (note ?), November 28, 1274, comes from the inscription on the grave of the Prince in Villalcázar de Sirga copied by F. de Rades y Andrada, *Chrónica de las tres órdenes de Sanctiago*, fol. 35v; and quoted by E. Flórez, *Reinas Cathólicas*, I, p. 25. Cf. R. Kinkade, "Alfonso X, *Cantiga* 235," p. 302, note 65.

[57] Desclot, *Llibre del rei En Pere*, p. 454; *Anales toledanos III*, p. 419.

August) 1275. Probably by then he only knew of the deaths caused
by the North African Moorish invasion, but not of the deaths in the
family that the chronicler accumulates in the quoted text in connection with the return, but which in reality Alfonso would learn about
gradually as he made his way, although he knew of many before his
arrival in Spain.

The return trip was very taxing, for he fell ill several times, and
his spirits were oppressed by the failure of his conversations with the
pope, and the news of the North African Muslim invasion, which he
probably felt responsible for, since he had left to seek the empire before
settling the question of the *arraeces*. This was a thorny question he had
deliberately not wanted to solve, because it was a way of keeping the
king of Granada on tenterhooks.[58] The king knew this, so he did not
remain idle during Alfonso's absence.

The Florentine Codex of the *Cantigas* preserves in a beautiful miniature a souvenir of the return from Beaucaire.[59] In vignette 2, Alfonso is
portrayed wearing a large travel hat decorated in red and gold inside,
and riding, like all other companions, a strong mule, the animal of
choice for long treks. As has been shown, the miniatures in the *Cantigas* follow a strict chronological order as regards the scenes, so we
can deduce it was the return trip, for the preceding vignette shows
Alfonso's illness at Montpellier on his return from his meeting with the
pope. The following vignettes also show events occurring after 1276.
Several court figures accompany the king, as well as a troop of soldiers
bearing the shields and banners of Castile and León. Several figures
of the royal family and nobility come to meet him. A very young one
in front and with a bare head, kisses his hand. He is probably Prince
Fernando, because, among those surrounding him, the representatives
of Lara (identified by two kettles in their caps and the banners) stand
out. These were his protectors, and would also go on to serve his children.[60] Documentation confirms the version of the *Cantiga* that says
Alfonso was accompanied on his return trip by his inseparable brother
don Manuel and his secretary don Gonzalo, bishop of Cuenca, who

---

[58] See the text further on in chap. 11, p. 376, note 21.

[59] This is the *Cantiga* 71bis, fol. 92r. See illustration 8.

[60] The shield of the Laras was: "On a red field, two caldrons checkered in gold and
black, hanging from a stick; from each end, seven snake heads sticking out, three
inwards and two outwards" (*Diccionario heráldico y nobiliario de los reinos de España*,
comp. by F. Gonzalo-Doria, Madrid: Editorial Bitácora, 1987, p. 603).

could be the two characters appearing to the left and right of the king. From Vienne, the pope, following Alfonso's suggestion (another small concession), named don Gonzalo, bishop of Burgos.[61]

The return itinerary, though much more generic than the trip there, is described by Muntaner, who points out he did not take the same route but went via Lérida and Aragón to Castile.[62] We know that on October 24 and November 11–14 and 19–26, don Jaime was in Lérida, where he probably went to in order to meet his son-in-law, daughter, and grandchildren who were on their way to Castile.[63] Although few details are known of the trip from Lérida to Brihuega, the place that appears for the first time in a document from December 10, 1275 after the return from Beaucaire, it is clear the that pace of the entourage was slow.[64] On December 22, the group was in Burgos for Christmas and the New Year.[65]

Despite all adversity, Beaucaire was good training for what was in store for him. Historians still do not understand how Alfonso, the wisest, most famous, and powerful king of Christendom, hurled himself into this absurd adventure, knowing the German electors had chosen Rudolf of Habsburg and that the pope had approved it. Despite this, and his father-in-law's advice to the contrary, Alfonso was intent on meeting the pope to present his rights to the crown. According to C. de Ayala Martínez, the main reason for attending the meeting at Beaucaire was internal propaganda, to attract all Ghibellines, not only in Genoa and Lombardy, but also in Aragón, Cataluña, and the French Midi, to Alfonso's cause. The scholar proves this by arguing that before his trip to France, he toured Aragón to promote his image among the

---

[61] *Les Registres de Gregoire X*, fasc. 3, p. 270. Cf. Ballesteros, *Alfonso X*, p. 774 note 47.

[62] *Crónica*, chap. 24, p. 61.

[63] Cf. J. Miret i Sans, *Itinerari de Jaume I "el Conqueridor,"* Barcelona, 1918, pp. 524–526). The *CAX* mistakenly traces the return route through Barcelona, going later through Valencia, Requena, Cuenca, Huete, and finally towards Alcalá de Henares on the way to northern Castile (chap. 67, pp. 216–217). There's no evidence of such itinerary at the time. Cf. Ballesteros, *Alfonso X*, p. 775.

[64] On December 10, he was in Brihuega, and on the 22, in Alcalá de Henares, as can be gleaned from privileges issued to both towns. Cf. Ballesteros, *Sevilla en el siglo XIII*, Madrid, 1913, p. 208; and E. González Díez, *Colección diplomática del concejo de Burgos (884–1369)*, Burgos, 1984, no. 44, pp. 129–130. Brihuega is 50 km northeast of Alcalá, which means Alfonso was traveling south from Lérida, and not north, from Cuenca or Requena, as stated in the *CAX* (cap. 67, p. 216).

[65] Ballesteros, *Alfonso X*, pp. 772–774; C. de Ayala Martínez, "Alfonso X, Beaucaire y el fin de la pretensión imperial," *H*, n. 165, 47 (1987), pp. 20, 31.

king's subjects there.[66] C. Estepa holds a similar view, drawing a parallel between the kingdom of Sicily and the empire of Frederick II, with Alfonso's Castile and his imperial aspirations: "Just as the case of Frederick II, it was a matter of developing his power as a feudal monarch, in this case of Castile... We can assume that Alfonso of Castile, with access to the imperial throne, intended to gain supremacy over other Christian princes and also to acquire the patrimony of the German royal family (*Reichsgut*), which was difficult to distinguish from what belonged to the Staufens."[67]

Those were indeed Alfonso's aspirations, as well as those of all other candidates. But against the opinions regarding the propagandistic nature of the tour, Muntaner describes the enthusiastic welcome Alfonso received from Jaime de Aragón, a man who was hypersensitive to Castile's hegemonic aspirations and would not have tolerated the presence of his son-in-law, had he perceived even remotely such political propaganda.[68] We discussed above don Jaime's reaction to Alfonso's proclamation as King of the Romans by the Pisans. Though Muntaner states that the motive of Alfonso's meeting was because "he wanted to be emperor of Spain" (*Crónica*, p. 61), he indicates that Alfonso's motives for touring Aragón were twofold: the desire that he, his wife, and children had to see don Jaime, and Alfonso's own need to hear his opinion about the meeting with the pope (p. 55).

---

[66] Cf. "Alfonso X, Beaucaire y el fin de la pretensión imperial," pp. 5–31. A. Steiger went even further, arguing that Alfonso's intention on his trip to Beaucaire was to be crowned emperor and thus create "a Roman Empire with a Hispanic nationality" ("Alfonso X y la idea imperial," *Arbor*, 18, 1946, p. 393).

[67] C. Estepa, "Alfonso X en la Europa del siglo XIII," en *Alfonso X. Aportaciones de un rey castellano a la construcción de Europa*, pp. 27–28. W.F. Schoen also thinks that for Alfonso, "imperial dignity had an incalculable value [...] [as a means] to impose himself on his own unruly vassals, as well as on his neighbors, the kings of Aragón and Portugal" (*Alfonso X de Castilla*, Madrid, 1966, p. 101).

[68] And the said king [don Jaime] and the said princes [of Aragón] were very pleased by this, and immediately, with the messengers of the king of Castile, they sent others with the message that they were very pleased with his visit and that he should think about accepting in his service all the territories as if they were his, and that via those messengers he should let them know where he wished to enter their lands and what day he would arrive. (*Crónica*, p. 55)

Knowing the political ideology of don Jaime "that he should think about accepting in his service all the territories as if they were his," can only be understood from the desire to host his son-in-law, his daughter, and their grandchildren as if they were at home, and never as an act of vassalage to the king of Castile, whom Jaime I knew would never be crowned emperor of the Holy Roman Empire.

Other aspects of the failed encounter are harder to understand. Given Alfonso's arrogance and the virtually null possibilities of obtaining the title through an election, it is unclear how he would subject himself to such humiliation by the pope. If he did go to Beaucaire to improve his public relations, and to appear among his fellow countrymen and foreigners worthy of the crown because of his meeting with the pope, the refusal must have dealt a severe blow to his personal pride and reputation. According to the *CAX* (chap. 66 pp. 214–215), despite his prestige, wisdom, and power, his failure made him look like a fool in the eyes of his enemies and supporters. But whether or not hegemony over the Peninsula was the goal, Alfonso had invested a great deal of his energy and his subjects' money in the project, and had been struggling for twenty years, so he was convinced he had as much of a right to it as any other candidate, and thought that this was the time to obtain it. Obviously, it was a miscalculation.

The accumulation of news of death and calamity overshadowed the disappointment caused by the disagreement with the pope. Adding to this string of calamities the very serious illness he suffered at Montpellier and which almost killed him, we could have a faint idea of the events surrounding "la ida al Imperio" (the journey to the Empire) which must have forever remained impressed in his memory as one of the darkest periods of his life. That ill-fated journey also marked the twilight of his reign. Alfonso would never mention again his "ida al Imperio" or his meeting with the pope.

In the field of public relations, if we believe the chronicler, the failure of his visit to the pope, which circulated by word of mouth in Spain as the rest of Europe, was a true disaster, for it made the wisest king the object of ridicule: "[F]or this reason [namely, the deaths of family members and devastation by the North African Moors], and also because he had learned that concerning the matter of the empire they were mocking him, and that he had wasted a very large fortune on this journey, he departed from Beaucaire and set out for Castile" (chap. 66, pp. 214). Alfonso, upon his return, must have felt overwhelmed.

CHAPTER SEVEN

ILLNESS AND INTELLECTUAL PURSUITS

Beginning with his ascent to the throne, Alfonso X's life became a true personal drama he had to confront daily if he wanted to outdo his father. This drama developed simultaneously in three main acts: the first, psychological and political, was the struggle for the imperial crown discussed in previous chapters; the second, physical and personal, had to do with the serious illnesses that afflicted him during long periods of his life; the third, social and family-related, were the rebellions in the kingdom, first by Muslim subjects, and then, unbelievably, by the nobility, his family (siblings and wife), and finally, his own son and heir, don Sancho. If the first two only took up certain moments of his life, the last one plagued him from the day he acceded to the throne, to the day he died, and it was the worst ignominy of his life as king and father, for it deprived him of his human dignity and it followed him beyond the grave, casting him as a learned man in stars and books, but as an idiot when it came to the management of his own self, house, and kingdom.

But for the student of Alfonso's life, it is precisely this triple drama that made his work as a man of letters even more admirable, for it seems almost a miracle that a man with his woes and adversities could carry out such immense literary, scientific, and legal production, which in the opinion of scholars, was at its height precisely between 1269 and 1278, a period in which he also had to fight against those three insurmountable obstacles. G. Menéndez Pidal writes, "The creative streak is precisely what marks this second period in Alfonso's life. He was not happy to just support and direct translations, but rather he made an effort at a syncretic total task… It is in this second period when he wrote his most original and personal works."[1] After having dealt with the first act in the preceding chapter, we will devote the following two to the second, leaving the rest of the book to the dramatic final one.

---

[1] "Como trabajaron las escuelas alfonsíes," *NRFH*, V (1951), p. 369.

1. *Illness and Literary Creation*

"Grande doloris / Ingenium est miserisque uenit
sollertia rebus"

(*Metamorphosis*, VI, 574–575)

"Mas dize Ouidio que grant es el engenno e la sabe-
duría del qui el dolor [h]a, et que el artería e la sabe-
duría estonces uiene a ombre quando se uee en la
mesquindat"

(*GE*, II, 1, p. 253a17–21)

["But Ovid says there is much wit and wisdom in
pain, and that sagacity and wisdom come to man in
the midst of suffering."]

"Ovid says…" Few writers in the 13th century would have thought to
open a treatise on suffering and knowledge, and how the former leads
to the latter, with a phrase from a pagan author. Alfonso, a passionate
admirer of Ovid, the poet of love, pain, and exile, does so without difficulty and great pleasure as he did before and on many other subjects.
The text appears in the second part of the *General Estoria*, where the
Learned King, paraphrasing a passage from the *Metamorphosis* (VI,
574–575) in which the Latin poet speaks of adversity as the source of
knowledge, comments: But Ovid says there is much wit and wisdom
in pain, and that sagacity and wisdom come to man in the midst of
suffering" (*GE*, II, 1, p. 253a17–25). If Ovid's words were not entirely
clear, Alfonso glosses them with the opinion of "another sage" who
maintained "that man becomes wise in his suffering, and that he who
suffers from something becomes sharper in his learning."[2]

It is worthwhile to summarize the context of the Ovidian myth to
understand Alfonso's paraphrase and the point of his comment, which
is double-edged. It is the story of Tereus and Philomena, whose tongue
was cut by the traitor Tereus after which he locked her up in a shepherd's
hut to conceal her rape. Loneliness and suffering, however, stimulated
Philomena's wit and she managed to subtly weave into a tapestry
the story of Tereus's crimes and secretly sent it to her sister Progne,

---

[2] This "sage" was probably Arnulf of Orleans, called the "frayre" ["Friar"] and
"esponedor" ["commentator"] of Ovid by Alfonso. He composed *Allegoriae super Ovi-
dii Metamorphosin*, which Alfonso used extensively in his Works. See the edition of
Allegoriae in F. Ghisalberti, "Arnolfo d'Orléans, un cultore d'Ovidio nel secolo XII," in
Memorie del R. Istituto Lombardo di Scienze e Lettere, XXIV, 4 (1932), pp. 157–234.

queen of Thracia and Tereus's wife. Progne's revenge was atrocious. She personally beheaded Itis, her five-year old son with Tereus, cooked his body except for the head, and fed it to Tereus in a lavish banquet. At the end of the banquet, the mute Philomena appeared with the head of the boy in her hands, which she hurled at Tereus's chest. Tereus went mad, and according to the Ovidian fable, he turned into a foul bird, an *upupa*, while Progne and Philomena turned into a sparrow and a mockingbird, respectively (*GE*, II, 1, a5–33).

Alfonso freely manipulates the Ovidian fable to turn it into a kind of short novella, complete with plot and its tragic denouement. This part of the *GE* was completed before 1280, and Alfonso actively worked on it during the revolt of the nobles headed by his brother Felipe, one of the greatest adversities of his political life, as well as during the 70s when he suffered some of his worst illnesses. We cannot rule out that this fable, with certain rich details added by Alfonso, may contain a secret message when he says "sagacity and wisdom come to man in the midst of suffering". Alfonso is telling us that he learned all of his craftiness and skill, both in government and in the acquisition of knowledge, in adversity and pain, as did Philomena.

Recent scholarship on Alfonso points to the importance of his health problems as a way to explain his erratic and even callous behavior in decisions made in the last two decades of his life. As possible causes of his excesses, scholars cite a list of physical ailments he suffered and which might have caused his mental imbalance. Faced with this situation, those responsible for the kingdom (his son and heir don Sancho, the nobility and the clergy), decided to depose him.[3] But scholars stress much less the other side of the coin, that is, the positive aspects of physical illnesses (of which the mental ones, despite his son's accusation of insanity, have not been proven) on his intellectual production.

Without ignoring the possible influence of physical ailments on Alfonso's psyche and how his imbalance may have influenced certain decisions, I believe it's appropriate here to emphasize how, as stated in the *Metamorphosis* commentary, illness and pain led him at times to

---

[3] For instance, R. Kinkade writes, "Alfonso's ailments must have constituted a major impediment to his successful management of the affairs of state and one of the principal causes of the political chaos which characterized the turbulent decade between 1269 and 1278," "Alfonso X, *Cantiga* 235, and the Events of 1269–1278," *Speculum*, 67 (1992), pp. 284–323, p. 283.

withdraw from public life to cure himself and to seek refuge in solitude, where he could more freely devote himself to scholarship and the composition of his works. Clearly, certain of his works must be associated with periods in which there are no signs of Alfonso's external activity, either military or political, periods in which he was either ill or convalescing.

Following the political failure in Beaucaire and the very serious illnesses that followed, it would seem Alfonso may have tried to compensate for his political defeat and the fragility of his physical health with a stronger effort in his intellectual activities, not simply commissioning a translation or the composition of works, but putting forth an organic concept of knowledge which would extend to all the fields of his cultural activities, juridical, historiographical, and scientific, including the natural sciences. He also continued collecting poems for his Marian songbook, begun in 1257 and which would continue to grow into various collections to the end of his days. We should also not exclude that in this same period he compiled a Galician-Portuguese songbook of profane poetry, which sadly has not come down to us. For Filgueira Valverde, "This activity, unified as a concept but varied in its directions, is not a compensatory derivation of his political misadventures, but rather, the most definitive aspect of royal politics, the only achievement of his program. For every work was determined both by an individual desire to know, systematize, and give to others the results, which through a complex we could symbolize with highly charged words, in 'Toledanism' and the 'Charlemagnism' of Alfonso X."[4]

It is not our purpose here to arrive at medical conclusions founded on a certain clinical diagnosis that we do not have sufficient data or adequate qualifications to evaluate. The purpose of this chapter is to examine what precious little historical sources and Alfonso's works themselves tell us about his illnesses, to determine to what point some crucial decisions may have been influenced by them, but also to illustrate how during long periods of illness and convalescence he withdrew from the bustle of public life to devote himself to his literary passion. As his nephew and admirer, don Juan Manuel, points out, it was to these that he devoted "much time to studying the subjects about which he wanted to compose his books, for which purpose he spent a year or two in some places and sometimes more, and according to those who

---

[4] *Las Cantigas de Santa María*, Madrid: Castalia, Odres Nuevos, p. XIX.

lived from his favor, whoever wanted could speak with him, whenever they wanted and whenever he wanted, and in such a way he had time to study what he wanted on his own and even to supervise and finish the works of knowledge he commissioned from learned men and teachers he had at his court for this purpose."[5] Don Juan Manuel also reports that his uncle learned to use his time in these activities from Ovid, confirming how he practiced the ideal of the man-of-letters.

2. *The Testimony of the* Cantigas

Since this chapter focuses on several *cantigas* and specifically on the topics of illness and literary creation, I would first like to discuss the transcendental meaning of Alfonso's prime poetic work as a personal historical testimony of the first topic (illness) and as an artistic manifestation of the second (literary creation).

The *Cantigas de Santa María*, containing 420 compositions and 2400 miniatures, constitute the richest Marian songbook of the entire Middle Ages and "the most important musical repertoire in European medieval lyric poetry."[6] The *Cantigas* are preserved in four lavish manuscripts most probably composed for the royal chambers and for the king's personal use and that of his court. The first of these manuscripts, the codex known as *To*, from the Toledo Cathedral (number 103–23), today housed in the National Library in Madrid (number 10.069) and written in a beautiful 13th-century French script, contains the first 100 poems in the collection; it does not contain any miniatures.

The second is the codex *E*, from the Monastery at El Escorial (number j.b.2), also known as "Códice princeps" (Princeps codex) or "Códice de los músicos" (Codex of the musicians) because of its miniatures depicting musicians and musical instruments. It is the only complete copy of the *Cantigas*, with 401 songs and 41 miniatures, including also the notation for musical performance. The distribution

---

[5] *Crónica abreviada*, Prólogo, in J.M. Blecua, *Obras completas*, 2 vols. Madrid: Gredos, 1983, II, pp. 575–576. See the commentary to the eulogy of Alfonso by don Juan Manuel in M. Alvar, "Alfonso contemplado por don Juan Manuel," in *La literatura en la época de Sancho IV (Actas del Congreso Internacional "La Literatura en la época de Sancho IV," Alcalá de Henares, 21–24 de febrero de 1994)*, Universidad de Alcalá, 1996, pp. 91–106.

[6] H. Anglés, *La música de las Cantigas de Santa María del rey Alfonso el Sabio.*
Facsímil, transcripción y estudio crítico, 4 vols., Barcelona: Diputación Provincial, 1943–1964; II, p. 11.

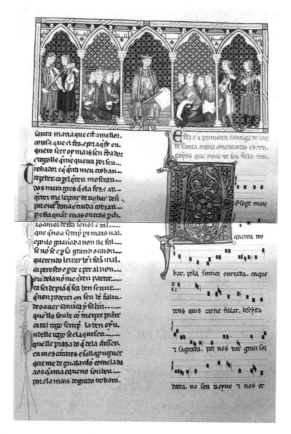

1. King Alfonso sitting with an open book directs a group of singers and musicians in front of a small audience. The Manuscript contains both text and music. Códice de los músicos, Bibl. Escorial, Ms.b.I.2, fol. 29r.

is one miniature per every ten *cantigas de loor* (of praise) plus one of presentation in the fol. 29r which fills the space of the two columns in which the folios are divided (see the reproduction in illustration 1). In this miniature there are five ogive-shaped arches supported by columns. Alfonso is seated in the middle arch, wearing a golden crown, mantle, and shoes. In the arch to the left of the king, there are four men, who are about to sing lyrics written on a parchment they have in their hands, and in the one to the right, there are four women who attend the concert. In the arches on the far ends, there are two musicians with string instruments known as *vihuelas de arco* (bow citherns) and *vihuelas de péñola* (plectrum citherns). In the miniatures inserted every ten cantigas appear one or two musicians playing *vihuelas de arco*, tubas, timpani and other instruments. In the last folio of the codex (361v), in a smaller italic script, appears the phrase "Virgen bien auenturada / ser de mi remembrada / Johannes gundisalui" ["Most blessed Virgin / remember me / Juan González"]. This was indeed the copyist of the manuscript, Juan González.

The third manuscript is codex *T*, in the Library at El Escorial (number T.j.1), known as "Códice rico," and although incomplete, it is considered the most important from the point of view of the miniatures. It is made up of 256 pages of parchment in the elegant French script of 13th-century codices. Originally it contained 200 *cantigas*, but the loss of some folios has reduced the count to 195. This codex was lavishly illustrated with 1257 miniatures in 210 folios. Only one of the illustrations is divided in eight vignettes (the one belonging to the first *cantiga*), while the others all have six. Two of these miniatures portray important aspects of Alfonso X's life and cultural activities. The first one is in fol. 4v and it fills up the entire first column (see illustration 2). Under an ogive-shaped arch supported by two columns, the king is seated with a parchment in his hand with the inscription "Because composing songs is an art which requires great understanding, therefore he who undertakes it must have this quality" (*Songs of Holy Mary*, p. 2), which are the words that begin Prologue B. There are three singers in each of the side arches, four holding parchments in their hands. The second miniature is in fol. 5r where the king is also represented seated under a central arch, with an open book on a table, and in the adjoining arches two scribes write the *cantigas* the king is dictating to them. The writing shows letters on a musical staff. In the last arch, to the right of the king, stand three musicians with *vihuelas de arco* and *vihuelas de péñola*; and in the left one, there are four singers with tonsure (see illustration 3).

Finally, in codex *F* at the Nacional Library in Florence (Banco Rari, 20), there are 131 parchment folios with late 13th-century script, currently containing 104 *cantigas*. Apparently, it originally had 166 folios and 200 *cantigas* in total, which means that many of the poems and illustrations have been lost. In this codex too Alfonso appears in fol. 1r in a miniature divided in two scenes, in which he is represented in the act of instilling in the faithful the cult and devotion of Mary (see illustration 4). The structure of the illustrations is a bit different than in other codices: here, apparently each *cantiga* had to be followed by its respective illustration, laid out in one or two pages (only the illustrations to *cantigas* 22, 35, 45, 51, and 103 span two pages, but according to some scholars every tenth one was supposed to have two).

2. Alfonso reading from a roll dictates to his scribes the text of the first *cantiga* which begins: "Because composing songs is an art that requires great understanding...". Códice Rico, Bibl. Escorial, Ms. T.I.1, fol. 4v, Cantiga 1, Prólogo A.

It was thus an impressive project that was not completed. Many miniatures have been lost and others were never finished. In fact, only 48 folios have the complete miniatures. Others only have the frame of the vignette. Still others contain only the design of the heads of the figures, while in some cases there is a complete miniature but the *cantiga* has been lost (as is the case of *Cantiga* 235, fol. 71bis, which we will discuss below). All this was the result of mutilations suffered by the codex.[7]

---

[7] The codices are described by A. Paz y Melia in the edition *Cantigas de Santa María de Don Alfonso el Sabio*, ed. L. de Cueto, Marqués de Valmar, Madrid: Real Academia de la Historia, 1889; pp. [35]–[41]; H. Anglés, *La música*, II, pp. 16–31;

3. A young king Alfonso in great splendor gets ready to perform a *Cantiga*.
Códice Rico, Bibl. Escorial, Ms. T.I.1, fol. 5v, Cantiga 1, Prólogo B.

Some scholars argue that El Escorial's "Códice rico" and the Florentine
one were part of one work that was to contain 200 *cantigas* in two
volumes, "accompanied each by a full-page miniature in a system of
six small vignettes around a single frame. In most of the miniatures,
the iconography sticks to an illustration of the *cantiga* narrated in the
successive frames".[8] But as we said, this project remained unfinished,
and successive mutilations and other calamities have left these codices

---

G. Menéndez Pidal, "Los manuscritos de las *Cantigas de Santa Maria*: Cómo se elaboró
la miniatura alfonsí," *BRAE*, 150 (1962), pp. 23–51; M. López Serrano, *Cantigas de
Santa María de Alfonso X el Sabio, rey de Castilla*, Madrid: Patrimonio Nacional, 1974;
N. Aita, *O codice florentino das Cantigas do rey Alfonso, o Sabio*, Rio de Janeiro, 1922;
A. Garcia Solalinde, "El códice florentino de las *Cantigas de Santa María* y su relación
con los demás manuscritos," *RFE*, 5 (1918), pp. 143–179; J. Guerrero Lovillo, J., *Las
Cantigas de Santa María del rey Alfonso X el Sabio. Estudio arqueológico de sus min-
iaturas*, 2 vols., Madrid, 1949; C. Scarborough, "A Summary of the Research on the
Miniatures of the *Cantigas de Santa María*," *BC*, 1 (1987), pp. 41–50.

[8] A. Domínguez, "Imágenes de un rey trovador de Santa María (Alfonso X en las
Cantigas de Santa María)," in *Il Medio Oriente e l'Occidente nell'Arte del XIII secolo*,
Bologna: Hans Belting, 1982, p. 237; G. Menéndez Pidal, "Los manuscritos de las
Cantigas de Santa María," pp. 23–51.

4. Alfonso shows his courtiers how the doors of Heaven are opened by the intercession of Mary. Codex F, Library of Florence, Ms. Banco Rari 20, fol. 1r, Cantiga 1.

(especially the Florentine) in a state that is only a pale shadow of the splendid work conceived to be used by the most learned and liberal king of the Middle Ages.

The *Cantigas de Santa María* and the *Setenario*, it has been argued, are the only two works written personally by Alfonso X.[9] His direct and personal participation in both has to be assumed in terms of the topic selection, in the composition of the lyrics and music as well as in the revision and correction, which, as we will see, he continued until his death.[10] However, we should also recognize that the collection of Marian poems, composed in various stages and throughout a period of some thirty years, does not have the stylistic coherence that would point to a single author. Chiefly, the quality of the composition and

---

[9] W. Mettmann, one of the major experts in the *Cantigas*, affirms that "it is the only work not written in Castilian, and it is above all, his most personal one," *Cantigas de Santa María*, ed. W. Mettmann, 3 vols., Madrid: Castalia, 1986–1989, I, p. 8. All citations from the *Cantigas*, unless otherwise noted, are quoted from this edition.

[10] There is proof everywhere of these direct interventions. In the *cantigas* 27, 31, 59, 60, 74, 77, and 81 of the *To* codex, which contains the first collection of 100 poems, there are some marginal corrections and additions in a small italic script attributed to Alfonso X. In the "Códice rico" at El Escorial, on fol. 85, there is another note in italic script similar to the one in the *To*. Cf. W. Mettmann, *Cantigas*, I, pp. 27 and 29 and the cited *cantigas*.

poetic technique, which can vary greatly from one *cantiga* to another, is what betrays a multiplicity of authors.[11] Next to nothing is known about the participation of collaborators in the *Setenario*, as we will see at the end of this chapter; if we take into account that it was probably also composed in two different periods, it seems logical to assume the collaboration of numerous specialists.

The topic of numerous collaborators in the *Cantigas*, excluding for the moment the acquisition of material, focuses in two main areas of expertise: doctrine or theology and poetics. The Franciscan Fr. Juan Gil de Zamora, Alfonso's confessor, is thought to have collaborated in the first. We know Alfonso commissioned him to write *Officium Almiflue Virginis* in honor of the Virgin, and perhaps also *Liber Mariae*, where he gathers 70 of Mary's miracles, 50 of which coincide with the ones narrated in the *Cantigas*. This seems to indicate his collaboration in the selection of themes as well as in the active composition of the poems.[12] Fr. Gil himself tells us he wrote a *Liber de miraculis Almiflue Virginis*, which has not come down to us.[13] Apparently he also wrote "Leyendas de los Santos" (Legends of the Saints), a topic that Alfonso was interested in as material for the sixth part of the *General Estoria*.[14] In the *Cantigas* too there's a new spirituality disseminated mainly by the Franciscans, and it is believed it was Fr. Gil, a Franciscan disciple of St. Bonaventure in Paris, who introduced it in the court and in Alfonso's *scriptorium*. Given his musical skill, it is highly probable that he also participated in composing the music for the *Cantigas*, as the eulogy of

---

[11] Cf. W. Mettmann: *Cantigas de Santa María*, I, p. 17. Regarding the endpoints for the composition of the *Cantigas*, we can say they go from 1257, when Alfonso assumed the title "King of the Romans" (Prologue A, l. 17), until 1281, when the last historically datable event appears in *Cantiga* 386 (cf. E. Procter, *Alfonso of Castile: Patron of Literature and Learning*, Oxford: Clarendon Press, 1951, pp. 42–45).

[12] Cf. F. Fita, "Cincuenta leyendas por Gil de Zamora combinadas con las *Cantigas* de Alfonso el Sabio," *BRAH*, 7 (1886), pp. 54–144; J. Filgueira Valverde, *Cantigas de Santa María*, Madrid: Castalia, Odres Nuevos, p. XXXI; M.R. Vílchez, M.R.: "El *Liber Mariae* de Gil de Zamora," *Eidos: Cuadernos de la Institución Teresiana*, 1 (1954), pp. 9–43.

[13] Cf. *De preconiis Hispanie*, ed. M. de Castro y Castro, O.F.M., Madrid, 1955, p. LXXXIII.

[14] See the work of M. Díaz y Díaz, "Tres compiladores latinos en el ambiente de Sancho IV," in *La literatura en la época de Sancho IV (Actas del Congreso Internacional "La literatura en la época de Sancho IV," Alcalá de Henares, 21–24 de febrero de 1994)*, eds. C. Alvar and J.M. Lucía Megías, Universidad de Alcalá, 1996, pp. 35–52, esp. pp. 46–49. The article deals precisely with Fr. Bernardo de Brihuega, Fr. Rodrigo de Cerrato and Fr. Juan Gil de Zamora.

his commissioner says: "He also composed in the manner of King David many and very beautiful songs in honor of the Virgin, accompanying them with many adequate and well-proportioned melodies."[15] Fr. Gil was indeed very familiar with the music of the *Cantigas*, probably because he was the author of many of their melodies, but, as we can expect from the quoted passage, following the concept of authorship at the time, their composition is attributed to the commissioner of the work.

Also in the theological realm, Alfonso must have received a great contribution from the distinguished 13th-century hagiographer, Bernardo de Brihuega, court clergyman who collected codices for his king and wrote *Gestae et vitae sanctorum* (h. 1256–1260). El Briocano, as he was known, along with the Dominican Rodrigo de Cerrato, known as *el Cerratense*, also author of a collection of *Vitae sanctorum*, were also in charge of collecting and composing hagiographical texts that Alfonso meant to include in his great work, *General Estoria*.[16]

In the second area, poetics, the number of collaborators must have been much higher. There were many Galician-Portuguese poets that frequented the court of the Learned King, whose names and poetic features have already been identified by R. Menéndez Pidal, J. Filgueira Valverde, J. Montoya, and other scholars.[17] Within this group of autochthonous poets, Walter Mettmann notes the presence of one troubadour, who, on account of his style, must have been responsible for the greater part of the *Cantigas*: "Although it's untenable that the *Cantigas* are an individual work, it is however probable that the majority of poems maybe owed to a single person and that the number of authors was not more than half a dozen."[18] Mettmann believes he can identify this main collaborator as the Santiago cleric Airas

[15] In F. Fita, "Biografías de San Fernando y de Alfonso el Sabio por Gil de Zamora," *BRAH*, V (1885), p. 321. See the edition of his treatise *Liber de musica*, ed. M. Gerbet, in *Scriptores ecclesiastici de musica sacra*, II, Saint-Blaise, 1784, pp. 370–393; and see R. Mota Murillo, "El *Ars musica* de Juan Gil de Zamora. El Ms. H/29 dell'Archivio Capitolare Vaticano," in *Archivo Iberoamericano*, 42 (1982), pp. 651–701.

[16] Cf. M. Díaz y Díaz, "Tres compiladores latinos en el ambiente de Sancho IV"; and the extensive bibliography in the Castilian version of this work.

[17] R. Menéndez Pidal, *Poesía juglaresca y juglares*, p. 81 and ff; J. Filgueira Valverde, *Alfonso X el Sabio. Cantigas de Santa María*, Madrid: Castalia, Odres Nuevos, 1985, pp. XXX–XXXIV; y J. Montoya, *Alfonso X el Sabio. Cantigas*, Madrid: Cátedra, 1988, pp. 22–27.

[18] W. Mettmann, *Cantigas de Santa María*, I, p. 18.

Nunes, whose name, the only one, appears between the two columns of *Cantiga* 223.[19]

In the early seventies, the famous Provençal troubadour Guiraut Riquier (1270/71) arrived and stayed until 1279.[20] Along with Riquier, a great admirer of Alfonso and to whom he dedicated a flattering eulogy,[21] arrived also many other Provençal poets who, fleeing the war against the Albigensians and Charles of Anjou's harsh repression, sought refuge at Alfonso's court.[22] His influence in the poetics of the *Cantigas* and in the Alfonsian lyric in general, including profane poetry, perhaps is greater than acknowledged. It has already been pointed out, for instance, that *Cantiga* 349 is an imitation of the *aubade* by the Provenzal troubadour Cadenet.[23] Despite being surrounded by Galician-Portuguese troubadours, Alfonso always showed a marked preference for Provenzal poets. In a famous satirical poem, debating with Pero da Ponte, a minstrel at his court and previously his father's court, he accuses him "Vós non trobades come proençal, / mais come Bernaldo de Bonaval; / por ende non é trobar natural, / pois que o del e do Dem' aprendestes" ("You do not write poetry the Provenzal way, but rather like Bernardo de Bonaval; therefore is not natural poetry-writing, for you learned it from him and from the Devil.")[24] This accusation of the famous minstrel may have to do not only with the new Provenzal poetic technique, but also with the fact that, apparently, Pero da Ponte was a supporter of the House of Haro,

---

[19] *Cantigas*, I, p. 20; cf. Mettmann, "Airas Nunes, Mitautor der '*CSM*'?," *Iberorromania*, 3 (1971), pp. 8–10.

[20] Cf. V. Beltrán, "Los trovadores en la corte de Castilla (II): Alfonso X, Guiraut Riquier y Pero da Ponte," *Romania*, 76 (1987), 230–247.

[21] Cf. V. Bertolucci Pizzorusso, "La supplica di Guirault Riquier e la risposta di Alfonso X di Castiglia," *Studi Mediolatini e Volgari*, XIV (1966), pp. 9–135; and Ballesteros, *Alfonso X*, p. 815; E. Vuolo, "Per il testo della supplica di Guiraut Riquier ad Alfonso X," *Studi Medievali*, 3rd series, IX (1968), pp. 376–394.

[22] Cf. A. Jeanroy, *La poésie lyrique des troubadours*, 2 vols., Paris, 1934, vol. I, p. 186; I. Frank, "Les troubadours et le Portugal," in *Mélanges d'études portugaises à M. Georges Le Gentil*, Lisboa, 1949, pp. 199–200; M. de Riquer, *Los trovadores. Historia literaria y textos*, 3 vols. Barcelona, 1975, III, pp. 1556–1564; A. Gier, "Alphonse le Savant, poète lyrique et mécène des troubadours," in *Court and Poet* (Selected Proceedings of the Third Congress of the International Courtly Literature Society), ed. G.S. Burgess, Liverpool: Francis Cairs, 1981, pp. 155–165; C. Alvar, *Poesía trovadoresca en España y Portugal*, Madrid: Cupsa, 1977, pp. 181–258. V. Beltrán, "Los trovadores en la corte de Castilla," pp. 235–242.

[23] Cf. H. Spanke in I. Anglés, *La música de las Cantigas*, III. 1, pp. 216–217.

[24] In M. Rodrigues Lapa, *Cantigas d'escarhno e de mal dizer dos cancioneiros medievais galego portugueses*, Coimbra: Editorial Galaxia, 1970, no. 17, p. 30.

as it is hinted at in other satirical poems that go beyond satire and other poetic games played at by court poets.[25] The Provenzal influence in Alfonsine poetry is clearly seen in the several versification schemes used in the *Cantigas* where two-thirds (306 cantigas) follow the *virelai* (AA/bbba), which was typical of Occitan poetry. However, there are also many examples of *rondel* (*rondeaux*), where the stanza is composed of three lines in unison, alternating with one of the lines of the refrain. There are also some "ballads" (no. 10) and other zéjel-like stanzas (nos. 4 and 40).[26]

Alfonso must have been helped by many of these Galician-Portuguese and Provenzal poets, both in collecting materials as well as in the composition and poetic expression techniques.[27] There's proof of this teamwork in the *Cantigas* themselves, where there are expressions such as "quero que seja colocado" ["I shall have this miracle placed"][28] (in the cantiga 219 referring to a miracle), or "e fez tod' est escrebir" ["and had all this written down"][29] (*cantiga* 295). In other cases, collaboration involved the performance of the *Cantiga*: "E desto cantar fezemos que cantassen os jograres" ["And we ordered that this song be sung by the troubadours"].[30] The miniatures also offer clear examples of the Alfonsine team working in the *scriptorium* under the king's supervision.[31]

[25] Cf. F.R. Holliday, "The Relations Between Alfonso X and Pero da Ponte," *Revista da Faculdade de Letras*, Lisboa, 3a Serie, IV (1970), pp. 25–37; S. Panunzio, "Le poesie storiche. Rapporti poetici tra Pero da Ponte e Alfonso X," in his ed. of *Pero da Ponte. Poesie*, Biblioteca di Filologia Romanza, X, Bari: Adriatica Editrice, 1959.

[26] Cf. Cf. V. Beltrán, "Los trovadores en la corte de Castilla (II)," p. 238; and his studies on poetics "Rondel y refram intercalat en la lírica gallego-portuguesa," *Studi mediolatini e volgari*, XXX (1984), pp. 69–90; and "La balada provenzal en la poesía gallego-portuguesa," in *La lengua y la literatura en tiempos de Alfonso X*, pp. 79–90; see also D.C. Clarke, "Versification in Alfonso el Sabio's 'Cantigas,'" *Hispanic Review* XXIII (1955), pp. 67–78.

[27] Cf. G. Bertoni, "Alfonso X di Castiglia e il provenzalismo della prima lirica portughese," *Archivum Romanicum*, VII (1923), pp. 75–87.

[28] *Songs of Holy Mary of Alfonso X, The Wise: A Translation of the* Cantigas de Santa Maria, trans. Kathleen Kulp-Hill, Tempe, Arizona: Arizona Center for Medieval and Renaissance Studies, 2000, p. 263. All translations of the *Cantigas*, unless otherwise indicated, come from this work.

[29] *Songs of Holy Mary*, cantiga 295, p. 358.

[30] In the *Cantiga* 284 and less so in *Cantigas* 64, 188, and 206 he describes the compilation and writing process which is also very similar to the one described by D. Catalán in the case of the historiographic works ("El taller historiográfico alfonsí. -Métodos y problemas en el trabajo compilatorio-," *R*, 89, 1963, pp. 354–375).

[31] The most prominent example in the miniature in codex *TJ1*, fol. 4v and fol. 5r (illustrations 2 and 3). Life and the cultural activities in Alfonso's court are described

But along with these *cantigas*, there are others, especially profane ones, which exhibit Alfonso's most personal production. Today few scholars would deny that at least the *cantigas* written in the first person were penned by Alfonso himself, as the expressions he uses reveal: "que eu compuse" ["which I composed"[32]], "que eu fiz" ["which I commissioned"], "que hei de fazer" ["that I have worked on"], "Pois cen cantares feitos acabei e con son" ["Later I finished one hundred songs with their music"].[33] Alfonso is so sincere about this that he even confesses at some point that he prayed to the Virgin so he could narrate one miracle without help from others:

> Porend' un miragre vos direi muy grande
> que Santa Maria fez; e ela mande
> que mostra-lo posa per mi e non ande
> demandand' a outre que m'en dé recado. (65, 5–8);

> [Concerning this, I shall tell you a great miracle which Holy Mary performed. She commands that I tell it myself, without asking anyone else for assistance.][34]

while elsewhere (at least once), Alfonso claims the work, including the music, is entirely his ("con son meu"):

> Desto direi un miragre / que en Tudia aveo
> e porrei-o con os outros, / ond' un gran livro e cheo
> de que fiz cantiga nova / con son meu, ca non alleo
> que fez a que nos / amostra/por ir a Deus muitas vias. (347, 5–8)

> [Concerning this, I shall tell a miracle which happened in Tudia and shall put it with the others which fill a great book. I made a new song about it with music of my own and no one else's. She who shows us many ways to find God performed it.][35]

---

by an exceptional witness, his nephew, don Juan Manuel, as a place teeming with artists and scholars entirely devoted to the study of "the sciences of knowledge" (the "seven liberal arts"), cf. *Crónica abreviada*, en *Obras Completas*, ed. J.M. Blecua, Madrid: Gredos, 1983, vol. II, pp. 78–100.

[32] *Songs of Holy Mary*, cantiga 47, p. 263.
[33] *Songs of Holy Mary*, *Petición* [Petition], in T100, p. 482.
[34] *Songs of Holy Mary*, cantiga 65, p. 83.
[35] *Songs of Holy Mary*, cantiga 347, p. 422.

Internal features and content also indicate that other *cantigas* written in the third person were nevertheless also entirely (text and music)
composed by Alfonso.[36]

So, despite collaboration, scholars hold that a great part of the *Cantigas* was composed by Alfonso himself. Hence, just as a careful reading
of the historical works, particularly the *General Estoria*, reveals unexpected personal and clearly autobiographical allusions, many *cantigas*
also contain personal and intimate details that could only have been
written or dictated by Alfonso. These details involve not only political
issues (the quest for empire, the revolt of the nobles, the rebelliousness
of the king of Granada, the invasion of the North African Moors, the
ungratefulness and betrayal of his relatives), but also personal issues
such as his illnesses, physical and psychological suffering, included in
the *Cantigas*, just as in the historical works, through the rewriting of
myths (such as the commentary on Ovid quoted at the beginning of
this chapter). But this tracking method would take us too far in the
exploration of a reflection of the Learned King's personality in his
work, and would go beyond the limits of this chapter that seeks mostly
historical facts and not an exploration of hidden corners of his work
where Alfonso's life and thought could be explored, going beyond the
goals of the present work.

Given the testimonial value and autobiographical content noted
by scholars in the *Cantigas*, we will focus on Alfonso's life, analyzing these texts for what they reveal of his personality, illnesses, and
profound psychological crises created by adversity in his personal and
public dealings. We will attempt to determine how the mental conditions brought about by these situations affected his ability to govern
and his cultural project.

The personal nature of the *Cantigas* is indeed the clearest and only
proof that Alfonso suffered many serious illnesses. But as lyrical poetry,
they leave the historian with serious doubts about their imaginary
nature. What is the historical value of statements in a poetic work such

---

[36] The great defender of Alfonso's authorship of most of the *Cantigas* has been
J.T. Snow in a series of well-documented articles, among which: "Alfonso X: sus 'Can-
tigas…' Apuntes para su (auto)biografía literaria," in *Josep María Solá-Solé: Homage,
Homenaje, Homenatge (Miscelanea de estudios de amigos y discípulos)*, ed. A. Tor-
res-Alcalá, Barcelona: Puvill Libros, S.A., 1984, pp. 79–89; "Alfonso as Troubadour:
The Fact and the Fiction," in R.I. Burns, *Emperor of Culture*, pp. 124–140. See also
J. García Varela, "La función ejemplar de Alfonso X en las cantigas personales," *BC*,
4 spring (1992), pp. 3–16.

as the *Cantigas*? The topic, which was not much discussed by his early biographers, has been much debated by current scholars. The common opinion is that his poetic works reveal historical reality in images and words much more faithfully than the documents themselves. Thus, there are specialists in the *Cantigas*, such as J. Snow, who argue "it may be said the *Cantigas* precede the most perfect 'biographies' of Dante's *Vita nuova* and Petrarch's *Canzoniere*;"[37] and J.E. Keller says about *Cantiga* 209 in the Florentine codex, that it is "autobiographical writing" when it pictorially and poetically tells of Alfonso's healing by the Virgin in Vitoria.[38]

The *Cantigas* are thus an invaluable historical source to learn about certain aspects of Alfonso's personal life, such as the illnesses he suffered. The fact that the king would deal with his illnesses in his most personal work can be a clue for gathering important clinical data, which, along with forensic analysis, may help us understand the general conditions of his physical and mental health, and the probable causes of his death.

Scholars note *Cantigas* 200, 209, 235, 279, 366, and 367 as indispensable sources to reconstruct certain episodes in Alfonso's life when he was afflicted by very serious ailments.[39] The fact that the events narrated in *Cantiga* 235 follow a strict chronological order is proof that the episode effectively took place on the date and in the manner that

---

[37] "Self-Conscious Reference and the Organic Narrative Pattern of the *Cantigas de Santa Maria* of Alfonso X," *Medieval, Renaissance and Folklore Studies in Honor of John Estern Keller*, Newark, 1980, pp. 53–66, p. 66. Cf. J.F. O'Callaghan, "Image and Reality: The King Creates His Kingdom," in Burns, *Emperor of Culture*, pp. 14–32.

[38] "Iconography and Literature: Alfonso Himself in *Cantiga* 209," *Hisp.*, 66 (1983), pp. 348–352; cf. J.E. Keller and R.P. Kinkade, *Iconography in Medieval Spanish Literature*, Lexington: University of Kentucky Press, 1983. The great specialist of the life and works of the Learned King, Evelyn Procter, who has studied the *Cantigas* from a historian's point of view, says about *cantiga* 235, which we are focusing on here:

> [...] it might more justly be described as the king's complaint of the treachery of his nobles and his own difficulties, disappointments, and illnesses, for it is only after a long catalogue of woes and in the seventeenth stanza that we reach the king's illness at Valladolid. Every incident given can be identified and dated, and the poem provides an historical epitome from 1272 to 1278. (*Alfonso X of Castile: Patron of Literature and Learning*, Oxford: Clarendon Press, 1951, pp. 37–38; in her panoramic view of Alfonso's oeuvre, she deals with the *Cantigas* on pp. 24–46.)

On the *Cantigas* as historical document, there is today a vast bibliography that can be consulted in the Spanish version of this book.

[39] For the dates of the *cantigas* in question, all composed between 1272 and 1279, see E. Procter, *Alfonso X el Sabio*, pp. 37–40.

other historical sources also reveal. In fact, in many other cases, the *Cantiga* is more reliable than the historical documents.

The second aspect of this chapter, literary creation, can also be discussed in light of these *cantigas*, especially *Cantiga* 235, for it contains a synthesis of Alfonso's physical ailments and personal misfortunes (as well as in the kingdom) between 1269 and 1278 which chronologically match key dates in his literary, juridical, and historical production.

3. *Marian Devotion and the* Cantigas

Marian devotion is a religious practice that goes back to the beginnings of Christianity, but spread widely throughout Europe at the end of the 12th and throughout the 13th century with the growth of mendicant orders. A literary consequence of this devotion was the compilation of large volumes of miracles of the Virgin Mary in vernacular, both in poetry (Adgar, 1190–1200; Gautier de Coinci, 1177–1236; Berceo, 1240–1250), and in prose, mainly in Latin (Vicente de Beauvais, *Speculum historiale*; a. 1264; Gil de Zamora, *Liber Mariae*, 1275).[40]

Historical criticism, particularly the history of the miniatures in the *Cantigas*, has changed radically since H. Guerrero Lovillo wrote in his influential work, *Las Cantigas. Estudio arqueológico de sus miniaturas* (Madrid, 1949), that the art of the *Cantigas* ignores "[...] the speculations of theologians and is wholly indifferent to mystics [...] They are far from the intricate concepts of theologians. A charming simplicity and ingenuousness transpires in the entire work, from both the artistic and literary points of view [...] This is an entirely lay art despite being a religious songbook" (p. 25). Nowadays there are not many scholars who agree with H. Guerrero Lovillo. On the contrary, recent studies show the *Cantigas* are permeated by a profound and innovative, complex and conceptually refined theological thought.

At the root of Marian devotion manifested in the *Cantigas* are several theological-biblical concepts that underlie the widespread popular devotion to Mary in the 13th Century. One concept is *compassio* and

---

[40] Cf. J.A. Sánchez Pérez, *El culto mariano en España*, Madrid: CSIC, 1943; J. Montoya Martínez, *Las colecciones de milagros de la Virgen en la Edad Media (El milagro literario)*, Universidad de Granada, Colección Filológica XXIX, 1981; L.A. Ruiz y Ruiz, "Gonzalo de Berceo y Alfonso X el Sabio: los 'Milagros de Nuestra Señora' y las 'Cantigas'," *Universidad de San Carlos*, XXIV (1951), pp. 35–75.

co-redemptio.[41] Mary enjoys extraordinary powers of intercession not only because she is the Redeemer's mother, but also because she is the Co-redeemer. This concept derives from the doctrine of Mary as universal mediator of all graces, laid out eloquently by Saint Bernard in his celebrated sermon on Mary's nativity (*De Aqueductu*). Bernard says Mary is the channel through which the waters of grace reach us, for God wants us to obtain everything though Mary. Between Christ and sinful mortals stands Mary as intermediary. She intercedes before the Son and the Son before the Father. The Son listens to his Mother and the Father to his Son: "If the divine Majesty frightens you, seek Mary [...] She is the ladder of sinners."[42]

The idea of an intermediary mediator is iconographically accompanied by a new concept in 13th-century spirituality disseminated mostly by the Franciscans. They preached the idea of Christ's humanity in all its manifestations, from the re-enactment of the Nativity by Saint Francis in Greggio, to the flagellation and crucifixion scenes by Giotto and Cimabue.[43] Franciscan preaching and mysticism are centered on Christ's suffering and redemptive death and the parallel passion of his mother.[44] A new sensibility towards Christ's more human aspects, such as his childhood, suffering and death is thus disseminated, together with the participation of the Mother in all the phases of the Son's life. The *Cantigas* portray this spirituality in an extraordinary way. Images

---

[41] This topic has been addressed by A. Domínguez, " 'Compassio' y 'Co-redemptio' en las *Cantigas de Santa María*. Crucifixión y Juicio final," *Archivo Español de Arte*, no. 281 (1998), pp. 17–35. The topic of "compassio Mariae," or the passion of Mary, parallel to that of her Son, had a long theological tradition when Alfonso takes it up in his Marian songbook. The expression was coined by Saint Bernard of Claraval (1090–1153).

[42] San Bernardo, *Obras completas*, IV, Madrid: BAC, 1986, pp. 425–427; and in P. Perdrizet, *La Vierge de Misericorde. Étude d'un thème iconographique*, Paris, 1908, pp. 237–252.

[43] I'm not sure how this news reached the Alfonsiene *scriptorium*, but in *Cantiga* 1, vignette 2, there is a beautiful representation of the Nativity which could be clearly related to the re-enactment of the event by Saint Francis at Greggio. Cf. M. Chico Picaza, *Composición pictórica en el códice rico de las Cantigas de Santa María*, Madrid, 1987.

[44] Alfonso learned about the new Franciscan spirituality through *Meditationes vitae Christi*, preserved in a 14th century manuscript, a key text attributed to Saint Bonaventure (1221–1274). How this text or a precursor or derivation of it arrived at Alfonso's court is unclear, but it is certain it was known. It was probably brought to Spain by the Franciscan Fr. Juan Gil de Zamora, considered by some as the author of the *cantigas decenales* and who studied in Paris, perhaps as a disciple of St. Bonaventure himself.

of Christ crucified and the Virgin who accompanies him in his passion, suffering with him, were familiar in Alfonso's court. As part of
this tender Franciscan humanity, Mary as co-redeemer and mediator
appears in a scene as dramatic as the Final Judgment, showing her
bare breast to the Son to indicate her participation in the Redemption
though the act of breastfeeding him. All these *cantigas* exude this new
spirituality made of a human affection profoundly lived by the protagonists of the Redemption's iconography.

These theological concepts and new spirituality may be expressed
in several *cantigas* with "simplicity" and "ingenuousness," according
to Guerrero Lovillo, but no less effectively through poetry, image, and
music. I would like to quote only two *cantigas* that make direct reference
to Christ's passion and crucifixion, two of the prime moments of the
Redemption process, namely, *Cantiga 50* and 140, where the concepts
of "Redemption" and "Co-redemption" are dramatically visualized.

Vignette 4, in *Cantiga 50*, depicts Mary as was customary in medieval
iconography—next to the cross (as sung in the popular hymn *Stabat
Mater dolorosa / iuxta crucem lachrimosa*), while her son, still alive, is
being nailed by the executioners to the erect cross (illustration 5)—
and also on her knees, keeled over by pain, embracing the cross and
the feet of her son (illustration 6). As Ana Domínguez reminds us, this
image, unprecedented in the history of art, and the equally unique one
in vignette 5 of *Cantiga 140*, (both from Códice rico at El Escorial),
where the Virgin appears alone once again (though both depict crowds
next to the cross) embracing the cross and Christ crucified, constitute
an original representation of the theological concept of Mary as "co-
redemptrix." By embracing the cross and the Crucified Redeemer, and
accepting the divine will, Mary becomes a Co-redeemer.[45] We still do
not fully understand the relationship between the "verbal text" and the
"pictorial text" in general, and particularly in these two *cantigas*, as

---

[45] In *De septem donis Spiritus Sancti*, Saint Bonaventure (1221–1274) states that
the Virgin, at the foot of the cross, accepts the divine will, and offers the fruit of her
womb for man's Redemption. He sees in Mary the priest of the sacrifice, something
comparable to the heroic figures of Judith, and of Abraham ready to sacrifice his own
son (cfr *Opera omnia*, XXXVII, Paris, 1898, pp. 81 and 214 and ff.). Saint Albertus
Magnus (1193–1280), a contemporary of Saint Bonaventure and a teacher of Saint
Thomas Aquinas (1225–1274), had also affirmed following Saint Bernard that Christ
wanted to make his Mother a participant in the benefits of Redemption.

5. Scene from the Passion of Christ and the "Com-passion" of Mary. Vignette 4 Mary embraces the Cross, thus participating in the act of Redemption of mankind. Códice Rico, Bibl. Escorial, Ms. T.I.1, fol. 74v, Cantiga 50, vignette 4.

there does not seem to be much in common between the two. Perhaps in this case the vignette was painted before the text was composed.[46]

The participation of Mary, the new Eve, in human salvation as Co-redeemer gives her extraordinary powers over her Son, who cannot

---

[46] A. Domínguez writes: "The text of each *cantiga* of praise does not justify at all the evangelical image, because the image could be interpreted in various ways. There are no rules that explain the text-image interrelation" ("'Compassio' y 'Co-Redemptio'," p. 20, note 15). Luis Beltrán, however, thinks he can explain the images of these two *cantigas* on the basis of the texts themselves (*Las cantigas de loor de Alfonso X el Sabio. Estudio y traducción*, Madrid: Ediciones Júcar, 1990, pp. 131–133). But see the article by J.W. Marchand and S. Baldwin, "Singers of the Virgin in Thirteenth-century Spain," *Bulletin of Hispanic Studies*, LXXI (1994), 169–184; and G. Greenia, "The Politics of Piety: Manuscript Illumination and Narration in the *Cantigas de Santa Maria*," *Hispanic Review*, 61 (1993), pp. 325–344.

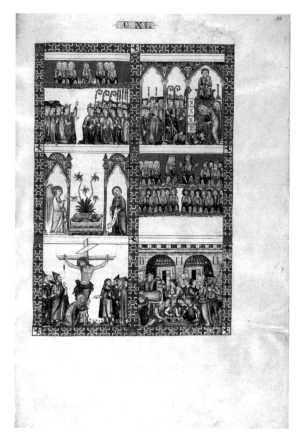

6. Mary as "co-redeemer" from the scene of the Annunciation (vignette 3) to the tragic embrace of the Crucified Son (vignette 5) and his glorification (vignette 4). The beautiful miniature begins with king Alfonso pointing to bishops and the faithful the power of mediation of Mary and ends with a scene in a tavern where drinking, gambling, and moral corruption are presided over by the Devil. Códice Rico, Bibl. Escorial, Ms. T.I.1, fol. 196r, Cantiga 140.

refuse a favor when requested via Mary.[47] The *Cantigas* also illustrate this concept in an original and dramatic way. The new Franciscan spirituality enhance religious sensibility and human emotion in the *Cantigas'* iconography, reaching new, unsuspected heights. In vignette

---

[47] On the typology Eve-Ave (Maria) there is also a beautiful song written in shorter lines (*Cantiga* 60) where Eve the sinner is contrasted with Mary the redeemer. In the sixth vignette, Mary, as the new Eve, opens the gates of Paradise through which the redeemed enter. On this cantiga, see the exhaustive study by E. Guldan, *Eva und Maria. Eine antithese als Bildmotiv*, Graz – Köln, 1966, pp. 58–59 and 178–179.

2 of *Cantiga* 50, we also find a representation of the Last Judgment (illustration 5). The artist wanted to express the concept of Mary as universal "Co-redeemer" and "Mediator" in a dramatic fashion. Christ is depicted in the center with open arms showing his wounds; to his right, kneeling but crowned as queen, the Virgin Mary opens her garments showing her Son the naked breast that fed him as an infant.

There are other *cantigas* for which no illustration has been found, and which where not copied in the "Códice rico" (such as 360, 403, and 422), where the text itself supports the doctrine of Mary's co-redemption on the basis of the breasts that fed the Redeemer. The theme of breasts and milk, with all its human associations of motherly love and tenderness, also appear in *Cantiga* 110 (the Virgin of the Milk) where Baby Jesus stops sucking for a moment, but hangs on to the Mother's breast with one hand while he caresses her with the other while angels and three female saints are watching the scene. There are many of these scenes of love and tenderness in the *Cantigas*. The sixth vignette of *Cantiga* 30, for instance, portrays Mother and Son sitting on a step, joined in a tight embrace.

All this clearly shows to what extent Alfonso and his collaborators were familiar with certain surprisingly advanced spiritual and theological currents, which, in some cases, bordered on heterodoxy or were nonconformist vis-à-vis traditional theological thought.

Considering other elements of Alfonsine culture, the presence of innovative theology on the margin of ecclesiastical institutions (as for example in the *Cantigas*, where it is Alfonso, rather than a member of the clergy, who serves as intermediary, priest or teacher between Mary and the people), leads us to conclude that Alfonso's thought, despite its dispersion in countless works, was very consistent and uniform, characterized by a lay vision of culture, even in works with high religious content. The sources and channels for these new theological-spiritual ideas still remain to be explored, but we may assume that the Franciscan Fr. Juan Gil de Zamora probably played an important role, for he, as art historian Ana Domínguez points out, had probably been in contact with Italian spiritual thinkers during his student days in Paris.[48]

---

[48] A. Domínguez, *quoted art.*, p. 24, note 30.

4. *Illness and the Miracle*

Medieval people saw healings worked by the Virgin not only as a sign
of divine favor, in a truly religious sense, but also as a literary motif, a
sufficient pretext to dedicate delicate compositions singing her praises
or, as Alfonso states in the Prologue to his *Cantigas*, to be her troubadour in love:

And that which I seek is to praise the Virgin, Mother of Our Lord,

> Holy Mary, the most wondrous of His creations. Therefore, I wish from
> this day forth to be Her troubadour, and I pray that She will have me
> for Her troubadour and accept my songs, for through them I seek to
> reveal the miracles She performed. Hence from now on I choose to sing
> for no other lady, and I think thereby to recover all that I wasted on the
> others.][49]

The second stanza clearly indicates the poetic conscience of the author,
who was ready to relinquish poetic devotion to any other woman to
sing instead the miracles of the Virgin Mary. This leads us to wonder
whether the author of the *Cantigas* was not using illness and healing as
metaphors to further emphasize Mary's power of intercession in favor
of her faithful, instead of as a narrative of real historical events. But
the historical value of the *Cantigas*, especially the more personal ones,
seems to dispel such doubts. So beyond the rhetorical use of the topics of sickness and death, for the medieval poets, as men of faith, such
miraculous events really did happen. Hence, the miracles in the *Cantigas* cannot be seen as merely a beautiful literary fiction. Death and
illness—excluding catastrophes such as plagues, earthquakes, floods,
and famines—were everyday realities that terrorized medieval people.
In a time when antibiotics were unknown and diagnoses were difficult,
disease was seen as the prelude to an imminent death, and healing,
especially when sudden, was often attributed to divine intervention.[50]

---

[49] *Songs of Holy Mary*, p. 2. On the topic of Alfonso as the Virgin's troubadour, see
J.T. Snow, "Alfonso as Troubadour: The Fact and the Fiction," in R.I. Burns, *Emperor
of Culture*, pp. 124–140; and "The Central Role of the Troubadour Persona of Alfonso
X in the *Cantigas de Santa Maria*," *Bulletin of Hispanic Studies*, LVI (1979), pp. 305–
316.

[50] As Ronald C. Finucane states, "to be ill was not a trivial matter, and to recover
from illness was not considered the usual outcome" ("The Use and Abuse of Medieval
Miracles," *History*, 60 (1975), 7–8; quoted by M. Presilla, *The Image of Death in the
Cantigas de Santa Maria of Alfonso X, el Sabio*, II, p. 473).

Recent studies have shown that medieval people did not have a clear idea of the degree of seriousness of an illness. Scholars who have studied this issue for medieval England have good reason to think the majority did not know if one was dead or alive.[51] The confusion was not geographically specific; Alfonso's *Cantigas* reveal a similar situation in Spain.[52] Twenty-four *cantigas* deal with the miraculous resurrection of dead people; nine of them refer to adult resurrections (nos. 26, 45, 54, 111, 142, 144, 182, 241, and 311), and fifteen to those of children (nos. 21, 43, 76, 118, 122—dealing with Alfonso's sister Berenguela-, 133, 167, 168, 171, 197, 224, 269, 331, 347, 381). The resurrection of animals is also noted (no. 178 mentions the resurrection of a mule).[53] Statistics on child mortality were staggering: twice that of the adult population. Again, regarding the confusion between life and death, some *Cantigas* tell of cases where dead children were resurrected after three days (*Cantiga* 168), after four (*Cantiga* 347), and still one more after six days (*Cantiga* 43).[54] Commenting on *Cantiga* 235, we will suggest that at least twice, the poet seems to hint at the fact that Alfonso too was resurrected and perhaps not metaphorically.

We do not intend to contradict the popular belief in divine intervention in favor of the faithful nor the power of prayer as a potent therapeutic remedy, which some contemporary physicians have postulated. What we do want to emphasize is that healing was seen exclusively as the result of divine intervention (the ability of humans to fight off infections and be healed on their own did not spread until the Renaissance). Recovering from a serious illness in the Middle Ages was only possible thanks to the miracle of God's intervention in human life. Sometimes this grace was requested and obtained thanks to a saint's or

---

[51] Cf. Finucane, op. cit., pp. 6–7.

[52] Cf. L. García Ballester, "La circulación de las ideas médicas en la Castilla de Alfonso X el Sabio," *Revista de Occidente*, 43 (1984), pp. 85–107; and "Medical Science in Thirteenth-Century Castile: Problems and Prospects," *Bulletin of the History of Medicine*, 61 (1987), pp. 183–202.

[53] For the thematic classification of *cantigas* telling of miracles, cf. J. Filgueira Valverde, *Las Cantigas*, pp. LX–LXIII; M. Presilla, *The Image of Death in the Cantigas de Santa María*, II, p. 494, note 1.

[54] *Cantiga* 167 also tells of the resurrection of the child of a Muslim woman. This poem is decorated with an exquisite miniature where the mother and the father, dressed as pilgrims, follow a mule carrying the child's coffin on their way to the sanctuary of the Virgin of Salas, imitating what Christians did. Cf. H.S. Martínez, *Convivencia en la España del siglo XIII. Perspectivas alfonsíes*, Madrid: Ediciones Polifemo, pp. 330–331, and illustration 42.

a religious image's intervention, but above all thanks to the intercession of the Virgin Mary, which in the 13th century, under the influence
of the doctrine of Mary as Mediatrix, was sought with the conviction
that one's plea would be heard and the favor granted. Alfonso himself
dedicated many *cantigas de loor* to singing the greatness of Mary as
a helper ("ajudador") and mediator ("rezõador") between the faithful
and God (cf. for instance *Cantigas* 140, 150, 180, 310, 360, and especially 279, which we will describe below).

Considering this idea of Mary's intercessory power, in the midst of
grave illnesses that were not cured by the best physicians of the time,
a man as devout as Alfonso had to pray to Mary and implore to be
healed (*Cantiga* 279). If he recovered, he could not but attribute the
cure to a miracle worked by the Virgin. Excluding the *cantigas* narrating resurrection, 359 *cantigas* narrate miracles, twenty-five of which
involved several family members or persons closely connected to the
royal family. Five of those twenty-five tell of miracles that occurred to
Alfonso himself, and are therefore highly autobiographical.[55]

5. *Fitero in Navarra*

The first news of a serious illness of Alfonso X happened during Ibn
el-Ahmer's rebellion in the South (1263–1265), *Cantiga* 366 makes reference to this illness:

> Quand' este feito fezerom, tornaron pera Sevilla.
> E el Rei mui mal doente foi y a gran maravilla,
> mais guariu pela merçee da que é Madr[e] e Filla
> de Deus, que o guareçera ja d'outras grandes doores. (ll. 15–18)

> [when they had finished the deed, they returned to Seville. The king fell
> very seriously ill but recovered by the mercy of Her who is Mother and
> Daughter of God, who had already cured him of other great afflictions.][56]

---

[55] J.T. Snow discusses some aspects of Alfonso's autobiographical writing in the
Cantigas in "A Chapter in Alfonso X's Personal Narrative: the Puerto de Santa Maria
Poems in the *Cantigas de Santa Maria,*" *La Corónica*, VIII (1979), 10–21; C. Scarborough, "Alfonso X: A Monarch in Search of a Miracle," *KRQ*, 33 (1986), pp. 349–354;
and the work by J. O'Callaghan, *Alfonso X and the Cantigas de Santa María. A Poetic
Biography*, Brill: The Medieval Mediterranean Series, 16, Leiden-Boston-Cologne,
1998.

[56] *Songs of Holy Mary*, cantiga 366, p. 445.

Criticism generally maintains that this *cantiga* makes reference to the war Alfonso waged in 1264 against the king of Granada to crush the rebellion in the South. Upon his return from war, as the *cantiga* relates (lines 7–15), both he and his brother Manuel fell ill. Nothing is known about the nature of the illness, but the *CAX* seems to indicate that it was perhaps a depression caused by the betrayal of the king of Granada, whom Alfonso considered a faithful and firm ally. In the *cantiga*, the expression "que o guareçera ja d'outras grandes doores" [who had already cured him of other great afflictions] indicates former cures we do not know about. Based on these works, other critics maintain that *Cantiga* 366 references an event happening later than 1282, and not the rebellion of 1264. But *Cantiga* 200, which closed the second collection finished around 1274, also mentioned "great illnesses" (l. 14) in which the Virgin had helped him: "la que no yerra me ayudó en toda guerra, y no me faltó cuando la llamé...A mí me libró de desgracias, de peligro de muerte y de lesiones; de donde sabed, varones, que por ella moriré" (ll. 30–37) ["For She who does not err nor ever erred made me lord of a fine land and helped me in every war when I called on Her... She delivered me from misfortunes, death, and injury. Therefore know, good men, that I shall die for Her."][57] These can only refer to the Moorish rebellion of 1262–1264, when Alfonso was nearly assassinated in a plot against him and his family by the king of Granada (the line "She delivered me from misfortunes, death, and injury" alluded to in the *cantiga*).

News about a serious illness of Alfonso's that appears in the documents as happening during Christmas 1269 can be dated more precisely. It happened after the Burgos Cortes, as the nobility was gathered for the wedding of the Castilian heir to the throne, don Fernando, with Blanche, daughter of Saint Louis of France (1214–1270). Jaime I in his *Llibre dels feyts*, tells that Alfonso set out to accompany him until Tarazona where they celebrated Christmas together. During his return trip to Castile, Alfonso fell gravely ill at Fitero in Navarra, where he had probably arrived December 28. Knowing of the great illness of his son-in-law, Jaime returned to Fitero with some of his knights and his personal physician, "Mestre Ioan," to help him because "he was very ill of a kick which a horse have [sic] given him in the leg at Burgos." After comforting him and giving him medical help three or four days,

---

[57] *Songs of Holy Mary, cantiga* 200, lines 30–37, p. 240.

Alfonso, writes Jaime, entreated him to continue his trip, for he was perfectly well.[58]

The reason for such grave illness, according to don Jaime's text, would have been the horse's kick in the leg. Nothing is said about an ailment of the eye or the face. But some claim he must have been kicked in the face, since it took him a long time to recover, and that the fracture caused him chronic sinusitis, and eventually, carcinoma of the maxillary cavity.[59] The diagnosis, according to some oncologists, would match this type of carcinoma.[60] It is possible, albeit very rare (very few oncologists indeed admit this) that a horse's kick could cause cancer at the site of the injury. But even if it had been so, the textual difficulty we pointed out remains unexplained. Hence, we must guess that the illness at Fitero must have been a different one. As the *Llibre* hints at, perhaps it was a serious accident causing a leg fracture which prevented him from riding a horse and even moving during the entire month and a half when we lack documentation from the chancellery. Notably, *Cantiga* 235, which we will discuss below, does not mention the illness at Fitero de Navarra, perhaps because it was an accident that was not cured by the Virgin's intervention, and hence

---

[58] This is the complete passage from *Crònica de Jaime I*:
The King of Castile then left Tarazona and went to Fitero, whence came word to me that he was very ill of a kick which a horse have [sic] given him in the leg at Burgos. I immediately went there, and with me four or five knights and my own train. I saw him and comforted him. I had with me at the time a surgeon doctor named Master John; I besides carried with me everything that was needed, and stayed with him three or four days, when he begged me earnestly to go back, as he considered he was cured. He thence went into Castile, and I went to Calata-yud for a month or more. (John. Forster, trans., *The Chronicle of James I, King of Aragón, Surnamed the Conqueror*, London: Chapman and Hall, 1883, vol. II, pp. 618–619)

[59] R. Kinkade writes:
I believe we may reasonably infer that Alfonso had been kicked in the face by a horse and that the resultant fracture led to chronic sinusitis, caused by an obstruction of the maxilary sinus ostium into the nasal cavity, or perhaps even by osteomyelitis of the maxillary bone. An injury of this kind is consistent with the subsequent development of a squamous-cell carcinoma of the maxillary antrum, as described by Maricel Presilla. ("Alfonso X, *Cantiga* 235," p. 290)
According to the author of the article, the English translator of *Cronica de Jaume I*, John Forster, "gratuitously adds that Alfonso was kicked 'in the leg'" (ib., note 21). There is nothing "gratuitous," or arbitrary, in Forster's translation, for that is exactly what the Catalan text says ("era fort malalte de la cama de un colp que un cavall li havia dat en Burgos"), which Kinkade himself quotes on p. 289, note 17. "Cama" in Catalan means "leg" in English.

[60] See the opinion of Dr. Shimm from the Oncology Department of the University of Arizona, quoted by R.P. Kinkade, "Alfonso X, *Cantiga* 235," p. 290, note 20.

is unmentioned in a miracle *cantiga*. Whether Alfonso suffered a skin carcinoma, which seems plausible from forensic analysis, is a topic to be debated by experts. What we do know for sure is that the carcinoma was not caused by the horse's kick, for this was in the leg, and not on the face.

The convalescence that followed the accident, during which Alfonso suspended his public activities, was a period of great cultural activity, to which Alfonso devoted as much energy as he did to the administration of the kingdom.

6. *Alfonso X in the* Cantiga *235*

The decade described in *Cantiga* 235 coincides with what scholars have termed Alfonso's second period of cultural activity.[61] The topic of *Cantiga* 235 (*narrative*) had already been dealt with more briefly and generally in *Cantiga* 200 (*de loor* or *of praise*), where the poet unexpectedly threatens traitors with giving them their due (ll. 19–22). The threat seems to be carried out in *Cantiga* 235. The events narrated in these two *cantigas* fill voids in the historical documentation where there is no evidence of the King's external political activity, and allow us to confirm dates and places that surprisingly coincide with the production of many of his most important works.

Cantiga 235, and less so 200, above all, allow us to reconstruct five concrete instances in which Alfonso almost lost his life to grave illnesses, but was miraculously cured by the Virgin Mary. Written in the third person, to render it more objective, the *cantiga* is a good summary of the adversities Alfonso had to confront, reflecting also his view of Divine Providence and human ungratefulness toward the end of his reign. It also reveals how he was forsaken by his closest relatives and collaborators and bitterly laments the lack of gratitude and rebellion of the nobility as well as the disenchantment at the loss of the imperial crown. His mental state fluctuates between feelings of gratitude to the Virgin for sparing him from the betrayal of his

---

[61] Cf. G. Menéndez Pidal, "Cómo trabajaron las escuelas alfonsíes," p. 369; O. Gringerich, "Alfonso the Tenth as a Patron of Astronomy," in F. Márquez Villanueva, ed., *Alfonso X of Castile the Learned King (1221–1284)*, pp. 30–45; W. Freiherr von Schoen, *Alfons X. von Kastilien. Ein ungekronter deutscher Konig*, Munich, 1957, chap. VII, pp. 49–53.

enemies and from other illnesses, and at times expresses hard feelings of disdain and righteous anger toward those who tried to dethrone him. The Virgin liberates him both from his illnesses (lines 31–88) and from his political enemies (lines 20–30). Alfonso expresses time and again these feelings in the very phrases used in the *Cantigas* and in the concepts around which it is structured, the traditional binomials: betrayal-ingratitude and loyalty-devotion. Although these same concepts also appear in other *cantigas*, such as 200, 300, and 401, and are the *leitmotif* of his entire oeuvre, especially his historiographical works, here they appear expressed with particular zeal. For this reason, *Cantiga* 235 may be directly attributed to him, for it accurately reflects the great disenchantment of his life: the betrayal by don Sancho and his own destitution. This also suggests that it may have been written, or edited, after the dramatic events of 1282.[62]

a. *The Illness at Ávila*

After attending the assembly at Ávila on April 24 1273, Alfonso left in early May for Segovia, where we find him June 18.[63] In Segovia he wrote a long letter to his son Fernando, in response to one his son had sent him, detailing various problems in the kingdom resulting from the noblemen's rebellion.[64] Among several personal details in the letter, there is what could be seen as the first indication of his physical ailments: "E sabed, Don Fernando, que cuando estas cartas me llegaron, yo era en Ávila por fablar con los concejos de León e Extremaduras, *e hobe ahí enfermedad de romadizo, e frío e calentura*, e pesóme mucho, porque en tal tiempo acaescía; e hobe gran pesar cuando entendí lo que las cartas decían" ["And be informed, Don Fernando, that when your letters arrived, I was in Ávila to speak with the councils of León and the Extremaduras, and there I was ill with *romadizo* (a respiratory infection) and cold and a fever, and I was very sorry at that time these things happened; and I was very saddened when I understood

---

[62] The last datable historical events in the *Cantigas* are found in *Cantiga* 386, where there is a probable reference to 1281 (cf. E. Procter, *Alfonso X of Castile*, Oxford, 1951, p. 42); or perhaps in *Cantiga* 393 (1282), as J. Montoya argues.

[63] On the nature of the gathering (or "ayuntamiento") at Ávila, cf. J. O'Callaghan, *Cortes of Castile-León*, p. 25, note 27; Ballesteros, *Alfonso X*, pp. 646–47 and 676–677.

[64] See the edition by P.K. Rodgers, "Alfonso X Writes to His Son: Reflections on the *Crónica de Alfonso X* (together with a commentary on and critical text of the unique Alfonsine letter that it preserves)," *Exemplaria Hispanica*, 1 (1991–1992), pp. 58–79.

what the letters said."[65] R. Kinkade, in the work quoted on the *cantiga*, associates the symptoms in the letter with chronic maxillary sinusitis which provoked a fever that forced him into bed rest, preventing him from traveling to Córdoba to meet the rebels as intended, sending instead his wife Violante and his son Fernando.[66]

We do not know anything about the seriousness of the illness that Alfonso suffered at Ávila, although, in the letter to don Fernando, he complains it was something critical that stopped him from traveling to Córdoba to conclude negotiations with the king's rebellious nobles. Alfonso uses a technical term to describe his illness, namely, *romadizo*, which is an inflammation of the nasal mucous tissue, an illness that was a prelude to, or a sign of, the maxillary cancer he suffered in his last days. The four-month interval between the meeting at Ávila and the meeting with don Jaime at Requena, with long stays in Segovia, Guadalajara and Cuenca, may be a good indication that the king was not in good health. But he was not mentally incapacitated, for the illness or convalescence did not hinder his intellectual efforts.

The meeting at Ávila was followed by a new convalescence (or perhaps a relapse), which may have lasted longer than is believed. There are no reports of the king's whereabouts between April 24 and June 18. We only know, lacking dates, what the *CAX* indicates: "We have now related how King Alfonso departed from Ávila to go to meet with King Jaime of Aragón. He brought with him to the meeting Prince Don Sancho, Archbishop of Toledo and the son of King Jaime; Prince Manuel; Prince Sancho, son of this King Alfonso; and his nephew don Alfonso, whom they called Molina; and other companies of prelates,

---

[65] Compare with the text in the *CAX*:
Don Fernando, when these letters reached me, was in Ávila, for he was coming there to speak with the councils of the land of León and Extremadura that I had assembled. I was sick with catarrh and a low fever, and I was very sorry that it had befallen us at that time, but I even received more grief when I realized what the letters were saying." (*Chronicle of Alfonso X*, p. 165)
The *CAX*, hence, essentially coincides with the letter's text; and regarding the illness, the coincidence is literal, which proves the chronicler had the letter at hand.

[66] Cf. R. Kinkade, "Alfonso X, *Cantiga* 235," p. 296. The *CAX*, accurately describes the political situation at that moment:
The king, realizing how convenient it was for him to appease the affairs of the noblemen in order to go to the empire—which was something he coveted much—considered it good to send his wife, Queen Violante, to Córdoba so that she and Prince Don Fernando could resolve the affairs of the noblemen and bring them back to the king's service. (*CAX*, p. 173)

noblemen, knights, and citizens from the cities."[67] Alfonso must have considered the interview with his father-in-law of great importance in order to surround himself with some very influential people, such as don Sancho, archbishop of Toledo and son of the king of Aragón.

The journey to the south was slow. On June 24, Alfonso was in Guadalajara, and on July 18, in Cuenca. It was during his stay in this city when he learned of the conflict between don Jaime and his son don Pedro: "and for this reason King Alfonso remained in Cuenca for a few days, sending his messengers to the king and Prince Pedro to work out peace and appeasement so that both of them could come to the meeting."[68] In Cuenca too, he received an urgent message from the queen and her son don Fernando to arrive as soon as possible in Córdoba to talk with the rebels.[69] There's no evidence Alfonso made it to Córdoba for the negotiations, perhaps, as suggested by R. Kinkade, because he was ill somewhere, or preparing for the meeting with his father-in-law.[70] His whereabouts between July 18 and the end of August are unknown.

b. *Requena*

During the month of August 1273, between the 22nd and 28th, Alfonso met his father-in-law at Requena.[71] The *CAX* provides the agenda and a summary of the talks: the rebellion of the nobility in both kingdoms, the summoning of the Lyon Council by the pope, the possibility of an invasion of the Peninsula by the emir of Morocco, and Alfonso's request for help from his father-in-law in case of the feared invasion by Ibn Yûsuf (chap. 57, pp. 187–190). The meeting was also attended by prince Sancho, Jaime's favorite grandson, and his presence certainly aided in the negotiations and concessions on the part of the King of Aragón. Following the conversations, the *CAX* states: "After this, King Alfonso departed from the meetings, and King Jaime went to Valencia. King Alfonso fell ill with tertian fever at Requena [...]"[72]

---

[67] *CAX*, p. 180.
[68] *CAX*, p. 180.
[69] Cf. *CAX*, chap. 55, pp. 180–182.
[70] "Alfonso X, *Cantiga* 235," p. 296.
[71] Ballesteros, *Alfonso X*, p. 670. The date coincides with the itinerary of Jaime I, cf. J. Miret i Sans, *Itinerari de Jaume I, "el Conqueridor,"* Barcelona, 1918, p. 485.
[72] *CAX*, p. 188.

Lack of historical documentation does not allow us to establish a relation between the tertian fever at Requena and the other two incidents at Fitero and Ávila. But it is clear that the Requena illness was a lot more serious than what the laconic text of the *CAX* indicates, for the chancellery did not produce any document the rest of the summer. Ballesteros quotes several documents from the Aragón chancellery regarding Jaime I's expenses in relation to the meeting that, according to him, "don't have any other date than 1274". Two items indeed have to do with the king of Castile's illness.[73] From theses details, we glean that don Jaime incurred several expenses in relation to the "malatia" (illness) of his son-in-law, but we are not told what illness it was and the word seems to indicate a serious, perhaps chronic condition.

The Requena episode is also the subject of the first miracle of *Cantiga* 235. The entire first part of the *Cantiga* is set against the background of the noblemen's revolt: "[m]ost of them were related to him by blood ties."[74] Thus, this coincides with the historical period we are discussing. The Virgin, however, comforted him by saying, "Mas eu o desfarei todo o que eles van ordir, / que aquelo que desejan nunca o possan conprir; / ca meu Fillo Jhesu-Christo sabor á de sse servir, / e d'oi mais mui ben te guarda de gran pecado mortal" (lines 30–33) ["However, I shall undo all that they are scheming, for they can never accomplish that which they seek. My Son, Jesus Christ, is eager to serve His ends and from this day on defends you from grave mortal sin"].[75] The poet goes on to say:

> Tod' aquesto fez a Virgen, ca deles ben o vingou;
> e depois, quand' en Requena este Rey mal enfermou,
> u cuidavan que morresse, daquel mal ben o sãou;
> fez por el este miragre que foi comec' e sinal
> Dos bees que lle fezera e lle queria fazer. (lines 35–40)

> [The Virgin did all She said and took vengeance on them for him. Later, when he was in Requena, the king became gravely ill, and just as they thought that he would die, he recovered from that malady. She worked this miracle for him, which was an indication of the blessings She had bestowed and would bestow on him.][76]

---

[73] In Ballesteros, *Alfonso X*, p. 671.
[74] *Songs of Holy Mary*, p. 281.
[75] *Songs of Holy Mary*, p. 281.
[76] *Songs of Holy Mary*, p. 281.

The Requena miracle presents itself therefore in the context of what the Virgin did for her devotee Alfonso, first, undoing the revolt of the nobles, and secondly, healing him from that life-threatening illness. The text of the *cantiga* seems to indicate that the Requena healing happened after ("e depois") the noblemen's rebellion was resolved, which would be historically accurate, but the conjunction could also express deduction. Whether it was a miracle or not, the king's activity following the Requena tertian fever is puzzling when it comes to determining how serious the illness was, as well as its nature and causes (unless one admits of the miracle). On the other hand, there's no reason, based on the documentation we possess, to associate it with the tumor in the maxillary cavity, as R. Kinkade suggests.[77] An attack of tertian fever could have had a countless number of causes.

But if the illness was as serious as the *Cantiga* suggests, his quick passage from a life-threatening condition to very intense activity seems inexplicable. In fact, a few days after the meeting with don Jaime, on September 15, 1273, he was at Brihuega, near Guadalajara, which is more than 200 kilometers from Requena. Only a miracle could explain such a complete recovery that allowed him to travel so swiftly. Even more surprising is the fact that in the following three months, Alfonso traveled at a very fast pace, touring a great part of his kingdom, from Guadalajara to Burgos and, in December of that same year, from Burgos to Seville, and then returning again to Burgos; in sum, he traveled 775 kilometers in less than 8 days.[78] Either the tertian fever was not as serious or the Virgin worked a miraculous cure, for only a miracle could explain such busy travel activity at a time when roads and means of transportation were very rudimentary, slow, and uncomfortable. If he recovered from a cancer relapse, as some claim, this would be even more prodigious and Alfonso's motives to believe in a miracle, greater still.

At Requena, besides meeting Jaime of Aragón, he also met with representatives of Lombardy, headed by count Ventimiglia.[79] According to the *CAX*, the meeting took place at the same time as the tertian

---

[77] "Alfonso X, *Cantiga 235*," pp. 297–298.

[78] Cf. details in the *CAX*, chap. 57, pp. 187–190; and the documentation in Ballesteros, *Alfonso X*, pp. 678–681.

[79] "and being so [that is, ill with tertian fever], the Count of Ventimilia and other Lombards came there to the king with a message from those who had elected him as emperor" (*CAX*, p. 188).

fever, which might contradict the grave illness the *Cantiga* speaks about, unless this fever, that struck every three days, was so strong that it threatened his life every time it happened but allowed him to function normally in between. In any event, given the tight itinerary Alfonso had after the cure, we must conclude that the meeting with the Lombardians must have happened before the meeting with don Jaime, that is, between August 15 and 22, for Alfonso did not return to Requena the rest of that year.

Two major lacunae exist in Alfonso's itinerary south in 1273. The first goes from April 24, when he was in Ávila, until June 24, when we find him in Segovia; the second goes from July 18, in Cuenca, to the end of August, when he's in Requena with his father-in-law. Where was Alfonso during those periods?

7. Cultural Activities

Alfonso disappears from the public sphere between the incident at Fitero and his reappearance in Burgos on March 7, 1270.[80] Although it is unknown where he was, it is possible he may have been convalescing at Logroño (there's a letter dated January 28 sent from that town), or elsewhere in the area, under the care of his personal physician, Alonso Martínez, who arrived from Toledo to treat him.[81] But we can be sure he was not idle in that period. We can establish his presence in certain places. Thus we know that during January and February 1270, he toured several monasteries in La Rioja looking for books and manuscripts, since he knew that those places, not far from where he had grown up, were centers for the preservation of learning where he could find the materials he needed for his great cultural project. For that reason, time and again he would tread their stone floors and seek his lodging there. Among those monasteries, Silos is noteworthy as it was visited by Alfonso several times and possessed one of the best libraries of the 13th century.[82]

---

[80] For his cultural activities during 1258–1269, see below chap. 9, pp. 313–314.

[81] Ballesteros, *Alfonso X*, p. 497. In the first half of February, Alfonso issued several diplomas and letters to various people and institutions, which indicates the chancellery had resumed its regular activities.

[82] A document from Silos, precisely dating to the 13th century, mentions 18 works that had been recently lent to other monasteries and individuals, among which is the following entry: "10. *Paulo Osorio* [obviously this is Paulo Orosio], [to] the king," that is,

First he stayed at the Albelda Monastery (today Albelda de Iregua), some 15 km south of Logroño, where he spent several days with the monks consulting several codices from their vast library. From there he visited the Colegiata de Santa María de Nájera, where he also perused the excellent library for several days and before leaving requested the loan of several works to be copied.[83] On Saturday, February 22, he was at Santo Domingo de la Calzada, accompanied by some abbots and priors of the local monasteries. It was at Santo Domingo de la Calzada where the prior of Albelda requested the king to sign a receipt for the loan of several precious codices. Aware of their incalculable material and cultural value, Alfonso readily signed the receipt, promising to return the codices as soon as his scribes copied them.[84] On February 24th, again in Nájera, he issued a similar receipt listing the titles of the borrowed works.[85] During one of his visits to Silos, he borrowed a "Paulo Orosio" and El Silense's *Crónica*.[86]

All these works, along with many others that became part of Alfonso's virtual library, reappear in the sources of the *Estoria de España* and the *General Estoria* which he himself quotes in the respective prologues, a clear indication that both projects were conceived at the same time and developed in parallel.[87] In any event, both receipts attest to the fact that during his illness at Fitero, Alfonso was actively gathering materials and working on his historiographic projects, for which

Alfonso X. This document's texts can be seen in D.M. Férotin, *Histoire de l'Abbaye de Silos*, Paris, 1877, p. 273; and cf. J. Martial Besse, *Histoire du Dépôt Littéraire de l'Abbaye de Silos*, Société de Saint-Augustin, 1897; and L. Rubio Garcia's article, "En torno a la biblioteca de Alfonso X el Sabio," in *La lengua y la literatura en tiempos de Alfonso el Sabio*, pp. 531–551.

[83] Cf. *MHE*, I, pp. 257–258; R. Menéndez Pidal, *PCG*, 3a ed., 1977, pp. 856–857; Ballesteros, *Alfonso X*, p. 311. For identifying information on the borrowed works, see the following note.

[84] The receipt can be seen in the Archivo de Albelda, today in the Archivo de la Colegiata de Logroño; it was published in *Memorial Histórico Español*, I, Madrid, 1851, p. 257. Alfonso made use of the works mentioned in the receipt in the composition of the *Estoria de España* and the *General Estoria*, which he had begun that same year.

[85] Text of the receipt in the *MHE*, I, p. 258; and cf. Biblioteca Nacional, Madrid, Ms.7365, fol. 64.

[86] Cf. Ballesteros, *Alfonso X*, pp. 309–310.

[87] On "Alfonso X's library" see: M. Alvar, "Didactismo e integración en la *General Estoria*. Estudio del *Génesis*," in *La lengua y la literatura en tiempos de Alfonso el Sabio*, pp. 25–78; and L. Rubio García, "En torno a la biblioteca de Alfonso X el Sabio," pp. 531–551.

he probably already had a translation of the Bible, the backbone of both works.

1273 was Alfonso's epistolary year. Besides the long letter to his son from Segovia, where he carefully analyzes the political situation of the kingdom, displaying good knowledge of the people he had to contend with for his projects to succeed, Alfonso also wrote several letters during his stay in Cuenca, which are summarized in chap. 55 of the *CAX*.

But correspondence was probably not Alfonso's main occupation during the long rest periods of his political activities. According to G. Menéndez Pidal, "...creativity is the main feature of this second period in Alfonso's life. He is no longer happy with commissioning and directing translations—his efforts are now directed towards a total syncretic task... Alfonso's most original and personal works are written during this second period".[88] Alfonso spent a calm and quiet period in Murcia between January and June 1272, devoted to his cultural projects. In this time he must have written a large part of the *Estoria de España*.[89] Scholars hold that it was during the noblemen's revolt (1272–1274) when the *"Versión primitiva,"* or *"regia"* ("Primitive" or "Royal version"), of the *Estoria de España* (up to chap. 616) and the *"Versión concisa"* ("Concise" or "Vulgar version"), or *"Vulgar,"* (up to chap. 801) were finished. Both versions must have been drafted in 1272, while the *"Versión enmendada"* ("Amended version"), including the story of the discovery and transference of King Wamba's remains in April 1274, was probably finished shortly before this date.[90]

But he did not only work on history. In these three years (1272–1275) he redrafted the *Libro del fuero de las leyes*. The chronology of Alfonso's juridical works is still a controversial matter, but there are good reasons to believe that the project begun on June 2, 1256 and concluded on August 28, 1265 with the title *Libro del fuero de las leyes*, as stated in the most important manuscript containing it, became

---

[88] "Cómo trabajaron las escuelas alfonsíes," *NRFH*, 5 (1951), p. 369.

[89] Cf. Ballesteros, *Alfonso X*, pp. 551–561.

[90] Cf. D. Catalán, *De Alfonso X al Conde de Barcelos. Cuatro estudios sobre el nacimiento de la historiografía romance en Castilla y Portugal*, Madrid: Gredos, 1962, p. 24; and *De la silva textual al taller historiográfico alfonsí: codices, crónicas, versiones y cuadernos de trabajo*, Madrid: Fundación R. Menéndez Pidal-Universidad Autónoma de Madrid, 1997, chaps. II and III, pp. 33–284; I. Fernández-Ordóñez, *Las "Estorias" de Alfonso el Sabio*, Madrid: Istmo, 1992, esp. chap "VII. Las secciones elaborativas de la *Estoria de España*," pp. 205–220.

during the seventies the basis of a new work that from 1275 on would be called *Primera Partida* (*First Partida*).[91] As is well known, both the Alfonsine *historiographic corpus* (*EE* and *GE*) and the legal one were completed and promulgated by his great-grandson, Alfonso XI.[92]

Finally, it is also in the seventies that various Marian compositions are actively collected to be included in the first collection of 100 *cantigas*, begun in 1257 and completed 1272–1274. In reality, neither physical illnesses nor political or family adversities were able to stop his intellectual labors, which were much more important to him than life itself.

---

[91] Primera Partida (Manuscript Add. 20787 in the Bristish Museum), ed. J.A. Arias Bonet, Valladolid: Universidad, 1975, esp. p. 3. Cf. J.R. Craddock, "La cronología de las obras legislativas de Alfonso X el Sabio," AHDE, 51 (1981), pp. 365–418, esp. p. 391; and his bibliographic essay The Legislative Works of Alfonso X, El Sabio. A Critical Bibliography, London: Grant and Cutler, 1986.

[92] The *Siete Partidas* were not promulgated until 1348 with the *Ordenamiento de Alcalá* (in *Códigos españoles*, I, pp. 427–485).

CHAPTER EIGHT

THE BLACK DECADE (1269–1279)

Cantiga 235, which we began to discuss in the previous chapter, presents, according to many scholars, what could be Alfonso X's "black decade" due to the many adversities he had to confront and which the *Cantiga* describes in a surprisingly chronological order.

1. *Montpellier*

The illness that afflicted Alfonso during the trip he took to Beaucaire to meet the pope was more serious than the one he suffered at Requena, which we discussed in the last chapter. For unknown reasons, the chronicles of the period, notably the *CAX* (chap. 66, pp. 214–215) omit the conversations between Alfonso and the pope and also do not deal with details of his personal life during the trip, such as his illnesses. R. Kinkade, who argues that Alfonso met with the pope for mere propaganda reasons, concludes: "In that case Alfonso would have made every effort to conceal the nature and extent of his illness, which may well account for the lack of official records alluding to his condition."[1] Thus, the only source we have regarding the illness at Montpellier is *Cantiga* 235, according to which:

> Later, when he left his land and went to see the pope of that time, he fell so gravely ill that they thought he would surely die from that affliction.
> …
>
> Then he arrived in Montpellier and became so seriously ill that of all the physicians there, each and every one, firmly believed that he was surely dead. However, the Holy Virgin Mary completely cured him, faithful Lady that she is.
> …
>
> She caused him to be able to ride in a few days and to go back to his own land to recover there. He passed through Catalonia, where he had to cover great distances each day as one does on a long journey.
> …

---

[1] "Alfonso X, *Cantiga* 235." p. 304, note 77.

When he entered Castile, all the people of the land came to meet him
and told him: "A very good day to you, my lord."[2]

The general tone of the narrative gives the impression that the *Cantiga*
was composed some time after the events ("went to see the pope *of
that time*"). This indeed had to do with the fact that it is written in the
third person, giving the reader and potential listeners the impression
that the poet has a relatively vague idea about the events he was speaking of and that he had not witnessed them first hand, as would have
been the case if Alfonso had authored the *Cantiga*. But all contemporary scholars who have written about this poem consider it personal
and "absolutely autobiographical."[3] So, to begin with, if there was an
illness, it probably was not very serious, and the expression, "o teve-
ron por morto" ["they believed he was dead"] rather a literary device
used by the poet to exalt the Virgin's power in favor of her devotee,
Alfonso, which is the ultimate goal of this *cantiga de loor* (*cantiga* of
praise).

It is not entirely clear if Alfonso's lapse happened on the way there,
as the first stanza seems to indicate and R. Kinkade postulates, in
which case it would make sense that it was the pope who suggested to
meet Alfonso in Beaucaire instead of Lyon, to avoid the complications
of a trip five times as long and its return.[4] Against the idea that this
happened during the trip there, we have the testimony of Muntaner,
a careful observer, as we have seen, and who accompanied Alfonso
at Montpellier for two weeks until he left for Beaucaire. Muntaner
does not mention at all the very serious illness but only the celebrations. This leads us to believe the relapse happened on his return from
Beaucaire to Montpellier, although this hypothesis too seems to be
in conflict with the text, which states in a separate stanza: "Then he
arrived in Montpellier," as if this was another episode. The two enu-
merative phrases "Then" (lines 41 and 45) seem to indicate two separate episodes, that is, one on the way there ("when he left his land"),
the location of which we ignore, and the other one upon his return
("And later at Montpellier"), which indeed happened in that town, as

---

[2] *Songs of Holy Mary*, pp. 281–282.
[3] According to the editors of the facsimile edition of the Florence Codex, p. 91.
Ballesteros thought that this *cantiga* was "one of the most personal ones by the king,
and in it, the king sings the favor of the Virgin to whom he dedicates all his devotion
in the most heartfelt verses" (*Alfonso X*, p. 771).
[4] "Alfonso X, *Cantiga* 235." p. 303.

can be gleaned from the explicit allusion to the famous "physicians" of the most celebrated school of medicine in Europe.[5]

We believe the *Cantiga* refers to two distinct episodes, one during the trip there, which probably occurred during the stay in Beaucaire and which would explain why Muntaner does not mention it, since he was not in Beaucaire, and which would also explain why Alfonso was there for four months, when he knew in advance he would not get anything out of his conversations with the pope.[6] Both relapses were very serious, but it seems that only the second saw the intervention of the Montpellier physicians, who pronounced him terminally ill ("he fell so gravely ill that all the physicians present there thought that he was indeed dead," lines 45–47, in *Songs of Holy Mary* translated as: "he fell so gravely ill that they thought he should surely die from that affliction" p. 281). If the most celebrated learned man of the period thought that Alfonso was dead, would we admit that the cure, in reality, was seen as a resurrection? Only the intervention of the Virgin would have saved him from death and helped him recover to the extent that he was able to ride a horse and continue his journey towards Spain in long stretches, "as one does on a long journey" (line 53). However, if it was indeed the Virgin who cured him, it seems that the cure was not as quick or long-lasting as the *Cantiga* suggests, for there were no documents issued by the chancellery between July 10 and December 10, a period of some five months that Alfonso might have spent at Montpellier under medical care, or more probably, as the *Cantiga* suggests, traveling "back to his own land to recover there"(line 51). The silence of the chancellery, given the many troubles in the kingdom, has no other explanation: during those five months Alfonso was convalescing or incapacitated, as the chronicler Desclot suggests.

The illness at Montpellier is remembered in a splendid illustration of the Florence Codex of the *Cantigas* (illustration 7).[7] The text of the

---

[5] About Montpellier and its famous medical school, see L.E. Demaitre, *Doctor Bernard de Gordon: Professor and Practitioner*, Studies and Texts. 51, Toronto, 1980. Mestre Nicolás, Alfonso's personal physician who also treated him at the moment of his death, had also studied at Montpellier (cf. Ballesteros, *Alfonso X*, p. 1049).

[6] This is also the opinion of E. Procter, who writes:
> The illness at Beaucaire and Montpellier which are recounted in the Cantiga thus help to account for the otherwise puzzling six months' gap between Alfonso's audience with Gregory X in May and his return to Castile in December 1275 (*Alfonso X of Castile*, p. 38).

[7] Codex *F*, Biblioteca Nazionale Centrale de Florencia, Banco Rari, 20, *Cantiga*, 71bis, fol. 92r; facsimile edition by Edilán, Madrid, 1989.

7. Miracle at Montpellier and Valladolid. Holy Mary heals Alfonso at Montpellier (vignette 1); Alfonso returns to Castile from the meeting with the pope (vignette 2); Mary and her infant Son heal Alfonso at Valladolid (vignette 5). Codex F, Library of Florence, Ms.Banco Rari 20, fol. 92r Cantiga 235.

Cantiga in this codex has been lost, but one of the two folios of the miniatures survives, whose ending in 5 indicates it must have had 12 vignettes, as was the norm. But this one contains only six. Fortunately, the surviving folio contains the miniatures relative to the episodes narrated in the text of the Rico Codex in El Escorial. The first vignette indeed illustrates the miracle at Montpellier described in lines 45–49. Alfonso, lying with the king's crown on his head, eyes half-closed, a stiff facial expression and arms under the covers, seems to be in a coma, or dead, as the most celebrated physicians of Europe at the time thought. Next to the bed, under the two arches on the left, we can see the Virgin with a crown and a blue halo, in the company of an angel and a female saint, blessing him with the right hand while she touches his chest with the left. The last two arches on the right contain a weeping figure, a courtier (perhaps his brother Manuel) who is praying, and two physicians observing a flask with urine. The physician on the right, judging from his dress and demeanor, represents a great authority and seems to be pointing to the symptoms of the illness in the urine.

The *Cantiga* does not tell us anything new about the nature of the illness; but if we take into account that years later Alfonso would suffer from dropsy, a symptom of cardiac or kidney failure, we can perhaps surmise that he had a very painful renal dysfunction which may have sometimes left him unconscious, at which time his contemporaries, even the most celebrated physicians, might have confused his state with death. According to others, the illness at Montpellier would have been another sign of his heart failure.[8] After the attack and after the kidney stones were out, Alfonso recovered his health and could continue his return trip.

The Montpellier illness was only one of the great adversities of this unfortunate trip. The report about the Moorish invasion probably reached him will he was in Beaucaire, and his heart was filled by grief by news of the deaths of close relatives, such as his nephew, Alfonso Manuel, son of his brother Manuel, which he received upon arriving in Montpellier, where he also learned of the death of his last daughter, doña Leonor, who had stayed in Perpignan with doña Violante and part of the entourage. All these events justify Desclot's phrase that he arrived in Castile "irritated and ill".[9]

2. *The Illness at Vitoria and* Cantiga *209*

During the fall of 1275, Alfonso was finally able to return to Castile after crossing the Pyrenees and passing through Lérida and Aragón. On December 10 he was in Brihuega and on the 22nd in Alcalá de Henares, as is evidenced by the privileges issued in both cities.[10] *Cantiga* 235 confirms what Muntaner had already said, namely that when Alfonso returned to Castile, he was received with great joy by all:

---

[8] "An illness that for several years had been causing occasional edemas. (Logically we must think of a heart problem with growing periods of failure)" F. Torres González, "Rasgos médico-psicológicos de Alfonso el Sabio." p. 135.

[9] *Llibre del rei En Pere*, chap. 66, p. 454.

[10] See chap. 6 above, note 64.

> When he entered Castile, all the people of the land came to meet him
> and told him: "A very good day to you, my lord." (lines 55–57, *Songs of
> Holy Mary*, p. 282)

Alfonso spent the rest of the autumn recovering from the serious illness that struck him on his way back from Beaucaire and planning the
defense of the southern border, which in his absence and following the
death of don Fernando, his heir, young prince don Sancho had cour-
geously secured, forcing Yûsuf to return to Algeciras and from there
to Africa in mid-November.[11]

Alfonso spent Christmas of that year most likely in Alcalá. Here
he would have received the news that on October 15, the pope had
announced to all the princes of Europe that the king of Castile had
finally given up the crown of the King of the Romans and, consequently, his aspirations to the Holy Roman-Germanic Empire. He also
would have learned about the death of Gregory X, which happened
in December of that year. The death of such an illustrious pope with
whom he had recently interacted seemed the recapitulation of a year
of misfortunes in his personal life and in the kingdom. The disappearance of such an enterprising pope from the scene of European politics must have led him to reflection on his enormous personal losses,
namely, the recent death of his son and heir, don Fernando, and of
his brother-in-law, don Sancho, archbishop of Toledo, as well as of
his daughter, princess Leonor and the illustrious Commander of the
Frontier, don Nuño González de Lara, who had died in the battle of
Écija on September 7 of that same year. These losses and his absence
from the kingdom indeed made the Moorish invasion easier and at the
same time created enormous internal problems that plunged Alfonso
into a deep depression that he would overcome by immersing himself
in his cultural projects. Illness and a passion for culture would be the
double motif of Alfonso's life in this calamitous decade.

In early January 1276, Alfonso began with renewed interest to take
up the matters of state, going first to Toledo. The scene the *CAX*
locates in Camarena actually took place in Toledo on January 4, as
we will discuss below. It was at this time when the nobles who had
accompanied the young prince don Sancho in his campaign to contain
the Moorish invasion of Yûsuf, appeared individually before Alfonso
in order to ask him to name as legitimate successor his oldest son,

---

[11] Cf. *CAX*, chap. 65, pp. 211–213.

don Sancho. The king answered that he "loved don Sancho and held him in high regard," but did not commit to a formal answer, saying he would respond to the matter after consulting his advisors. Alfonso left Toledo for Valladolid, stopping for a few days in Camarena, near Toledo. The benign climate and serenity of the place certainly helped him recover his health.

Alfonso was in Valladolid on February 25, 1276. On April 26 he was back in Burgos, where he summoned a new Cortes that must have been celebrated between May and July of that same year. It was at these Cortes that don Sancho was officially named heir to the throne of Castile.[12]

The spring and summer of that year were no less tumultuous than the winter. In May, the war in Navarra flared up again, where, since the death of King Enrique, on July 22, 1274, things had gotten progressively worse. Soon after Enrique's death, his widow, Blanche of Artois, had fled with their daughter and heir, Juana, to France, seeking the protection of her brother, Philip III, *the Bold*, who practically became the ruler of Navarra. The only peninsular power with any influence up to that point in Navarra politics was the kingdom of Aragón, but on July 29, 1276, Jaime I, a matchless supporter of Alfonso and his foreign policy, died, and his heir, don Pedro, had not had the time to formulate his policy regarding Navarra. It was thus that Navarra started to become a nightmare for the king of Castile, especially after don Sancho's proclamation as heir during the May-July Cortes. When the king of France found out that his nephew, Alfonso de la Cerda, son of the deceased don Fernando de la Cerda, had been excluded from the throne of Castile, he ordered an invasion of the territory of Navarra and at the same time sent Robert d'Artois, Blanche's brother, to head an army in defense of the interests of the king of France in Pamplona.[13] Alfonso responded to the aggression by also dispatching

---

[12] Cf. O'Callaghan, *Cortes de Castile-León*, pp. 83–84; Procter, *Curia and Cortes*, pp. 138–143. The chroniclers of the period point to the 1276 Burgos Cortes as the moment when don Sancho was proclaimed heir to the throne, cf. Jofré de Loaysa, *Crónica*, pp. 20–21; *Anales toledanos III*, p. 419; Desclot, *Llibre del rey En Pere*, chap. 66, p. 454.

[13] Cf. Ballesteros, *Alfonso X*, pp. 796–800. For the French sources, cf. Ch.V. Langlois, *Le Regne de Philippe III le Hardi*, Paris, 1857, p. 105; and the rhymed chronicle of an eyewitness, Guillaume Anelier of Toulouse, *Histoire de la guerre de Navarre en 1276 et 1277*, ed. F. Michel in *Collection de documents inédits sur l'histoire de France*, Paris, 1856.

a considerable army to Pamplona commanded by his brother don Fadrique, and Fadrique's son-in-law don Simón Ruiz de los Cameros. The expected battle did not take place; instead, the Castilian army, unexpectedly and for unknown reasons, stopped at Monreal, a few kilometers to the southeast of Pamplona, while the Castilian supporters in Navarra were defeated by the French.

On September 5, 1276 and in order to better control movements in Navarra, Alfonso settled in Vitoria, where, according to *Cantiga* 235, he spent a year and a month seriously ill (line 66). During that year, the second attack by the French king took place, "with a very large army" (line 67).[14] But later, according to the *Cantiga*, the king "behaved more courteously,"[15] because God undid his plans the way water dissolves salt (lines 67–68).[16]

Alfonso dedicated an entire *cantiga* to this relapse in Vitoria and his miraculous cure, namely, *Cantiga* 209 (illustration 8).[17] The Learned King tells us how during his stay in that city he fell gravely ill and everyone thought he would die:

> Therefore, I shall tell you what happened to me while I lay in Vitoria, so ill that all believed I should die there and did not expect me to recover.
>
> For such a pain afflicted me that I believed it to be mortal and cried out: "Holy Mary, help me, and with your power dispel this malady."
> …
> The doctors ordered hot cloths placed on me, but I did not wish it and ordered Her Book to be brought. They placed it on me, and at once I lay in peace.
> …
> I never cried out nor felt anything of the pain but at once felt very well. I gave thanks to Her for it, for I know full well She was dismayed at my affliction.

---

[14] *Songs of Holy Mary*, p. 282.

[15] *Songs of Holy Mary*, p. 282.

[16] His stay in Vitoria did not really last "one year and one month," but rather from August 1276 to March 1277. Cf. Ballesteros, *Alfonso X*, p. 811; E. Procter, *Alfonso X*, p. 40.

[17] This *Cantiga* is found both in the codex *E* in El Escorial (j.b.2), as in codex *F* in Florence (Banco Rari, 20), *Cantiga* 95, fol. 119r. In the codex at El Escorial it is entitled: "Como el rey don Affonso de Castela adoeçeu en Bitoria e ouv'hũa door tan grande que coidaron que morresse ende, e poseron-lle de suso o Livro das Cantigas de Santa María, e foi guarido" ["How King don Alfonso of Castile fell ill in Vitoria and had such a severe pain that he thought he would die of it. They laid the book of the *Songs of Holy Mary* upon him, and he was cured," *Songs of Holy Mary*, p. 251]. Cf. E. Procter, *Alfonso X of Castile*, p. 40.

8. Miracle at Vitoria. Alfonso requests that the *Book of the Cantigas of Holy Mary* be placed on his chest and he is healed. Codex F, Library of Florence, Ms.Banco Rari 20, fol. 119v, Cantiga 95.

...

> When this happened, many were in the place who expressed great sorrow at my suffering and began to weep, standing before me in a line.

> When they saw the mercy that the Holy Virgin, Lady of Great Worth, showed me, they all praised Her, each one pressing his face to the earth. (lines 17–45)[18]

In contrast to *Cantiga* 235, this one is written in the first person, which, as we noted, is a good indication that the composition was

---

[18] *Songs of Holy Mary*, p. 251.

truly penned by the king. The illness, as noted, happened between September 5, 1276, when he arrived in Vitoria, and the month of May in 1277, when he left for Burgos, hence not a year and a month, but eight months, unless the poet meant he stayed for a year and a month in the region of Vitoria, which could also include the nearby city of Burgos.

Fortunately, this *Cantiga* was lavishly illustrated in the Florence codex along with *Cantiga* 71bis in the same codex, both of which are the only illuminated *cantigas* on the subject of the king's illnesses.[19] The illuminations reflect quite accurately and faithfully the story narrated in the poem, especially what pertains to the king's person. In the case of *Cantiga* 209, as has been repeatedly noted, we are faced with a composition that, more than any other, reveals the most intimate and personal aspects of Alfonso's private life and his courtiers, both in images and words.

The first vignette portrays the king lying on his back in a lavish bed with a pink brocade decorated with the shield of León-Castile (a black lion on a white background and a golden castle on a red background), a motif that repeats itself on the four corners of the six panels and on the fringes of the bed covers. Lying in bed, Alfonso is wearing a tunic with tight sleeves, and his body is covered by a bedspread, except for the right arm and shoulder, which are exposed, folded on his chest. His head, as was customary in the Peninsula, is resting on a high pillow decorated with blue and golden stripes; at the head of the bed, in the six panels of the illustration of this *cantiga*, there is always a servant stirring the air with a fan made from peacock feathers. Although the King is lying in bed sick, the miniature artist represented him always wearing his crown, so that he would be immediately recognizable in the illustration. The entire scene takes place in a sumptuous chamber divided by three arches: the first, twice as big as the other two, is a round arch, while the other two are pointed arches and are occupied by the bed with the king, extending all the way to the third, where two court physicians are in conversation.

In the second vignette, likewise divided into three similar arches, the king appears upset, with his face turning right while he pushes away the hot compresses two doctors offer him (in the second arch);

---

[19] Codex *F*, Biblioteca Nazionale Centrale of Florence, Banco Rari, 20, *Cantiga* 95, fol. 119r (text), 119v (illustration 8).

under the third arch, two characters from the court cover their faces with dark cloths and cry.

In the third vignette, the caption reads: "How the king asked for the *Book of Songs* he made in honor of Holy Mary to be brought to him." Alfonso appears facing those present, and a cleric hands him the *Book of Songs* decorated in red and gold, while physicians and courtiers contemplate the scene. In the fourth vignette, we see Alfonso in the same position as before, but here he is holding the book over his chest while his right hand rests on the pages; his face appears serene and his body relaxed; the courtiers, now numbering eight, watch the scene in amazement, while others kneel in prayer. In the fifth vignette, Alfonso appears seated on the bed, wearing a blue chamber cape over a white tunic; in both hands he raises the codex of the *Cantigas* and kisses it devoutly, while those present fall on their knees. The inscription reads: "How the king was cured instantly without feeling any pain, and he praises Holy Mary," or as the *Cantiga* says: "[...] and at once I lay in peace. I never cried out nor felt anything of the pain but at once felt very well. I gave thanks to Her for it, for I know full well She was dismayed at my affliction." Alfonso's face is beaming with joy and devotion. In the sixth and last vignette, Alfonso is still sitting up in bed in the same position, but now the closed book rests on his lap, his clasped hands are reaching to the sky in thanks for being healed, while some of those present also pray with joined hands, raising their eyes to the sky, and others are prostrate with their faces to the ground.[20]

The Florence codex, as is known, is an extremely valuable source of knowledge on the daily life of Alfonso's court and of peninsular society in the 13th century. It contains numerous illustrated *cantigas*, where the narrated scenes are pictorially complete, although the heads of some of the characters, particularly the king, appear unfinished. This probably indicates that there was an artist who exclusively painted the portraits of Alfonso X and his immediate family and collaborators, which, evidently, due to a lack of time, he was unable to finish. None of the recently published facsimiles or printed photographic reproductions of the codex can compare with the brilliance and accuracy of detail of the six splendid panels in the original, which, when seen

---

[20] For more details about the architecture, the furniture, and the clothes of the characters in the *Cantigas*, see J.E. Keller, *Iconography*, pp. 6–40; and *Daily Life*, pp. 8–52.

up close and under a magnifying glass, progressively reveal the king's face during different stages of the illness: the anguish and pain of the first scene, to the joy of healing in the final one. All portraits of the king, in this and other illustrations, show him with the same physical characteristics: bright blue eyes, an aquiline nose, a well-groomed beard, red lips, blonde hair, and fair skin. In the case of *Cantiga* 209, besides the consistency and quasi-photographic precision of the portrait, the artist captured in Alfonso's features the anxiety and pain of an ill man, the uselessness of medical remedies, the hope for a miracle, the joy of being healed, and the gratitude to the Virgin who, through the *Book of Songs*, worked a miracle to restore his health. The expressions and gestures of the other characters in the scene also correspond to the dramatic tension of the moment. Each panel has a narrative inscription, but the scene represented is so eloquent that, in reality, no explanation is necessary. Yet the image and caption allow us not only to see Alfonso, but also to hear him, so to speak.[21]

As in previous *Cantigas*, Alfonso does not discuss the nature of his illness, although here he adds that the doctors recommended hot compresses, which does not say much, because that could have corresponded to an swelling in any part of the body as well as to a high fever that they tried to bring down. According to the *cantiga*, Alfonso did not follow the doctors' advice and, instead, asked for "Her book," art. cit the *Cantigas*, to be brought and placed on him, which cured him.[22] As in previous illnesses, we cannot reach a conclusion on the

---

[21] As J.E. Keller and R.P. Kinkade aptly note:
Viewers may well have been so thrilled at the series of scenes in the intimacy of the royal bedchamber amid so much luxury and pomp, that other effects may have been diffused. The point of view is most unusually personal and like no other found in either verbal of visual form, since King Alfonso allows the reader to hear him speak, and through the visualization and their captions, to see that he is speaking. The king has actually versified a vignette straight from his own personal experience, from a mortal illness he himself suffered. The mood or tone is one of deep religiosity. Of all the Cantigas in which Alfonso appears, none is more intimate. (*Iconography in Medieval Spanish Literature*, p. 31)

[22] The codex placed on Alfonso's chest at the time only contained the first one hundred *cantigas* and should be identified as the one known as *To* in the Toledo Cathedral (call number 103–23), housed today in the Biblioteca Nacional in Madrid (call number 10.069), which was carefully described by A. Paz y Melia in the edition of the *Cantigas* by Marqués de Valmar, pp. 35–41. The physical appearance of the codex, as can be seen in panels 3, 5, and 6, corresponds to that of the extant codex, according to Paz y Melia's description: "It is bound in red leather with brass clasps." The artist clearly copied the scene from life.

nature of the illness at Vitoria based on the miniatures, but if these do reflect historical reality, as it is commonly believed, we must conclude that his illness did not affect his head or face, as nothing abnormal is depicted in that part of the body in the miniatures.[23]

As we will see later on, when discussing *Cantiga* 279, there's a Seville tradition that Alfonso ordered the construction of the Church of St. Anne in the Triana neighborhood to give thanks for the miraculous cure of his illness at Vitoria. According to this tradition, it was an eye condition, which could confirm the hypothesis of a maxillary cancer. But neither the text nor the miniatures confirm this interpretation.

Perhaps the miniatures of the *Cantiga* reveal not only the king's private state, as many scholars have pointed out, but also the nature of the illness that afflicted him at Vitoria. In searching for such a message, I decided to consult a professional artist, Ángel Aragonés. Without explaining what I suspected, I asked him if he saw anything peculiar in the horizontal figure of the king. After carefully examining the six vignettes, the first thing he said was, "There seems to be something abnormal in the representations of the king's left leg. It appears bent and a lot thicker than the right one, as if it were swollen." That was precisely what I suspected. He then offered to sketch a drawing on onionskin paper to depict the real shape of the king's naked leg.[24] We do not want to overly insist on this point we present as a mere hypothesis, yet it is worthwhile to note some expressions in the text such as "extirpa este mal" ["dispel this malady"], or the fact that he tells us the pain would make him scream and that they brought him hot compresses to ease the pain. All this could point to the acute symptoms of an incipient edema, which coincides with the chronology that indicates he was incapacitated in Vitoria and unable to travel for several months.

Following this digression about the illness at Vitoria described in *Cantiga* 209, and before returning to *Cantiga* 235, which we have

---

[23] R.P. Kinkade, however, holds that, "the monarch's rapid recovery is consistent with the gradual accumulation and sadden release of pressure characteristic of a squamous-cell carcinoma" "Alfonso X, *Cantiga* 235," p. 313, note 115; and *Iconography*, p. 31.

[24] Besides being a famous artist who regularly shows in New York and various European cities, Ángel Aragonés is a professor of art history at New York University's program in Madrid. I would like to gratefully acknowledge his opinion and his permission to publish the sketch, which appeared in the Appendix of the Spanish edition of this work.

chosen as a our guide in this chapter, we would like to note, in passing, that lines 70–78 of the latter, apparently allude to the execution of his brother, don Fadrique, and of his son in law, don Simón Ruiz de los Cameros, during Alfonso's stay at Vitoria. We will address this bloody incident later on in the chapter on don Sancho's rebellion (p. 387 and ff). The illustration of *Cantiga* 235 in the Florence codex does not depict the illness at Vitoria. But there is an empty space left for the third vignette (illustration 7), which might have been meant for such an illustration, although, as we will see, perhaps that space was also reserved for the execution of his brother, Fadrique. Alfonso, however, never commented on that sorry decision and evidently also did not approve the miniature meant to depict it.

After recovering his health, Alfonso was able to celebrate a new Cortes at Burgos in May 1277.[25] Alfonso's greatest worry was the new attack by Ibn Yûsuf, whose troops had already been in the Peninsula for several months. The Moorish leader himself arrived in Tarifa on July 1 to personally launch the final offensive. The Christian resistance was minimal, so the Moorish leader arrived in Seville on August 3, where he met the forces of Alfonso Fernández, Alfonso's representative in the south. The Castilians were defeated and Yûsuf followed up with an attack on Jerez, which fell on September 15, and on Cordova, which surrendered October 30.[26] The Moorish conquests alarmed the participants at the Cortes and Alfonso who was still weak from his last illness. Faced with the bad news, following the Cortes, Alfonso was forced to travel south to organize the resistance, but he did not make it very far.

The following stanza of *Cantiga* 235 seems to reference this trip south to counter the Moorish offensive:

> After leaving Castile, the king was eager to go to the frontier, but the Virtuous Lady did not wish him to go there just then, until he recovered more fully.[27]

---

[25] The Cortes took place before the feast of Pentecost, that is around May 16. Cf. O'Callaghan, *Cortes of Castile-Leon*, p. 67, note 17.

[26] Cf. Ballesteros, *Alfonso X*, pp. 827–835, who uses *Rawad al-Qirtas* as his main source, given the lack of information in the Christian chronicles.

[27] *Songs of Holy Mary*, p. 282. Independent documentation confirms the precise phrase of the *Cantiga* almost verbatim: "el Rey con mui gran sabor ouve d'ir aa fronteira" [the king was eager to go to the frontier]. The document is a letter sent to the town council of Cordova on March 24 from Peñafiel, on the way to Valladolid: "Et agora sere yo ayna alla en la tierra, si Dios quiere" [And immediately I will be there in the land, God willing] (in Ballesteros, *Alfonso X*, p. 867).

In other words, the Virgin prevented Alfonso from leaving for the border until he had properly recovered, and hence brought about in him a "general fever in the entire body," which held him up at Burgos for the rest of 1277. This was a unique way in which the Virgin (or the narrator of the *Cantiga*) managed to look after the beloved Alfonso in order to allow him to devote himself to other matters. This fever and the illness that ensued kept the king in the North until well into the following year (1278), while Ibn Yûsuf and his soldiers caused irreparable damage to the towns and economy of the South. The ways of the Lord are mysterious indeed.

Finally, on March 11, the king was able to set out towards Valladolid, where he arrived April 10, Palm Sunday. It was precisely between Palm Sunday and Easter Sunday 1278, when the Virgin gave him "a taste of death."

3. *The Miracle at Valladolid*

Once again we must refer to *Cantiga* 235 to learn more of the trial to which Alfonso was subjected:

. . .

> With this illness She caused him to be cured of the others. When they thought he would die, he went directly to Valladolid, and the worthy Lady cured him of his remaining illness. However, before She made him well, She caused his condition to reach such severity

> that no judge would have pronounced him alive. The Holy Empress caused him to experience death. However, on the happy day of Easter, when they make the paschal candle,

> She began to relieve him, for he had suffered greatly, and delivered him peacefully and fully from all his torments, stroking him with Her hands. She did not wear a veil and seemed more bright than ruby or crystal.

. . .

> All this was done on Easter Day by Her and Her Son, Who was nailed on the cross, Whom She cradled in Her arms and Who, for our sakes, bestows His mercy and grace amidst the perils of the world (lines 80–103).[28]

---

[28] *Songs of Holy Mary*, pp. 282–283.

Based on diplomas and other documents issued by the chancellery we can date the miracle narrated in the *Cantiga* as happening on Easter Sunday 1278, which that year was on April 17.[29] The narrative tone of the *Cantiga* reaches an allegorical-mystical level when it alludes to the redemptive value of suffering. But the analogy with the resurrection of Christ prompts the question of whether the poet is perhaps describing the king's resurrection brought about by intercession of the Virgin. This motif appeared as well during the illness at Montpellier, when, according to the poet "[he] became so seriously ill that all the physicians there, and each and every one, firmly believed that he was surely dead" (lines 45–47).[30] Would this be another instance in Alfonso's life when a loss of consciousness led those around him to think he was dead? What does the line "The Holy Empress caused him to experience death" mean?

Let us examine the details of the cure, which are particularly interesting and revealing. In stanza 85, the poet says that the Virgin cured all other illnesses along with this one. When everyone thought he would die, he went straight to Valladolid, where the Virgin, worthy of praise, also cured him of a previous affliction, but "before She made him well, She caused his condition [illness, death?] to reach such severity that no judge [witness] would have pronounced him alive [...] The Holy Empress caused him to experience death. However, on the happy day of Easter, when they make the paschal candle, [stanza 90] She began to relieve him, for he had suffered greatly, and delivered him peacefully and fully from all his torments, stroking him with Her hands. She did not wear a veil and seemed more bright than ruby or crystal [stanza 95]."

Cantiga 235, obviously, is articulated in a crescendo of the healing process, the illnesses becoming progressively more serious to the point that, in the quoted stanzas, it is suggested that Alfonso entered a coma, which in literary terms is the climax of the narrative and the final objective of the composition: death and resurrection. According to this narrative strategy, illnesses came and went, a horse's kick, a cold, a tertian fever, two more serious relapses during the trip to Beaucaire, the very serious illness at Vitoria, and, finally, this one,

---

[29] Cf. E. Procter, *Alfonso X of Castile*, pp. 39–40. Procter also gives the date of the miracle as Easter Sunday 1278.

[30] In *Songs of Holy Mary*, p. 282, this is translated as: "he fell so gravely ill that they thought he would surely die from that affliction."

during which, apparently, Alfonso was [like] dead for some time. No other *cantiga* mentions the Virgin taking him to the brink of death to later restore his life ("She began to relieve him"). This poetic climax is properly capped with the metaphor of the passion, death, and resurrection of Christ: like Christ, Alfonso, spent Holy Week on the brink of death, to the point of even getting "a taste of it," only to be, like Jesus, raised from the dead on the very day that Christians celebrate the resurrection.

What parts of this narrative could be historically accurate? The use of a specific literary technique to tell of historical events in the life of a society or an individual, *per se*, does not exclude the veracity of what is narrated. Specifically, the use of the metaphor of death to add dramatic tension to the narrative is evident in *Cantiga* 235, where it is used in order to exalt the mediating power of the Virgin. In medieval times, the appearance of death or phenomena such fainting or the loss of consciousness were frequently confused with death itself given the high mortality rate. Hence the metaphor of death was not simply metaphorical but a sad reality faced by people every day. This is why, as perhaps in no other period in history, illness and pain were seen as a metaphor for other realities, in which pain represents death as imminent and inevitable, and illnesses, particularly those such as leprosy, were seen as the worst of all deaths: the death of the soul.

The Florence codex (*Cantiga* 71bis, fol. 92r) contains a unique illustration of the miracle at Valladolid, which essentially confirms the text (illustration 7). The fifth vignette depicts the Virgin in front of the bed, not behind as in other illustrations, dressed in a resplendent [white] dress, "like crystal," offering the Child Jesus to Alfonso lying in bed. The scene is full of drama. At the head of the bed, two powerless physicians lament the occurrence, while the four other figures cover their faces and weep. It is an original way of representing the Virgin, as if she were an immaterial reality, a vision or apparition. In contrast, the Baby Jesus does seem to have a physical reality, and it is he who, contradicting the text, imposes his hands on the chest of the ill king (in *Cantiga* 235 it is His Mother), although He is still held by His Mother, the mediator and intercessor. As we noted, the illustration has an oneiric or vision-like quality. Lying motionless with his arms under the covers, as if in his coffin, Alfonso stares with open eyes at the Virgin in a state of ecstasy. He contemplates the airy, transparent figure, which is apparently invisible to the other weeping characters. The layout of the scene parallels exactly the third panel of *Cantiga* 95 in the same Florence codex (illustration 8, vignette 5), which, as we

noted, narrates in images the miracle at Vitoria. Even the bed Alfonso
is lying in appears to be the same, with the exception of the pillow,
which is more simply decorated here. As in the illustration of *Cantiga*
95, here too Alfonso wears a white chamber tunic, the crown is on his
head, and he stares intently at the Virgin, the same way she stared at
"Her book." But instead of a cleric offering her the "Book," the Virgin
here offers her own Son. The symbolism is clear: the miraculous power
of the "Book" is similar to that of the Son, and in both cases the mediator is the Virgin Mary.

As in other cases of healing we discussed, we also do not know for
certain what was the illness that afflicted the king at Valladolid. The
Cantiga only mentions a "general fever" that affected his entire body,
which is not very revealing if we consider the possibility of maxillary
cancer, for the fever could have had many other causes. Comparing
Cantiga 235, where the Virgin imposed her hands on his body to heal
him ("stroking him with Her hands"), with what we know about the
deformities of the king's face determined through the analysis of his
remains, we would have to conclude that the illness did not affect his
face, for that was not where the Virgin applied the cure. *Cantiga* 209
leads to the same conclusion, since in it the Virgin used the codex of
the *Cantigas* to work the miraculous cure by placing it on the king's
chest, according to his explicit request.

Both the text and miniatures seem to rule out any illness in Alfonso's face, at least until this period. The miniatures of the Florentine
codex, which show the cure at Vitoria, do not show any sign of dete-
rioration of the king's face: it appears in perfect condition and his eyes
are beautiful and bright. But Dr. Delgado Roig's 1948 report regarding
the deformities of his maxillary antrum, including a perforation of the
left nasal bone, and don Sancho's remark that his father looked like a
"leper," which are used as arguments for Alfonso's maxillary cancer,
present a serious discrepancy with the version portrayed in the *Cantigas*. Therefore, based on the text and the miniatures, we can conclude
that if Alfonso suffered from maxillary cancer, it only developed after
1278, the date of the last miracle discussed. If it did happen before this
date, there is only one explanation to justify the miniatures' version:
out of respect for the king, the artist chose not to represent him in a
way not matching the dignity of his lord and patron.

Of course, if indeed on April 17 Alfonso had one foot in the grave, a
fairly certain thing, and "[a]ll this was done on Easter Day" (line 100),
the cure must have been instantaneous and total, that is, miraculous.
This because in mid-May he was already in Segovia presiding over

an important meeting of the Cortes, in which he handed over a fair amount of his responsibilities to his son, don Sancho, appointing him co-regent. Clearly, the last relapse, despite his cure, must have made him think of the need for a successor who could at least govern the kingdom during his illnesses, which were becoming more and more frequent and preventing him from ruling with the same energy he had before. Hence, he conferred extraordinary powers on don Sancho during the Cortes held in Segovia from May to July that same year.[31]

The chain of illnesses and other political and family misfortunes (Beaucaire, the rebellion of the nobility, senseless executions, etc.) which afflicted Alfonso during the seventies undermined his physical health and his image as an even-tempered king dedicated to the well-being of his subjects. His external appearance at certain times must also have caused his enemies to mock and malign him. The accusation by his son Sancho that he was a "leper," given the moral accusations implied by the word, was more than an insult; it was a veritable moral reproof that placed a man like Alfonso, at times wise and learned and at times naïve, in the category of perverts.[32]

Starting in 1278 there are fewer and fewer references to Alfonso's delicate health in the chronicles and the documentation. The problem must have been well known, as confirmed by a letter from Nicholas III (1277–1280) dated July 15, 1278, that is, soon after the Segovia Cortes. In this letter sent from Viterbo, the pope, in an affectionate tone, invited him to meet the king of France in order to reach a peace agreement on Navarra and the question of succession, topics that had created a state of constant war between the two Christian kingdoms. The pope also said that he had heard, not without some bitterness and fatherly compassion, about his serious illnesses, and therefore asked, if he was unable to attend the meeting, to send prince don Sancho to represent him.[33] Thus, despite the miraculous cures, Alfonso was still ill. For reasons we will discuss below, however, he did not go to meet the king of France nor did he send don Sancho in his stead.

Despite his constant ailments, in August 1278, Alfonso was in Seville preparing the siege of the port of Algeciras, which took place August

---

[31] Cf. *CAX*, chap. 68, pp. 219–220; Ballesteros, pp. 852–857; J. O'Callaghan, *Cortes of Castile-León*, pp. 25, 84; E. Procter, *Curia and Cortes*, p. 143.

[32] Frequently in the Middle Ages, leprosy was seen as the external manifestation of, or the divine punishment for, moral corruption. See S.N. Brody, *The Disease of the Soul: Leprosy in Medieval Literature*, Ithaca, 1974, pp. 25–35.

[33] See the Latin text in Ballesteros, *Alfonso X*, p. 844.

6.[34] Two years later we have the first indications that Alfonso suffered of an eye condition. The *Crónica de Alfonso X* tells us that during a war against the king of Granada, in June 1280, the king had to abandon the field and remain in Cordova because of an eye problem:

> King Alfonso had agreed to enter the Vega through Rute and Prince Sancho through Alcaudete so that he could join the armies in Alcalá de Benzaide. It happened that King Alfonso had fallen ill with a pain in his eye, and for this reason he was unable to go. So he sent all his army to his son Prince Sancho so that he could enter the Vega.[35]

In contrast to the *Cantigas*, here the chronicler confirms he had an eye problem, referring concretely to one eye ("had fallen ill with a pain in his eye"), as if it were something chronic and well known. The phrase in the *CAX*: "de que le oviera a perder" ["[illness] that would cause him to lose it"] seems to indicate that between 1280, the date of the incident, and 1284, when he died, Alfonso lost an eye. We can assume it was always the same eye, the left, to which Dr. Delgado Roig's report also refers.

An inscription in the Seville church of Santa Ana de Triana recalls a tradition according to which Alfonso had the church built to give thanks for this miraculous cure brought about by the Virgin:

> ...The above mentioned don Alfonso, having a serious ailment of the eyes, had his right eye pop out of its orbit, and he made a promise to Our Lady, the Holy Virgin Mary, and within the hour, his eye was healed and back in its place, and when the most noble king don Alfonso saw the great miracle performed by Our Lord God, came to this place and asked the neighbors of Triana why they didn't build a church there, and they said, "Lord, we want to build it now." And he asked them what they wanted to name it, they said, "We want to call it Santa María." And then the noble king don Alfonso said, "It is my will that a church should be built here dedicated to the blessed Saint Anne, mother of our Lady, the Virgin Mary, who I am devoted to because I know how many favors she has bestowed on me, so that without her I would be unable to obtain what I beg of her precious son, Our Lord..."[36]

---

[34] *CAX*, chap. 69, pp. 221–222; cf. Ballesteros, *Alfonso X*, pp. 866–885 and 885–889.

[35] *CAX*, chap. 74, p. 234.

[36] J. Alonso de Morgado, *Historia de Sevilla. Libro Quarto*, Sevilla, 1587, p. 110. Text reproduced by Ballesteros, *Alfonso X*, pp. 851–852. Cf. M. Presilla, "The Image of Death." pp. 432–440; J.F. O'Callaghan, *The Learned King*, p. 235.

This eye disorder that the inscription of the painting hanging on the left wall of the church of Saint Anne, near the entrance from Vázquez de Lara street, refers to would be the same illness that Alfonso X was healed from in Vitoria in 1276, and which would come back in 1280 during the Granada war when the construction of the Church was finished.[37] However, we would like to point out a small discrepancy between the inscription and the result of the examination of his remains. The inscription mentions the "right eye" while Dr. Delgado Roig's report indicates that the skull had notable changes in the entire area of the left eye's orbit, with a perforation of the left nasal bone and a large necrosis area in the upper inner part of the maxillary bone.[38] The first examination of the remains performed in 1579 only speaks in general terms describing "the brow and head [as] inordinately large."[39] As mentioned, the inscription along with the analysis of his remains leads some contemporary scholars to conclude that the cause of his illnesses and his eventual death was an epidermal carcinoma of the maxillary cavity. Others believe that his death was due to heart problems.

4. Cantigas *279, 366, and 367*

The last three *cantigas* dealing with the illnesses of the Learned King and how they were cured by the intervention of the Virgin are numbers 279, 366, and 367. None of the three have been accurately dated, but it seems clear that they describe episodes in the last years of Alfonso X's life (1280–1284), and they describe his worsening health, although none give any specific details, but rather general symptoms that signal a variety of ailments that undermined the king's health.

Cantiga 279, which appears as *Cantiga* X in the Toledo (*To*) codex, corresponds one of the sixteen miracles that were added to the initial core of 100 *cantigas* in the Toledo manuscript. This codex is considered a copy of the original manuscript that contained the first 100 *cantigas*. We lack reliable sources to date it, but based on the description of Alfonso's physical condition—the *cantiga* mentions certain specific

---

[37] Cf. D. Ortiz de Zúñiga, *Anales eclesiásticos y seculares*, Madrid, 1795, I, pp. 317–318. According to our chronology, and as held by Ballesteros, the episode narrated in the inscription could only have happened in 1279 and not in 1276 (*Alfonso X*, p. 852).

[38] J. Delgado Roig, "Examen médico-legal...." p. 151.

[39] In J. Alonso de Morgado, *Historia de Sevilla*, p. 108.

symptoms—and the little we know through the documentation, it must have been composed toward the end of his life, probably between 1280 and 1282. It is entitled, "How the king asked Holy Mary to have mercy on him and cure him of a grave illness he had. She, powerful Lady that She is, cured him."[40] It is a lyrical/narrative composition. In his favorite role as "troubadour," Alfonso invokes her protection:

> Holy Mary, have mercy, My Lady, and come to the aid of your troubadour, for he has need.
>
> …
>
> Since God made you best of all His things, and gave you as our Advocate, *Holy Mary, have mercy, My Lady,* and be my kind benefactor in this struggle
>
> …
>
> with death, which I sorely fear, and in this illness which has me in its grip and makes me green as Cambrai cloth. *Holy Mary, have mercy, My Lady.*
>
> And what then did She who bestows all goods and heals all ills do? She took away his fever and the vile and noxious humor (14–27).[41]

The *cantiga* reveals one of the main feelings of medieval man: the terror of pain and its inevitable consequence, the "assault" of death ("in this struggle with death, which I sorely fear"). Alfonso is scared of his color "green as Cambrai cloth,"[42] thus exclaiming:

> Holy Mary, have mercy, My Lady, and come to the aid of your troubadour, for he has need,

imploring that his "rezõador" ("advocate") may liberate him from that "fever and the vile and noxious humor." This *cantiga* is indeed one of the most personal and intimate ones in the entire collection, where Alfonso, like any other mortal, afflicted by many ailments and scared

---

[40] *Songs of Holy Mary*, p. 338.

[41] *Songs of Holy Mary*, p. 338. This *cantiga* is a personal work by Alfonso with a marked Provenzal influence, both in form (it is written as a "rondel") as in vocabulary "vosso loador" ("your singer" Alfonso calls himself, "trobador," troubadour); "nossa rezoador" ["our Advocate"]; "est'enssay" [this essay or trial; from ancient Occitan], "cambrai" ["Cambrai cloth"]. On the figure of Alfonso as troubadour, see J.J. Rey, "El trovador don Alfonso X," *RO*, 43 (1984), pp. 166–183.

[42] This refers to the refined textiles produced in the French city of Cambrai, characterized by their bright colors, in this case, green.

of death, finds solace in the only person he trusts, for she has always been his "bõ' ajudador" ("great help") in moments of crisis.

In the process of opening his soul to hope, Mary's "troubadour" reveals some of the symptoms that, according to supporters of the theory of maxillary cancer, oncologists attribute to the advanced state of the carcinoma when the tumor bursts creating a constant drainage ("humor") which was expelled through the nose and which in turn produced the infections that caused ulcers on the nose and face, as well as the "fever" and discoloration of the skin the *Cantiga* mentions.[43] But in this case too it could be something less serious, from our current clinical perspective, for instance, food poisoning or another serious liver dysfunction such as jaundice, which medieval physicians labeled *morbo regio* (kings' illness).

There are also no details on the disease the king suffered upon his return from Seville, after participating in the war against Granada described in *Cantiga* 366. The main theme of this *Cantiga* is to narrate how don Manuel, the king's brother, lost a prized falcon he owned and recovered it thanks to the Virgin's intercession.[44] But this theme is preceded by a three-stanza preamble in which the poet situates his composition in the historical context of the war against Granada:

> On such a theme as this, a great miracle occurred in Seville in the time the king was there. He had come from making war in Granada on the Moors of that land who were living there (lines 5–8).[45]

Some scholars believe the *Cantiga* relates incidents from the Fall of 1265. If that is the case, it would be the first allusion to a serious illness of the king in the *Cantigas*, not the illness at Fitero. We do not agree with this opinion. The allusions to the illness ("fell very seriously ill"), and the fact that the king had already been miraculously cured of other illnesses ("who had already cured him of other great afflictions"), seem to indicate a chronic condition, something we should think happened only starting from the second half of the seventies, and more intensely during the period of the war of 1280–1281.

---

[43] On the various opinions regarding the symptoms, see M. Presilla, *The Image of Death*, pp. 478–480.

[44] I. Montoya, "La caza en las *Cantigas de Santa María*." BC, 5 spring (1993), pp. 35–48; D.P. Seniff, "Falconry, Venery, and Fishing in the *Cantigas de Santa María*," in *Noble Pursuits: Literature and the Hunt*, ed. D.M. Wright and C.L. Scarborough, Newark, Del.: Juan de la Cuesta, 1992, pp. 76–87.

[45] *Songs of Holy Mary*, p. 445.

When they had finished the deed, [they] returned to Seville. The king fell very seriously ill but recovered by the mercy of Her who is Mother and Daughter of God, who had already cured him of other great afflictions (lines 15–18).[46]

The last phrase clearly refers to the other cures described in the preceding *cantigas*: 209, 235, and 279.

Finally, *Cantiga* 367, entitled "How Holy Mary of the Port cured King don Alfonso from a great sickness which caused his legs to swell so much that they would not fit inside his shoes,"[47] is one of the 24 *cantigas* naming the famous sanctuary of the Virgin of Puerto de Santa María (Cádiz), that Alfonso X himself had built in 1260.[48] In the *cantiga* Alfonso tells how on his way to the sanctuary ("he went to see the beautiful church he had built in Andalusia, lines 18–19)"[49] to give thanks to the Virgin for being healed from "a grave illness" he had suffered in Seville (lines 26–39, also mentioned in *Cantiga* 366, just noted), he fell so gravely ill "that all thought he would be long in recovering from that ailment" (lines 43–44).[50]

...

While the king was traveling by sea, both his legs swelled so alarmingly and became so inflamed that all thought he would be long in recovering from that ailment

...

They had swollen to such an extent that they no longer fit into his boots, and, what is more, the skin on them split, and yellow fluid came out.

...

However, the king, who held all his hope in the Virgin and doubted not, would not delay because of this and went on to the Port as fast as he could.

...

---

[46] *Songs of Holy Mary*, p. 445.

[47] *Songs of Holy Mary*, p. 447.

[48] The details and historical circumstances of the construction are also described in the *Cantigas*, especially in number 328. Cf. L. Torres Balbás, "La mezquita de Al-Qanatir y el Santuario de Alfonso el Sabio en el Puerto de Santa María," *Al-Andalus*, 7 (1942), pp. 417–436; J.T. Snow, "A Chapter in Alfonso X's Personal Narrative: The Puerto de Santa María Poems in the *Cantigas de Santa María*," *La Corónica*, 8 (1979), 10–21; H. Sancho de Sopranís, *Alfonso X y El Puerto de Santa María*, El Puerto de Santa María, 1984.

[49] *Songs of Holy Mary*, p. 447.

[50] *Songs of Holy Mary*, p. 445.

He arrived on Friday at the church of this Virgin, may She be blessed, and with this grave affliction went to Her altar to hold vigil.

…

When Her priests began the matins, which they sang very well, at once both his legs lost their swelling, and he recovered from that disease.

The king and all his company, as soon as they saw the great miracle, fervently praised Her who wins health for us from God and gives us joy (lines 41–69).[51]

In this case, it seems relatively clear that the illness in question was dropsy or water retention, an illness that had also afflicted his father and caused his premature death.[52] The details of the *Cantiga* reveal that it must have been a chronic condition in an advanced state, for we are told that while he made the journey across sea to reach the sanctuary, his legs became so swollen and red that everyone thought he would take long to recover from that illness. His skin broke, oozing a yellow fluid, probably pus. But as M. Presilla notes, dropsy is not a disease but rather a symptom produced by a great variety of illnesses that go from renal dysfunction and gout to heart anomalies. Despite this, it should not be related to the tumor that the king had on his face, but rather to another disease that afflicted him.

The disease and miraculous cure described in *Cantiga* 367, must have happened immediately after the cure alluded to in *Cantiga* 366; that is, the spring and summer of 1281, ("E macar l[l]' o tempo fez mui gran guerra." ["although the weather gave him much difficulty"] *Cantiga* 367, line 37, *Songs of Holy Mary*, p. 447), and therefore during the attack on the city of Granada on June 25 of that year.

There's confirmation that it was a chronic illness because a year later it was still around. In his first will, dated November 8, 1283, he speaks of his gratitude towards Ibn Yûsuf, the emir of Morocco, for the gracious assistance he received from him during his campaign in the autumn of 1282 to quash the rebellion of his son Sancho: first, because with the emir's help he was able to emerge "from the shadow of our treacherous enemies who were contrary to us and drowned us with their great betrayal," and second, because "we recovered our

---

[51] *Songs of Holy Mary*, p. 447.

[52] Alfonso does not use the term "dropsy", though he clearly knew the condition, since in *Cantiga* 308, he tells of the miraculous cure of a woman afflicted by dropsy in the French city of "Rara" (Cala, today Chelles en Seine-et-Marne). Alfonso X spoke of the illness that his father had suffered when he was a child in the beautiful *Cantiga* 221.

health and began to ride and walk,"[53] which he was unable to do in the last year, on account of the swelling in his legs.

Both the text and the iconography of the *Cantigas* provide us with snapshots of Alfonso's private life, his court, and the world in which he lived, and they are useful in reconstructing certain aspects of his person and kingdom that we would otherwise not know. Alfonso himself wanted to leave us as an epilogue, a synthesis of his life from the point of view of his role as devout and confidante of Mary in his "Petiçón" ["Petition"] that closes the collection (*Cantiga* 401). In that *cantiga*, the Learned King reviews the themes and moments in which he felt the mediating hand of Mary, while imploring at the same time her protection in the future. This *Cantiga* already appeared at the end of the first collection of one hundred poems preserved in the Toledo (*To*) codex, but was retouched and adapted to the final version of four hundred *cantigas*. It is very probable that it would have been retouched again at the end of Alfonso's life, since it seems to refer to events that happened before 1282. It is a personal and intimate confession, when he did not have much left to lose, since he had already lost almost everything, having only his soul to save. It is in this *cantiga* where he first recognizes some of his main mistakes as a ruler while remaining firm about certain fundamental topics such as the defeat of the Moors, the punishment for the rebellion and the treason of his son and the nobility.

Following the style of a typical narrative prayer, in ten stanzas made up of ten 14-syllable single-rhyming lines with no refrain, Alfonso asks the Virgin, as reward for having sung her glory and power in the *Cantigas,* to intercede before her Son to obtain the pardon of his sins (stanza 1). In stanza 2, he requests to be received among the saints in Paradise and "that in this world I may be able to destroy the infidel Moors, who are Philistines, just as Judas Maccabaeus, who was long ago the leader of the Jews, destroyed his enemies."[54] In the third stanza he asks to be protected from the devil, who looks for opportunities to make him sin, and to be given the power and strength against the Moors "who hold the Holy Land and great portions of Spain, to my great regret, so that I may drive them out."[55] After these requests, Alfonso implores Mary's

---

[53] In García Solalinde, *Antología*, p. 230.
[54] *Songs of Holy Mary*, p. 482.
[55] *Songs of Holy* Mary, p. 482.

help to protect him from other ills more closely related to ailments and misfortunes in the kingdom (stanzas 4, 5, and 9).

In this Petition, Alfonso touches the nerve of the topics that would consume him toward the end of his days: the reconquest of the territories held by the enemy (the Muslims), his personal health, his fear of death and eternal damnation, the squandering of his kingdom's riches, and his concern with ruling in a fair and equitable manner. All these themes worried him in the past and continued to worry him in his last days. The request for "sanity" has more to do with the virtue of "prudence" to govern fairly than with the state of his mental health, which had been called into question by his son, to which we now turn.

5. *Alfonso's Madness and the* Setenario

Our Lady, Holy Mary [...] I beg you that, since your Son made me King, please obtain from him the sanity I need [...]

At this point, we must ask ourselves how a man afflicted by all these ailments and physical tribulations was able to carry out such important cultural work. Because Alfonso was involved in everything: law, history, politics, science, art, and literature. In the field of law, we can say that he legislated about everything, from institutions of State and Church, to food, entertainment, and urban sanitation, environmental protection, and the garments to be worn by his subjects, the nobility, and the plebeians, the Jews and the Moors. He dictated norms for proper speaking, poetics, and guidelines to avoid not only the breaking of grammar rules but also offensive expressions, as when he issued a judgment on "This is what happened to a man who took another man to court because he had called him a traitor and an asshole." The word in the original, "fudiduncul," is more offensive and vulgar and has the connotation of sodomy.[56] His historiographic oeuvre is a monument of 13th-century humanistic culture, and his astrologic/astronomic

---

[56] Cf. Ballesteros, *Alfonso X*, p. 853. Nowadays, it seems unthinkable that laws and prescriptions as detailed as those formulated in the Cortes of 1256 and 1272 or in the *Ordenamiento de las Tafurerías* could be carried out. Alfonso is credited with the invention of "tapas," for it was stipulated that inns should not serve wine unless it was accompanied by some kind of food to prevent alcohol from damaging the stomach.

treatises served as the vehicle whereby Eastern culture crossed over to the Christian West.[57]

In the midst of all this cultural activity at all levels, the Learned King also had to confront the limitations of his own nature. For it is certain that the illnesses and political setbacks he suffered must have caused him at various times serious psychological and mental instability, to which we now briefly turn.[58] I am not certain what clinical value this may have, but all historians mention that the Learned King in the sentence of disinheritance of don Sancho, which we will address later on, bitterly complained about his son's animosity against him, who, driven by his ambition for power, had called him a "madman" and a "leper." Ballesteros believes that the "madness" had to do with his "prolonged aspirations to Empire" and the accusations of "leprosy" had to do with the "last disease he suffered in which his legs were swollen, a probable symptom of dropsy."[59] Evidently Ballesteros was not aware of the results of the postmortem forensic examination that gives us an idea of the incredible pain and the cranial disorders from which the Learned King must have suffered.

It seems that there is more in don Sancho's accusation than his modern biographer would have us believe. The fact that "madman" is associated with the act of killing "without a cause" his brother Fadrique, Simón Ruiz de los Cameros, the Jewish financier Çag de la Maleha and, at the beginning of his reign, Rodrigo Fernández de Sahagún (April 17, 1255), a judge in the court and an official of the king, is a clear sign that his son and many of the nobles surrounding him detested the arbitrariness that according to them he had shown in all these cases.[60] At least in the case of don Çag, there seems to be a disproportion between the cause of the king's anger and the punishment he inflicted. The great Jewish financier, who was a close collaborator

---

[57] See the superb essay by J. Vernet, *Lo que Europa debe al Islam de España*, Barcelona: Círculo de Lectores, 1999.

[58] F. Torres González, "Rasgos médico-psicólogicos de Alfonso el Sabio," in *Alfonso X y Ciudad Real: Conferencias pronunciadas con motivo del VII centenario de la muerte del Rey Sabio (1284–1984)*, ed. M. Espadas Burgos, Ciudad Real, 1986, pp. 107–140.

[59] *Alfonso X*, p. 995.

[60] The reason for the execution of this illustrious court official would have been his disobedience on three occasions and his rejection of Alfonso's authority (there's no proof Alfonso had anyone executed before having tried him first, although he was accused in general terms of killing "men without a cause," an expression which is also meant to include don Çag and perhaps also don Rodrigo Fernández).

of Alfonso's and a dear friend, was executed only to show to his son, don Sancho, who held power.

The charge of being a "leper", in addition to arising from the condition of Alfonso's legs, which might not have been obvious to those around him, could also have derived from the deformity of his face and the truly repugnant appearance it must have sometimes presented as a result of the ulcers caused by the maxillary tumor. A man with a bloody eye protruding from its orbit with ulcers on the nose and cheeks and cracks and pustules on his legs must have appeared to his son and those around him like a leper.

Thus undoubtedly the physical illnesses and the accompanying, debilitating agony must have profoundly affected Alfonso's psyche, producing unexpected reactions of anxiety, depression, and fear, hence his need to act impulsively when faced with a real or imaginary danger, especially when he felt personally threatened.[61] Some of the apparently most misguided decisions, such as the executions mentioned, were made precisely at times when the king was suffering or emerging from those very serious illnesses. That was the case of the execution of don Fadrique and don Simón, which happened when he was getting over the very serious illness at Vitoria (April–May 1277), described in a dramatic way in *Cantiga* 209. Don Çag's occurred during the anti-Moorish campaign in September 1280, another memorable time in the history of the king's illnesses, when he had to leave the battleground and stay in Cordova. Hence, don Sancho and those who knew him must have thought Alfonso acted with capricious, impulsive, and irrational behavior, improper for a great king, and like a true madman. In other words, must we conclude that the manifestations of the illness altered Alfonso's personality and behavior?

Some modern biographers, considering Alfonso's haughty temperament and inability to accept defeat, together with the huge blunders he committed—the brutal executions, his obsessive pursuit of the imperial crown, the squandering of money to obtain it, his willingness to seek the protection of his Muslim enemy, and finally, his attempt to

---

[61] On the effect of chronic pain on the psyche of cancer patients, see S. Lack, "Total Pain," in *Clinics in Oncology*, 3 (1984), 33–35, quoted by M. Presilla, op. cit., p. 484, note 29. R.P. Kinkade adds: "The symptomatology of his illness, with its circle of agonizing pain and abrupt remission, was simply not conducive to forceful and deliberate action but rather predisposed the monarch to bouts of depression, indecision, and frequently bizarre behavior" ("Alfonso X, *Cantiga* 235." pp. 299–300).

leave his kingdom to the French king—have concluded that physical ailments and political harassment indeed led the king to madness.[62] Based on J. Craddock's work on the *Setenario*, which he assumes was written towards the end of Alfonso's life, Peter Linehan states, "True, the text of the *Setenario* as we have it (in a quite early manuscript of the work) shows all of the signs of a fine intelligence in a state of terminal disintegration, loss of contact with reality, and, above all, a pathological obsession with the number seven."[63] Linehan's diagnosis of this obsession, which J. Craddock also mentions, would also be confirmed by the fact that when he wrote the *Setenario,* Alfonso was also contemplating leaving his kingdom to the king of France, another sign of his insanity.

If the *Setenario* truly reveals this obsession with the number seven, and was written, as some surmise, towards the beginning of his reign, this would mean that Alfonso had more than one obsession (with the number seven, the imperial crown, peninsular hegemony, and other matters) throughout his life. In other words, he was demented, which is a synonym of insane, throughout his entire adult life as a king. But if we bracket out the "insanity" (which, as we will see, was not so irrational) of renouncing his throne in favor of the French king, Alfonso did not suffer from a pathological obsession with the number seven, or any other number for that matter. This matter has been the source of great misunderstanding.

J. Craddock's hypothesis has not been universally accepted; many scholars still hold that the *Setenario* was a work written early in Alfonso's reign and presumably started during that of his father. The *Setenario*'s date of composition is a matter of controversy, and although this is not the place to discuss that, I believe the work as we know it today was not written in a single period, but rather that it was started under Fernando III and finished by Alfonso X.[64]

---

[62] See, for example, F. Pérez Algar, *Alfonso X, el Sabio. Biografía,* Madrid: Studium Generalis, S.L., 1997, pp. 289–290.

[63] *History and the Historians,* p. 440; and J. Craddock, "El *Setenario*: última e inconclusa refundición alfonsina de la *Primera Partida.*" *AHDE,* 56 (1986), pp. 441–466.

[64] See a discussion of this problem in F. Gómez Redondo, *Historia de la prosa castellana,* pp. 304–330, which has an up-to-date bibliography. Cf. F.J. Flores Arroyuelo, "El *Setenario* una primera versión de los capítulos introductorios de *Las Siete Partidas,*" in *La lengua y la literatura en tiempos de Alfonso X. Actas,* ed. F. Carmona and F.J. Flores, Murcia: Universidad de Murcia, 1985, pp. 169–180; G. Martin, "Datation du *Septénaire*: rappels et nouvelles considérations." *Cahiers de Linguistique Hispani-*

There is also good reason to doubt that the *Setenario* is a book of laws and that, therefore, it could be the foundation of the *Primera Partida*, and even less, its "final draft." I believe, as do many others, that laws I–XI were written after Alfonso X assumed the throne in order to explain what had already been done during his father's reign, that is, laws XII–CVIII. When Fernando died, his "Treatise on the Communion" was already being drafted, although it was never completed. Internal references allow us to deduce that if the project was not completed before Fernando III's death, its general plan was well established. It provided for a division into seven parts: "the king don Fernando ordered the composition of this work, and that he and the kings who would follow him would hold it as a treasure…And to eliminate these seven [previously described] evils, he divided this book in seven parts. And he showed in each one of them how men should understand what was convenient for them to do and what was convenient for them to avoid" (p. 17)

It seems, then, that Alfonso had very little to do with this seven-part division, though he did complete the work that his father was unable to finish: "And we, don Alfonso, since we received this book composed and ordered, we called it *Setenario*, a title we found fitting according to the nature of the arguments and the method of their exposition" (p. 25, 18–20). This clearly indicates that he gave it such a name based on both its content and the manner of its exposition. Matter and form are two of the four Aristotelian causes around which Alfonso, a great admirer of Aristotle, structured not only the *Setenario* and the *Seven Partidas*, but also his two large historical compilations. The choice of "seven" is based on a simple reason: seven is the number that leads us to wisdom, which is man's goal:

> Wisdom, according to what the sages have said, is to lead man to the fulfillment of all the things he wishes to do and achieve. And that is why the sages ordered the seven arts of knowledge, which they called the arts, and these are subtle and noble skills they invented in order to know things with certainty and to act accordingly, both in heavenly as in earthly matters. (*Setenario*, pp. 29, 19–24)

Although Alfonso was not responsible for the seven-part structure and internal division of the work, this does not mean that he was not a

---

que *Médiévale*, 24 (2001), pp. 325–342; and "De nuevo sobre la fecha del *Setenario*," *e-Spania*, 2, December 2006.

true enthusiast of a numerological conception of knowledge in general and of the number seven in particular, as can be gleaned from the explanation he gave of the title: "We called this book *Setenario* because all things in it are ordered according to the number seven" (p. 25, 23–29).

Given these precedents, I am not convinced by those who think the writing of the *Setenario* signals mental dysfunction. That Alfonso, like many men of great genius had, so to speak, a poetic touch of madness should not surprise us. For only a man with ideas that were out of the ordinary could accomplish a cultural revolution such as his, daring to launch into that sea of Latin culture the fragile vessel of Castilian as the language of science, history, and law. But his choice of the number seven as a structuring agent of his works does not seem to me a sign of mental disintegration, especially since he was able to dispassionately articulate the reasons for it. On the other hand, an arithmologic conception of knowledge was indeed an essential component of allegorical rhetoric.[65]

Alfonso was not alone in using the numerological system. The allegoric/symbolic use of numbers was as old as the use of allegory itself (St. Augustine's commentary of the Gospel of John is an example). Medieval writers followed this ancient tradition of "numeric composition" in their rhetoric.[66] Alfonso divided his most important legal treatise in seven parts, the *Siete Partidas*, following the model begun in the *Setenario*. The number also has a primary structuring function in the *Cantigas*, where Alfonso plays with several units but gives special emphasis to the number 10-considered the perfect number since antiquity—in the distribution of compositions in three collections.[67]

---

[65] On this subject, see the reflections of J. Perona, "Espesores simbólicos de la glosa del mundo: el *Setenario* alfonsí, una aritmología sagrada," *Glosae. Revista de Historia del Derecho Europeo*, 1 (1988), pp. 35–96.

[66] Cf. E.R. Curtius, *European Literature and the Latin Middle Ages*, trans. W.R. Trask, New York: Bollingen Foundation, 1953, esp. pp. 52–509 (Excursus XV: "Numerical Composition"). J. Perona, "Espesores simbólicos de la glosa del mundo," pp. 35–96.

[67] Ten is of particular significance in the *Cantigas* numbered 10 and 100, and the successive hundreds: 200, 300 and 400. All of these *loor* or praise *cantigas* follow nine narratives in which the miracles dominate, while the *loor* ones emphasize the theological doctrine of the mystery of Mary's virginal motherhood and her power as mediator of all the graces. The *cantiga* number 100 and those that close the collections (200, 300, 400) are exclusively devoted to personal requests by Alfonso, while *Cantigas* 1, 10 and all multiples of 10 up to 100 are *loor cantigas*. Scholars have also noted the symbolic presence of the number 5 in the codices of illuminated histories (*Tj1* and *F*), where,

But the number 7, as we could expect, also has an unusually symbolic value in the *Cantigas*: *Cantiga* 1 deals with "The Seven Joys of Mary"; number 403 with "The Seven Sorrows of Mary"; 418 explains how "The Seven Gifts of the Holy Spirit" correspond to "The Seven Gifts that God Granted to Mary," etc. The Learned King also made use of the symbolism of the number 3 in *Cantiga* 414 where he discusses the triple virginity of Mary through an analogy with the Trinity.

Alfonso not only enjoyed the hermetic symbolism of numbers but also that of names, and his entire scientific, historiographic, juridical and poetical oeuvre is full of that display of this allegoric technique: the use of names. The *Setenario* would also be a good example of this technique when it allegorically explains the seven letters of his father's name, FER[N]ANDO, and of his, ALFONSO.[68] But he also employed this technique, for instance, in *Cantiga* 140, where he explained the five letters of the name MARIA; and in his premier legal work, the *Siete Partidas*, he begins each one of the seven divisions of the work with the seven letters of his name. Would all this signal that he was obsessed with the numbers 7, 3, and 10, as well as with letters and names, and that he was therefore insane? Undoubtedly, Alfonso, who was passionate about science, was a tireless student of the world around him. His intellectual curiosity had no limits: he was interested in everything, from the value and meaning of stones (he wrote four *Lapidaries*), to that of stars (he composed sixteen *Books of the Wisdom of Astronomy*). We should therefore not be surprised that as a good Pythagorean, he would see the key to the knowledge of reality in numbers and their meaning.

---

in contrast to the normal praxis of including only six vignettes in the illumination of a *cantiga, cantigas* ending in 5 include twelve miniatures. Regarding the symbolism of 5, Alfonso dedicated thirteen *cantigas* to the 5 feasts of the Virgin, all of them in successive order from *Cantiga* 410 to 422. For Pythagoras, the perfection of 10 stemmed from being the sum of other digits (1+2+3+4=10); hence the ten fingers of man, the ten commandments, etc. Cf. Curtius, *European Literature*, p. 225.

[68] For FER[N]ANDO, cf. pp. 20–21; for ALFONSO, "…whose name God's mercy willed it would begin with an A and end with an O, that it would have seven letters, and that according to the language of Spain, similar to his name. Through those seven letters he sent us the seven gifts of the Holy Spirit, which are these…" (pp. 7, 23–28). The observation about the beginning and the end of the name, A and O, alpha and omega, could not be more meaningful, for that was what Alfonso thought he represented for his subjects as a legislator and wise man.

6. Diagnosis

The *Cantigas* we have examined, just as the little information that appears in the historical documentation, do not speak of the causes or nature of the illnesses of the Learned King, and rarely do they mention any symptoms. Alfonso himself in his last will, drafted five months before his death, speaks in general terms about the "many ailments and many burdens of great illnesses of many sorts in our body" he had to suffer. Among those symptoms are fever, changes in the color of his skin, pus, edema or swelling of the legs, and above all sharp pains and loss of consciousness, which so terrified medieval people for they saw it as a prelude to an imminent death, and with which they frequently identified it. These symptoms could have been caused by a great variety of illnesses. In fact, Alfonso X was burdened in his last years by not one but several conditions, all of them serious, very painful, and potentially fatal.

Although it is very difficult and risky to make any definite statements about the illnesses that afflicted Alfonso and their causes, according to the clinical examination of some physicians of our day gathered by Maricel Presilla in her doctoral thesis, Alfonso suffered most probably from a squamous-cell carcinoma of the maxillary antrum that, with time, extended to the entire bone structure of the face.[69] The author based her conclusions on the data from forensic exams on the remains of Alfonso X carried out in 1579 and in 1948, which she submitted to several oncologists.[70]

---

[69] Cf. *The Image of Death in the Cantigas de Santa María of Alfonso X (1252–84): The Politics of Death and Salvation*, New York University, 1989, 2 vols., II, pp. 473–484. Maricel Presilla, who besides her doctoral thesis dedicated a long paper to the illnesses of the Learned King, defines it as:

> [...] a squamous-cell carcinoma of the maxillary antrum, a slow-growing cancer which inexorably spread through the bony structure of his face, alternately exerting great pressure from the accumulation of fluid within the sinus followed by a rapid remission of symptoms when the abscess drained.

("The Image of Death and Political Ideology in the *Cantigas de Santa Maria*." in *Studies on the Cantigas de Santa María: Art, Music and Poetry*, ed. I.J. Katz, J.E. Keller, et al., Madison: Wis., 1987, pp. 403–459, 435.)

[70] We know about the 1579 exam through J. Alonso de Morgado, *Historia de Sevilla*, Seville, 1587, Book IV, pp. 107–108; the 1948 exam was reported by the forensic physician Dr. J. Delgado Roig, "Examen médico legal de unos restos históricos: los cadáveres de Alfonso X el Sabio y Doña Beatriz de Suabia." *AH,* 9 (1948), pp. 135–153. The opinions of the various specialists consulted by M. Presilla can be seen in her doctoral thesis, *The Image of Death in the Cantigas de Santa María* II, pp. 473–484. The author also used as a guide two well known works on squamous-cell carcinoma of the maxillary antrum: L.V. Ackerman and J.A. del Regato, *Cancer. Diagnosis, Treatment and*

The first examination of Alfonso X's remains we know of happened on "Saturday, June thirteenth of the year fifteen hundred seventy-nine at seven p.m." following "the mandate and approval of his Highness [Felipe II]" and before the presence of all the ecclesiastic and secular authorities of Seville: "Jurados y Titulados," that is, judges and forensic doctors.[71] Although the celebrated historian of Seville witnessed the event first hand, he does not deal with the medical/scientific aspects of the examination; he simply describes succinctly what he saw: "The King Don Alfonso the Learned also had [like his father] a sword in hand, with a scepter, crown and other imperial insignia, and he wore old-fashioned shoes with silver buckles. *And it was noticed that his forehead and head were unusually large,* and his beard was a bit longer than a cleric's" (fol. 108r, emphasis added). The 1579 exam, therefore, shows that the skull of the Learned King showed signs of deformity in the front part of the head: "*his forehead and head were unusually large.*"

According to the 1948 exam that was carried out at the same time as that of his mother, doña Beatriz, Alfonso was not wearing the clothes described by Morgado, but rather, much simpler ones which were obviously from a period after his death.[72] The body was practically complete but in an almost complete skeletal state, with few remains of muscle tissue in some places. In contrast to that of his mother, which preserved all teeth and had the elegantly groomed nails almost

---

Prognosis, St. Louis: The C.V. Mosby Company, 1985; and J.G. Batsakis, *Tumors of the Head and Neck. Clinical and Pathological Considerations,* Baltimore: The Williams and Webins Company, 1979. See also, R.P. Kinkade, "Alfonso X, *Cantiga* 235, and the Events of 1269–1278." *Speculum,* 67 (1992), pp. 284–323, espec. p. 290, note 20, where he quotes the opinion of another specialist who relates the possible origin of the cancer to a blow Alfonso received in that part of the face.

[71] Morgado, op. cit., fol. 107. Until it was placed in its definitive location in the Seville cathedral, Alfonso's body was moved several times. During all these relocations, it appears that the remains were examined by prominent physicians of the period, whose names are known, but not their reports, if any were drafted at all (cf. Delgado Roig, art. cit., pp. 136–137).

[72] When the coffin was opened and after lifting the sheets that covered the body, it was found lying face up, with the head leaning heavily towards the right side. He was wearing a lavish embroidered tunic, had folded arms, the right lying on the left. The arms were lacking hands, the bones of which appeared at the bottom of the coffin and probably had fallen off during a violent change in the position of the coffin...The inferior maxillary was found in the right angle of the coffin. The skull was covered by an elegant black cap embroidered with threads with gold rings, corals, and jet. The trunk was complete, as were the spine and pelvis. The femurs and leg bones were bent, with the right leg on top of the left, and the left foot was separated from its joint, placed under the right one. (Delgado, p. 137)

intact, Alfonso's had no finger or toenails and was missing all teeth. His hair was light blonde with gray patches in the distal extremity. There were no signs in his body of spine injuries or any other bone degeneration of any interest (p. 143). But it did have two transverse cuts on the left lateral region of the thorax, "possibly [made] to extract the viscera from this cavity, especially the heart, which is mentioned in his will and preserved in Murcia" (p. 147). On the right side of his body, near the forearm, the jaw of a small dog was found, while other bone remains of the dog were found at the bottom of the coffin (pp. 138–142). According to Dr. Delgado's calculations, Alfonso would have been 5'9" tall. "He was, therefore, of superior height without being overly tall" (p. 141).

Regarding the skull, a matter of great interest for Alfonso X's medical history, Dr. Delgado describes in great detail anthropometric and other characteristics, concluding that it was "rather small in relation to his height. The only noteworthy aspect of the general skull structure was the great size and curved shape of the frontal sinuses" (p. 150). Regarding the face, he notes its elongation and narrowness. "Another feature worthy of note," the report reads, "was the length of the nose, its posterior overlapping and the obtuse, yet somewhat closed angle it forms with the forehead. This makes us think that king Alfonso had a long, overlapping and narrow nose" (p. 150). The report goes on to describe the front part of the head thus:

> The left orbit cavity presents an abundant hypersexostosis, located in the orbit antrum, more profuse in the cheek region than in other areas. The left bone of the nose proper appears to have a perforation. The lesion is perfectly localized, with the upper inner edge of the maxillary exhibiting a large necrosed area. In our view, these signs of exostosis, with hard, exfoliated leaves with remains of vascularization in the bone mass itself, clearly indicate the king may have suffered from a tumor—a sarcoma?— localized in the upper cheek and maxillary, which caused a disturbance in the function of the left eye (and perhaps also the right), and perhaps could have caused the King's death. This neoplasia necessarily produced a deformity of the face, since the left orbit appears to have a larger opening than the right one, and the height of the zygomatic arch emphasizes the left frontal area, producing an acute asymmetry of the face due to the displacement of the bone mass pushed by the tumor. The tumor must have produced the loss of sight in the left eye at least, due to the pressure it exerted on the optic nerve. (p. 151)[73]

---

[73] Dr. Delgado's analysis of the remains included a measurement of the skeleton, a microscopic analysis of the hair and bones, and a chemical analysis of the resins

As we saw, during the winter 1276–1277 and later in the summer of 1280, the pressure exerted by the tumor was so great that the left eye was pushed out of its orbit, which coincides with the description of the carcinoma of the maxillary antrum, according to the specialists mentioned by M. Presilla.[74] We do not know exactly when the first symptoms of the illness emerged, but everything seems to indicate that already in 1269 the king was suffering from a serious illness, although we cannot specify what it was. If a radiological exam, which was not performed in 1948, could confirm that it was cancer, then it would be plausible, as some specialists hold, that the illness caused inflammation in that part of the face making his eye protrude from its orbit and producing a constant oozing and pus he expelled from the nose, forming pustules and other infections that made him look like a leper, as his son Sancho claimed. This kind of cancer (as opposed to the sarcoma mentioned by Dr. Delgado Roig in his report) grows slowly and may have frequent remission periods without any treatment, whereas a sarcoma would have killed Alfonso in a few months.[75] In the medieval concept of illness-cure mentioned above, this type of cancer, with unexpected flares and quick remissions, made it easy for Alfonso and his contemporaries to interpret a period of remission as an authentic miracle worked by the Virgin, for it was impossible to be cured overnight from such a serious and obvious illness except by divine intervention.

The various specialists we consulted from the Móstoles Hospital in Madrid—Dr. Carlos Barros Aguado, from the Infectious Diseases Unit, Dr. Miguel Méndez Ureña, from the Oncology Service, Dr.

---

used in the embalming process. But no radiological analysis was performed which could have determined more accurately the illnesses he suffered from and the cause of death.

[74] Cf. Ackerman and Del Regato, *Cancer. Diagnosis*, p. 238; Batsakis, *Tumors of the Head and Neck*, p. 183. According to these scholars 80% of the tumors in this part of the head are squamous-cell carcinomas and primarily affect men (90% of the cases) who are over 40, which was Alfonso's case. Sarcomas in this part of the head are very rare (10%).

[75] Cf. Presilla, *The Image of Death in the Cantigas de Santa Maria of Alfonso X, el Sabio*, p. 479, where the opinión of Dr. Rubén Oropeza, a specialist in cancer surgery at Mount Sinai Hospital in New York, is cited; on p. 481 she quotes the opinion of the pathologist, Dr. Ackerman, who thought that it was also a cancer of the maxillary antrum and not a sarcoma. Members of the Oncology Department of New York University's Medical Center agree that the slow development of the illness, along with one more symptom such as the total loss of the teeth, seem to indicate that it was effectively a cancer of the maxillary antrum, which probably did not kill him. Instead, he probably died of kidney or heart failure.

Carlos Barra Galán, from the Nose, Ear and Throat Service, and Dr. Ángel Lavín Cobo, Director of the Cardiology Service—agree that the possibility of a maxillary-facial cancer is quite remote, and that there are other more plausible reasons to explain the symptoms we know though the documentation and forensic medical exam. Dr. Ángel Lavín Cobo summarized for us the detailed report of his other colleagues regarding the diseases suffered by Alfonso X in the following way: "Given the analysis of the data obtained from the remains of the Learned King, and the consultation with the aforementioned specialists, we could conclude the following: 1) The King may have suffered from a recurrent sinus infection complicated by a suppuration process, that is a facial/orbital secondary cellulites to an ostheomelitis of the area, which got better when the corresponding abcess drained, which would explain the remissions. 2) It may have been a chronic granulomatous process, either infectious—with a high probability of tuberculosis—or rather, non-infectious, perhaps a malignant mid-range granulomatosis, with a torpid evolution and the corresponding remissions, which could explain the improvements cited in the *Cantigas*. 3) A cancer of the maxillary sinus secondary to the malignant evolution of an inverted papiloma, with secondary infections and purulent rhinorrheas, which would explain the spectacular remissions cited in the *Cantigas*. On the other hand, the possibility of a squamous-cell carcinoma, sarcoma, etc., in the area seems remote because the evolution was too long for this types of processes and, likewise, the remissions were also too prolonged."[76]

In any event, whether it was a tumor, a chronic sinus infection, or a chronic granuolmatosis in the maxillary region of the skull with sporadic flare-ups and remissions, Alfonso must surely have suffered terrible pains, given the primitive state of painkillers at the time, along with mood swings that would have certainly alarmed those around him, as were his wife, doña Violante, who abandoned him, and his children, who rebelled against him. Recent studies have shown the

---

[76] I wish to express my gratitude to Dr. Lavín for his gracious collaboration in obtaining the opinion of his colleagues who, in the midst of their busy work schedules, found the time to go over the materials submitted and issue their opinion. I would also like to express my sincere gratitude to my good friend, Dr. Mario Verna, a distinguished surgeon at Hackensack Medical Center (New Jersey, USA), for his advice regarding the treatment of medical issues in this biography of Alfonso X.

consequences of pain in cancer patients, ranging from anxiety, depression and violent and uncontrollable behavior, to suicide.[77]

In the last years of his life, perhaps since the illness at Vitoria in 1276, Alfonso also suffered from a very serious dropsy condition, which is not an illness but the symptom of a problem with the heart or kidneys; as noted, it may have manifested itself at Montpellier, and as was the case with his father, it was with him until his death.

The *Cantigas* we have analyzed never abound in the clinical details of the Learned King's illnesses, nor does the *Crónica de Alfonso X*. In fact, the text and especially the illustrations of the *Cantigas* seem to contradict what we know about the king's last illness from the analysis of his remains. In the miniatures, Alfonso's face is represented in a conventional way, always in a beaming, perfect state, with no trace of illness or imperfection, as could be expected of the works destined for the king's daily use and produced by artists under his supervision.

As noted, the mental health and stability of the king was quite another matter. The diagnosis in this case proves more difficult and conflictive, since it must be based on speculative data and theoretical clinical principles about which there is no agreement. Still, in order to reach a better understanding of the subject of this biography, it is important to consider what a specialist in our days has said about this matter.

According to Dr. Francisco Torres González, Director of "La Atalaya" Psychiatric Hospital, in his 1984 address on his admission to the Instituto de Estudios Manchegos, Alfonso was an *introverted* and *immature* intellectual. He attempts to apply these two terms of modern psychology to the personality of the Learned King, not always with complete success, although in general his analysis helps us to better understand certain attitudes and behaviors of don Alfonso.

Dr. Torres arrived at this psychological diagnosis of the personality of the Learned King based on the somatic data detected by

---

[77] Cf. Sylvia Lack, "Total Pain," *Clinics in Oncology*, 3 (1984), 33–34; and the insightful essay of a famous cancer patient: Susan Sontag, *Illness as Metaphor*, New York: Farrar, Straus and Giroux, 1988. Dr. Torres writes that, "In the meantime, Alfonso, at 62, had already fallen ill with 'an ailment of the soul,' to use a contemporary expression. He certainly had motives for such an ailment of the soul (namely, the many betrayals and troubles he suffered), but there was also another reason: the depression typical of cancer patients. In addition to the old ailment of the heart, as the studies of his skull have revealed, there was now a sarcoma in his left orbit that had also deformed his face" ("Rasgos médico-psicológicos." p. 136).

Dr. Delgado during the forensic medical examination of the remains. As mentioned, Alfonso was 5'9" tall, "of superior height without being overly tall" (Delgado, p. 141). From this physical characteristic, Dr. Torres concludes he had an elongated body, in the leptosomatic or endomorphic-cerebrotonic categories. "This seems particularly evident when studying the skull, which is very much within this typology: a doliocephalic skull, a long-line nose (slightly curved), and an elongated face. These physical features help explain Alfonso's introverted nature" (p. 110). From these physical features, he concludes that, "tall slender types, in general, have introverted temperaments, are not very realistic, and tend to be solitary" (p. 111).

The second characteristic of the Learned King's personality, namely, his *immaturity*, as diagnosed by Dr. Torres, began primarily during his childhood, "the period of indelible marks." It sometimes emerges as a result of a medical problem affecting the brain. At other times, more frequently, it is due to family influences. In Alfonso's case, Dr. Torres believes his immaturity was caused mainly by lack of contact with his father between the ages of 4 and 10 (pp. 119–120). As we noted in Chapter 1, not much is known about this period in Alfonso's life, but everything seems to indicate that his father's absence was not as long as Dr. Torres believes. From his childhood until his father's death, Alfonso truly venerated his father.

His immaturity, according to Dr. Torres, may also have been the cause of his love affairs and extramarital adventures, although this practice was widely accepted and even admired at the time, at least among the nobility, and Alfonso himself recognized it as normal, rather than as a personal psychological problem. (Regarding this matter, Alfonso would also go on to legitimize the children of religious men and their concubines.) Therefore, I do not feel that his unstable love relationships are a good standard by which to judge Alfonso's psyche. Mental instability, as some of his biographers have noted, can also be seen in his indecisive personality. He has also been accused of having a weak character, which made him dependent on others. First, in his early years, he was dominated by an authoritarian grandmother; later by his wife, on whom he bestowed ample powers when he discovered her talent for negotiation; and, in the end of his life, by his son, don Sancho, *the Brave*, "the violent genius" (in the words of Dr. Torres, p. 135). According to the Marquis of Lozoya, don Sancho "came to dominate his weak and indecisive father, and managed to proclaim himself heir, possibly against Alfonso's secret preference for the Infantes de la Cerda."[78] That was the last irony in the life of this kind and very talented man who, nevertheless, had a physically and metaphorically weak heart.

7. Cultural Parenthesis

In the period from his return from Beaucaire in July 1275 to his departure from Valladolid after his cure on April 17, 1278, there were two long gaps with little public activity due to the two serious illnesses he suffered, first in Vitoria (1275–76), and then the relapses in Burgos and Valladolid (from mid-1277 to after April 17, 1278). Once more we see how Alfonso combined, as was his habit, physical pain and moral adversity with intense intellectual activity. During the first period (July 20–December 10, 1275), despite the many setbacks of that year and while he physically and mentally recovered, Alfonso continued to work on his historiographic project, *Estoria de España*, on which, as mentioned, he had probably already made much progress. He was also actively working on the revision of the *Libro del fuero de las leyes* (*Book of the Code of Laws*), which after a new draft circa 1275 would be entitled, *Primera Partida* (*First Partida*). Between 1274 and 1277 he was also busy with the second collection of *cantigas,* which would end up including close to 200 new compositions.

During the second interval, he commissioned and supervised the composition of new legal works geared towards the need to establish norms of behavior in all aspects of his subjects' social life. Hence on September 1276, Maestro Roldán, by order of Alfonso, concluded *Ordenamiento de las Tafurerías* (*Regulations on Gambling Houses*), a legal code that regulated gaming and gambling disputes, one of the most original pieces of legislation of the Learned King's reign.[79] The author/compiler of this work states in the preamble, "This is the book that I, Master Roldán, ordered and composed about gambling houses by request of the most noble and high lord don Alfonso, king of Castile by the grace of God…And the king determined, as a wise and

---

[78] *Historia de España*, 2 vols., Barcelona: Salvat, II, p. 106.
[79] See the excellent edition by R.A. MacDonald, *Libro de las Tahurerias. A Special Code of Law, Concerning Gambling, Drawn Up by Maestro Roldan at the Command of Alfonso X of Castile*, Madison: Seminary of Medieval Studies, 1995.

learned man in all matters, that each person should be punished for impiety and for acting as false witnesses in gambling houses."[80]

Between 1276 and 1279, despite the growing political and family adversities such as the crisis around the succession of the throne of Castile and doña Violante's flight to Aragón along with her grandchildren, the compilation of the 16 astrological treatises that conform the *Libros del saber de astronomía* (*Books of the Wisdom of Astronomy*) were completed, most preceded by a preface written personally by Alfonso himself.[81] Around the same time, *Libro de las formas et de las imagines* (*Book of the Forms and Images*) was completed.[82] The various treatises on magical astrology, including *Picatrix*, were completed towards the end of the seventies.

During this period of convalescence, Alfonso also composed several of his astronomical works. In 1276 he put the final touches on *Cuatro libros de las estrellas fijas de la ochava esfera* (*Four Books on the Fixed Stars of the Eighth Sphere*), a work by Abd al-Rahman the Sufi, translated into Spanish by Yehuda Mosha-Cohen, a learned Jew in Alfonso's court, and Guillén Arremón d'Aspa, a Sevillian clergyman, in collaboration with Juan de Mesina, Juan de Cremona, and Samuel ha-Levi. It is precisely in the prologue to this work where we find one of the most immediate testimonies of the direct intervention of the Learned King in the composition of his works:

> In the name of God, Amen. This is the book of the figures of the fixed stars found in the eight heaven, that king don Alfonso had translated

---

[80] *Libro de las Tahurerias*, quoted ed., p. 286.

[81] A. Cárdenas, "Hacia una edición crítica del *Libro del saber de astrología* de Alfonso X: Estudio codicológico actual de la obra regia (mutilaciones, fechas, y motivos)," in *Homenaje a Pedro Sáinz Rodríguez*, II, Madrid: Fundación Universitaria Española, pp. 111–120; and his edition *A Study and Edition of the Royal Scriptorium Manuscript of El Libro del saber de astrologia by Alfonso X el Sabio*, 4 vols., Doctoral Dissertation, Madison: University of Wisconsin, 1974. Regarding the prologues, see R. González-Casanovas, "Alfonso's X Scientific Prologues: Scholarship as Enlightenment," in *Medieval Perspectives*, 6 (1991), pp. 113–121; and "Alfonso X's Rhetoric of Humanist Education: Professional Literacy in the Scientific Prologues," *Romance Languages Annual*, 2 (1990), pp. 434–441.

[82] R.C. Diman y L.W. Winget, *Alfonso el Sabio, Lapidario and Libro de las formas & ymagenes*, Madison: Hispanic Seminary of Medieval Studies, 1980, pp. 151–178. A.J. Cárdenas, A.J.: "Alfonso X's *Libro de las formas e de las ymagenes*: Facts and Probabilities," *Romance Quarterly*, 33 (1986), pp. 269–274. For translations of the other astronomical works, see Ballesteros, *Alfonso X*, pp. 816–819; and A. Cárdenas, "A Survey of Scholarship on the Scientific Treatises of Alfonso X, el Sabio," *La Corónica*, XI, 2 (1982–1983), pp. 231–247.

from the Chaldean and the Arabic to the Castilian language…and it was translated at his request by Yhuda Cohen, his *alfaquí* [learned man in Islamic law], and Guillén Arremón d'Aspa, his cleric…And later he had it ordered, the abovementioned king, and he removed the arguments he thought were superfluous and that repeated themselves and that were not in correct Castilian, and he put in others that he thought fit in; and in regards to the language, he corrected that himself […][83]

Following the introduction of his collaborators, Alfonso devotes himself to writing the prologue. The King's intervention in his works was therefore direct and personal, and covered all aspects of composition, including minimal details such as corrections of language usage and style.

In the same prologue, written personally by Alfonso, he left the following reflection, which is witness to his attitude towards illness and the many setbacks he was suffering during its composition:

> […] Likewise, we must love him [God] because thanks to his virtue and mercy he gives us and sustains our life in this world while He wants us to be alive, and protects us and frees us from many evils we receive and would receive, according to our natural penchant to behave badly rather than well. (*Ochava esfera*, pp. 180–181)

In this prologue too, Alfonso addresses the main theme of his entire humanistic-didactic enterprise, where he stresses God's will that man, through scientific knowledge of his surrounding world, profit from the things that God has made available to him (Ib., p. 181).

The activities of the court and the Alfonsine *scriptorium* in all areas of knowledge and cultural life were also evidenced by the many poets who followed it and expressed their affiliation to it. In September 1276, Guiraut de Riquier, who as mentioned was present at Alfonso's court, wrote and dedicated a poem to him in which he praised his love for the sciences, the arts and his generosity towards artists and scientists.[84] This eulogy would constitute a perfect finale to life dedicated to patronage and the tireless pursuit of knowledge.

---

[83] *Ochava esfera*, in A. García Solalinde, *Antología*, p. 180; and see the commentary by A. Cárdenas, "Alfonso el Sabio's 'castellano drecho'," *La Corónica*, 9 (1980).

[84] Cf. V. Bertolucci Pizzorusso, "La supplica di Guirault Riquier e la risposta di Alfonso X di Castiglia," *Studi Mediolatini e Volgari*, XIV (1966), pp. 9–135; Ballesteros, *Alfonso X*, p. 815.

CHAPTER NINE

THE NOBLES' REBELLION

1. *A New Concept of Royal Power*

As we saw in the last chapter, the last decade of Alfonso's life was marked by an endless chain of setbacks and misfortunes, both personal and relative to the kingdom. The first one in order of occurrence was the nobles' rebellion, which had catastrophic consequences for his internal politics and vis-à-vis the kingdom of Granada.[1] This predicament was followed by others equally serious: the failure to obtain the imperial crown, the death of his son and heir, don Fernando, which caused family rifts (the abandonment by his wife and don Sancho's rebellion) resulting in civil war and the Moorish invasion and the devastation it caused in the south. The last thorn in this crown of sorrows was his own deposition by his son don Sancho, supported by the nobility and the Church in a climate of anarchy and chaos on all levels of society. *Eppur*, to quote Galileo, in the last two years of his life, despite all these adversities and in the midst of the chaos of civil war, Alfonso, in his Seville retreat, would continue to work on the important projects that constitute his great cultural legacy.

The origins of the nobles' rebellion against Alfonso X, like the hostile attitude of a large portion of the Church, his own family, his subjects, and of society in general, are not as a whole easily traceable, because it was not something that began from one day to the next,

---

[1] In this chapter and throughout this book, by "nobles" we mean not only the "high nobility," made up of some thirty families whose last names appear in the diplomas and chronicles of the period (the Lara, Castro, Haro, Cameros, Manrique, Mendoza, Ponce, Meneses families, etc.), but also the "lower nobility" (gentleman, knights, etc.) and those bearing the title of "ricoshombres." The distinction between these three groups is not entirely clear, especially between the last two categories. The "high nobility," according to Moxó, is defined by these characteristics: patrimony, lineage, and favor at court ("De la nobleza vieja a la nobleza nueva," *CHE*. Anexos de *Hispania*, 3 (1969), pp. 1–210). As we will see, all the leaders of the rebellion owned considerable patrimony, were descended from illustrious families, and in some way participated in the life of the court, because they were related to the royal family or they occupied high offices, that is, they belonged to the "high nobility."

but rather the result of a slow process of discontent slowly accumulating for years, until it erupted in the form of violence on the surface of society. Wounded feelings and trampled rights and privileges produced this political trauma that devastated the reign of the Learned King.[2] So, when reflecting on the causes of the rebellion, it might seem that certain attitudes of the nobles vis-à-vis Alfonso escape all rational explanation and clearly border on ungratefulness. But upon closer examination, it becomes evident this was not always the case: the nobles often had serious motives for dissent, even if they were not always right.

In general terms, it could be said the rebellion of the Castile-León nobility against Alfonso X should be seen in the wider context of the profound changes that took place since the end of the 12th century regarding the concept of royalty as a social institution. The traditional view of the king as a feudal lord who enters into a personal vassalage relationship with his subjects was being quickly substituted by a new relationship in which the king was responsible for a corporate entity. His function was more of a *primus inter pares* (first among equals), with the three other estates of the kingdom, the clergy, the nobility, and the representatives of the cities, along with him, responsible for the common good and the security of the kingdom.[3] From this perspective, what happened to Alfonso with the nobility of his kingdom was not different from what happened to all the other peninsular and European kings, all of whom were bound by blood ties.[4]

In the mid-12th century, with the adoption of Roman Law, and the elimination of traditional privileges, the monarchy went from being a feudal institution with very limited powers, which only sustained itself

---

[2] One could quote, as a typical case, the spite felt by Diego López de Haro, Alfonso's ensign, when Alfonso favored his childhood friend, don Nuño González de Lara, in a land possession dispute ("on the inheritance of a mountain"). De Haro abandoned his king and became a vassal to the king of Aragón in August 1254. For similar motives, his brother don Enrique rebelled and went into exile. Cf. *CAX*, chap. 30, pp. 112–115.

[3] On this problem, see: W. Ullman, *Principles of Government and Politics in the Middle Ages*, New York, 1966; E. Kantorowicz, *The King's Two Bodies: A Study in Medieval Political Theology*, Princeton, 1957; and S. Barton, *The Aristocracy of Twelfth-Century León and Castile*, Cambridge: Cambridge University Press, 1997.

[4] On the blood ties of the European nobility starting with Alfonso VIII, see: J. González, *El reino de Castilla en la época de Alfonso VIII*, 3 vols., Madrid, 1960, I, pp. 185–188, 206–207; and G. Daumet, *Mémoire sur les relations de la France et de la Castille de 1255 à 1320*, Paris: Bibliothèque de l'École des Hautes Études, 1913.

with the support of the nobles, to a more centralizing and powerful institution. The creation of a strong and integrative monarchy was not only Alfonso's idea; it also appears throughout the 13th century in other European monarchies.[5] Alfonso also adopted in his political ideology the absolutist conception of royal power to which he attributed a divine origin: "Kings, each one in his kingdom, are the vicars of God," he says in the *Partidas* (II.1.5);[6] and in the *Espéculo de las leyes* (*Mirror of the Laws*), he declares: "By the grace of God we have no higher authority over us in the temporal realm" (I.13). For the Learned King, that is, royal power stemmed directly from God, and the king was only accountable to God, or as he says in the same work, "Christ...gave the king power to administer justice and make the laws, and he left him as his judge...and the king is obligated to render accounts for what Christ entrusted him" (IV.7.29). Alfonso was not the only European king who adopted this independence-minded legal principle that rejected the pope's and the emperor's authority in the temporal matters of the kingdom ("The king is emperor in his kingdom"),[7] but he did go the farthest in justifying that supreme dominion when he assumed the position that the king is the origin and source of the law.[8] In his legislation, he even formulated this theoretical position using the same metaphor that Pauline theology used to express the relationship between the faithful and Christ: "Christ is the head of the church: and he is the savior of the body; For as the body is one, and has many members, and all the members of that one body, being many, are one body: so also *is* Christ" (*Eph.* 5:23 and *1 Cor.* 12:12), which Alfonso applies to the legal/moral union between the king and his subjects:

> [T]he king is the head of the kingdom, for, as from the head originate the feelings by which all the members of the body are controlled; so also by the commands which originate from the king, who is the lord

---

[5] See R. Fedou, *El Estado en la Edad Media*, Madrid, 1978; and L. Genicot, *Europa en el siglo XIII*, Barcelona, 1970.

[6] *Las Siete Partidas*, 4 vols., ed. Robert I. Burns, trans. By Samuel Parsons Scott, Philadelphia: University of Pennsylvania Press, 2001. All quotations in English from this work come from this edition, unless otherwise noted; vol. 2, p. 271.

[7] Cf. J.A. Maravall, "El concepto de Monarquía en la Edad Media española" and "Del régimen feudal al régimen corporativo en el pensamiento de Alfonso X," in *Estudios de historia del pensamiento español*, I, Madrid, 1983, pp. 73–75 and 102–109.

[8] The king's exclusive right to legislate stems logically from this principle: "An emperor or king may make laws for the people of his dominions, but no one else has the power to make them with regard to temporal matters" (*Partidas*, I, 1.12), *Las Siete Partidas*, vol. 1, p. 5.

and head of all the people of his kingdom, they should be directed and guided, and act in harmony with him, to obey him, and support, and protect, and aggrandize the kingdom, of which he is the soul and head, and they are the members. (*Partidas*, II.1.5)[9]

This conception of royal power must have seemed to the Castilian nobility and the Church hierarchy as an authentic revolution that disrupted the balance these two institutions traditionally maintained with the monarchy, hence the precipitation of the crisis.

But at the same time, as we suggested above, we should also consider that to compensate this somewhat absolutist view of the king, Alfonso also actively promoted the participation of the other two estates of society in the administration (not the legislation) of the kingdom. This other face of his administrative policy, which envisioned the kingdom as a corporate entity, was expressed in the institution of the Cortes and other minor manifestations such as the "councils" and "assemblies," which became very important in determining fiscal policy, solving economic problems, financing his "road to Empire," his war against the North African Moors, and even the selection of his successor. No other king ruled his subjects based on consultation, consensus, and the active participation of the governed and their representatives as effectively as Alfonso X. It could thus be said that Alfonso was an absolutist yet not an authoritarian king.

In the analysis of the relations between nobility and monarchy, which Alfonso made in his famous letter to his son and heir don Fernando in 1272, the terms of the conflict almost appear to be personal and from a historical perspective of the past. He explained that, "the reason why they did it [to rebel] was this: because they wanted to always have the kings oppressed and seize what was theirs, thinking of and finding ways to dispossess and dishonor them as their ancestors have done before...and just as the kings gave them possessions and honored them, they struggled to dispossess and dishonor them in so many ways, that it would be very long and very embarrassing to tell."[10]

Immersed in his absolutist vision of royal power, Alfonso was unable to remotely admit that the rebels, in their opposition to his

---

[9] In the *Fuero real* the metaphor of the Church as the "mystical body of Christ" is extended, conceiving of the structure of the king's court in the same way as the Heavenly court (*Fuero real*, I, 2.3, ed. A. Palacios Alcaine, Barcelona: PPU, 1991, p. 6).

[10] In Mondéjar, *Memorias*, p. 306; and A. García Solalinde, *Antología*, p. 219.

vision, perhaps also had legitimate intentions and an interest in the common good: "Likewise, they don't do it for the sake of the kingdom, because no one could want this [the common good] more than I do, since I'm the heir, and therefore they have very few benefits, except those that we grant them" (letter to don Fernando). But, as we will soon see, there were also valid and specific reasons why the nobility dissented from the monolithic Alfonsine concept of the king and his relations with the kingdom.

2. Dissidence

The first signs of political disagreement between Alfonso and the Castilian nobility took place during an incident narrated in the *Crónica de Alfonso X*. Although this source is not always reliable when it comes to chronology and sometimes too in its content, we must acknowledge that the section dealing with the nobles' rebellion, the topic it treats with the greatest accuracy and detail (30 of its 77 chapters are devoted to it), proves a reliable guide to many of the events and must be considered credible given the sources it employed, which, as far as can be seen, were mostly firsthand.[11]

That incident, which occurred in Seville in 1267, was brought about by a visit by his grandson, don Dinis, future king of Portugal. But even before this, several run-ins with the nobility had already called into question Alfonso's authority and jurisdiction in many aspects of his administrative policy, and they had already attempted to free themselves from its shackles. One example was what happened two years after his accession to the throne, in 1254, when, on April 22, pope Innocent IV ordered the bishop of Segovia to absolve from oath all those who had illicitly agreed to fight against the Castilian king's rights and jurisdiction. Up until that point the Church considered this agreement as subversive and punished it by excommunication.[12] But now, the lifting of the excommunication sanctioned by the pope

---

[11] For a historical work dating back to the beginning of the 14th century, the number of documents the *CAX* literally reproduces and carefully summarizes is very impressive. I was unable to consult the new edition by M. González Jiménez, *Crónica de Alfonso X según el Ms.II / 2777 de la Biblioteca del Palacio Real de Madrid*, Murcia: Real Academia Alfonso X el Sabio, 1998.

[12] In *Registres d'Innocent IV (1243–1254), (Les)*, 4 vols., ed. E. Berger, Paris, 1881–1921, III, no. 7.497, p. 410.

meant the hierarchy's approval of the nobles' conspiracy. This showed that not only a group of nobles (for who else except them could start a rebellion?) even before 1254 had sworn to rebel against the king if he somehow violated their rights, but also that the Church blessed their initiative, becoming thus an accomplice in the conspiracy. In fact, in the beginning of August of that same year, one of the most trusted men in the court (for he was the royal ensign of Castile), don Diego López de Haro, lord of Vizcaya, declared himself *desnaturado*, which means that he abandoned the oath of allegiance to his king in order to kiss the hand of another lord, in this case the king of Aragón, don Jaime I.[13]

To these past incidents that clearly showed the traditional conflict between the nobility and the monarchy, which Alfonso mentioned in his letter to his son don Fernando, we must add some important legal measures taken by Alfonso, which were perceived by the nobility as an assault on their traditional position of privilege. These were the promulgation in the spring of 1254 during the Toledo Cortes of a new code of laws known as the *Espéculo de las leyes* (*Mirror of the Laws*).[14] In the prologue, Alfonso states the objective of this work and the motives that led to its composition.[15]

The *Espéculo* is a work full of legal resonances from the entire Alfonsine oeuvre. Both in its prologue and the prologue to the *Fuero real* (I.6.1–5) and ten years later in the one to the *Partidas* (I.1.11–12), the Learned King held that only the king can make laws, for only he is the source of the law ("The king is the law and the judicial power and the entire kingdom," he would even say in *GE*, II, vol. II, p. 252b14–15); but, at the same time, he also upholds the legal axiom of Roman Law: "quod omnes tangit, ab omnibus debet approbari" (that which affects all, must be approved by all).[16] Thus, following this tradition according

---

[13] Text of the homage presented by don Diego López de Haro to Jaime I in Estella on August 8, 1254 in A. Huici – M.D. Cabanes Pecourt, *Documentos de Jaime I de Aragón*, III (1251–1257), Zaragoza, 1978, and IV (1258–1262), Zaragoza, 1982. III, no. 657, pp. 147–148.

[14] R.A. MacDonald, "Law and Politics: Alfonso's Program of Political Reform," *The Worlds of Alfonso*, pp. 150–202. J. O'Callaghan holds that both the *Espéculo* and the *Fuero real* were promulgated during the 1255 Palencia Cortes, see below note 19.

[15] *Espéculo. Texto jurídico atribuído al Rey de Castilla Don Alfonso X, el Sabio*, critical edition and introduction by R.A. MacDonald, Madison, 1990, pp. 5a–b.

[16] Cf. J.A. Maravall, "Del régimen feudal al régimen corporativo en el pensamiento de Alfonso X," *BRAH*, 157 (1965), pp. 213–268; and in *Estudios de historia del pensamiento español. Serie I. Edad Media*, Instituto de Cooperación Iberoamericana,

to which, to ensure the acceptance of laws among the subjects, the legislator must obtain their approval (*Partida* I, 2.9), Alfonso, before promulgating the *Espéculo*, acquired the consent of the various estates of society and recruited for its composition "the most honest sages we could obtain and find and others who were in our court and in our kingdom."

Alfonso goes on to say that the new collection aimed at gathering in writing or 'reflecting' (hence the name, *Espéculo de las leyes*, or *Mirror of the Laws*) an entire series of customs and habits that were thought to be common throughout the kingdom; as justification he noted that the collection would facilitate the judges' task of applying the law in a more uniform way. But Alfonso went further: he expressly wanted it to be based on Roman law rather than on Castilian common law, and he required that henceforth, royal judges were to be experts in Roman law.[17] The establishment of "ius commune" [common law], as it was called, was one of the components of the rebirth of 13th-century humanism. For Alfonso, as a king and legislator, adopting Roman law also meant, as Maravall has noted, that not only legal concepts but also political ones could be conceived "using a more accurate legal technique."[18] And although it may not be asserted that Alfonso was already thinking about his imperial project, this was indeed a great step towards constituting, in the future, the basis for legislation common to all the peoples gathered under one imperial crown. In any event, it is clear that in Alfonso's concept, the administration of justice following the promulgation of the *Espéculo*, would be in the hands of experts in Roman and canonical law, and not in the hands of nobles who ruled themselves according to common law.

A year later, on August 25, 1255, Alfonso put into practice the laws contained in the *Espéculo* (though some scholars question whether the *Espéculo* was ever promulgated) by issuing the *Fuero real*, which he

---

Madrid, 1968, pp. 103–171; and "La corriente democrática medieval en España y la fórmula *Quod omnes tangit*," in ib. pp. 157–175.

[17] On the reception of Roman law in Spain, see: A. García y García, "En torno al derecho romano en la España medieval," *Estudios en Homenaje a Don Claudio Sánchez Albornoz, CHE*, Anejos, 3, pp. 59–72; J.M. Font Rius, "La recepción del derecho romano en la península ibérica durante la Edad Media" in *Recueil des mémoires et travaux publiées par la Société du Droit et des Institutions des anciens pays de droit écrit*, 6 (1967), pp. 85–104.

[18] J.M. Maravall, "Del régimen feudal al régimen corporativo," in *Estudios de historia del pensamiento español. Edad*, p. 116.

granted to Burgos as its compilation of laws for the city, and successively to the most important cities and towns in León and the Castilian Extremadura.[19] By giving all the cities essentially the same laws by which to be governed, the Learned King attempted to achieve uniformity in the administrative policy of all towns. In case of disagreement, they could always consult a copy of the *Espéculo* kept at the court, from which all laws of the *Fuero real* were derived and which served as the standard for all royal judges (also known as *alcaldes de corte*).

The history of the genesis of the *Fuero de Sahagún* could be a good example of how Alfonso proceeded in disseminating the new legal norms of the *Espéculo* in situations of conflict. We know through the anonymous chronicler of the monastery that Alfonso arrived in Sahagún on March 24, 1255, from Burgos where he had celebrated the Cortes (see chap. 3 above) and that he stayed in the monastery for a month. On Easter Monday, March 28, 1255, after the religious celebrations, Alfonso asked the abbot to show him all the privileges of the monastery in order to examine and confirm them, as the abbot had requested. According to the contemporary chronicler, "the lord king, taking both from the old code of law as from the new, according to the best information he could obtain, the parts of the constitutions in which [were contained] the documents and the privileges, besides other freedoms contained in them, in the ways that seemed best to him, had two documents and privileges drafted about the code of laws of the city, and protected and made strong by his lead seal and the seals of the convent's abbot and the council's, gave the abbot full powers he did not have before."[20] According to the anonymous chronicler, who must have been present during the compilation process, Alfonso would have compiled the *Fuero de Sahagún* during his stay in the monastery, between March 24 and April 25, 1255, leaving

---

[19] Cf. J.F. O'Callaghan, "On the Promulgation of the *Espéculo* and the *Fuero real*," in *Alfonso X, the Cortes, and Government in Medieval Spain*, Aldershot – Brookfield: Ashgate, 1998, III, pp. 1–12). There is great disagreement among specialists on the dates of composition and promulgation of these important legal works by Alfonso, which is discussed by J. Sánchez-Arcilla Bernal, "La obra legislativa de Alfonso X el Sabio. Historia de una polémica," in J. Montoya Martínez and A. Domínguez Rodríguez, *El Scriptorium alfonsí: de los libros de Astrología a las "Cantigas de Santa María,"* Madrid: Editorial Complutense, 1999, pp. 17–81.

[20] *Anonimo II*, quoted ed., pp. 189–190. "Fuero viejo" probably refers to *Fuero juzgo*, while "fuero nuevo" would be the laws by Alfonso VI (1085) and which were probably granted to the monastery by Alfonso VII in 1152.

two copies, which were given to the town council and abbot and the monks, respectively.

But the king's legislative activity did not end here. According to the *Anonymous*, "he also gave to the monastery and the council a book of judgments, authorizing it with his lead seal, whereby the town residents would be judged and ruled forever, except for the things discussed in the documents and privileges mentioned above" (pág. 190). This "libro de juicios" [or "book of judgements"] was probably the *Fuero real*. Procedures on how to judge mayors and judges found in the *Fuero real* also appear in the town's statutes, modifying previous laws that evidently Alfonso did not consider adequate, in such a way that he established a new legal hierarchy that went from the town council to the abbot, and finally to the royal court. A.M. Barrero writes that "In this respect, the aspirations of the town council were thwarted because the abbot's authority prevailed as supervisor and recipient of non-royal taxes."[21] From Sahagún, Alfonso continued on, as the *Anonymous* notes, "very happily" to Palencia, where, according to some scholars, he celebrated the new Cortes and officially promulgated both the *Espéculo* and the *Fuero real*.

The *Fuero real* abrogated the *Fuero viejo de Castilla*, where all the privileges and prerogatives of the nobility and the clergy were codified. With the new code, the king's court received the prerogative of the exclusive jurisdiction of certain specific cases, on top of the power to operate as a royal court of appeals in cases of conflict. The king undoubtedly acknowledged the need for ecclesiastic courts, but he also frequently intervened directly in matters of ecclesiastic jurisdiction. This angered bishops and abbots, and those who refused to accept royal decisions were exiled. Alfonso also established other civil courts that had an independent jurisdiction from ecclesiastic courts and those pertaining to the nobility, and he appointed royal judges who would deal with the cases relative to the conflicts of the Mesta, the large cattle and wool corporation of Castile.[22] From a practical point of view, what Alfonso intended with these two works was the compilation of a code of laws for ruling cases in the king's court (*Espéculo*), and a municipal

---

[21] "Los fueros de Sahagún," *AHDE*, 1972, p. 527.
[22] Cf. J. Klein, "Los privilegios de la Mesta de 1272 y 1276," *BRAH*, LXIV (1914), pp. 202–219; and his work, *La Mesta*, Madrid, 1936.

code derived from the previous one to rule on cases in the city courts
(*Fuero real*).[23]

The legislation in both of these works displayed a completely new
attitude on the part of the legislator towards the privileged classes by
trying to unify the legal norms and rules and to render, inasmuch as it
was possible, all subjects equal under the law. According to J. Valdeón,
"Alfonso was, above all, a king who fiercely defended the uniformity
of his kingdoms in the area of norms."[24] This entailed truly radical
changes in certain legal and constitutional concepts that would only
fully develop centuries later. In the midst of the 13th century, Alfonso
directly intervened in the feudal relationships between lord and vassals, which was a great step for his time.[25] From the point of view of
the nobility, the simple fact that a royal judge who did not belong to
the estate of the nobility could rule on the basis of laws written in a
book and not according to common-law norms was simply unacceptable.[26]

Naturally, the nobles who defended the "fueros antiguos" (old
codes) and had a diametrically opposed ideological stance on royal
power (the king being the first among equals) to that of Alfonso's (the
king is the "head and beginning of the entire people," *Fuero real*, I,
2.2), despite the fact that the new legislation had been drafted and
issued with their consent, soon realized that this was a policy against
the nobility. Hence a rebellious seed was planted from the very beginning. Meanwhile, Alfonso would continue to grant his *Fuero real* to
more and more towns.

Many years later, when the 1269–1272 second rebellion of the nobles
was well underway, the Learned King, in a letter written in the third
person to a childhood friend, Nuño González de Lara, complained
bitterly about his unexpected abandonment. In the letter, he explained

---

[23] A. Iglesia Ferreirós, "Las Cortes de Zamora de 1274 y los casos de corte," *AHDE*,
XLI (1971), pp. 845–873.

[24] "Las cortes medievales castellano-leonesas en la historiografía reciente," in
W. Piskorski, *Las cortes de Castilla en el período de tránsito de la edad media a la
moderna 1188–1520*, trans. C. Sánchez Albornoz, Barcelona, 1930. Repr. 1977, pp.
V–XXXV; and cf. "Las cortes castellanas en el siglo XIV," *AEM*, 7 (1970–1971), pp.
633–644.

[25] For the relations between the nobility and the monarchy established in the *Espéculo*, cf. J.M. Pérez Prendes, "Las leyes de Alfonso el Sabio," *Revista de Occidente*, 43
(1984), pp. 67–84.

[26] The *Fuero real* is also known in the documentation as *Fuero del Libro*. Cf. below
note 70.

the fundamental motives why the most faithful don Diego López de Haro had become a *desnaturado* or defector, that is, to protest against the favors granted by Alfonso to Nuño de Lara to his own detriment. Alfonso also reminded don Nuño of the high price he had to pay to keep him in his favor, including the loss of the old friendship with don Diego and the anger of his father, don Fernando, who disapproved of the new friendship with de Lara. Alfonso told don Nuño this story of the breakup of an old friendship in confidence in order to show his generosity towards him and to illustrate how ungratefully he had behaved in that critical moment when all others were abandoning him.[27] Hence, upon closer inspection, the reason for the nobles' defection in 1254–1255, namely, the elevation of a political rival, would have been much more petty and immaterial than the motives derived from changes in the legal structures or the privileges of the nobility. And yet, both were the cause or excuse for the rebellion.

3. *Unexpected Opposition*

The rise of the Lara clan and the fall of the Haros caused the desertion of all their noble supporters, who also went on to join the king of Aragón. Also, as soon as don Enrique, Alfonso's brother, found out about the massive rebellion of a great number of the Castilian nobles, he wasted no time in getting in touch with some of them.[28] Don Jaime I's degree of involvement in this rebellion remains to be determined: Did he actively instigate the Castilian nobles to rebellion as a way to quell Alfonso's hegemonic aspirations, or did he passively benefit from the pressure caused by them in his son-in-law's kingdom? In any event, it is clear that don Jaime was a lifesaver for the rebels who defected from Castile and he ended up becoming a problem for Alfonso.[29]

There had always been bad blood between Enrique and his brother Alfonso. Fernando III's third son was indeed the best warrior among

---

[27] *CAX*, chap. 30, pp. 112–115; the complete text of the letter is in pp. 112–115).

[28] The coalition between Enrique and the rebels is described in the *CAX*, chap. 8, pp. 43–45.

[29] It appears that Alfonso did the same with the Moors who, led by the rebel al-Azark, stood up in arms against don Jaime in Valencia, generously welcoming them when they were driven out of their lands by don Jaime, as told by Jaime in his *Llibre dels feits* (ed. F. Soldevila, in *Les Quatre Grans Cròniques*, chap. 369, p. 138).

the brothers and contributed more than any other to the conquest of
Andalusia. But he was not a king, and this bothered him to such an
extent that he never accepted the authority of his brother. While don
Fernando was alive, Enrique was recognized for his courage and tact
in public relations. Towards the end of 1239 or beginning of 1240,
according to the *Anonymous II* of Sahagún, he was sent to accompany
the abbot of Sahagún on a diplomatic mission that, under Fernando's
orders, would take them first to the court of Frederick II and then to
the pope in Rome, in order to reconcile the emperor with the pope.
The mission clearly failed, but Innocent IV thanked the Castilian king
all the same by making the abbot of Sahagún into a cardinal, while the
young don Enrique acquired a good reputation as mediator with the
pope and his court.[30]

But when Fernando III died, Alfonso confiscated from Enrique
many of the gifts he had deceitfully received from his father. This decision angered Enrique even more. The relations between the two brothers worsened when Alfonso found out that Enrique had become the
lover of doña Juana of Ponthieu, Fernando's second wife, for Alfonso
respected and admired Fernando and had promised him on his deathbed that he would protect his mother-in-law. Enrique's relations with
doña Juana dishonored the memory of Fernando III, so Alfonso took
drastic measures against his brother. Enrique never forgot this action
of Alfonso's and awaited the right moment to take revenge. Joining
the rebels, Enrique hoped not only to extract revenge from Alfonso
but also to recover the lost possessions.[31]

The presence of prince don Enrique at the Aragón court produced
other complications. Jaime I and Violante of Hungary had a very
beautiful daughter named Constanza. As soon as Enrique met her,
he fell madly in love with her and immediately asked don Jaime for
her hand. But, because of a previous promise made to his wife, Violante, he was not able to give his daughter in marriage to anyone who
was not a king. The explanation for this unusual agreement between
spouses was given by none other than a son of Constanza's, the illustrious writer, don Juan Manuel.[32] Constanza was the sister of Violante

[30] Cf. R. Escalona, *Historia del Real Monasterio de Sahagún*, p. 144.

[31] On don Enrique, see below, note 33 and cf. chap. 3, pp. 20–21, note 62, and
chap. 5, pp. 27–30.

[32] Cf. *Libro de las armas*, ed. Blecua, *Obras completas de don Juan Manuel*, I,
Madrid, 1982, pp. 128–130.

of Aragón, the wife of Alfonso X and queen of Castile. As between Alfonso and his brother Enrique, also between the two sisters, Violante and Constanza, there was bad blood, presumably, according to their mother, because of the envy Violante had of Constanza's beauty, and of Constanza's envy of Violante's crown. The matter was so serious, that the mother feared Violante would kill Constanza. To prevent this, she thought of the following scheme: to have Constanza also marry a king so that both sisters would be forced to live separately from one another. Violante made her husband don Jaime swear he would only give Constanza in marriage to a king. Not being one, Enrique, there-fore, could not aspire to Constanza's hand. But the courageous and adventurous prince was not deterred by this obstacle. On the contrary: if he had to become a king, he would find a way to do it.

In considering the various kingdoms he might conquer, Enrique, for obvious reasons, could not attack the powerful kingdom of his brother Alfonso, nor the kingdom of the father of his beloved, nor the kingdom of Navarra, for it was also protected by Aragón. He had thus to set his hopes on one of the Muslim kingdoms to the South. He astutely picked a kingdom dependent on his brother Alfonso. Niebla, an independent kingdom that was nonetheless subjected to Castile and to whom it paid tribute, would become the victim of the rest-less prince's whims. The conquest of Niebla was the perfect goal: he would manage to wrest a tribute-paying kingdom from his brother, whom he hated, depriving him of income, and he would finally obtain Constanza's hand.[33] Jaime I, a warrior, liked the idea because it would teach Alfonso a lesson about his hegemonic aspirations, since he had recently tried to militarily attack Navarra. If Alfonso attempted to take over Navarra, the king of Aragón, Jaime thought, could also attempt to take over territories in the south, such as the small kingdom of Niebla.

Enrique actively recruited troops all over Castile. As soon as the Laras, who owned extensive property in Niebla, heard of the prince's intentions, they sent their own troops to oppose him. The clash of the two armies, according to the CAX, took place in the surroundings

---

[33] According to don Juan Manuel, who narrates these events:
And for this reason Enrique headed to Niebla, which was a Moorish kingdom, and surrounded it, and considering it subjected, he sent news to the king of Aragón that since he had the kingdom, he should give him his daughter, as he had promised. (*Libro de las armas*, quoted ed., p. 129)

of Lebrija.[34] The battle was very hard, but the fearless don Enrique stepped amid the fighting troops in order to find don Nuño González de Lara. Suddenly, the troops on both sides stopped fighting in order to watch the fight between the brother of Alfonso and Alfonso's best ally. Both men were seriously wounded when news came about the fresh arrival of reinforcements to support Alfonso's troops. Faced with the possibility of being captured and suffering the consequences of his brother's justice, Enrique decided to flee, beginning a long exile.[35]

It does not seem very probable that the chronicler was right in affirming that "king don Jaime did not want to protect him against the will of the king don Alfonso, and he sent him away from the king-dom," given the 1254 Estella agreement and the fact that he had prom-ised to help both leaders of the rebellion. However, it is also true that around that time don Jaime was also taking the first steps to settle his differences with Alfonso.[36] In any event, it's worth asking why Jaime I did not intervene in support of his protégé if he was truly interested in marrying his daughter Constanza to the prince. There is no logical answer. It's quite possible that the suspension of military help would

---

[34] For Ballesteros the battle took place in Morón, based on a *cantiga* by Gonzalo Eanes do Vihnal. The relevant stanza is worth quoting because it gave rise to the famous legend of doña Juana's coif that don Enrique always carried with him:

Friends, I have heard
The Moors from Morón fought
Against the supporters of the king
And I could not know in truth
If my friend is alive,
The one who carried my coif with him.

Cantigas de amigo, were usually in the voice of the woman in love, which in this case was none other than the queen, Juana of Ponthieu, as was also explained in a note that accompanies the composition in the *Cancioneiro da Vaticana*: "This *cantiga* was made by don Gonçal[o] Eanes do Vihnal for don Enrique in name of the queen, doña Juana, his stepmother, because they say he was her lover, when he fought in Morón against don Nuño and don Rodrigo Alfonso" (in J.J. Nunes, *Cantigas de amigo dos trovadores galego-portugueses*, II, Lisboa, 1973, 132). In another one of his *cantigas*, Gonzalo Eanes has doña Juana begging the king, don Alfonso to forgive "her friend," prince don Enrique (cf. *Id.*, 133).

[35] *CAX*, chap. 8, pp. 43–45. Before entering in the service of the sultan of Tunis, it seems he attempted to serve the king of England and of France but did not receive a favorable welcome. Cf. T. Rymer, *Foedera, conventiones, litterae et cuiuscumque acta publica inter reges Angliae et alios quovis imperatores, reges, pontifices, principes*, 20 vols., London, 1704–1735, I, p. 667.

[36] See, for instance, the agreement with Ramiro Rodríguez, one of the noble Castil-ians who defected, where it is specified that he will help him until "we come to an agreement with the king of Castile," in Huici-Cabanes, *Documentos...*, III, no. 687, pp. 176–177.

have been due to a possible intervention by his daughter Violante, who, according to the *CAX*, suddenly appeared at Calatayud before her father with her children and riding a donkey. Don Jaime could not believe what he saw: his daughter, the queen of Castile, without previous announcement or messenger, jumping off a donkey, moaning and crying. It was a startling scene. The king of Aragón asked her what had happened and whether Alfonso had died. When Violante recovered, she said that because of him she was going to lose the crown of Castile, and that by supporting the marriage of her sister Constanza with Enrique, and the Niebla conquest to justify it, the prince would continue to plot with the other nobles until he managed to steal all of Alfonso's territories and, in the end, seize also his crown. At such accusations, the king of Aragón was horrified, and he assured her that he would never allow her or any of her offspring to be deprived of the crown. As a result of this meeting, Jaime decided to abandon the Niebla project. Following Enrique's flight, Constanza married another one of Alfonso X's brothers, don Manuel. Although Manuel too was not a king, to solve the question of Jaime's promise to his wife, they found the very original solution that Alfonso X would grant him his rights over the kingdom of Murcia, but that it would remain subjected to Castile's power.[37]

That is how, in 1256, it was possible to reach a period of peace and quiet between the two main peninsular kingdoms, Castile and Aragón, especially after Thibault II of Navarre, always protected by Aragón, decided to kiss Alfonso X's hand. This first attempt at rebellion by the nobility was over. The two leaders had disappeared from the political scene: don Diego López de Haro died a few months after abandoning his king, and prince Enrique had to leave Castile to become a mercenary for various kingdoms.[38] Once the problem of Enrique was solved,

---

[37] The meeting between father and daughter is dramatically narrated by don Juan Manuel in *Libro de las armas* (ed. J.M. Blecua, I, pp. 129–130).

[38] After spending some time in the court of Aragón, with the help of Jaime, who even paid for the horse he used in his exile journey, don Enrique went to the court of Henry III of England who welcomed him generously. Relations between Enrique III and Alfonso had recently become colder as a result of Alfonso's threat to intervene in Gascony and the candidacy of Henry's brother, Richard of Cornwall, for the imperial crown. The English king attempted to use the rebellious prince as a threat against Alfonso X if he intervened militarily in Gascony (cf. Ballesteros, *Alfonso X*, pp. 171–173). But Alfonso maintained political pressure on Henry III, allying himself to the two leaders of the rebellion in Gascony, Gaston de Bearn and Guy de Limoges, who practically resided at the Castilian court (the first one at least confirmed by documents

the nobles who defected began to return to Castile, and the new successor of the Haros, don Lope, seemed momentarily more disposed towards reconciliation that towards a confrontation with Alfonso.

Alfonso's relations with the nobility in the following years would have their ups and downs until, toward the end of the summer of 1267, when he received the visit of his grandson, prince don Dinis (1261–1325), the son of Beatriz and Alfonso III, king of Portugal.[39] Soon after assuming the throne, Alfonso X had reached an agreement with the king of Portugal regarding the Algarve, in which he granted that territory to Portugal, retaining its profit until the future heir would reach age 7, at which time the territory would be completely ceded to the king of Portugal. But, in 1262, as a consequence of the conquest of Niebla, Alfonso took control of the entire Algarve and it was not until the treaty of 1264 that he relinquished his rights, keeping a mostly symbolic "tribute" of 50 lances, whenever he deemed it necessary. Now, during his visit, his grandson asked for two things: to be knighted, and "the favor of removing the tribute that the kings of Portugal were obliged to make to the King of León, namely, that they were to come to his help every time he asked them" (*CAX*, chap. 19, p. 72). Regarding the first request, despite the prohibitions in the Order of Knighthood against admitting such young kings, Alfonso agreed, "Because this prince was the king's grandson—and also because other princes, heirs of kingdoms, had come to receive knighthood from him—King Alfonso was very pleased with him and with his coming, and he did him much honor with his knighthood" (ib.) The second request was more difficult, hence Alfonso replied that "he could not do it on his own, but that he would have the princes and noblemen who were there with him called, and would speak about it before them, and that if they were to advise it, he would gladly do it" (p. 72). The next

---

until 1274, in Ballesteros, *Sevilla en el siglo XIII*, no. 85, pp. LXXXVII–LXXXVIII). The political tension between the king of England and the king of Castile lasted until Henry III, due to the internal instability of the kingdom, had to yield to Alfonso's diplomacy and arrange for the transfer or expulsion of don Enrique to Africa, ordering the Bordeaux City Council to give the prince the necessary resources to allow him to leave the territories of the English crown without any troubles (cf. Rymer, *Foedera...*, I, 2, p. 49).

[39] M. González Jiménez (*Alfonso X*, p. 100, note 17) denies that there ever was such a visit. He believes instead that "This event was in all likelihood a piece of orally transmitted history." "Oral history", however, does not necessarily mean fiction, and there are good reasons to believe in what the *CAX* tells in great detail, given its undeniable reliability regarding the topic of the nobles' rebellion.

day, Alfonso summoned his advisors, the princes don Manuel and
don Felipe (the *CAX,* erroneously also includes don Fadrique), and
the representatives of the three most powerful families of the kingdom:
don Nuño González de Lara, don Lope Díaz de Haro, don Esteban
Fernández de Castro, and other gentlemen and knights, to hear the
request directly from his grandson. Apparently, the child was intimidated, so a Portuguese gentleman had to speak for him. The speech of
the skillful Portuguese nobleman did not mention at all the Algarve
but only the question of the tribute. The *CAX* goes on to say:

> King Alfonso ordered the princes and noblemen of his council who were
> with him there to speak to speak to him and advise him about what he
> should do about this. But all of them were silent for a long time without
> saying anything. The king again asked them why they did not answer
> to the plea that was spoken by the prince and became angry with all of
> them; but he showed more anger against don Nuño than against any of
> the others who were there. (p. 73)

The scene became tense. The silence of the king's brothers and nobles
and Alfonso's loss of patience chiding them for their cowardice seem
to be a clear indication that Alfonso suspected they were against the
demand and that they were perhaps already planning a conspiracy
against him. Finally, after that endless silence, don Nuño stood up to
say that as a grandfather who loved and was proud of his grandson,
Alfonso could not grant him everything that he requested, "But Lord,
that you take away from the Crown of your kingdoms the tribute that
the King of Portugal and his kingdom are obliged to give to you, I
shall never advise you." The chronicler concludes by saying: "As soon
as don Nuño said this, King Alfonso showed that what don Nuño
said did not please him, and the king ordered the others to speak.
And don Nuño left the meeting and went from the palace."[40] Alfonso's
brothers and the rest of the nobles present there, upon witnessing the
king's anger vis-à-vis don Nuño, said that the king "had cause to grant

---

[40] *CAX,* chap. 19, pp. 73–74. The *Crónica* quotes the date of the visit as 1269; but
this is obviously a mistake, since the Treaty of Badajoz, where the concession is formalized, was only concluded a few months after the visit (on February 16,1267). See
J.F. O'Callaghan, *A History of Medieval Spain,* Ithaca, N.Y, 1975, pp. 368–369. According to Ballesteros, the visit took place between May 7 and September 4, 1267 (*Alfonso
X,* p. 431).

the prince what he was requesting."[41] Obviously, all who were present were simply pretending, as will be shown below.

Don Nuño's opinion, self-interested as it may seem, was indeed quite sensible, since what the king was doing was an infraction of the kingdom's rights and damaged the interests of his subjects. During the 13th century and especially during Alfonso X's reign, the perception of the king's relationship to his kingdom changed, with the kingdom being considered less the property of the king—like his horse or his sword—than the property of his subjects, an idea Alfonso was always reluctant to accept. Don Nuño made it very clear that the payment of tribute was not a personal but rather a state matter. Although Alfonso was a man with a great sense of duty and always desired consensus about his decisions, as the summoning of the assembly shows, he was also a very humane individual in considering his grandson's request. He thus found don Nuño's opinion offensive, and became angry. Alfonso, however, would pay dearly for his generosity towards his grandson, for this would be the last straw that unleashed the nobles' rebellion.

4. The Promoters of the Conspiracy

The incident of the Portuguese kingdom's release from tribute at the assembly in Seville was thus the immediate antecedent that clearly signaled to the nobles Alfonso's plan to completely absorb the kingdom's power. It was the last in a series of decisions made by Alfonso that irritated his brothers and his close advisors from the nobility. It is believed that on the basis of that incident the first conspiracy to depose him was organized.

The promoters of the rebellion were his brother, prince don Felipe (c. 1231–1274) and don Nuño González de Lara, governor of the border and a relative of the king through his marriage with Teresa Alonso de León, Alfonso X's cousin. The *CAX* is clear about this point, establishing a direct causal connection between the release from tribute and the conspiracy (19, pp. 74–75).

---

[41] At the head of those who were eager to please Alfonso was his favorite brother, prince don Manuel, who publicly declared that "the tribute that the King of Portugal and his kingdom had to make to the King of León was very small, and that because Prince Dinis had such great family ties the king should do more for him than this, and that if he did not it would not be a good thing" (ibid.).

The *CAX* does not state who the "prince" was, but it is clear that it could be no other than don Felipe, who inexplicably turned against his brother. A historian like González Dávila holds that the reason for Felipe's mistrust of his brother was that in 1258 Alfonso had promised him great sums of money and noble titles to make him renounce his bishopric in Seville, to which he had been elected, in order to marry princess Christina of Norway, but that later Alfonso had not kept his promises.[42] This explanation entirely contradicts what Alfonso X said in his letter to don Fernando, where he explains that it was precisely don Felipe who had entreated him to free him from his ecclesiastic commitments. As we shall see further on, when speaking of this letter, the reasons for don Felipe's rebellion were, according to Alfonso, more than absurd. He had always been incorrigibly ungrateful.

Regarding don Nuño, according to the *CAX* (chap. 16, pp. 63–64) he had probably already been in touch with the king of Granada through his son before that incident at the court. This meeting and secret pact, narrated after the one Ibn el-Ahmer established with Alfonso regarding the return of the *arraeces* (Moorish rulers) to Moorish obedience, probably took place outside of Seville in Ibn el-Ahmer's tent in 1266, after the Moorish subjection promoted by the king of Granada himself. In the general context of the story the central theme seems to be the king of Granada's discontent at Alfonso's denial to return the *arraeces* and the discontent of the Laras for "all the complaints they had against him."

It was therefore a real alliance and mutual help agreement between the nobles and the king of Granada. Although the *CAX* does not give a date for the meeting, from the context and other documents we can assume it happened in January 1266. Ibn el-Ahmer was not willing to give up the two *arraeces* Alfonso had promised to return to his obedience in the treaty of Alcalá de Benzayde and who now, out of political-economic convenience and military strategy, Alfonso clearly refused to return. It was expected that the Moorish king would do anything he could to exact revenge using the same tactics: if Alfonso

---

[42] G. González Dávila, *Theatro eclesiástico de las iglesias de España*, 2 vols., Madrid, 1647, II, p. 50. However, the *CAX* clearly implies that Felipe abandoned the bishopric of Seville freely in order to marry Christina of Norway, while at the same time hinted that his studies in Paris led him to abandon his ecclesiastic career. Cf. A. Hernández Parrales, "El Infante Don Felipe primer arzobispo electo de Sevilla, después de la reconquista," *AH*, 31 (1959), pp. 195–204.

took advantage of his Muslim subjects to launch them against him, he would do the same using his Christian subjects against Alfonso. In his talks with the king of Granada, Don Nuño González did not give any specific reasons for the betrayal and rebellion of the nobles (none is actually acknowledged), remaining instead along very general lines ("some wrongs and injustices"). But in light of the above, it seems obvious that the revolt had to do with the threat of new legislation that threatened their class privileges and prerogatives.

These two initiators of the revolt, prince don Felipe and don Nuño de Lara, were followed by other famous individuals, sometimes in conflict with one another, such as the Lord of Vizcaya, don Lope Díaz de Haro, and the governor of Galicia, don Esteban Fernández de Castro, who would nonetheless come together in a common cause in order to dethrone Alfonso.[43] There were too many conspirators for their alliances to be secret for long. News of the planned rebellion must have soon reached Alfonso, because before their return to Castile, the four main conspirators requested a meeting with Alfonso during which, the chronicler states, don Nuño attempted to discredit any rumors about their intentions: "There, don Nuño spoke to the king and to don Pero Lorenzo, Bishop of Cuenca, who was also there, and don Nuño told King Alfonso that never had he such willingness to serve the king as he had then and that he asked a favor: not to believe anything they said about him. Then he took leave of the king, and Prince Felipe, and don Lope Díaz, and don Esteban did the same, and they departed from there and went to Castile" (*CAX*, chap. 19, p. 75). All of them were lying through their teeth. The bishop of Cuenca, a friend of Alfonso's, knew about this, but he chose to remain silent for the moment. The seed of the rebellion had been planted and would soon bear fruit.

The decade from 1258 to 1269 had been a period of relative serenity for Alfonso X, amid the political turmoil that never was lacking in his life as a king. Alfonso resided continuously during those years in Seville, where he actively devoted himself to his scientific works.[44] On February 26, 1259 he finished drafting the astrological work *Libro de las cruzes* (*Book of the Crosses*) and soon after he finished the *Libro de la Alcora* (*Book of the Alcora*). In 1260 he finished the *Cuatro libros de las*

---

[43] Cf. *CAX*, chap. 19, pp. 71–75.
[44] This decade is the "first period" of cultural activity of the Learned King, according to G. Menéndez Pidal, "Cómo trabajaron las escuelas alfonsíes," p. 369.

estrellas fijas (*Four Books of the Fixed Stars*) and he also worked on collecting and preparing materials to compile the famous *Tablas alfonsíes* (*Alfonsine Tables*) and the *Estoria de España* (*History of Spain*). In 1261 the revision of the translation of the work on Oriental fiction *Calila e Dimna* (*Calila and Dimna*) was finished. But amid all these literary and scientific works, Alfonso never abandoned his legal and juridical projects. In 1263 he finished drafting the *Partidas*, in 1264 he concluded *Ordenamiento de las Extremaduras* (*Ordinances of the Extremaduras*), and in 1265 the *Libro del fuero de las leyes* (*Book of the Collection of Laws*, later known as *Siete Partidas*) was completed. The last years of this period of serenity were altered by the war against the king of Granada and the revolt in the south, which lasted until the end of 1267 or beginning of 1268. During those years of military activity, Alfonso's literary pursuits diminished noticeably, but this does not mean that the *scriptorium* diminished the rhythm of its activities. As we will see, Alfonso was still very active in the field of foreign relations, receiving princes, magnates, and intellectuals from all over Europe and the Orient in his palaces in Seville. The prestige of his court reached the most remote corners of Europe and the Muslim world.

5. *New Perspectives*

The rebellion was brewing with greater strength every day, in secret and even in open confrontations with Alfonso. In his autobiographical chronicle, *Llibre dels feyts*, don Jaime I tells us that during the Burgos Cortes in December 1269, which had been summoned on the occasion of the wedding of the heir to the throne in order to find a solution to the kingdom's problems, don Nuño approached him to speak to him in private. The conversation took place in the sandy field of Arlanzón, on the way to Hospital del Rey, where don Jaime resided. Don Jaime, a man of great diplomatic skill, sent off his companions in order to allow Nuño to speak openly. Nuño began the talk by offering him the services of one or two hundred knights. Before Nuño addressed the real topic of the meeting, namely, the complaints against Alfonso, don Jaime interrupted him saying he knew perfectly well the king's displeasure with the nobles' rebellious attitude as well as their complaints against him. He promised he would speak with Alfonso the next day to solve the conflict. Don Jaime went on to say that Alfonso told him he could not understand how that man whom he had showered with privileges like no lord ever bestowed on a vassal could behave so ungratefully. Don Jaime concluded his story by telling us that upon seeing that Alfonso was right, he did not wish to intervene more in the matter.[45]

The *Crónica de Alfonso X*, a first-hand source on the rebellion of the nobles, tells us that, headed by don Nuño and shortly after the Burgos Cortes, they held a secret meeting where they agreed on a plan of action and also dared to seal the agreement with a marriage, as was customary with the nobility (chap. 18, pp. 68–70). This action, clearly lacking the king's consent, was a challenge to Alfonso's authority. Alfonso, despite knowing about the plot and the provocation of the marriage of one of his cousins to one of the leaders of the rebellion (an act requiring his consent), agreed to everything. Those who criticize Alfonso's submissive attitude see this as evidence of his naïveté and the extent to which he was a victim of circumstance. Threatened by the Moors at his doorstep and lacking other resources, he had no choice but to tolerate those rebellious nobles because he was convinced that they were the only ones who could help him both contain the Muslims in the south and obtain the imperial crown. He was wrong, or as the *Crónica* states: "he did not see the disservice that came to him later," losing his crown and the kingdom itself, not because of the Muslims, but rather because of the Christian nobles who he thought would be his salvation. If instead of being affable and understanding with the conspirators, he had used the *iron rod*, as Saint Dominic had suggested during a vision in Silos in 1255, perhaps he would have lost neither his kingdom nor the Empire.[46]

For his part, don Jaime of Aragón, after some fifteen or twenty days in Burgos, set out on his way back to Aragón. In his *Llibre* he tells how Alfonso accompanied him to the border of his kingdom and tells also about his meeting with Alfonso in Tarazona, before his return

---

[45] Jaime I: *Llibre dels feyts*, ed. F. Soldevila, *Quatre grans cròniques*, Barcelona: Selecta, 1971, chaps.497–498. English translation: John. Forster, trans., *The Chronicle of James I, King of Aragón, Surnamed the Conqueror*, London: Chapman and Hall, 1883, vol. II, pp. 614–618.

[46] This vision was narrated by the prior of Silos, Pero Marín, according to which Saint Dominic appeared to Alfonso with an iron rod in his hand saying, "Did you not read in the *Psalms*: *Reges eos in uirga ferrea et tanquam vas figuli confringes eos*? [You shall break them with a rod of iron, you shall shatter them like a clay pot"?], *Psalm*. 2:9. That is how you should live with the kings and the princes you have around you" (*Los "Miraculos romanzados" de Pero Marín*, critical ed., introduction and indexes by Karl-Heinz Anton, Studia Silensia, XIV, Abadía de Silos, Studia, 1988, p. 44.

to Castile. Don Jaime invited him to spend Christmas with him and prepared a sumptuous welcome for his son-in-law. According to don Jaime, Alfonso was deeply worried about the nobles' rebellion, but at the same time he was torn about quashing it, for he knew he would need their support for his imperial project and to safeguard the conquered territories.

Alfonso stayed with his father-in-law for seven days in Tarazona, during which time he discussed the most urgent political matters prompted by the nobles' rebellion and the state of the economy. As a senior and experienced statesman, don Jaime offered the king of Castile seven useful hints on how to govern the kingdom: 1. Never to promise what he would be unable to fulfill; 2. Once a concession was made in writing, never to revoke it; 3. To keep the love of all subjects God had given him; 4. If the love of all subjects could not be maintained, to keep at all costs the love of the Church, the people, and the cities, for God loves them more than He loves knights, and with the love of the former you will always conquer the latter. In other words, the crown's natural allies are the Church and the people, or their representatives, for these were formed by the three groups that actively participated in the Cortes; while the nobility was the common enemy, always ready to challenge the king's authority; 5. To always act with justice in the partition of the kingdom of Murcia in order to keep all his subjects happy (apparently, the Catalans who had helped in reconquering that territory, had been shortchanged in the partition and had complained to don Jaime about this); 6. In the newly conquered cities, justice should be administered by men of great integrity and who would govern rightly; 7. Justice should not be done in the dark, in the palace, or in a secluded place, but rather in public, under the sun, so the good may feel honored and the criminals corrected.[47] This meeting between the two most powerful kings of the Peninsula must have been very useful to clarify many past misunderstandings, to get to know each other more, and to forge a new friendship and future alliances. As we will see, Alfonso would have avoided many troubles had he followed the advice of this man who was well seasoned in war and politics.

---

[47] *Llibre del feyts*, ed. cit., chaps. 498–499. Don Jaime's personal narrative gathers various moments in the confidential relations between the two kings where don Jaime, on his own or responding to his son-in-law's request, offered Alfonso his advice (chaps. 432–433, 474–475, 494–499, 505–507, and 607).

Alfonso left Tarazona on January 26 or 27 for Castile. On the 28th, he must have arrived at Fitero de Navarra, where he fell ill. When a messenger informed don Jaime about his illness, he went back with his personal physician, Mestre Joan, to help Alfonso. Four days later, Alfonso told him he could return to Aragón, for he was cured. Alfonso spent practically all of 1270 in la Rioja, mainly in Vitoria and Logroño, with some trips to Burgos, Santo Domingo de la Calzada, Caleruega, and other monasteries in the area, perusing manuscripts and listening to miracles of the Virgin Mary for his collection of *Cantigas*. On November 2, he was in Salvatierra, on his way to Murcia, where he had to solve urgent issues regarding the territory's partition.

6. Murcian Sojourn

In February 1271, while Alfonso was in Murcia, the rebels gathered at Lerma for the first time with the purpose of planning his deposition. The anonymous author of the *CAX*, who consulted a great variety of documents, adds to the four names of the rebels we already know two more, also relatives Alfonso's brother Fadrique: a son-in-law, don Simón Ruiz de los Cameros, and a brother-in-law, Ferrán Ruiz de Castro. The *CAX* also explicitly outlines the reasons for and objectives of the meeting:

> ... since King Alfonso had gone to the kingdom of Murcia, Prince Felipe and don Nuño, and many noblemen and knights, and those of noble descent, and all others got together in Lerma and made a pact and agreement: to assist each other in opposing King Alfonso, harming him however they could if he did not grant and fulfill to them the things they would go and demand (which we will relate further along).[48]

During the meeting, which was also attended by representatives of the towns and cities,[49] the rebels agreed to send prince Felipe to Navarra in order to strike an alliance with the king of Navarra or his regent,

---

[48] *CAX*, chap. 20, pp. 78–81. Don Fadrique was married to princesses Malespina; they had a girl, Beatriz Fadrique de Castilla, who became the second wife of don Simón Ruiz de los Cameros. When, on examining the list of the conspirators, one sees that they were all related by marriage or birth, the rebellion seems more like a family feud.

[49] Any speculation to the contrary by modern historians based on Mondéjar (*Memorias*, pp. 287–288) seems to me fault-finding in an area where the chronicler is well informed.

for king Thibault II was not in the kingdom, busy at the Crusade of Tunis alongside Saint Louis.[50] Felipe's embassy would prepare the way, in case the nobles had to defect, for them to find protection under the neighboring king of Navarra, who at the time was Alfonso's enemy, rather than having to turn to an enemy of Christendom such as the king of Granada, an action that Alfonso might consider not only a personal offense, but an offense against the kingdom. If the king of Navarra did not accept the proposal of the nobles, then they had no choice but to seek refuge with the Muslim king of Granada.[51] In fact, the king of Navarra, through his regent, Henry of Champagne, who was married to Blanche, the niece of the king of France and daughter of Robert of Artois, Saint Louis's brother, did not agree to ally himself with rebels, or rather, as the *CAX* states, he set a condition they could not fulfill: he asked them, in exchange for their help, to return to Navarra the Castilian territories that had once belonged to it.[52] The rebel nobles thus saw the last door to a refuge in the Christian territories slam shut.

Alfonso, who was very aware of the movements of the conspirators, feared the new alliance with Navarra. He therefore asked Jaime de Aragón, his father-in-law and trusted advisor, for a new meeting. The meeting took place in Valencia in the second half of February 1271. Deep down, what Alfonso wanted to know was whether don Jaime supported him unconditionally should the rebels reach an agreement with the king of Navarra. Don Jaime recommended he negotiate a truce with the king of Granada in order to prevent another node of conflict. During the truce he would be better able to concentrate on the problem of the rebels. In any event, the king of Aragón promised he would support him on two fronts, the rebellion and in Granada, and meanwhile Alfonso should begin contact with the rebels.

Alfonso's patience and his desire to reach an agreement with the rebels was indeed admirable: it is hard to understand how he could tolerate such a conspiracy at a time when rebellion was punishable by death. Did he not want to or was he unable to take more drastic measures? Did he really hope to appease them so he did not have to fight two enemies (the king of Granada and the nobles) at once?

---

[50] Don Felipe's presence among the rebels has not yet been fully clarified, but it appears that he too had serious complaints against his brother Alfonso.

[51] Cf. *CAX*, chap. 20, pp. 78–81.

[52] *CAX*, chap. 24, pp. 95–98.

At the end of the day, it seems that if the Learned King did not take drastic measures against the rebels it was because he never believed the nobles, especially his closest friend don Nuño and his own brother Felipe, could commit such treason. Alfonso was indecisive and naïve, and such immature personalities place endless trust in others.

From Murcia, where he had arrived before March 24, 1271, feigning not to know what had been discussed at Lerma, Alfonso merely sent his friend and confidante Ferrán Pérez, the deacon of the Seville cathedral, to inquire with his brother about what had happened at the Lerma meeting and what the intentions of the participants in the "council" were.[53] Both don Felipe as well as the other rebels shamelessly deceived the messenger in their answers, saying there had been no such meeting: "Dean Fernán Pérez went to don Nuño and don Lope Diaz and spoke with them, but they denied that they had any agreements. He had King Alfonso told everything, and in order to know more about this matter, he remained in Castile" (*CAX*, chap. 20, p. 78).

When he received the answer of his brothers and the nobles to the deacon's query, Alfonso sent another trusted messenger to reinforce the deacon's negotiations. This was his *repostero mayor* (main baker), don Enrique Pérez de Harana. The baker was to meet alone and in secret with don Nuño, for whom he was carrying a long document from Alfonso. The document, partially reproduced in the *CAX*, reveals how Alfonso was truly familiar with the tricks and falsity of the rebels, for he "knew he [don Nuño] had discussions and meetings with all the noblemen and many knights who were against the king because of the wrongs and downright injustices they said he was doing to them; and that don Nuño could not do more against the law, since in that lay disinheritance, and that all other evil could come to him, and that he was surprised that he promoted such uproar among his kingdoms and their inhabitants, encouraging enmity between them and him, and that he erred much in this, the king having done all the good he had done him" (chap. 20, pp. 78–79). Alfonso insisted on how shameful it must have been for don Nuño, to whom he had granted many favors, to rise up in arms against his king and lord. Alfonso closes the document with a clear warning to his former friend, saying that if he was

---

[53] *CAX*, chap. 20, pp. 76–81. Cf. Ballesteros, *Alfonso X*, pp. 527, 531.

doing all that to instill fear in him, he "should know that he was not afraid of a proud man who was wrong." (ib.).

Don Nuño ignored all of this because as a man who was experienced in matters of state and was well acquainted with the king's temperament, he knew perfectly well that Alfonso would do nothing to repress the revolt, first, because he needed the nobles, who held the true military power, to contain the king of Granada and his supporters across the Strait, and second, because peace with the rebels was the precondition for his "road to Empire." However, on the other hand, Alfonso was always unpredictable, even for those who thought they knew him well, like don Nuño. Nobody could be certain of Alfonso's reactions, who could with the greatest ease make use of one of the norms in the traditional laws that they themselves invoked, such as: "it is the law in Castile that if anyone wages war against the king and harms the land on account of a gift he has granted, then the king is lawfully allowed to seize it,"[54] in order to confiscate all his property and throw him into a dungeon.

Despite all evidence to the contrary and the requests from all parts of Castile to go there and quell the rebellion, Alfonso did not leave Murcia. The Learned King had a magnificent court there and he also managed his interests in Italian politics and his aspirations to the imperial crown from there. He probably did not go to Castile at the time because he was convinced that don Nuño and his followers would not lend themselves to the king of Granada's scheme to destroy the largest Christian kingdom of the peninsula which also stabilized all the others. In the end, keeping Christian unity in the south, where the nobility—especially don Nuño—had great economic interests, was something that mattered both to the nobles and Alfonso.[55] Alfonso's true concern during his sojourn in Murcia was, on the one hand, to obtain the imperial crown (his rival, Richard of Cornwall had died on April 2, 1272), and on the other, the possible and feared alliance of the king of Granada, his usual enemy, with the two other Muslim rulers of Málaga and Guadix (the *arraeces*), who had been on his side up to that point. In his truly infantile naïveté, Alfonso was convinced, despite the

---

[54] Letter to don Lope Díaz de Haro, in *CAX*, chap. 31, p. 117.

[55] The Alfonsine chronicler confirms that this was also the nobles' position when he says that they would have preferred a deal with the king of Navarra rather than having to turn to the king of Granada: "in order not to embolden the Moors, who through their efforts might come to harm the Christians" (*CAX*, chap. 20, p. 76).

bad news that reached him daily, that the nobles' conspiracy would not materialize.

During his magnificent sojourn in Murcia, Alfonso also devoted time to his favorite passion: letters. He created an important Muslim school that he placed under the direction of the scholar Ahmed Ibn Abu Bakr, also known as *el-Ricotí*, after the valley of Ricote from which he hailed. Many of the Arab language scholars who later worked in Alfonso's *scriptorium* must have been educated there. In the *Repartimiento de Murcia* (Partition of Murcia) the following names are mentioned: Ferrán Domínguez *del Aráuigo* (Arabic specialist) and the teacher Bernaldo *del Aráuigo,* who also worked for Alfonso doing translation work. But the court also included historians, troubadours and poets, law scholars, commentators and rhetoricians, with many Italians in this latter category.[56]

During this period, Rabi Çag finished drafting the *Tablas astronómicas alfonsíes* (*Alfonsine Astronomical Tables*) in Toledo; the first collection of 100 *Cantigas* was completed and the *Estoria de España* was begun, including the "*Versión primitiva*," or "*regia*" (Original or regal version, up to chap. 616), and the "*Versión concisa*," or "*vulgar*" (Concise or vulgar version, which went up to chap. 801). At the same time, he also devoted a fair amount of time to matters of international politics. In August 1271, he welcomed there the Marquis of Monferrato, who had arrived from Italy to ask for the hand of his second-born, princess doña Beatriz, who had turned 17 that year. On November 10, the Marquis and his wife set on their way, arriving in Italy in early January 1272. Alfonso, who gave his daughter a generous dowry, thought the presence of young Beatriz among the Italian nobility would help him maintain relationships with his supporters, who were diminishing by the day.

At the beginning of 1272, Alfonso asked don Jaime for a new meeting. Don Jaime, who was in Zaragoza, sent a messenger, Jaime de Daroca, who was the king of Aragón's trusted ally and a man in whom he could confide about any matter, explaining that at that moment, he could not meet him personally in Murcia. Alfonso answered that

---

[56] J. Torres Fontes, *Repartimiento y repoblación de Murcia en el siglo XIII,* 2nd ed. Murcia: Academia Alfonso X, 1990; and "Los Repartimientos murcianos del siglo XIII," in *De Al-Andalus a la sociedad feudal: los repartimientos bajomedievales, AEM,* Anejo 25, Barcelona: CSIC, 1990, pp. 71–94; and "El poblamiento murciano en el siglo XIII," *Murgetana,* 18 (1961), pp. 89–99, where he discusses Bernardo *el Arábigo.*

what he wanted to consult with him about could not be revealed to anyone except him. Don Jaime left his most urgent business and set on his way to Alicante where Alfonso was waiting for him. The king of Aragón went back there between February 6 and 14, 1272. The matter was indeed very serious, as don Jaime recounts in his *Llibre dels feyts*. Alfonso informed him that he had learned about an alliance the Castilian rebels had struck with some gentlemen from Aragón and with the Moors in order to rise up against don Jaime. At the same time had emerged the problem of the king of Granada, who was asking for his help against the *arraeces*, while they too were asking for his protection against the Granada sultan.[57] Alfonso was, so to speak, between a rock and a hard place, because as the lord of both, he had defense agreements with both rivals. Regarding the king of Granada, don Jaime counseled him to keep his agreement so long as the other did not break it. In case he did, Alfonso could seek an alliance with the *arraeces* against him. The *Llibre dels feyts* does not give us much detail regarding the measures taken by don Jaime against the rebellious gentlemen. However, Ballesteros, with a good basis, holds that during the meeting and on the occasion of the recent marriage of Beatriz to the Marquis of Monferrato, they must also have discussed another matter that worried Alfonso, his quest for empire as well as other problems of Alfonso's politics in Italy related to the quest for the imperial crown.[58]

On February 26, 1272, Alfonso's brother Fadrique arrived unexpectedly in Murcia from Tunis, where he had been living since the defeat of the Ghibellines in Tagliacozzo in 1268. Alfonso saw this as the perfect opportunity to seek reconciliation with his brother, to keep him away from the Castilian conspirators, and to use him in support of the Angevin cause. We do not know much about Fadrique's life in Italy, but according to P. Flórez, it seems that he had married Catalina, daughter of the Romanian king. They had a daughter, Beatriz, who first married don Tello Alfonso de Meneses, and then married the unfortunate don Simón Ruiz de los Cameros.[59] Alfonso behaved very generously with his brother, who, following the reconciliation, gave considerable contributions to Murcia and Andalusia. However,

---

[57] *Llibre dels feyts*, chap. 376.
[58] *Alfonso X*, p. 546.
[59] Ballesteros, *Alfonso X*, p. 547.

all was in vain, for Fadrique ended up joining the rebels, who would ally themselves with the king of Granada and the emir of Morocco to promote a new invasion of Alfonso's territories.

According to the *CAX*, in Murcia Alfonso continued receiving letters from the rebels in which they hypocritically professed: "that they had never made an oath or pact with the Moors nor with the Christians that might do disservice against him" (*CAX*, chap. 21, p. 82). This was utterly shameless. They also requested their sums of money and offered to fight the Moors and Christians, but in reality what they were doing was to demand the new "service" tax to finance their own revolt while at the same time plotting a rebellion against the king of Granada.

In his unbelievable naïveté, Alfonso took a long time to convince himself that all that was happening could take place: "he was amazed about all of this they told him; and it seemed so absurd that he could not believe it" (*CAX*, chap. 21, 17a, Spanish version). But he only snapped out of his amazement when the rebels tried to win over to their side the crown prince himself, who in a letter to his father told how don Nuño González de Lara had appeared before him making claims against Alfonso and inciting him to also rebel. Faced with all this incontrovertible proof, Alfonso gathered a council made up of a group of close advisors, doña Violante, don Fadrique, the bishops of Cádiz and Córdoba, don Pérez de Harana, don Jofré de Loaísa and two or three more. They discussed what should be done, and Alfonso, always because of the imperial quest, decided to make peace with the rebels by sending them the money they requested and explaining how he intended it to be spent: "exempting them from the sums they had from him, for he did not need them for the war against the Moors the, that he thought that now, with those sums he then ordered given them, some of them would prepare to go with him to the empire where he wanted to go, and the others would stay to serve Prince Fernando, however he might need them"(*CAX*, chap. 21, p. 83). This was wasted time and money, as the chronicler says in the detailed chapter 21. As soon as they received the money sent by Alfonso through his envoy don Pedro Laurencio, bishop of Cuenca, "they divided it among their vassals, and they gathered as many men as they could have as knights. With those sums they supplied themselves with weapons and horses, and many of them wandered throughout the land and seized food from many places they should not have, and they did great damage in the land" (p. 83) So, notwithstanding that a new visit by the prince don Felipe to the king of Granada had been futile once more, "[t]hen they sent their messengers to the King of Granada and to the King of Morocco, and they also sent letters to the King of Portugal, in order to encourage them to wage war on Castile. Prince Felipe once again went to have meetings with the King of Navarre so that he could make firm with him the things that were being discussed" (ib.) The rebels were indeed looking desperately for an alliance with a Christian king before surrendering to a Muslim one. But in view of the king of Navarra's refusal, they had no choice but to throw themselves in the arms of the king of Granada, their natural ally, so to speak. The Moorish king must have reasoned that if Alfonso was taking away his *arraeces*, he intended to deprive him of the nobles. When Alfonso returned the *arraeces*, only then would he reciprocate.

7. On the Road to Castile. The Showdown with the Rebels

After finding out through his heir, don Fernando, and his faithful brother don Manuel, that the troops of Ibn Yûsuf had disembarked on the Andalusian coast to help the king of Granada, on June 16, 1272 Alfonso was forced to leave Murcia for Castile looking for help and also to resolve the discontent of the nobles.[60] Alfonso wrote to the rebels from Huete, saying that it was the time to make good on their promises by joining their forces to don Fernando's in order to repel the common enemy. The answer sent by the rebels reveals the drama they were staging: Prince Felipe and the noblemen had him told though their letters that they could not go immediately to the border, but that all of them as one and with their vassals, would go to Alfonso and speak with him about some things they had to tell him" (chap. 22, p. 85). Meanwhile, they continued their negotiations with the king of Granada.

In Huete, on the way to Castile, Alfonso visited Ferrand Gudiel, mayor of Toledo, who gave him some "Arabic letters" that had been intercepted and confiscated by Alfonso's spies from Lorenzo Rodríguez, don Nuño's squire. The letters—reproduced in the *CAX* in the translation done by Alfonso's translators, Alfonso Pérez de Toledo and Vasco

---

[60] The journey from Murcia to Castile is described by the *CAX*, chap. 22, pp. 85–90, in great detail, but it again errs in the chronology, placing it in 1271, when it really happened in June–September 1272. Cf. Ballesteros, *Itinerario*, pp. 276–277.

Gómez—were from the emir of Morocco, Ibn Yûsuf, to the main leaders of the rebellion: prince don Felipe, Nuño González de Lara, Lope Díaz de Haro, and Esteban Fernández de Castro, among others, and the correspondence revealed the plot of Alfonso's enemies. Using privileged information obtained through spies and perhaps through don Felipe himself, the emir discussed in these letters other more pressing issues that were being debated by the conspirators and Alfonso: excessive taxes, the devaluation of the currency ("false coins"), etc. But above all the emir reminded the conspirators that "[Alfonso] broke the good statutes you used before" (chap. 22 p. 87). In other words, the Moorish king was perfectly aware of the most controversial matter between Alfonso and the rebels. Alfonso needed no greater proof of the betrayal that his ungrateful subjects were plotting. Through the bishop of Cuenca Alfonso thus warned them once more in clear terms "to consider what they were doing in that matter, for they knew well that it was against the loyalty to which they were bound and that they should preserve."[61]

The time of warnings was past, and a new solution had to be sought against the rebellion. Alfonso once more did nothing. The noble rebels sent him a messenger requesting a meeting in Roa to speak with and welcome him "as their king and natural lord." Alfonso thought he might reach an agreement with them, so he waited at Roa for five days (August 25–30, 1272), but the rebels never showed up and he continued his journey to Burgos.

On his way to Burgos, while he was hunting, "a large number of mounted men met him on the road. They all came armed and with a great crowd, and don Felipe did not come there, because he had gone to the King of Navarre. When the king saw that they were coming in such fashion, he considered it very strange, because they were not coming as men who go to their lord but like those who come to look for their enemies" (*CAX*, chap. 23, p. 91). He nonetheless invited them to travel with him as far as Burgos to discuss their complaints, but they did not trust him, for they knew the people of Burgos were against them and in favor of the king. They therefore suspected it was a trap to capture and imprison them, and they chose to remain outside

---

[61] *CAX*, p. 89. The betrayal of his old friend Nuño de Lara was particularly painful for Alfonso, who still wrote him in a friendly and personal tone, as if it the matter were a quarrel between teenagers (ib., p. 89).

the city walls on the sandy lands next to the river. There they laid out their complaints, first to the delegates of the king. The next day, after much negotiation, they sent eight representatives to the royal palace to formally present their complaints to Alfonso. The delegation was headed by don Nuño de Lara, who appeared before his childhood friend surrounded by eight heavily armed knights, which surprised Alfonso. Alfonso said that "in his court all men were safe and they had no reason to demand a truce or to come armed" (*CAX*, chap. 25, p. 99).

The two old friends now had to confront each other fact to face. Alfonso told don Nuño that "he knew well he had never done anything to him or to the other noblemen by which they should be as upset as they were, and that they were doing him a great wrong." Don Nuño replied, saying "that Felipe and the noblemen, the knights, and the others of noble descent from Castile perceived themselves wronged by the king in some matters, which were these: that the statutes the king had given to some cities ruled by those of noble descent were oppressive to them and to their vassals, and that they had been forced to adopt the statutes; and also that the king did not keep in his court governors from Castile who might judge them" (*CAX*, p. 93).

According to don Nuño, the nobles' complaints had to do mainly with the legislative and administrative reforms carried out by the Learned King in his *Fuero real* and in the *Espéculo*. The nobles were also complaining about the new repopulation policy that evidently not only took lands away from their jurisdiction, but which, by granting the legal status described in the *Fuero real* to the new settlements, planted the seed of rebellion in the bordering territories that were under the nobles' jurisdiction. But above all, they were very resentful about having to be judged by royal judges (*alcaldes de corte*) who were experts in Roman law, as the *Espéculo* established, rather than by the *alcaldes de los fijosdalgo* (judges of those of noble descent), which they were requesting and which better reflected their status.[62] Through their representative, don Nuño, they also asked for an elimination or reduction of the taxes approved during the 1269 Burgos Cortes, where

---

[62] Some scholars claim that both the *alcaldes de corte* and the *alcaldes de los fijos-dalgo* never really were instituted or at least not in the way envisioned in the *Fuero real*. Cf. M.A. Pérez de la Canal, "La justicia de la corte de Castilla durante los siglos XIII al XV," *HID*, 2 (1975), pp. 387–481; D. Torres Sanz, *La administración central castellana en la Baja Edad Media*, Valladolid, 1982.

Alfonso taxed his subjects with a special "service" tax to pay for the extravagant and costly expenses of the wedding of his firstborn, don Fernando, and other expenses related to his "quest for empire."[63] Don Nuño went on to list a long series of violations of their past rights and privileges as well as the excessive taxes.[64]

Overwhelmed by the problems in the south and worries about the loss of the imperial crown, Alfonso was amenable to the demands of the nobles and ready to make concessions. The nobles then demanded that the changes and concessions be solemnly declared in the Cortes that were about to be celebrated. The chronicler concludes the narrative of this first encounter between Alfonso and the noble rebels by quoting don Nuño as saying that "if the king corrected these things, all of them would serve him gladly. King Alfonso told them that he wished to reflect on these matters and would send them his answer. And don Nuño went to the other noblemen who were staying in the villages" (*CAX*, chap. 23, p. 94).

In a concise chap. 24, the *CAX* quotes Alfonso's response to all the accusations of violations of the nobles' traditional rights and privileges. Ballesteros comments that "[t]hese answers are a model of sound judgment and equanimity. Lacking other proof, they would suffice to demonstrate the ruler's wisdom and the extraordinary administrative ability of a sovereign ahead of his time" (*Alfonso X*, p. 577). The answer regarding the weight of the taxes ("servicios" or services) is particularly interesting and probably did not please the nobles. Alfonso argued that such taxes had not been imposed by him, but rather had been granted by the Cortes in order to pay for the expenses of the war against the Moors and the quest for the empire. Also, many of those taxes had ended up in the nobles' coffers as payment for their "soldadas" or military services.

---

[63] This was a tax on wandering cattle: "Servicio de los ganados que fue demandado por toda la tierra para las bodas del Infante don Fernando", *MHE*, I, no. CXL, p. 314.

[64] Cf. *CAX*, chaps. 22–24, pp. 85–98; Ballesteros, *Alfonso X*, pp. 568–577; E. Procter, *Curia and Cortes*, p. 133; J. O'Callaghan, *The Cortes of Castile-León*, pp. 117–120.

8. *The 1272 Cortes. Confrontation*

Arriving in Burgos at the beginning of September to celebrate the Cortes, Alfonso received bad news on all fronts. There he learned from his delegates that on the 16th of the month, pope Gregory X had finally rejected his demand to be crowned emperor. But above all he had his first great confrontation with don Nuño and the rebellious nobility, with whom he needed to maintain good relations with in order to contain the Moroccan invasion and at the same time pursue the imperial crown.

Before the inauguration of the Cortes, Alfonso sealed an important agreement with the king of Navarra. It was a well-calculated political move because it opened the door to peace between the two kingdoms while at the same time definitively closing the possibility of defection by the nobles to that kingdom. It was an alliance of mutual help between the two kings "against all the men in the world except the kings of Aragón and France." The agreement was sealed with the marriage of the heir to the throne of Navarre, Thibault, to a daughter of Alfonso X, princess doña Violante (1272).[65]

The Cortes to which don Nuño had appealed had been summoned by Alfonso for the day of St. Michael (September 29), and we know that they lasted until the day of St. Martin (November 11). According to some scholars, these were the most important Cortes of Alfonso X's reign. During the Cortes, Alfonso reiterated all the promises made to the nobles outside the city walls, but the rebels were not satisfied and presented new demands, such as removing the royal judges or participating in the kingdom's management and the levying of taxes on its subjects, which seemed almost absurd. Nevertheless, Alfonso considered with great acumen and magnanimity all their requests, conceding them for the most part. During several sessions of the Cortes, the king had to repeatedly confront various groups: the rebels; the aristocracy, who were unhappy on account of the taxes and elimination of their privileges; the clergy, who vehemently protested against the king's intervention in fiscal and jurisdictional matters; and

---

[65] The text of the agreement can be seen in J. Zabalo Zabalegui, *Colección diplomática de los reyes de Navarra de la dinastía de Champaña. 3: Enrique I de Navarra (1270–1274)*, no. 31, in *Fuentes documentales medievales del País Vasco*, vol. 62, Donosti-San Sebastián, 1995.

the rural landowners, who complained about the new regulations on repopulation.[66]

Alfonso indeed must have expected that political storm, but he was not afraid to confront the problems that his malcontent subjects presented. The purpose of the Burgos Cortes was precisely to come to an agreement about the matters under dispute. The *CAX*, which describes in great detail such Cortes and the entire process of rebellion, presents the various demands of the nobles which, in the end, could be reduced to one: the restoration of their old privileges and the *fueros viejos* (old legal codes) by which the nobility wanted to be ruled in judicial cases (chap. 25, pp. 99–102).

The clergy, for its part, demanded among other things, the revocation of the payment of a tax known as *tercias reales*, which had been suppressed when pope Clement IV had conceded to Alfonso in June 1265 one-tenth of all Church income for three years but that Alfonso continued to collect. The bishops, upon seeing that Alfonso had no intention of renouncing the *tercias*, found this particularly irritating, especially after the concessions they had to make to the pope in 1262 to raise funds for the reconquest of the Holy Land.[67] In reality, the clergy, who had been in general quite submissive during Alfonso's reign, took advantage of these Cortes to air a long list of complaints that had accumulated over the past years, most of which had to do with their tax and jurisdiction exemptions.

In the end, what these two constituencies expected through these complaints and demands, was to return to the status quo they had enjoyed until the recent Alfonsine legislation promulgated in the *Fuero real*, in relation to which not only the nobles but also the clergy had great complaints and demands, such as the abolition of *ius spolii* (the right of the king to appropriate the goods of the diocese upon the death of the bishop), his interference in Church censorship, the appointment of bishops, the violations of Church jurisdiction, the prosecution of criminal clergymen by secular judges who at times

---

[66] *CAX*, chaps. 25–26, pp. 99–104; and cf. J. O'Callaghan, *Cortes of Castile-León*, pp. 117–120; E. Procter, *Curia*, pp. 133–134; Ballesteros, *Alfonso X*, pp. 579–587. For the problems of repopulation see. J.I. Ruiz de la Peña, "Los procesos tardíos de repoblación urbana en las tierras del norte del Duero (siglos XII–XIV)," *Boletín del Instituto de Estudios Asturianos*, 30 (1976), pp. 765–766.

[67] Cf. *Regist. Clément IV*, 350–352, nos. 890, 896; and P. Linehan, "The 'Gravamina' of the Castilian Church in 1262–1263," *EHR*, 85 (1970), pp. 730–734.

condemned them to capital punishment, etc.[68] It also became evident that the king's excessive expenses, occasioned by his imperial ambitions, were bankrupting the kingdom and were considered by his subjects unbearable and devoid of any benefit to the kingdom.[69] Alfonso, however, as we will see, justified such expenses with an unexpected argument: the honor of his subjects (*CAX*, p. 96).

Alfonso, as any politician of our day, when he felt attacked from all sides, appointed a commission of 42 members made up of the queen doña Violante, the prince don Fadrique, six magnates, four knights, four bishops, four clergymen, five Franciscans and Dominicans, and seventeen citizens. The commission did its work and presented a series of recommendations. Following the recommendations, Alfonso gave in on everything, confirming "good habits and customs" and the traditional privileges of the nobility, just as he had done with *fueros* of many of the cities to which he had recently granted the *Fuero real*.[70] In the interests of the king's good will, the assembly voted in favor of granting him a new *servicio* tax that would be in effect for as long as Alfonso considered necessary, following approval by the Cortes. Alfonso granted practically all the demands of the rebels, so that the *Fuero real* was no longer in effect and was substituted by the *Fuero viejo de Castilla*.[71] The only point about which Alfonso was firm were the expenses relative to his quest for the empire, which, according to his nephew don Juan in the eulogy of his uncle, he justified by saying: "it was to bring honor to the people of his kingdoms...[for he] had a great predisposition for knowledge and very much desired the honor

---

[68] Many of these complaints would be later transmitted to the pope, who presented them to Alfonso in his *Memoriale secretum* discussed below.

[69] The *Crónica* is not very explicit about this point. It implies that the nobles complained about the expenses of the imperial aspirations and the quest for the empire, but they did not denounce Alfonso explicitly during the assembly: "those noblemen were saying that the king was impoverishing the land by giving wealth to men of other kingdoms and also for the matter concerning the empire" (p. 96).

[70] The complete list of recommendations by the commission headed by the queen and the archbishop of Toledo appears in chap. 39, pp. 131–32 of the *CAX*. Cf. O'Callaghan, *The Cortes of Castile-León*, p. 119 and in note 21.

[71] The story of this concession by Alfonso is narrated in the prologue to the *Fuero Viejo de Castilla* (ed. Galo Sánchez, Barcelona, 1924, p. 1): "And they judged according to this code of law...and according to these customs until king Alfonso...gave the *Code of the Book* [see above note 25] to the councils of Castile [...] and the judged according to this book until the feast of St. Martin in November, which was in the era of one thousand three hundred and ten years [1272]."

of his kingdoms."[72] That is, as part of the ideal Alfonso had conceived for his kingdom, he wanted his subjects to be known and respected for their wisdom and for their generosity, virtues that increased their honor and prestige.

In his reasoning, Alfonso does not point to what could be considered legal reasons supporting his claim to the imperial crown, for example his Hohenstaufen ancestry, although he does mention his election as the new basis for his rights. Alfonso seems to have forgotten his ancestry himself, which leads us to ask whether he really wanted to be emperor, or simply advanced his candidacy due to external pressures. Was he so proud that he feared disappointing those who had expectations of him? Was he really obsessed with the imperial crown? Apparently, all of Castile thought so, including his representatives at the Cortes and even his chronicler ("which was something he coveted much" *CAX*, chap. 53, p. 173). Of course it was this firm conviction that pushed the nobles and others present at the Cortes to exploit the situation, convinced as they were that if they supported his quest for the imperial crown, he would agree to everything else. This led them to increase their demands to the point that if he had satisfied them, Alfonso would have ended up destroying the constitutional structures of the kingdom.

The *CAX* concludes the section on the commission's recommendations and how they were rejected by the nobles, who had already left Castile, with these words: "All of these things the king grants to them so that they go along with him on the matter of the empire and serve him just as they promised. And the prince and the noblemen, having heard and seen the writ regarding what don Fernando and the other good men who were there with him told them, were not satisfied by what the king was telling them. And they had a letter written concerning the things that they requested the king do for them, and they gave it to the archbishop and to don Manuel. And they departed from Sabiote and went to Granada, carrying along all they had seized from Castile" (chap. 39, p. 132).

Regarding the demands of the clergy at the Cortes, Alfonso had to use a subterfuge in order not to blow up against the hypocrisy and *auri sacra fames* [the sacred hunger for gold] of the two-faced Church officials implicated in the conspiracy to dethrone him. The anonymous

---

[72] *Crónica abreviada*, ed. J.M. Blecua, *Obras completas*, II, p. 57.

chronicler, who almost always sides with the rebels, shows some empathy for Alfonso here (pp. 99–104). We do not know what "estoria" the chronicler refers to (perhaps the *CAX* itself) when he accuses the prelates of being responsible for the defection and rebellion, denouncing at the same time the base motives by which "they acted in this fashion thinking that the king would grant them everything they requested." In any event, given the delicate circumstances regarding his imperial aspirations and to ingratiate himself with the new pope, Alfonso preferred to stay calm and satisfy the clergy's demands, deferring the matter to the commission and accepting their decision, rather than openly confronting the representatives of the Church.[73] He had not forgotten the advice of his father-in-law at Tarazona: do not oppose the Church.

And yet he could have achieved this, for he was completely convinced of the rebellious attitude of those prelates who, with their protest, knowingly destabilized the peace and social order of the kingdom. With such behavior, they also exposed their true nature as feudal lords, sharing the same interests of the secular lords whom they joined to maintain their privileges.[74]

Despite Alfonso's good will in reaching an agreement, the clergy's demands persisted, and the Church's opposition due to fiscal matters became one of the most serious political issues of the kingdom at the end of Alfonso's life. It was indeed the clergy who first helped Sancho take the throne away from his father and who later were instrumental to him in ending the Alfonsine cultural enterprise and turning radically, under the regency of María de Molina, to a religious view of culture matching the previous century's canon.[75]

It is unclear how much support the rebels received from another very powerful institution, the Military Orders. A letter from Alfonso to don Fernando, discussed below, only mentions the Master of the Order of Santiago, don Pelay Pérez Correa, warning that don Fernando should

---

[73] Ballesteros identified the rebellious bishops, all of whom hailed from León: Astorga, León, Ciudad Rodrigo, Lugo, Mondoñedo, Orense, Túy, Coria, and Badajoz. Cf. *Alfonso X*, p. 584.

[74] On Alfonso X's conflict with the Church in León-Castile, see J.M. Nieto Soria, *La relaciones monarquía-episcopado castellano como sistema de poder (1252–1312)*, Madrid, 1983; and P. Linehan, *The Spanish Church and the Papacy*, pp. 175–176.

[75] Cf. G. Orduna, "La elite intelectual de la escuela catedralicia de Toledo y la literatura en la época de Sancho IV," in *La Literatura en la época de Sancho IV*, ed. C. Alvar and J.M. Lucía Megías, Universidad de Alcalá, 1996, pp. 53–62.

be wary of him since he was a dangerously duplicitous character who had advised the nobles to do what they did. Although Alfonso's new legal and administrative rules did not affect them directly, given their social status, the Great Masters of the Orders, noblemen and related to noblemen, must have indeed sympathized with the rebels, although they too sided with the dispossessed, perhaps out of a desire to protect them from royal abuse or due to political opportunism, a possibility yet to be explored.[76]

During the Cortes that autumn of 1272, one of the most important moments of his legal career, Alfonso was at his best displaying his knowledge of past legislation and putting forth a vision for the future unification of laws. Even the usually critical author of the *CAX* confessed: "The king argued so well concerning these matters that all of those who had assembled there understood that he was just and lawful and that don Felipe and those noblemen were causing the uprising unjustly. As soon as don Felipe, don Nuño, and all the noblemen heard what the king told them, they did not respond. They all left the palace and departed in the midst of their rebellion, even though they were armed" (chap. 25, p. 101).

---

[76] On the Military Orders in Alfonso X's time, see E. Benito Ruano, "Establecimientos de la Orden de Santiago durante el maestrazgo de D. Pelay Pérez Correa," in *Homenaje al Dr. Juan Reglá Campistol*, I, Valencia, 1975, pp. 93–101; M. González Jiménez, "Relaciones de las Ordenes Militares castellanas con la Corona," *HID*, 18 (1991), pp. 209–222; and D.W. Lomax, *La Orden de Santiago. 1170–1275*, Madrid, 1965, esp. p. 31.

CHAPTER TEN

DESNATURACIÓN

1. *Alfonso's Reaction: The "Justice-Seeking Letters"*

In view of Alfonso's triumph in the Burgos Cortes, according to medieval practices the rebels faced a dilemma: either to accept the authority and decisions of their king or to *desnaturarse*, that is, to break the vassalage bond that linked them to their lord and leave the kingdom to go into exile. According to feudal customs, that was the most drastic measure, other than declaring war, that a noble could take against his lord, and it was precisely the option that the rebels chose, requesting from the king the usual 42 days to leave their kingdoms, which they did at the end of November 1272.[1]

The reasonableness, flexibility, and willingness to please that Alfonso had shown them during the Cortes and the final deliberations were of no use. Despite the irrational attitude of the conspirators, Alfonso, egged on by the queen and the archbishop of Toledo, confirmed once more the nobility's codes [*fueros* or *privileges*], granting most of their demands and having to personally be reproached by the rebels who told him in his face that if he wanted to squander wealth to benefit foreigners, he should do so out of his own coffers.[2]

Among the rebels who refused to accept Alfonso's sovereignty and who even signed a pact of alliance and submission with Ibn el-Ahmer, the king of Grananda, becoming his subjects and abandoning his king, the names of prince don Felipe, Nuño González de Lara, Lope Díaz de Haro, Esteban Fernández de Castro, Fernán Ruiz de Castro, Simón Ruiz de los Cameros, and Alvar Díaz de Asturias are explicitly mentioned in the *CAX*.[3] On their way to the kingdom of Granada, from Atienza, where they were gathered, they destroyed towns and lands in

---

[1] *CAX*, chap. 27, p. 105.
[2] *CAX*, chap. 40, pp. 133–36.
[3] One copy of the pact with the king of Granada has been included in the *CAX*, chap. 43, p. 140. Cf. Ballesteros, *Alfonso X*, pp. 626–633. This pact of alliance with the enemy and their submission as vassals was an incredibly serious offence that entailed the loss of all their possessions, and in case of a war and capture, execution.

such a way that Alfonso had to confront them militarily, in order to stop their devastating fury.[4] These acts violated the rules of the royal assurance they had obtained from Alfonso, turned them into criminals, a legal condition that authorized the king to use his goods to compensate those who had suffered the consequences of their *malfetrías* or wrongdoings.

When Alfonso learned of the insolence of the rebels and their desire to defect despite his accommodating attitude, he was enraged, especially against his brother don Felipe. But that spontaneous reaction soon had to be repressed and curbed because he was aware that without the support of the nobility, among whom he recruited most of his army in case of war, he was unable to face his enemies. The king of Castile therefore found himself alone and powerless against his feared enemies to the south. Taking severe measures against the rebels who, besides the king's brother, belonged to the three most important families in Christian Spain (the Laras, the Haros, and the Castros), must have seemed to Alfonso as an aggravation of an already difficult situation in which he had much to lose militarily.

I therefore believe that this was not a case of indecisiveness, as some do, but that realistically, Alfonso could have done no better. It was a political compromise where Alfonso was too generous, preferring to be accommodating instead of defeating his rivals. Such an attitude in the context of harsh times and unscrupulous warriors must have been, and still is for other reasons, seen as a weakness characteristic of an "immature introvert."[5] However, there is sufficient proof to demonstrate the realistic attitude and practical sense of the Learned King. The letter he wrote to his son Fernando (that will be discussed below, pp. 334–351) would be sufficient to reveal to what extent he was on firm footing regarding the political realities and knowledge of his adversaries. It is a priceless document permitting us to know this complex man, whose personality was dominated by his desire for concord and the wellbeing of his subjects, even when they were his enemies.

---

[4] *CAX*, chap. 37, pp. 128–29; Ballesteros, *Alfonso X*, pp. 587–590. On the activities of the rebels before leaving for Granada, see M. González Jiménez, "Alfonso y la revuelta nobiliaria de 1272–1273. Notas y comentarios a propósito de unos documentos navarros," *Fundación* 1, Buenos Aires, 1997–1998.

[5] Cf. F. Torres González, "Rasgos médico-psicológicos de Alfonso X el Sabio," pp. 118–121.

Having exhausted the diplomatic route (for to make war against them would have been political suicide), Alfonso had only one route left: to try to convince them with his most powerful weapon: the pen. It was an excellent opportunity to put into practice the epistolary talents learned in his youth from great masters. As a true intellectual humanist, instead of attacking them with the sword, he preferred to convince them with very rational and even moving arguments. But these were not times for sensible and humane methods. This episode in the Learned King's life gave him the occasion to write his "cartas justicieras" (justice-seeking letters), as Ballesteros termed them, in which, in a poignant tone, he reveals his anguish and disenchantment with the attitude of his own brothers and the inexplicable ungratefulness of those men he had showered with favors. From this moment on, ungratefulness and betrayal were the themes he would repeat tirelessly in all of his works.

The letters were written in Toledo during his stay there when he was busy with his cultural projects and following the movements of the rebels in their march to the south. They are written in the third person and they are a kind of oral message that Alfonso's representatives, Gonzalo Ruiz de Atienza, mayor of Toledo, and Sancho Pérez, scribe and notary of the king's chamber, relayed to the rebels on their stopover in Atienza (January–February 1273) on the way to Granada. The *Chronicle* reproduces the text of these eight letters or messages that according to Ballesteros, the anonymous chronicler "copied from the royal archives." The first one is addressed to all the rebels in general and the other seven to each of the leaders of the rebellion individually.[6]

Among these letters, the ones sent to his brother, prince don Felipe, and to don Nuño de Lara, who were on their way to Granada with the rebels destroying towns and villages, are worth singling out. Alfonso sends out his last call to save them from that embarrassing act of treason. In the letter to don Felipe, which is a kind of biography of the unfaithful brother from his youth and studies in Paris to his high positions and appointments (the archbishopric of Seville to which he was elected, etc.), Alfonso insists on the many favors he had granted

---

[6] The collection begins with the letter to his brother, prince don Felipe, followed by the ones to his close friends, don Nuño González de Lara, don Lope Díaz de Haro, don Fernán Ruiz de Castro, don Esteban Ferrández, don Juan Núñez and don Alvar (*CAX*, chaps. 27–36, pp. 107–127).

personally to him and the many signs of preference he had displayed, such as the marriage he arranged for him to Christina, daughter of the king of Norway, which liberated him from an ecclesiastical post he resented. Alonso urges his brother to consider how his actions not only degraded him personally, turning him into an ungrateful traitor, but also degraded his lineage:

> [...] Moreover, he sends word that they told him you were going to the kingdom of Granada to be on its side, knowing that the King of Granada is the enemy of God and of the Faith, and of the king and his kingdoms, and the enemy of all of noble descent who are in Castile and León, and of all of those from these other kingdoms. And you, being the son of King Fernando and of Queen Beatriz, and brother of King Alfonso, he considers that you ought to protect better the lineage from which you come and the duty you have toward him. In all of these things you deprived the land and you disinherited yourself, and he did not deprive you nor is he disinheriting you. (*CAX* chap. 29, pp. 110–111)

In the letter to don Nuño, who was known as "the Andalusian Raven" for his skill and effectiveness in battle, Alfonso insistently reminds him of the many favors he had granted him since childhood: "[y]ou know that you received from him [art. cit. Alfonso himself] much honor and favor, more than any man of your station ever received from any other king. For being a child, you grew up with him, and being Prince, when he began to rule, because of the love he felt for you, he placed Gonzalo Nuñez, your brother, under his protection and favor ..." (*CAX*, chap. 30, p. 112). This attitude vis-à-vis the Laras, according to Alfonso, had put him in conflict with his father, king don Fernando, who held in contempt all relations with the Laras because of betrayals committed by their ancestors. It also damaged his relations with the nobility when, to favor don Nuño, Alfonso started a feud with the Haros, which was perceived negatively in the kingdom and provoked the rebellion of his own royal standard-bearer, don Diego López de Haro.[7] Alfonso closed by insisting on the countless favors he had bestowed on don Nuño, reminding him that he was fleeing to Granada with the king's money which he had illegally collected from his subjects, and warning that "[you] should ponder what might come to you from this deed" (*CAX*, chap. 30, p. 115).

---

[7] *CAX*, chap. 30, pp. 112–13.

The letters survive as a historical and literary document and a faithful testimony of the attempts of the Learned King to salvage the integrity of his kingdom, although, despite their rhetorical skill and the warnings issued, they were completely ineffective. All efforts were in vain.

The *CAX* tells us that after hearing the king's messengers, the rebels "withdrew in order to reach an agreement, and they sent for the king's messengers and gave them this answer" (chap. 37, p. 128) The answer is short but clear: The rebels informed Alfonso that they had no intention of heeding him regarding the service they were obligated to render nor regarding the money they had taken with them when they left Castile, nor did they think about repairing the damage they left in their wake, "because we left good properties there; and according to what they find in the investigation, they should order them handed over" (*CAX*, chap. 37, p. 128). In other words, they asked Alfonso to make an assessment of the damage they had caused and to compensate the affected with the properties they had left behind in Castile.

Despite the enormous political adversities, Alfonso had decided what his priorities were: the quest for the Empire, and the Muslim danger to the South. But he understood that reaching these two goals depended on an adequate solution to the conflict with the powerful rebels, so he continued his efforts to reach an agreement with them, sending a sizeable delegation headed by his son Fernando, his wife Violante, his brother Manuel, and the archbishop of Toledo, don Sancho, to negotiate at all costs a compromise with the defectors.[8]

The delegation met the fugitives at Sabiote (Jaén) near Úbeda in the vicinity of the kingdom of Granada, where they had arrived "with all of the plunder they carried along with them—which was more than five thousand horses, and clothes, and cattle, and other things" (*CAX*, chap. 38, p. 130). According to the *CAX*, once more, Alfonso's delegates "spoke with them, telling and showing them the error and wrong that they were committing, and doing what they could in order to convince them not to go on that journey. No matter how much they said to them, they were not able to stop Prince Felipe and the noblemen nor return them to the service of the king, even though they promised many things" (*CAX*, chap. 38, p. 130). In a dramatic scene, Alfonso's representatives showed the rebels a document "which was sealed with

---

[8] *CAX*, chap. 53, pp. 173–174.

the king's seal" (*CAX*, chap. 38, p. 130) which read thus: "These are the things that the queen, the archbishop, and the bishops asked of the king through his grace so that he might grant them to Prince Felipe and the noblemen concerning the demands they made" (*CAX*, chap. 39, p. 131).

This document, conceived and executed with the best of intentions by his brothers don Manuel and don Sancho, archbishop of Toledo, and his wife doña Violante, left Alfonso in a difficult situation because it gave the impression that Alfonso wanted to reward rebelliousness. Still, the Learned King consented to those embarrassing conditions according to which all of his recent legislation was abolished and returned to the status quo of the era of Alfonso VIII and Saint Fernando. Perhaps the only reason that pushed Alfonso to such an arrangement was the desire to internally pacify the kingdom, a *sine qua non* condition to obtaining the imperial crown. At that moment in the Learned King's life, all seemed to depend on his quest for the Empire.

But unfortunately, not even the acceptance of such humiliating conditions satisfied the rebels, who, upon seeing Alfonso's weakness, increased their demands in a long *Memorial* they delivered to don Manuel and don Sancho to take to Toledo where Alfonso was residing.[9] According to the chronicler, Alfonso was dumbstruck when he was shown the demands in text of the *Memorial*: "it seemed to the king very strange to grant these things that the noblemen sent to demand from him, and that it was very grave to authorize them, particularly because they requested them in arrogance. Nonetheless, he handed this matter over to don Fadrique and don Manuel, his brothers. And the king sent them his letters in this fashion..." (*CAX*, chap. 40, p. 134). In these letters to the leaders of the rebellion, transcribed in the *CAX*, Alfonso reluctantly had to give up everything in order to save his imperial ambitions. But he had to make it abundantly clear, discharging all responsibility, that he did so under the pressure of his advisors: "Hence, I tell you that I consider it a good thing and it pleases me to do all of those things that they told me, and regarding this I send you my ordinance with legal security for it all" (*CAX*, chap. 40, pp. 134–135). The *CAX* concludes that: "All of these things the king grants to them so that they go along with him to the empire and

---

[9] It is in this *Memorial* that they finally articulated their demands. Cf. *CAX*, pp. 30–31. (chap. 40, pp. 133–136).

so that they may serve him just as they promised him" (*CAX*, chap. 39, p. 132).[10]

The discontent and rebellion of the nobles had to do with the proposal of exchanging the common law legislation for a centralized and uniform justice system for all the kingdoms, and with the exorbitant taxes that had been put in place as economic support for his quest for the Empire and were bankrupting everyone. In his response to the nobles' *Memorial*, Alfonso finally realized that his recent legislation, especially the fiscal system, was meeting with fierce opposition not only among the nobles exiled in Granada, but also from a majority of the nobles, bishops, knights, and even the most humble citizens of the kingdom. It was now time to do something so that the structures of society would not collapse.

Meanwhile, the nobles had reached their destination, Granada. But before entering the city, the *CAX* writes, they sent letters to the king of Granada to clarify the terms of their vassalage. It was perfectly natural that the terms of the agreement would be put in writing, as the request for protection was not unconditional. The agreement in Castilian and Arabic has been preserved in the *CAX* (chap. 43, pp. 140–143). The signatories were, on the one hand, Mohamed Ibn Yûsuf Ibn Nasr, known as Ibn el-Ahmer (or the *Son of the Red*) and his successor Alamir Aboabdille, and on the other hand, the prince, don Felipe and the noble *ricohombre*, Nuño González. The document, as Ballesteros states, is a "striking example of a disloyalty seldom committed in history".[11] Even today, after more than seven centuries, we cannot understand how a motley crew of Christian warriors and skilled political strategists such as all the rebels could have signed an alliance pact with the enemy of Christendom to overthrow their king, aware that they were thus signing their own demise. The agreement on the part of the nobles consisted in putting themselves at the service of the king of Granada to make valid the Alcalá de Benzayde's agreement: "I [...] promise to help you against all men in the world, Christians or Moors, in war as well as in peace" (*CAX*, chap. 43, p. 141). The king of Granada, for his part, agreed "that we are making a treaty of fealty in good faith, without evil and deceit; and that if the King of Castile were to seize the land you hold from him or your inheritance, or if

---

[10] The capitulation letter can be seen in the *CAX*, chaps. 47–48, pp. 151–156.

[11] *Alfonso X*, p. 627.

he were to come to us, may we be obliged to assist you with our territories, our men, and our might and wage war against him" (*CAX*, chap. 43, p. 141). We do not know for sure when the agreement was signed, but, as we said before, it was before the arrival of the nobles in Granada and during the life of Ibn el-Ahmer, who died shortly thereafter, in January 1273.

The death of the elderly and seasoned king of Granada gave a new twist to the nobles' rebellion. He was succeeded by his son Mohamed Ibn Yûsuf Ibn Nasr II (1273–1302), also known as Amir Amus Lemin, or "Miramamolín", as he is known in the Christian chronicles. But the succession was not an easy affair, since it was opposed by several rivals, in particular by his own brother, who was supported by the two *arraeces*, subjects of Alfonso. But according to the *CAX*, "the noblemen of Castile and León took their plea to Alamir Abboadille and made him the king" (*CAX*, chap. 43, p. 143). In other words, they managed to place on the throne the son chosen by the late Ibn el-Ahmer, although they had to fight the faction supported by the *arraeces*. From the beginning, the new king of Granada, Mohamed Ibn Yûsuf, showed his desire to solve the issue of the noble rebels and the contentious king of Castile. But, like his father, he kept a firm position regarding the *arraeces* and did not release the noble Castilians from their oath of fidelity until Alfonso guaranteed the return of the *arraeces* as agreed at Alcalá de Benzayde. But it was precisely the hostility of the *arraeces* that forced him to ask don Nuño to send his son, Juan Núñez, to Toledo to present a solution to Alfonso (*CAX*, chap. 45, pp. 147–149).

2. *"Assemblies" at Almagro and Ávila*

Between March 23 and 28, 1273, in the midst of negotiations with the rebels carried out on several fronts by the queen, the crown prince and Alfonso's two brothers, don Fadrique and don Manuel, Alfonso gathered the entire nobility at Almagro in order to discuss the state of negotiations with the rebels and to clarify his position regarding the special "servicio" tax which was the immediate cause of all the commotion (*CAX*, chap. 47, p. 151).

It was during this "assembly" at Almagro (the *CAX* does not term this meeting a "Cortes" but rather an "ayuntamiento") that Alfonso finally acknowledged the economic troubles caused by the "servicio" approved at the 1269 Burgos Cortes, but at the same time apologized that he could not avoid it because he needed it for his quest for the Empire.[12] But he was willing to forgo two of the four years he still expected to collect, although he continued to levy road taxes and a special tax ("diezmos del mar," an import tax on foreign goods) to compensate those who would accompany him on his trip.[13] The nobles present at Almagro, among whom were queen Violante, prince Fernando, and the king's brothers, don Fadrique and don Manuel, together with the Masters of the Orders of Uclés, Calatrava, Alcántara, and the Templars, agreed with the king, who, perhaps under the advice of the commission, also confirmed the codes known as "fueros, customs and traditions" (fueros, e usos e costumbres") that had been in use under other kings.[14]

The "assembly" was not attended by the noble rebels, who had exiled themselves in Granada, nor by the bishops and clergymen present at the 1267 and 1272 Cortes. The nobles once more showed their discontent, demanding that the tribute paid by the king of Granada should be paid to them to compensate them for the losses incurred in their exile. Furious, Alfonso responded with an order to demolish their homes (CAX, chap. 50, pp. 160–161).

As we hinted above, things began to change favorably for Alfonso in his relationship to Grananda with the death of its astute king and the succession of Mohamed II. In fact, during the "assembly" at Almagro, Alfonso received news from the king of Granada proposing a new friendship agreement that showed his desire to establish the good relations his father had maintained in the past with the Castilian king, promising to pay back taxes and contributing the sum of 250,000 maravedís to help Alfonso in his quest for the Empire. The only condition was the return of the arraeces to his obedience. Alfonso must have been happy about this unexpected good news that allowed him to be more flexible with his Castilian subjects on the controversial tax issue.[15]

---

[12] CAX, chap. 47, p. 152.
[13] CAX, chap. 47, p. 152; J. O'Callaghan, Cortes of Castile-León, pp. 24–25, 52; Ballesteros, Alfonso X, pp. 637–646.
[14] CAX, chap. 47, p. 152; Ballesteros, Alfonso X, pp. 638–641.
[15] Cf. CAX, chaps. 48–51, pp. 154–164; O'Callaghan, The Cortes, pp. 25–26; E. Procter, Curia and Cortes, p. 135; Ballesteros, Alfonso X, pp. 646–680.

Alfonso now had an advantage over the rebels, namely, the favor of the new sultan of Granada, and the rebels were aware of this. They thus began to fear for their situation, which this new rapprochement made ever more precarious. If the two kings reached an agreement, they would certainly pay the consequences. The dissent among them began, and the coalition of the rebels began to disintegrate. But the new dynamic in the relationship between the two kings seemed to be resolving in favor of the rebels, when their emissary, Juan Núñez, returned from his meeting with Alfonso in Toledo. Juan brought with him a new proposal by Alfonso that was more inflexible on the matter of the *arraeces*, the crucial point of Alfonso's negotiations with the sultan. This gave the rebels new hope that no agreement could be reached without them.

After the "assembly" at Almagro, the king set out on his way to Toledo, arriving there on March 27. Between April 21 and May 28, 1273, Alfonso visited Ávila where he celebrated a meeting or "assembly" with the representatives of the town councils of León and the two Extremaduras in order to reach an agreement on the controversial topic of the establishment of new settlements in the areas where the nobles opposed it. It was during this visit to Ávila when, as we saw above, he fell ill with a fever and *romadizo* (respiratory infection), being miraculously cured by the Virgin. The king took this opportunity once more to inform the assembly of the state of negotiations with the rebellious nobles: "[b]eing there and showing them the making of the treaty that he had with the Moors, and likewise, the wrong and outrage that don Felipe and the nobles who were in Granada had done him in departing to his enemies and pillaging the land from him, and proclaiming all the other things that they had done to him (as the *History* has related)" (*CAX*, chap. 50, p. 160). During the assembly, Alfonso promised he would not go forward with the repopulation except in lands belonging to the Crown.[16]

During the "assembly" of Ávila, the cause of the rebels received a harsh blow with the defection of one of the main conspirators, Ferrán Ruiz de Castro, brother-in-law of prince don Felipe, who defected to the side loyal to Alfonso together with many of his knights: "[...] don Fernán Ruiz de Castro, who had parted from the King of Granada and

---

[16] *CAX*, chap. 50, pp. 160–161, chap. 52, pp. 165–72; J. O'Callaghan, *Cortes of Castile-León*, p. 25, note 27; Ballesteros, *Alfonso X*, pp. 646–650, 676–677.

the friendship of the nobles, came to his protection. He came with many knights from there, and the king was greatly pleased with them and received them well and favored them greatly" (*CAX*, chap. 50, p. 160). The defections had begun.

As if to counter this piece of good news, another one arrived through the royal messenger, Gonzalo Ruiz, who informed Alfonso that the nobles, together with the Muslims from Córdoba, had begun attacking the Christian borders "seizing food and other things for which they had need" (*CAX*, chap. 51, p. 162). The crown prince, don Fernando, who was at the time in Córdoba, called an emergency meeting of his council and sent against the rebels the Master of the Order of Calatrava in order to stop their advance. The Master, Juan González, left Córdoba for Porcuna where he sent representatives to Granada to invite the nobles to meet with him and negotiate a solution to the conflict. The *Crónica* tells us that González met with the *ricoshombres* (gentlemen) in Alcalá de Benzayde, where they were all assembled and ready to attack the Christians. The Master, changing the command of the prince, agreed to all they asked for (*CAX*, chap. 51, pp. 162–163).

The Master's agreement could not have been more disastrous for Alfonso's cause, since it was in direct conflict with his entire policy towards the Moorish kingdom and the negotiations carried out until that moment. Only an incompetent man or a traitor could have agreed to that dishonorable pact. In fact, the chronicler notes that "the Master signed with them the treaties as best he could, *but not according to what King Alfonso wanted*" (*CAX*, chap. 51, p. 163 emphasis added). Naturally, after returning to Córdoba and informing don Fernando of the agreement, he refused to sign it because he knew it was against his father's will. He also, as the chronicler notes, "sent to tell the king to carry out what he considered good" (*CAX*, chap. 51, p. 163), that is, he wrote to his father asking for advice in this delicate matter.

3. Alfonso Writes to his Son

Soon after these events, in late spring of 1273 and after leaving Ávila, Alfonso wrote his famous letter in response to the one his son Fernando, then in charge of the Granada border, wrote him about the political situation in the kingdom due to the nobles' revolt.[17] Written

---

[17] The beautiful letter of the Learned King to his son and heir is entirely reproduced in the Appendix of the Spanish version of this work. It can also be found in the *CAX*,

in a direct style, this letter is a key political document for understanding the rebellion from Alfonso's perspective. It also gives a panorama of the problems being debated in the kingdom, but above all, it is an exceptional testimony of the Learned King's personality as a father concerned about the future of his heir and as a seasoned ruler, revealing "his skill in gauging the truth of human relations."[18]

The letter begins precisely with a short summary of don Fernando's letter in which the prince informed him of the state of negotiations by the Master of Calatrava with the rebels and the king of Granada: "Don Fernando, when these letters reached me, [I] was in Ávila, for he was coming to speak with the councils of the land of León and Extremadura that I had assembled. I was sick with catarrh and a low fever, and I was very sorry that it had befallen us at that time, but I even received more grief when I realized what the letters were saying" (*CAX*, chap. 52, p. 165). Alfonso was very unhappy with the state of the negotiations and the agreements by the Master, telling his son that if the letter had upset him because of its timing (Alfonso was sick at the time) "I was even much more saddened when I understood the content of the letters"

Don Fernando was right not to sign because he knew his father well. Alfonso cast doubt on the impartiality of the advice from those who were with him in Córdoba regarding sending the Master to Granada. Among such advice-givers were, for instance the Master of Uclés (about whom Alfonso writes, "you should beware of the art of the Master of Uclés in believing such a piece of advice, because he is one of the men in this world who counseled these gentlemen to do what they did") and the Master of Calatrava himself (about whom "I say that even if I love him and regard him as a good man, I know that he is on the side of Lope Díaz [de Haro] due to his lineage"). Alfonso's attack against don Pelay Pérez Carrea, Master of the Order of Santiago

---

chap. 52, pp. 165–72. On this letter, see. K. Rodgers, "Alfonso X Writes to His Son: Reflections on the *Crónica de Alfonso X* (together with a commentary on and critical text of the unique Alfonsine letter that it preserves)," *EH*, 1 (1991–1992), pp. 58–79.

[18] F. Gómez Redondo, *Historia de la prosa medieval castellana*, p. 972, note 205. According to Ballesteros:
> We must thank the chronicler for having saved some of the most beautiful documents of that period. This precious epistle in which a father entrusts his son with state secrets, granting him supreme trust, is one of the most important clues into Alfonso's personality, the most intimate aspects of his psychology and perhaps his merit as a historian. (*Alfonso X*, p. 650)

is even stronger: he accused him of infidelity and of having broken an old friendship in order to join the conspirators.

From the harsh criticism of these personalities, it can be deduced that Alfonso was fully aware of their connivance, which was understandable given the affinities of class and interests between the Master of Calatrava and the noble defectors. Alfonso reveals to his son how knowledgeable he was about the contact of the Masters of the Military Orders with the noble rebels, but he explains how political prudence and the awareness that antagonizing those who had military power meant the risk of losing his crown had stopped him from reproaching them for their betrayal. Reading these paragraphs of the letter, it is surprising how these natural allies of Alfonso's, whom he had favored generously in the distribution of the new conquered territories, broke away from their king.[19]

Then, a desperate Alfonso goes on to analyze the causes of the rebellion, describing to his son, in a very intimate and personal tone yet with the objectivity of a seasoned historian, how he had arrived at this critical juncture:

> And just as kings made [the nobility] powerful and honored them, they strove to make the kings less powerful and to dishonor them in so many ways that it would be long and very shameful to relate [...] Now you can understand this, for all things that led me to do what they wanted, they rejected—particulary the journey to the empire, which is the most important [...] Besides, they desire that we be unable to make any kind of agreement with the Moors without them, so that they might gain one firm foothold there and another here, which will stand if God is willing. (CAX, chap. 52, pp. 166–167)

This was indeed a very negative vision of the Castilian nobility of all times, conditioned, according to Alfonso, forever to destroy the monarchy and pursue its own profit. It is clear that this analysis of the rebellion contains much truth that Alfonso tried to impart to his son, but we also discover a fundamental error in Alfonso's arguments if we consider the fact that Alfonso did not believe that the rebels were sincere when they claimed that their rebellion was "for the sake of the land", that is, the economic wellbeing of the kingdom. Alfonso

---

[19] C. de Ayala Martínez attempted an answer in "La monarquía y las Ordenes Militares durante el reinado de Alfonso X," *Hispania*, 178 (1991), pp. 409–465; and *La Orden de Santiago en la evolución política del reinado de Alfonso X (1252–1284)*, Madrid: Universidad Autónoma, 1983.

argued that when it came to seeking the wellbeing of the country, he had nothing to learn from anyone, for in the end, he was defending what was his own; at best, the rebellious nobles could only defend what had been given to them. This traditional view that the king is the source and origin of all justice stood in contrast to the new currents of thought holding that the kingdom was a corporate entity wherein all subjects participated via their representatives. In Castile, these were the monarchy, the nobility, the clergy, and the officials of the cities.

We are once more faced with the same problem that had surfaced in the first rebellion of the nobility on account of the concessions made to his grandson, don Dinis of Portugal. On that occasion, it had been precisely his childhood friend, don Nuño de Lara, who had had the nerve to tell him that as a loving grandfather, proud of his handsome grandson, he could grant him everything he wanted, "But Lord, that you take away from the Crown of your kingdoms the tribute that the King of Portugal and his kingdom are obliged to give to you, I shall never advise you" (*CAX*, chap. 19, pp. 73–74).

If Alfonso's position was not sufficiently clear at the time, in this confidential letter to his heir it is crystal-clear: the Learned King continued to uphold the old concept according to which the kingdom was the king's private property, and he could make use of it as he would of his sword, his goshawk, or his horse.[20] From this perspective, it is clear that Alfonso did not even remotely accept that anyone could suggest how to administer what was his. If he was right in his rule, the merit was his only, and if he was wrong, only he would suffer the consequences. Nobody had the right to intervene in his decisions.

Since this was a confidential letter obtained directly from Alfonso's archive, the chronicler therefore does not reproduce any reply or challenge by don Nuño because there simply was not one, but his ideology and that of his followers was clear from the beginning of the rebellion (recall the reaction in the episode with don Dinis). But to what extent the position of the nobles was honest and disinterested is another matter. If don Nuño and the rest of the nobles were committed to

---

[20] The confidential nature of the letter is obvious: "And when you read this letter, my son, may Alfonso Fernández be there with you; and don Jofré de Loaysa, Diego de Corral, and none other be with you" (*CAX*, chap. 52, p. 172). These were two close associates of the king; in the first case, Alfonso Fernández, known as "el Niño" who was his illegitimate but much beloved and trusted son; the second was a greatly esteemed man of the court who was also don Fernando's caretaker; the third was don Fernando's valet.

preserving their privilege, which was certain, we can also think that in order to defend their personal interests they would want to promote a concept of the kingdom in which the property of the crown was property of all subjects and thus the king could not make indiscriminate use of it without previous approval from all kingdom representatives.

One of the aspects of the king's complete domination with which the rebels most found fault with was his fiscal policy. In a moment of economic crisis, Alfonso, in order to finance his imperial electoral campaign, was burdening his subjects with taxes they could not pay. According to the rebels, subjects were aggravated by the fact that their taxes were being used for a purpose that only benefited the king personally. Nobody believed anymore what Alfonso had said at the Burgos Cortes in defense and as justification of the expenses for the Empire: "he told the nobles that if he was giving wealth to men of other lands, it was to bring honor to the people of his kingdoms, and that because of it, those of his realm were the most loved and valued men who ever lived in the whole world" (*CAX*, chap. 24, p. 96). But in the letter, Alfonso insists that the opposition to his fiscal policy was not so much for economic reasons, which he recognized were clearly precarious, but rather for political ones. The nobles' opposition to his imperial ambitions, according to Alfonso, was due to the same old reasons: the animosity of the nobility to the institution of the monarchy. If they now were opposing the kingdom, much more so would they oppose "the quest for the Empire, which is even greater".

The second point that Alfonso touches upon in his letter is the matter of the alliance of the nobles with the king of Granada and his potential Moroccan allies, who believed they had a military capacity that Alfonso doubted. He advises his son not to fear the king of Granada and to consider that his forces are inferior to those of Castile ("for you have three for every one of them, and better than them"). He also should not fear a possible invasion or help from Africa "because of which I believe he [Abenyuzaf] cannot cross over, as those [Alfonso does not even mention them by name] who are in Granada are saying. Let's say he wants to cross: where could he find ships to carry across so many knights, and will he bring food to feed those and the others who are here? I cannot believe this could be, nor as much help as they say he will have, for it is a custom among the Moors to write skilful and false letters and to send them to each other in order to obtain some advantages for themselves" (*CAX*, chap. 52, p. 168). Alfonso assures his favorite son, who at the time was in Córdoba securing the border to the south, that the nobles' and the Muslims' threats are feigned and with propagandistic goals: "to obtain some advantages for themselves" (*CAX*, chap. 52, p. 168).

Alfonso goes on to explain to the young and inexperienced heir a possible strategic plan using the two *arraeces* to spearhead the action (for they knew the territory well and they hated the king of Granada), while at the same time placing ships on the Strait: "I also think that the first thing you should have examined was how the galleys might be readied, for if they were not in the straight, neither Aben Yuzaf nor any other could cross even if they wanted to" (*CAX*, chap. 52, p. 170). With this psychological advice and his defense plan, Alfonso attempts to encourage his son, perhaps exaggerating a bit the power and capacity of the Christian forces. From then on, it will become clear how wrong Alfonso was regarding the force and ability of the enemy. For obvious security reasons, he does not say much to don Fernando regarding the help he was preparing ("I cannot say much to you by letter," *CAX*, chap. 52, p. 171); but he does tell him: "I immediately will come there as soon as I can; and I do not delay at all, except to wait for the King of Aragón, because I do not know when he will come" (*CAX*, chap. 52, p. 171).

Besides the reference to the Moors' claims of superiority, one of the most interesting aspects of the letter from the point of view of psychological warfare (namely, the demonizing of the enemy) is the psychological portrait Alfonso paints of some of the rebels, such as the main leader, don Nuño de Lara, and his uncle, don Felipe, for whom the young don Fernando perhaps felt some admiration as seasoned warriors. Alfonso not only demythologize them, but also degrades them, presenting them as intellectually inferior beings who have made fools of themselves through their behavior:

> If they make us think that they are wise, consider don Nuño, who is considered to be the wisest of them, who did not know how to thank God for the good He had done to him nor serve me in that estate and honor in which I placed him. He knew how to lose it through this madness in which he got involved, and hence, you can see what his wisdom is; moreover, he comes from a lineage of those who always lost what they had and for this reason died in misfortune. About my brother, don Felipe, I do not have to talk about his wisdom, for you know well what he did to God and what he forsook that he had from the Holy Church, and what he did to us, in which he fully manifested his wisdom—and he appears as he is today. (*CAX*, chap. 52, p. 169)

The use of derogatory irony is impressive. We should not forget that don Nuño was considered the "más sesudo" (literally, "brainiest" translated here as "wisest") nobleman of Castile, "hence, you can see what his wisdom is [...]," Alfonso tells his son. About don Felipe's "seso" (literally, "brain") it is enough to recall the high-ranking position in the Church he had given up in order to get married.

It is surprising that Alfonso here would reproach his brother with "what he did to God" (an obvious allusion to the fact that he left the clergy to marry princess Christina of Norway), when, as has been noted, Alfonso either the promoted the marriage or at least gave his consent to it. It is obvious that Alfonso alludes to this matter not because he finds fault with the marriage to Christina itself, but rather to assert that it was Alfonso who helped Felipe to a future worthy of a Castilian prince when he left the bishopric of Seville.[21]

However, not everything in the letter was negative, and there are also passages where Alfonso encourages his son to feel confident and proud, simply because he is on the side of truth, justice, and the law:

> For, don Fernando, I trust in God that we will quickly have great justice over them, for we would not want anything greater. For we hold with the law, and we want to expand it and defend it as much as they diminish it. Moreover, we have justice and truth, which they do not have; but they are in manifest wrong and in falsehood, and we have justice over what is ours, for they want to seize from us to our harm and dishonour, and desire that we give it to them; and that should not be done if the whole world should come against us and we should know that we would die a thousand deaths. Don Fernando, when a man receives harm by force, there is no surprise; but when he does it by his own hand, this is the greatest harm that can be. We should fight to protect ourselves as much as we can, for I trust in God that He will protect us, for He always protected those from whom we came. (*CAX*, chap. 52, p. 168)

This enormous moral strength against adversity was supported by two firm pillars of Alfonso's psyche: his conviction of being on the side of truth and a just cause, and the thought of keeping the honor of his elders. He thus counsels his son to maintain moral integrity and his political convictions, although the entire world may turn against him

---

[21] A passage in the *CAX* (chap. 29, pp. 109–110) seems to clarify this apparent contradiction. Reportedly, Alfonso was against don Felipe abandoning the Church, but once he did it, it was Alfonso who helped his brother find a wife appropriate to his status.

or if he should have to die a thousand deaths in order to not violate his principles.

This exceptional document, full of emotion and practical wisdom that Alfonso wishes to impart to his son and heir, ends with the following advice: "I beg you that you ponder the things that these letters say and that you dedicate yourself vigorously to them, and you will immediately see that the news and rumors will change in a different manner" (*CAX*, chap. 52, pp. 171–172).

4. *Agreement in Seville*

Alfonso's extensive discussion of the nobles' rebellion and their presence in Granada is a clear indication that, despite the recent rapprochement with the young sultan, Granada continued to be a thorny issue in his policy to contain the feared African Islam. It was no longer a simple arrangement with Mohamed regarding the *arraeces*—everything was suddenly more complicated due to the presence of the Castilian nobles at the Granada court and their opposition to such an agreement. Also, the royal supporters who accompanied don Fernando to Córdoba began to show signs of impatience and weariness due to the lack of economic resources and military help from the king which was slow to arrive.[22]

On the other hand, there were also promises that had not been kept by Alfonso's supporters in Italy who, as his brother-in-law the Marquis of Monferrato reported, also displayed impatience over the lack of pledged military help and Alfonso's unfulfilled promise to visit them. As time went by, Alfonso began to realize his imperial quest was impossible if he did not first resolve the issue of the nobles which was paralyzing his foreign policy initiatives and jeopardizing the well-being of his kingdom.

In August 1273, Alfonso met with his father-in-law Jaime I in Requena to discuss the Granada issue. The king of Aragón promised him help should the hostilities with the king of Granada begin anew or should the feared invasion by the king of Morocco take place.[23] When king Jaime left Requena, Alfonso X fell so gravely ill that nobody

---

[22] *CAX*, chap. 53, p. 173.
[23] *CAX*, chaps. 53 and 57, pp. 173–174, 187–190. Cf. Ballesteros, *Alfonso X*, pp. 668–671.

thought he would survive.[24] Unable to travel personally to Granada to reach an agreement with Mohamed, he sent his wife doña Violante and his son Fernando to negotiate with the king of Granada and the rebels represented by Nuño González de Lara, don Lope Díaz de Haro, and don Esteban Fernández de Castro.[25]

After many difficulties and threats on both sides, an agreement was reached in which Alfonso agreed to respect the 1265 Alcalá de Benzayde treaty on condition that the king of Granada would pay the two years of tribute in arrears (450,000 maravedís) and would provide the 250,000 maravedís he had promised as a contribution towards expenses incurred in the quest for the empire, "plus one-year's rent in advance" (*CAX*, chap. 54, p. 176). Through his representatives, Alfonso agreed that following a two-year truce, he would return the *arraeces* to the king of Granada, a concession he made reluctantly, for it prevented him from controlling Granada in case of a new North African invasion.[26]

Realizing he could not fight the joint Castilian and Aragonese armies, Mohamed responded positively to the proposals of Alfonso's representatives, showing his willingness to respect the terms of the new agreement, which contemplated the king of Granada becoming a new vassal of the Castilian king, with all the consequences that that entailed, including the liberation of the rebels from the oath of vassalage, and the obligation to assist their lord in case of attack by any enemy. The nobles who were the key to all the negotiations also put forth their demands, which, as in the past, had to do with reestablish-

---

[24] See above, chap. 8, pp. 41–42.

[25] The terms of the negotiation appear clearly in the *CAX*, chaps. 53–54, pp. 173–179.

[26] The following year, because of his quest for the Empire, Alfonso left the reins of the kingdom in Fernando's hands. Among the advice he gave him, he continued to insist on the need to keep the *arraeces*.

> He ordered him even more to make great effort to have as help and in his service the leaders of Málaga, Guadix, and of Gomares and to protect them; and that with these he would conquer the land belonging to the Lord of Granada and would always have him under pressure so that he would never rebel nor leave his rule. (*CAX*, chap. 59, p. 196)

Alfonso's use of the Banu Asqilula *arraeces* as currency in the political negotiations stemming from the Moorish rebellion of 1264 would be a source of continuous conflict among the various political forces operating in the south of the peninsula and the north of Africa. Cf. F. García Fitz, "Alfonso X, el reino de Granada y los Banu Asqilula. Estrategias políticas de disolución durante la segunda mitad del siglo XIII," *AEM*, 27.1 (1997), pp. 215–237.

ing the privileges and exemptions they had enjoyed in the times of Alfonso VIII and Alfonso IX of León. The queen and don Fernando assured them that the king would accept the terms and would confirm their legal codes or "fueros" by letter, which he did, as the chronicler tells us.

The nobles who truly wanted to return to Castile and be reconciled with their king accepted the terms saying that "they were pleased with the discussion and agreement and that they were authorizing it and would be in favor of it" (*CAX*, chap. 56, p. 183) but they were also very conscious of the damage they had caused in their flight from the kingdom. They thus feared for their personal safety, since they suspected that Alfonso would probably want to retaliate or at least demand compensation. The queen, nonetheless, assured their personal safety would be safeguarded, "for they considered that because of her they were assured of their heads" (*CAX*, chap. 56, p. 183)

News about the agreement was communicated to Alfonso at Cuenca by Gonzalo Ruiz, the queen's and prince don Fernando's messenger who had arrived from Córdoba. Encouraged by this, Alfonso immediately sent a letter back to the queen and don Fernando with the same messenger thanking them for their help.[27] Alfonso acknowledged that he could count himself lucky to have two such skillful negotiators as were his wife and son. Doña Violante, in particular, played an extraordinary role during the entire crisis. She resembled her father in her tact at negotiating political and economic agreements. She was the one to persuade her husband to be more flexible and make agreements that would benefit all. Alfonso trusted her to such an extent that when he delegated to her the mission of reconciling the nobles at Ávila, he only gave her the points that she had to resolve, but not how to resolve them, leaving that matter entirely up to her (*CAX*, chap. 53, p. 173). Doña Violante did not disappoint him for, as he admitted, "he ordered and pleaded with her to resolve it to his honor [...and] she resolved it better that what the king ordered her" (ib.).[28]

For Alfonso, besides positive aspects such as the return of the nobles and the lifting of that obstacles to his quest for the Empire, the agreement meant renouncing all of his ideas to restructure the legal and

---

[27] *CAX*, chap. 55, pp. 180–182.
[28] On doña Violante, see R.P. Kinkade, "Violante of Aragón (1236–1300): An Historical Overview," *EH*, 2 (1992–1993).

social life of the kingdom according to the principles listed in the *Espé-culo* and the *Fuero real* and having to reactivate the old measures of the traditional "fueros" of Castile. Regarding the king of Granada, the agreement also contained a fundamental flaw, unnoticed at the time by the Learned King, which would eventually cause much trouble. The agreement was not a permanent solution, but rather a truce that liberated him for a time from the troubles of the kingdom, and allowed him to continue dreaming about the imperial crown.

Once the terms of the agreement had been set, Alfonso's presence in Córdoba was necessary for the ratification of the agreement and to appease the "ricoshombres" and the armed retinue that had accompanied don Fernando to Córdoba, where they had been already for eight months, the last three of them without receiving a cent in pay. But the king had other important matters to resolve both in Castile and internationally. His half-sister Eleanor of England had written requesting a meeting. Doña Violante insisted that he postpone the encounter with his sister and not delay his arrival in Córdoba lest he should lose the trust of the few nobles and warriors who still supported Fernando.

As mentioned, between August 22 and 28, 1273, Alfonso met with king Jaime in Requena. The subject of the talks was the rebellion of the nobles and the agreement negotiated by Violante, still unsigned by Alfonso although he agreed to all that his wife and son had negotiated.[29] Alfonso expressed his worries to his father-in-law regarding rumors about an imminent invasion by Ibn Yûsuf of Morocco, with whom don Jaime had recently signed a friendship and compliance agreement, sending him 500 men to help in the invasion of Ceuta.[30] Alfonso's worries and his request for aid in the case of a Moorish invasion presented a dilemma to don Jaime. To help Alfonso, Jaime had to break his agreement with the Moroccan, something he was not fond of doing. But he too had his priorities when it came to safeguarding the inheritance of his grandchildren: "King Jaime answered King Alfonso that if Aben Yuzaf were to cross hither, and King Alfonso had to do battle with him, he would come to the conflict in his succor. Concerning the noblemen who were in Granada, he told him that because the queen and his son had negotiated with them peace and accord on behalf of King Alfonso, he should consider it well to give

---

[29] See *CAX*, chap. 57, pp. 187–190.
[30] *CAX*, chap. 57, p. 188.

the opportunity time so that they could settle their differences with the noblemen" (*CAX*, chap. 57, p. 188). Don Jaime therefore was willing to help Alfonso unconditionally, but wanted to first give his daughter a chance to negotiate a solution with the nobles and the king of Granada (ib.).

After his miraculous recovery, Alfonso left Requena four days after the meeting with his father-in-law, and on September 2, he was already in Guadalajara. On September 15, we find him in Brihuega, some 15 kms from Guadalajara, on the road to Burgos, where he arrived October 15 after going though San Esteban de Gormaz (September 27). It was probably during his brief stay at Burgos that he received the news that the German electors had elected Rudolph of Habsburg as emperor of the Holy Roman Empire. For Alfonso, as we saw, it was a tough blow, but he did not despair, thinking he could still convince the pope about the validity of his candidacy. With such an objective in mind, he hurried to gather funds for his "quest for the empire."[31]

Given the financial situation of Castile, Alfonso indeed attempted to find these funds in the south, as a result of his agreement with the king of Granada. On November 9, we find him at Cuenca on the road to Seville, where he arrived on December 16.[32] According to the *CAX*, Alfonso prepared a splendid reception for the king of Granada, who had presented himself at the royal palace carrying more than a million *maravedís*. Alfonso knighted him in the same way that his father, Fernando III, had knighted the new sultan. To reciprocate this great honor, Muhammad II of Granada accepted the vassalage: "The king of Granada also granted to King Alfonso to be always his vassal and to give him from his revenues three hundred thousand *maravedís* in the currency of Castile each year" (chap. 58, p. 192). Alfonso sealed the agreement with the Moorish king of Granada, which granted him a considerable sum of money for the most important journey of his life. The matter of the nobles' rebellion was also in principle resolved, for the king of Granada had released them from their oath of fidelity and vassalage, allowing them to return to Alfonso's jurisdiction.[33]

---

[31] *CAX*, chap. 69, pp. 221–222; Ballesteros, *Alfonso X*, p. 678.

[32] The documentation on Alfonso's trip to Seville the fall of 1273 is unclear. We know that on October 15 he was in Burgos and we find him again in the same city on December 24. Obviously between these two dates he had enough time to go to Seville, as we and Ballesteros have suggested (*Alfonso X*, p. 681).

[33] *CAX*, chap. 48, pp. 154–156; Ballesteros, *Alfonso X*, pp. 631–633.

But the tension between the nobles and Alfonso persisted. Don Nuño insisted he would not support him in his journey to seek the empire, unless he would enlist 1000 knights. Alfonso replied this was a breach of the agreement that had just been signed and that only 500 were needed, which was what he had asked of the Count of Ventimiglia during his visit. Obviously, the nobles wanted to protect themselves from potential retaliation by Alfonso and to increase his expenses so that they could keep the funds supplied by the sultan. Alfonso was so irritated about this matter that, according to the *CAX*, he told the nobles that, "[i]f they had the willingness to come to his service, they should not want things that seemed proper to them but rather as he saw that were advantageous to him. Those who refused this should abandon the journey to the empire and remain in Castile" (chap. 57, p. 189). The expenses of the journey would be paid with the funds from the king of Granada, which through Alfonso's express will had been deposited by the king of Granada in the hands of the Order of Calatrava so that the nobles would not use them as before for subversive purposes (pp. 187–88, 191–92).

As we have previously suggested, it was Alfonso's promise to return the *arraeces* that had driven the king of Granada to this agreement, although in the negotiations with the king, no agreement had been reached. But during his stay in Seville, when it seemed that all was solved, including the nobles' release from fidelity and vassalage to the king of Granada, and sultan's money transferred to Alfonso, according to the *CAX* the queen who had crafted the agreement took the king of Granada to a remote location of the palace and began to speak to him about the difficult matter of the *arraeces*, attempting to explain that Alfonso knew nothing of that private meeting and the talks they were holding. In other words, she was telling him that the *arraeces* were not part of the agreement. The king of Granada must have been astonished, especially because the queen, who was accompanied by don Felipe and don Nuño de Lara and in the presence of don Fernando, requested a truce of two years for Alfonso to return the *arraeces* (*CAX*, chap. 58, pp. 192–193).

The chronicler says that Violante had not mentioned this matter earlier for fear that the king of Granada would refuse to accept the terms of the agreement with the nobles, which was a distinct possibility. Hearing this now after having delivered a considerable sum of money must have seemed to him a hoax. The *CAX* tells us that "[t]he King of Granada was very grieved with this plea, for he realized that they [Queen Violante and the Prince] wanted to protect [the *arraeces*] from him and that they had taken from him the sum that he had given so that they would forsake the chiefs, and he had not wished to do it willingly; but because of the great insistence of the queen and the prince, he had to grant this truce to the chiefs for a year" (*CAX*, chap. 58, pp. 192–193). On the return trip from Granada, the young Moorish sultan must have reflected on the chances of negotiating with such disloyal rivals. If he still had any hope of reaching an agreement with the king of Castile, the experience of the visit and the trick they played on him to steal from him a million *maravedís* made him abandon it. Ballesteros writes that "[t]hat trip to Seville had been disastrous for him and in his heart he vowed revenge,"[34] which he would soon achieve.

Between misunderstandings, subterfuges, and tricks, the Seville agreement must have seemed useless and exorbitantly expensive to the king of Granada. For his part, Alfonso obtained a large sum of money, reconciliation with the nobles, and their support in his quest for the empire, but he had to pay a high price: he had to revert the legal and constitutional reforms to the system used during his father's time. The nobles' rebellion was thus highly effective because Alfonso had to repeal the magnificent legal and constitutional edifice he had been building since his accession to the throne.

Meanwhile, swift as the wind, Alfonso was back in Burgos on December 24, where he would spend the first three months of 1274, preparing the Cortes that were held in March before his trip to France to meet with the pope.[35]

5. *The North African Moors in the Peninsula*

The revenge of the king of Granada was swift. We know through the *CAX* that as soon as he arrived in Granada, he was in touch with the Muslims in North Africa to explore how he could strip the Christians of the territories that through tricks and broken agreements they had seized and still held under their control. The chronicler very clearly traces the causes of the North African invasion:

---

[34] *Alfonso X*, p. 682.
[35] See above pp. 294–296; *CAX*, chap. 58, p. 191; Procter, *Curia and Cortes*, pp. 135–136; Ballesteros, *Alfonso X*, pp. 683–687.

The King of Granada was very aggrieved because of the truce he granted
to the chiefs while he was in Seville, for he had given King Alfonso a
great fortune and had destroyed the letter of the treaty that the noblemen had with him. All of this he had done thinking that the chiefs would
remain in such fashion that he could conquer them and take them from
the land they held. [...] In order to seek vengeance for this, he immediately left Seville and sent his messengers to Aben Yuzaf, king from
beyond the sea; he sent word of the harm he had received from those
chiefs, who held the land forcefully [...] They were letting him know that
the land of the Christians was now in such situation that if Aben Yuzaf
crossed, he would be able to conquer a great portion of it with the help
the King of Granada would give him—for King Alfonso was outside the
kingdom, traveling to the empire. All the other people were guaranteed,
and thus he could seize a great portion of the land of the Christians in a
very short period of time. (*CAX*, chap. 61, pp. 199–200)[36]

The brief but substantial summary of the letter from the king of Granada
to the Emir of Morocco, which coincides with what we know from
Muslim historiography, shows that the chronicler was well informed
of the events of the period. During the spring of 1275, there was a
new invasion of the Peninsula by of the emir of Morocco Abû Yûsuf
Ya'qûb b. 'Abd al-Haqq, chief of the Marinid tribe, and the sultan of
Fez (1258–1286), which had disastrous economic and political consequences for Castile and its Andalusian territories.[37]

Abu Yûsuf arrived in Spain at the request of the king of Granada,
who, taking advantage of the fact that Alfonso was away from the
kingdom in Beaucaire and frustrated by the breach of the Seville agreement on the part of the Castilian king, asked the emir for help, offering him forts in Algeciras and Tarifa to facilitate the landing.[38] The
cunning king of Granada, as the letter indicated, took advantage of a

---

[36] According to the *Rawad al-Qirtas*, this exchange between the king of Granada
and Yûsuf took place in September 1274. See Ibn Abi Zar', *Rawad al-Qirtas*, 2 vols.,
trans. A. Huici, 2nd ed., Valencia: Anubar, 1964, II, p. 591 and ff.; and Ballesteros,
Alfonso X, p. 742.

[37] *CAX*, chaps. 61–64, pp. 199–210. Cf. Ballesteros, *Alfonso X*, pp. 827–835; M.A.
Manzano Rodríguez, *La intervención de los benimerines en la Península Ibérica*,
Madrid, 1992.

[38] According to the *Rawd al-Qirtas* on May 13, 1275 a smaller contingent with
5000 horses commanded by Abu Zián, Ibn Yûsuf's son, crossed the Strait and occupied Algeciras and Tarifa in order to prepare a larger scale invasion which occurred
Thursday, August 16, with the landing in Tarifa of the great emir Ibn Yûsuf with
an army of "seventeen thousand knights" (chap. 61, p. 200) and many other people
(*CAX*, chap. 61, p. 200). More details in Ibn Abi Zar, *Rawd al-Qirtas*, ed. A. Huici
Miranda, II, p. 591; cf. Ballesteros, pp. 746–747; and M.A. Manzano, *La intervención
de los benimerines*, pp. 15–18.

moment of distraction and the loosening of the Christian forces. The opportunity could not have been better, with Alfonso away from the kingdom and prince don Fernando equally distant, touring cities and towns in Castile-León with don Nuño de Lara and the archbishop of Seville, don Remondo.[39]

The emir of Morocco arrived in the peninsula with preconceived ideas and a hostile and vindictive attitude. He had already confronted the Castilians in the major raid of Salé. Then and in the following years, busy with internal strife over control of the Western Maghreb, he had been unable to avenge that effrontery by the Castilian king. This was the occasion awaited to collect the pending debt. The *arraeces* of Málaga and Guadix, who were under Alfonso's command, did not resist Yûsuf's troops, appearing instead before the emir, fearing for their lives. But he was generous with them on condition that they vowed obedience to the king of Granada, signing pledges of allegiance with him in Yûsuf's presence.[40]

Although the Christian leaders were a long way from the battlefield, Yûsuf's arrival did not entirely surprise the Christian armies: a North African invasion was a permanent threat in their minds and strategic plans. As the *CAX* informs us, between the arrival of the invaders in May and the reaction of the first Christians led by don Nuño de Lara, in September, they had time to recruit troops and organize the defense. The number of troops and Yûsuf's personal command of them, however, did surprise them.[41]

The only two sources we possess on the armed encounter are the *CAX* and the more detailed narrative of the *Rawd al-Qirtas*, a work by the court chronicler of the Banu Marin sultans, Ibn Abi Zar. The Christian defense plan can be reconstructed using these two sources. It was centered on three points: the capital, Seville, was defended by don Alfonso Fernández *el Niño*; Écija and its territories, by his lieutenant, don Nuño de Lara; and Jaén and its bishopric by don Sancho de Aragón, archbishop of Toledo.[42]

---

[39] Cf. *CAX*, chap. 69, p. 198; and Ballesteros, *Alfonso X*, pp. 736–738, who discusses Fernando's itinerary in the first months of 1275.

[40] *CAX*, chap. 61, pp. 200–201.

[41] Don Nuño's participation in that war in which he died, makes it doubtful that he accompanied Alfonso in Beaucaire.

[42] More details and historical reconstruction in F. García Fitz, "Los acontecimientos político-militares en la frontera en el último cuarto del siglo XIII," *Revista de Historia Militar*, 64 (Madrid, 1988), pp. 9–71.

Yûsuf remembered the actions of the Christians at Salé, and desiring revenge, he stormed the cities of the South, looking to conquer the capital, Seville. However, it seemed that the Moorish army, despite its weapons, was not prepared to assault the cities, so it had to resort to killings, terror, and starvation, destroying crops and capturing the greatest number of Christians.[43]

According to the *CAX*, as soon as don Nuño learned of the invasion, he sent his letters to don Fernando to round up the Christian army. For his part, "[a]fter don Nuño had sent these letters to don Fernando, he sent to call all of those from the frontier to come to him at Écija, for he knew that Aben Yuzaf was coming to attack the land of the Christians through that region; and some men from the frontier came to him, and also his vassals who were with him" (*CAX*, chap. 62, p. 202). The chronicler, probably basing himself on oral reports as well as written documents, writes that Don Nuño, upon seeing that Yûsuf's troops were more numerous, thought of retreating, but his companions begged him to fight the enemy so it would not seem that "[they were] fleeing" (*CAX*, chap. 62, p. 202). He adds: "Some say this was the manner in which it was related, but it is not found written if the battle took place because of this or not. It is true that don Nuño and those who were with him fought the Moors that came with Aben Yuzaf, that the Christians were defeated, and that don Nuño and many of those with him died in the battle. More would have died, but they had the town of Écija close by where they could find refuge" (chap. 62, pp. 202–203) The story in the *CAX* ends by saying, "Aben Yuzaf showed that he was sorry about don Nuño's death, for he said that he wanted to take him alive, and he ordered the severing of the head. He then sent it to the King of Granada and sent to tell him that he should take his share of the foray. The King of Granada replied to Aben Yuzaf that he was pleased with the portion he had sent him, but that he was very sorry about don Nuño's death, for he had done much so that he could become king; and this head was sent to Córdoba, with word that it should be buried with the body. The day on which don Nuño died

---

[43] The atrocities of the war were graphically described by Ibn Abi Zar, *Rawd al-Qirtas*, trans. A. Huici Miranda, II, p. 596; they are also mentioned in the *Cantigas*, among which 323 narrates a miracle occurred in Coria del Río, a village near Seville, "at the time Aboyuçaf passed through the Strait of Algeciras and rapidly invaded all the land of Seville, and many villages were burned by the Moors" (*Songs of Holy Mary*, *cantiga* 323, p. 392).

was a Saturday, during the month of May, in the year one thousand
and three hundred and thirteen of the Era" (*CAX*, chap. 62, p. 203).

The account of the Moroccan chronicler coincides in essence with
the one in the *CAX*, but as could be expected, there is more emphasis
on the feats of the North Africans, though don Nuño too is praised:
"The Christians who were under his command were fortunate, because
he was never defeated, and was the scourge of the Muslim kingdoms
he devastated for the most part, not hesitating in his advances either
by day or by night."[44] The descriptions of the Muslim chronicler are
unmatched: he was impressed by the armor of the Christian troops,
who had the appearance of a fierce war machine, ferrous, dark, com-
pact and impenetrable, which contrasted with the light clothes of the
Muslim warriors who rode light horses and were equipped only with
their fearsome scimitars.[45] The account continues with the ritual prayer
of the troops to Allah, and concludes with the description of the battle,
full of the hyperbole typical of Arabic historical prose.[46]

Once victorious, "The emir of the Muslims had the dead Christians
beheaded and the heads counted. More than 18,000 knights were dead,
and they formed a mountain. The muezzins climbed on top and called
the faithful to prayer; the Muslims said the midday and the *aser* (after-
noon) prayer in the middle of the battlefield, among the dead and
covered with blood[...]"[47] The account of the *Rawd al-Qirtas* ends with
the account of the fabulous booty that Yûsuf took to Algeciras, where
he divided it among his followers.[48] As in the *CAX*, here too it is said
that Yûsuf sent the head of don Nuño to the king of Granada "so he
would see what God had done to his enemies and the help He had
given his defenders. Aben Alahamar placed it in musk and camphor
and sent it to Don Alfonso as a gesture of serving him and to win
him over."[49] The final observation indicates clearly that the king of
Granada realized that after Yûsuf's military activities were over, Yûsuf
would return to Morocco and that he himself would have to live with
the hostility of the Christians at his doorstep every day of his life. He

---

[44] Ibn Abi Zar, *Rawd al-Qirtas*, II, p. 597.
[45] *Id.*, II, p. 596; and cf. Ballesteros, *id.*, p. 751.
Rawd al-Qirtas, II, p. 598 and cf. Ballesteros, op. cit., p. 753.
[46] *Id.*, II, p. 597. According to the *CAX*, many Christian warriors survived and
sought refuge in Écija (chap. 62, pp. 202–204).
[47] *Id.*, II, p. 598 and see Ballesteros, op. cit., p. 753.
[48] *Id.*, II, p. 598.
[49] *Rawd al-Qirtas*, II, p. 598.

therefore tried to win Alfonso over by sending him the embalmed head of his former rival.[50] But things had changed at Alfonso's court since the king had made peace with the rebellious nobility, and, despite their divisions, the Christians would not forgive the betrayal of the king of Granada.[51]

When don Sancho, archbishop of Toledo, heard of the defeat and death of the *Adelantado de la Frontera*, as don Nuño was known, he immediately began to recruit troops and organize an army to contain the invasion. Don Sancho, the son of a great warrior, Jaime I of Aragón, brother of the queen of Castile and primate of Spain, certainly had the prestige, economic means, and authority to launch a campaign against Yûsuf.[52] But he did not have the military experience. The *CAX*, which devotes much space to this minor incident in the war to expel the North Africans from the peninsula (the *Rawd al-Qirtas* does not even mention it), tell us that the Muslims were represented by two leader brothers (Hanojanatali and Uzmen) and by the *arraeces* of Málaga and Guadix and two more from the kingdom of Granada, Ascauuaela and Aben-Macar, but does not mention Yûsuf. Don Sancho, who was short-tempered and impatient, was ill advised by those who did not know the enemy well, such as the Comendador of Martos, and unwisely confronted the enemy near that town without the proper preparations. His army was defeated in a short time without Yûsuf's participation.[53] Don Sancho on account of his rashness and don Nuño for the sake of his honor were the victims of haste and bad advice.

The archbishop was captured by the Muslim troops. There was a debate about what should be done with the illustrious prisoner. Some wanted him to be handed over to the king of Granada and others to Yûsuf. Finally, Aben-Macar, *arrayaz* of Granada, mounted his horse, "and went to the archbishop where he was naked, and he struck him over his shoulder with a spear, which penetrated his body and killed

---

[50] According to the *Memorias de Cardeña*, don Nuño's body was buried in Burgos at the monastery of Predicadores (in Berganza, *Antigüedades de España*, Part 2, p. 589); and later, once the head was recovered, in the convent of San Pablo in Valladolid, which he had favored in his life.

[51] The *Rawd al-Qirtas* is right to quote the date of the battle at Écija as September 8, 1275, coinciding with Christian sources such as the *Anales Toledanos III* and the *Memorias antiguas de Cardeña*; but not with the *CAX* that as we noted, incorrectly quotes the date as a Saturday in May.

[52] *CAX*, chap. 63, pp. 205–207.

[53] *CAX*, chap. 63, pp. 206–207.

him." He then gave the following explanation: "'May it not be the will of Allah that on account of one dog, so many good men as are here kill each other'; and they cut off his head and the hand on which he wore the ring, and they moved from there with their plunder and left" (*CAX*, chap. 63 pp. 206). This battle, according to the most reliable text, the *Anales toledanos III*, took place on October 20, 1275.

Soon after the defeat of the archbishop's small army, don Lope Díaz de Haro's much larger one arrived on the battlefield. The Muslims showed him the cross of the archbishop and the battle resumed immediately until night came and it had to be suspended. The next morning, neither Christians nor Muslims decided to attack, but don Lope was able to recover the body of don Sancho, although it was missing the head and the right hand on which he wore his bishop's ring. But thanks to the mediation of the Comendador Mayor of Calatrava, don Gonzalo Romero, the Muslims readily returned the remains and left the battlefield with the booty. Don Sancho was buried under the main altar of the Toledo Cathedral wearing lavish pontifical garments.[54]

If the death of don Nuño González de Lara deprived Spain of one of its most skillful and powerful military leaders, the death of don Sancho, primate of the Spanish Church, son of Jaime I of Aragón and brother of doña Violante, queen of Castile, left the Church and the nobility in a panic caused by the possibility of a return to the situation in the reconquest prior to 1212. With the king absent from the kingdom and in the dark or at least unable to respond to what was happening in the Peninsula—Alfonso was either still in Beaucaire, arguing his imperial cause before the pope, or on his return journey—those responsible for the defense turned to his son and heir, don Fernando.

The disastrous news from the border pushed the young prince to organize an army capable of confronting the Moors who now, from Algeciras, had started to attack the area around Seville again, arriving at the city gates. Fernando needed the support of all of the kingdom's grandees whom he summoned in Ciudad Real before heading out south. On his way to Ciudad Real he learned of the deaths of don Nuño (September 8) and of his uncle don Sancho (October 20). It was precisely in Ciudad Real, waiting for the Christian forces who would

---

[54] Cf. Ballesteros, *Alfonso X*, p. 759. Cf. F. García Fitz, "Los acontecimientos político-militares en la frontera en el último cuarto del siglo XIII," *Revista de Historia Militar*, 64 (Madrid, 1988), pp. 9–71.

join those commanded by his uncle don Fadrique and his brother don Sancho, that he was felled by a "serious illness" and died shortly thereafter.[55]

The chronicles of the period do not say anything about the cause of death or the funeral of the heir to the throne of Castile. The *CAX* simply records the place where he was buried: "They took this prince to be buried in Huelgas de Burgos, for he had chosen his burial there, and don Juan Núñez traveled with the body of this prince in order to have it buried" (*CAX,* chap. 64, p. 210). But thanks to the archaeological findings in his sarcophagus discovered in 1943 (the only one respected by the French troops during the pillage and devastation that included the profanation of all the tombs in the Monastery of Las Huelgas), we must conclude the funeral was fitting for a king.[56] In the absence of his parents, someone from the court, probably his tutor, the famous courtier, Jofré de Loaysa, or don Juan Núñez de Lara, who according to the *CAX* always attended him and never left him" (*CAX,* chap. 66, p. 209) had him dressed in the most lavish garments, which fortunately have been preserved intact, as can be seen in the splendid Textiles Museum of Las Huelgas, where they have been on display since 1988.[57] As heir to the throne, before his death Fernando made an important disposition that would greatly affect the succession crisis that Alfonso X's death unleashed. According to the *CAX,* Fernando made his inseparable advisor and confidant, Juan Núñez de Lara, don

---

[55] Fernando was about 20 years old. The sources contradict each other regarding the date of his death: Jofré de Loaysa, son of Fernando's tutor, asserts it was July 24 (*Crónica de los reyes de Castilla,* ed. A. Ubieto Arteta, Valencia, 1971, p. 18); the *CAX* states: "and soon after, this Prince Fernando passed away during the month of August" (chap. 64, p. 210), something that is chronologically impossible.

[56] The same can be gleaned from the iconography sculpted on the sarcophagus that depicts the temple of Solomon and other Solomonic motifs that hint at Fernando's royal lineage proclaimed by his father for the Hohenstaufen dynasty. Cf. A. Domínguez Rodríguez, "El *Officium Salomonis* de Carlos V en el monasterio de El Escorial: Alfonso X y el planeta Sol: Absolutismo monárquico y hermetismo," *Reales Sitios,* 22/83 (1985), 14 and ff.

[57] The remains and garments revealed that the prince was not very robust, but was very tall, almost 6′6″ and extremely thin, perhaps due to illness, but no bone exam that would confirm this was performed. For a study of the garments he was shrouded in see C. Herrero Carretero, *Museo de telas medievales. Monasterio de Santa María la Real de Huelgas,* Madrid, 1988; and the volume *Centenario del Infante don Fernando de la Cerda: Jornadas de estudio,* Ciudad Real, Abril, 1975, Madrid, 1976.

Nuño's eldest son, promise he would defend the succession rights of his children. Don Juan kept his promise in earnest.[58]

6. *Don Sancho's Intervention*

The Christian army did not do anything until don Sancho, Alfonso's second son, arrived in Ciudad Real. He was about seventeen, having been born in 1258. The *CAX* is the only source that narrates in detail what happened after don Fernando died and Sancho assumed the leadership of the Christian forces. Before taking command, the young prince asked the collaboration of the nobles, in particular of his best friend don Lope Díaz de Haro, with whom he made an agreement that went beyond what the circumstances demanded.[59]

It could be argued that Don Sancho was preparing the way to succession. Under don Lope's advice, he addressed the nobles and the army to inform them that "his father, King Alfonso, was not in the kingdoms and his brother Prince Fernando was dead, that he wanted to go to defend the land, and that he ordered and begged them to go with him, and that they would serve him and help him in such fashion that the frontier could be protected while his father, the king, was returning or was sending to order what to do, and that with this, Prince Sancho would earn the love of his father the king, for he would realize that Prince Sancho had the willingness to stand and defend the kingdom and that he deserved to inherit it after the king's days. He would also win the hearts of all those of the kingdoms, and they would regard it as right to receive him as heir after the days of his father; and don Lope Díaz advised that Sancho immediately should call himself in his letters the oldest son and heir" (*CAX*, chap. 65, p. 212).

It is obvious that the strategist behind the accession of Sancho to the throne of Castile was don Lope even from this moment on, and according to the chronology in the *CAX*, he profited from the favorable absence of Alfonso to convince him "that Sancho immediately should call himself in his letters the oldest son and heir" (*CAX*, chap.

---

[58] *CAX*, chap. 64, pp. 209–210.

[59] The text is in the *CAX*, chap. 65, pp. 210–213. Don Sancho's agreement, together with the promise made by Juan Núñez de Lara to don Fernando before his death to defend the succession of his children, fired the first shot in the battle for the succession of Alfonso X: the Infantes de la Cerda, children of Fernando, against their uncle don Sancho, a matter discussed below.

65, p. 212). That he was the oldest surviving son was true, but not that he was the heir. That was a true provocation, when all the Alfonsine legislation to that point established that the heirs were the children of the late don Fernando, the Infantes de la Cerda. But, as Ballesteros notes, don Lope was as violent as the prince and his ambition had no limits: "He saw an opportunity in the death of the firstborn and tried to exploit that friendship, which was not anymore a second-degree friendship, but a friendship with the heir to the throne of Castile."[60] Despite being roughly the same age as don Sancho, don Lope, Ballesteros goes on to remark, "was a distinguished personality, trained in diplomatic battles by his father don Nuño, and with more sense and complexity than his father... From that time one his advisors and even the dark soul of don Sancho, Lope, the young lord of Vizcaya, would become the prototype of the bold and unscrupulous nobleman" (ib.).[61]

Headed by don Sancho, the army set out for Córdoba. From there he sent a letter to all the noblemen, knights and councils of Castile who had not yet arrived telling them "that they should immediately come to him at Códoba so that they could help him to defend the land. In this letter Prince Sancho immediately called himself the oldest heir, son of King Alfonso, and the very same from then on in all of the regions [...]" (*CAX*, chap. 65, pp. 212–213). From Córdoba he sent don Lope to help the defenders of Écija who had heroically held on to the city but were in precarious conditions and depressed by don Nuño's and especially don Fernando's death. With the reinforcements arrived from Castile, don Sancho headed to Seville "because Aben Yuzaf had crossed to that region, and also in order to have the fleet armed and to make them go to guard the sea, for it was unprotected" (*CAX*, chap. 65, p. 213). The strategy was to occupy the Strait with the Castilian fleet and thus cut communications between Africa and Spain. Yûsuf realized what Sancho's strategy was, and he retreated to the forts of Algeciras and Tarifa, where he would be better able to monitor the Strait, and if need be, return to Africa. Obviously, the strategy of the Castilians together with the exhaustion of the emir's troops and problems with supplies as well as the real danger of losing Algeciras and

---

[60] *Alfonso X*, p. 767.
[61] This was also proved by his attitude towards don Sancho himself when the critical moment arrived and don Lope had to once more choose sides.

Tarifa which would cut off supplies from the other side of the Strait forced Yûsuf to accept a two-year truce, returning to Morocco in mid-January 1276.[62]

As with all pacts and agreements, with this one too, something was gained and something was lost. In the truce agreed, the Christians gained some time to reorganize the defense and think about a new strategy now that Alfonso had returned from Beaucaire. Yûsuf's Moroccan army, for their part, besides earning a large booty also continued to control Tarifa and Algeciras, two strategic locations for repeating the invasion with impunity. Don Sancho and his advisors who at that time probably were in a good position to take control of both places, let go of them, because they ignored Yûsuf's true motives for the truce: we know through other sources that internal pressures in his kingdom demanded his presence if he did not want his African dominions to collapse internally. During that truce, don Jaime de Aragón met with Alfonso when passing through Catalonia on his way back from Beaucaire, and grieved the loss of his son don Sancho, archbishop of Toledo, he put at Alfonso's service an impressive contingent of 1000 knights and 5000 foot soldiers headed by his son and successor, don Pedro.[63]

Towards the end of 1275, Alfonso returned to Castile. He had been absent in France for less than a year, but the kingdom's military and political scene had drastically changed with the death of his heir and his *Adelantado Mayor* as well as that of his brother-in-law the archbishop of Toledo. As a result of all these events, new political forces were coming into play. The clan of the Haros took advantage of such favorable circumstances to openly support his son, don Sancho, while the Laras had sworn to defend the interests of his grandchildren, the Infantes de la Cerda. In foreign relations, the king of France continued to aspire to control Navarra. The most alarming political news was the breach of the truce by the king of Granada, who had taken sides with the emir of Morocco and had invited him to occupy the Christian territories. But, on the other hand, the kingdom was at peace thanks to his son Sancho and a united nobility, and for the time being the most

---

[62] The terms and strategic motives that Ibn Yûsuf had to negotiate the truce are abundantly acknowledged by the *CAX*, chap. 67, pp. 216–218.

[63] Cf. F. Soldevila, *Pere el Gran*, 3 vols., Barcelona, 1253, pp. 472–473.

important thing was that Ibn Yûsuf's return to Morocco gave him a respite and the possibility to reorganize his defense.

Ill and depressed by the results of his meeting with the pope and the negative string of news from the kingdom, Alfonso must have been encouraged by the decisive and vigorous actions of his son Sancho. The *CAX* reflects his change of attitude towards don Sancho which took place in the mind of the Learned King. While at Alcalá in early January 1276, Alfonso learned "...how his son Prince Sancho and the noblemen of the kingdom had reinforced the land so that it could be protected and not be lost. What Sancho had done pleased him greatly, and notwithstanding that before he loved him as his son, from then on he had better disposition toward him and he loved him and appreciated him much" (chap. 67, p. 216).

CHAPTER ELEVEN

THE PROBLEMS OF SUCCESSION

1. *The Dilemma*

In the Middle Ages, the periods of transition of power from one king to another were always traumatic and often tinged with blood.[1] The relative peace enjoyed by Alfonso and his reign starting in 1258 that led him to accelerate the implementation of his cultural enterprises also made him reflect on his succession. This was a topic that, apparently, he had dealt with two years after his accession to the throne, when he did not yet have a male child.[2] It was actually in 1255 when Alfonso of Castile and Louis IX of France had conceived the project of unifying the two kingdoms by marrying Berenguela, Alfonso's oldest daughter and at the time heir to the throne of Castile, to Louis, the king of France's firstborn. The project was not accomplished because at the end of that same year a male child was born to Alfonso, and the king of France prematurely lost his heir.[3]

Alfonso again attempted to deal with the issue of succession before leaving the kingdom to go meet the pope at Beaucaire. He then left the kingdom in the hands of his first-born, and though the Alfonsine chronicler does not describe how don Fernando ruled during his father's absence, he suggests he did it properly, telling us that he "ruled and preserved all of the land in justice and in such fashion that all of those from the kingdom were very pleased with him."[4]

---

[1] R. Gibert, "La sucesión al trono en la monarquía española," *Recueils de la société Jean Bodin*, 21, 2 (1969), pp. 447–546.

[2] Up until the birth of don Fernando, his daughter Berenguela had been the heiress, proclaimed by oath of the kingdom during the 1254 Toledo Cortes.

[3] Don Fernando was declared the heir two months after his birth, during the Vitoria Cortes in January 1256. Cf. Ballesteros, *Alfonso X*, p. 146.

[4] *CAX*, chap. 60, p. 198. The documents of the brief government of don Fernando that have been preserved are numerous. Through them, Ballesteros has been able to reconstruct a brief summary of his activities and concludes that by all standards he was a fair and impartial judge. Cf. *Alfonso X*, pp. 734–765. See also the volume *VII Centenario del Infante don Fernando de la Cerda: Jornadas de estudio, Ciudad Real, Abril, 1975*, Madrid, 1976.

Upon his return from Beaucaire, and after the death of his first-born and declared successor, Alfonso had to reconsider once again the question of his succession, an issue that would haunt him to the end of his life. In principle, everything was clear. According to Castilian tradition, the father was succeeded by the eldest son; if the latter died, the second-born followed, and so on. This meant that after Fernando's death, he would be succeeded by his brother Sancho. But Alfonso himself had established both in the *Espéculo* (2.16.1, 3), issued in 1255, as well as in the *Partidas* (2.15.2), published before 1265, the "right of representation," according to which the children of the heir, in this case the grandchildren of Alfonso X, had the right to the crown, since they had the right to inherit the rights of the firstborn directly from their father; thus the right of succession went from father to son and on to grandson.[5]

Thus following this new succession principle, Alfonso, according to research by J.R. Craddock based on the *Crónica general de 1344* (a text which, in my opinion, is not very reliable regarding Alfonsine matters due to its great prejudice against the Learned King), would have carried out a pact with Louis IX of France even before Fernando and Blanche were married (November 30, 1269), in which he promised as a condition for marriage that the offspring would inherit the throne of Castile.[6] The agreement was successively renewed under the successor of Saint Louis, Philip III, when he acceded to the throne in 1270, and, once again, after the birth of don Alfonso de la Cerda, son of Fernando and Blanche and grandson of Alfonso X, that same year. Both in the original agreement and in the successive renewals, it was stipulated that the children born of the marriage of Fernando and Blanche would inherit the crown of Castile and would have priority over the children of Alfonso X himself.[7] As a consequence of this agreement, the wife of Fernando and mother of Alfonso de la Cerda, who was the sister of

---

[5] *Part.* II, 15, 2. Cf. J.L. Bermejo Cabrera, "Notas sobre la Segunda Partida," in *VII Centenario del Infante don Fernando de la Cerda, 1275–1975*, pp. 265–273. Cf. R.A. MacDonald, "Alfonso the Learned and Succession: A Father's Dilemma," *Speculum*, XL (1965), pp. 647–653; J.R. Craddock, "Dynasty in Dispute: Alfonso X el Sabio and the Succession to the Throne of Castile and León in History and Legend," *Viator*, 17 (1986), pp. 197–219.

[6] *Crónica General de 1344*, ed. D. Catalán, p. 236. Cf. J.R. Craddock, "La cronología de las obras legislativas," *AHDE*, 51 (1981), p. 403.

[7] J.R. Craddock, "Dynasty in Dispute"; and "La cronología de las obras legislativas," pp. 401–403.

King Philip III of France, upon the death of her husband, began the claim for the rights of her son by travelling to France to request the protection of her brother the king. Likewise, as a result of these agreements, France also allied itself with those who defended the rights of the child, don Alfonso de la Cerda, in the event that the crown was denied to him.[8]

According to J. Craddock, given these precedents, both from the theoretical/legal point of view (the laws in the *Espéculo* and the *Partidas*) as well as from the practical/political perspective (the need to maintain the agreement with the King of France), in 1274, during the Burgos Cortes and before leaving for Beaucaire, Alfonso would have been forced to declare himself in favor of his grandson, don Alfonso de la Cerda, and would have had the nobles of León and Castile pay homage not only to the heir, don Fernando, but also to Fernando's son, Alfonso de la Cerda. The *CAX*'s narrative of these events however does not mention this (chap. 59, pp. 195–197). On the other hand, there is good reason to suspect that Alfonso had no intention of respecting such a pact with the king of France.[9]

The conflict of succession was also caused by recent events in internal politics that further complicated the situation. Among these, according to the *CAX*, were on the one hand, the vow that don Fernando, on his deathbed, had exacted from Juan Núñez de Lara, son of the *Adelantado Mayor*, don Nuño, who had died in the battle of Écija fighting against the Moors.[10] According to such an oath, the Castilian nobleman had promised to defend at all costs the right of succession to the throne of Castile of don Fernando's firstborn son, who at the time was five years old. On the other hand, there was also an agreement that Lope Díaz de Haro had made with prince don Sancho, at

---

[8] For this entire debate, see, cf. R. Kinkade, "Alfonso X, *Cantiga* 235," p. 309; J.R. Craddock, "La cronología de las obras legislativas," pp. 365–418; and "Dynasty in Dispute," *Viator*, pp. 197–219.

[9] Two years later, on April 30, 1276, he writes a letter to the council of Salamanca "ordering this town to nominate two good men from their town council who would go to Burgos to appoint the heir prince of these kingdoms and answer to the king of France that D. Alfonso, grandson of Alfonso X, claimed to have rights to them." From this it can be gleaned that if the Cortes, in violation of the pact had supported don Sancho, he also did not feel obligated to respect it. The summary of the letter's content preserved in the Municipal Archive of Salamanca and now lost, is due to J. Sánchez Ruano, ed., *Fuero de Salamanca*, Salamanca 1870.

[10] *CAX*, chap. 64, pp. 209–210.

the time a young man of 16 years but a seasoned warrior, to defend his rights of succession against Alfonso de la Cerda.[11]

Once more, a dynastic struggle unfolded, promoted by the two powerful clans: the Laras against the Haros. Deep down, what the nobility attempted to do was to control royal powers through the control of the person of the king by one of the two clans. Thus, if Alfonso chose his son, he had to ally himself with the Laras, and if he chose his grandson, he had to side with the Haros, hence the importance that both clans would acquire in the process of determining the succession and in the future politics of the kingdom. The proverbial rivalry between the Laras and the Haros only aggravated the succession conflict.

2. Alfonso Changes the Rules

Despite these complications, it could be argued that at least from the legal point of view and that of social commitments, the succession was clear: after Alfonso X's death, he would be succeeded by his grandson, Alfonso de la Cerda. But with the enemy at home, the courage that Sancho had demonstrated during his father's absence in Beaucaire and his subsequent skill in negotiating a truce, Alfonso's advisors must have pressured him to change the rules. In other words, given the current circumstances, Sancho's supporters sought a political solution that would annul the legal status of succession by representation.

In January 1276, Alfonso moved temporarily to Toledo, where he resided for a couple of months. While he was in the city, don Sancho arrived with the noble gentlemen who had accompanied him in the defense of the territory to the South from the fearsome Moorish invasion. The *CAX*, which shows that the meeting happened at Camarena (January 4), a few kilometers from Toledo, tells us the motives behind the presence of these men in Toledo: to petition Alfonso so that, following the death of don Fernando and the victories of don Sancho in the South against Yûsuf, the young prince be declared Alfonso's successor. The agent and promoter of this candidacy was don Lope Díaz de Haro, who secretly asked all of his followers there present to insist before the king on the need to nominate don Sancho as an heir to the throne (*CAX*, chap. 67, pp. 216–218).

---

[11] See the text of the pact in *CAX*, chap. 64, p. 210; and cf. E. Procter, *Curia and Cortes*, p. 139 and 230; Ballesteros, *Alfonso X*, pp. 769 and 785.

In other words, according to the text, don Sancho's party, headed by don Lope Díaz de Haro, was formed without the young prince's knowledge. Alfonso, despite his fatherly love and although he recognized his son's merits, was very cautious about immediately agreeing to the petition of don Sancho's supporters, saying to don Lope that he was in agreement with what they were asking, but that he had to consult with his council first (*CAX*, chap. 67, pp. 216–218).

The council, headed by his brother, don Manuel, reminded Alfonso of the rules of the common law of Castile, according to which, after don Fernando's death, don Sancho should become ruler ("if the greatest that comes from the tree dies, the branch that is the highest should remain. And there are three things that are not under question") insisting that certain things, despite promises made to the contrary, should not be compromised: "[neither] law, nor king, nor kingdom." The author of the chronicle continues: "In the writing that is found from that time it is stated that in that council only these words were spoken." (*CAX*, chap. 67, p. 218). By this the chronicler means that the text he had before him did not include dissenting opinions presented during the council meeting, probably because there were none.[12] Although the chronicler silenced him, it is obvious that the words of don Manuel insinuated "other questions"; that is other agreements or dispositions, such as prenuptial agreement between Fernando and Blanche, and perhaps the queen's own position which favored the candidacy of the grandchildren.

Armed with this resolution, Alfonso, from Segovia, summoned a new Cortes: "and sent letters to all of the cities and towns of his kingdoms so that they might immediately send their solicitors to him in Segovia with certain powers in order to make an agreement and fealty to Prince Sancho; to have him as king and as lord after his days" (*CAX*, chap. 67, p. 218). Thus from this moment on, Alfonso's will regarding succession was clear. But besides paying homage to don Sancho, Alfonso intended that these Cortes also serve as the official response of all representatives of the kingdom to the king of France in matters of succession, as is obvious from a summons sent to the representatives of Salamanca, where Alfonso explains his intentions: "to appoint the

---

[12] *CAX*, chap. 67, pp. 216–218.

heir prince of these kingdoms and answer to the king of France that
D. Alfonso, grandson of Alfonso X, claimed to have rights to them."[13]

These Cortes, as Ballesteros has shown, were held in Burgos and not
in Segovia, as the *CAX* holds, in June 1276.[14] During the celebration,
the leaders of each of the two noble clans, the Laras and the Haros,
defended the cause of their respective candidate. It must not have
been an easy situation for the Learned King. In view of the dilemma,
Alfonso, considering the actual situation of the kingdom (the need to
contain the Moorish invasion and to allay the discontent of the people,
the nobility, and the clergy) realized that what was needed was a more
prominent figure than Alfonso de la Cerda who was a five year-old
boy. He thus had to lean towards his son, declaring him "his first son
and heir," and not towards his grandson, as he had up to that point
legally stipulated. This decision clearly contradicted all his previous
legislation and positions.[15]

The *CAX* erroneously locates these Cortes in Segovia, but accurately
describes what was decided then:

> The king having arrived at the city of Segovia, the princess, masters, all
> the high noblemen, *infanzones*, and knights of the cities and towns of his
> kingdom came to him. The king ordered that they should make a pledge
> and do homage to Prince Sancho, his first heir, so that after the days of
> King Alfonso they would have him as king and lord; and all of them did
> what the king ordered them. (*CAX*, chap. 68, p. 219)[16]

Neither the documents related to the celebration of the Cortes nor the
CAX explain what motivated the change of heir. But years later, when

---

[13] Cf. J. Sánchez Ruano, *Fuero de Salamanca*, p. XXIV; and note 9 above.

[14] *CAX*, chaps. 67–68, pp. 216–220. We know that Alfonso was not in Segovia, neither in 1276 nor in 1277. His first visit to Segovia after returning from Beaucaire was
in the summer of 1278. On the celebration of the 1276 Burgos Cortes, see Ballesteros,
Alfonso X, pp. 789–793.

[15] Ballesteros held that Alfonso did not arrive at a final decision until the Segovia
Cortes in April 1278 (*Alfonso X*, pp. 785–787 and 852–857); but his opinion conflicts with all early historiography. In a document dated June 10, 1276, Sancho already
appears as a "eldest son and heir," something that is also affirmed by some of the most
reliable texts such as the contemporary Jofré de Loaysa (*Crónica*, chap. 219.20–21, pp.
90–92). The fact that the sucession was decided at the 1276 Burgos Cortes is confirmed
by Bernat Desclot (*Llibre del rey En Pere*, chap. LXVI, III, p. 454), Jaime I (*Llibre dels
feyts*, chap. IX, 7–8), and above all, the *Anales Toledanos III*, whose testimony is irre-
futable (*España Sagrada*, vol. 23, p. 420). Cf. E. Procter, *Curia y Cortes*, pp. 138–143.
J. O'Callaghan, *Cortes of Castile-León*, pp. 83–84.

[16] Cf. R.A. MacDonald, "Alfonso the Learned and Succession," 647–653; Procter,
Curia and Cortes, pp. 140–142; J.F. O'Callaghan, *The Cortes of Castile-León*, pp. 82–84.

dictating his last will, Alfonso himself revealed the real motives that led him to do this, or at least, to justify from the legal point of view why he did it:

> And because it is the custom and natural right as well as a code and law of Spain, that the eldest son should inherit his father's kingdoms and dominion, not doing things against these above mentioned rights whereby he might lose them, therefore, we, following this custom, after the death of don Fernando, our eldest son, [...] granted don Sancho, our eldest son, to obtain the rights of don Fernando, our eldest son, because he was more directly related to us than our grandchildren, the children of don Fernando.[17]

Despite this brilliant legal explanation that allowed him to muddle through the issue and at the same time appease the majority of his subjects who demanded don Sancho as successor, with such a change, Alfonso actually contradicted himself and the innovative legislation he had promulgated up until that point in the *Fuero real* and the *Partidas*, returning instead to the old traditions and common law of the Peninsula.[18] We do not know to what extent the Learned King felt satisfied with the change at the time he implemented it. But the fact that ten years later, when drafting his last will, he referred to it as an extraordinary deed that illustrated to what extent he had aided his ungrateful son, is a clear signal that such a change was made without firm conviction and only to muddle through the social needs and difficulties of the moment.

Such a radical change in terms of succession when everything was already established and even legislated, would bring about unexpected conflicts in the kingdom and in relations with the neighboring kingdoms: France, Aragón, and Navarra. Also, the thorny question of personal relations between father and son, which had never been very good, remained to be solved. In contrast to the late don Fernando, who had a peaceful, serene, and agreeable demeanor, Sancho had a volatile, indomitable, extreme, and even violent temperament, which earned him the nickname *el Bravo*. From childhood he appeared to be a free spirit. He was similar to his father in many ways, especially

---

[17] Last will dated November 8, 1283, in A. García Solalinde, *Antología*, pp. 225–226; and cf. the Appendix at the end of the present work.

[18] Cf. J. O'Callagham, *Alfonso X, the Cortes and Government in Spain*, III: "On the Promulgation of the *Espéculo* and the *Fuero Real*," Aldershot-Brookfield: Ashgate, 1998, pp. 1–12.

in his love of culture and his hot-headedness, often prone to sudden
fits of anger. A sign of such an imbalanced and unruly personality is
recorded in the *CAX*, which was written during Sancho's reign: on
the occasion of the wedding of his brother Fernando in Burgos in
1269 (when Sancho was 11), his father wanted Fernando to knight his
three younger brothers, the princes Sancho, Juan, and Pedro.[19] Sancho
refused to be knighted by his brother, declaring that only his father
could do it. Such an unexpected decision from a young boy must have
alarmed those present. Don Jaime of Aragón, who directly influenced
the decision of his grandson Sancho, tells us somewhat differently in
his *Llibre dels feyts* how the events unfolded. He noted that it was him
(Jaime) who pointed out to Alfonso X the personal ties that the fact
of knighting someone entailed, and that being knighted could be the
cause of future conflicts between the brothers, when they were subjected to the supremacy of the one who had knighted them.[20] He goes
on to say that when his grandson Sancho was next to him, he whis-
pered in his ear: "let yourself be knighted by your father and no other
man."[21] In other words, the idea was the grandfather's and not the
grandson's, because only the former knew that according to medieval
customs, to be knighted by his brother meant recognizing his primacy
over him. Sancho was, therefore, not knighted by his brother; indeed,
there is no record that he was knighted by his father either, although
Jofré de Loaysa's chronicle mentions him along with his brother Fernando among the many figures who, "because of his great fame," came
from many parts to receive "the military belt" from Alfonso X. The fact
that Jaime was mainly responsible for Sancho's refusal to by knighted
by Fernando does not change the verdict on Sancho's independent,
haughty, and impulsive character.[22]

---

[19] *CAX*, chap. 18, pp. 68–70.

[20] Ed. F. Soldevila, chap. 495; cf. Ballesteros, *Alfonso X*, pp. 487–488. Alfonso did
not really need to be reminded of this point because he himself had declared something similar to this effect in the *Partidas*.

[21] *Llibre del feyts*, chap. 495; cf. Ballesteros, *Alfonso X*, pp. 487–488.

[22] On don Sancho's temperament, see *Crónica de Sancho IV*, despite its partiality,
the best testimony to the extremely violent temperament of the prince even before
becoming king (cf. chap. XV) and more so thereafter. In 1286, while passing through
Sahagún, on his way to Santiago on pilgrimage, don Sancho clubbed to death a royal
judge who had disobeyed him (p. 74a). The Sahagún incident was but a pale reflection
of what happened in Alfaro on June 8, 1288, when he discovered the treachery and
infidelity of his powerful court minion, don Lope Díaz de Haro, who fell dead at his
feet, killed by one of Sancho's halberdiers because Lope Díaz accosted Sancho, while

Alfonso's attempt to make his heir knight his brothers and the other nobles reveals, on the one hand, the degree of attention Alfonso accorded to the symbols of feudal investiture with which he wanted to honor his favorite child as legitimate heir. On the other, they show the distance that from this moment on was established as a result of that paternal preference between Fernando and his brothers, especially don Sancho, who was next in the line of succession. This was so much the case, that, from this moment on, the temperamental don Sancho began to interact more with the maternal family circle and the court of Aragón, which would end up having great political influence and moral support at the moment of the rebellion and succession following the death of Fernando.

3. *Civil War in Navarra*

The change of heir, besides fundamentally contradicting Alfonso's political and legal ideology, also, as we suggested, conflicted with his agreements and commitments with the king of France. The support of Sancho, in terms of international politics, meant a break with France; and in terms of internal politics, the alienation of the nobles who supported Alfonso de la Cerda, Fernando de la Cerda's oldest son. The decision provoked a predictable reaction among his supporters, who, under the leadership of Juan Núñez de Lara, sought the protection of the king of France, Philip III *the Bold*. Philip was the brother of doña Blanca (Blanche), wife of the late don Fernando, and was married to Isabel of Aragón, daughter of Jaime I, *the Conqueror*, and sister of the young king of Aragón, don Pedro III.[23] Philip of France was, therefore, Alfonso's brother-in-law, as they were both married to daughters of Jaime I of Aragón. All these family ties of the house of Aragón with

---

Sancho himself killed another supporter of don Lope, Diego López de Campos, with his own knife (pp. 78–79). For these, and other episodes of violence, see M. Gaibrois, *Historia del reinado de Sancho IV*, I, pp. 90, and 118–120.

[23] Don Pedro III *el Grande*, brother of Violante, Alfonso X's wife, acceded to the throne of Aragón upon the death of his father, don Jaime I, which occurred in Valencia on July 29, 1276. On Philip III, his kingdom and relations with Navarra and Castile, see the excellent study by Ch. V. Langlois, *Le Regne de Philippe III le Hardi*, Paris, 1857. Cf. G. Daumet, *Mémoire sur les relations de la France et de la Castille de 1255 à 1320*, Paris: Bibliothèque de l'École des Hautes Études, 1913, pp. 244–246; and M. Arigita y Lasa, *Cartulario de don Felipe III, rey de Francia*, Madrid, 1913, n. 5, 65, and 116.

the reigning houses of France and Castile placed don Jaime, and later his successor, don Pedro, in a difficult political position at the center of the conflict for the succession to the Castilian crown. It was therefore logical that the supporters of that five year-old boy, when they saw themselves cornered, turned to the king of France for help to defend the rights of the Infantes de la Cerda (sons of Fernando), swearing loyalty to him at the same time.[24] This is how unexpectedly the change of heir, due to agreements and family ties, created great national, international and even dynastic uproar, such as the flight of Violante of Aragón with her two grandchildren, the Infantes de la Cerda.

Things became unexpectedly complicated for Alfonso because Philip III, who undoubtedly was pleased to see his sister Blanche on the throne of Castile even as a regent, had also presented his demand for rights to the kingdom of Pamplona, following the death of its king, Henry of Champagne, who was married to Blanche of Artois, cousin king Philip III of France. (The two Blanches, one, a cousin—married to the late Henry—and the other, a sister—married to the late don Fernando—were now under Philip's protection.) Navarra had been and still was essentially Castilian and enjoyed extraordinary *fueros* or legal codes. However because of the marriage of Henry with Blanche of Artois, an extensive population of French burghers had come to occupy the center of public life. These burghers attempted to end the Navarra *fueros* and seek protection exclusively from the king of France. Strained relations between Navarrese and French caused the civil war described day by day by an eye-witness, the poet, Guillaume Anelier.[25]

At the end of 1275, Eustache of Beaumarchais, seneschal of Toulouse, a key figure of the French court, entered Pamplona. He had been named governor of Navarra. Not surprisingly, one of the first decisions he made was to suppress the Navarrese codes of law and to substitute the *sanchetes* for the French Tours pound as currency.

---

[24] This happened in September of that same year, 1276, when don Juan Núñez de Lara rendered homage in Angoulême to Philip III of France and put at his service an army of 300 knights; soon afterwards, his brother Nuño González would do the same. Cf. G. Daumet, *Mémoire sur les relations de la France et de la Castille*, pp. 157–159, no. 7–8; *MHE*, I, no. 143, pp. 325–326; and M. Arigita y Lasa, *Cartulario de don Felipe III*, n. 5, 65, and 116, where the various contracts with the rebellious Castilian nobles have been published. Cf. Ballesteros, *Alfonso X*, pp. 824 and 841.

[25] G. Anelier de Toulouse, *Histoire de la guerre civile de Navarre*, ed. F. Michel, in *Collection de documents inédits sur l'Histoire de France*, Paris, 1856, pp. 651–655.

These actions ignited the civil war that bloodied the streets and squares of Pamplona during the months of May and June in 1276. Faced with the danger that the luck of the supporters of France might be reversed, Philip III had no choice but to intervene with all of his armed forces, which he entrusted to the command of Robert of Artois. The struggle for the succession to the throne of Castile had unforeseen repercussions.

Alfonso X, unable personally to attend to the defense of Pamplona due to an illness, had no choice but to defend his interests in the kingdom of Navarra by sending a considerable army (40,000 knights and 4,000 horses) under the command of his brother Fadrique and Fadrique's son-in-law, Simón Ruiz de los Cameros. The Castilians were easily defeated three leagues from Pamplona by the more numerous troops of the king of France. But at Alfonso's court it was suspected that the defeat had been caused, in great part, by a betrayal plotted by Alfonso's two old enemies and the other rebellious nobles.[26]

Alfonso could not understand how the Pamplona supporters of Castile had been defeated, but he quickly discovered the real reasons. The noble Castilians conniving with the two Lara brothers, Juan and Nuño, sons of Nuño González de Lara, plotted once more against Alfonso, appearing before Philip III in Angoulême in order to render homage to him and put themselves at his service.[27] Things were clear: don Sancho's appointment as successor to the throne of Castile had bothered not only the king of France, but also Juan Núñez de Lara, who, as we saw, had sworn to don Fernando de la Cerda that he would defend the rights of his son Alfonso. Now it was the time to make good on his word.

I believe that this rebellion of the nobility is also narrated in *Cantiga* 235, when Alfonso himself affirms:

. . .

However, later, believe you me, King don Sancho in Portugal was never betrayed so vilely.

---

[26] Cf. P.J. Moret, *Anales del reino de Navarra*, vol. V, ed. 1912, p. 68; G. Anelier de Toulouse, *Histoire de la guerre civile de Navarre*, pp. 651–652; Ballesteros, *Alfonso X*, pp. 793–797, 801–804.

[27] Cf. Ballesteros, *Alfonso X*, p. 805; and G. Daumet, *Mémoire sur les relations de la France*, pp. 157–158. Cf. *Cartulario de Don Felipe III*, no. 25, p. 21, where the correspondence between Philip III and the Castilian nobility appears, also cited by R. Kinkade, "Alfonso X, *Cantiga* 235" p. 311, note 107.

...

> For the greater part of the nobles conspired, as I know, to throw him out
> of the kingdom so that it would belong to them, and they could divide it
> among themselves. However, they failed in their attempt, for God raised
> him to the summit and drove them down into the depths. (*Songs of Holy
> Mary*, 235, p. 282)

"However, later," that is, after Alfonso returned from his meeting with
the pope in France and was warmly received by his subjects, believe
me, the poet says, not even the king don Sancho of Portugal was sold
in a baser manner. Although the text of the *Cantiga* is sufficiently
vague to refer to any of the rebellions of the nobility during the reign
of Alfonso, the fact that this rebellion took place upon his return from
France, during his stay in Vitoria (lines 65–67), seems to indicate that
this refers to the events of the Navarra civil war, where don Fadrique
and Simón de los Cameros played a vital role along with other nobles.
On the other hand, the comparison that Alfonso draws here between
the betrayal of his nobles and the betrayal plotted by the Portuguese
nobility and the Church against his relative and close friend Sancho II
of Portugal (1223–1248) is very meaningful. The Portuguese king, as
mentioned above, was practically deposed by the betrayal plotted by
the Portuguese nobility to get rid of him, convincing pope Innocent
IV to depose him, which he did during the Lyon Council on July 24,
1245. The pope urged the Portuguese nobility and people to deny their
loyalty to don Sancho II and to render homage to his brother don
Alfonso, Duke of Boulogne.[28]

The topic of the deposition of don Sancho II of Portugal had become
almost proverbial when some 30 years later the poet composed the
Cantiga, clearly trying to establish a parallel between the betrayal of
the king by the Portuguese nobility and that of Alfonso by the Castilian nobility, Alfonso being a distant relative of Sancho II, who ended
his days deposed and exiled in the city of Toledo.[29] There is, thus, a
bitter critique not only of the rebellious nobility, but also of the attitude of the Church both in Sancho II's and in Alfonso's case. But the

---

[28] Cf. *CAX*, chap. 7, pp. 41–45; J. O'Callaghan, *A History of Medieval Spain*, pp.
349–351; Ballesteros, *Alfonso X*, pp. 146–147; E.M. Peters, "*Rex inutilis*: Sancho II of
Portugal and Thirteenth-Century Deposition Theory," *Studia Gratiana*, 14 [*Collecta-
nea Stephan Kuttner*, 4] (1967) pp. 255–305. Cf. above Chapter 3, pp. 92–94.

[29] Sancho II of Portugal died in Toledo in January, 1248. His wife, doña Mencía de
Haro, lived the rest of her days in Ciudad del Tajo under Alfonso X's protection. Cf.
CAX, chap. 29, pp. 109–111; and Ballesteros, *Alfonso X*, pp. 146–147.

poet also emphasizes how Divine Providence watched over the king of Castile, raising him to the top and casting his enemies into the depths of the valley (line 63). In reality only Divine Providence could have stopped the large army of Philip III, which did not manage to go beyond Sauveterre-de-Béarne, some 50 km from Bayonne, where the French were stopped by a pouring rain. Later, the lack of supplies forced them to return home and give up the invasion.[30]

Evidently, for the Learned King, deposing a king legally instituted, simply because he disobeyed the will of the pope and the nobles, was a true betrayal, a model *par excellence* of all betrayals. The difference, however, between the betrayal of Sancho Capelo of Portugal and the one plotted by Alfonso's nobles supported by the ecclesiastical hierarchy was that Sancho's was successful, while the one against Alfonso, according to the *Cantiga*, ended badly, because God, through the intercession of the Virgin, "raised him to the summit" and "drove them [his enemies] down into the depths." Six years later, time would witness the bitter surprise that lay in store for him.

If we consider that these events were taking place when Alfonso had just returned from his meeting with the pope, where everything turned out badly and that the Peninsular Church hierarchy was siding with the rebels, one cannot avoid seeing these lines of verse as an allusion to the events in Beaucaire and a plot of the nobility and the Church, as the *Cantiga* says, "to throw him out of the kingdom so that it would belong to them, and they could divide it among themselves," a goal that the rebels in 1272–74 did not have. Therefore, we should interpret the text of the *Cantiga* as an explicit allusion to a betrayal related to the war in Navarra, to which we now turn.

On September 5, 1276, Alfonso retreated to Vitoria, with brief visits to Burgos and surroundings, where he could more carefully follow the development of the political and military situation of the kingdom of Navarra. Navarra and the French territorial expansion towards the Ebro had been one of the political problems Alfonso discussed with the pope in Beaucaire and which he had not been able to solve. The pope

---

[30] Cf. Langlois, *Philippe III*, pp. 105–107; Ballesteros, *Alfonso X*, pp. 800–801; more sources can be seen in R. Kinkade, "Alfonso X, *Cantiga* 235," pp. 281–283, where he also points out how Philip III's campaigns against Castile and then against Aragón were parodied in a contemporary French chronicle entitled *Chroniques de Saint Magloir* (c. 1300), ed. E. Barbazan, in *Fabliaux et contes des poètes français*, 4 vols. Paris, 1808; repr. Geneva, 1976, II, pp. 221–235.

supported the marriage of Philip III's second son, who later became Philip IV, *the Handsome*, and Juana, daughter of the late Henry of Champagne, and heiress to the throne of Navarra.[31]

From his retreat in Vitoria, Alfonso looked for the best way to block the expansion of France. We know that Alfonso remained in Vitoria, according to the poetic expression in the *Cantiga* 235, "a year and a month" (in reality, from September 5, 1276 to March 7, 1277). The reason for this lengthy stay in this city of Navarra was a relapse of a serious illness ("while he lay gravely ill"), during which time the French king attacked. It was also during this period when Alfonso sent letters and messengers to Philip III, treating him in a very haughty manner and with a tone of defiance. The king was shocked at the Castilian monarch's irresponsibility when faced with the threat of an army of more than 300,000 men ready to crush him at any moment.[32] We know, however, that besides the pouring rain mentioned above, it was precisely the large number of warriors, also alluded to in the *Cantiga* ("the King of France attacked him with a very large army" [*Songs of Holy Mary*, 235, p. 282]), which forced him to retreat, facing the impossibility of providing for them and never going beyond Salvatierra. To a physically debilitated and militarily inferior Alfonso, the failed invasion must have seemed a true miracle from God, who, in the words of the *Cantiga*, dissolved the plans of the king of France "as water dissolves salt" (*Songs of Holy Mary*, 235, p. 282).

During the period Alfonso spent in Vitoria he also met with count Robert of Artois, who, in the king of France's name, signed a treaty with Alfonso X on November 7, 1276. In this agreement, obviously signed after the Castilian defeat, a truce was established between Castile and Navarra until doña Juana, heiress to the throne of Navarra, reached legal age. But what the French king really had in mind was a solution to the problem of the succession to the throne of Castile. With this agreement, Alfonso had to commit to revoking the pledge and homage paid by the nobles and the Church to don Sancho, and to summon a royal ecclesiastical tribunal in one year, during which time

---

[31] In May 1275 the Treaty of Orléans was signed, in which, despite the marriage that was sanctioned by the pope, the very peculiar conditions of the union between Navarra and France were stipulated. Doña Blanca ceded the government of Navarra to the king of France, but only until her daughter reached legal age.

[32] See the details on the preparations for and participants in the great military campaign to invade Alfonso's kingdom in Ballesteros, *Alfonso X*, p. 800.

the Church officials and nobles would chose a successor between his son, don Sancho, and his grandson, Alfonso de la Cerda. If Alfonso was not able to revoke the pledge and homage paid by the nobles and Church to don Sancho during this curia, he promised to name "other barons and prelates," the wisest that could be found and who had participated in the oath-taking at the Burgos Cortes, so they would impartially decide on the case. The implicit intention of this clause was to make Philip III understand that Alfonso's will was to return to the original dispositions, proclaiming his grandson, Alfonso de la Cerda, as heir. Finally Philip of France would commit to respecting the decision of the Castilian courts, regardless of the outcome, and at the same time waived his right to appeal to a higher authority, including the pope. The agreement was signed by Robert of Artois, on behalf of Philip III, and by the *repostero* (baker) don Enrique Pérez de Harana on behalf of Alfonso X.[33]

The agreement at Vitoria, however, was never ratified by Philip III, indeed because he found it unfavorable, and therefore had no effect. But for Alfonso it was a great diplomatic triumph—he won in the terrain of negotiation what he had lost in the battlefield. Don Sancho, in fact, continues to appear in the documents from the fall of 1276 and throughout all of 1277 as the "eldest son and heir." The state of war between France and Castile continued, but now with the certainty that Alfonso would have a successor, even if it did not please the opposition.

4. *Mysterious Executions*

Alfonso spent the entire winter and part of the spring of 1276–77 ill at Vitoria. When he reappears in the political scene to celebrate the May 9 Cortes, one of the most hair-raising and mysterious events of this humane and justice-loving king had already taken place. The events are narrated thus in the anonymous *Chronicle of Alfonso X*:

> The king departed from Segovia, and Prince Sancho with him, and they went to Burgos; and because the king found out some matters about his

---

[33] The text of the agreement or convention was published by Francisque Michel in his edition of G. Anelier de Toulouse, *Histoire de la guerre civile de Navarre*, Paris 1856, p. 652. See also G. Daumet, *Memoires*, n. 7 and 8. Cf. E. Procter, *Curia and Cortes*, pp. 140–141; Ballesteros, *Alfonso X*, pp. 804–806.

brother Prince Fadrique and about don Simón Ruiz de los Cameros, he
ordered Prince Sancho to go and seize don Simón Ruiz de los Cameros
and to immediately have him killed. Don Sancho immediately left Burgos and went to Logroño and found don Simón Ruiz there and arrested
him; and this same day that they arrested him, Diego López de Salcedo
arrested don Fadrique in Burgos by the king's order. Don Sancho went
to Treviño and ordered don Simón Ruiz burned there, and the king
ordered don Fadrique strangled. (*CAX*, chap. 68, pp. 219–220)[34]

The text, as can be noted, leaves many issues unresolved, and the main
one is the reason for the executions. What grave action did these two
nobles perform that merited such a summary execution, apparently
without due process? We do not know. As the only explanation, the
Chronicle says, "because the king found out some matters" (*CAX*,
chap. 68, p. 219) The first thing that comes to mind is that the phrase
may simply refer to the fact that it was around that time when Alfonso
discovered the true reason for the defeat of the Castilian troops by
the French, namely, the betrayal plotted by his close relatives whom
he had so trusted in that moment when he was incapacitated. That
is, the execution was a way of settling accounts, or rather, a punishment for the betrayal. After a long series of personal conflicts with
Fadrique, Alfonso had lost his patience with him. As many chroniclers attest, Fadrique was prone to plotting, despite his intelligence and

---

[34] The *Crónica* mistakenly dates the events as occurring in 1276. The exact date is
given by the *Anales Toledanos III*: "Anno domini MCCLXXVII; nobilis rex Alfonsus
mediante justitia occidit domnum Fredicum et dominum Simonem Roderici de los
Cameros" (in A. Huici, *Las crónicas latinas de la reconquista*, I, p. 370). The events
happened therefore in 1277; according to Ballesteros, at the end of April or the beginning of May (*Alfonso X*, p. 823). The *CAX* is also wrong when it states that the King
and don Sancho were coming from the Segovia Cortes, which were held almost two
years later in 1278. Regarding the details of the execution, the anonymous *Anales del
reinado de Alfonso X*, say: "It was in 1316 [AD 1278] when the prince don Sancho,
son of king Alfonso and heir, captured don Simón Ruiz de los Cameros in Logroño
by order of the king, his father. And in that year the king don Alfonso captured don
Fadrique, his brother, in Burgos, and he had him put in the castle and placed in a
coffer that was full of sharp iron rods and there he died" (in M. González Jiménez,
"Unos anales del reinado de Alfonso X," p. 477, 19). Don Fadrique's body was buried [thrown] in a "shameful place" according to don Sancho's subsequent accusation
against his father. Sancho, once king, ordered that Fadrique's body be transferred
to the Church of la Trinidad in Burgos, where he received a more dignified burial.
When this Church was destroyed, according to Osma, don Fadrique's cenotaph was
transferred to the portico of the Monastery of Las Huelgas. Cf. Ballesteros, *Alfonso
X*, p. 271.

good qualities.[35] He had indeed a rash personality that upset Alfonso many times, allying himself with his enemies and seeking adventures in the South of Europe and Northern Africa.[36] Fadrique and his alliances with the enemies of the pope not only caused Alfonso many diplomatic problems, but also contributed to Alfonso being associated in the eyes of the papacy with his adventurous brother and the entire clan of the Hohenstaufen, thus damaging his aspiration to the imperial crown.

The animosity between the two brothers had a long history. Fadrique, according to some historians, had received as inheritance from his mother, Beatriz of Swabia, the lands and estates of the Swabian duchy. When he was only seventeen, he was sent by his father, don Fernando, to the imperial court of Frederick II to officially claim his maternal inheritance. The emperor, however, did not support the request. While in Italy, he married a Romanian-Greek princess, and upon his return to Spain, he took part in the conquest of Seville, for which he received great rewards in the *Repartimiento*. In 1246, pope Innocent IV denied him the title of the Duchy of Swabia, granting it instead to Alfonso X. Fadrique would never forget this effrontery. In 1255, he joined his brother Enrique in the conspiracy against Alfonso. When the conspiracy failed, he had to seek the protection of the sultan of Tunis, as did his brother Enrique. Alfonso confiscated from both all the properties his father had granted them for their participation in the conquests of the south. Following the adventures in Tunis and his return to Spain, Alfonso was reconciled with Fadrique, returning his property and welcoming him at the court. But don Fadrique continued to plot against him. During the 1276–77 crisis of Navarra, when he saw how his sick brother was faltering under the pressure of the French, the Navarrese and the Muslims to the south, he must have thought that, as the second-born, his time had come to seize the throne,

---

[35] Gil de Zamora describes him as: "…gifted with great discretion, sharp intelligence, shrewd at business, brave in battle, and prudent in all his civil and military actions" (*De praeconis*, p. 215). Given that Fr. Gil was a courtier of Alfonso X's and the tutor of don Sancho, the material executioner of the sentence, it is not clear how he could have praised Fadrique in such terms.

[36] There's a brief summary of these adventures in R. Kinkade, "Alfonso X, *Cantiga* 235," pp. 314–315, note 119; more details in Ballesteros, *Alfonso X*, pp. 270–272; 465–475, 537, 546–547.

heading a plot to dethrone him.[37] Perhaps it was Fadrique's aspirations
to the throne that led Sancho, who at the time also had his eyes set
on the succession, to collaborate with his father to eliminate the two
plotters. Later, as we will see, he would side with the victims in order
to revile his father for disinheriting and murdering his uncle.

According to this reconstruction, therefore, all seems to indicate
that the cause of the executions would have been the nobles' attempt
to depose Alfonso and divide up the kingdom amongst themselves and
perhaps among the French, granting them Navarra, and maybe also to
place the nephew, don Alfonso de la Cerda, on the throne. However
not everything is clear in this dark tale of plots and murders, hence
the various hypothesis on the possible causes of such an unexpected
execution. Jerónimo de Zurita, for instance, believed, based on an "old
Portuguese writer" [perhaps the *Crónica de 1344*], that Alfonso had his
brother killed on account of an astrological prediction according to
which a member of his own family would dethrone him (don Simón
was also related to Alfonso X because he was married to a daughter
of don Fadrique).[38] Mondéjar for his part insisted on the plot and the
opposition of the two brothers, Fadrique and Enrique, to the idea of the
empire, which, at this point, Alfonso was not concerned about. Ballesteros believed that "[t]he proof of the plot is to be found in France,"
in the sense that there was a wide conspiracy of the nobles to depose
Alfonso, and that they had sold themselves to the king of France, as
the extant documents clearly show.[39] Other scholars hold that Alfonso
probably discovered that his brother was directly involved in a plot to
assassinate him, thinking that he as the older brother would inherit
the throne. This theory would explain why don Sancho actively collaborated in executing his father's command, simply because his own
succession to the throne was threatened. Traditional historiography
(Zurita, Mariana, Mondéjar, Lafuente, Ballesteros), in general, points
to various reasons that, in some way or another, indicate some kind
of plot to depose Alfonso.

---

[37] Mondéjar, *Memorias*, p. 344; Ballesteros, *Alfonso X*, pp. 164–165, 731, 820; and
in the biography by G. del Giudice, *Don Arrigo, Infante di Castiglia*, Naples, 1875,
pp. 169–173.

[38] *Anales de la Corona de Aragón*, book IV, chap. III, ed. A. Ubieto and M.D. Pérez
Soler, Valencia: Anubar, 1967.

[39] Cf. Ballesteros, *Alfonso X*, pp. 821–823; and *Sevilla en el siglo XIII*, Madrid: Impr.
Juan Pérez Torres, 1913; Daumet, op. cit., pp. 33–34; cf. also M. González Jiménez,
M. Borrero Fernández, I. Montes Romero-Camacho, *Sevilla en tiempos de Alfonso X*,
Seville, 1987.

Of course, the two simultaneous detention orders in two different places as well as the fact that both executions were carried out with great speed and in secret in two different places suggest not only a plot to depose Alfonso (something that at this point he was already used to), but also an imminent attempt on his life. Based on Alfonso's temperament, only this motive could have led him to such a drastic and devastating action. In his legislation, the Learned King clearly had established punishments for anyone who would threaten the life, health, honor, or lordship of the king, as well as against traitors. All these crimes were punishable by death or at least by blinding.[40]

Alfonso never made any declaration about the cause of the executions or remotely attempted to justify them, which shows that he had a firm intention of hiding them. It was a zealously kept secret, even in the moments of greatest pressure, as when his son Sancho, who was witness to and executor of the deeds, accused him of many things including the murder his brother. He did respond to some of the accusations but never to the one about the murder of his brother. The closest thing to an explanation is found in *Cantiga* 235, where, after having spoken of the various illnesses of which the Virgin miraculously cured him, and of the betrayals of his relatives and friends, he continues in a sibylline tone:

> [...] in Castile [...] the Son of God granted him vengeance on those who were His enemies and hence the king's also. Just as a candle burns, so did the flesh burn of those who shunned women. Others went to the devil, and may it please God to take anyone there also who commits such a deed. I care not a whit for the evil which befalls them. (*Cantiga* 235, p. 282)[41]

We do not know the identities of the enemies of God and Alfonso to whom Alfonso refers in lines 71–72, and against whom he exacted "a great revenge." But the historical circumstances of the moment (Alfonso was in Vitoria, as the context of the *Cantiga* reveals) seem to indicate that, in effect, the revenge he alludes to may be the one of the executions (no other one is known). Given this theory, we can go on to the analysis of the rest of the *Cantiga*.

The Learned King, without preambles, goes on to say: 1) "Just as a candle burns, so did the flesh burn of those who shunned women." 2) "Others went to the devil, and may it please God to take anyone

---

[40] *Fuero real*, ed. A. Palacios Alcaine, Barcelona: PPU, 1991, I, 2.2, p. 5.
[41] *Songs of Holy Mary*, p. 282.

who commits such a deed there also." (235, p. 282) What "deed" is he referring to? Richard Kinkade, in the frequently cited article, based on this *Cantiga* has proposed as the reason of such a radical and unexpected decision that Fadrique and Simón Ruiz de los Cameros may have been discovered in the act of sodomy, an action that was punishable by death.[42] It would not be very difficult to reach this conclusion if we were certain that the *Cantiga* is referring to the execution in question and that the "deed" was sodomy. The only thing we can be certain of is that the *Cantiga* seems to give as the motive of the sentence Alfonso's "many serious illnesses, which he suffered in Castile, where the Son of God granted him vengeance on those who were His enemies [...]" (*Cantiga* 235, p. 282). This statement, given the historical circumstances, can only be understood as referring to the political problems of Castile caused by the rebellion of the two noblemen and, consequently, the loss of Navarra. The topic of homosexuality, however, leaps into view, albeit expressed in metaphorical language, when the punishment inflicted is mentioned: "Just as a candle burns so did the flesh burn of those who shunned women" (235, p. 282). In other words, the poet, in the process of informing us about the punishment applied, i.e., fire, would be suggesting the nature of the crime, homosexuality. How this crime may also have caused both God and Alfonso "many serious illnesses [...] in Castile" (*Cantiga* 235, p. 282) is harder to explain (while this is a lot easier if we accept that "the deed" was the betrayal). But we can suppose that this sin, and perhaps the renunciation of Fadrique's Christian faith while he was serving in Muslim Africa, or the rebellion and betrayal of his own king, were also considered sins and offenses against God.[43] The poet also identifies the enemies of God and Alfonso as "those who shunned women,"a euphemism, according to some scholars, for heretics and indirectly the vice of homosexuality.[44]

---

[42] Commenting on the words of the *Cantiga*: "Just as a candle burns so did the flesh burn of those who shunned women." (*Cantiga* 235, p. 282), Kinkade writes: "Those of his enemies who did not love women, a not-so-veiled allusion to the crime of sodomy, were burned at the stake, perhaps the most often prescribed punishment for this much-feared crime. The implication would seem to be that Simon Ruiz and Fadrique were discovered *in flagrante delicto* and summarily dispatched without benefit of trial," "Alfonso X, *Cantiga* 235," pp. 315–316.

[43] In the *Partidas* it is clearly stated that whoever attacks the king or lays hands on him directly offends God (II, 1, 5–6).

[44] For J. Montoya Martínez, the words in the *Cantiga* "daqueles que non querian moller" ["those who shunned women"] are code language for Cathar heretics, thus

If sodomy is accepted as the cause of the execution, the expression on line 77 could also be interpreted in the same way, following a long tradition of euphemisms in Peninsular letters: "Others went to the devil, and may it please God to take anyone who commits such a deed there also" (cant. 235, p. 282), where the "deed" would clearly allude to sexual activities. Though chronicles of the period are, like the *Cantiga*, quite discreet in the discussion of homosexuality, they could indirectly confirm the sexual nature of the crime by their use of a euphemism that makes us suspect the accused had committed a crime of this sort (whether as converts to Catharism or by simply practicing its doctrines). The *CAX* uses the expression "because the king found out certain little things [*cosillas*] about his brother Prince Fadrique and about don Simón Ruiz de los Cameros" (*CAX*, chap. 68, p. 219), where the term *cosillas* traditionally is a veiled allusion to the crime of sodomy.[45] The contemporary and well-informed writer Jofré de Loaysa suggests the same thing in his *Chronicle*: "...because of *certain little things* the king knew."[46] The fact that they were rebels was known by all, so it makes sense to ask, what else did the king "know" ("as I know," *Songs of Holy Mary*, *Cantiga* 235, p. 282) that the others did not? We can be certain that Alfonso knew a great deal, especially

---

concluding that the two victims of execution would have adopted such a heresy ("La 'gran vingança' de Dios y de Alfonso X," *BC*, 3 [1990], pp. 53–59). We know that Cathars rejected marriage and all sexual contact with women, and, as was general practice for all heretics, were punished by burning at the stake. There is however no proof that don Fadrique (who was strangled and not burnt) professed any heresy or had contacts with this religious sect, although given his unruly temperament, anything is possible. On the other hand, the hypothesis of the Cathar heresy would explain the expression: "those who were His enemies and hence the king's also" (p. 282). I also do not believe that as precedent of a certain antifeminist and misogynist tendencies one should mention the fact that 24 years earlier don Fadrique supported the translation from the Arabic of *Sendebar* or *Libro de los engaños et los assayamientos de las mujeres*, one of the most misogynist books of medieval Castilian literature, although it is not difficult to associate the misogyny in this work with the expression "those who shunned women" in the *Cantiga*. Against this possible explanation, however, is the fact that both were married and had children. On misogyny and the *Sendebar*, cf. J.E. Keller, ed., *El libro de los engaños*, Valencia and Chapel Hill, 1959; and M.J. Lacarra, ed., *Sendebar*, Madrid: Cátedra, 1989; A.D. Deyermond, "The *Libro de los engaños*: its Social and Literary Context" in *The Spirit of the Court: Selected Proceedings of the Fourth Congress of the International Courtly Literature Society*, ed. Glyn S. Burgess and Robert A. Taylor, Cambridge: D.S. Brewer, 1985, pp. 158–167.

[45] Recall the meaning of *"cosillas"* in the *Lazarillo de Tormes*: "Because of this and because of other *little things* that I won't tell, I left him", in the episode of the friar of the Order of Mercy (Treatise IV).

[46] J. de Loaysa, *Crónica*, p. 21.

if it was a matter of betrayal or homosexuality. The trouble was that he never said anything. The fact that the king did not want to declare anything specific about the motives of the execution may also be an argument for the case of homosexuality, because his reticence regarding this topic in his works is well known: "[...] we're sorry to have to speak about something that must be approached with great caution and is even more dangerous to commit [...]" he writes in the *Fuero real* (see note 49 below).

Finally, we must consider the type of punishment applied and the apparent secrecy of the execution, matters which, again, suggest some crime of sexual perversion or religious deviance. The artist who illustrated *Cantiga* 235 in the Florence Codex (*Cantiga* 71bis), which, as we saw, contains six illustrations of great historical value, very probably would have destined two panels (the third and the fourth) to this bloody incident with the intention of setting an example for all viewers of the miniatures about the consequences of rebelling against the authority of the king (see illustration 7). Of the two vignettes planned, only one (the fourth) was completed. It shows a human head burning at the stake. Around the fire stands a crowd of armed warriors (among them don Sancho), but there are no Church officials as witnesses, which would have been normal when a heretic was burnt at the stake. This seems to indicate that it was instead the burning of a criminal or traitor who had just been captured and sentenced, not a heretic, although burning at the stake was the punishment typically applied to heretics. These details match what we know about the capture and execution of Simón Ruiz de los Cameros. The possible reference to the burning of a nobleman was depicted because, in the end, the scene could be interpreted allegorically as an allusion to the punishment that awaited all heretics or all who did not live according to the principles of the Decalogue, including obedience to the king (in this context, Simon's hypothetical connection to Catharism could be included), otherwise such a scene would not appear in a religious work such as the *Cantigas*.

But the other vignette (the third), where the punishment and execution of don Fadrique should have been depicted in some manner, was left blank.[47] As we noted, don Fadrique was strangled and his body

---

[47] I do not believe, as some scholars do, that in the third vignette the miracle at Vitoria should have been depicted. I see no rational motive to justify the absence of a

was thrown in "un lixoso lugar" (a latrine or dung heap) a punishment that typically was not applied to a prince, a king's brother, even one accused of treason or political conspiracy.[48] For the miniature artist, illustrating the strangulation of the prince or the shameful disposal of the body of the king's brother would have been too violent for a work destined for the royal chamber and Alfonso's private use. The presence of such an image would have been an unbearable reproach, reminding him constantly of an episode of his life about which he never wanted to speak and which he would much rather forget.

We nevertheless believe that, despite all these signs of possible sexual or religious motives, according to the *Cantiga*, the cause of the execution was not the sodomy of the accused, but rather the "many serious illnesses" (*Cantiga* 235, p. 282) that they had caused him (treason, a plot to depose or murder him). But it is possible that if the homosexuality of the executed was not the cause, it could just as easily have been the pretext, and a convenient one indeed, perhaps as valid as the crime of rebellion or attempted rebellion against the king, given the attitudes towards homosexuality in the period. Furthermore, the executions for these crimes, especially when the perpetrators were high-ranking figures, were usually performed clandestinely and quickly, to avoid scandal and popular unrest, while common traitors were publicly executed to serve as an example for all.[49]

---

miracle in the third, when both the vignette above it (the first) and the one below (the fifth) deal with miracles. Why then was a miracle not also depicted in the third? I believe the reason is that this vignette was reserved to depict don Fadrique's punishment.

[48] The author of the *CAX* may exaggerate regarding the disposal of don Fadrique's body, because it seems an extreme punishment that he would not have been buried in a holy place. After all, he was the king's brother, and by all accounts, a loved one. Also, if he had been thrown into a latrine, it would have been difficult for don Sancho to transfer the body five years later (1282) to the Monasterio de la Trinidad in Burgos, when he violently seized power and accused his father of such an irrational deed (*CAX*, chap. 76 , pp. 244–249).

[49] Laws against homosexuals in this period were extremely severe. Normally, once the facts were ascertained, the sentence was applied without the need of a trial. In the *Fuero de Alarcón*, for instance, it was stipulated that: "any man who is found fucking another man shall be burned" quoted by J.R. Craddock, "The Legislative Works of Alfonso el Sabio," in *Emperor of Culture*, pp. 182–197, p. 186. Alfonso X in his legislation sentences to death "those who commit the sin of lust against nature" (*Partidas*, 7.21.2); and in the *Fuero real*, compiled between 1252 and 1255, he decrees:

Although we're sorry to have to speak about something that must be approached with great caution and is even more dangerous to commit, but which, unfortunately happens sometimes when a man covets another man to sin with him against nature, we order that whoever it is who commits this sin, that it should immediately be reported, that both be castrated in front of all the people, and

Still, we cannot deny that the two executed men, married and with children, were not known to be promiscuous, and that Alfonso did not use the accusation of homosexuality as a pretext to eliminate them without the need of a normal trial, as the accusations of rebellion, plotting, or treason would have required.[50] On the other hand, it was a common belief at the time that sodomites, traitors, and heretics (almost always named in that order) attracted the wrath of God over their kingdoms, and for this simple reason, according to Goodich, homosexual licentiousness was punished with the same rigor as subversion.[51]

Alfonso was much criticized in his day for this monstrous action. Is there an explanation? As we will see later, the *CAX* recalls the episode of the execution immediately after the flight of doña Violante with her daughter-in-law and her grandchildren to Aragón, something that profoundly depressed Alfonso because he felt abandoned not only by his relatives, but also by his subjects, who did nothing to prevent the flight despite his instructions regarding it. All these family affairs, added to the adversities in the field of international politics in a difficult moment personally (he had just overcome a serious illness) and politically (he was threatened by the French king's troops in the North and by the emir of Morocco's in the South) may have led him to a rash decision, but not for this reason less justified according to the current legislation, because treason, an attempt on the king's life, and sodomy were all capital crimes.

This type of reaction, violent and unexpected on Alfonso's part, would correspond, according to the psychological analysis of his personality, to the nature of his character, if we accept Dr. Torres's theory that he was an immature introvert. But there is also historical evidence that the execution was not as arbitrary or capricious as early

---

then, on the third day, that they should be hanged from their legs until they die, and that the bodies should never be removed from there. (2, 134)

For the intolerant attitude towards homosexuals in the rest of Europe, see M. Goodich, *The Unmentionable Vice: Homosexuality in the Later Medieval Period*, Santa Barbara, Calif., 1979, esp. pp. 77, 83; and J. Brundage, *Law, Sex and Christian Society in Medieval Europe*, Chicago, 1987, esp. p. 473.

[50] The presence of don Fadrique for almost ten years at the court of the sultan of Tunis, where it was believed that as in all Muslim courts homosexuality was widespread, earned Alfonso's rebellious brother his scandalous reputation. Cf. R. Kinkade, "Alfonso X, *Cantiga* 235," p. 317, note 127.

[51] "Charges of sexual immorality were linked with political nonconformity," *The Unmentionable Vice*, pp. 84–85.

anti-Alfonsine historiography would have us believe. It was rather the result of a judicial process, summarily as it may have been carried out. Unique among the documents quoted above (note 34) is perhaps the *Anales Toledanos III*, which explicitly says: "the noble king Alfonso killed *according to justice* don Fadrique and don Simón Rodríguez de los Cameros." The words "according to justice" clearly indicate that there was a trial against the accused. Such was also Alfonso's own sentiment, repeated often until the end of his days.

In any event, for Alfonso, a man of liberal ideas, very tolerant and according to the opinion of the psychiatrist Dr. Torres and of Ballesteros himself, "incapable of holding any grudges," the execution of his younger brother, for whom he always felt a great love, was a truly traumatic experience that depressed him psychologically and aggravated his physical illnesses. Fadrique, the only one of his brothers who was a kindred spirit to Alfonso: he loved culture and art and, as mentioned, he was responsible for the compilation of the celebrated *Libro de los engaños et asayamientos de las mujeres*. Still, the *Cantiga* for all its sibylline, metaphorical, and elliptic language reveals a mood in the poet found nowhere else. Alfonso, undoubtedly the author, does not appear as the tender and devout troubadour of the Virgin Mary, but rather as a man hardened and embittered by life, one who never regretted such a brutal decision, given the chilling closing commentary: "Others went to the devil, and may it please God to take anyone who commits such a deed there also. I care not a whit for the evil which befalls them." (235, p. 282) The evil here can be no other than the punishment imposed and, ultimately, eternal damnation. I do not believe that this *Cantiga*, in which the Christian humaneness and compassion of a man as devoted to the Virgin as was Alfonso is less than evident, was ever sung before an image of Mary and surrounded by Christian people.

As a result of the executions, as Ballesteros thinks, some of the nobles (such as Fernán Pérez de Ponce, cousin of the king, the aforementioned Nuño de Lara and several more), who were probably also implicated in the conspiracy to dethrone Alfonso and feared the same fate, switched over to support the French king.[52] The most remarkable and perhaps revealing aspect of the case was that even the main proponent and defender of don Sancho's candidacy, don Lope Díaz

---

[52] Ballesteros, *Alfonso X*, pp. 803–804.

de Haro, also put himself at the service of the king of France. Thus, in mid-May 1277, both the supporters of Alfonso de La Cerda and those of Sancho went against their king, Alfonso, pledging fidelity to Philip III and imploring his protection.

Given the interests of the king of France in this plot, and given his generosity towards the rebels, we must conclude that the conspiracy consisted not only of deposing Alfonso, but also of denying the right of succession to don Sancho, placing one of the de la Cerda princes on the throne of Castile. The matter was so serious and so much beyond the course of the decisions of the Cortes, that Alfonso, with the unconditional cooperation of Sancho (although Sancho would later deny it), had to react suddenly. Why did don Lope Díaz de Haro flee to seek the king of France's protection? Was Sancho's protection not enough? What did he fear? Perhaps he feared the same fate as don Fadrique and don Simón, which means he also was implicated in the conspiracy of the two executed men and that the conspiracy went beyond the deposition of Alfonso X.[53] The extent of the conspiracy among the nobility was indeed much greater than what the documents transmit and had as its final objective to place one of Alfonso's grandchildren on the throne, or as the *Cantiga* literally says, to divide the kingdom up amongst themselves:

> For the greater part of the nobles conspired, as I know, to throw him out of the kingdom so that it would belong to them, and they could divide it among themselves.
>   However, they failed in their attempt, for God raised him to the summit and drove them down into the depths. (*Cantiga* 235, p. 282)

At a moment when Alfonso's enemies among the nobility must have been numerous, the effect of these executions was devastating. If the king could at will have his own brother and one of his best generals killed, only God knows what he would be capable of doing to the majority of the nobles who were hostile to him politically and were not related to him by blood. Many defected to go serve the king of France, and others began to think how to remedy such a desperate situation,

---

[53] Don Lope switched sides to serve the king of France at around the same time that the plot was discovered and Fadrique and Simón were executed. In September 1277, Philip III had already granted him "lands" valued at 2,000 Tours pounds (cf. M. Arigita, *Cartulario*, n. 34). This document and others lead us to believe that don Lope had sold himself to the supporters of Alfonso de la Cerda (in Daumet, *Memoires*, pp. 254–256).

turning to the heir, don Sancho.[54] In any event, the *CAX* is very clear regarding the main motive of the rebellion of the nobles who had remained in the kingdom: it was "[...] due to the many deaths and outrages that he caused—especially in that he killed both Prince Don Fadrique, his brother, and likewise killed don Simón de los Cameros, our uncle" (chap. 76, p. 248).[55]

5. *New Marinid Invasion*

The truce signed by Yûsuf and Sancho in early 1276 did not last long. When the Moroccan sultan found out about the state of self-destruction of the Castilian kingdom following the execution of one of the king's brothers and one of the best warriors in Christendom, together with the defection of the majority of the nobles that supplied soldiers to the Christian forces, he decided to take advantage of the situation, breaking the truce and occupying the entire south of the Peninsula. As the *CAX* says very little about this second campaign, the only narrative source is the *Rawd al-Qirtas* and a document that the bishops of Castile sent to the pope during the 1277 Burgos Cortes.[56]

On June 28, 1277, the great Marinid sultan, Abû Yûsuf Ya'qûb, once again landed in Tarifa. From there he quickly moved on to Algeciras and Ronda. This is where the children of Axkilula, the *arraez* of Guadix and Málaga, joined him. Together with his Peninsular allies, Yûsuf left Ronda on August 2 with the intention of reaching Seville. As was expected, he did not encounter any resistance. He realized that there was no Christian army to fight. If he had wanted to, he could have conquered not only Andalusia, but also crossed the old frontier of the Sierra Morena, perhaps taking Toledo and even in Burgos. Historians still do not understand why he did not do so. The Marinid leader was satisfied with Andalusia, using his old strategy of raiding the country, the crops and the cattle. The same evils of the previous invasion were

---

[54] Some of these defections or alliances, as with those of the most prominent figures of Castilian politics, were actually purchased. We know Philip III paid 14,000 Tours pounds to Juan Núñez de Lara and his 300 knights, while Juan's brother, Nuño, and his 106 warriors received 8,000 pounds. The king of France used this method to attract the favor of the opposing camps in the issue of succession.

[55] *CAX*, chap. 76, p. 248.

[56] The text of the plea in *RABM*, 1 época, tomo II, p. 58; and cf. Ballesteros, *Alfonso X*, p. 837); and J. O'Callaghan, "The Ecclesiastical Estate in the Cortes of León-Castile, 1252–1350," *The Catholic Historical Review*, 67 (1981), pp. 185–213.

repeated: assaults and kidnappings of women and children, murders, and, above all, the burning of fields, agricultural villages, and towns. The entire region of Córdoba, which supplied the majority of products that supported the Andalusian population, was devastated. At the end of the same month, the Muslim armies were already at the gates of Seville. But Yûsuf did not attempt to conquer the cities, which, for lack of supplies, automatically fell into his hands.

The first great encounter with the defenders of Seville, according to Ibn Abi Zar, took place outside the city, on the banks of the Guadalquivir, on August 3, the day of the Prophet.[57] The Christian army, led by Alfonso Fernández, was no match for Yûsuf's more numerous forces; it had to retreat and seek refuge in the city, where a vigorous defense was launched, preventing conquest by the emir's troops.[58] On August 29, Yûsuf returned to his base, Algeciras, carrying a great booty and many prisoners. But not for long, for on September 15, he was already again on the battlefield, attacking and raiding the region of Jerez. According to the *Rawd al-Qirtas*, after returning to Algeciras with the booty and dividing it up, on October 30 he launched the campaign to conquer Córdoba, joined also by Ibn Alahmar of Granada. This time, the Christians were unable to contain the Muslim avalanche. At the end of 1277, practically all of Andalusia, except Seville, was again under the power of the great Muslim leader. The map of the reconquest resembled again that of the times of Alfonso VIII and Fernando III.

However, at the end of this campaign, an event took place that led to the falling out of Ibn Yûsuf and the king of Granada. While the Marinid sultan was in Algeciras resting, following the expedition in September, Abû Mohamed ben Axkilula, *arraez* of Málaga died. The sultan, instead of granting the territory to the king of Granada as expected, occupied the city. This unforeseen decision led the king of Granada to break relations with the leader he thought had come to liberate him.

---

[57] The details of the battle, the speeches by Yûsuf, the remarkable participation of his son Abû Jacoub in the initial attack, and other details are meticulously described by Ibn Abi Zar, *Rawd al-Qirtas*, in Huici, II, p. 589.

[58] Despite its well-known hyperbole regarding Muslim victories, the *Rawd al-Qirtas* acknowledges that the great leader, after spending the entire night on horseback, decided to retreat but not before "sending out soldiers throughout the entire region in order to murder, capture, burn, and raid" (in Huici, ib.).

During the Córdoba campaign on October 30, according to the *Rawd al-Qirtas*, a delegation of "priests and religious men" arrived in Yûsuf's tent, "humble and dispirited," requesting peace. It is not known that the Castilian Church on its own or in the name of Alfonso made such a request. Therefore, it is believed that the "religious men" mentioned by the Muslim historian were perhaps representatives of the Military Orders. Suddenly, and contradicting what he had done after the death of the *arraez* of Málaga, the sultan, putting himself on the side of the king of Granada, replied to the "religious men": "Here I am a guest, and I cannot offer you peace if Aben Alahmar does not grant it." Hence, the Christian representatives went to the king of Granada with their proposal begging for peace. Mohamed II said that he not only wanted to grant the truce they requested, but that he supported a "firm peace that may last for centuries and will remain while days and nights pass." The emissaries could not believe what they were hearing. The king of Granada asked them what would happen if Alfonso was not willing to ratify the peace signed by them. Then, according to the Muslim historian, the monks "swore by their crosses that if Alfonso did not accept, they would depose him, because he did not defend the Cross, nor did he secure the borders or the country, but rather had left his subjects at the mercy of their enemy."[59] The king of Granada certainly must have been relieved when he heard from his enemies that the sultan had entrusted him with the peace negotiations. But he must not have been very certain of the Marinid leader's trust, because he invited the Christians to sign the agreement in the presence of Ibn Yûsuf: "Come with me, he said, to the presence of the emir of the Muslims, and before him we will conclude the peace and will both sign it, God willing."[60]

Clearly, the peace of which the Muslim historian speaks was not negotiated by Alfonso, but rather by the "monks," that is, the representatives of the Military Orders who bore the title of "freyres" and who were the front line of the Christian defense. Yûsuf delivered the booty to the king of Granada saying: "the Moors will have no other prizes from this expedition than divine reward". And he then left for Algeciras, were he fell ill. The king of Granada, following this apparent change in attitude, could think that the *arraeces*, who had been the

---

[59] *Rawd al-Qirtas*, ed. Huici, II, p. 587.
[60] *Rawd al-Qirtas*, II, p. 589.

cause of the break with Alfonso, would return to his control. But that was not the case. Abu Isha, the brother and successor of Ibn Mohamed of Málaga, appeared before the ill sultan, asking him to take possession of the city, saying: "I am unable to sustain it, and if you do not come here, to receive it from my hands, I will deliver it to the Christians so that Aben Alhamar may never occupy it".[61] The sultan had no choice but to send to Málaga his son Abû Zian, who took possession of the city on February 24, 1278. All efforts by the king of Granada to recover his arraeces had been unsuccessful. On June 3 of that same year, the great sultan Yûsuf returned forever to Morocco.

It was not the first time in the history of the Christian-Muslim conflict that a leader arriving from Africa, being in the best position to seize a good portion of Christian territories, suddenly decided to go back to his base in the Maghreb. The Christians were never able to understand this behavior or its logic and therefore considered it a miracle worked by Divine Providence watching over the interest of the Christians. But what had really happened?

Two main motives seem to have pushed Yûsuf to return to Morocco. As we said above, the military strategy of the Marinid leader of raiding the countryside so that the famished cities would surrender was indeed very efficient, but the weaknesses in it soon began to surface. With the destruction of the crops, his very large army had to get supplies from the foodstuffs stored in the cities, especially in the capital of the kingdom of their ally, Granada. This situation could not go on for long. Muhamed began to worry that the presence of the Marinid warriors was devastating the economy of his kingdom without producing compensatory results such as the return of the *arraeces*. Furthermore, it was already the case that *arraez* of Málaga, the more important of the two officials whose return to obedience Muhamed had sought by requesting Yûsuf's intervention, had instead switched sides over to Yûsuf himself. This was a clear indication that the Marinid leader could make use of the kingdom of Granada at any moment and in any way he pleased. Faced with this dilemma, Muhamed decided that it was better for him to continue under the protection of the king of Castile than to have to depend on the whim of a Marinid sultan. Hence his proposal for permanent peace with Alfonso, behind the sultan of Morocco's back.

---

[61] *Rawd al-Qirtas*, II, p. 588.

Another element that indeed must have influenced Yûsuf's decision to return to Morocco was the presence of the Castilian navy in the area of the Strait of Gibraltar. Alfonso could not count at the time on a land army, for which he almost completely depended on the cooperation of the nobles, but he did have a naval fleet that was entirely at the king's command. We know that in the summer of 1278 the Castilian navy was blocking the port of Algeciras, a situation that must have alarmed Yûsuf, because he ran the risk of being isolated in Grenada, which, with its permanent peace proposal with Castile, had to be considered hostile territory.

As we have noted, the *CAX* and the rest of Christian historiography completely ignores this return of the Moors. Yet numerous reminders of the deaths and the devastation caused by the Muslim armies during these campaigns exist in the *Cantigas*, among which *Cantiga* 215 stands out. It contains the narrative of how a statue of the Virgin, which had been stolen from a church near the village of Martos (Jaén), was unharmed by the various trials to which it was subjected by the invaders. One Muslim, the poet tells us, cut off one of its arms with a blow of his sword, but in retribution, his own sword arm fell off; later they stoned the image, but the stones would not touch it; thereafter they cast it in the fire for two days, but it would not burn; finally, they hurled it into the river with a large stone attached to the neck, yet the image floated. At the sight of so many prodigies, the terrified Muslims took the image to the king of Granada, who secretly sent it to Alfonso, who was then in Segovia. The story of the *Cantiga* is perfectly set in the context of Yusuf's second campaign of 1277–78, for other sources confirm that Alfonso was indeed in Segovia, to celebrate the 1278 Cortes.[62]

---

[62] Cf. Montoya, "Historia de Andalucía en las *Cantigas de Santa Maria*," in *Actas I Congreso de Historia de Andalucía*, Córdoba, 1978, pp. 259–269.

CHAPTER TWELVE

DON SANCHO IS DECLARED SUCCESSOR

1. *The Burgos and the Segovia Cortes*

Ill in Burgos and deprived of the support of the majority of his nobles and allies who had fled to France to seek the king's protection following the executions of don Fadrique and Simón de los Cameros, Alfonso summoned new Cortes in Burgos in order to request the military and economic support he would need against the feared invasion. The documents show that these Cortes had already begun May 9. None of the dissident nobles alluded to above (such as Lope Díaz de Haro, Núñez de Lara, etc.) were present, nor are the names of Fadrique or Simón mentioned, which confirms that the execution had already taken place. Don Sancho's name does not appear either, because, Ballesteros argues, "he was fulfilling his mission of justice in la Rioja and in the county of Treviño" (*Alfonso X*, p. 837).

During the Cortes meetings, the representatives of the nobility, the towns, and the Church sent a plea to pope John XXI relating the deplorable state of the economy as a result of the flight of capital, for the most recent coinages had contained a large amount of silver and the powerful were obviously hoarding them to the detriment of the population, who no longer had currency with which to pay for their basic needs.[1] In other words, the opposite of what happened at the beginning of Alfonso's reign was now taking place. Then, to increase the circulation of the currency, Alfonso had reduced the silver content, a monetary policy decision that caused inflation and rising prices. The same document reports something not mentioned in the *CAX*, namely, how Alfonso found out about the second invasion of the North African Moors.[2] In order to counter the lack of currency, and to collect the funds necessary to defend the southern border, the representatives at the Cortes sent their plea to the pope imploring that they be absolved

---

[1] The text of the plea in *RABM*, 1 época, tomo II, p. 58.
[2] See above chap. 11, note 54; and Ballesteros, *Alfonso X*, p. 837.

from their oath to not coin any other currency except the "dineros prietos" (i.e., money with low silver content).

Despite the complaints at the Cortes regarding the economic situation of the country and the poverty of all who did not have enough to afford the high prices, let alone to pay new taxes, Alfonso was still able to have a new annual tribute approved that no future king would be able to collect.[3] The new tribute would help finance the defense of the South from Moorish attacks. At the end of 1277, the assemblies at the Cortes were finished, and Alfonso remained in Burgos at least until March 11, 1278. Surprisingly, these Cortes did not deal with the matter of succession, which had caused so many problems in the kingdom and was still not completely resolved.

During this period, the popes—first the Portuguese Pedro Julião Rabello, who took the name John XXI (1276–1277); and later the Italian Giovanni Gaetano Orsini, who called himself Nicholas III (1277–12800—began the first initiatives to broker a truce between the kings of Castile and France. But Alfonso, who besides being ill was not very willing to negotiate what he believed belonged to him by legal right, did not attend the meeting, sending instead a delegate, Juan of Galicia, who excused his sovereign saying that the city where the meeting was scheduled, Toulouse, was too far and was not on neutral territory. On the other hand, the pope's suggestion that if the king of Castile were too ill to attend the meeting, he should send don Sancho, did not sit well with Alfonso; at that moment the issue of the succession was at stake, and although Alfonso had decided to name don Sancho his heir, knowing his son, the king was afraid he would dethrone him. Alfonso deemed it counterproductive to send his son to negotiate what as already non-negotiable. Alfonso may have been ill, but regarding the succession he had very clear ideas, and to safeguard them, he had even broken his promise to the king of France to submit the nomination to a royal Church tribunal of prelates and barons before Christmas 1277.[4] Nicholas III did not appreciate this, sending to Alfonso, according to Ballesteros, "one of the strongest letters found in the Vatican

[3] Ballesteros, *Alfonso X*, pp. 835–841; O'Callaghan, "The Cortes and Royal Taxation during the Reign of Alfonso X," *Traditio*, XXVII (1971), pp. 379–398, p. 391.

[4] Cf. F. Michel, ed., *Histoire de la guerre de Navarre par Guillaume Anelier*, in *Collection de documents inédits sur l'Histoire de France*, Paris, 1856, pp. 651–655.

archives."[5] Alfonso had other more pressing matters to attend to in those days of crisis in the South.

Regardless of his plans and his good will, however, due to illness Alfonso could not go out to meet the Muslim hordes, therefore entrusting the defense of Seville to Alfonso Fernández, who was defeated by the troops of Abû Yûsuf on August 3. The Muslims moved on to Jerez and Córdoba, which they also conquered on September 15 and October 30, respectively. In his Burgos retreat, Alfonso continued to receive bad news from the front, unable to do anything himself. In the spring of the following year (February 24, 1278) he was finally able to obtain a truce from the unstoppable North African Moors. In mid-March 1278, at great risk to his own life, Alfonso had himself transported to Valladolid where, as he said, the Virgin, before curing him, gave him a taste of death (April 17).[6] During the months of May and June 1278 Alfonso planned to celebrate a new Cortes in Segovia. The truce with the king of Granada and the return of Yûsuf to Morocco now allowed him a moment of respite that he would use to solve the most urgent and serious internal problems of the kingdom, the most important of them the succession.

Given the king's state of health, the royal advisors believed it was imperative to relieve him of part of his government duties. In fact, Alfonso took advantage of that free time to devote himself to his cultural activities, which increased considerably in these years.[7] According to the testimony of Fr. Gil de Zamora, tutor and advisor to don Sancho, it was in the Segovia Cortes when Alfonso finally decided to declare the young prince his heir and successor. That year in May, Sancho had turned 20 and "began to co-reign" with his father.[8] The

---

[5] The letter is dated at St. Peter's on November 29, 1278. The most important passages can be read in Ballesteros, *Alfonso X*, pp. 845–846. At that time, Alfonso was in Toledo on his way south to contain Yûsuf's invasion.

[6] A letter to the council of the Córdoba cathedral, dated at Peñafiel on March 24, 1278, confirms hat Alfonso was on his way south to fight back the invasion: "agora seré yo ayna en la tierra, si Dios quisiere" ["now I will be in the land, God willing"] (Biblioteca Capitular de Córdoba, in M. González Jiménez, *Diplomatario*, n. 436).

[7] Cf. Ballesteros, *Alfonso X*, pp. 853–855. Thanks to the Cortes notebooks, we know that new laws were drafted regarding usury by the Jews, ordering that interests should not go above "three times four" (12%) and other norms of conduct that applied to all subjects. There is also a rich correspondence on legal matters from this period.

[8] *Liber de preconiis civitatis numantine*, ed. F. Fita, in "Dos obra inéditas de Gil de Zamora," *BRAH*, 5 (1884), 146. Cf. Procter, *Curia*, p. 143; J. O'Callaghan, *Cortes of Castile-León*, pp. 25, 84.

CAX, sympathetic to don Sancho, is much more emphatic when stating that the matter of the successor's election was not even debated, but that Alfonso simply ordered the representatives to pay homage to don Sancho (*CAX*, chap. 68, pp. 219–220).

Don Sancho, however, did not receive the title of king, which could only be borne by one person. He did however receive extraordinary powers to decide on many matters, so that as a result of these Cortes, many royal diplomas say that he was "ruling in Castile and in León."[9] The documentation, therefore, reveals the absolute trust that Alfonso had put in don Sancho beginning with his nomination as successor. In his testament, when analyzing the treason of his son, Alfonso himself confirmed the extraordinary powers that he had granted him as heir.[10]

At the end of the Cortes, and following the acknowledgement of don Sancho as heir, the Haros, don Lope Díaz de Vizcaya, and don Lope Díaz de Haro, returned to Castile. This is confirmed by a letter from Alfonso to the Segovia City Council dated September 26, where their names appear as witnesses.[11] This quick return would seem to indicate that the reason for their departure was the frustration they felt at Alfonso's hesitation in naming don Sancho as successor. Once he did it, it would not have been difficult for Sancho to obtain the pardon for his allies so they could return to Castile.

2. *The Queen's Flight*

At the beginning of 1278 or during the Segovia Cortes, as Ballesteros holds, or after the Cortes, as others argue, one of the most embarrassing episodes of Alfonso's life took place: doña Violante, his wife, along with their two grandchildren, the Infantes de la Cerda, and doña Blanca, the children's mother, fled the court to seek refuge at the court of her brother, Pedro III of Aragón (1276–1285), imploring his

---

[9] There are indeed fourteen documents and diplomas from 1278–79 where the name of don Sancho appears as intervening in fiscal matters. He even managed to pronounce the sentence in three legal cases of individuals who had resorted to royal justice (texts in J.A. Bonachía Hernando, y J.A. Pardos Martínez, *Catálogo documental del Archivo Municipal de Burgos. Sección Histórica (931–1515)*, vol. I, Burgos, 1983.

[10] See the complete text of the testament in the Spanish version of this book, Apénd. VIII, p. 610.

[11] Cf. Ballesteros, *Alfonso X*, pp. 855–856.

protection.[12] It was well known in court circles that Violante preferred as successors the children of the late don Fernando rather than don Sancho, and that she never accepted her husband's change of the rules of succession. Hence the flight described in the *CAX* (chap. 68, pp. 219–220).[13]

It is not entirely clear why Violante took her grandchildren to Aragón and not France, especially since the mother was also with them, but it seems that the official nomination of Sancho as "eldest son and heir" had much to do with the queen's decision. The queen, who knew Sancho's temperament, must have deemed it dangerous for her grandchildren to remain in the court. Did she flee to protect them from a potential attack by her son Sancho, who would clearly feel threatened by the princes' candidacy since they had been previously declared heirs; or was it a ploy on the part of the queen to distance them from the court, and given the fact that Philip III's troops were at the border, to prevent them from being captured by the king of France and declared successors to the throne of Castile, thus seizing the throne from don Sancho, who had just been declared successor? We do not know, but it is safe to assume that a woman with the diplomatic and political experience of Violante, who knew well all the court intrigues, would not have resorted to such a radical decision had it not been that she feared for the life of her grandchildren or the political future of her son, whom she had raised more in contact with the court of Aragón than that of Castile.[14]

It is probable that (whether the flight took place before or after the Segovia Cortes), the queen would have expressed to her husband her opposition to the changes made two years earlier at the Burgos Cortes, leaving the kingdom to don Sancho, rather than to her grandson, don Alfonso de la Cerda, as had been stipulated thus far. Realizing now at the Segovia Cortes that the change was definitive and seeing how her husband confirmed and expanded his decision by conceding

---

[12] Cf. *Anales Toledanos III, ES*, XXIII, p. 76. Ballesteros, on the contrary, believes perhaps rightly that the flight must have happened during the Segovia Cortes (May–July 1278), hence the *Anales Toledanos* would be wrong about the month. Cf. O'Callaghan, *Cortes*, p. 84.

[13] The Aragonese historians and Muntaner himself speak of this unexpected flight of the queen. Cf. *Crónica*, chap. 40, pp. 90–91; and J. de Zurita, *Anales de la Corona de Aragón*, II, p. 12.

[14] On the temperament and personality of doña Violante, see R.P. Kinkade, "Violante of Aragón (1236–1300): An Historical Overview," *EH*, 2 (1992–1993), pp. 36–48.

even greater powers to don Sancho, doña Violante must have thought only of saving her grandchildren's lives. From what we know about the personalities of Alfonso and Violante, the dispute must have been unpleasant, hence Violante's decision to take her grandchildren away from Castile to protect them both from her son and husband.[15]

According to the *CAX*, in the flight of the queen also arose from a conspiracy by don Sancho and don Pedro de Aragón. The conspiracy went against the political interests of doña Violante and her grandchildren, for it consisted in making the two de la Cerda princes disappear from the political scene and preventing them from falling in the hands of the king of France, who still aspired to place one of his nephews on the throne of Castile:

> Concerning the negotiation of the queen's return, Prince Sancho's messengers spoke with King Pedro of Aragón saying that as soon as the Queen Violante had returned to Castile, the King of Aragón would order don Alfonso and don Fernando held as prisoners so that they could not be taken to France, nor could Prince Sancho face any obstacles because of them. King Pedro loved much his nephew Prince Sancho, and he sent to promise him that as soon as the queen went to Castile, he would fulfill what Prince Sancho was begging him to do. (*CAX*, chap. 71, p. 225)[16]

Besides this passage, which clearly refers to the periods of negotiation between don Sancho and don Pedro to make the queen return to Castile, Ballesteros, reproduces an entire series of letters between uncle and nephew where it becomes clear that in the months preceding the Segovia Cortes both were plotting regarding a matter of interest to both parties, but the matter itself is never explicitly mentioned. What is more, in one of the letters, don Pedro does not deem it appropriate to put the matter in writing, given the love he felt for his nephew, but rather entrusts the message to his sister, to transmit orally to her son,

---

[15] Jerónimo Zurita, the illustrious Aragonese commentator who knew both sides of the controversy, writes:
> ...the Queen of Castile, who was at the Segovia Cortes during the oath taken for Don Sancho, her son, feeling gravely that don Alfonso and don Fernando, her grandchildren, whom she said had the right of succession the throne of Castile and León, might be disowned, considering the great danger that could follow if they remained in Castile under the power of the prince, their uncle, who was taking over the entire government, decided to bring them to the kingdom of Aragón and go with them and with the princess doña Blanca, her daughter-in-law. (*Anales de la Corona de Aragón*, qtd. ed., II, p. 15)

[16] Cf. Ballesteros, *Alfonso X*, p. 862.

Sancho.[17] All of this means that the queen herself was not unaware of the conspiracy. In light of these events that would take place during don Sancho's period of rebellion, it seems difficult to admit that doña Violante would have withdrawn her support of don Sancho, even if for a brief time, to give it to her grandchildren. On the other hand, all the interest that Sancho would show in the return of his mother to Castile was perhaps compensation for her support in the conspiracy against the princes, his nephews.

I believe the text of the *CAX* quoted above clarifies the content of the letters, showing that the flight of the princes was undertaken to prevent their capture by the king of France and thus to prevent one of them from acceding to the throne of Castile.[18] Although according to the text of the *CAX* we cannot know if doña Violante was an accomplice in this plan or not, one of the letters makes it clear that she was aware of the arrangement between her son and her brother, because she served as their messenger. Of course, the plan to keep the children in don Pedro's custody worked, because the *CAX* itself confirms that, once the queen returned to Castile,

> [...] King Pedro of Aragón ordered seized don Alfonso and don Fernando, sons of Prince Fernando and doña Blanca, and they put them in the Castle of Játiva, where they were imprisoned during the whole lifetime of this King Pedro. Doña Blanca, mother of don Alfonso and don Fernando, as soon as she saw them imprisoned, spent a short time in Aragón at the monastery for ladies; afterward she departed from there and went to France. (*CAX*, chap. 71, p. 226)[19]

The presence of Blanca among the fugitives makes one think of a different explanation for the reasons of the flight. We know that Blanca, following Fernando's death, had repeatedly asked Alfonso to allow her to return to France with her two children, but the Castilian king was opposed to this for the simple reason that once the princes were at

---

[17] Cf. Ballesteros, *Alfonso X*, pp. 849–850.

[18] Muntaner dedicates a good portion of Chapter 40 of his *Crónica* to the agreement of mutual help between Pedro III and the prince don Sancho (pp. 91–92); but insisting that it was don Sancho who implored his protection, to which Sancho responded generously, but with conditions:

> Nephew, I have understood well what you have said, and I answer you that, if you want to be for me the one you should be and that I know, you can be certain that I will not be your opponent, as long as you do what I want, and that you make an oath about this and pay homage to me. (p. 91)

[19] This information is also confirmed by Jofré de Loaysa, *Crónica*, p. 9, and by the comments of the editor on pp. 112–114.

Philip III's court, they could be manipulated at will for Philip's political interests, which at the time were contrary to Alfonso's. Therefore, according to this hypothesis, the entourage would have planned, not doña Violante's flight with her grandchildren, but rather Blanca's, who expected to leave her children under the care of the king of Aragón and continue on to the court of her brother, Philip, as she would do later on.[20] Perhaps this is what is alluded to in the following passage of the *CAX*: "When King Alfonso found out how the queen and doña Blanca were gone, it grieved him. He ordered his advisors to watch the roads and to not let them pass or go out of the kingdom, and because of these letters and this order their journey was hindered" (*CAX*, chap. 68, p. 219).

Some historians, supporters of the queen's position, attribute the queen's flight to the fact that Alfonso did not treat her with the due respect, hence don Pedro had to enter Castile with his troops and escort his sister and grandchildren to Aragón.[21] It is unclear how much of this is true, but the copious correspondence between Alfonso X and Pedro III, and between the latter and his sister, does not confirm such a foray, other than the meeting between Violante and Pedro, at Violante's request, planned for the Monastery of Santa María de la Huerta, on the border of Soria, which never took place. What is clear is that the queen disagreed with her husband on the matter of succession, supporting her grandchildren, although later, when Alfonso too would favor them, Violante would then support her son Sancho.

Recent studies of Alfonso's illnesses and the consequences for his mental stability have led scholars to think, in line with the Catalan historian, that the reason for the queen's flight was not so much political as personal, that is the possible break up of her marriage to Alfonso as a result of his erratic and unpleasant behavior caused by the cancer that was undermining him.[22] That they had trouble in their marriage

---

[20] Cf. G. de Nangis, *Gesta Philippi Tertii*, en *Recueil des historiens des Gaules et de la France*, ed. E. Martin Bouquet et alii, 24 vols., Paris: Academie des Inscriptions et Belles Lettres, 1738–1904, vol. 20, pp. 498–499.

[21] *Crònica general de Pere III el Ceremoniòs, dita comunament Crònica de Sant Joan de la Penya*, ed. A.J. Soberans Lleó, Barcelona: Alpha, 1961, chap. 36, pp. 130–131). In his *Crónica*, chap. 40, p. 90, Muntaner says something similar.

[22] O'Callaghan writes: "It would seem that Alfonso X, now apparently suffering from a cancerous growth in his head, was becoming increasingly irritable and so estranged his wife that she returned to her native Aragón, where she remained for about a year and a half. This event was another sign that the king's illness was having an untoward effect on his behavior and his relations with the closest members of

around this time and in connection with the problems of succession can be clearly gleaned from the *CAX*, which narrates the efforts of don Sancho to reconcile his parents and make his mother return to Castile, something he achieved the following year (July 1279) after much negotiation and payment to the king of Aragón for all expenses incurred by doña Violante, plus "something" for her.[23] But I do not believe that the marital problems had anything to do directly with the flight, which seems to have been caused by the desire to save her grandchildren and the throne of her son.

Whatever the cause of the flight, for Alfonso, that sudden, semi-clandestine departure of his wife from the kingdom was an unexpected humiliation and, undoubtedly, a cause for profound irritation. The *CAX* which erroneously dates the flight in 1276 during the sojourn of the kings at Segovia, says: "When King Alfonso found out how the queen and doña Blanca were gone, it grieved him. He ordered the advisors to watch the roads and to not let them pass or go out of the kingdom, and because of these letters and this order their journey was hindered" (*CAX*, chap. 68, p. 219). Yet no one did anything to stop them. On the contrary, there is evidence that they were helped by Church officials, such as the bishop of Segovia, don Rodrigo Tello, who accompanied the fugitives to Aragón. Don Tello would not have had it easy when returning to his seat. He instead prudently remained in Aragón where, following Alfonso's death, he became Archbishop of Tarragona (1289).[24]

This complicity of the militia of the councils and the clergy in the queen's flight is a clear sign that Alfonso was losing his authority, perhaps another element that may have influenced his decision to execute his brother don Fadrique and Simón Ruiz de los Cameros. We know Alfonso reacted severely when he felt his royal authority was being threatened, as we shall soon see in another bloody incident. In fact, the

---

his family" (*The Learned King*, p. 245). Also Dr. Torres, in his psychological essay on Alfonso, points to the difficulties in living with people with an introverted personality, given to sudden anger attacks and unexpected mood changes ("Rasgos médico-psicológicos," pp. 133–134).

[23] See the text of the *CAX* further on, p. 11. The text there alludes to the fact that Alfonso, when he discovered the flight, in a moment of exasperation confiscated the property Violante owned in Castile. Therefore, before returning to Castile, she wanted to make sure she would not be effectively destitute (cf. chap. 14, pp. 58–59).

[24] Cf. Mondéjar, *Memorias*, p. 234; G. González Dávila, *Teatro eclesiástico de las iglesias metropolitanas y catedrales de los reinos de las dos Castillas*, 3 vols., Madrid, 1645–650, III, p. 225; but see Ballesteros, *Alfonso X*, pp. 864–865.

CAX narrates the executions immediately following the flight of the queen. According to this theory, Alfonso needed to make an unusual gesture so that his subjects would know who still was in command of the kingdom. These violent and uncontrolled, yet quite human actions would characterize Alfonso X's immature and introverted personality, according to Dr. Torres.[25]

In any event, as Zurita informs us, Alfonso also acted in the diplomatic sphere, sending embassies and letters to don Pedro asking him to do what was necessary so that his wife would return to Castile as soon as possible, promising to return all property and goods she possessed there.[26] We can therefore conclude that the return of the queen was not a pleasant surprise for Alfonso, prepared secretly by his son, although actively promoted by don Sancho.

Before returning to Castile, Violante asked her brother to allow her two grandchildren to return with her, but the king of Aragón refused categorically giving no explanation.[27] We could assume he wanted to keep them hostage for the purposes of his political struggle with Sancho of Castile and Philip of France. Don Pedro also had political ambitions that his brother-in-law, the king of France, could either thwart or further. Pedro had recently married Constance of Hohenstaufen, daughter of Manfred, the illegitimate son of Frederick II. The Staufen children that remained in Italy, including Manfred, were all in conflict with Charles of Anjou, who had dethroned them, proclaiming himself sovereign of the two Sicilies. Charles was uncle by blood of Philip III of France, and it is certain that Constance was also doing everything in her power to prevent the king of France from imposing on Aragón and Castile an Anjou government. Pedro III, brother of the king of France's wife, therefore, had several reasons to keep the two de la Cerda princes in his control, maintaining the balance of power between various political forces: the king of Castile and his successor, don Sancho, and the king of France and his uncle, Charles of Anjou. A letter from don Pedro to Blanca, mother of the princes, makes it clear that it was she who requested the king of Aragón to continue protecting the children, meaning that he should not allow them to be taken to Castile, as their grandmother wanted, nor to France, as Blanca's

---

[25] "Rasgos médico-psicológicos," p. 134.
[26] Cf. Ballesteros, *Alfonso X*, pp. 864–865 and pp. 891–892.
[27] Thanks to don Pedro's letter dated June 19, 1279, we know the reasons: the pact with don Sancho to not release them (text in *MHE*, II, p. 34).

brother did. Clearly, the king of Aragón did not want to do otherwise, as the letter openly states.[28]

3. *The Siege of Algeciras and the Return of the Queen*

During the meetings of the Segovia Cortes, another very important matter was discussed, namely, the defense of the realm against the North African Moors who were attacking the south and always a threat. Alfonso proposed at the Cortes that, to avoid the errors of the past, the Strait be blocked and Algeciras be put under siege, and "[t]hose who were there with King Alfonso told him that it was right, and for this they gave him two of the tributes from all of the kingdoms" (*CAX*, chap. 69, p. 221).[29]

Alfonso left Segovia for the south, stopping at Toledo for the rest of that year and the first months of 1279. From Toledo he coordinated the preparations of the southern defense, including the construction of ships in the shipyards of Seville and other war machines to defend or take cities by force. While in Toledo he also launched a large campaign to raise troops and funds, entrusting his son don Sancho with a tour of the cities of Castile for the purpose of "recruiting all the noblemen and councils of the land." He also issued many legal rules and granted privileges to institutions and individuals.[30] Part of the time he used to write letters, including one to his brother-in-law, Pedro of Aragón, requesting his help to fight the invaders.[31]

With no few sacrifices on the part of everyone, on August 28, 1278, the Christian forces under the leadership of the royal captain Pedro Martínez de Fe, who had already led the unsuccessful attack on Salé, attacked Algeciras by sea, while other contingents led by don Pedro

---

[28] In Ballesteros, *Alfonso X*, p. 870. In another document that Ballesteros calls the "draft" of the letter, don Pedro clearly told doña Blanca that he could no longer prevent his sister from returning to her "man," but that he would do everything possible to avoid that the children would remain in her care (ib., p. 871).

[29] The *CAX* tells of the decisions made at the Cortes and the preparations for the attack on Algeciras in the same chap. 69, pp. 221–222; but it mistakenly dates those events in the year 1277. The date (August 6, 1278) and the strategy of besieging Algeciras to block access through the Strait is confirmed by the *Rawd al Qirtas* (in Huici, II, p. 598; and cf. Ballesteros, *Alfonso X*, p. 868).

[30] Among other things, he ruled over matters as detailed as insults and he banned vulgar, offensive, and denigrating language (cf. Ballesteros, p. 882).

[31] The correspondence of this period between Alfonso and don Pedro de Aragón is discussed by Ballesteros, *Alfonso X*, pp. 876–877.

with the consent and perhaps the active participation of the king of Granada, also attacked it by land. Some months later (February 27, 1279), the fort was completely surrounded by Christian troops.[32]

At the beginning of May, Alfonso left Toledo, arriving in Córdoba on the 14 of the month. He stayed there until the end of June, at which time we find him in Seville (where on the 28th he issued a privilege to the clergy of Córdoba). Towards the end of the year, the Christian forces began to experience difficulties due to lack of supplies. The *CAX* describes the situation in dramatic terms:

> [...] Those of the army fulfilled the time for which they were paid in their contracts. Also, those at sea who were with the fleet safeguarding the sea during all of winter spent many days in which they went unpaid; and all of those at sea and on land sent to tell King Alfonso to send them something so that they could stay there. (*CAX*, chap. 72, p. 227)

The money Alfonso had allocated for the defense, however, did not arrive, and the king had to resort to bankers in Seville to obtain the necessary funds to keep up the attack. Alfonso gathered all he could, but all efforts were in vain: hunger and illnesses caused many deaths daily (*CAX*, chap. 72, pp. 227–231). The Christians, despite knowing that conditions inside the attacked city were even worse,[33] had to lift the siege, forced by an attack of 72 ships sent by the emir of Tangiers, Abû Ya'qûb, when he found out about the deplorable state of both warring parties. Ya'qûb's attack took place July 19, 1279 and the defeat of the Chrisitans, who had continued the attack with great sacrifices for almost a year, happened six days later, on July 25.

The chronicler of the *CAX*, who knew of oral versions of the events and often mentions also an "escripto" (document), has left us a good narrative of the final battle, or rather, of the precipitous withdrawal of the Christian troops when Abû Ya'qûb launched the naval assault.

---

[32] The description of the preparations and the attack in the *CAX* (chap. 70, pp. 223–224) coincides essentially with the narrative of the *Rawd al-Qirtas*, but is wrong about the date. It is also incorrect in placing Alfonso in Seville, when he was still in Toledo. The description of the attack and its consequences in the narrative of the Muslim historian is a lot more flowery than the sparse narrative of *CAX*, although it is just as accurate (in Huici, II, p. 599).

[33] "Notwithstanding that those of the army and the fleet were very stricken by disease and that they were surviving on reduced wages and rations, the Moors who were in the city of Algeciras had used up and eaten all of the bread they had, and they had reached such a state of hunger that they were falling dead in the streets of the city." (*CAX*, chap. 72, p. 228).

According to the narrator, prince don Pedro ordered the siege lifted and retreated to Jerez, abandoning all remaining war supplies.[34] Once again, Alfonso, despite all preparations, must have felt frustrated and incapable of defeating the invaders. He had no alternative but to request a new truce from Yûsuf, which would allow him to organize his defenses. But in view of the general unrest among the nobility and the people, any new request for help would find serious resistance. For Alfonso and his dedicated warriors it was an unprecedented catastrophe.

We can think that deep down, at the bottom of this military disaster, was an issue of poor planning or bad government, perhaps a result of "co-reigning", where the right hand does not know what the left one is doing. But it was not so. If there was any of this, it should only be considered a minimal contributor to the disaster of the Christian troops. Alfonso's plan for the attack was impeccable. The failure came from an unexpected direction. The defeat at Algeciras coincided with the return of doña Violante to Castile. This event was initially a cause of great joy for the distressed Alfonso, but only because he did not know what was behind the return of the queen. Happiness must have turned into anger and despair when Alfonso realized the price he had paid for that desired reunion with his spouse. Alfonso was completely in the dark regarding how his son Sancho had managed to obtain the return of his mother. The *CAX* insists that during the siege of Algeciras, don Sancho continued in Castile, doing everything possible so that his mother would return: "[...] Prince Sancho made an effort during that time so that his mother, the queen, might return to the kingdom. He was not doing this without his father's order, and he sent his very insistent letters to his mother, the queen, and King Pedro of Aragón, his uncle and the queen's brother, so that the queen might return to Castile" (*CAX*, chap. 71, p. 225).

Obviously the absence of the queen damaged the cause of the succession, otherwise it is hard to understand why don Sancho was so interested in arranging the secret return of his mother. The *CAX* does not mention the Infantes de la Cerda, but we can be sure that they were the main motive for don Sancho's interest in Violante's return:

---

[34] Cf. *CAX*, chap. 72, pp. 230–231, which contains very detailed descriptions; Ibn Abi Zar, *Rawd al-Quirtas*, II, p. 602 and Ibn-Khaldun, *Histoire des rois chrétiens de l'Espagne*, trans. R. Dozy, *Recherches sur l'histoire et la littérature de l'Espagne pendant le Moyen Age*, 2nd ed., Leiden, 1860, IV, pp. 101–103.

Concerning the negotiation of the queen's return, Prince Sancho's messengers spoke with King Pedro of Aragón saying that as soon as Queen Violante had returned to Castile, the King of Aragón would order don Alfonso and don Fernando held as prisoners so that they could not be taken to France, nor could Prince Sancho face any obstacles because of them. King Pedro loved much his nephew Prince Sancho, and he sent to promise him that as soon as the queen went to Castile, he would fulfill what Prince Sancho was begging him to do. (*CAX*, chap. 71, p. 225)

Don Pedro must have been happy about the request of the nephew, for he knew now that the Infantes de la Cerda had no claim over Castile and were entirely under his control. This was a great gain in his negotiations with Philip of France. What is less clear is what the *CAX* says regarding the excessive demands that Violante made as condition for her return to Castile:

When the queen saw the messengers and the letters that her son Prince Sancho was sending King Pedro and also the assurances that her brother, King Pedro, was giving him concerning this, she said she could not leave Aragón nor go to Castile until they paid a great amount of money that she owed in Aragón–this she had spent during the two years that she had been there–and also that they should give her something with which to go. So Prince Sancho, in order to bring her to Castile, considered how that money might be paid. In Castile and León there was a Jew, a collector of the king's rents, whose name was don Zag de la Malea. The sum that this Jew and the others who went with him collected was sent to the frontier for the maintenance of the army and fleet that were at Algeciras. When Prince Sancho learned how this don Zag had a great amount of *maravedís* to send, he sent for him and ordered don Zag to give the money to him so that the prince could give it to his mother, the queen, by means of which she might come to Aragón. So the Jew gave the *maravedís* to him, and Prince Sancho immediately sent them to his mother, the queen, and she then came to Castile. (*CAX*, chap. 71, pp. 225–26)[35]

It is hard to understand how doña Violante could have demanded from Castile payment of the expenses of her stay at the court of her brother,

---

[35] The *CAX* continues:
After she had come, King Pedro of Aragón ordered seized don Alfonso and don Fernando, sons of Prince Fernando and doña Blanca, and they put them in the Castle of Játiva, where they were imprisoned during the whole lifetime of this King Pedro. Doña Blanca, mother of don Alfonso and don Fernando, as soon as she saw them imprisoned, spent a short time in Aragón at the monastery for ladies; afterward she departed from there and went to France. (*CAX*, chap. 71, p. 226)

but it is even harder to understand how she would have demanded something for her "with which she might come to Aragón." Of course her brother did not demand any payment, and in a letter sent approving her return, don Pedro told her she could stay as long as she wanted in the kingdom, although he also added that he thought it more useful and honorable for her to return to Castile to her husband.[36] Why did Violante make these demands? Did she not have enough with what she had access to in the Castilian court where she was queen? The greed of her ancestors is well known, but we cannot imagine that in those moments of crisis in the kingdom, doña Violante would demand extraordinary amounts for her personal use. For her part, the irresponsibility of don Sancho in forcing Alfonso's treasurer to surrender the monies destined for the Algeciras campaign reveals to what extent he was thinking more about his succession, which he felt was at risk, than about the integrity of the kingdom. His father never forgave him such intervention. On the other hand, it seems fairly clear that Sancho's exaggerated interest in the return of his mother was not based on maternal affection or the desire to bring her back to his father, but rather on the fact that he needed her as support to inherit the crown. With the queen on his side, it would be much harder for his father to change his mind again. In fact, the venal doña Violante switched over to Sancho's side (possibly for good) and distinguished herself for her pro-Sancho activism in Alfonso's deposition. Doña Violante, probably accompanied by her son, returned to Castile at the end of July 1279, where according to the *CAX*, "The queen and the Prince Sancho went through the cities of Castile carrying out justice" (*CAX*, chap. 71, p. 226).

The *CAX* does not speak of Alfonso X's reaction. But we can imagine it, as the events will prove soon enough. The return of the queen for the defeat at Algeciras! And all that such a defeat entailed. It is not surprising that Alfonso, in his son Sancho's opinion, would go mad. It was understandable.

---

[36] Letter dated June 19, 1279 from Valencia, in Ballesteros, *Alfonso X*, pp. 891–892. It is in this same letter that he says he is willing to comply with her wishes, except in the matter of taking her grandchildren with her, because they were to remain in Aragón for the time being, as we know.

4. *New Initiatives against the North African Moors*

As we suggested above, the loss of Algeciras renewed the danger of losing many of the territories in the south. Alfonso therefore had no choice but to agree on a truce with Ibn Yûsuf, as the *CAX* informs us: "Prince Pedro and those of the army went to Seville. As soon as King Alfonso learned of the destruction of his fleet and saw his men coming in that fashion, he was very grieved by it. Realizing that he could not obtain that city nor remove from this side of the sea Aben Yuzaf's might, he looked for a way to reconcile himself with this Aben Yuzaf so that he could wage war on the King of Grenada. And King Alfonso and King Aben Yuzaf made their agreement together and remained in truce and peace for a while" (*CAX*, chap. 72, p. 231)

The *CAX* does not explain what led the Moroccan king to accept the truce, when in reality he could have won the battle. However, we know through the *Rawd al-Qirtas* that he too had good reason to seek an alliance with the king of Castile, because the Moorish king of Granada, who had recently taken control Málaga after fighting for it for many years, had refused to grant it to Abû Ya'qûb, the liberator of Algeciras. This conflict between the two leaders was used by Alfonso to his advantage because it gave him the opportunity to take revenge on the king of Granada for having called the North Africans to the peninsula. Alfonso allied himself with his enemy Abû Ya'qûb to punish the king of Granada and take control of his dear Málaga.

Between October 14 and 20, 1279, Alfonso traveled to Badajoz to meet his grandson, don Dinis, an 18 year-old who had acceded to the throne of Portugal on February 16 of that year, when his father, Alfonso III, died. The meeting was to be held at Elvas, "a town in the kingdom of Portugal that is three leagues from Badajoz" (*CAX*, chap. 73, p. 233).[37] The reason for the meeting apparently had to do with the fact that the young king did not agree with his mother, Beatriz, Alfonso X's most beloved daughter, who had taken control of the regency council after her husband's death. It was probably doña Beatriz who requested the intervention of Alfonso, who was much admired and respected by her son. Don Dinis, therefore, "suspecting that King Alfonso wanted to place him under the authority of this

---

[37] There's good reason to think that this meeting did not happen until February 1280, as Ballesteros argues (*Alfonso X*, p. 912).

mother, Queen Beatriz, and by which he was not pleased", refused to come to Badajoz to meet his grandfather and instead went to Lisbon. When King Alfonso learned that his grandson the King of Portugal did not wish to receive him, he returned to Seville; and Prince Sancho and his brothers returned to Castile to prepare their men to go with the army to the frontier. (*CAX*, chap. 73, p. 233)

While Alfonso was in Elvas, awaiting the return of his grandson, he called his brother Manuel and his sons, the princes don Sancho, don Pedro, don Juan, and don Jaime, to inform them of the agreement with Abû Ya'qûb, requesting them to recruit new forces to fight the king of Granada, whom he blamed for the Algeciras disaster, for "he wanted to return to the war with the King of Granada so that he could serve God and regain this land that the Moors held on this side of the sea. King Alfonso immediately called up all of his armies so that they might go with him to Córdoba in order to enter the *vega* of Granada. He also ordered Prince Sancho to return to Castile to draw out all of his armies, including those of noble descent as well as his advisors, so that they might all arrive at the frontier in order to invade the Vega of Granada to cut the wheat" (*CAX*, chap. 73, pp. 232–233). So great was his desire to topple the Moorish traitor that Alfonso also sought very actively the help of his brother-in-law, Pedro de Aragón.[38]

Don Pedro was indeed interested in keeping the integrity of Castile's territories in the South because of the repercussions that the hostile presence of Muslims in his immediate borders would mean for his own lands. So he promptly replied to Alfonso from Valencia with a long and very friendly letter dated December 4, 1279, where he proposed an interview to be held between Ariza and Huerta on the day of St. John the Baptist, June 24, of the following year. A few days later (December 20), Alfonso also wrote to Sancho, announcing the date of the meeting with the king of Aragón and inviting him to attend.[39]

In the first weeks of May, Alfonso moved to Córdoba, where he would establish the general garrison, so to speak, of his Granada campaign. The chronicler gives many details of the preparations, attributing

---

[38] See his request for help in the letter he wrote to don Pedro III on October 3, 1279 in Ballesteros, *Alfonso X*, p. 907.

[39] The text of don Pedro's response to Alfonso in Ballesteros, *Alfonso X*, pp. 910–911. The meeting, however, could not take place on the appointed date because the war against the king of Granada had begun exactly two days before.

to don Sancho both the recruitment of troops and the planning and combat strategy (*CAX*, chap. 74, pp. 234–237).

Thus Don Sancho was at the head of the Christian troops on their way to Alcalá de Benzayde, near where they arrived on June 22, 1280. Upon arriving at "a Moorish castle named Moclín, which is two leagues from Alcalá," the Christian troops stopped to gather hay for the horses and wood for the campfire. The man in charge of protecting the provisioners was the Master of the Order of Santiago, don Gonzalo Ruiz Girón. Suddenly, one hundred Moorish fighters appeared; when he confronted them, the Moors pretended to flee, leading the pursuing Christians into a disastrous trap manned by more than 1000 Moorish soldiers. Gonzalo himself died, and "[t]hey slew on that day one thousand eight hundred knights and foot soldiers, and most of the friars of the Order of Santiago; and they captured their knights and many others" (*CAX*, chap. 74, p. 235).

This unexpected adversity generated panic among the troops, who attempted to desert. But don Sancho, the historian tells us, "took in his hand a javelin and went out on a horse and passed through all the camp. He ordered all the men to be calm" (*CAX*, chap. 74, p. 235). After the feast of St. John, the Christian army attacked Moclín and moved on to Granada: "The next day, Thursday ["*martes*" in the original] Prince Don Sancho went out from there with all his people and set out for the castle Moclín. From there he set out for the *vega*, and he approached Granada, burning wheat and laying waste, and tearing down all that he found. As soon as the entire *vega* had been devastated, Prince Don Sancho went back with all of his army to Jaén, and from there to his father the king in Córdoba. The way Prince Don Sancho had managed the army so well pleased the king greatly. The king and his sons with him moved from Córdoba and went to Seville, and Prince Sancho lodged in San Francisco" (*CAX*, chap. 74, p. 235).[40]

The expedition to punish the king of Granada therefore had the desired effect, but Alfonso, as a result of the destruction of his naval fleet the year before and now the loss of the Master of Santiago and other knights of Order (the *CAX* quotes the loss as 2,800), decided to dissolve the Order of Santa María de España, which he himself had

---

[40] The *Anales Toledanos III* confirm the historian's statement: "That thanks to the efforts of don Sancho, the Moors were defeated at the gates of Granada. So many died that they could not be counted" (sect. 67).

founded at the beginning of the seventies with the name Orden de la Estrella (Order of the Star), and integrate it to the Order of Santiago.[41] The dissolution of this Order, which had been founded as a marine force for the defense of the Strait, also meant the end of Alfonso's dream to create a powerful navy that could confront that of the Muslims.

5. *Don Çag de la Meleha*

During the anti-Moorish offensive, Alfonso suffered another attack in his eye, which, as noted in the *CAX*, he would eventually lose. This time the attack was so strong that the eye popped out of its orbit, rendering him unable to participate in the battle. The illness must have been much more serious than what is recorded in the *CAX*, because he was ill in Cordoba until the middle of August, when he was finally able to travel to Seville.

In the recent campaign to punish the king of Granada, don Sancho had distinguished himself in battle like a real hero despite his youth, which much pleased his father. But around this time too Alfonso must have discovered the real reason that the funds designated for the attack on Algeciras never arrived at their destination. Hence, despite the recent heroism of Sancho, the king was very dissatisfied and angry at his son for arranging the payment of such a huge sum to persuade doña Violante to return to Castile. This caused the loss of Algeciras and many political disasters deriving from it. Alfonso had not forgotten Sancho's misdeed, and he must have now been furious when another key yet innocent figure in the case of don Sancho's abuse of power arrived in Seville. This figure was Alfonso's *almojarife mayor* or senior treasurer, don Çag (Isaac) de la Meleha, the son of another distinguished treasurer of Alfonso's, don Zulemán (or Salomon) ben Sadoq.

We do not know what led Alfonso to attempt to settle accounts with his son at such an ill-timed moment. Perhaps it was don Çag's presence in Seville or perhaps Sancho's recent military victory had stirred jealousy in Alfonso, who, in ill health, feared the loss of his crown. It could also have been his sense of justice, not wanting to leave any

---

[41] Cf. J. Torres Fontes, "La Orden de Santa María de España," in *Miscelánea Medieval Murciana*, 3 (1977), pp. 75–118, esp. pp. 94–95. The knights of Santa María de España appear with their colorful clothes and insignia in several *cantigas*.

crime unpunished. We do not know, but the fact is that he wanted to teach don Sancho a lesson ("In order to punish Prince Don Sancho for this annoyance he had done him" [*CAX*, pp. 235–236].)

The occasion chosen to execute such cruel punishment seems to have been a bad one in terms of timing, because it was not advisable at a moment when don Sancho was acquiring popularity as a warrior and merited praise, not punishment. Besides distinguishing himself in combat, the young prince had worked tirelessly to recruit troops and funds, sometimes using threats and somewhat extreme methods to satisfy the desires of his father. The attack against Granada, despite the loss of many lives, had had the expected positive results: the devastation of the Vega of Granada. Ignoring all this, at the beginning of September 1280, Alfonso had all the Jewish tax collectors arrested. It seems that, before this detention order, he had already stripped don Çag de la Meleha of his title of treasurer and had confiscated all his goods. Now, when don Çag was in Seville, Alfonso had him arrested and executed in the residence where don Sancho was staying. This is the narrative in the *CAX*:

> The king and his sons with him moved from Córdoba and went to Seville, and Prince Sancho lodged in San Francisco. The king had the Jews, who were collectors of rent, arrested, including the greatest of them, don Zag de la Malea—who had been ordered to bring succor at the siege of Algeciras and had not done so. The misappropriation of the funds don Zag de la Malea collected that he had given to Prince Don Sancho—who was here in the land—to give to Queen Doña Violante, his mother, when he brought her from Aragón to Castile, did not please his father the king. In order to punish Prince Don Sancho for this annoyance he had done him, the king commanded this don Zag de la Malea be taken to San Francisco, where the Prince Don Sancho was residing with all of his brothers, and that they drag don Zag up to the outskirts. As soon as Prince Don Sancho found this out, he wanted to go forth and take him, but those who were with him did not agree to it. But Prince Sancho remained in great belligerence against the king because of the death of this Jew, and he believed that the king had done it all on account of the service don Zag had rendered him. (*CAX*, chap. 74, pp. 235–236)[42]

---

[42] Don Çag's execution must have occurred at the end of September 1280. Cf. Ballesteros, *Alfonso X*, pp. 918–919. The episode has been much discussed by all historians of Spanish Jews in the Middle Ages. Cf. Y. Baer, *A History of the Jews in Christian Spain*, 2 vols., Philadelphia: Jewish Publication Society, 1966; vol. I, pp. 124–130; D.E. Carpentier, *Alfonso X and the Jews: An Edition and Commentary on Siete Partidas 7.24* "De los judíos," Berkeley: University of California, 1986.

What was the motive for the execution? To have delivered to don Sancho the collected monies without the king's consent. Disobeying the king's command in fiscal affairs, especially in such critical moments, was a crime punishable by death. Sancho, however took the execution of don Çag as a personal affront, and wanted to oppose his father's decision. But the advisors and his brothers, who were there with him in San Francisco, warned that that was not the most appropriate moment to challenge his father, as he was likely to lose. However, this execution was the straw that broke the camel's back in the conflict between father and son. The public execution of such a distinguished figure of the court was not so much a punishment of don Çag's disobedience as a lesson for Sancho and his supporters about who still held power.[43]

Meanwhile, Alfonso's coffers were empty and he was deeply in debt to the bankers and merchants of Seville, so he was forced to take drastic measures to collect new funds. He therefore had all the Jews in the country arrested without cause and forced them to pay 12,000 *maravedís* as ransom.[44] The *CAX* mixes this information with other news around Alfonso's desire to leave one of his kingdoms to his de la Cerda grandchildren, noting that Alfonso wanted to keep both pieces of news secret in order not to further irritate his son Sancho. This does not make much sense, since the letters of detention and ransom were disseminated widely throughout Castile.

6. *The* Memoriale Secretum *and International Politics*

If the military and economic situation of the kingdom was serious as a result of the Moorish victories and the insubordination of the king of Granada, the state of international relations was worse, because Alfonso, due to internal politics, had had to abandon all efforts in that area.

---

[43] J.M. Nieto Soria has advanced the theory that Alfonso took such a drastic measure, among other reasons, because he had lost his trust and affection for don Çag after he established links with, and began to "rely more and more with the support of, another family of Jewish tax-collectors and money-lenders, the Abenxuxén" ("Los judíos de Toledo en sus relaciones financieras con la monarquía y la Iglesia [1252–1312]," *Sefarad*, XLI (1981), 7.

[44] *CAX*, chap. 74, pp. 236–237. Cf. Baer, *A History of the Jews*, I, pp. 124–130; the amount of the ransom, 4,380,000 maravedís, was more than double the annual tribute paid by Jews in Castile. Cf. O'Callaghan, *The Learned King*, p. 342, note 60.

As if the political and military crisis were not enough, in May 1279, while he was in Córdoba, bishop Pietro de Rieti, messenger of Pope Nicholas III (1277–1280), appeared at the court and delivered a papal document known as the *Memoriale secretum*, which listed a number of complaints lodged by the Peninsular church hierarchy, especially by the archbishop of Santiago, don Gonzalo García, and the bishop of León, don Martín Fernández, who had been exiled by Alfonso. The seven very detailed parts of the document dealt mainly with the unbearable economic burdens that Alfonso had imposed on the churches, and above all, with his intervention in Church elections.[45] The pope's complaints were very serious and, although they were mostly related to matters of Church jurisdiction (6 of them), the seventh had to do with the oppression of his subjects, including among them several bishops and the clergy in general.[46]

Couched in the dry language of papal diplomacy, the *Memoriale secretum* reveals the long history of complaints of the Peninsular Church hierarchy against Alfonso, including interference and abuse in Church matters, appointment of bishops, preservation of the vacant seats on the part of the king in order to collect their rent, etc., and above all the inappropriate collection of taxes known as *gravamina* (*media*, *tercia*, and *vicesima*). This topic had already been debated and partly resolved at the 1272 Burgos Cortes, when the prelates of the kingdom, according to the *CAX*, sided with the nobles and even recommended they defect as a way to obtain what they wanted from Alfonso. This advice amounted to an act of subversion, which Alfonso chose not to punish.[47] On that occasion, given the urgency of the matter and despite the obvious hostility of the prelates, in order to appear impartial towards them, Alfonso named a commission of lay people led by doña Violante and of members of the clergy led by don

---

[45] J. Gay, *Les Registres de Nicholas III (1277–1280)*, Paris: Bibliothèque des Écoles Françaises d'Athènes et de Rome, 1898–1932, pp. 338–340, 341–344, nos. 739–741, 743 (text of the *Memoriale*). The topics of each of the chapters were: 1. The *tercias*; 2. The custody of vacant churches and monasteries; 3. The oppression of the archbishop of Compostela; 4. The oppression of the bishop of León; 5. The complaints of the prelates; 6. Ecclesiastic freedoms in Portugal; 7. The oppression of the subjects.

[46] Cf. P. Linehan, *Spanish Church and the Papacy*, pp. 209, 217–220; and his articles "The 'Gravamina' of the Castilian Church in 1262–1263," *Economic History Review*, LXXXV (1970), 730–754; and "The Spanish Church Revisited," pp. 141–147; J.F. O'Callaghan, "Alfonso X and the Castilian Church," *Thought: A Review of Culture and Ideas*, 60 (1985), 417–429.

[47] See above chap. 9, pp. 328–333.

Sancho, archbishop of Toledo and brother of the queen, "[…] for all of them to examine the demands those prelates were making, and that whatever they found that he had to correct, he should compensate them for it, and likewise, they should amend that for which they were at fault with him. Concerning their demands, he said he would grant those things that were granted to them during the time of the king whence he came" (*CAX*, chap. 26, p. 104). The matter was discussed again after the nomination of don Sancho as successor, in a meeting in Salamanca in 1279. Naturally, the events that followed—the defection and rebellion of the nobles, supported by the clergy—forced Alfonso to break his word regarding the recommendations of the commission. This and the successive demands of the king to refinance his quest for the Empire led the prelates to raise new complaints with the pope, hence the *Memoriale*.

Alfonso's relations with the Church of Castile-León had been quite strained since the king formulated the Ghibelline notion of king and kingdom, according to which the clergy, as other social strata, was simply an instrument the king could use at any moment to rule more effectively.[48] The presence of the bishops and abbots and many religious men at the court meant more than just picking the best and most learned men of his kingdom for the tasks of the chancellery and the *scriptorium*. Alfonso also employed Church officials and civil servants in lay matters, such as the *repartimientos* or land grants following the conquest of new territories. But it was not so much the use or abuse of the best Church officials in the business of the court, which deprived the dioceses sometimes for years of their invaluable pastors, which led the Castilian Church to complain to the pope, but rather the abuses in taxation.

The levying of taxes gave rise to such complaints to the pope because over the past 20 years, popes had often authorized such taxes; this was the case for example of the *décima*, approved by Clement IV in 1265 and renewed by Gregory X after his meeting with Alfonso at Beaucaire. In this matter, regardless of the complaints of the Peninsular church, popes had agreed more with Alfonso than with their own clergy. At the papal court of the previous eleven popes (1252–1294), it

---

[48] J.M. Nieto Soria, *Las relaciones monarquía-episcopado*, pp. 78–120; P. Linehan, *The Spanish Church and the Papacy*, esp. chap. 9; J.F. O'Callaghan, "Alfonso X and the Castilian Church," *Thought*, 60 (1985), 417–429.

was well known that the Church of Castile-León had been economically squeezed by papal tax-collectors and royal officials under the pretext of a wider vision of international politics than the short-term view of unruly Castilian bishops and abbots could begin to see. A good part of such papal "international politics" was shrouded under the pretence of the need to fight the Muslim infidels at home, and had been carried out to keep Alfonso happy. In fact, we know that despite everything, Alfonso had enjoyed better relations with the popes than with the vast majority of his own bishops.[49]

But now, suddenly, Nicholas III, the simoniac pope whom Dante placed writhing in the Eight Circle of Hell (*Inferno*, XIX, 70), wanted to change things. He wanted to defend the *"libertas Ecclesiae"* (freedom of the Church), showing himself inflexible with the Castilian king not only in matters of Church discipline, but also in fiscal policy.[50] The pope's instructions to the delegate to present the document and desires of the pope to the Castilian king in a certain order and little by little were extremely detailed, a true example of papal diplomatic finesse. Above all, part seven was to be discussed at the end and secretly.[51] The presentation of the document, which lasted several sessions, was to be followed by the king's consent and the appropriate reparation, not by flowery language and vain promises, but by concrete and fitting actions.[52]

Alfonso did not aspire any longer to the empire and therefore it is possible that he did not need the pope much. It is not known if he replied to the pope but on July 29 he wrote from Seville to his son don Sancho, whom he had entrusted with the government of the northern territories, asking him to consult with a commission of bishops, Church officials and good men and to prepare a response to the first six chapters.[53]

---

[49] P. Linehan, *The Spanish Church and the Papacy*, pp. 188–221.

[50] Already in February 1278, soon after acceding to the throne, he had warned Alfonso about the persecution of the archbishop D. Gonzalo of Santiago of Compostela; and some months later he had done the same regarding Gregory X's *decima* (*Regest. Nich.*, III, 5). But now, in the section "gravamina prelatorum" of the *Memoriale*'s fifth part, the pope denounced with impressive detail each and everyone of Alfonso's abuses regarding everything from graft in the election of bishops and the sacking of the treasures of cathedrals, to the placing of Jews above the Christians, from which "many evils derive", as the bishops had stated in 1267.

[51] *Les Registres de Nicolas III*, ed. Gay, p. 342.

[52] Ib., p. 343.

[53] The text of Alfonso's letter to his son can be read in P. Linehan, "The Spanish Church Revisited," p. 133; on pp. 141–147, the author publishes what is considered

Some of the specific accusations, such as the irregular appointment of bishops (an infringement on the "freedom of the Church", about which the pope had spoken), already had been justified and addressed in Alfonsine legislation, at least in principle. This legislation was based on certain particular circumstances that distinguished the Peninsular church from other national churches in other European countries. As is well known, the foundation or renovation of many of the Peninsular dioceses had been carried out by kings as a result of the reconquest of territories. Along with the creation of a new diocese and the appointment of a trustworthy bishop, the king made concessions of land, serfs, and at times entire towns, which would serve the bishop. The bishop held all the new properties of the new diocese as lord and feudal appointee of the king. Hence, upon his death, the king thought had the right (*ius spolii*) to repossess what in the end was his. As legislator, Alfonso was very clear on this point, so that neither his son nor his advisors dared alter what he had laid out in the *Partidas* on this practice (I, 5.18).

It is not known if a response was drafted to the seventh part, where there was a long list of accusations including the use of astrologers and soothsayers at the court and the preference given to Jews over Christians in royal appointments, all of which insinuated the king's lack of orthodoxy, although this was precisely the theme in which Alfonso had distanced himself most from the doctrine and praxis of the Church.

But the last papal document went further, launching in the final part an unexpected and unusual accusation against Alfonso, namely, that of having established a "novum ordinem seu religionem" ("a new order or religion"). At first sight, it seems that the pope could have been referring to the founding of the Order of the Star or of Santa María de España, as the maritime order founded by Alfonso for the defense of the southern coasts against Muslim attacks was known. But we soon realize that the "new order" refers to a new way of conceiving of the social structure of Church-State relations and Christian culture in general. The *CAX* and primitive historiography have been very skillful at silencing the possible unorthodoxy of Alfonso X, but court figures and contemporaries who were acquainted with him personally, such as abbots and bishops, knew perfectly well that Alfonso's thought

---

don Sancho's and his advisor's response to parts 1, 2 and portions of part 5 of the *Memoriale*.

and attitudes were profoundly Ghibelline, that is lay and secular. This behavior was clearly in conflict with the religious and ecclesiastical spirit that permeated medieval society.

If we ignore the works compiled and illuminated under Alfonso's commission, which may have led us to attribute to him extreme unorthodox positions, including the writing of astrological works that include prayers to the Sun or Mercury (such as the *Libro de Astromagia* or *Picatrix*), and if we exclude also the positions of spiritual Ghibellines associated with Salimbene da Parma and Gerard of Borgo, who, using Joachite prophecy, identified Alfonso X with the new Antichrist who would redeem the Lombard Ghibellines, it is obvious that also the rest of the Alfonsine books, including the *Cantigas de Santa María*, were filled with pagan tendencies and a rebellious conception of power and religion vis-à-vis the papacy, Church doctrine, and the Peninsular bishops. The informants and authors of the *Memoriale* were aware of this.[54]

In Rome, the popes would never forget that the king of Castile was descended from that "cursed breed" of the Staufens "that had by nature a hatred towards the Catholic Church." The astrology disseminated by Alfonso X was part of a set of hermetic doctrines that were transmitted secretly and were based on an absolutist concept of the royalty. The Church of Rome saw in Alfonso a high priest or magus of that "new order" of knowledge. Alfonso was very aware of the risk he ran of being misunderstood or that his knowledge could be misused due to incompetence or ignorance. The book of *Astromagia* therefore issues the following warnings for the preservation and correct interpretation of the work:

> But we pray, command and recommend, on God's behalf and ours and all of our goodness, to those in whose hands this may fall after our days, that this book should be kept in three ways. Firstly, with honor, because man is beholden to honor the things that God himself honored greatly, such as these, which he made for the purpose of honoring in particular

---

[54] Cf. A. Domínguez, "'Compassio' y 'Co-redemptio' en las Cantigas de Santa María. Crucifixión y Juicio final," *Archivo Español de Arte*, no. 281 (1998), pp. 17–35; E. Mitre, "Hérésie et culture dirigeant dans la Castille de la fin du XIIIe siècle. La modèle d'Alphonse X," *Heresis*, 9 (1987), 33–47; J. Paul, "Le joachinisme et les joachinites au millieu du XIIIe siècle d'après le témoignage de Fra Slimbene," in *1274. Annèe Charnière. Mutations et continuités. Colloques internationaux del CNRS (Lyon, 1974)*, Paris, 1977, pp. 786–823. Cf. L.R. Funes, "La blasfemia del Rey Sabio: itinerario narrativo de una leyenda," *Incipit*, 13 (1993), pp. 51–70 and 14 (1994), pp. 69–101.

man above all other creatures, because for this reason he gave him understanding and power of action, to understand and do whatever he wills. The other, that he may keep it in counsel, because God made knowledge noble in itself and made man noble by granting it to him, therefore it is in this manner to be kept noble and not made vile by revealing it, because in this way, whoever reveals it will become vile. The third reason is that man should be careful to act by it, in such a way that he does not err in his works, because if he errs, he will never attain what he strives for, and he would blame his failure on knowledge, from which no failure or blame can come. And keeping it in these ways we have stated, whoever honors it will be made noble by God, receiving from him good sense, kindness and above all, he will be able to accomplish all he desires, which is something greatly esteemed. And to others who would go against this, God will have him dishonored and reviled and will make him err in all his actions. And therefore he who would hear this book or read it, pay attention to all these things and pray to God and ask his mercy to guide and orient him in it. (*Libro de astromagia*, IV.1, ed. A. D'Agostino, p. 229)

Astrology, as a supreme science that encompasses all other sciences of nature, is only for the initiates and should not be presented to incompetent people or charlatans. Alfonso saw no conflict between this attitude of the wise man or magus dedicated to the knowledge of nature through rational methods, and the official teachings of the Church based on faith. In fact, bringing together astrology with faith seemed perfectly natural and spontaneous for a rational Alfonso. But Rome had a different opinion. As this biography shows, not only his astrological works but the entire Alfonsine corpus, including the *Cantigas*, conveys the lay and secular spirit in which they were conceived. To the Peninsular church officials who sent their complaint to the Pope, this spirit bordered on heresy. In the words of Ana Domínguez, a distinguished scholar of the *Cantigas* iconography, "[t]he king was the philosopher, the magus, but he also possessed semi-divine characteristics; he was the representative of the Divine, usurping the role of the priests and interpreted religion. Thus appears Alfonso X in those images of the king as a troubadour, constituting a manifesto in which the king presents himself as a 'new Solomon' and sings to Mary and Christ, just as his forebear did in the Song of Songs."[55] Alfonso presents himself

---

[55] "Originales astrológicos de Alfonso X, el Sabio y copias del siglo XVI," in *Originalidad, modelo y copia en el arte medieval hispánico. Actas del V Congreso Español de Historia del Arte*, Barcelona, 1984, p. 40.

in the *Cantigas* as an intermediary between God and the faithful, dispensing with the clergy, who alone were to perform such functions.

This lay attitude, given the precedent of another Staufen, Frederick II, raised serious doubts in Rome about the orthodoxy of the king of Castile. Alfonso was indeed the first medieval Christian king who secularized the state and all its institutions, uncoupling them from Church links but not breaking openly with the Church, as his relative Frederick II had done. The Alfonsine secular spirit manifests itself in his wide-ranging cultural oeuvre and is portrayed visually in many miniatures as well as in religious, and more obviously, in secular works, for instance, in the celebrated vignette of the codex of the *First Partida* in the British Library. In the illustration of a capital letter of fol. 1v, Alfonso is portrayed receiving from or perhaps offering to God his work, which is seen emerging from the sky above. The illustration corresponds exactly to the idea expressed in the prologue of the work by Alfonso himself, where he insists that the power to legislate is granted to the king directly by God.

As we will more clearly illustrate in another work in preparation, it is with Alfonso that the lay, secular, and rationalist spirit in European culture is born, though this spirit would not solidify definitively until many centuries later. The vicissitudes of the Alfonsine corpus and the radical shifts in the cultural policies of his successors, which swung between secularist rationalism and religious dogmatism, disrupted the continuity of the concept for an open and free society designed by the Learned King. But the flame never went out completely. Following the anti-Alfonsine reaction that followed his death, eleven years later, when his grandson Fernando IV acceded to the throne, a radical change in his favor took place. In the 1295 Valladolid Cortes, the regents of the kingdom (Fernando was then nine years old), pushed by doña María de Molina, decreed the expulsion of bishops and religious officials from the offices of the kingdom's government, with the exception of the royal chapel, and their replacement by lay officers. Alfonso X's secular and vernacular humanism survived against all odds, though it has taken some time to discover and recognize it in all its phases and nuances throughout the centuries.

It seems that Alfonso or his courtiers did not lose much sleep over the *Memoriale secretum*, partly because the accusations of the clergy did not have popular support. In the subsequent meetings of the king with his subjects it seems that whenever the topic of the abuses of the clergy came up, the representatives in the councils, who were opposed to ecclesiastical privileges, always sided with the king. On the other hand, at the moment when the *Memoriale* arrived, the Learned King was worried about other matters, not the least of which was protecting his own kingdom. Therefore, despite all the good intentions of pope Nicholas III to correct Alfonso X's abuses against the privileges of the Church and its clergy, the realities of Peninsular politics dominated, so that only very little in the mysterious and threatening *Memoriale* was actually carried out. But the aggrieved bishops of Castile-León did not forget the affronts, and although they would have to wait three years to vindicate their rights, when the appropriate occasion arrived to claim them, they did not hesitate to support the rebellion of don Sancho against his father. As P. Linehan explains, "Political rebellion was the result of ecclesiastical repression."[56] Alfonso had ignored the wise advice of his father-in-law at Fitero: "do not mess with the Church." He would soon have to pay the consequences.

7. Negotiations with Philip III of France

Following the tragic event of don Çag's execution, Alfonso continued in Seville, working assiduously in matters of state. There is a rich correspondence from this period corroborating the intense activity of his chancellery both in national and international matters. The correspondence with his half-brother-in-law, Edward I of England (married to Eleanor, daughter of Fernando III and his second wife, Juana of Ponthieu), is particularly revealing. Edward was doing everything possible to achieve peace between Alfonso and Philip III of France, ending the war between the two kingdoms. The two crucial points of the conflict were the Navarra issue, which remained unresolved, and the dispute over the Infantes de la Cerda.

On May 22, 1280, Alfonso wrote from Seville to Edward to tell him that through his messengers, Guillermo of Valencia and Juan of Greyley, seneschal of Gascony, he had conceded a truce with the king of France until Christmas of that year. Later, via other envoys of Alfonso's, "master Geoffrey of Eversley, our faithful notary" ("magistrum Gaufredum de Everle, nostrum fidelem natarium") and the noble *milite* Talliferum de Monte Oserii, he extended the truce one more

---

[56] *The Spanish Church and the Papacy*, p. 221.

year, starting on Christmas of 1280. Two weeks later, on June 1, 1280, he wrote again to Edward to tell him that, responding to his insistence, he had decided to extend the truce from the feast of St. John's that year until the feast of St. Martin's 1282.[57]

Alfonso did not limit himself to the mediation of Edward of England. Inexplicably, while he maintained that intense epistolary and diplomatic activity with the English king, Alfonso took the initiative to seek out another mediator, and a surprising one: prince Charles of Salerno. This idea could have been motivated by a request of the pope (who always sought to maintain peace between the kings of Castile and France) that the two kings meet to resolve their differences. Aware that Pope Nicholas III (Orsini), despite his well-known anti-Anjou attitudes, was not on his side as other popes had been, and remembering the demands and threats listed in the *Memoriale secretum*, Alfonso reluctantly accepted the pope's proposal, thinking that perhaps he could use the meeting with the French and English kings to launch an invasion of Morocco and from there continue the conquest and liberation of the Holy Land in the great crusade that had been his dream and his father's before him (cf. below note 59). Alfonso must have quickly seen the advantages of such a meeting, which, if it produced the results he expected, would allow him to forever eliminate the danger of the Muslims beyond the Strait and at the same time, satisfy the pope. In Alfonso's mind, relations with the papacy were always intimately connected to his own international interests and those of his supporters in Italy. Thus, knowing of Nicholas III's anti-Anjou sentiment, he welcomed any opportunity to advance his cause.

As we have noted, Alfonso selected as mediator a figure as distinguished as he was unknown at the Castilian court, Charles of Anjou, prince of Salerno, named for his father, King Charles of Sicily, and a cousin by blood of the king of France. It is not clear what Alfonso's secret motives were in contacting a member of the opposing side. But regardless of the motive, we can assume that he did not want to bet only on the mediation of Edward, who also had had his run-ins with the king of France and, therefore, could be an obstacle to the success of the meeting. The young Charles of Anjou, on the other hand,

---

[57] Regarding this correspondence, see Ballesteros, *Alfonso X*, pp. 920–923; and T. Rymer, *Foedera*, I, pp. 235–238. "*Magistrum Gaufredum,*" as we pointed out above (chap. 2), is the famous author of the *Ars Epistolarium*, Geoffrey of Eversley.

belonged to the family of Philip III, and as an Angevin, also had the pope's support.

Alfonso sent his ambassadors to Aix-en-Provence. They left Seville secretly on Easter Sunday (April 21), while Alfonso was in the midst of negotiations with Edward. The messengers were the archdeacon of Astorga, Pelayo Pérez, the knight Bellus of Arculis, porter of the royal chamber of Castile, and his protonotary, Peter of Regio. His mission was to ask Charles of Salerno to set a time and place to hold the meeting with the king of France, with the goal of solving the dispute over Navarra and other pending matters, including the political situation of the de la Cerda princes. A surprised Charles immediately assumed the role of intermediary, accompanying the ambassadors of the Castilian king to Paris in order to present them to his cousin. The embassy arrived in Paris on June 24, 1280. Philip III accepted his cousin as mediator, setting the feast of St. Michael, September 29, as the date for the meeting. The negotiators would stay in different but nearby places: Mont-Marsan would be the seat of the king of France's group while Alfonso's representatives would stay at Bayonne. Charles of Salerno, who would mediate between both groups, would stay in Dax. Both Mont-Marsan and Bayonne were under the control of Edward of England, who had to be informed so he could allow the presence of both delegations, which would no doubt be accompanied by a large number of troops. Edward was extremely accommodating, giving timely instructions to his local representatives so they would welcome and protect both parties. The English king behaved like a true gentleman, for despite having promoted the meeting, he was now being excluded without adequate explanation. In several letters, Philip of France tried to excuse himself saying that it was not a decision he had made. In any event, when Philip asked him to at least accompany him to Mont-Marsan, Edward politely declined (letter dated July 13).[58]

At the end of the summer, Alfonso left Seville headed north. On November 4, we find him in Burgos, and on December 25 he was in San Sebastián, on the way to Bayonne, where his representatives were waiting. We must take into account that, as the *CAX* reminds us, even

---

[58] For all this correspondence, see G. Daumet, *Memoires sur les relations de la France et de la Castille*, Paris, 1913 [Spanish trans. in *Revista de la Facultad de Derecho*. Universidad Complutense, 9 (1985), Apéndice, doc. XIV]; T. Rymer, *Foedera*, I, pp. 237–238; Ch. V. Langlois, *Le Regne de Philippe III le Hardi*, Paris, 1857; and Ballesteros, *Alfonso X*, pp. 923–925.

before the meeting, the king of France had repeatedly asked Alfonso not to leave his grandchildren dispossessed of the crown that belonged to them.[59] The well-informed historian behind the *CAX*, though erring in some of the details, tells us succinctly: "King Alfonso was in Bayonne with all his sons, and the King of France came and reached Salvatierra in Gascony and sent the Prince of Morea, son of King Charles of Sicily, to treaty with King Don Alfonso about the pact of agreement concerning Prince Don Fernando. He had come to certify that King Alfonso would give him the kingdom of Jaén and that he would be his vassal and the vassal of Prince Don Sancho" (chap. 74, p. 236). In other words, Charles, the negotiator between the two parties, had managed to have Alfonso X name prince Alfonso de la Cerda king of Jaén, but under the proviso that he would hold the kingdom as a vassal of Castile. It was similar to what Alfonso had done with his brother Manuel and the kingdom of Murcia. Clearly, the offer to grant the kingdom of Jaén to his grandchildren, while keeping it under his sovereignty and, after his death, under Sancho's, was not exactly what the king of France expected. Philip demanded no less than the throne of Castile or León for his nephews. Thus the parties were far from reaching an accord.

Naturally, Philip III rejected Alfonso's proposal, saying that his nephews did not have to accept such an arrangement when, in reality, they had the right to inherit the kingdoms of Castile and León. The meeting ended, therefore, without an agreement, since Alfonso told Philip of France he could not make concessions that were not acceptable to the declared heir, who, when he found out about the negotiations, vigorously complained to his father. By the time the meeting at Bayonne ended in total failure, Pope Nicholas III had already passed away.

The meeting was also attended by don Sancho, heir to the throne, and if we believe the *CAX*, he had much to do with his father's proposals. If the king of France thought that Alfonso's concessions were not sufficient, to his son they seemed excessive and unacceptable (*CAX*, chap. 74, pp. 236–37). There was therefore a consultation and

---

[59] *CAX*, chap. 74, pp. 235–236. Alfonso's response to Philip seems to have been his agenda for the meeting. Regarding the matter of the de la Cerda brothers, Alfonso wanted to leave something to both, and not just to don Alfonso, as the king of France has suggested.

an intense debate between father and son, whose positions are well laid out in the text of the *Crónica*. In a certain way, Sancho's position prevailed when he invoked first the indivisibility of the kingdom which should be maintained at all costs, then by his father and later by himself; and second, when he resorted to the fact that the de la Cerda princes were in the hands of the king of Aragón, on whom both Alfonso and Philip had to rely to determine the future of those children. Therefore, the young Sancho advised his father to negotiate with his neighbor, the king of Aragón, and to remain calm regarding the demands of the French king because, if he managed to agree with his brother-in-law, he had nothing to fear from the king of France. The author of the chronicle writes, "King Don Alfonso had to agree to this advice" (*CAX*, chap. 74, p. 237). Philip of France, for his part, did not waste any time, meeting with Pedro of Aragón in Toulouse. This meeting, however, did not take place at the most appropriate moment, given the tensions between Anjou and Aragón in Sicily. Still, Philip did not hesitate to ask the king of Aragón to hand over the two princes. Don Pedro, accompanied by his bother, the king of Mallorca, refused categorically to allow the children to leave Aragón.

The year 1280 ended without a resolution to the conflict between Philip and Alfonso, as both pope and Alfonso would have wanted. But the Castilian king had other pending problems to attend to, among them, the complicated situation in the south, which had turned into a continuous war, although it was mostly a war of attrition, punishment and retaliation against the king of Granada for previous offenses, rather than an open war with great display of troops and battles. The young Sancho was in charge of this guerrilla war.

After the meeting with the king of France, Alfonso returned to Burgos, beginning 1281 by lavishly celebrating the double wedding of two of his sons, don Pedro and don Juan: "King Alfonso came to Burgos and held the marriages of his sons Prince Pedro and Prince Juan. Prince Pedro wed the daughter of the Lord of Narbonne, and Prince Juan married the daughter of the Marquis of Monferrat, who was wed to Princess Beatriz, his daughter" (*CAX*, chap. 75, p. 238). The daughter of the Lord of Narbonne was named Marguerite, and the wife of don Juan was Juana of Monferrato, and she was the daughter of William IV of Monferrato and Elizabeth of Cornwall, who was the daughter of count Richard of Cornwall, Alfonso's first rival in the fight for the imperial crown. The world of the European nobility was indeed small.

As if these weddings did not suffice to leave the coffers of the kingdom in bad shape, at the end of that year, the heir prince, don Sancho, would marry (against the will of his father) doña María de Molina. On the occasion of his wedding, Alfonso knighted his youngest son, Jaime, whom he named señor de los Cameros, a title he had granted him after the execution of Simón Ruiz.

Alfonso was always very splendid in his celebrations. He sent invitations to all corners of Europe, still naming himself "Elected King of the Romans". Weddings were a good occasion to maintain and repair international relations, which around this time were quite neglected, if not broken. In the midst of the celebrations, Alfonso did not forget his international commitments, and the presence of personalities from the south of France and several Italian republics must have encouraged him to renew his contacts. All those present benefited from Alfonso's generosity. The *CAX*, clearly critical about this tendency, mentions only the case of the father of prince don Juan's wife, the Marquis of Monferrato, to whom Alfonso was particularly openhanded. The Marquis requested his economic help to fight against his enemies in Italy. Alfonso responded generously. According to the *CAX*:

> And the Marquis of Monferrat asked King Alfonso to give him something for the land he had in Normandy. So the king gave him in pay two tallies in coin, which amounted to fifteen coins per *maravedí*, and he also gave him many horses and many gifts. When Prince Sancho and his brother saw what he gave to the Marquis, they took it to heart and considered it bad. It was one of the practices of King Alfonso that later was to be used against him. (*CAX*, chap. 75, p. 238)

We do not know if the information in the second part of the quote is true or not. It is not clear how Alfonso's generosity could have bothered the newlyweds, at least not at that moment when they were the center of attention and the object of their father's generosity. It could perhaps be true of don Sancho, with whom the chronicler often sympathizes; here the *CAX* already hints that Alfonso's generosity was excessive. On the other hand, we also should not forget that the stranger who was the beneficiary, the object of don Sancho's anger, was not a stranger at all, but rather Alfonso's son-in-law to whom he owed much for keeping alive the Alfonsine cause in Italy against the Guelfs and the Angevin faction.

8. The Campillo Treaty

Just as Philip of France had done, Alfonso too met with Pedro of Aragón. But from the correspondence that preceded the meeting, we know that the two kings were united by common interests ("we have a similar will," writes don Pedro) other than those that had brought the kings of France and Aragón together. The meeting took place on March 27, 1281 in Campillo, a town between Agreda and Tarazona. In attendance were don Sancho and his uncle don Manuel and a great number of nobles on both sides. Among the signatories of the agreements appears also the Marquis of Monferrato. Many topics were to be discussed at that meeting, but above all was the matter of the joint conquest of Navarra. Alfonso promised Pedro the valley of Ayora, between Valencia and Murcia, while the king of Aragón recognized the dominion of Castile in Albarracín, "and [they] made their covenants in such a way that through it they remained friends" (chap. 75, p. 238).[60] The signed documents contain many declarations and mutual promises of peace and help.[61]

The next day, March 28, don Sancho met personally with Pedro III to sign a separate friendship and alliance agreement. During this meeting, which was not attended by Alfonso, the positions and concessions of the previous day were revised, with don Sancho making new territorial concessions to the king of Aragón. The most important one was the granting of all rights to the kingdom of Navarra, which would become effective only upon his accession to the throne following the death of his father. Don Pedro, for his part, promised his nephew unconditional help in order to conquer it.

All scholars agree that the peace at Campillo was the first instance that revealed how don Sancho's presence was already significant to the future of the kingdom of Castile, because Pedro III signed an agreement with him without the participation of Alfonso. On the other hand, the alliance of Sancho and Pedro, while the latter was in possession of the de la Cerda princes, automatically neutralized the king

---

[60] *CAX*, chap. 75, p. 238. Cf. C. de Ayala Martínez, "Paces castellano-aragonesas de Campillo-Agreda (1281)," in *En la España medieval*, 5.2 (1986), pp. 153–160; Ballesteros, *Alfonso X*, pp. 937–939, 956–957.

[61] The four documents signed at Campillo can also be seen in A. Bejarano Rubio, "La frontera del reino de Murcia en la política castellano-aragonesa del siglo XIII," in J.C. de Miguel Rodríguez, *Alfonso X el Sabio, vida, obra y época*, pp. 199–212, texts on pp. 210–212.

of France, with or without Navarra, leaving the road clear for Sancho to accede to the throne following his father's death. The beneficiary in the short term was indeed don Pedro, who got all he asked for, but in the long run it would be Sancho, who would receive the throne from his father without interference from the de la Cerda princes, while at the same time obtaining the unconditional support of his uncle in case of conflicts with his father. Without this support, the de la Cerda princes were like the sword of Damocles, and Sancho knew it. Hence his territorial concessions.

In June of that year, Alfonso, accompanied by his children, don Sancho, don Pedro, don Juan, and the illegitimate but beloved don Alfonso, *the Child*, launched a new military offensive to punish Granada and its king, Mohamed II, who had sided the year before with the invaders, an action that amounted to treason in Alfonso's mind. Free of commitments in the north, and certain of his friendship with his brother-in-law, don Pedro of Aragón, Alfonso thought it was the moment to set the record straight with the rebel Moor. The *CAX* is very clear on this episode, even describing the battle plan:

> King Alfonso demanded all of his armies to be summoned to go to enter the *vega* of Granada again, and all of the armies were assembled in the month of June. He moved with all of his armies. Prince Sancho led the vanguard, while Prince Pedro led another part, and Prince Juan another, and a son of King Alfonso who was illegitimate and who was named Alfonso the Child, and was the lord of Molina, led the rear; King Alfonso went in the middle. So they entered the *vega*, waging fierce war and laying siege to the city of Granada. (*CAX*, chap. 75, pp. 238–239)[62]

The chronicler narrates a truly heroic episode headed by don Sancho, who with very few men, was assailed by "fifty thousand [Moors] bearing leather shields, and twice as many archers, and all the people in the city, well-mounted Andalusians [...]. But he showed himself to be so strong and so ardent that through his strength alone he protected everyone, and after this danger he made evident his honor and great prowess" (*CAX*, chap. 75, p. 239).

Disregarding the obvious partiality of the anonymous chronicler, there is no doubt that don Sancho, as other documents confirm, was the architect of the victory that frightened the king of Granada, who

---

[62] *Anales Toledanos III* corroborate to the slightest detail the narrative of the *CAX*. Cf. Balleteros, *Alfonso X*, p. 942.

immediately asked Alfonso for new peace negotiations. Alfonso sent Gómez García Díaz de Toledo, who had been the notary of prince don Fernando de la Cerda and would later become abbot of Valladolid and don Sancho's confidant, to establish with the king of Granada, the conditions of the truce. Mohamed II told Alfonso's envoy that he was willing to give him "one-third of all the rents he had from treaties, and King Don Alfonso said that he would give the King of Granada the castles and fortresses that he was already giving, and nothing more. With this he departed, and King Don Alfonso came to Córdoba with all his host, and he and the entire cavalry departed for the frontier castles to fulfill the time they were to serve" (*CAX*, chap. 75, p. 239).[63]

Just as after the campaign of 1279, Alfonso settled in Córdoba, which served as the base of operations and the watchtower from which he controlled the rest of the territories of Andalusia. Peace was not only attained by military victories but also through vigilance and a firm hand, necessary to keep order in the midst of the social chaos and criminality that had spread everywhere. The *CAX* recounts a curious episode that occurred during the war against the king of Granada, which reveals the flux of life on the frontier and the militant and justice-seeking spirit of the Learned King:

> Likewise, a large company of rogues had been going about in the mountains, killing and stealing all they found, since King Alfonso had pardoned them so that they could accompany him to the *vega*; and as soon as they were out of it, they demanded of the king many things with which to support themselves. Because he did not give those things to them, they went about threatening that they would go to the mountains and commit every evil they could in the land. When King Alfonso learned of this, he ordered all of them seized and slain. (*CAX*, chap. 75, p. 239)

---

[63] The places demanded by Alfonso were, apparently, the ones occupied by Granada since 1275 (Rute, Benamejí, Huelma, and others); but Alfonso must have also demanded territories that would allow direct access to the Strait. This, naturally was not entirely under the control of the king of Granada. They could therefore not reach an agreement at that point. Cf. M. González Jiménez, *Alfonso X*, p. 161.

CHAPTER THIRTEEN

DEPOSITION AND CIVIL WAR

1. *The Seville Cortes (1281)*

While in Córdoba, Alfonso summoned a new Cortes to be held in Seville the following year. At this time the king's health began to worry don Sancho, who conveyed this to his father. In the fall of 1281, on the feast day of Saint Martin (November 11), a document tells us that Alfonso opened the announced Cortes in Seville, the city where he habitually resided.[1] These were probably the best-attended Cortes of all his reign. Prelates, nobles, and *ricoshombres* from various parts of the country were in attendance.

Cantiga 386, which we can also use to date the Cortes ("[he] summoned a great council. This was the time when he returned from the invasion of the *vega* of Granada, subjecting it and all the lands about, the lowlands as well as the mountains, to tribute" *Songs of Holy Mary*, p. 471), describes how, faced with the scarcity of staples to feed so many participants, the Virgin helped Alfonso, providing him with fish to satisfy the needs of all those present. The *Cantiga* also informs us that the king "granted them without delay all they had asked in their petitions which they rightfully presented, for it is seldom that anyone asks his lord for anything without just cause" (*Songs of Holy Mary*, p. 471). The last line clearly hides the conflict that emerged during the Cortes. According to the *Cantiga* the king granted what were the 'reasonable' requests ("rightfully presented"), which, considering that the author of the *Cantiga* was the king himself, is a polite way of saying how irrational some of their demands might have been. *Cantiga* 386, most probably, is the last of the *cantigas* that allude to a historical fact narrated in the collection.[2]

---

[1] Cf. *CAX*, chap. 75, pp. 238–242; Procter, *Curia*, pp. 146–147; J. O'Callaghan, *The Cortes of Castile-León*, p. 105.

[2] J. Montoya Martínez, on the contrary, thinks that *Cantiga* 386 refers to the assembly of 1264, "Historia de Andalucía en las *Cantigas de Santa María*," *Andalucía medieval*, 1 (1978), pp. 259–269; but the *Cantiga* explicitly mentions the "Cortes," not an "assembly," such as the one held in 1264.

The Seville Cortes, held in the middle of the campaign against the king of Granada, dealt firstly with how to finance the campaign so that it would not lose the gains and momentum of the last weeks.[3] Alfonso, his historian tells us, did not want to burden the kingdom with new taxes, since it was already in a deep economic crisis (a letter from prince don Juan states that the representatives of the kingdom had asked don Sancho to make it clear to his father "what were the real facts of the kingdom, and how men were very poor and taxes very high", *CAX*, chap. 75). But instead he proposed to the attendees the adoption of new economic measures, among which was monetary reform, which according to him had not been done since the time of his father, Fernando III.[4]

To finance the campaign against the Moroccan invasion and to enable his subjects to purchase their basic necessities in that period of economic crisis, the Learned King had two types of coins minted, one in silver and the other in copper.[5] Regarding this matter, the Cortes, according to the *CAX*, "replied to King Alfonso more through fear than with affection that he should do what he considered good and what he pleased" (*CAX*, chap. 75, p. 240).

Although the historian's words hint at some disagreement between the Cortes attendees and the king, I do not believe they support J. O'Callaghan's theory that the double minting of coins in silver and

---

[3] In a long and very interesting letter from prince don Juan, Alfonso's son, written in Seville on August 26, 1281 to the city of Burgos, the younger brother of don Sancho asks the citizens of Burgos to send their representatives to Seville to present to don Sancho any request they have for king Alfonso. This extraordinary document suggests, on the one hand, the very important role that don Sancho played as coordinator of the proceedings, and on the other, that before the Cortes were held, there were preliminary meetings in which Alfonso was presented with a report on the economic state of the kingdom and its most urgent problems (text in Ballesteros, *Alfonso X*, pp. 946–947).

[4] Alfonso very eloquently argued his point of view (*CAX*, chap. 75, pp. 238–242). Cf. E. Procter, *Curia and Cortes*, pp. 146–147; M.A. Ladero Quesada, "Las reformas fiscales y monetarias de Alfonso X como base del *Estado moderno*," in *Alfonso X. Aportaciones de un rey castellano a la construcción de Europa*, Murcia: Región de Murcia, 1997, pp. 33–54; and "Aspectos de la política económica de Alfonso X," in *Alfonso X. VII Centenario, Revista de la Facultad de Derecho. Universidad Complutense*, 9 (1985), pp. 69–82.

[5] *CAX*, pp. 239–241. The meaning and economic consequences of this reform have been studied by J. Gautier Dalché, "La politique monetaire d'Alphonse X," in *Homenaje al profesor D. Claudio Sánchez Albornoz en sus 90 años*, vol. I, Buenos Aires, 1988, pp. 75–95. For the technical characteristics of coins in the time of Alfonso X, see J.F. Todesca, "The Monetary History of Castile-León (ca. 1100–1300) in Light of Bourgey Hoard," *American Numismatic Society Museum Notes*, 33 (1988), pp. 129–203.

copper was planned by don Sancho and his supporters in a kind of sinister plot to discredit his father, knowing perfectly well that the copper coin was worth nothing, and would thus be useless to humble people for acquiring basic goods. They would then be the first to rise against Alfonso.[6] Although I do not think that there is a valid reason for this hypothesis, there is a document that attests to the low value of the copper coin, which a contemporary historian has called "paper money": "Likewise, the king, while in Seville, had a copper currency coined which had no silver content, and in this way he did away with the little that was left in the kingdom."[7] It should also be mentioned that one of the first economic measures adopted by Sancho after the deposition of his father was to restore the monetary system that had been in place since the monetary reforms of his great-grandfather.[8] On the other hand, the *CAX* (pp. 241–242) speaks about the recommendation that don Sancho made to the representatives of the town councils to not oppose the monetary decisions of his father, hinting that he would later change all the rules, as he in effect did.

2. *The Conflict between Alfonso and Sancho Erupts*

Alfonso was less worried about the economic challenges facing the kingdom than the political ones, in particular, solving the controversy with Philip III over the de la Cerda princes and the return of the best part of the Castilian nobility, who had sought refuge and compensation from the French king.[9] As the grandfather of these innocent princes, whom he himself had declared heirs to the throne, the Learned King felt a profound obligation to grant them, even if only as an honorific title, a small part of his kingdom. In his mind, it did not represent a division of the kingdom, but rather a concession of vassalage, like

---

[6] *The Learned King*, p. 306.

[7] In M. González Jiménez, "Unos Anales del reinado de Alfonso X," *BRAH*, 192 (1995), pp. 461–491, p. 479. Cf. F.J. Hernández, *Las rentas del rey. Sociedad y fisco en el reino castellano del siglo XIII*, Madrid, 1993, p. clxxxiv.

[8] "The *burgaleses*, *leoneses*, and *salamanqueses*, the currency from Burgos, León, and Salamanca, and that known as *pepiones*, which used to circulate in the times of the king don Alfonso VIII, my great-grandfather, and the king Fernando III, my grandfather," in E. González Díez, *Colección diplomática de Burgos*, n. 118.

[9] On October 13, 1281, for example, the famous Lord of Vizcaya, don Lope Díaz de Haro, in a document signed at Estella, declared himself vassal of Philip III. In return, he would receive 14,000 Tours pounds to be paid over three years.

many others. With this small concession he also thought he might be able to please the French uncle of the princes and thus make peace with him. Peace with the French king, Alfonso thought, might allow him to concentrate on the military campaign in the south. The benefits of such a concession to his grandchildren were, from his perspective, many and quite desirable. Don Sancho, however, did not see things in this way. For him, the de la Cerda princes were not just any kind of vassals. Behind them were powerful interests: France and Aragón were not about to abandon the aspirations of those children so easily. For the heir to the throne of Castile, as we know, any decrease of his sovereignty was a violation of the kingdom's unity, and therefore a threat to the Christian unity in his dominions.

Given the polarizing nature of the issue, rather than discussing it openly in the Cortes before all the representatives, Alfonso cautiously presented it to a select group of Castilian nobles so that Sancho would not find out ("But he hid the treaty from his son Prince Don Sancho so that Prince Sancho was unaware of it" (*CAX*, chap. 75, p. 240). Alfonso announced to those gathered that he would begin new negotiations with the pope and the king of France about the future of his grandson, don Alfonso de la Cerda, "who was in prison in Játiva under the power of the King of Aragón" (*CAX*, chap. 75, p. 240), to whom he wanted to leave the kingdom of Jaén subject as vassal to Castile. This was the solution proposed to the king of France during the meeting at Bayonne. The nobles in attendance had no choice but to agree with the king's will. Nobody dared to go against his wishes at that point.

Immediately after this meeting, Alfonso sent don Frédulo, bishop of Oviedo (who was from Provencal, not Tuscany, as the *CAX* states) to the pope to arrange a new meeting with the king of France in order to discuss a proposal regarding the de la Cerda princes. The possibilities of an agreement with Philip were better than in the previous year, because there was a new pope, Martin IV (1281–1285) who, in contrast to Nicholas III (Orsini), was French (Simon de Brie) and a declared supporter of the Anjou faction. Alfonso expected from him more persuasive power vis-à-vis the king of France.

When don Sancho found about don Frédulo's trip to Rome,

> [...] Prince Don Sancho immediately suspected the message concerning this treaty, since don Frédulo was not his subject. And don Sancho suspected that the king, his father, was sending him contrary to his interests with the treaty he had begun concerning don Alfonso [de la Cerda]— Prince Don Fernando's son—and Prince Don Sancho brought it up to

> King Don Alfonso. The king answered Prince Sancho that he was only sending the bishop because he was in favor with the pope and was the right one for collecting those blessings for the war with the Moors. But no matter that he said this, Prince Don Sancho kept his suspicion of the king, his father, concerning the treaty. (*CAX*, chap. 75, pp. 240–241)

Alfonso must have realized that don Sancho did not believe the explanation. He therefore had to look for a way to communicate to him the real motive of the messenger's trip, and of the proposal discussed with the nobles, without creating a controversy at the Cortes: "[a]nd when King Don Alfonso asked his counselors if there was anybody there who wanted to share this treaty with Prince Don Sancho concerning don Alfonso [de la Cerda], none of his counselors wanted to commit themselves to it, nor did they dare to tell him so" (*CAX*, chap. 75, p. 241).

Knowing the impulsive temperament of the young prince, nobody dared to break the news to him. Finally, the only one who would do so was the Dominican Friar Aimar, bishop-elect of Ávila: "[t]his Friar Aimar went to Prince Don Sancho and talked with him in secret" (*CAX*, chap. 75, p. 241). Upon hearing the news, don Sancho was so incensed he told the friar "he was crazy and brash and that if it were not for the habit he wore, he would make an example of him so that no one else would dare to say such a thing" (*CAX*, chap. 75, p. 241).

When Alfonso found out that don Sancho had given such an insensitive answer to such a dignified figure and a defender of his court, he decided to deal with the matter himself:

> As soon as King Don Alfonso learned about this reply that Prince Don Sancho had given, he said that he would tell him everything even though he did not want to. The king came to speak with Prince Don Sancho, and Prince Sancho replied that he beseeched King Alfonso not to speak out about this treaty nor to order him to accept it, because there was nothing in the world in it to which he would agree. King Don Alfonso was enraged at this reply and told him that even though he did not want the agreement, he would have it and that he would not desist from having it, neither because of Sancho nor because of the homage the people of the realm had paid him, and that he, Prince Sancho, should agree to it or be disinherited. (*CAX*, chap. 75, p. 241)

Things got bad between father and son: Sancho insisted on not wanting to hear about the matter, because he would never consent to such a proposal. And the father answered, incensed, that he would do it anyway, and if Sancho did not accept his recommendation, he would disinherit him regardless of any oath or homage paid to him by the nobles to accept him as heir.

Upon hearing this from his father, don Sancho exploded in a long tirade:

> When Prince Don Sancho heard this reply, he turned against King Alfonso and spoke these words: "Sire, you did not make me, rather, God made me, and He did much in creating me. But He killed my brother, who was older than I and who was to inherit the kingdom from you, if he had lived longer than you. God did not kill him so that I could inherit from you after your days are ended. I could well excuse the word that you used [disinherited]. There will come a time when you will regret having uttered it." With all this, the two departed from one another very angry. (CAX, chap. 75, p. 241)[10]

This violent verbal altercation, given the temperamental nature of both father and son, is quite probable. The author of the CAX must have learned about it only through one of the many eyewitnesses that must have been present at the scene. With this open confrontation, relations between father and son deteriorated beyond repair. From this moment on, Sancho saw his right to succession as a design of Divine Providence, and had the arrogance to disown his own royal descent, affirming that he, the heir to the throne was not created by his father, but by God, because God, in "killing" his brother Fernando, had prepared the way for Sancho to inherit the throne. From the providentialist perspective that Sancho assumed, Alfonso had little to do with the succession.

I am not sure that such a categorical answer from don Sancho to his father in justifying his right to the throne was entirely his and not an elaboration by the chronicler, who, as is known, belonged to an extreme wing of the so-called "Toledo mafia", a group of reactionary thinkers who became advisors to Sancho. This intellectual elite always attempted to legitimize the succession of their king appealing to divine will, because they knew that according to human laws he was illegitimate. It is hard to imagine that such a young prince already had, at that moment, very clear ideas about his "divine right" to the throne. But his mentors and advisors did. The Franciscan Fr. Gil de Zamora

---

[10] Cf. J. de Loaysa, Crónica, 14, p. 96; E. Procter, Curia and Cortes, pp. 146–147; J. O'Callaghan, "The Cantigas de Santa Maria as an Historical Source: Two Examples (nos. 321 and 386)," in Katz and Keller, Studies, 387–402. M. López-Ibor, "El pleito de sucesión en el reinado de Alfonso X," RO, 43 (1984), 55–66.

no doubt had indoctrinated him from childhood regarding the divine origin of royal power. In any event, this line of thinking appears seven years after his accession to the throne in Sancho's celebrated work, *Castigos e documentos* (Instructions and Documents), where we know his court advisors intervened as redactors of the work. When trying to explain to his son Fernando how being the firstborn is part of the plan Divine Providence has chosen to transmit royal power, don Sancho (or rather his intellectual advisors) illustrates his point by telling him the story of his grandfather, Fernando III, who inherited the throne of Castile from his grandfather (Alfonso VIII), and not from his father (Alfonso IX), and he adds:

> And we, the king don Sancho, who ordered this book, inherited the kingdoms that our father, king don Alfonso, possessed, because prince don Fernando, who was older than we, being married and having children, died much earlier than the king, our father, because if he had lived one more day than our father, we would not have had any right to the kingdom. But it was God's will that it be so, and what He commands, no one can or should contradict, because He is the one who knows what He does.[11]

What is said here, and even more, what is *not* said is extremely sharp. It is not said, for instance, that Fernando III acceded to the throne because his mother, doña Berenguela, relinquished her firstborn rights. The matter of the right to representation is not touched upon, which, according to the ruling of his father in the *Partidas* (2, 15.2), would have given the throne to the de la Cerda princes, and, above all, nothing is mentioned regarding the curse his father cast on him, disinheriting him. But it does attempt to subtly establish a similarity between Fernando III's succession and his own, as if they both had reached the throne through the same legitimate process, which was not true. However, the comparison with his saintly and illustrious grandfather was something his zealous advisors were very keen on.[12]

We can certainly imagine the impact of these words on the mind of a man like Alfonso, obsessed with succession lines and genealogies.

---

[11] *Castigos e documentos para bien vivir ordenados por el rey don Sancho IV*, ed. A. Rey, Bloomington, Indiana: Indiana University Publications, Humanities Series, 24, 1952, pp. 100–101.

[12] Cf. García Gallo, "El *Libro de las Leyes* de Alfonso el Sabio: del *Espéculo* a las *Partidas*," *AHDE*, XXI–XXII (1951–1952), pp. 345–528; P. Linehan, *Histories and the Historians*, pp. 496–497.

The Learned King must have thought that his son's angry words were a sign of unbelievable ignorance, or that he stood before a monster in human form. In any event, they were an unforgivable insult. But the argument did not end there. Don Sancho also allowed himself to launch a none-too-subtle threat: "I could well excuse the word that you used [disinherited]. There will come a time when you will regret having uttered it." If Don Sancho did not already have a rebellion planned against his father, from that moment on, he would do everything possible to have him deposed. The animosity between father and son would not end during Alfonso's life, at least not on don Sancho's end.

But the threats of the outraged prince did not discourage Alfonso, and according to the *CAX*, "King Alfonso kept his plan to finish what he had begun with the pope and with the King of France; and he again had the council who were there summoned to give him advice, and he asked that they agree to mint those coins as has been said" (*CAX*, chap. 75, p. 241). In other words, regardless of the crisis between father and son, Alfonso ordered the work of the Cortes to move forward to the discussion of negotiations with the king of France and the topic of the new minting of coins.

According to our chronicler, who here seems clearly partisan if not manipulating the facts, it was precisely the matter of the new coinage that worried the representatives of the town councils, who, rather than complaining to Alfonso as they normally would have done, requested don Sancho's intervention. As we know from don Juan's letter mentioned above (note 3), Sancho had offered to mediate on behalf of, and defend the interests of, the representatives of the towns and cities of the kingdom.[13] The representatives pleaded with don Sancho to intercede with his father so that the proposed change in currency would not take place, explaining their rationale (*CAX*, chap. 75, pp. 241–242). Up to this point, turning to don Sancho seemed within the mandate the prince had received from his father, according to don Juan's letter. But given the recent altercation between father and son and the fact that, according to the chronicler, "the two departed from

---

[13] According to Ballesteros, the chronicler not only exaggerates, but he also lies, holding that it was not the representatives who spontaneously sought don Sancho, but rather that his many agents were the ones who "created discord among the representatives of the councils, inciting them to resistance and laying before their eyes the disasters that would occur by what they called an alteration of the currency" (*Alfonso X*, pp. 950–951).

one another very angry" (*CAX*, chap. 75, p. 241) the possibilities of a successful negotiation through don Sancho were null. Hence the veiled threat to seek another solution when the representatives of the councils affirmed that "they could not get along without finding some other way to avoid enduring all the harm they were experiencing with the king" (*CAX*, chap. 75, p. 242). But the advice they received from don Sancho was not within the functions assigned to him:

> Understanding what they were telling him, which was true, and distrusting the king, his father, concerning the treaty he had agreed to—because perchance the people of the realm might act in such a way that he might lose his inheritance of the realms—Prince Sancho had to say that he desired that they go back and be with his father, the king, in Seville. He wanted them to grant King Alfonso whatever he wished and said that he would go back to Córdoba and would tell them what to do. (*CAX*, chap. 75, p. 242)

The pretence and dissimulation that don Sancho advises to the representatives of the town councils—accepting all that Alfonso would propose at the Cortes with the implication that Sancho would later undo it in their favor—was an undignified action on the part of a future heir, and it constituted a crime of high treason, as Alfonso himself would declare in his famous sentence of curse and disownment. But, as the chronicler says, at this point too don Sancho already had his rebellion planned out, employing the old stratagems used in the past by all traitors of the Christian cause: an alliance with the enemy, who in this case, was none other than the king of Granada, against whom Sancho himself had fought a few months before. In this way, secretly and under the pretext of negotiating a truce with the king of Granada that his father had asked for, Sancho, with his father's permission, left for Córdoba.

This episode presents the first incontrovertible proof that in the process of rebellion, Sancho's two brothers, Pedro and Juan, were implicated from the very beginning. (Juan in particular spread throughout the kingdom the advantages of Sancho's political-economic program over the abuses and neglect of his father.) The two intended to prosper under the shadow of their rebellious brother, as did the king of Granada, always ready to sell himself to the highest bidder in order to survive.

The end of these Cortes, perhaps the best attended during Alfonso's reign, also signals the beginning of the last period in the politics and life of the Learned King. It was characterized by conflict and endless recriminations between father and son. After the close of the Seville Cortes, Alfonso retreated to his lavish palaces and stopped traveling, perhaps due to declining health. His mind was still lucid, but his physical health deteriorated with the last ailments, his eye illness and his dropsy. In his Sevillian retreat, he concentrated on the administration of the kingdom, as many letters and privileges show. He also devoted himself again to international relations, but, above all, he diligently dedicated himself to the composition of new kinds of works of leisure and to the completion and correction of those he had already begun.

The *CAX* does not say so, but according to the document that contains Alfonso's curse against don Sancho (published by Zurita, and to which we will turn below), the version of don Sancho's visit to Córdoba was a bit different.[14] According to that version, don Sancho headed to Córdoba under the explicit command of his father to negotiate the truce with the king of Granada, which he achieved while at the same time as making him a vassal of Castile once more. But the conditions of the peace agreement were not even remotely what his father expected. In fact, what don Sancho did was to take the first steps towards a coup d'état against his father, making a deal with the king of Granada in which the latter promised not to take advantage of the crisis between father and son to attack Christian territory while the coup was unfolding. Once Muhammad II's cooperation was secured, Sancho met with the representatives of the city and with his two brothers, Pedro and Juan, and they agreed to depose their father. It must not seem surprising, then, that when Alfonso found out about the conditions of the agreement, he accused don Sancho of being a "liar and a traitor" and of having reached an agreement with the Moorish king, among other reasons, to keep the tribute money.

In the end, the two texts, the *CAX* and the "curse" document, both point clearly towards don Sancho's betrayal. Ballesteros writes that, "[t]he prince negotiates with the enemy asking for the king's permission as mediator in order to sell, later and to his personal gain, the interests of the monarchy. He did not only employ deceit when dealing with the most serious and momentous matters of state, but also to achieve his own purposes more carefully, he asks his father for carteblanche, which he will use against him. No greater felony and treach-

---

[14] *CAX*, pp. 241–242. Text of the "curse" in Ballesteros, *Alfonso X*, p. 993.

ery can be imagined. The labels of liar and traitor used by Alfonso do not seem excessive."[15]

3. Don Sancho's Rebellion

From Córdoba, Sancho left for Castile to recruit new supporters for his cause. He began by directing his epistolary campaign to the nobles and clergy, the towns and villages of the kingdom, openly inciting them to rebellion against his father and inviting them to an assembly, which would take place in Valladolid in the month of April 1282.

> To all the counselors, all the prelates, and all the others of the realm of the king, Sancho sent his letters to tell them that he wanted to speak for them with the king, his father: to ask him not to kill them, not to dispossess them, nor encroach upon them, as he had done up until then. All of them should go to Valladolid in the month of April, for he wanted to meet with them all. (CAX, chap. 76, p. 245)[16]

The support was almost general, beginning with the nobility, whose heads of household had almost completely defected, among them the Lord of Vizcaya, don Lope Díaz de Haro, with the most representative members of his lineage: don Fernando Pérez Ponce, don Ramiro Díaz, don Pedro Pérez de Asturias, and don Fernando Rodríguez Cabrera, together with many more.[17] But the powerful leader of the Lara clan did not join them, since he had sworn to don Fernando in his deathbed that he would defend the rights of the de la Cerda princes. The clergy—archbishops, bishops, abbots, and superiors of the religious

---

[15] Alfonso X, p. 993. The quoted Cantiga 386 (lines 20–28) also seems to allude to the crime of high treason. But as if it wanted to contradict the narrative of the CAX, the Cantiga also deals with the good and cordial relations between Alfonso and the representatives that attended the Cortes, portrayed in the final banquet and the miracle of the Virgin, who, when food supplies ran out, provided the king's table with three boats of fish that appeared in the canal next to the royal palaces. With this Cantiga, "we are faced with a more truthful poetic source than the historical testimony in prose" (Ballesteros, Alfonso X, p. 952).

[16] The chronicler was well informed about the history of the rebellion of don Sancho, as he was of the nobles, although he does not devote so much space to it. In the quote he presents a good summary of the oral message that accompanied those letters, because the letters themselves, it could be said, were the credentials that served to officially authenticate the messenger who carried them. Ballesteros gathers some of these letters, Alfonso X, p. 959.

[17] Cf. CAX, pp. 244–249; and M. Gaibrois de Ballesteros, Historia del reinado de Sancho IV de Castilla, I, p. 9.

orders—also sided with him. Except for the archbishops of Toledo and
Seville and a few others, practically all bishops of Castile and León
who had suffered abuses, deprivation, and burdensome taxes during
the entire reign of Alfonso X, switched over to don Sancho's side.[18]
Surprisingly, among them were some councils of the south (Andújar, Jaén, and Úbeda) and the Masters of the most important military
Orders (Calatrava, Uclés, Santiago, Hospitallers and Templars), who,
because they possessed large territories in the south, had suffered the
most from the consequences of the North African attacks.[19] These
Masters, as we saw above, were probably the same ones who during
the first uprising in the south achieved a truce, promising Yûsuf that
if Alfonso did not ratify it, they would depose him. Now, although the
circumstances and motives were different, it was the time to carry out
their promise.

The overwhelming participation in the rebellion of the military
orders, which constituted the largest and best of the Christian forces,
must have given Sancho the confidence that he would prevail.[20]
Because they were unexpected, the alliances of the king of Portugal,[21]
and Aragón[22] must have seemed more alarming to Alfonso, as did
those of his children, don Pedro and don Juan, and even the incomprehensible one of his brother don Manuel, who had always been his
great confidant.

---

[18] We know this in retrospect from the "letter of brotherhood" signed by the religious men gathered at the Sahagún monastery on July 8, 1282, when the plot had
already taken place (cf. below note 48).

[19] The Order of Alcántara and the Templars of León and Castile apparently
remained faithful to Alfonso.

[20] Cf. C. de Ayala Martínez, "Monarquía y órdenes militares en el reinado de
Alfonso X," 459–465.

[21] The CAX says that don Dinis "was in disfavor with his grandfather, King Don
Alfonso, because the latter was holding his mother, [and he] made a treaty with Prince
Don Sancho to support him against King Don Alfonso" (CAX, chap. 76, p. 245). Doña
Beatriz, as we mentioned, had abandoned the court of Portugal and had sought refuge
with her father in Toledo, at first, and later in Seville, where she probably already was
at this point.

[22] Likewise, Prince Don Sancho quickly sent his messengers to King Don Pedro of
Aragón, telling him the stance he was taking and begging him to let them love
each other so that he would help him if there were need. This greatly pleased
King Don Pedro, and he immediately signed the treaties with him. (CAX, chap.
76, p. 245)
However, see note 24 below.

Above and beyond the support of the powerful military orders and the kings of Portugal and Aragón, Sancho was concerned, for obvious reasons, to attract the cause of the nobility. To this effect, he sent letters too to the defecting nobles who were in France. The *CAX* records that among others who returned were don Lope Díaz de Haro (leader of the clan favorable to don Sancho), his brother don Diego, don Fernando Pérez Ponce, don Ramiro Díaz, don Pedro Páez de Asturias, don Ferrán Rodríguez de Cabrera and "other noblemen and many knights who had been cast out of the realm. Prince Sancho sent the messengers to say that they should all come to Valladolid and he would hand over to them all their inheritances that the king, his father, had taken from them. He also said he would restore their lands and soldiers very well and would act with much goodness and grace" (*CAX*, chap. 76, p. 245).

Don Sancho traveled to all cities of the kingdom in the company of his mother, who, according to the *CAX*, was in Valladolid, a city she ruled, and "[s]he was very pleased with this position that he had taken against King Don Alfonso, her husband" (*CAX*, chap. 76, p. 246). The young prince made everyone happy with his gifts, benefits, and privileges. In Burgos, the chronicler writes, "[h]e learned that King Don Alfonso had killed his uncle Prince Don Fadrique, who lay buried in a foul place where King Don Alfonso had ordered him buried. Prince Sancho removed him from there and buried him in a very honorable sepulcher that he built in the monastery of the Monks of the Trinity in Burgos" (*CAX*, chap. 76, p. 246). The chronicler had no reason to mention here this act of Christian piety, which was no doubt worthy of praise but out of place, precisely at that moment when don Sancho was persecuting the members of the family who did not support his cause, as was his aunt Berenguela, the abbess of Las Huegas, sister of his father, whom he would expel from the monastery. The reason to mention this must have been no other than to denigrate Alfonso, forgetting to mention that don Sancho himself had participated actively in the death of his uncle and the material execution of don Simón.

No less active in León and Castile was his brother, prince don Juan, who according to the *CAX*, obtained the support of practically all the towns and councils: "Prince Don Juan went everywhere urging that they support Prince Don Sancho; and they all, every town and council, made a pact and covenant by letters and fealty to support Prince Don Sancho" (*CAX*, chap. 76, p. 244). The *CAX* however paints a negative

portrait of don Juan when it describes in detail the violent and terrifying methods he used in order to get their support.[23] I do not believe
that the anonymous chronicler sympathized too much with the "tortuous prince," as Ballesteros calls him (*Alfonso X*, p. 958), for the simple
reason that he knew that one not too distant day, he would betray his
brother Sancho too.

While all of this chaos was going on in the kingdom, Alfonso was
still in Seville, receiving alarming news and taking care of business,
granting letters and privileges and even keeping up an important correspondence with don Pedro de Aragón, who in a letter asked his help
to expel the Angevins from Sicily and requested the support of the
Marquis of Monferrato, Alfonso's son-in-law. This letter is dated at
Valencia on January 15, 1282, which leads us to believe that his support
of don Sancho must have taken place some time later after his return
from Sicily, and not as early as the *CAX* states.[24] Something similar
may be said of don Dinis's support, although because of the conflict
with his mother, he had more reasons to disagree with his grandfather.

4. *Deposition of Alfonso X*

In Valladolid, on April 21, 1282, a particularly unusual event in the
history of the Castilian monarchy took place: the deposition of a king.
Gathered there were "all the people of the land and the *ricoshombres*
who were outside" of Castile and León as well as the wife of Alfonso X,
doña Violante, his dear brother don Manuel, "prince of traitors" (Ballesteros p. 967) together with all of king don Alfonso's children, beginning with the promoter of the revolt, don Sancho, and his younger
brothers, Pedro, Juan, and Jaime.[25] Many bishops, abbots, and members

---

[23] E.g., blackmail and the kidnapping of minors used to subject Zamora (*CAX*,
chap. 76, pp. 244–246).

[24] Text of the letter in Ballesteros, *Alfonso X*, pp. 959–960. Because of the chronology of the events in don Pedro's life it does not seem that his support of don Sancho
discussed above took place before mid-September, that is, when the meeting of the
nobles, clergy, and representatives of the town councils had already taken place in Valladolid, when don Sancho wrote to his uncle to tell him that, fulfilling the agreements
of Campillo, he would deliver Requena. Don Pedro answered by thanking him, but
declined the offer probably because he did not believe that his nephew had the power
to carry out such a grant.

[25] Ballesteros gathers the names of all the participants in the "plot" (*Alfonso X*,
p. 970). The abandonment by his entire family caused Alfonso unparalleled distress.
He must particularly have been hurt by the betrayal of his brother Manuel, who had
been by his side as advisor from the day he acceded to the throne.

of the religious and military orders also participated, but the bishops of Toledo and Seville and some others stayed away, remaining loyal to Alfonso.[26] And, of course, the only person who could legitimize that assembly and turn it into a Cortes was also absent, namely, Alfonso the king. After no dearth of intrigues, struggles, and blackmailing, the *CAX* states:

> Then Prince Sancho went to Valladolid and found there Queen Doña Violante, his mother, who was awaiting him there. She was very pleased with the position that he had taken against King Don Alfonso, her husband. When Prince Sancho arrived there, all of the realm and the nobles who were outside were united. They all agreed that they would give him the kingdom's power. Prince Sancho did not wish to agree that he be called king of his realm during his father's lifetime. About this they reached an agreement, and they agreed that they would require that King Don Alfonso yield all the fortresses and that they gave Prince Don Sancho the rule and the wealth of the kingdom. And Prince Don Manuel, King Don Alfonso's brother, declared this decree in the *Cortes* of Valladolid; and then Prince Don Sancho gave Prince Don Manuel as an inheritance Chinchilla, Porquera, Almansa, Aspe, and Beas. Prince Don Sancho granted to the people of the land the petitions they made for whatever they wanted, in which he gave them his letters with leaded royal seals. He divided the rents; he divided parcels of land among all the princes and nobles, just as they used to have them; and besides, he gave them what was for the maintenance of the king, to wit, the rents from the Jewish quarters, the *diezmo* tax, and the ancient duties on exports to Toledo, Talavera, and Murcia, and the rents of all the Moorish quarters. He did not keep for himself anything, so as to be sure that they were paid. (*CAX*, chap. 76, p. 246)[27]

The author of the *CAX*, as we've repeatedly stated, is clearly a supporter of don Sancho's, and in this situation, which will determine

---

[26] Through the archbishop of Toledo, don Gonzalo Gudiel, who always remained faithful to Alfonso, we know that "[t]he archbishop worked very hard in different ways to pacify [don Sancho], trying to make the relatives who were following the prince's faction return to the service of the king" (doc. De la Real Academia de la Historia, *Colección Salazar*, vol. R–1, fol. 302r. About don Gonzalo, see the monumental study by F. Hernández and P. Linehan, *The Mozarabic Cardinal. The Life and Times of Gonzalo Pérez Gudiel*, Florence: SISMEL / Edicioni del Galluzzo, 2004.

[27] For the author of the *CAX*, therefore, that meeting was doubtless a summoning of the Cortes, but not for some of the participants or the majority of the historians that have dealt with the matter throughout the centuries. Cf. J. O'Callaghan, *The Cortes of Castile-León, 1188–1350*, p. 84; E. Procter, *Curia and Cortes*, pp. 146–148; J.M. Pérez-Prendes, *Las Cortes de Castilla*, Barcelona, 1974, p. 76 and ff. For the various opinions on the nature of this assembly, cf. P. Lineham, *History and the Historians*, p. 529 note 78.

not only the prestige but also the legitimacy of the future king, he will express it more than ever, hiding how that coup d'état was actually achieved, that is, with threats, blackmail, and above all by buying support with money and gifts, as this passage states. It should be noted that the passage contradicts itself when it says that don Sancho "did not wish to agree that he be called king of his realm during his father's lifetime" (*CAX*, chap. 76, p. 246). One could then ask why Sancho held that meeting. What role did he expect to play while his father was alive? The *CAX* does not speak openly of the deposition, although it does affirm, "[t]hey all agreed that they would give him the kingdom's power" (*CAX*, chap. 76, p. 246). Wanting to prove next the generosity of don Sancho towards his uncle don Manuel, the architect of that farce or simulacrum of the Cortes, together his brothers and all the nobles who had supported don Sancho, the *CAX* unconsciously uncovers the embarrassing aspect of the agreement with those responsible for the politics of the kingdom, to whom Sancho gave everything: "Prince Don Sancho granted to the people of the land the petitions they made for whatever they wanted, in which he gave them his letters with leaded royal seals. He divided the rents; he divided parcels of land among all the princes and nobles, just as they used to have them; and besides, he gave them what was for the maintenance of the king [...]" (*CAX*, chap. 76, p. 246).

It is obvious that the *CAX* only gives us a half-truth. In fact, according to Zurita, don Sancho, as we suspected, wanted to name himself king, and exerted a great deal of pressure on his supporters so they would confer the title on him. But those present at the meeting unanimously chose not grant it to him, simply authorizing him to govern the kingdoms and administer justice in them. They also ordered that all fortresses, royal castles and royal income in Castile and León be granted to him, but they did not authorize him to use the title of king.[28] Therefore it is not that don Sancho did not want to use it, but rather that he did not receive it.[29] According to Mondéjar, this was the sentence "given by prince don Manuel, king Alfonso's brother,

---

[28] J. de Zurita, *Indices rerum ab Aragoniae regibus gestarum ab initiis Regni ad annum MCDX*, Zaragoza, 1578, p. 173; J. de Loaysa, *Crónica*, 298, p. 102; Ballesteros, *Alfonso X*, pp. 966 and 996.
[29] In fact, there is evidence that don Sancho used the title of king in several documents starting from the meeting at Valladolid (in J.M. del Estal, *Documentos inéditos de Alfonso X el Sabio y del infante su hijo don Sancho*, Alicante, 1984, p. 119).

while he was at the Valladolid Cortes," which the *CAX* speaks of.[30] This could lead to the conclusion that all the invectives of the biographers of the Learned King against his brother don Manuel were perhaps undeserved, because it seems that he was rather an element of moderation in that meeting that threatened to become civil war. Giving don Sancho the official responsibility of the administration of the kingdom in Castile and León in reality was nothing new, since that was what he had done with the express will of his father, practically since he began to co-reign. No summoning of a royal assembly was necessary for that. In Valladolid, don Sancho had wider concessions than what the *CAX* indicates. In any event, it is clear that the version of events in the *CAX* is incomplete and highly partisan.

To fill in the lacunae and distortions of the *CAX* and have a more complete picture of that plot, we fortunately also have the detailed testimony of several high-ranking Church figures, who courageously opposed the intrigue at great risk to their lives. One is a document of protest against the abuses and violence of don Sancho's henchmen, as well as against the tactics he used to obtain the support of all.[31] This document also narrates how the deposition took place, which, of course was not held in a very solemn meeting of Cortes, as the *CAX* would lead us to believe, but rather semi-clandestinely and before a very small ecclesiastical court of the king, summoned *ad hoc* and in which evidently only his supporters took part. Written by the Franciscan bishop of Burgos, Francisco, and Juan of Palencia, along with the Provincial of the Dominicans of Castile and León (Muño of Zamora), and three superiors of the same order, the document presents a completely different version of the deposition.

These Church officials tell how, when they were staying in the houses belonging to a certain Domingo Gómez de Monzón, where don Sancho too was staying, "subito et inesperato" (suddenly and unexpectedly), several nobles, town council representatives, and the princes Pedro and Juan showed up at the inn, asking them to immediately go to don Sancho's palace, since he was going to issue a sentence depriving don Alfonso of his royal functions, stripping him of the right to exercise

---

[30] Marqués de Mondejar, *Memorias*, pp. 409 and 412.
[31] The document is found in the Burgos cathedral. It was issued at the convent of the Dominicans of Valladolid and is dated April 21, 1282. It was published in the *MHE*, II, no. 198, pp. 59–63 and thoroughly discussed by Ballesteros, *Alfonso X*, pp. 967–969.

justice, and banning him from ownership of the cities, towns, castles, and fortresses, through himself or others. He would also be banned from receiving rent or any benefit in Castile and León. All of these rights, following the sentence, would be handed over to Sancho.[32] The authors of the document tell us that they replied that that was not a decision that could be made lightly and that required a careful thinking, because such a sentence, in the absence of solid proof, seemed unjust. The envoys replied there was no time for careful thinking. They threatened the clerics, saying that if they did not accompany them immediately to the palace, they would be beheaded on the spot. The prelates had no choice but to accompany them (*"mortis timore compulsi"*, for fear of being killed).

When they arrived at the palace, the envoys made them wait in a hall adjoining the other one where don Sancho was having a meeting behind closed doors with some men from military and civil circles with the goal of issuing the sentence that deprived Alfonso of his functions and declared Sancho as the only one capable of administering justice and governing the towns. When they opened the doors, the sentence of the king's deposition was announced to them.[33] The authors of the document go on to say that they vigorously protested against the clandestine nature of the meeting and the deposition of Alfonso and his substitution by Sancho, but everything was in vain.[34]

Based on this document, it is obvious that the meeting at Valladolid was not a convocation of the Cortes, but rather, a true plot as Ballesteros called it: "At that meeting, he writes, without a previous summons and without being convicted, the king don Alfonso was deposed of his royalty and from then on would no longer administer justice nor exercise sovereign functions."[35] But both the *CAX* and the abundant correspondence of don Sancho during this period shamelessly call the meeting a "Cortes," and it is not hard to see why. One thing, however, became clear at the end of the meeting at Valladolid: Alfonso, according to the *CAX* and the other document mentioned, had been completely abandoned by the clergy, the nobility, the representatives

---

[32] Text in *MHE*, II, pp. 59–63. Cf. Ballesteros, pp. 967–969; and "Burgos y la rebelión del Infante Don Sancho," *BRAH*, CXIX (1946), pp. 93–194, p. 175.

[33] *MHE*, II, pp. 59–63; Ballesteros, *Alfonso X*, p. 960.

[34] *MHE*, II, p. 62.

[35] *Alfonso X*, p. 969.

of the town councils participating in the assembly, and his entire family: wife, children, and brother.

In his distinctive style, don Juan Manuel concludes his passionate eulogy of his uncle, king Alfonso X, lamenting: "But because of the sins of Spain and specifically of the ones who were present then and even today belong to his lineage, he had an end that is sad to tell."[36] This constitutes a condemnation of the behavior of all of his uncle's lineage, including those who "were present then" (such as his dead father, don Manuel) and "and even today," that is, his cousin don Sancho. And even if in the *Libro de las armas* he writes about his father as "a loyal man [who] loved the king very much,"[37] don Juan knew perfectly well that his father had been disloyal and a traitor to the king.

What happened a few months after the famous meeting is not so clear. It seems that the support began to vanish relatively quickly. There's good reason to believe that alliances either with don Sancho or his father, especially among the high nobility and clergy, fluctuated considerably in the following months. There was much switching around of loyalties. This would explain why, in fact, Alfonso remained king until the end of his days. As M. González Jiménez has pointed out, there are several privileges dating from after the date of the deposition that indicate that practically all who participated at the meeting and were in favor of the positions of don Sancho, a few weeks later had turned in favor of their legitimate king don Alfonso. For instance, in a diploma dated July 13, 1282, Alfonso dispossesses the Order of Santiago from the town of Montemolín and delivers it to Seville. The cause of this decision, according to the document, was that the master of the Order, Pedro Núñez, and the friars had turned against the king, "rising up with our land and with their councils they also made those belonging to our lineage rise up and rebel against us and take away our power and our dominion."[38] The most surprising thing about this document, this scholar notes, is that, "in the lists of those confirming the diploma [...] few if any of the usual figures are missing, except for don Sancho and the Master of Santiago. All of the others figure there, as if the meeting and sentence given at Valladolid had not taken place: the princes don Pedro, don Juan, and don Jaime, children of the king,

---

[36] *Crónica abreviada*, ed. J.M. Blecua, *Obras completas*, II, p. 576.
[37] In *Obras completas*, ed. J.M. Blecua, I, p. 132.
[38] In M. González Jiménez, *Diplomatario*, n. 501; and *Alfonso X*, p. 187.

and his brother prince don Manuel. Of course, no noble is missing, nor are the bishops of Castile and León."[39] From the diploma it can be gleaned that not only the Master had risen up, but also that Alfonso blamed him for the rebellion of his children ("our lineage").

5. *Causes of the Deposition*

Alfonso X's deposition has been the subject of much controversy since the moment it happened. Historians will continue to debate the most ignominious event in the life of the Learned King. For some, it was "divine punishment," the logical consequence of his pride, which, as was said of his uncle Frederick II, intended to amend the Creator's work (see p. 26). According to them, don Sancho was the instrument that divine justice used to punish Alfonso's pride. However, most scholars, at least today, believe that is was the product of don Sancho's boundless ambition perhaps manipulated by a courtly elite who made him believe that he had been chosen by divine providence, as he himself expressed it during the confrontation with his father at the Seville Cortes discussed above. On the other hand, we cannot rule out other real and objective causes and motives that derive from poor administration and all kinds of abuses committed by Alfonso himself.[40]

The *CAX*, when announcing the deposition at what it terms the "Cortes" of Valladolid, does not give details as to its cause. But all post-Sancho literature repeats them almost in unison. The immediate cause of the conflict between father and son, in the days preceding and causing the Valladolid meeting, was the altercation between don Sancho and his father when Sancho found out that Alfonso wanted to leave one of his kingdoms to his grandchildren, the de la Cerda princes. It was indeed don Sancho's fear that the kingdom would be divided if his father truly carried out those plans that led him to a confrontation with him. The other motive, the discontent among the attendees of the Seville Cortes regarding the change in currency, also a result of the confrontation at Seville, was merely the excuse used by don Sancho to incite the town council representatives against his father. (The nobility and the clergy needed no agitators.) The aversion

---

[39] *Alfonso X*, pp. 187–188.
[40] M. Rodríguez Gil, "Para un estudio de la sentencia de deposición de Alfonso X," *Revista de la Facultad de Derecho.* Universidad Complutense, 9 (1985), pp. 103–113.

to his father, the cause of the rebellion, was produced by the fear of having to share the crown with one of his nephews, a prospect which made him beside himself with anger "[…] and Prince Sancho replied that he beseeched King Alfonso not to speak out about this treaty nor to order him to accept it, because there was nothing in the world in it to which he would agree." (CAX, chap. 75, p. 241)

This leads us to consider don Sancho's personality and ambitions. If we ignore for the moment how real was the waste of the kingdom's riches and Alfonso's abuse of power, it is clear that a major factor in the political process that led to the deposition of the Learned King was rightly identified in the king's formal malediction against don Sancho: "because he was blind with ambition".

For more than five years, the prince had been the declared heir, but there had already been several instances in which, when the moment of truth arrived regarding important decisions or ones which Sancho did not agree with (don Çag's execution, the concessions to the de la Cerda princes, the extravagance toward the Marquis of Monferrato during his sister's wedding, the negotiations with the king of France, etc.), his father had had the last word. On the other hand, it was also true that he had risked his life to contain the North African Moors at his father's request. For someone with Sancho's impetuous and proud temperament, this state of things could only cause dissatisfaction. His desire to be declared king at the Valladolid assembly in order to obtain total control of the kingdom's politics (for we should not doubt that that was the purpose of the meeting)[41] must have been a new source of frustration and resentment when he did not achieve the desired nomination and may very well have led him to the coup d'état. Of course the ambition to obtain the crown was the reason to use all kinds of tricks: the corruption of rivals, threats, blackmail, and other ignoble acts.

Having said this, we can still consider the problem of the doubt that, as we will see further on, also assailed in his day don Pedro de Aragón. In other words, how to explain the fact that all of Alfonso's children, his wife and his brother don Manuel, just as practically all of the

---

[41] His father expressed this clearly in the document where he cursed and disinherited him:

And besides this, insisting all he could, both by himself and through his servants and followers, he did everything he could to be called king of Castile, of León, and of Andalusia from that point on. (In Ballesteros, *Alfonso X*, p. 994).

nobility and the representatives of the cities and the town councils
of Castile would rise up against him? Was it that there were legitimate motives for this? What could those have been? What was it, for
instance, that led six bishops and fifty-four abbots, two weeks after
the deposition, to meet in that same city to express their agreement
with the sentence? Or what was it that led those civic brotherhoods
in the cities of León and Castile to come together for the first time as
a new social force to vindicate the rights that the king had stamped
out? According to a contemporary biographer of the Learned King,
the reason for the opposition of all these groups was to "reach a specific political objective: that Alfonso X would no longer occupy the
throne. Does this mean that the prince had bribed practically all the
inhabitants of the state? Evidently not. There were other reasons for
rebellion."[42]

The first time the *CAX* dealt thoroughly with the causes of the deposition was on the occasion of the attack that the joint forces of Alfonso
X and Yûsuf launched against Córdoba the summer of that year, 1282.
Alfonso sent a message to don Sancho's appointee in charge of the
city, Ferrand Muñiz (or Muñoz) telling him to give up supporting the
position of the rebellious prince and to consider the favors received
from his king and lord. Alfonso asked him to deliver the city and
abandon the cause of the rebels. Ferrand Muñiz, through his representatives who obviously also represented Sancho, delivered this message
through Diego López:

> Tell the king, our lord, that we, Diego López and don Álvaro, who are
> here with Prince Don Sancho, due to the many deaths and outrages that
> the king caused—especially in that he killed both Prince Don Fadrique,
> his brother, and likewise killed don Simón de los Cameros, our uncle,
> who reared us and was very good to us, and for the many other deaths
> he caused with violence to the nobles, and for the many encroachments
> he made upon our vassals in the entire realm—for these reasons, we had
> to appeal to the grace of Prince Don Sancho, who is his son and heir, to
> speak with us, and he did so. If King Alfonso should come as a king and
> lord should come, we and Prince Don Sancho would open the gates of
> the city and would receive him as king and lord. (*CAX*, chap. 76, p. 248)

The emphasis here is on two main causes: "due to the many deaths
and outrages that he caused" in particular that of his brother and
of don Simón de los Cameros, imposed "con desafuero" ("with vio-

---

[42] F. Pérez Algar, *Alfonso X, el Sabio*, p. 327.

lence"), and the many and outrageous taxes with which he burdened his subjects.[43] Neither of these complaints are new, and the rest revolve around those two.

Both causes, from a much wider social perspective in which are implicated not only the two highest strata, the clergy and the nobility, but also the cities, towns, and burghers, are described in greater detail in the foundational documents of a new political-social institution that, although it already existed in its initial form, began to acquire new power as a vehicle of social vindication: the *communal brotherhood*.[44] It is also through the foundational and other documents of these organizations that we can delve into the causes of and motives for Alfonso's deposition.[45]

The brotherhoods, both ecclesiastical and civil, that emerged in this period were organized, mostly, for the defense and promotion of Sancho's cause, but also as institutions that promoted the solidarity and interests of their members. The ecclesiastical brotherhoods led by very powerful bishops and abbots were particularly active. The two founded on May 2 and 3, 1282 in Valladolid and discussed above, had forty abbots (Benedictine, Cistercian, Cluniac, and Premonstratensian) and six bishops (Astorga, Zamora, Mondoñedo, Tuy, Badajoz, and Coria), respectively. The latter was joined by 25 abbots of the most important monasteries in Castile, León, and Galicia (Benedictine, Cistercian, and Premonstratensian).[46] The bishops of Castile-León, with a couple of exceptions, and a few more bishops in the South, were all in favor of don Sancho. Among abbots and heads of monasteries, there were even fewer supporters of Alfonso.[47]

---

[43] The first cause has been discussed almost exclusively by R. Kinkade, "Alfonso X, *Cantiga* 235, and the Events of 1269–1278," *Speculum*, 67 (1992), pp. 284–323. On the second, Alfonso X's economic and fiscal policy, as a cause of his downfall, there are many studies, see, in particular, J.F. O'Callaghan, "Paths to Ruin: The Economic and Financial Policies of Alfonso the Learned," in R.I. Burns, *The Worlds*, pp. 41–67.

[44] Cf. A. Alvarez de Morales, *Las hermandades: Expresión del movimiento comunitario en España*, Valladolid, 1974. pp. 267–268; L. Suárez Fernández, "Evolución histórica de las hermandades castellanas," *CHE*, 16 (1952), pp. 14–15; and J. O'Callaghan, *The Cortes of Castile-León*, pp. 85–87.

[45] Some of the foundational charters have been published in the *MHE*, II, no. 202, pp. 67–68.

[46] Cf. Ballesteros, *Alfonso X*, pp. 971–972. For the texts of the meetings, see *MHE*, II, no. 203, pp. 68–70.

[47] See the long list of the abbots and monasteries in favor of don Sancho in Ballesteros, *Alfonso X*, pp. 971–972; for the list of the bishops, cf. *id.*, p. 972. Cf. L. Fernández Martín, "La participación de los monasterios," pp. 5–35.

We must ask again what led the entire hierarchy to oppose Alfonso and support his deposition? Historians have discussed the various causes, but if we want to find out the reasons directly from the testimony of his rivals, whether truthful or not, we need to go back and peruse the various foundational documents of the brotherhoods. Here, for example, is the document of the brotherhood founded at the Sahagún monastery:

> In the name of God and of Holy Mary, Amen. To all who may read this letter, be it known that on account of the many illegal actions, the many damages, and violence, and death, and incarcerations, and excessive tributes, without a hearing; and on account of much dishonor and many other endless things against God, and against justice, and against the law, and which were of great damage to all the kingdoms, carried out by the king don Alfonso, therefore, the princes, the prelates, and the noblemen, and the councils, and the Orders, and the knights of the kingdom of León and Galicia, seeing that we were deprived of our rights and mistreated as we mentioned above, and since we could not tolerate it any longer, our lord, prince don Sancho, decided we should all unite with one will and one heart. He with us, and we with him, in order to safeguard our rights, our privileges, our customs and our traditions.[48]

Although this letter was written in the context of a religious institution by a group of Church officials gathered at the monastery of Sahagún, it is clear that it reflects the wider perspectives of a "general" brotherhood that covered much wider and diverse interests, from don Sancho's to those of the *ricoshombres* of the town councils ("He with us, and we with him"). Hence, when explaining the reasons that led them to such a shameful action—one that still caused embarrassment to the historian of the monastery five centuries later—they cited the common motives that brought together clergy and laity, nobles and commoners to reject their legitimate king and embrace the cause of the rebellious son.

The first part of the quote is explicit: "the many illegal actions, the many damages, and violence, and death, and incarcerations, and exces-

---

[48] In R. Escalona, *Historia del Real Monasterio de Sahagún*, Apéndice III, doc. no. 264, pp. 616–617; and the much more extensive Castilian version dated at Valladolid on July 8, 1282 (doc. 266, pp. 618–622). The well-known historian of the monastery cannot hide his disapproval of the participation of the abbot in the brotherhood, whose purpose was to support don Sancho's party against the legitimate king (ib., p. 156).

sive tributes."[49] Although the deaths of don Fadrique and don Simón are not mentioned explicitly, we can assume that they were among the "deaths," because the phrase "without a hearing," is repeated constantly when mentioning the executions. The newest aspect in the long list of causes may appear above, where the text says "and many other endless things against God, and against justice, and against the law, and which were of great damage to all the kingdoms". For the triple accusation: "against God, and against justice, and against the law," is the key to understanding why representatives of every level of society, and above all the clergy and the nobility, supported don Sancho and the deposition of his father. The general perception was that Alfonso, in killing his brother without due process or explanation, had gone against nature, God and justice all at the same time.

Other important pillars of medieval society were the *fueros* or codes of common law, and in this case Alfonso was guilty of issuing new laws that had eliminated them all (although it was also true that from 1272 on, any city or town could recover their traditional *fueros* if they so wished). To this effect, the foundation charter of the brotherhood was very clear and eloquent: it was founded as an institution precisely to safeguard the *fueros*, privileges, customs, and traditions of the clergy and nobility from the abuses that Alfonso had committed against them. We can infer that such abuses were the reason for their union or brotherhood with don Sancho, who promised to safeguard "our rights and our privileges, and our customs and in our traditions," in other words, to maintain the status quo that they had enjoyed thus far. It was in the field of the *fueros* and the rights of their members that the brotherhood had an attitude of reclaiming rights, and could become a two-edged sword: today against Alfonso, and tomorrow, or whenever luck would change, against Sancho, which happened when Sancho attempted to do what his father had done. But as one might imagine, in the majority of foundational documents of these brotherhoods that emerge with Sancho's rebellion, Alfonso is accused of having

---

[49] The best list of Alfonso's fiscal blunders, specifically against the ecclesiastical hierarchy, appears in part 5 of the *Memoriale secretum*, of which the pope was evidently informed by the Castilian-Leonese bishops; with one phrase, it demolishes Alfonso's behavior in all aspects: "Peccat ergo graviter in percipiendo, peccat etiam in modo percipiendi" ["He, sins gravely by imposing [taxes], and he also sins in the way he imposes [them]" (*Reg. Nich. III*, 343).

committed great injustices, and the protection of the rebellious prince is sought to defend and preserve the codes of law of the members.[50]

Both in Ferrand Muñiz's list of accusations and in the letter of the Sahagún brotherhood, we find frequent mention of "many illegal taxes" and "violations of the codes of law," in other words, unjust and excessive taxes. From what we know, the deaths and the violations of the law codes affected a limited, albeit the most powerful sector of the population. But the overall discontent with Alfonso's fiscal policy produced many more victims, because taxes affected everyone and were felt more severely in the humble sectors of the agricultural towns, villages, and fortresses. It was this oppressed social class that, through its representatives, raised its cry to the heavens, resorting to don Sancho to end the abuses. In fact, according to his contemporary, Jofré de Loaysa, this was the fundamental cause of the coup d'état: "The prince don Sancho...seeing that the king his father taxed the kingdom with enormous taxes and services, convinced the barons and nobles and the councils to ask the king not to loot their land in such a way with unbearable taxes...and gathering the nobles and the councils in Valladolid...they agreed firmly among them, that King Alfonso would not be received in any town and that no other taxes or services should be paid to him."[51] In other words, even a figure as close to Alfonso's court as this supporter and ally identifies and acknowledges the king's poor fiscal policy, and to such an extent that he passes over in silence the other accusations mentioned in the *CAX* and pro-Sancho historiography. Historically, abuses of this sort frequently caused rebellion; the case of Alfonso was one more.

The deposition of the Learned King must have had a tremendous impact on literature at the time. A historical event of that magnitude could not be ignored. There are echoes of that unprecedented crisis in the history of the kingdom of Castile-León not only among the historians and chroniclers, but also among the poets and fiction writers. I will cite only one example from a work composed during the events or shortly thereafter, which illustrates the new vision of politics and culture typical of Sancho IV's court.

---

[50] This case of conditional support (*do ut des*), becomes obvious in an explicit way in the long document that the brotherhood of bishops, abbots, and representatives of the kingdom's churches would issue at the end of the assembly gathered at Benavente on May 9, 1283.

[51] *Crónica*, no. 28.

I am referring to the *Libro del Caballero Zifar*, (*The Book of the Knight Zifar*) whose author reflects the same line of thinking as the historian Jofré de Loaysa by attributing the cause of the rebellion to excessive taxes. This work, according to the opinion of the scholars who have dealt with it, is properly set in and connected to the political realities at the end of the 13th century, although it is written as a work of fiction. The author was most probably Ferrán Martínez, a secretary at Alfonso X's court at least since 1274, the year his signature appears in a grant from don Gonzalo García Gudiel, who was then bishop of Cuenca and notary of the king. Don Gonzalo would subsequently become archbishop of Toledo, rising to become cardinal, and would die in Rome towards 1299. In 1300, on the occasion of the papal jubilee, as is stated in the prologue of the work, Ferrán Martínez went to Rome to pick up the mortal remains of the cardinal and transfer them to Toledo. He also served as secretary at the court of Sancho IV, until, after Sancho's death, the Valladolid Cortes (in the summer of 1295) decided to end the intervention of the clergy in government through control of the kingdom's chancellery, ordering that the notaries of the court must henceforth be laymen.[52]

Ferrán Martínez therefore would have been a direct witness to the historical events that led to don Sancho's rebellion and Alfonso's deposition. The topic must have been the subject of heated discussions between the courtiers and the supporters of both sides. Scholars of this work have found many important reflections of life and the attitudes of Ferrán Martínez in *El Caballero Zifar*. For example, in the section entitled "Castigos del rey de Mentón" ("The Instructions of the King of Mentón"), which constitutes a veritable treatise on the education of princes, much space is dedicated to the theme of social justice, and future kings are instructed not to overburden their subjects with taxes if they want to be loved by them.[53] The author even adopts relatively

---

[52] *El Libro del Cavallero Zifar*, ed. Ch.Ph. Wagner, Ann Arbor: University of Michigan, 1912; English translation from which passages of this work are quoted: *The Book of the Knight of Zifar. A Translation of El Libro del Cavallero Zifar*, trans. Charles L. Nelson. Lexington, Kentucky: University Press of Kentucky, 1983; and cf. F.J. Hernández's scholarly articles, "Ferrán Martínez, 'Escrivano del rey', canónigo de Toledo y autor del *Libro del caballero Zifar*," *RABM*, 81 (1978), pp. 289–325; "Noticias sobre Jofré de Loaisa y Ferrán Martínez," *RCEH*, 4 (1979–1980), pp. 281–309; F.J. Hernández and P.A. Linehan, *The Mozarabic Cardinal. The Life and Times of Gonzalo Pérez Gudiel*, Florence: SISMEL / Edicioni del Galluzzo, 2004.

[53] Among the works in this section, a majority are oriental, and some of them, such as *Flores de Filosofía* (Philosophy Flowers), coincide with the education manuals for

rigid positions in this matter, justifying the imposition of taxes only when they are absolutely necessary to defend the kingdom.[54]

In the same section we find the story of what "happened to the Emperor of Armenia, who appeared very powerful and wise to all men" (*The Book of The Knight Zifar*, p. 220). But it so happened that

> [...] through the scheming of evil counselors, who thought they would have a great share in what the emperor would exact from his land, they advised him to burden his people with taxes, although it was against his own laws. They advised him to order money of base value made that could be used in purchases and sales, and other coins of great value that his taxpayers, the privileged as well as the non privileged, could pay him and in this way he would acquire all the wealth of the land and would be able to give and to spend as extravagantly as he wanted; and so he did. And when the people realized it and understood this great oppression that came to them from all these things, they rose against the emperor and refused to welcome him in any of his towns. And what was worse, those who advised this, sided with the people against the emperor, so that he died fallen from favor and sorely afflicted. (*The Book of The Knight Zifar*, p. 220)

It appears that here the author was alluding to the events that led to Alfonso X's deposition, at times literally reproducing expressions from Jofré de Loaysa's chronicle. But unlike Loaysa's historical account, which makes explicit mention of "a rebellious prince" who deposed his father for fiscal abuses, in the account by Ferrán Martínez, who was a priest from the Toledo elite working Sancho IV's chancellery while writing his book, there is no mention at all of the deposition of the emperor by a rebellious son. All the blame is laid on the treacherous advisors and nobles who use the popular discontent they themselves provoked by advising the emperor to impose disproportionate taxes, adding "[a]nd what was worse, those who advised this, sided with the people against the emperor" (*The Book of The Knight Zifar*, p. 220).

This behavior is perfectly understandable. No courtier of Sancho IV's, especially a Church official, would have ever dared to delegitimize his king by accusing him of having acceded to the throne through the deposition of his father. On the contrary, in all the works that were produced under Sancho's patronage, the legitimacy of the succession

---

princes that Alfonso X used during his own formative years. Cf. Ch.Ph. Wagner, "The Sources of *El Cavallero Zifar*," *RH*, X (1903), pp. 5–104.

[54] *The Book of The Knight Zifar*, p. 220.

is made abundantly clear. We are thus faced with a work that was the product of a post-Alfonsine culture, as can be gleaned too from the positive attitude of the author towards the Church and its hierarchy, which is generally apparent in all the works that were produced during the reign of Sancho IV.[55] Such an attitude is completely different from what emerges from the works of Alfonso X and from those composed during his reign or under his patronage. For example Chapter 149 ("How the king of Mentón told his sons that all kings sought [sic] to hold counsel with the prelates of the Holy Mother Church", *The Book of The Knight Zifar*, p. 187) concludes thus: "it is fitting for the king to pay honor to the priest just as to a father, and to respect him the same as his doctor and the people's doctor, and to love him as a guardian of the faith. And know, my sons, that it is never found in the Scripture that the king should be without a priest, not even in the era of the gentiles. And every Christian king ought to have with him some good man of the Holy Church and to request advice from him for the body and for the soul" (*The Book of The Knight Zifar*, pp. 187–188). Attitudes such as this would have been inconceivable in the cultural milieu of Alfonso's reign.

6. *Alfonso Defends Himself*

We cannot have a complete picture of the causes of the deposition without asking ourselves what the deposed thought, and therefore we must explore what, according to Alfonso, led his friends and family to that coup d'état. Fortunately, about Sancho's rebellion and the meeting of the nobles and the clergy at Valladolid, there is an invaluable document containing a detailed analysis carried out by Alfonso himself. It is a text that, in its impressive drama and wealth of detail, reveals the deep knowledge of the Learned King about the political situation of the kingdom, the temperament of his faithless son, and the most prominent figures in Peninsular politics in the 13th century who

---

[55] Ideologically, it seems that indeed, *The Book of the Knight Zifar* was mostly written during the reign of Sancho IV (1284–1295), especially the section "Los castigos del rey de Mentón" ("The Instructions of the King of Mentón"), that is, before 1300, the date mentioned in the prologue. However, everything seems to indicate that it could not have been composed before March/May of 1302, the probable date on which the body of don Gonzalo García Gudiel arrived in Toledo accompanied by don Ferrán Martínez.

betrayed him. This is the document that contains Alfonso's sentences of malediction and disinheritance against don Sancho. When speaking of what caused the usurpation of power, Alfonso states:

> We do not think we should fail to mention that the abovenamed don Sancho, in the speeches he gave to incite the people against us, often uttered very ugly words, both he and his followers very often saying, among other things: the king is insane and is a leper, and he is even more false and deceitful regarding many things, killing men for no reason, as he did with don Fadrique and don Simón.[56]

A year later, on March 4, 1283, in a privilege granted to his daughter Beatriz given in the city of Niebla, Alfonso emphatically denounces the rebelliousness of his son and those who supported him: "the said uprising was against God, and against justice, and against reason, and against the law, and against natural lordship," accusing don Sancho of spreading false and misleading information about him in order to incite people to rebellion: "because at the time, our other children and the majority of the men in our land rose up against us due to things they were told and informed about, which were not so."[57] We do not know what lies under the phrase "things...which were not so," but we can surmise that it refers to a version of the events surrounding the execution of his brother, in which don Sancho too had participated. He was one of the few who knew the truth about those events but neither he nor Alfonso ever wanted to reveal the true causes of the execution. He went around, according to Alfonso, spreading false information and accusations because it was undignified or shameful to reveal the truth.

The image of Alfonso that don Sancho and his supporters promoted, presenting him as a "leper madman"—labels that Alfonso considered particularly "ugly" because in medieval times they had the connotation of "horrible" and "monstrous"—was an indecorous and undignified image for a son to present of his own father in public. But the most interesting thing about the passage is that Alfonso, perfectly aware of all the documents, did not do anything to defend himself. As we said

---

[56] In Ballesteros, *Alfonso X*, p. 994. The same accusations of insanity (and leprosy?) also appear in the letter that Alfonso sent to Yûsuf requesting his help: "They say: 'he's an old man who has lost his mind and whose reasoning has been impaired'" (Ibn Abi Zar', *Rawad al-Qirtas*, trans. A. Huici, II, p. 635).

[57] In Ballesteros, *Alfonso X*, p. 1015 and further on chap. 15, note 9. For the complete text of the privilege, cf. M. González Jiménez, *Diplomatario*, n. 508.

above, he took this secret to the grave. We will never know whether the execution was justified or not. The fact is that in this document, and even when the facts were undeniable, Alfonso rejects the accusation of fratricide. This can lead us to two possible conclusions: either Alfonso was lying, or he was convinced that the execution was fair, and that don Sancho knew it had been so, though he would later maliciously spread the horrible accusation of fratricide against his father, which is what would remain in the minds of his subjects, chroniclers and later historians who did not find out the truth. To all those who did not know the motives for the execution, Alfonso left a puzzle: How can a king be fair if he kills his own brother for no reason? Only a monster or a madman could commit such a transgression. In any event, this was exactly the image of Alfonso that don Sancho wanted to promote, although to do so, as Alfonso's document hints, he had to twist the truth. A sign of his success is that fratricide remains the most consistent accusation against the king in the later documentation and historiography.

In another passage of the same document cursing don Sancho, Alfonso seems to suggest that he was informed about the complaints about his excessive taxes, admitting that perhaps he was unfair in extending them beyond what the Cortes, or the pope, had authorized. This is what the expression "false and deceitful regarding many things" probably refers to, in the sense that after the concession of a new tax, Alfonso would promise not to ask more, though he did not stick to his word (for as the pope said in his *Memoriale secretum*: "He sins gravely by imposing [taxes], and he also sins in the way he imposes [them]"). Regarding this accusation, however, Alfonso declares: "We were ready to completely revoke, according to his decision, and that of the prelates, gentlemen, and other good men, any grievance, if there was one; to amend everything that needed amending, and to restore all things to a state of peace and calm."[58]

It is clear that Alfonso was excessive with taxation. The needs of the reconquest, the expenses of his quest for the Empire, the investments in scientific and cultural projects, his patronage of artists and poets, and also his boundless generosity, bordering on wastefulness in some cases—all of this was paid for through the sweat and deprivation of

---

[58] In Ballesteros, *Alfonso X*, p. 995.

his subjects, and it was getting to a point that they could no longer bear it.[59]

Although taxes themselves were not a sufficient reason to depose a king, when this was added to popular discontent over the injustices and homicides, especially the execution of his brother, the impression his subjects must have had was that they were ruled by an irrational, unfair, and heartless king. His frequent excesses must have left the impression on those observing him up close that he was in fact insane. At the same time, the advanced maxillary cancer, which caused the deformity of his face and left eye, must have made him look like a leper.

As final testimony, although it was written sixty years later, we would like to cite the *Crónica de 1344* (*Chronicle of 1344*), composed by the count don Pedro of Barcelos, the illegitimate son of king don Dinis of Portugal, grandson of Alfonso X, which is one of the most anti-Alfonsine texts we know of. The Count of Barcelos justifies the deposition with a series of charges similar to those laid out by the brotherhood, previously noted. Significantly, however, he places the sentence of deposition, as the *CAX* does, in the mouth of prince don Manuel:

> Because king don Alfonso killed don Fadrique, his brother, and don Simón Ruiz, lord of Los Cameros, and many other noblemen without justice, as he should have done, may he lose control of justice.
>
> Because he disinherited the noblemen of Castile and León and the citizens of the town councils, may he not be received in towns or castles and may he be disinherited from them.
>
> Because he deprived the noblemen and the town councils of their codes of laws, may they not fulfill what is requested in his letters and may his orders not be respected.
>
> And because he expropriated the land and coined bad currency, may not receive payment of taxes or services, nor […] tributes, nor any other rights over land, even if he demands it.[60]

---

[59] Alfonso's generosity and wastefulness were, according to the Catalan historian Bernat Desclot, the main cause of the deposition (*Crónica*, ed. M. Coll i Alentorn, 5 vols., Barcelona: Barcino, 1949–1951, II, chap. V, p. 39). E. Procter quotes several contemporary testimonies of those who benefited from his generosity (*Alfonso X of Castile, Patron of Literature and Learning*, Oxford, 1951, pp. 137–139).

[60] Quoted by D. Catalán, *La Estoria de España de Alfonso X. Creación y evolución*, Madrid: Fundación Ramón Menéndez Pidal – Universidad Autónoma, 1992, p. 12 (according to the Mss. U).

This elaborate list of Alfonso X's crimes and excesses is the most complete summary of the accusations traditionally leveled against the Learned King. Written in the style of a trial document, in which to each charge a punishment is accorded, it is clearly an attempt to denigrate Alfonso, although the accusations essentially correspond to what we have examined. The text returns to the topic of the deaths ordered by Alfonso, stressing in particular that of his brother and Simón de los Cameros, and adds a new cause, the coining of "bad currency", which had not appeared explicitly in any of the previous documents. But like other texts previously quoted, the Count of Barcelos also does not mention explicitly the waste of funds involved in Alfonso's quest for the Empire. In another passage, however, the Portuguese historian does emphasize the fact that Alfonso deprived his subjects of their common law, the reason why the pope, apprized by the bishops of León and Santiago, denied him the imperial crown: "And the pope learned the truth from the bishop of Santiago, don Gonzalo Gómez, and through the bishop of León, about how he deprived his subjects of their *fueros* and for this reason he did not want to grant him the empire."[61]

The topic of the oppression of the people that the Portuguese historian speaks of, together with the bad treatment accorded certain members of the clergy was also the chief accusation in the *Memoriale secretum*, a document based on the complaints of the Peninsular Church hierarchy, who, because of their position, were the ones who accused Alfonso before the pope. Although the *Memoriale* did not advocate deposition (in fact, the pope would later condemn don Sancho's rebellion and excommunicate him), it is clear that the pontifical document must have encouraged the high Church officials, unhappy with Alfonso's government, to support Sancho and his coup d'état.

All of these causes of the deposition and one more besides reappear in the list of Father Mariana's opinion, which is famous because of its absurdity:

> A punishment from heaven, indeed, deserved for other reasons and because he dared with a loose and unruly tongue, trusting his wit and ability, to find fault in the works of Divine Providence, and in the design and shape of the human body, such is the testimony and common opinion of the people, handed down from father to son from long ago. This

---

[61] Quoted by Linehan, *Histories and the Historians*, p. 509, note 10.

insolence God punished by treating him in this way, a misfortune they say he had reached through the art of Astrology in which he was well-versed, if it can be called an art at all and not a deceit and hoax which will always be reprehended and will always have supporters.[62]

A skillful historian, Mariana levels the accusation, but he washes his hands of the truthfulness of what he's telling by attributing to it to "the testimony and common opinion of the people". According to Ballesteros, who has analyzed better than anyone else the causes of the deposition, "[t]he legal life of the Learned King completely contradicts the words of the Jesuit historian" (*Alfonso X*, p. 969). And regarding the charge that in his palace of Toledo Alfonso had committed blasphemy about the divine creation and design of the human body, it was a "false story already rejected by healthy criticism" (p. 969).

Whether the list of complaints from the peoples of Castile and León was true or not is not very important at this stage. What does matter is to know what those grievances were, which according to his subjects had rendered him unfit to continue ruling as king. In the end, as we will see later on, it was not even concrete grievances that led the members of the nobility and the clergy to oppose Alfonso, but rather the perception that he was trying to change, on the one hand, the privileged position of the nobility by unifying the law codes and making all his subjects equal before the law, and on the other, that he was extricating civil society and the power of the monarchy from the control of the Church. In the final analysis, the affair was a desperate struggle pitting the two traditional strata of society trying to preserve their status quo against a progressive monarchy that wanted to give society new directives.[63] As the letter from the brotherhood formed at the Sahagún monastery suggests, I believe that this was the ultimate reason for the opposition by the nobility and the clergy. Clearly, attempting such a socio-cultural revolution in the 13th century was premature, and therefore, Alfonso ended up losing.

---

[62] Quoted by Ballesteros, *Alfonso X*, pp. 969–970.

[63] The rebellious bishops, as we saw, went as far as demanding that don Sancho organize even his own chancellery according to the criterion of his grandparents and great-grandparents (in *MHE*, II, p. 70).

CHAPTER FOURTEEN

DON SANCHO SEEKS THE CONSOLIDATION OF POWER. THE CURSE

1. *Political Propaganda and Change*

Excited by the power he had received from the nobility, the clergy, and the representatives of the city councils at the assembly at Valladolid and in the days following, Sancho began a southbound tour of Castile, leaving Valladolid in mid-May, while his chancellery, headed at his request by his brother Pedro, began an intense propaganda and public relations campaign.[1]

According to some, that same month he obtained the support of don Gonzalo García Pérez (Gudiel), archbishop of Toledo and primate of Spain (1280–1298), on whom his father had bestowed many favors, having taken him along to Beaucaire, for example, and later naming him Chancellor of the Crown of Castile (1280–1284). But these allegations do not seem very likely, since by all accounts don Gonzalo remained faithful to Alfonso throughout the king's life, and did not even participate in Sancho's coronation, which was conducted in his bishopric but presided over by four bishops who supported the rebel.[2] Don Gonzalo, the "extraordinary Toledan," was a prominent figure in the Spanish Church of the 13th century. He became cardinal-bishop of Albano, 1298–1299. In collaboration with a group of priests belonging to Toledo's intellectual elite he would also become the chief architect of Sancho IV's international and domestic policies, to the point that, according to the historian of the archbishops of Toledo,

---

[1] This activity has been studied by M.I. Ostolaza, "La cancillería del infante don Sancho durante la rebelión contra su padre Alfonso X el Sabio," *HID*, 16 (1989), pp. 305–313.

[2] The bishops were Fr. Fernando, bishop of Burgos; Gonzalo, bishop of Cuenca; Alfonso, bishop of Coria; and Gil, bishop of Badajoz. Cf. *Crónica de Sancho IV*, p. 69b; and P. Linehan, *History and the Historians*, pp. 471–476. On don Gonzalo Pérez Gudiel, see the monumental work by F. Hernández and P. Linehan, *The Mozarabic Cardinal. The Life and Times of Gonzalo Pérez Gudiel*, Florence: SISMEL / Edizioni del Galluzzo, 2004.

Diego Castejón, Sancho "was ruled by him."[3] But perhaps where don Gonzalo's influence was seen most was in promoting the extensive cultural change that occurred after Alfonso X's death. Don Sancho would repay his services to the Crown by naming him, first, his chancellor in León, Castile, and Andalusia (1290), and in October of that same year, by appointing him to the highest position of the kingdom, chancellor general of all the kingdoms.[4] He died in Rome in 1299 and was buried in a lavish Cosmatesque mausoleum in the basilica of St. John Lateran, and in 1301 his remains were transferred to his bishopric in Toledo.

Expressions of support for Sancho were dampened by less pleasant news from his uncle, don Pedro of Aragón, who, in a letter dated May 18, 1282, suggested that he reconcile himself with his father for the good of the kingdom. On the same date, Pedro wrote also to Alfonso, in a dilemma because both father and son had requested help from him, and the terms of the treaty of Campillo obliged him to aid them both.[5] Don Pedro's concerns were twofold: first, that not only Sancho but "all of the children", together with Alfonso's wife and many of his subjects, had rebelled against the father; second and perhaps much more, the likelihood that Alfonso would take drastic and irreversible measures against them all.[6] The king of Aragón was at the time preparing to depart for Sicily, and he feared that during his absence, the Peninsula might turn into a powder keg, with civil war breaking out in Castile. Given this situation, the North African Moors could take advantage of the chaos to launch a new attack, called back by the discontent of the king of Granada. Therefore, he promised Alfonso that, before leaving the kingdom, he would send his eldest son, don Alfonso, to him and to don Sancho in order to negotiate reconciliation between the two.[7] From the context, it can be deduced that, in a previous letter, Alfonso X had asked him for asylum in case things went badly and he was in danger. Don Pedro had replied saying that Alfonso could count on his hospitality, adding that he was ready to extend it to don Sancho as well. Don Pedro truly behaved like a family member and friend and,

---

[3] D. Castejón y Fonseca, *Primacía de la Iglesia de Toledo*, pp. 777–778.

[4] Cf. J.M. Nieto Soria, *Iglesia y poder real*, p. 36.

[5] For the texts of the correspondence see Ballesteros, *Alfonso X*, pp. 973–974.

[6] Therefore, he repeatedly pleaded with Alfonso to use moderation in punishment, because he knew perfectly well that he could be implacable (*ib.*). Don Pedro evidently was thinking that an inflexible attitude on Alfonso's part could lead his children to regicide, which would be detrimental to all.

[7] In Ballesteros, p. 974.

at the same time, as an exceptional politician who rose to the occasion at that moment of crisis in Castile.

While they were heading south, don Sancho was picking up new supporters and making good on the reform promises he had made during the campaign prior to the assembly at Valladolid. One of the reasons for the rebellion, as we know, had been the change in the currency introduced by Alfonso at the Seville Cortes, which had created panic among the representatives of the northern cities. Don Sancho had sworn he would do everything possible to go back to the state of things during the times of his grandfather and great-grandfather. The time to make good on his promises had arrived, and that is what he did when he passed through Cuéllar. In a privilege granted to that city, he ruled on the currency norms, and according to his own testimony, he did so after consulting "teachers and wise men, knowledgeable about currency [...] and according to what they told me and advised me, I made the decision and decided to do as follows: that the new *burgalés* and *pepión* currency would be coined in Burgos, and the new *leonés* currency would be coined in León, and the new *salamanqués* currency would be coined in Salamanca."[8] In other words, instead of the two currencies his father had set up for the entire kingdom, he ordered that only one be used, but that each city should have its own. The change must not have been that easy, because barely two months later the first protests against the new rules began. From Toledo, on June 6, don Sancho sent a letter to the Burgos town council to reproach them for having banned "any man from changing the currency that circulated then or from melting it. I cannot believe [he says] that you would have carried out or commanded such a thing without informing me, since all people in the land asked me to do this as a favor". At the same time, he commanded them: "proclaim that the ordered currency be coined, and may twelve of the ones I've now ordered to be minted be worth eighteen of the white coins that circulated before I had this coin minted."[9] It was therefore a revalorization of only 0.66%, but a new element of confusion was added when a new currency was created for each city.

From Cuéllar he headed to Toledo, where he arrived at the beginning of June. According to the *CAX*, "and when he arrived, he married

---

[8] In Ballesteros, *Alfonso X*, p. 975.
[9] Text of the document in Ballesteros, *Alfonso X*, p. 977.

doña María, daughter of the Prince of Molina" (*CAX*, chap. 76, p. 246), the brother of his paternal grandfather Fernando III. María, therefore, was a cousin by blood of his father and his aunt. Canonically, the marriage was not only incestuous but also bigamous, because in Burgos in April of 1270 Sancho had married Guillermina de Montcada, daughter of Gaston VII, viscount of Béarne, and that marriage had not yet been annulled.[10] To complicate things further, Doña María de Molina was godmother to an illegitimate daughter of don Sancho's, which created yet another canonical impediment: spiritual affinity. A very irregular situation indeed, this was a repetition of a familiar pattern: the blood ties between the groom and bride, the pope's condemnation, the decree of separation, and, of course, the proverbial story of the royal couple that goes on with their life as if nothing were the matter.[11]

During his stay in Toledo, his sister Violante, Alfonso X's youngest daughter, married don Diego Díaz de Haro. The political aim of this marriage was obvious to everyone. Don Diego was the nobleman with the greatest prestige who had not participated in the Valladolid meeting because he supported the succession of the de la Cerda princes. Giving her daughter in marriage to him was an easy way to get his support for his cause. The marriage, however, did not please the father of the bride, who, at the time, was not on good terms with the Haros because of their recent defection and because they had supported the cause of his rebellious son. It was also a new incident of abuse of power on Sancho's part, who, through this act of defiance, killed two birds with one stone.

The author of the *CAX* also reminds us that on the occasion of the wedding of don Sancho to María de Molina, he also served as the

---

[10] The marriage to Guillermina de Montcada, "rich, ugly, and fierce," effected through representatives when don Sancho had not yet turned twelve, was his only legitimate marriage and the only one canonically recognized by the Church, although it was never consummated, and husband and wife never lived together. Cf. A. Marcos Pous, "Los dos matrimonios de Sancho IV de Castilla," in *Escuela Española de Arqueología e Historia en Roma: Cuadernos de trabajo*, 8 (1956), 7–108. See also M. Gaibrois, *María de Molina, tres veces reina*, Madrid: Espasa Calpe, 1936; and *Historia del reinado de Sancho IV*, I, pp. 27–28.

[11] Sancho's married life was eventful. Besides the two marriages already mentioned, don Sancho also had several romantic adventures and had at least one illegitimate daughter (María de Meneses) with María Alfonsi de Ucera, to whom María de Molina was godmother (cf. Flórez, *Memorias de las reinas cathólicas*, II, p. 561). His marital case was considered so serious in Rome, that he did not even receive the pope's dispensation after his death. Apparently, in Rome Sancho IV's legitimacy was never accepted.

godfather to a son of his uncle's, prince don Manuel, who was born on May 5 in Escalona to countess Beatrice of Savoy, "and they named him Juan. Prince Don Manuel asked him to give him Peñafiel, and Prince Don Sancho gave it to him on the conditions that the royal privilege states" (CAX, chap. 76, p. 246). When don Manuel died, a year later after the birth of the child (1283), and when Beatrice died seven years later, don Sancho would become the guardian of that child who would grow up to be one of the most distinguished figures in 14th-century letters and politics.

In all of these actions, don Sancho was behaving as if he had complete control of the kingdom, but it was not so. In fact, if he did not want to lose what he had conquered, he had to act very quickly to consolidate power, which had begun to crumble. This was what he attempted with his trip to the south, and by setting up in Córdoba his base of operations. On August 5, 1282 he was already in the city of the caliphs. The first thing he did was to leave his wife doña María de Molina in the care of the Masters of Calatrava and Alcántara and the Prior of the Hospitallers, while he headed to Badajoz to try to quell the rebellion. This was his first setback, as he was unable to subject it, and the city went over to his father's side, joining Murcia and Seville, which never abandoned Alfonso.[12]

2. Alfonso Reacts

While Sancho was touring Castile, buying alliances, his father was ensconced in Seville, in a poor state of health, alone, and abandoned by all his relatives, including his wife, children, and even his dear brother, don Manuel, who, inexplicably, continued to support the cause of the rebel to his death. He had only the support of Seville, his beloved city, the region of Murcia, and the small kingdom of Niebla.[13] At the end of August, the city of Badajoz would also join Alfonso. The

---

[12] Don Sancho was at the gates of Badajoz on September 2, 1282. Cf. A. Ballesteros, "Burgos y la rebelión del infante don Sancho," BRAH, CXIX (1946), pp. 93–194, 167.

[13] Alfonso repeatedly showed his affection and devotion to Seville because of its fidelity, through not only a great number of privileges and concessions, but also in literary works (especially the Setenario, pp. 16–20, the GE, the EE). For the famous passage on Seville's loyalty in the city's privilege, see Ballesteros, Alfonso X, p. 1045. The case of Murcia's fidelity is similar, cf. J. Torres Fontes and C. Torres Suárez, La lealtad de Murcia a Alfonso X el Sabio, Murcia, 1984.

company of his inseparable and beloved daughter doña Beatriz, who was with him in Seville for similar reasons after having abandoned the Portuguese court due to conflicts with her son, don Dinis, must have been a great comfort to him in those days.[14] In his solitude, the Learned King began to desperately seek the support of all those who, because of blood or friendship ties or political agreements, could help him out. Nobody did.

His great worry was the state of the kingdom and its integrity. As a result of the irresponsible actions of his rebellious son, chaos and civil war were a threat similar to the plague. Alfonso had to quickly react and look for supporters if he wanted to save the few territories that remained faithful and even his own crown. To that end, as he tells us in the first version of his last will, he began an intense epistolary campaign, trying desperately to get in touch with his grandson, don Dinis, king of Portugal, his brother-in-law, don Pedro III, king of Aragón, his half-brother-in-law, Edward I of England, Philip III of France, and even pope Martin IV, pleading for their help.[15] In smooth prose and with impeccable arguments, the Learned King presented the reasons why he believed his correspondents were obligated to help him in this crisis, which threatened to end in the dissolution of his kingdom, something that would have disastrous consequences for all of Christendom.

The first two, don Dinis and don Pedro, besides being his relatives, had the absolute obligation to help Alfonso, according to the customs of the period, because they had been knighted by him. Following bad advice, don Dinis refused to do anything for his grandfather, "because we thought he was more a friend of our enemy than a friend of ours" (*Ant.*, p. 228). The king of Aragón, besides being his brother-in-law, was obligated through a formal commitment. But on the brink of his

---

[14] Regarding the presence of Beatriz in Seville, accompanying his father in those difficult moments, we have Alfonso's direct testimony in the privilege in which he granted Beatriz the city of Niebla as a reward for her daughterly love and dedication (in Ballesteros, *Alfonso X*, p. 1015). Cf. M. González Jiménez, *Diplomatario andaluz*, n. 508.

[15] For the correspondence with all these figures and the respective passages dedicated to them in the first of his two last wills, see the text in García Solalinde, *Antología de Alfonso X el Sabio*, pp. 228–230 and cf. Ballesteros, *Alfonso X*, pp. 978–981. It seems that the only positive reply together with some kind of help, despite his own difficulties, was Edward of England's, according to Lineham (*History and the Historians*, p. 500, note 138). This is not what Alfonso says in his last will. See now the edition by M. González Jiménez, *Diplomatario*, n. 518.

departure for Sicily, he used the excuse of his pledge to "the crusade to conquer Africa" (ib., p. 229). To Edward of England, Alfonso said, "we begged him to help us, for the love of God...but arguing that he was a long way from us and that, on the other hand, he too had great wars in his land, he skillfully excused himself in such a way that we did not receive any kind of help" (ib., p. 229).[16] The king of France, against whom Alfonso was then fighting, still had a serious obligation to help him, according to Alfonso, "because we know that it was he who raised this animosity between us and don Sancho." Also, it was thanks to Alfonso's good will that an agreement had been reached with the French king regarding the de la Cerda princes, which had pushed don Sancho to rebellion. Philip, therefore, had the moral obligation to recognize in that generous and disinterested gesture that Alfonso, "was asking for help in such a way that it made him sorry and that for the love of God, and on account of solidarity among kings, and because of a common debt, and for the sake of his prestige, he asked for help" (*Ant.*, p. 229). In other words, the reasons were the love of God that should exist among Christians, the solidarity that must exist between kings (this time for me, tomorrow for you, Alfonso seems to be saying), and, ultimately, because they were also relatives. Finally, in his plea to the pope, a desperate Alfonso made use of all the titles of honor that he and his ancestors had acquired fighting for the preservation of the true faith and the unity of the Church.[17] Nobody helped him out, although the pope did respond later to Alfonso's request with a brief dated August 9, 1283, in which he excommunicated don Sancho. Although the papal response gave Alfonso great moral satisfaction, in political terms, it arrived too late.

At that point, abandoned by all, in a last desperate move, Alfonso addressed his archenemy, the emir of Morocco, Ibn Yûsuf, to whom

---

[16] For the relations between Edward I and Alfonso, cf. J.C. Parsons, *Eleanor of Castile: Queen and Society in Thirteenth-Century England*, New York: St. Martin's Press, 1995 and 1998 (paperback).

[17] *Ant.*, pp. 229–230. The key points of the request were for justice, which as the vicar of Christ, the pope he was obligated to impose, and a reminder of the service that all Alfonso's ancestors had rendered to the Church at the expense of great sacrifices, including their lives. He himself says he had to suffer great ailments for this reason (perhaps an allusion to the illness he suffered during his quest for the Empire): "and we ourselves have always done our best for the faith and we have the steadfast will to live and die for it." For those in Rome, including some popes who had doubted the authenticity of Alfonso's Christian faith, such a profession of faith must have been a great satisfaction.

he wrote, "'Oh victorious king! The Christians have broken the oath of fidelity and with my son have rebelled against me. They say: he is an old man who has lost his mind and whose judgment has become unsound. Help me against them, and I will fight against them.' The Muslim emir took advantage of this and answered, 'I will come.'"[18] The emir's response, the content of which was summarized by Alfonso in his first last will, was the only positive one he received. In Alfonso's words,

> ...finding ourselves dispossessed of all the things in the world except the mercy of God, Ibn Yûsuf, king of Morocco and lord of all the Moors, understanding and remembering the mutual friendship that we had had, seeing the honor of the world, went ahead of the Christian and Moorish kings in order to obtain justice and truth, showing that he was sorry about the evils and pains we had been subjected to. (*Ant.*, p. 230)

Ibn Yûsuf was a lot less idealistic than Alfonso initially believed. The disintegration of Christian unity in the Peninsula was for the emir an unexpected opportunity that, as we will see, he would turn to his advantage. He did not help him out of sympathy, as Alfonso naively believed, nor even (surprisingly) to conquer territory, but only to plunder.

3. *Civil War*

Don Sancho, ignorant of his father's epistolary campaign and the emir of Morocco's promise to help, continued on his journey to the South, afraid that he might meet the offensive of his father's supporters there. He was not off track, but the counter-attack would not be what he expected.

The first signs against the unfair usurpation of power began in the autumn of 1282. The first city to rise up against the prince was Badajoz. Its people refused to be ruled by a rebel. It was the first shot fired in the civil war. In mid-September, Sancho hurried to recuperate the defiant city, crushing the rebellion, but not managing to seize it. There was general confusion on the battlefield, and Sancho had to retreat to Mérida.

---

[18] We know the content of Alfonso's letter through the summary by Ibn Abi Zar, *Rawd al-Qirtas*, II, p. 635; cf. Ballesteros, *Alfonso X*, p. 982.

While in Mérida, he began to receive increasingly alarming news:

> A message reached him there from Prince Don Juan, his brother, con-
> cerning how he was speaking with the councils of Toro, Zamora, Bena-
> vente, Villalpando, and Mallorca so that Prince Sancho might talk with
> them; likewise, that his brother Prince Don Pedro was speaking with the
> councils of Salamanca, Ciudad Rodrigo, and with all the people of the
> kingdom. A message also reached Prince Sancho as to how don Lope
> had spoken with the councils of Castile and was obtaining their treaty
> against the king. (*CAX*, chap. 76, p. 247)

In his absence from Castile, his two brothers, don Juan and don Pedro,
and even his recent ally, don Lope Díaz de Haro, took advantage of the
situation to divide amongst themselves large territories of Castile and
León, which had been from the beginning the object of their ambitions and the reason why they had joined Sancho against Alfonso. This
first crisis of the coalition helped Sancho reevaluate the true character
and interests of his two brothers who, taking advantage of the confusion, abandoned the cause of the rebel, attempting to get from their
father what their brother up to that moment had not been able to
grant them.

The crisis grew by the minute. A piece of news that don Sancho
could not have imagined also arrived in Mérida:

> Also there came to him a message about how King Alfonso, his father,
> and King Aben Yuzaf of Morocco had arrived at Écija and were com-
> ing against Córdoba. All their messengers took counsel so as to advise
> Prince Sancho what to do: some advised him to go to the kingdom of
> León lest he lose it; and others advised him to go to the kingdom of Cas-
> tile lest he should lose it; others counseled him to go to Córdoba, where
> he had left his wife, and said if he did not go, he would lose the city and
> his wife would be in great danger. (*CAX*, chap. 76, p. 247)

Ibn Yûsuf, the great Moroccan emir, had indeed made good on his
promise, coming to the rescue of his old enemy. He disembarked in
Algeciras in early July 1282. Alfonso went to meet him. They then
signed an agreement of mutual defense against all common enemies.
Alfonso was happy that his greatest enemy was willing to help him at
that time when not only all the Christian princes but also all of his
family and the majority of his subjects had abandoned him. According to the *Rawd al-Qirtas*, "The emir of the Muslims honored and
exalted him, and Alfonso explained his lack of resources and said,
'I have no one to help and defend me but you; I have nothing left but
my crown, and for this expedition I need money. This is the crown

of my father and my ancestors. Take it as guarantee of payment, and lend me what I need to spend now.' The emir of the Muslims gave him 100,000 dinars and with him raided the Christian lands until he arrived in Córdoba."[19] The armies met at Écija, and it was there where he received news that don Sancho was in Mérida. "Few scenes in history," Ballesteros writes, "suggest so many and so varied commentaries such as this one about the meeting of a Christian king who, only a few years earlier, was so powerful that he aspired to the most enlightened imperial crown of the planet and then fell into such penury that he had no resources to pay his small army and pawned his crown to finance the cruel war his own son was waging against him. Stranger still, and extremely surprising, was the fact that his protector was a Muslim king, his former enemy and now his generous supporter."[20]

To don Sancho this alliance of his father with none other than his greatest enemy from only a few months before must have seemed inexplicable. The chronicler goes on to say that "once he was certain as to the coming of from overseas of Aben Yuzaf, who was coming to aid King Alfonso, his father, he decided to go to Córdoba […] traveling in one day and one night the twenty-two leagues. He arrived there by night and entered the city" (*CAX*, chap. 76, p. 247). Don Sancho must have realized very quickly that, if he lost Córdoba, all of his plans would collapse, because he would not be able to contain both of his brothers and the other counter-rebels who were stirring up the territories in the north against him. A victory against Yûsuf, on the other hand, would give him the prestige he needed in order to impose himself as well in the north.

The next day, Yûsuf's army raided the city. Before attacking Córdoba, Alfonso wanted to send a delegation to ask Ferrán Muñiz, the Christian guardian of the city, to deliver it to him, "so that Muñiz remember how he had raised him and had wed him; and how he had knighted him and had appointed him high governor of the city of Córdoba; and how he had given it to him, and had given him its keys. Now King Alfonso was demanding refuge in it and that Ferrand Muñiz turn over its keys, warning that if not he would call him a traitor" (*CAX*, chap. 76, p. 248). Ferrán Muñiz's representatives responded with the list of changes cited above (chap. 13, p. 458), adding that

---

[19] *Rawd al-Qirtas*, II, p. 636.
[20] *Alfonso X*, p. 988.

now that he had joined the one who had killed Nuño González de Lara and prince Sancho of Aragón, archbishop of Toledo, and many more Christian heroes, they would under no circumstance "receive him in the town." Alfonso had no choice but to communicate his response to the emir, who ordered the attack, raiding the surroundings of Córdoba for 21 days. He later did the same in the surroundings of Andújar, Jaén, Úbeda, and many other cities in Andalusia, "making war and burning and wasting all they found; but they were unable to seize any of the towns, so they retreated. King Aben Yuzaf went across the sea with his army and King Don Alfonso remained in Seville" (*CAX*, chap. 76, p. 249).[21] This campaign by Yûsuf, according to Alfonso's first last will, must have lasted four months: "And seeing all that Yûsuf did, we trusted him so much that for about four months we were under his command with all the people we had, convinced of his love and his truthfulness" (*Ant.*, p. 230).

For Alfonso, as he declared in his last will, this was a brief period, albeit full of anxiety and trepidation. On the one hand, he recognized that "with the arrival of Yûsuf, many good things ensued. Firstly, because thanks to the mercy of God and his good efforts, and thanks to his good help, we were able to come out of the shadow of our treacherous enemies who had greatly offended us and stifled us with great treason. Secondly, because we recovered our health, since we began to walk and ride our horse again" (*Ant.*, p. 230). In other words, the prospect of recovering his prestige as sovereign, even if with the help of his enemy, gave him great hopes to live and continue fighting for his crown and kingdom. He recovered his health, recovered from the illness of his legs, and even began to walk and ride his horse again.

---

[21] According to the version of the campaign in the *Rawd al-Qirtas*, the devastation was greater than what the *CAX* recounts, because the troops of Yûsuf went all the way to Madrid:

> He camped out and fought against it [Córdoba] for some days, laying siege around Alfonso's son. He sent armies to Jaén, attacked the crops, and then left for Toledo, killing, capturing, stealing cattle, and destroying villages and castles. In that way, he arrived in Madrid, in the lands of Toledo, and the Muslims were so loaded with the booty and the cattle that for this reason the emir returned to Algeciras. It was a great expedition, as there had not been in past centuries. (II, pp. 636–637)

According to Ballesteros, the author of the *CAX* "fell short" in his narrative of the devastation by the Moroccans. What Ibn Abi Zar narrates corresponds to historical reality (*Alfonso X*, p. 989). Yûsuf returned to Algeciras in November 1282 (*Rawd al-Qirtas*, II, p. 637).

But, on the other hand, the great devastation caused by the Moroccan troops in those lands he so loved made him very bitter. In his struggle to recover the kingdom from the hands of the traitors, Alfonso accompanied the emir in the attack on Córdoba, where his son Sancho was. Córdoba, as mentioned, resisted the attack, and Alfonso, disheartened, abandoned the siege and returned to his dear Seville. As a father and Christian king, despite all, he was loath to fight against his own son beside the enemies of the cross. The Moroccan emir continued on his own, attacking and devastating the kingdom of his ally, Alfonso, to the point of reaching, in his destructive wrath, the cities of the central peninsula, Toledo and Madrid. When the winter arrived and he had amassed a large booty, Yûsuf went back to Algeciras.[22]

The news of the return of the great Moroccan emir to Morocco led don Sancho to sign a pact of alliance with the king of Granada. This gave the rebel a respite, which he used to attack Medellín and Talavera, thinking he would there capture the Master of the Templars, who had also switched over to Alfonso's side. But he was unable to do so because "he went to wage war against the castles, because he had the might of his father, King Don Alfonso, against him" (*CAX*, chap. 76, p. 249).[23]

Around the same time, in mid-September 1282, don Sancho received news that his brother Pedro, who was in Ledesma, "was on his way to desert Prince Sancho and to meet with King Alfonso, his father, because the king would give Prince Don Pedro the realm of Murcia of which they would name him king" (*CAX*, chap. 77, p. 250). The news was truthful and the offer was Alfonso's, who could not remain still while his kingdom was disintegrating. Seville, Murcia, and most probably Badajoz, which Sancho had been unable to conquer, were still under his command. Don Pedro's offer "to have himself be called king" under his crown, was quite credible because it was what he had tried to do also with the de la Cerda princes, the main cause of don Sancho's rebellion. As soon as he found out, the rebellious prince rushed to Ledesma, and "when he arrived there, he spoke with his brother don

---

[22] *CAX*, chap. 76, pp. 248–249; Jofré de Loaysa, *Crónica*, pp. 22–23. Many of the miracles narrated by Pero Marín in his *Miráculos romanzados* refer to the disasters of the Moroccan raids. They are the stories of those captured by the Muslims and liberated by Saint Domingo of Silos.

[23] Ballesteros believes it must have been the Master of the Templars, because all the other Orders favored don Sancho (*Alfonso X*, p. 999).

Pedro and told him that he knew very well how through his advice he had had this meeting with those of the realm and that now that he knew about the treaty he had with their father; he beseeched him not to wish to keep it, and that he ask him for whatever he wanted and he would give it to him" (*CAX*, chap. 77, p. 250). Then don Pedro, the chronicler tells us, asked him to give him the income of the Valladolid chancellery and the title of chancellor, as well as the "inheritance" ("heredamiento") of Tordesillas. Don Sancho pleased him in all. It was a good technique to permanently have his brother by his side and under his direct control, since the chancellor always followed the king. At the same time he would distance him from the potential influence of his father. Because of everything that don Pedro had done previously, taking control of towns and income, and what he was now asking from his brother, the Valladolid chancellery and the town of Tordesillas, we can conclude that the only thing that moved Pedro to support his brother was his desire and ambition to acquire lands and riches.

4. *Don Sancho Cursed and Disinherited*

On November 8, 1282, in the royal palace of Seville, Alfonso gave the formal response to the Valladolid deposition sentence, cursing and disinheriting his son:

> While the king was sitting on the platform prepared for that occasion and in the presence of all the people, the reasons for his sentence were publicly read from a written document; and then the king cursed prince Sancho, his son, saying that he subjected him to God's curse and his anger, and that prince Sancho would be subject to it like an impious, parricidal, rebellious, disobedient, and contumacious son. After this, he declared that he disinherited him of all rights to the crown, as a most ungrateful son.

This is in a nutshell the content of the celebrated "curse" and "disinheritance" sentence that, according to Jerónimo de Zurita, Alfonso X pronounced against his son Sancho.[24] It is a document of exceptional

---

[24] The Spanish text of the sentence has not been preserved. It survives only in the Latin translation made in the chancellery of Alfonso, destined for the pope and the kings of France and England. The analyst Jerónimo de Zurita included it in his collection *Indices rerum ab Aragoniae regibus gestarum ab initiis Regni ad annum MCDX*, Zaragoza, 1578, pp. 171–174. There is a modern Spanish translation in A. Canellas,

value for understanding the history of don Sancho's rebellion and the circumstances that led to the deposition of Alfonso X from Alfonso's perspective. With the coldness of an impartial judge, the Learned King, lists one by one all of the offenses and crimes against his majesty committed by his rebellious son after the Valladolid plot:

> Because of the many misdeeds and offenses he committed irreverently against us without warrant, we curse him, as someone deserving his father's curse, reproved by God, and deserving to be abhorred with good reason by men. And we subject him from now on to divine and human curse. And as a rebellious son, disobedient and contumacious, ungrateful and most ungrateful, and therefore degenerate, we disinherit him and we deprive him of any right that he may have had in our kingdoms, lordships, lands, honors, and dignities, or any other thing that in any way belongs to us, so that neither he nor any other nor any of his descendants may ever be able to succeed us in any way. We authorize through our royal seal everything stated in this irrevocable sentence promulgated in the presence of the undersigned witnesses. (p. 997)[25]

The document closes with an impressive list of witnesses. At the top appear the archbishop of Seville, don Remondo of Losana; don Suero, bishop of Cádiz, who upon Alfonso's death had to leave his diocese and seek refuge in France during all of Sancho's reign; don Ademar, bishop-elect of Ávila, who, as mentioned, was the one who dared bring the bad news to don Sancho during the Seville Cortes and whom Alfonso would send to Rome to negotiate the pope's intervention; Pelay Pérez, abbot of Valladolid; and Pedro Páez, archdeacon of Seville. Among the witnesses are also several Portuguese noblemen, including the ambassador to Alfonso, Gonzalo Pérez, and Castilian noblemen, among them Garcí Jofré de Loaysa.

Gestas de los Reyes de Aragón, I, Zaragoza, 1984, pp. 262–266. We quote the version by Balleteros, *Alfonso X*, p. 992 and ff. Cf. G. Martin, "Alphonse X maudit son fils," *Atalaya*, 5 (1994), pp. 153–157.

[25] In that same declaration, Alfonso even affirms that don Sancho tried to kill him:

> And to top off this evil, he not only threatened our life, but he also powerfully armed himself against us. Because thanks to advice that was premeditated and even disseminated by his servants and followers in such a way that it came to be known not only by those present, but also by many absent...in a hostile way he tried with them to arrive...in the city of Seville, to impiously and unjustly arrest us, making such an effort at this, that even on account this alone he could justly be deemed a parricide. (ib., p. 996)

The most impressive feature of the document is the elevated tone of the request, the logic of the argumentation, and the conclusions the Learned King reaches, which are peremptory and irrevocable. It is also surprising to note how well-informed Alfonso was about all the affairs, especially what had happened in Valladolid, a meeting about which he repeatedly said "if this name [Cortes] can be applied to it." Alfonso confirms beyond all doubt that don Sancho attempted to proclaim himself king at that meeting, thus contradicting the assertion of the *Crónica* which held that Sancho did not want to call himself king during his father's lifetime. The document also reveals some new facts, for instance the plot by Sancho and his followers to surprise Alfonso in Seville and assassinate him, something that was preempted by Alfonso's faithful Sevillian subjects. It is also admirable, and unknown through other documents although it could be suspected, that Alfonso made an extraordinary effort "with fatherly love" to steer don Sancho away from "such a great mistake," sending him qualified ambassadors and numerous letters, and even inviting him to a meeting where he could redress "any complaint" and please him in all his legitimate wishes:

> …we were ready to entirely revoke, according to his ruling, and that of the prelates, gentlemen and other good men, any complaint, if there was one, amend anything that needed amending, and restore all things to good peace and tranquility. And if he still had any suspicion that we might intend to diminish his honors, we would give him complete assurance and such that he from now on would have nothing to fear. When this was heard by don Sancho, he told our ambassadors that he would send his answer with his own emissaries. Nevertheless, he held our ambassadors by force so that they were unable to return to us. (p. 995)

Knowing of what his father had done during the negotiations to end the noblemen's rebellion, and of many other cases in which Alfonso had given generous terms to his opponents, it is not clear how don Sancho, who was his son and declared heir, could not accept such a magnanimous offer from his father. Given his precarious state of health, Alfonso probably would have renounced the throne of his own free will, for the love of his son and the sake of the peace and order of the kingdom. But Sancho's ingratitude, pride, and ambition had no limits.

It is not known how Sancho reacted immediately to the curse. Given the many problems that arose, as we will soon see, he probably did not have a lot of time to reflect on what his aged father had decreed in Seville. Whether as legitimate king or not, at the moment of his proclamation, Sancho believed he had the mandate to rule that his participants at the Valladolid meeting had confirmed on him, as well as the support of the great majority of his father's subjects. Therefore, he likely saw the curse of his father as another sign of the erratic behavior of a "crazy old man." But in reality, his father's curse would slowly start to profoundly eat away at Sancho's soul, unbalancing his mind and turning him at times into a true psychopath. Nine years of government could not satisfy his thirst for power or eliminate the torment that would not abandon him for a single day of his life, not even in his hour death, which occurred prematurely just before he turned thirty-seven.

At the end of January 1295, ill with consumption and very much aware of the imminence of his death, don Sancho had himself transported from Valladolid to Toledo, where he wished to die. When he passed through Peñafiel, his cousin Juan Manuel joined the entourage. On February 4, they arrived in Madrid, lodging at Santo Domingo el Real.[26] It was there that, as the great writer and politician don Juan Manuel relates in his *Libro de las armas*, the long conversation between the two cousins took place. In the memory of the brilliant teenager, when don Sancho received him in his room, he was lying in bed very ill and surrounded by physicians and courtiers:

> And after all of us were there with the king, and the rest of the people left the chamber, and the king being very ill in his bed, he took me by the arms and sat me next to him, and began his speech in the following way: "Now, don Juan, I would like to explain three things to you: first, I would like to beg you to remember and have pity for my soul, because through my sins I have behaved in such a way in my life, that my life is a shame before God... And now, you who are still alive and well, you can see that my sins kill me before you, without you being able to defend or help me. Because you can be certain that this death I am dying is not due to an illness, but to my sins, and particularly to the curse that my parents cast on me for the many offences I committed against them..."
> And saying this he coughed so violently that, unable to expel what was tearing apart his chest, twice we believed he was dead; first, because we saw how ill he was, and second because of the words he spoke. You can perfectly understand the sorrow and mourning we felt in our hearts...

---

[26] Cf. *Crónica de Sancho IV*, pp. 89a–90a–b. After the attack and conquest of Tarifa, the greatest military episode of don Sancho's reign, the historian follows closely the development of the king's illness and his death.

Having overcome the attack that was restricting his breathing, Sancho continued:

> Now, don Juan, after this conversation I have had with you, you will then go to the kingdom of Murcia, in God's service of God and mine, but before this, I want to say goodbye to you and give you my blessing. But unfortunately, I cannot give that you to or to anyone; for no one can give what he does not have…I cannot give you a blessing because I don't have it myself. On the contrary, because of the sins and the offenses I committed against my parents, I received instead their curse. My father cursed me many times when he was alive and well, and he cast his curse once more when he was dying…[27]

The scene has the marks of a personal tragedy because of the dramatic way don Juan Manuel retells it. If the death of Sancho's father was surrounded by anguish because of the heart-rending betrayal on all levels, the demise of the son was accompanied by the personal drama of impending death and the expectation of eternal damnation. This meeting between the two cousins, remembered in all its detail fifty years later by don Juan Manuel, is considered strictly historical by the majority of scholars.[28] Whether or not Alfonso forgave his son is something we will discuss later, but don Juan Manuel's remarks clearly show that Sancho never heard such a pardon, for he told his cousin that his father cursed him even "when he was dying."

5. The Rebellion Falters

That solemn scene in the patio of the Sevillian palace, during which Alfonso spoke of the terrible curse and sentence of disinheritance against don Sancho, together with his recent military triumphs achieved with the help of the emir of Morocco, began to have their effect on the subjects that had continued to believe in the legitimacy of the Learned

---

[27] *Libro de las armas*, ed. J.M. Blecua, *Obras completas*, I, pp. 137–138. Don Sancho died of tuberculosis in Toledo on Tuesday, April 23, 1295 "after midnight." According to his wishes, he was buried wearing the Franciscan habit in the tomb he himself had built next to that of Alfonso VII in the Toledo cathedral.

[28] Cf. D. Devoto, *Introducción al estudio de D. Juan Manuel y en particular de "El Conde Lucanor": Una bibliografía*, Madrid: Castalia, 1972, pp. 248–251; and A. Deyermond, "Cuentos orales y estructura formal en el *Libro de las tres razones* (*Libro de las armas*)," in *Don Juan Manuel: VII Centenario*, Murcia, 1982; M. González Jiménez, "La sucesión al trono de Castilla: 1275-1304," *Anales de la Universidad de Alicante. Historia Medieval*, 11 (1996–1997), pp. 201–212.

King. The two cities of Murcia and Seville, always very faithful to Alfonso, also created a brotherhood at the beginning of 1283 in order to defend the rights they thought belonged to their legitimate king.[29]

In his Sevillian retreat, Alfonso continued to be as active as always in the drafting of the politics of the kingdom and busy with his cultural projects. Proof of all these activities is the drafting of the so-called "critical version" of the *Estoria de España*, which reflects the contemporary political situation of the kingdom. When speaking of the succession to the throne of Castile and how it had been threatened throughout history, the Learned King writes:

> King don Alfonso, son of king don Fernando who won Seville, was dispossessed of his kingdom by his son, prince don Sancho. And all the people in the kingdom rose up with don Sancho and they plotted against the king to capture him and exile him from the land. But God helped him, and the people of Seville, and Ibn Yûsuf, king of the North African Moors.[30]

We could not hope for a better updating of the text.

In the days that followed the sentence of malediction, besides offering his son don Pedro the kingdom of Murcia in exchange for his obedience, Alfonso must of made many other initiatives to numerous lords of Castile, León, and Extremadura. Immediately after relating the narrative of Alfonso's negotiations with don Pedro, the *CAX* records a long list of declarations from many nobles in favor of Alfonso. Although he does not give us the dates, Ballesteros calculates that they must have happened during the month of February 1283.[31] Don Sancho, the chronicler says, lashed out against them, but the deserters, seeing that they could not defend themselves, said that "they wanted to depart their land and said Prince Sancho should give them someone to take them safely to Portugal. So Prince Don Sancho begged Prince Don Manuel, his uncle, to go with them, and he got them safely to Portugal. As soon as they were ready, they went to Portugal by way of

---

[29] The text of this brotherhood can be seen in J. Torres Fontes and C. Torres Suárez, *La lealtad de Murcia a Alfonso X el Sabio*, Murcia, 1984.

[30] In I. Fernández-Ordóñez, *Versión crítica de la Estoria de España. Estudio y Edición desde Pelayo hasta Ordoño II*, Madrid, 1993.

[31] *Alfonso X*, p. 1013, where he identifies the most prominent figures who declared themselves in favor of Alfonso. In a diploma issued in Seville on September 11, 1283, there are some thirty names of nobles and *hidalgos* who confirmed the document. See the complete list in M. González Jiménez, *Alfonso X*, p. 198, note 62.

Seville to King Alfonso" (*CAX*, chap. 77, p. 251).[32] It did not go easy for all of the nobles who declared themselves in favor of Alfonso. Don Sancho retaliated against some of them. He expelled his aunt, doña Berenguela, sister of his father and head of the Convent of Las Huelgas in Burgos, from the convent. In contrast, he reached an agreement with his younger brothers, Juan and Jaime, which allowed them to be reconciled with their father.

Don Juan unexpectedly arrived in Seville from Portugal. The deserter prince, who a year earlier had tried to slice a piece out of the future kingdom of his brother, was hoping to get from his father what his brother had been unable to give him. The chronicler, who is not very sympathetic toward don Juan, tells us in this section about the deserters that "Prince Don Juan went into the realm of León in order to watch those towns, and Prince Don Sancho sent to Prince Don Juan to make peace with him, and he came to him in Palencia and was welcomed by him. Then Prince Don Juan took his wife and his people from Palencia. He took the road to Portugal and thence to King Don Alfonso, his father, in Seville" (*CAX*, chap. 77, p. 251).[33]

That same spring, as part of his campaign of letters and ambassadors to recover those who had always been faithful allies, Alfonso must have also written to his old supporter, don Diego López Salcedo, who was in don Sancho's camp, probably more due to circumstances than to conviction. This is what can be gleaned from a letter written by don Sancho while he was in Burgos trying to reach an agreement of support with the city. (Burgos had always found it difficult to accept the prince and turn against the legitimate king.) In that letter to the city leaders, Sancho informed them of the state of relations with his

---

[32] In a privilege dated March 4, 1283, where Alfonso granted his daughter Beatriz the city of Niebla, most of the nobles who defected to Portugal appear listed as confirmants. They obviously did not do so, but instead left for Seville.

[33] As usual, the *CAX* does not tell us when the defection took place, but through Sancho's letter to the city of Burgos on April 3, 1283, which we will discuss below, it appears that don Juan's flight to Seville was not as quick, but rather that there was a period of negotiation. The submission to his father must not have taken place until after June 20, when the king of Aragón was still trying to dissuade the prince from returning to his father. According to Ballesteros, who gets his information from Diego Rodríguez de Almela, Alfonso at first did not want to welcome the rebel, but he appeared in the Seville Alcázar with his wife and child, they "entered [the palace] barefoot and implored the king's mercy on their knees. Moved by them, the father raised his son from the floor and crying with joy blessed the prince" (*Alfonso X*, p. 1016, and cf. p. 1017). The episode is also narrated in *Crónica Geral de Espahna de 1344*, qtd. ed., IV, p. 513.

father, telling them that many had advised him to reach an agreement with him.[34] Obviously the rebel had been forced to negotiate with his father due to pressure from some of his courtiers who saw the risk that his faction was running due to the continuous defections. He tells us in another passage of the letter that this was contrary to the truce, but that he wanted to know the will of the people of Burgos. He therefore sent them an emissary to receive their opinion in writing. Meanwhile, since he did not know how he would resolve the truce, he ordered them to prepare themselves to accompany him "to the border," that is Córdoba, or else be in violation of the oath of fidelity they had sworn (that is, he would declare them traitors).[35] This final threat, in a letter that, in the end, was announcing the news that the people of Burgos wanted to hear, was an obvious sign of mutual distrust. In fact, as we will soon see, don Sancho needed to recruit an emergency army to stop a new attack by the emir of Morocco, he resorted to the councils of the kingdom of León and not of Castile.[36]

At the end of March 1283, Yûsuf, who had remained in Algeciras all along, decided to attack Málaga and other towns and castles. "All of Al-Andalus was on fire and the cause was Málaga," says the *Rawd al-Quirtas* (II, p. 637). As a result of the alliance between don Sancho and the king of Granada the year before, the Moroccan emir was afraid of losing his influence in Andalusia, hence the new attack: "Once more the country of the idolaters was raided, and the emir of the Muslims sent columns to the country of the infidels, and they looted and captured [people]; then he himself left Algeciras for Córdoba, and this was the Talavera expedition."[37]

These campaigns of the Moroccan emir, as we suggested, were driven more by plunder than by the true conquest of the territory. So much so, that once the Moroccan armies had disappeared, the raided area often went back to the old alliances. Talavera, which had a long history of fidelity to Alfonso, was one of the towns that early on rose against don Sancho. The *CAX*, when narrating Sancho's "acts

---

[34] In Ballesteros, *Alfonso X*, p. 1017; and see his article, "Burgos y la rebelión del infante don Sancho," *BRAH*, CXIX (1946), pp. 180–186.

[35] Cf. E. González Díez, *Colección diplomática del Concejo de Burgos (884–1369)*, Burgos, 1984, p. 212, and see 214–215, nos. 125 and 128.

[36] Cf. *CAX*, chap. 77, pp. 251–252.

[37] *Rawd al-Qirtas*, II, p. 637; and cf. Ballesteros, p. 1021. More details on this campaign in the *Rawd al-Qirtas*, pp. 638–641 and in Ballesteros, p. 1022, who states that it lasted until September.

of justice", recounts among the most notable incidents of his brutality, one that occurred in a poor quarter of Talavera, where an obvious supporter of Alfonso, a certain Romero whom the *Crónica* calls a "thief," agitated the population against the prince. Sancho attacked him mercilessly and when unable to capture him, personally pursued him through roads and ravines, though without success. The fugitive took refuge in the fortified town of Cabañas del Castillo, near Trujillo. In his fury, the prince gave the order to devastate the poor quarter, "and slew all the men and women he found there who had given Romero and his knights shelter–and more than three hundred people were slain there" (*CAX*, chap. 77, p. 254). The act was clearly meant to serve as example to the rest of the population not to support those who "rose" against him.[38]

Ibn Yûsuf's new campaign (from May 11 to June 8, 1282) is also described by the *CAX* from the perspective of the problems it caused the Christians. According to the *Crónica*, when the emir arrived in Seville, Alfonso suggested a mutual attack the king of Granada, who had sided with don Sancho. Yûsuf agreed but asked Alfonso for a thousand Christian soldiers to go with him. Alfonso "gave him don Fernán Pérez Ponce, who was there with six hundred knights whom he had in his retinue. King Aben Yuzaf gave him wages for all who were with him, and they moved with their entire army and entered the land of the King of Granada" (*CAX*, chap. 77, p. 250). But conflicts soon arose between the Christian and Muslim warriors. Pérez Ponce was not used to fighting on the side of the Muslims, much less being commanded by one. Thus, the chronicler writes, "[he] did not wish to camp with the Moorish army, but separately, [and] this made King Aben Yuzaf suspicious that don Fernán Pérez was untrustworthy. Therefore, they had to separate the Christian soldiers from the soldiers of King Aben Yuzaf. When Aben Yuzaf saw this, he sent to demand from them the wages he had given them, and they gave them back rather than stay with him. They departed discordant from him and made their way to Córdoba and camped on the banks of the River of Guadajoz" (*CAX*, chap. 77, p. 251).

Thus the attack on the city of Córdoba had to be carried out jointly by Pérez Ponce's and Alfonso's troops, which, according to the

---

[38] The destruction of this poor quarter of Talavera on September 17, 1283 is also confirmed by the *Anales Toledanos III*.

chronicler's account, had been increasing in the last times, so that he was able to send substantial reinforcements to Yûsuf and still keep enough soldiers for the defense of Seville. There was no participation by the Moroccan troops. This was a combat between Christian forces, indeed a veritable civil war. "When Prince Don Sancho, don Fernand Anriquez, and those who were in Córdoba with Prince Don Sancho learned of it, they went out and fought them so that don Fernán Pérez Ponce and the others who came with him conquered the Cordovans. And they slew on that day Fernand Muñiz, Lord Mayor of Córdoba, and they cut off his head and took it to King Don Alfonso, who ordered it hung up on the scaffold of Seville on hooks. Likewise on that day they killed Rodrigo Esteban, Lord Mayor of Seville, and it greatly grieved King Don Alfonso. Then King Alfonso gave the mayorship of Seville to Diego Alfonso" (*CAX*, chap. 77, pp. 251–252).

The defeat of the supporters of don Sancho in the surroundings of Córdoba (the prince was not present there)[39] must have been a great incentive for the uprising against the rebel in several towns of Castile, especially Soria and Agreda. The dissident towns also received significant support from Navarra, where the French king had acted again, following Alfonso's disinheriting Sancho and naming the de la Cerda princes as heirs. Around the same time, Alfonso, from Seville, entrusted his youngest son, don Jaime, with the mission of traveling north accompanied by don Juan Alonso de Haro to support and encourage all those who were rising up against don Sancho. It was particularly difficult for the rebellious prince to reconquer the castle of Agreda and the Moorish quarter where all had risen up against him.[40] But he did not manage to take over Treviño, which was defended by don Jaime and don Juan Alonso de Haro.[41]

While don Sancho was doing everything possible to keep Castile under his control, some events in the field of international politics came to complicate things. Pedro III of Aragón had just returned from Sicily, where his intervention had enabled the rebellion of the populace against the tyrannical rule of Charles of Anjou. The rebellion, which

---

[39] But reportedly when he found out, he said: "They much deserved the defeat because they went out to fight against my father's banner, and they knew well that I never fought against it" (Mosén Diego de Valera, in Ballesteros, *Alfonso X*, p. 1023).

[40] Don Sancho was fighting in Agreda in May 1283 (from May 12 to June 2) when the city fell.

[41] *CAX*, pp. 251–252. On June 8 he was in Segovia on the way to Treviño.

began in Messina with the celebrated Sicilian Vespers, expanded to the territories controlled by supporters of Anjou in Italy, which then switched over to Aragón's control.[42] This change in the Italian political scene provoked the reaction of the king of France, Philip III, nephew of Charles of Anjou, who declared himself in favor of his uncle and against Pedro of Aragón, sending seven thousand knights to Navarra in order to challenge him.

Philip of France's war declaration, now supported by Alfonso, who, after the disinheritance of don Sancho, was even ready to cede one of his kingdoms to the de la Cerda princes, provoked a chain reaction also in Castile. Alfonso unexpectedly found himself in a quandary over alliances: at peace with his enemy Philip III, in conflict with his faithful supporter, the king of Aragón, and in violation of the Treaty of Campillo with the other signatory, don Sancho, whom Pedro III now openly supported against his father, because he needed him in order to fight the king of France. This new situation forced don Pedro to also intervene in Castile.

The *CAX* presents the war between Philip of France and Pedro of Aragón over conflicting policies on Sicily as a challenge expected to take place in Bordeaux between the two kings. But due to a ruse on the part of the king of Aragón, Philip did not show up at the meeting. In the war that followed, Philip of France was at a disadvantage because the Castilians who were fighting next to the Navarrese refused to fight against the coalition of don Pedro and prince Sancho. This is because in the coalition of Castile-Aragón, there were obviously Castilian troops, and although they supported don Sancho (which did not please the Navarrese-Castilians), still they were Castilian and preferable to the French, because among them fought don Sancho, who would one day become the king of Castile, regardless of the disinheritance sentence pronounced against him at that time: "When the French understood what the Castilians said, they abandoned the invasion and returned to Pamplona. Thus King Don Pedro was very grateful to Prince Don Sancho for what he had done, since but for him the French would have invaded his land" (*CAX*, chap. 77, p. 254).

---

[42] Cf. F. Soldevila, *Pere el Gran*, 4 vols., Barcelona, 1950–1962; J.N. Hilgarth, *The Problem of a Catalan Mediterranean Empire, 1229–1327*, EHR, supplement 8; S. Runciman, *The Sicilian Vespers: A History of the Mediterranean World in the Later Thirteenth Century*, Cambridge, 1958.

6. *The Pope's Intervention*

Alfonso remained all this time in Seville, following with great trepidation the course of events in Castile. His epistolary activity and his contacts through special envoys had earned him many supporters, among them, his two sons, don Juan and don Jaime. But he had also sought with great interest the support of foreign princes, especially the pope, to whom he sent letters and messengers to present the justness of his cause and the iniquity that his son and his supporters were committing against him, supported by the hierarchy of Castile-León. The new pope, Martin IV (1282–1285), who had risen to St. Peter's throne just before Alfonso's deposition, did not want to intervene at first, but he had a stake in the rebellion that since 1282 put the entire Church hierarchy of Castile-León on his side.

The new pope was not a stranger to peninsular politics. We can be certain that he had followed the situation very closely since, on September 28, 1266, he had participated as envoy of the Apostolic See in the marriage negotiations between the daughter of the king of France, Blanche, and the heir to the crown of Castile, Fernando. The cause of the children of this marriage, which was now at stake, must have been very familiar to him. As a Frenchman and a firm supporter of Charles of Anjou, Martin IV began to see things from a different perspective starting with the expulsion of the French from Sicily, especially after Alfonso tried to make peace with the king of France and leave part of the kingdom to one of his grandsons.[43] These changes, especially due to what has been noted about the war between France and Aragón, made it easier for the pope to side with Alfonso and against don Sancho, but there was still a serious obstacle: the peninsular church hierarchy who supported the rebel. To oppose don Sancho was to upset the Church hierarchy of Castile-León. That's why the pope, before declaring himself openly in favor of Alfonso, began an entire epistolary campaign, addressing several bishops and abbots as well as the Masters of the Military Orders of Calatrava, Santiago, the Templars and the Hospi-

---

[43] The letter to Alfonso, dated January 17, 1283, expresses in a mournful and very affectionate tone the extent to which the deposition had worried the pope (*Les Registres de Martin IV*, doc. 300 and cf. doc. 479; and A. Potthast, *Regesta Pontificum Romanorum*, nos. 21.931 and 21.932).

tallers, urging them to return to the obedience of the legitimate king.[44] It is quite possible that the long document issued by the high clergy of Castile-León at the end of the assembly at Benavente (see above, chap. 13, p. 462, note 50) was the fruit of these interventions and pressure by the pope. In that document, the abuses of don Sancho's supporters were denounced for the first time, and it is indeed the first indication of a certain will to distance themselves from the rebel. If don Sancho did not follow the warnings of the clergy, they would have good reason to denounce and abandon him.

After having prepared the way with letters and envoys, finally, on August 9, 1283, in Orvieto, pope Martin IV pronounced his sentence in favor of Alfonso X, condemning don Sancho's rebellion as an act of betrayal, excommunicating him, and placing the kingdom under interdict until the people returned to the king's obedience.[45] As executors of the sentence, the pope appointed don Remondo de Losana, archbishop of Seville, an unflinching supporter of Alfonso's; the deacon of Tudela, a Navarrese and thus presumably a supporter of the king of France; and the archdeacon of Nendín, in the diocese of Santiago de Compostela, perhaps the only impartial man among the three.

Sancho, however, had a very different temperament from his father. Taking as his excuse the fact that the rights of the subjects of the kingdom had been safeguarded, as a first move, perhaps only with the intention of being accommodating (although against the advice of some nobles), he also reached out to his father. At the same time, Sancho responded to the papal bull by ordering that whoever was found with a copy of the excommunication or the papal interdict would be executed, and that the interdict was not to be observed in any city of the kingdom. Further, according to the *CAX*, "[t]hen Prince Don Sancho, on behalf of himself and of those of the land, sought an appeal of this interdict either from a new pope, or from a council, or from God Himself" (*CAX*, chap. 77, p. 255).

In other words, Sancho took the excommunication as a personally, as an insult against his sovereignty and an affront against his subjects;

---

[44] This is what can be gleaned from the letter quoted in the previous note. On the attitude of the Church during don Sancho's revolt, see the important work by J.M. Nieto Soria, *Iglesia y poder real en Castilla. El Episcopado, 1250–1350*, pp. 79–83.

[45] *Regestum Martini IV*, 479. This document, written, like the letter mentioned above, in an anguished tone of imminent crisis, reveals the true concern of the pope over the devastation and social unrest produced by the civil war.

naturally, he would not tolerate such an offense. Sancho manifested here the same arrogant and shameless attitude he showed towards his father when he tried to prove his right to the royal crown. This attitude of defiance towards the papacy, which bordered on schism, was much more dangerous. As we know, to appeal against a pope's decision to a General Council or to God, as don Sancho does here, always entailed the risk of being accused of heresy, since it questioned the primate of Saint Peter's. I do not think that Sancho wanted to go that far, although it is possible that he was really unconcerned about it. In reality, what his act of arrogance and defiance reveals is that he was convinced that the pope had not excommunicated him for religious reasons, nor out of sympathy for his father, but rather for political reasons. The chronicler's version of this episode stresses the fact that Pope Martin IV was "French," which undoubtedly is meant to hint that the main reason for the excommunication was to remove Sancho's subjects from obedience to Sancho and return them to Alfonso, and in this way to promote the cause of the de la Cerda princes who, as we know, were the candidates to the throne of Castile supported by the French king.[46] Therefore, Sancho must have thought, what the pope intended with the excommunication and interdict was nothing more than an excuse to support the de la Cerda princes and, ultimately, the cause of the king of France.[47]

We have to recognize that, politically speaking, don Sancho and his supporters were not too much off track in their decision to oppose the pope's decrees. Martin IV, whose real name was Simon de Brie, was one of the popes who brought the most shame on the medieval Church. Placed on the throne of St. Peter's by a maneuver of Charles of Anjou, who had the cardinals of the opposition jailed during the conclave, he was indeed a pope entirely at the service of the king of France. And the despotic Charles of Anjou used him shamelessly for his political aims and cruel rapacity. He handed out excommunications at the request of the French king like a Sister of Charity hands out loaves of bread. There was good reason for his excommunication of prince don Sancho,

---

[46] *CAX*, chap. 77, pp. 252–258; Ballesteros, *Alfonso X*, p. 1039.

[47] This is very clear in chap. II of the *Crónica de Sancho IV*, a work by the same author who wrote the *CAX*. The attitude of contempt that Sancho had for religious institutions, including the papacy, during this entire period of rebellion stemmed from his conviction that they were manipulated by his enemies. Cf. *Crónica del rey don Sancho el Bravo*, ed. C. Rosell, *BAE*, LVI, chap. II, p. 73a.

not only because of his rebelliousness, but also because of his marriage irregularities. Yet he also excommunicated Michael VIII, Paleologus, emperor of Byzantium, only because Charles of Anjou had decided to conquer Constantinople, a very imprudent action that put the unity of Christendom at stake, reopening the wound of the Schism between the Catholic and Orthodox churches. He also excommunicated the king of Aragón, Pedro III, as a result of that tragic incident of Easter Monday 1282, the "Sicilian Vespers", when with a cry of "Death to the French!" the citizens of Palermo barbarically massacred all the French they could find, liberated the island from Angevin despotism, and delivered it to the pope. But Martin IV, who did not want to upset Charles of Anjou, refused to exert his sovereignty on the island. Instead, he imposed an excommunication on all Sicilians until they returned to the obedience of the French king, who at the time was in Naples preparing the expedition against Constantinople. Like don Sancho, the Sicilians did not heed the pope's condemnation, and wasted no time in offering their kingdom to Pedro III of Aragón, who was crowned king of Sicily on August 31, 1282. On November 18, Martin IV again issued an excommunication against the king of Aragón for having invaded Sicily and having attacked Charles of Anjou while he was preparing for the Constantinople crusade.[48] The partiality of this pope, who operated under the sign of France in all his public actions, must therefore have been well known among Sancho's supporters, who advised him to behave in such a reactionary way.

In any event, questioning the motives of the papal bull, and even more, disobeying the pope even if his sentence had been driven by political interests in his sentence, was always dangerous. The disobedient subject was termed a heretic, and the consequences of such an accusation, in the case of a king or someone who aspired to be king, were to risk losing the obedience and acceptance of his subjects and, therefore, the crown. Sancho's arrogant attitude was indeed what led the popes to never grant him the annulment of his first marriage, although, for reasons of social convenience and to mitigate Martin

---

[48] Potthast, *Regesta pontificum romanorum*, II, 1773, no. 21947; J. Zurita, *Anales de la Corona de Aragón*, I, pp. 252v–253r. Martin IV was also considered an enemy by Germans and Austrians. The *Continuatio Vindobonensis* of the *Anales Admutenses* tells us that "He had such hatred towards Germanic peoples, that he frequently wanted to be a stork, so if the Germanic peoples were frogs in the marshes, he might devour them all," in Potthast, *Regesta*, II, 1794.

IV's excesses, his successor, Honorius IV, who acceded to the papacy when Alfonso was already dead (April 2, 1285), decided to lift the excommunication and the interdict on the kingdom.[49]

7. Attempts at Reconciliation

Despite the drastic measures taken by don Sancho to counter the effect of the papal sanctions, the social consequences of the excommunication and especially of the interdict were devastating in the territories held by the rebel. Some cities, like Soria, despite the cruel retaliation, abandoned don Sancho's faction for fear of the interdict. At a time when social life revolved around the Church, worship and religious festivities, the prohibition of the solemn ceremonies, the administration of sacraments in public, the ringing of bells and the performance of liturgical songs, the burial of the dead according to the traditional rites, and the banning of pilgrims and foreigners from circulating in the streets left the city or kingdom completely paralyzed. In these circumstances, when the obedience owed by subjects was taken away from the authorities, crime and social chaos reigned. The *CAX* narrates several episodes of this sort and the retaliation ("the acts of justice") that don Sancho carried out (pp. 254–255).

Excommunication, social chaos, and the pressure of his advisors all began to chip away at the rebellious prince's strong will. Burgos, the capital of Castile, was still a problem: every time don Sancho appeared in the city, he was received very coldly and even had to do without the "conducho," or food tribute that lords could expect from their vassals, because the Burgos citizens refused to cooperate.[50]

Don Sancho's advisors thought that it was time to draft a political agreement with his father, which would give him more legitimacy in Castile. There is a document addressed to the Council of the Cathedral of León, where, after referring to his last visit to Burgos in the company of don Manuel, don Lope Díaz de Haro, don Diego Díaz

---

[49] Cf. *Les Registres d'Honorius IV*, doc. 808. The decree is dated November 7, 1286. Cf. A. Marcos Pous, "Los dos matrimonios de Sancho IV de Castilla," p. 54.

[50] See the letter to Burgos sent from Santo Domingo de Silos on September 16, 1283 announcing Sancho's upcoming visit to the city and asking for the food tribute, for which he promises to pay (in Ballesteros, *Alfonso X*, p. 1039).

de Haro, don Diego López de Salcedo and many other nobles and knights, Sancho says:

> And they said during the trip that we should find the way to go back to being friends and being agreeable with my father and with all others from the land. And I thought too it should be so. And we agreed on this matter: that all the others from the land should meet at Palencia the next All Saints' Day to determine how the king's right and my right could be respected the way you promised, and so that the codes of law belonging to those from the land would also be safeguarded according to your right, to each his own, as I promised you, in such a way that all are protected and secure, each according to his condition. (in Ballesteros, pp. 1039–1040)

He then asked them to name "two good and reasonable men" to represent the Council of the Cathedral at a meeting to be held in Palencia on All Saints' Day.

Don Sancho, faced with the pressure of his immediate allies, was looking for a way to make peace with his father, proof that the first initiative taken to Seville by Diego López de Salcedo had failed. At the Palencia meeting, however, there were surprises too. According to the author of the *CAX*, the promoter of the reconciliation plan with don Alfonso was don Sancho himself, but he was very surprised when he saw now that the nobles did not want peace, for personal reasons, "[a]nd even though they said that it pleased them, it was not so, rather it grieved them because they feared that the agreement would be against them. Then Prince Don Sancho made don Diego López de Salcedo go with a message to a nephew who lived with Prince Don Manuel whose name was Gómez Fernández de Maqueda, and then to King Don Alfonso to see if he wished a treaty, saying that the lordship and treaty with Prince Don Sancho should be protected, and also the lands and the inheritances of these good men" (*CAX*, chap. 77, p. 255).

The result of Gómez Fernández de Maqueda's proposal to Alfonso is unknown, but we can assume that, since the terms presupposed Alfonso's acceptance of the status quo both for Sancho and for his supporters, who did not want to lose any of their privileges, Alfonso probably did not even consider it. In any event, it seems quite clear that there were negotiations to reach an agreement between father and son on the division of power and the future of the kingdom. At the end of that year, don Sancho decided to travel to Seville to try to personally resolve with his father the matters that so troubled the kingdom.⁵¹ But apparently the trip did not take place. If it had happened, the rebellious son would have been very surprised at the number of magnates that had switched over to his father's side, among whom was his great protector don Gonzalo García Gudiel, archbishop of Toledo.⁵² Given this state of affairs, it is very probable that, had Alfonso lived one more year, he would have regained the throne, or perhaps a more submissive son would have renounced the crown in his favor.

The year 1283 closed with two tragic incidents that deeply affected don Sancho's future. The first, says the *CAX*, although tragic, was paradoxically a reason for the rebel to rejoice: "and when he came to Segovia, a message came to him concerning how Prince Don Pedro, his brother, had died in Ledesma; and it pleased him greatly, because he knew that don Pedro went about telling lies and that he wanted to go with the king, his father" (*CAX*, chap. 77, p. 255). The second was the death of his uncle, the prince don Manuel, who also passed away that year in Peñafiel.⁵³ Don Manuel had been a much-loved brother of Alfonso X's, but in the last two years, as we have noted, he had switched over to the side of the rebellious prince, serving him as a close advisor during the rebellion. His death was a clear setback for don Sancho and an irreparable loss, because after it occurred, there were many defections among his supporters.⁵⁴

The *CAX* connects don Manuel's death with an extraordinary event, which apparently happened at the end of May 1283:

> After this, Prince Don Sancho left Toro and went to Cáceres, and from there he went to Mérida and found Prince Don Juan with those noble-

---

⁵¹ There is proof of these negotiations, for instance, in the correspondence between don Pedro of Aragón and Queen Eleanor of England. In a letter written by don Pedro from Barcelona and dated February 7, 1283, to inform her of the state of negotiations between don Alfonso and his son Sancho, which she was anxious to know about, he tells her that it was always his intention to make peace between father and son, that he was doing everything possible to make them reach an agreement and that he expected very soon to be able to confirm positive results (in Ballesteros, p. 1047).

⁵² A list of these noblemen can be found in Ballesteros, *Alfonso X*, pp. 1045–1046.

⁵³ Don Pedro died on October 18, according to the *Anales Toledanos III*. The exact date of don Manuel's death in December is unknown, though the place is. Cf. Ballesteros, *Alfonso X*, p. 1042. Don Manuel is the only member of the royal family that Alfonso mentions by name in the *Cantigas*, as an advisor and confidant (366, 372, 382). Regarding the sincere love of Alfonso for his brother we have a good testimony in Alfonso's last will. Cf. D.W. Lomax, "El padre de don Juan Manuel," in *Don Juan Manuel, VII Centenario*, Murcia, 1982, pp. 163–176.

⁵⁴ Gaibrois, *Sancho IV*, vol. I, nos. 5 and 83.

men whom King Don Alfonso had sent there, and he considered going to him. But they did not think it was prudent to do so. Because he knew that the king, his father, was in Constantina, he went to Guadalcanal and tried to be with the king; but the noblemen did not consent to it nor did they want them to meet. When each of them understood this, they found another way to make a treaty so that they might meet. King Don Alfonso took his daughter Queen Doña Beatriz of Portugal, and Prince Don Sancho took Princess Doña María, his wife, and both of these ladies secretly began the bargaining between King Don Alfonso and Prince Don Sancho. They dealt with one another concerning the agreement of each of the lords. King Don Alfonso betook himself to Seville and Prince Don Sancho went to Salamanca. Prince Don Sancho was in very great pain and had no faith in the physicians. (*CAX*, chap. 77, pp. 256–257)[55]

This trip to the South to negotiate with his father, if it did indeed take place, would only have been psychologically possible for Sancho after the negotiations through mediators had failed. On the other hand, Sancho's mortal illness, which the *CAX* describes immediately after, would not fit with what we know about his itinerary. Yet the chronicler, who is quite reliable in this entire section, is very explicit in placing the illness of the prince at Salamanca, immediately after his return from the failed meeting with his father:

So don Gómez García, who as Abbot of Valladolid and the king's confidant, seeing how the prince had reached the point of death and was distrustful of physicians, sent a letter to his friend don Álvaro, who was with King Don Alfonso, to tell him how Prince Don Sancho was dead and should have King Don Alfonso's grace; and that he would have him given Toledo and many other towns. When the letter reached don Álvaro, he went to King Don Alfonso and showed it to him. When King Don Alfonso saw that it said in the letter that Prince Don Sancho, his son, was dead, he grieved greatly; and so as not to reveal it before those who were with him there, he withdrew to a private room so that no one dared to go [with] him in it. King Alfonso began to weep hard for Prince Don Sancho, and so great was his grief that he spoke very dolorous words, saying many times that the best man he had in his family was dead. When those of King Alfonso's house saw that he was so with-

---

[55] The *CAX* rarely give dates, and this case is no exception, but it does give us a piece of information that could be useful for dating Sancho's trip to Seville and the desired meeting with his father: "Prince Sancho left Princess Doña María, his wife, who was pregnant in Toro. And then Princess Doña Isabel was born there" (chap. 77, p. 256). In effect, doña Isabel, Sancho IV's and María de Molina's first born daughter, who later married Jaime II of Aragón, was born in the city of Toro in May 1283. Therefore, if the trip took place, it must have happened around that time or shortly after. Cf. M. Gaibrois, *Sancho IV*, II, p. 132.

drawn, they realized that he was demonstrating much great sorrow on account of the death of his son; so one of his confidants named Master Nicolás dared to go to him in the chamber, and he spoke these words to the king: "Sire, why are you showing such grief for Prince Don Sancho, your son, who has dispossessed you? For if Prince Don Juan and these other nobles who are here with you realize it, you will lose them all and they will make some movement against you." And so as not to reveal that he was weeping or grieving for Prince Don Sancho, King Alfonso concealed his grief from them; and he spoke these words: "Master Nicolás, I am not weeping for Prince Don Sancho, but I weep for myself, a miserable old man; because since he died, I shall never recover my realms, because the people of my towns and all of the nobles feared me so much for the orders I gave for the harm they did me that they will not want to give them back to me; and more quickly would I have recovered them from Prince Don Sancho, only one man, if he had lived, than from so many others." And with this reason he hid the grief for his son. (*CAX*, chap. 77, p. 257)[56]

A very clever explanation by the Learned King, though probably invented by the author of the *CAX* in order to exalt don Sancho who at the moment was losing ground on all fronts. (It was precisely around that time, at the end of 1283, when he lost the important city of Mérida, which switched over to Alfonso's obedience). The same kind of manipulation of history is also evident in the declaration he puts in Alfonso's mouth: "he spoke very dolorous words, saying many times that the best man he had in his family was dead" (*CAX*, chap. 77, p. 257). This was in obvious contradiction to what Alfonso had declared in his published curse and his last wills. It is indeed an attempt to legitimate don Sancho while his father was still alive. This does not exclude the possibility that Alfonso, aged, depressed, and abandoned by all, may have expressed his true paternal love in the face of this terrible news because, deep down, he still loved his son. It would also not be surprising if despite everything, and considering what kind of people the others were, Alfonso could consider Sancho "the best man he had in his family." Fortunately, however, the news about Sancho's death

---

[56] *CAX*, chap. 77, pp. 255–258. The "Master Nicolás" mentioned in the text is one of the three physicians who in the last years treated Alfonso. The other two were don Mair, a "Jewish physician," the one who most frequently cared for him and to whom he gave a house in Seville, and Alonso Martínez, probably from Toledo. Master Nicolás was a famous doctor who had studied in Montpellier. He was also a poet and an amateur musician, something the Learned King obviously admired. About Master Nicolás there are some humorous verses on his questionable healing arts.

must have been premature. Don Sancho had not yet died, although it is true that he had fallen gravely ill at Salamanca, and the physicians had declared him terminally ill. But he recovered soon, something that pleased Alfonso much, although he was careful not to show his happiness in public.[57]

---

[57] *CAX*, chap. 77, pp. 255–258.

CHAPTER FIFTEEN

THE LAST WILLS OF ALFONSO X

1. *First Last Will. The Great Surprise*

The harsh "curse and disinheritance sentence" of don Sancho is complemented, in terms of the Learned King's position regarding succession and the future rule of the kingdom, by two other documents: his two last wills.[1] On November 8, 1283, Alfonso drafted his first will. It is a complex document because it attempts to justify the change in the terms of succession he made in order to favor don Sancho, against what he had determined in his previous legislation, where he had favored the de la Cerda princes.[2] This first will is, besides a synthesis of his political thought, a personal confession that reveals his state of mind regarding the political crisis in the kingdom in the days in which he drafted it.

The dominant political themes are the contemporary ones: the betrayal of don Sancho and the search for a successor now that the declared heir had been cursed and disinherited. According to the Learned King, greed and disobedience were the two dominant vices that led don Sancho to betrayal, the reasons why he could not be his heir. Alfonso did not think even for a second that the discontent of the nobility and the people could have been the catalysts for the princes' rebellion. The Learned King insisted on the legal illegitimacy of don Sancho, basing his judgment on a charge of moral corruption:

> Because in all the evil deeds he performed against us, he clearly showed that his behavior was guided by these two vices [greed and disobedience]...Because divine justice requires and demands that whoever obstructs justice must lose the power over all things he might use to obstruct it. Likewise, since he goes against natural law, because not

---

[1] Both last wills were published in the *MHE*, II, nos. CCXXVIII–CCXXIX, pp. 110–122 and 122–134; and in Latin by G. Daumet, "Les testaments d'Alphonse le Savant, roi de Castille," *Bibliothèque de l'École des Chartes*, 67 (1906), pp. 70–99, with explanatory comments. See also the edition in *Diplomatario andaluz de Alfonso X*, n. 518. The Castilian text is reproduced by A. García Solalinde, *Antología de Alfonso X el Sabio*, pp. 224–242.

[2] See the passage of the last will quoted above, chap. 11, p. 375.

recognizing the debt that by nature he has contracted with his father, it is the will of God and the decree of law and justice that he be disinherited from what the father owns, and that he not participate in anything that would by natural right belong to him; and the son who inherits [something] from the father against the command of God and what the law prescribes, and the son who disinherits his father or mother, may he die for that. Therefore, don Sancho, because of the deeds he performed against us…may he be disinherited from God and Holy Mary, and we disinherit him…and may he be cursed by God and by Holy Mary and by all the heavenly court and by us…Thus we declare him a traitor in all the things he did against us, in such a way that he should not only receive the punishment accorded to traitors in Spain, but also in all lands, wherever he may be, dead or alive.[3]

Alfonso was directly countering the arrogant assertion by Sancho "Sir, you did not make me—it was God who made me," that the son used to challenge his dependency on his father to inherit the kingdom. The rebel, in Alfonsine thought, puts himself between God and his creation, hindering the functioning of laws established by the Creator. According to Alfonso, his son's belief that he did not need him in order to inherit the throne went against the principles of natural law, which established the dependency of child on the father, from whom he proceeds in all senses, and it also goes against divine and human law. Therefore, if the rebellious son attempted to alter such an order established by nature and by God, disowning his father or his mother, he would deserve the greatest punishment, namely, death: "may he die for that."

These ideas had also appeared in another document drafted on May 4 of that same year, 1283. It is a privilege on behalf of his daughter, Beatriz of Portugal, in which he grants her the city of Niebla as a reward for having accompanied him during his Sevillian retreat, when everyone else had abandoned him: "And when she saw this [Alfonso's abandonment] and recognized what others failed to notice, she left her children and her inheritance and all the things she had, and she came to share in our suffering, to live and die with us."[4] In the same privilege, the Learned King affirms once again the doctrine of the inviolability of natural law:

---

[3] *Antología*, p. 227. Cf. A. Domínguez Rodríguez, "El testamento de Alfonso X y la catedral de Toledo," *Reales sitios*, 21/82 (1984), pp. 73–75; cf. Linehan, *Histories and the Historians*, p. 497, note 131.

[4] In Ballesteros, *Alfonso X*, p. 1015.

> Considering the great and true love we found in our daughter, the very
> honorable doña Beatriz [...] because in that moment in which the rest
> of our children and most of the people of our land rose up against us
> because of things they were told or made to believe, but which were not
> so, their uprising was against God, and against the Law, and against
> reason and against the codes of law [*fueros*] and against natural lordship
> [...]⁵

In his last will Alfonso goes on to reflect on that moment in his personal life in which, when he saw that everyone else had abandoned
him, he must have reached the depths of depression as father, husband, and king: "And when we saw that our family and our natural
vassals had abandoned us, we turned to God, who had granted them to
us, and we asked him that in his mercy he would help us in some way
so that we might not perish when faced with such a great adversity"
(*Ant.*, p. 228). This is a very typical attitude of this man of great faith,
as many *Cantigas* witness. When all human hope had vanished, he
turns to God with his sorrow. But contrary to what many of his critics
believed, Alfonso was also a man of action, and therefore, following
the old saying, "God helps those who help themselves," he began his
long journey in search of human help as well.

It was then when, as we noted above, he turned to the Christian
princes (Portugal, Aragón, England, and France) and to the pope. Since
he did not find any support among the Christians, he had no choice
but to turn to the emir of Morocco. In his desperate state, Alfonso,
who had sworn to defend and protect the Christian faith,⁶ and whom
Bandino di Lancia had proclaimed as "[...] The most Christian and
faithful of all [...] aspiring with all his heart to expand the honor of Our
Holy Mother the Church, and of her pacific state as well as of the Holy
Roman Empire" (cf. above chap. 4, pp. 127–128), was now pleading
with his greatest enemy and that of Christendom, the emir of Morocco,
allying himself with him to fight against Christian armies and against
his own son. The passage of the last will in which the Learned King narrates the events that led him to such a desperate decision is dramatic:

> And seeing that we were dispossessed of all earthly things except for the
> mercy of God, and considering Ibn Yûsuf, king of Morocco and lord of

---

⁵ In Ballesteros, *Alfonso X*, p. 1015.

⁶ When he launched the attack on Salé, for instance, Alfonso, had given as his
motive: "Because of the great desire we have to carry forward the cause of the Overseas
Crusade in the service of God and for the greater glory of Christendom."

the Moors, and remembering the love that united us, and remembering the fame of the world, he acted before the Christian and Moorish kings in order to make justice and [speak the] truth, showing that he had compassion and regretted the evils and infringements to which we had been subjected to, saying that although we belonged to different religions and the house of Morocco had always fought against Spain, that he did not want to take this into account; knowing instead that our house had an honorable history, and because he considered that there was nothing more noble in the world and honorable for his law than to protect our house so that it would not be destroyed, nor we killed nor violated by such great treason that traitors had plotted against us. And he promised us that he would help us personally and with his family, vassals, power, and riches, until we recovered all that belonged to us previously. And this he did, for he not only sent first his children and relatives, but later also arrived himself with noble knights and great riches; in such a way that his arrival brought about many good things. Firstly, because thanks to the mercy of God and his good efforts, and thanks to his good help, we were able to emerge from the shadow of our treacherous enemies who had greatly offended us and stifled us with great treason. Secondly, because we recovered our health, since we began to walk and ride our horse again [...] And seeing all that Yûsuf did for us, we trusted him so much that for about four months we were under his command with the few people we had, convinced of his love and his truthfulness.[7]

One cannot help but think of the tragic figure of King Lear, a victim of betrayal by his own household, whose story Alfonso knew well, for he had commissioned a translation of Geoffrey of Monmouth's version and incorporated it into his own *General Estoria* (Part III, vii). Most probably he identified with it too.[8]

In the process of confessing how he could have reached the decision to ally with the emir, which even to Alfonso must have seemed like a veritable betrayal of his principles as a Christian king and a defender of the faith, he turns to a rational postulate which is beyond the differences of religion and culture: human solidarity with the oppressed, which all humans, on account of their reason, must respect. Used to dealing with Spanish Muslims, among whom he had met men of great integrity, Alfonso appreciated the emir's noble spirit and the motives that, according to him, led Yûsuf to help him. Although they belonged to different religions and in the past had been enemies, Yûsuf tells

---

[7] *Ant.*, p. 230.
[8] Cf. Lloyd Kasten, "The Utilization of the *Historia Regum Britanniae* by Alfonso X," *HR*, 38.5 (special issue, Nov. 1970), pp. 97–114.

him that he cannot allow such an old and noble lineage as Alfonso's
to disappear, "or that we...be killed or violated by such great treason
that traitors had plotted against us." After reading Yûsuf's letter, as
we said above, Alfonso was more than convinced of the sincerity and
generosity of his former rival.

Upon his return to Seville, after participating with his small army
in the attack on Córdoba, and when the emir had already returned to
Morocco after that campaign of looting and devastation, Alfonso, dis-
consolate, tells us that he expected to find "support in the pope and the
king of France and all the other kings whom we had informed of our situation, and we found nothing but good words and many promises that
helped us and comforted the few family members who were with us"
(*Ant.*, pp. 230–231).[9]

Despite the exquisite treatment received from the emir for four
months, during which time he recovered his energy and health and
was able to walk and ride his horse again, the Learned King was clearly
not happy. He must have realized that he had made a pact with the
enemy of Christendom, who was destroying and despoiling his own
kingdom. It was an agreement he was forced to accept, driven by des-
peration and the pressing needs of the moment. The last will reflects
the state of anguish of someone who is looking for a way out of that
necessary but undesirable commitment. He again sought the help of
the king of France. Philip III was more than willing to lend him aid,
but he set certain humiliating conditions he would be unwilling to
accept under normal circumstances: "[...] the king of France goes on
to tell us in his last will, informing us that if we gave his nephews, the
children of don Fernando, our son, what belonged to his father, all of
our problems would be resolved. When we learned of this, we understood that we had been abandoned by everyone in the world from
whom we could expect consolation and help" (ib., p. 231).

After this, in a move more incredible than the pact with the emir of
Morocco, a desperate Alfonso confesses that, "as someone who could
not take it anymore," he sent his delegates to the pope and the king of
France to sign the agreement "and grant the king of France what he
requested." In other words, Alfonso returns to his original idea of suc-

---

[9] To call "llagados" (hurt, dispossessed of their property) the "few" that had
remained with him in Seville is a way of expressing the state of depression the court
was in.

cession to the throne by right of representation, going on to explain, or rather justify, why he signed that agreement with someone with whom he had thus made war. And what is the explanation he offers? France, he argues, is the best nation in the world, under which one can serve Christendom as under no other:

> Therefore, we order, concede, grant, and command in this last will of ours that after our days, our greatest dominion [the kingdom] with all that we own and must own, be given to our grandchildren, the children of don Fernando, our firstborn and heir, in such a way that the eldest should inherit our dominion, and the other should receive its benefit as is fit, according to the tradition of Spain [...] And for these things to be more stable, firm, and valid, we establish and order also that if the children of don Fernando were to die without children who should inherit from them, that our dominion should go to the king of France, because he is descended in direct line from the same [family] from which we are descended, from the Emperor of Spain, and he is the great-grandchild of king don Alfonso of Castile, the same as us, because he is the son of his daughter [...] And we give and grant this dominion in such a way that it should be united to the kingdom of France, so that both kingdoms form a single one forever, and so that whoever is king and lord of France, should also be king and lord of our dominion of Spain. And because we present this offer to God so that He may be served and His law exalted, we place our decision in the hands and under the custody of the Holy Church of Rome, and so that it should always be obligated to perform and guard what is laid out in this our last will and through this document. (ib., p. 232)[10]

Alfonso continues to surprise us up until the end. Obviously such a radical solution as was the unification of the two kingdoms of France and Castile-León in the middle of the 13th century must have seemed absurd to all who knew the will, regardless of what how well-argued or grounded it was on genealogical arguments. The most important and surprising thing about the proposal was how Alfonso, in the midst of civil war and chaos in his kingdoms, toward the end of his days, was able to change successors once more. He would remain in this ambivalent and conflictive state between the traditional, time-honored Castilian principle of succession by the eldest surviving son and that

---

[10] Alfonso obviously is justifying once more his hypothetical surrender of the kingdom of Castile-León to France based on the blood ties that joined the dynasty ruling France with the kings of Castile-León. Philip III and Alfonso X were great grandchildren of Alfonso VIII, while their respective grandmothers, Blanche and Berenguela, were sisters and daughters of the victorious warrior of las Navas de Tolosa.

of succession by representation until the end of his days. Deep down, however, it was not his desire to renew the legal process of succession that led him to once more declare his grandchildren as successors, but rather the pressures of his day, namely don Sancho's rebellion and the firm conviction that his other children, besides being traitors, were incapable of taking the reins of the kingdom: "We do this also because we understand that none of our children will be able on their own to protect what is ours, given the state that it is in, and the destitution of the people, and the chaos in the kingdom, in such a way that whoever received it out of need, should seek help elsewhere to keep it; and nowhere could they find such good help as from the king of France" (ib., p. 232).[11]

The wish to deprive Sancho of the throne at all costs, as a punishment for his rebellion, and the inability of the other children to rule in such critical circumstances would be the reasons that, above all other considerations, would force the anguished father to adopt his initial choice, the de la Cerda princes. This seems to have been his last wish regarding the matter of succession. At least this is what he says when contemplating the possibility that his children, with the exception of Sancho, could one day return to his obedience: "... however, if any of our children, except don Sancho, whom we don't consider with the others, were to return to serve us, we could grant then some benefit, except for our greatest dominion [namely, the kingdom]" (ib., p. 231). In other words, he was willing to make concessions to his sons, but the "señorío mayor," the crown of Castile-León, he intended to give this one to the children of Fernando de la Cerda, or, in their absence, to the king of France.

Among the witnessing signatories of the last will were doña Beatriz, queen of Portugal and of the Algarve, whose name came first, followed by that of don Remondo, archbishop of Seville, and a list of well-known court figures. It was written by Juan Andrés, the king's notary.

---

[11] Regarding a previous attempt, cf. A. Rodríguez López, "*Quod alienus regnet et heredes expellatur. L'offre du trône de Castille au roi Louis de France*," *Le Moyen Age*, 105 (1999), pp. 109–128.

2. *Second Last Will*

Barely two months later, on January 24, 1284, Alfonso delivered a new last will, or *codicilo*, in which he introduced some changes to the one recorded in 1283.[12] His position toward Sancho, however, despite repeated attempts at rapprochement from both sides, was still inflexible due to Sancho's great betrayal. This would indicate that if there was a meeting, there had been no reconciliation as of that moment.

In contrast to the first will, which is a sort of synthesis of his political thought for governing the kingdom after his death, in this one he deals with several personal matters he had not mentioned in the previous one, such as the settling of his debts, which worried him to the point of obsession, since he ordered that his body not be buried until all debts had been paid. He demanded this despite the fact that he knew he had no money to pay them with: "And we order our children to be on our side and our vassals to observe and uphold this disposition, because we leave all to the mercy of God and his loyalty" (*Ant.*, p. 234).

He also dealt with the distribution of his personal belongings (the bed "with all the linen it may have at the moment of our death," for example he wanted to donate to the poor of the hospital of San Juan de Acre, together with one thousand silver marks), and, above all, he worried about the how his body was to be buried, a topic about which he gave detailed instructions:

> [we order] that our body be buried in our monastery of Santa María la Real of Murcia, which is the capital of the kingdom and the first place where God willed us to gain his service…Likewise, we command that immediately after our death, our heart be removed, and be taken overseas to the Holy Land, and that it be buried in Jerusalem, on the Hill of Calvary, there where some of our ancestors lie, and if it cannot be taken there, let it be placed somewhere else where it may lie until it is God's will that the Holy Land be recovered, and it may be safely taken there (ib., pp. 234–235) […] We also order that when our heart be removed in order for it to be taken to the Holy Land, as was mentioned, may the rest [of the viscera] also be taken from our body and buried in the monastery of Santa María la Real of Murcia, or wherever it is to be buried […] but

---

[12] This is the date that appears in the manuscript used by the editors of the *MHE*, II, pp. 122–134.

if it isn't possible, we order that all of this be done in the main church of Santa María of Seville. (ib. pp. 235–236)[13]

Perhaps anticipating future disputes about his body and the fact that it would be difficult to transport it to a Muslim-controlled Jerusalem (despite the detailed instructions to the Master of the Templars, who was charged with the transfer) Alfonso approved of burial in Seville, together with his parents, but under very clear conditions:

> And if our executors should decide to bury our body in Seville, we order that it be buried wherever they find it best, but in such a way that the tomb is not too high. And if they wish it, [may I be buried] near king don Fernando and queen doña Beatriz, in such a way that our head lies at their feet and that the tomb be simple, so that when the chaplain enters to recite a prayer for us and for them, that his feet should be on our tomb. (*Ant.*, p. 235)

It is worth noting that Alfonso, who was a great promoter of Gothic cathedrals, such as those at Burgos and León, did not chose as his mausoleum either one of these, nor even Toledo, where he had been born and where the traditional graves of many previous kings were located. He preferred instead to be buried in the old mosques of Murcia and Seville, which had been converted into Christian temples dedicated to Saint Mary, where he had also buried father and mother. It seems to be a very coherent attitude in relation to his independent view of Church tradition. Alfonso's remains were buried in several parts of the Seville cathedral before they were placed where they are today.[14]

---

[13] It is not known what ancestors he is referring to, for there is no record that any of his paternal forebears were buried in the Hill of the Calvary. Perhaps, according to Ballesteros, he was referring to "his Germanic lineage, since he was the son of Beatrice of Swabia" (*Alfonso X*, p. 1054). In 1948, on the occasion of the forensic medical examination of the remains of Alfonso X, it was discovered that, indeed, his heart was not found with the rest of his remains. According to the official report by Dr. Delgado, the body had two transversal incisions on the left side of his thorax, perhaps effected to extract the viscera from this cavity, especially the heart, which is mentioned in his last will and which is preserved in Murcia ("Examen médico legal," p. 147). Both the heart and the other organs were buried in the Murcia cathedral.

[14] Up until its final burial place in the Seville cathedral, where it is found today, Alfonso's body was moved several times. We do not know where he was initially buried, but we know that for some time his remains were in the high room of the Patio de los Naranjos, while construction work was going on in the cathedral. They were later transferred to the Chapel of St. Clement, and then to the Royal Chapel in 1579 to be buried next to the remains of his father. Finally, in 1677 they were transferred to the side walls of the Royal Chapel. During all of these transfers, they were examined by distinguished physicians of the period, whose names are known, though not

In the distribution of his material goods, numerous valuable objects are mentioned, including "the four books they call *Espejo historial*, which king Louis of France had made," an expensive brocade he had received from his sister Eleanor of England, "a large book [tabla] with a historical narrative in which there are many ebony images and the deeds and history of Saint Mary, [...] the two Bibles and three books with thick writing, silver covers, and the other history in three books that king Louis of France gave us and another book [tabla] with the relics, and the crowns with the stones and the cameo and rings and other noble things that belong to a king, may all this be received by whoever by right will inherit our greater dominion of Castile and León" (p. 236).[15] In this category of donations and legacies, the celebrated codex of the *Cantigas* is also mentioned: "Likewise, we order that all the books of the *Songs of Praise of Holy Mary* be taken to the church where our body will be buried, and that they be sung on the feasts of Holy Mary... We also give to whoever inherits our own, the book *Setenario* which we made. We also give him what we have in Toledo which was seized from us, whenever it is God's will that we recover it or that whomever inherits our kingdom may recover it; because these are very rich and very noble things that belong to kings" (p. 236).[16]

It is noteworthy that among the works composed under his direction and patronage, at the time of drafting his will, he only remembers two: the *Cantigas* and the *Setenario*, "which we made." Perhaps it was because only these two works were personally composed by him.

The second will fundamentally confirms the arrangements of the previous will in the matter of succession, but it does not specifically mention Alfonso de la Cerda as successor, nor the possibility that his kingdoms would be handed over to Philip III of France, in case the de la Cerda princes were unable to inherit them. Some new political dispositions are noted, however.

---

their reports, if indeed they wrote any. Cf. J. Delgado Roig, "Examen médico legal," pp. 137–138.

[15] J.A. De Morgado describes in great detail "Las Tablas Alphonsies, llamadas assi, por averlas dexado a esta Sancta Iglesia el Rey Don Alfonso el Sabio," which are indeed the same ones Alfonso mentions in his last will ("una tabla grande hestoriada," "e la nuestra tabla con las reliquias"). According to the illustrious historian of the city, this legacy of Alfonso's to his favorite city was preserved at the time with great honor (*Historia de Sevilla*, fols. 101r–v).

[16] More about the arrangements regarding the *Cantigas* codices in J. Guerrero Lovillo, *Las Cantigas de Santa María del rey Alfonso X el Sabio. Estudio arqueológico de sus miniaturas*, 2 vols., Madrid, 1949.

These were due to the changes that had taken place in the last months. To his son Juan, who had returned to his obedience, he bequeathed the kingdoms of Seville and Badajoz, but with a clause that guarantees the unity of the kingdom, "we order that don Juan and those that come from him may forever obey and receive the lordship from whomever inherits Castile and León and our other kingdoms from us" (p. 237). To don Jaime, who also had returned to his obedience, he left the kingdom of Murcia, under the same clause. To Queen Beatriz of Portugal, he renewed the gift of "the town of Niebla" in a different document dated in Seville, March 4, 1284.[17] He also bequeathed generous donations and gifts to other members of the family who had returned to his affection: to Princess Berenguela, "our daughter, all the inheritance we gave her in the kingdoms of Castile and León, after she came to be with us in Seville and don Sancho disinherited her of all we gave her" (p. 239); to his granddaughter Blanca, daughter of Beatriz of Portugal, he left 100,000 maravedís for her marriage; he also did not forget his other illegitimate children, Urraca Alfonso, and Martín Alfonso, to whom he left lands and considerable sums of money.[18]

In the second last will, as we just noted, the name of the successor is never mentioned. Instead, he is always referred to in general terms as "he who would inherit our own," or "he who would rightly inherit from us Castile and León, and our other kingdoms." Of course, this heir is not don Sancho, who was still cursed, to such an extent that even the thought that he might one day rule legitimately seemed to Alfonso a "misfortune." Faced with the possibility that Sancho might one day obtain the crown and that to pacify his brother Juan he would grant him Seville and Badajoz, Alfonso insists that don Juan should be wary of such an agreement, because Sancho would betray him also.

Despite these arrangements affecting his own children and heirs, in this second will there is also a trace of obsession on Alfonso's part that a future alliance or submission to France would be something "we could not excuse". This was perhaps out of fear that the de la Cerda princes would not be able to attain the throne. Speaking of the need

---

[17] The text of the diploma can be found in Ballesteros, *Alfonso X*, p. 1015.

[18] In a copy of the last will kept at the Archivo Nacional de la Torre do Tumbo, made directly from the original in Seville on April 16, 1283, among the beneficiaries is listed doña Inés, "mother of Ercules," whom scholars deem to be another one of the king's lovers. "Ercules" would be another illegitimate son of Alfonso's about whom we know nothing.

for don Juan to obey whomever inherits the kingdom (except don Sancho), among the various reasons why he should do it, Alfonso:

> [...] because it is convenient that the help that [the successor] receives is
> powerful and rich, and we don't know that this might happen without
> the support of the Church of Rome and of the king of France, who were
> always united as one, because France always served the Church in all
> the great deeds that it needed help in more than any other kingdom, it
> could rightfully be said; and because we belong to the same family from
> ancient and recent times, and therefore, we are not handing over our
> dominion to strangers...For all these reasons, we believe that this is for
> the best, and thus we counseled don Juan, and we begged and ordered
> him to do it so, and that he observe in every possible way, putting his
> love in the king of France, and that everything he does, he does with the
> counsel of the Church and of him. And we believe in this we are giving
> him great and good advice, like a father gives to his son, and a good
> lord to his vassal and good friend. And whoever obstructs this and gives
> him advice to the contrary, may he be called a traitor and receive God's
> anger and his. (p. 238)

What is happening here? Was the Learned King delirious? Perhaps
he was feeling remorse regarding his own legitimacy. Because it was
quite possible that he was being assailed by doubts about an old rumor
he thought he had cleared up and laid to rest when he wrote *Estoria de España*. The phrase he uses to justify his new position makes
us think that, as the historian he was, something was bothering him:
"and because we belong to the same family from ancient and recent
time, and therefore, we are not handing over our dominion to strangers[...]" Years earlier, there had been a rumor at court that his paternal grandmother, doña Berenguela, whom he had loved very much,
was younger than his sister doña Blanca, who was the mother of Louis
IX of France and grandmother of Philip III. If this was true, this meant
that at the death of Louis IX of France in 1274, the legitimate king of
Castile would have been Philip III of France, and not Alfonso X. This
must have been but a court rumor, because already don Rodrigo Jiménez de Rada, and later on Alfonso, in his *Estoria de España*, had set
out to defend Berenguela as the eldest daughter, affirming that Alfonso
VIII had issued a privilege, kept at the Burgos Cathedral, declaring
Berenguela the eldest.[19]

---

[19] *PCG*, chap. 1029, II, p. 713b42–44; R. Jiménez de Rada, *De rebus Hispaniae*, IX,
5. Cf. J. Craddock, "Dynasty in Dispute: Alfonso X el Sabio and the Succession to the
Throne of Castile and Leon in History and Legend," *Viator*, 17 (1986), p. 203.

Given these precedents, which Alfonso thought he had settled in his explanation in *Estoria de España*, and above all with the marriage agreement of 1269 between his son don Fernando and Blanche, daughter of Louis IX of France, and faced with the failure of his designated heir and that of the rest of his children, and the uncertainty over the de la Cerda princes, we may ask if Alfonso was not going back on his word and casting doubt over the truth of his great-grandfather's privilege. Did Alfonso actually believe that Philip of France had as much of a right as him, if not more, to inherit the crown of Castile and León?

It is worth pointing out that don Juan Manuel, in the famous meeting with the dying don Sancho discussed above, also quoted his cousin as saying that he himself could not give him his blessing because he had not received it from his parents, citing as cause, besides the evils he had committed against them, the fact that his parents had also not received it from their parents: "Because the holy king don Fernando, my grandfather, did not give his blessing to the king my father, except with certain conditions that he set, and he did not observe any of them. For this reason he did not receive his blessing. Likewise, the queen, my mother, I believe also did not obtain the blessing from her father because he disliked her very much because of the suspicion that he had about the death of princess Constanza, her sister. And thus, neither my father nor my mother received the blessing of their elders, and they were unable to give it to me."[20]

We cannot know for sure what words don Juan Manuel gathered verbatim from Sancho's mouth and what is his own elaboration. What is true is that the words he puts in his cousin's mouth about the circumstances of the blessing Fernando gave to his son Alfonso is something all documentation and chronicles pass over in silence. On the other hand, it is not clear what led Alfonso, who loved and defended the independence of his kingdoms, to a complete submission to France and the Church of Rome, and, ultimately, to Anjou Guelfism. In between the lines, we can read that what led him to this tardy conversion, which was in open conflict with his entire life as a fervent Ghibelline, was a desperate act to recover the royal authority that he saw was inevitably slipping from his hands. It was a behavior that very much resembled the desperate act of seeking help from the emir of Morocco. As a man without hope, let down by everyone, he threw

---

[20] *Libro de la armas*, quoted ed., p. 18.

himself into the arms of the enemy, perhaps thinking it preferable to have a French, Angevin, or Guelf king than having his kingdom in the hands of a traitor and his descendants. Clearly, the dynastic justification of his actions, saying that "we are not handing over our dominion to strangers" "because we belong to the same family from ancient and recent times," is not sufficiently convincing, despite the fact the two kings were related. He did not make use of this argument when he was at war with the king of France to defend his rights in Navarra. Therefore, given the international political situation at the moment, and the fact that in Rome (or rather, in Viterbo, because Martin IV never set foot in Rome) a pope at the service of the French king was occupying the throne of St. Peter, perhaps we should think that Alfonso acted under the pressure of the agents of Philip III, or perhaps that he wanted to respond in the best possible way to the flattering feelings of sympathy and understanding expressed by the pope in the letter of dated August 9, 1283.

In any event, Alfonso had lost his will to fight for the ideals that had always been his raison d'être as a statesman. In his last days, he seems to have been dazzled by the Angevin mirage that in Italy, with Manfred's death, had been the downfall of the Hohenstaufen. Of course, it is quite difficult to understand how Alfonso, who had felt throughout his life very connected to house of Swabia, would have become Guelf convert and accepted the possibility of introducing into his kingdoms, due only to the whim of a Francophile pope, an Angevin dynasty that had never had anything to do with the kingdom of the two Sicilies. Did the Learned King lose his intellect at the end of his days?

Perhaps the explanation of turning to France as last resort is given indirectly by one of his close collaborators who at the time drafted the Critical version of the *Estoria de España*. When talking about the disapproval of rebellion, the main motif of Alfonsine ideology insisted upon in all of the works, the writer of the *Versión crítica*, when explaining why the Visigothic kingdom was lost, quotes the opinion of don Rodrigo Jiménez de Rada, who attributed it to divine punishment brought about by the Visigoths themselves, when they did not respect the right to succession in the kingdom, committing several regicides (*De rebus*, III, 22, p. 70). The Alfonsine compiler of the *Version critica* [Ms. *Ss*] continues the list started by don Rodrigo, citing the assassinations of Fruela and Vímaro, and then those of the kings of Asturias and León, followed by those of the kings of Castile:

Prince don García seized the kingdom by force from his father, king don Alfonso the Great. King don Sancho II was treacherously killed by Vellido Adólfez, who was his vassal. King don Alfonso, son of king don Fernando, who won Seville, was dispossessed of the kingdom by force by his son, prince don Sancho. All the people in the kingdom rose up with don Sancho, and they plotted to capture the king and expel him from the land, but king don Alfonso was helped by God, and by the people of Seville, and by king Ibn Yusuf of the North African Moors, as will be told later on in due course. (*Ss.*, f. 66v)[21]

Could it be concluded from this text that, in Alfonso's last days, faced with his deposition and the political chaos caused by civil war and social disorders of all kinds, Alfonso's collaborators in the *Estoria de España* and his personal advisors thought that the only way to safeguard the unity of the kingdom and avoid its disintegration was to deliver it to the king of France?

The execution of this second will was entrusted to prince don Juan, to queen Beatriz of Portugal, and to don Remondo, archbishop of Seville, together with some other close associates. But, as in the first one, queen Violante's name is not mentioned anywhere.[22]

3. *Cultural Concerns until the End*

Despite all kinds of illnesses and political adversities, Alfonso, in the last years of his life, still found periods of calm and convalescence to devote himself intensely to his intellectual work. The number and quality of the works he supervised and personally wrote in the last years is such that it leaves us completely amazed, when we consider the enormous personal and family problems he faced. In 1280 he finished the first four parts of the *General Estoria*, and in the five years between 1277–1282, he concluded the collection of the *Cantigas de Santa María*, which contains over 400 (427) compositions. Between 1282 and 1284 he drafted the last version of the *Estoria de España*, known as the "Versión crítica." Finally, shortly before dying, during 1283, he begins and concludes the *Libro de Axedrez, Dados e Tablas* [Book of Chess, Dice, and Backgammon],[23] the *Libro del grant axedres, del alquerque*

---

[21] Quoted by I. Fernández-Ordoñez, *Versión crítica de la Estoria de España*, Madrid: Seminario Menéndez Pidal, 1993, pp. 54–55.

[22] Cf. Daumet, "Les testaments," pp. 87–99.

[23] Este libro fue començado e acabado en la cibdat de Sevilla, por mandado del muy noble rey don Alfonso, fijo de muy noble rey don Ferrando et de la reina

e del tablero que se juega por astronomía [The Book of Grand Chess, Checkers, and of the Chessboard Played Through Astronomy],[24] and perhaps also worked on a book entitled *Libro del fecho de los cavallos* [Book about Horses], whose attribution is unclear.[25] Finally it is believed that shortly before dying, he also supported the translation of the *Libro de Moamín* or *Libro que es fecho de las animalias que caçan* [Book of Moamín or Book about the Animals that Hunt].[26]

Without abandoning his serious works on historiography and his passion for collecting *cantigas*, in the last years of his life, he devoted himself to creating works he had not been very interested in until that moment. It was a way of soothing himself from the painful setbacks of the last years, precisely because they were works on pastimes, such as board games, falconry (which always fascinated him), or about the keeping of horses. The reason for all this intellectual activity in the twilight of his life is provided by Alfonso in the prologue to his *Libros de axedrez, dados e tablas*:

> Because God wanted men to naturally have all kids of joy so that they could endure the sorrows and toils whenever they should arrive. Therefore, men sought many other forms of leisure to properly satisfy this joy.[27] [...] There are other joys [...] that were invented to find solace from worries and woes whenever they should come. These are: hearing songs and the sound of instruments, playing chess, or board games, or other similar games... And even though each one of these amusements were invented for the sake of good, man should not make use of them except at a convenient time in such a way that he should benefit from them and not be harmed [by them]. (ib., V. XXI, 70)

---

doña Beatriz, señor de Castilla e de León...en trinta e dos años que el Rey sobredicho regñó. En la era de mill e trezientos e veint e uno año [1283]. (*Libros de acedrex, dados e tablas*, ed. by Arnold Steiger, Ginebra, Romanica Helvetica, 10, pp. 408–446)
A. Domínguez Rodríguez, *Libros del ajedrez, dados y tablas*, facsimile ed., Madrid-Valencia, 1987. This work is profusely illustrated with 150 miniatures that, together with the *Cantigas*, are the best display of painting at Alfonso X's court.

[24] Cf. F. Gómez Redondo, *Historia de la prosa medieval castellana*, pp. 833–838.

[25] See the ed. by G. Sachs, *El libro de los caballos. Tratado de albeitería del siglo XIII*, Madrid, Anejo XXII de la *RFE*, 1936; and more recently the ed. by M.I. Montoya, *Texto y concordancia del "Libro de los caballos," Escorial MS.b.IV.31*, Madison: HSMS, 1994.

[26] Cf. A.J. Cárdenas, *The Text and Concordance of Biblioteca Nacional Manuscript RES.270-217. Libro que es fecho de las animalias que caçan. The Book of Moamin*, Madison: HSMS, 1987. For the recent history of the manuscript containing this work, which is thought to be Alfonsine, see H.P. Kraus, "A Medieval Spanish Version of the Book of Moamin: Observations on Date and Sponsorship," *Manuscripta*, 31 (1987), pp. 166–180.

[27] *Libros de acedrex*, fol. 1r2–12, in *Concordances and Texts*.

They are therefore works destined to cheer up the life of those who for some reason cannot perform physical exercise, but still need to enjoy moments of leisure in their spare time or even in confinement.

Besides these works, all of which are ambitious and required careful and refined composition in which he must have invested much time, Alfonso, in those last years of his life, almost blind and physically handicapped, abandoned by all except his daughter Beatriz and a handful of faithful allies, also maintained an extensive epistolary correspondence, especially private, as we will later see. I also do not want to fail to mention here, even if in passing, the most important document of don Sancho's disinheritance, which, due to its length and detail, must have taken him a long time to prepare and draft. This too could be said of his two last wills, written at a moment of great anxiety and depression resulting from his deposition and abandonment by his closest family members and most of his allies. In reality, for Alfonso, as for Philomena in Ovid's fable, suffering and creativity were inseparable companions until the end.

When the end of his days arrived, Alfonso, despite his feverish pace of work up until the last minute, must have realized that his cultural oeuvre was far from being completed; it was not a feeling that surprised him suddenly at that moment when his life was slipping away, but rather one that had accompanied him throughout his entire adult life. As a writer, he had always been very conscious of the fleeting nature of time and the limitations of human beings. He reminds us of that frequently throughout his oeuvre, and very explicitly in *Cantiga* 110, where he uses a wonderful hyperbole to expose the insufficiency of human nature to sing the praises of Mary, but where, at the same time, he seems to be reflecting on the immense task lying ahead of him: "If the starry sky were made of parchment and the immense sea of ink, and a learned man lived forever writing, the greater part of Her virtues would remain untold" (*Songs of Holy Mary, Cantiga* 110, p. 137). Alfonso, like Cervantes centuries later, died with the pen in his hand, and like the author of *Don Quixote*, he too could have written "For me alone was Don Quixote born, and I for him; he knew how to act, and I to write; the two of us alone are one [...]" (part II, chap. 74).[28]

---

[28] Miguel de Cervantes, *Don Quixote*. Trans. Edith Grossman, Foreword by Harold Bloom, New York: Harper Collins, 2003, p. 939.

4. *Alfonso Forgives Don Sancho. The End*

In the last weeks before his death, according to the *Crónica* which had not mentioned at all the curse against his son, Alfonso forgave don Sancho, justifying his rebellion as a youthful act: "And when he was stricken by his illness, he said before them all that he forgave Prince Don Sancho, his son and heir, because he acted in that manner due to his youthfulness. King Alfonso also said that he forgave all of the subjects of the kingdoms who had worked against him; and he quickly ordered documents written concerning this, sealed with his golden seals so that all people of his kingdom would know that he had given up complaints against them and that he forgave them so that they would be safe from any vituperation whatsoever" (chap. 77, p. 258). In a letter to Pope Martin IV dated March 23, 1283, not only did Alfonso beg the pope to absolve his son who had confessed his crime and had repented of having strayed from the road of paternal devotion, but Alfonso also ends the letter by saying that he took back all the curses he had cast against Sancho, and he asks the pope to accept him in his grace.[29]

The letter to the pope does not specifically mention the curse or disinheritance sentence pronounced against don Sancho in October 1282, nor the last wills where the sentence was ratified. If the letter is authentic, then such a sentence would have been revoked. Some scholars doubt the authenticity of the letter, while others accept its validity.[30] It is very possible that in other documents besides the letter to the pope, which have not been preserved, Alfonso expressed a final wish to forgive his son and restore to him the right to the throne. This would explain why when prince don Juan asked Alfonso, shortly before his death, to confirm the inheritance he had left him in his will, namely, the kingdoms of Seville and Badajoz, Alfonso "did not want to [do so]" (*CAX* chap. 77, p. 258). This would have been so because Alfonso would have considered it a matter for his successor to decide. What we do not know is whether the successor was at that

---

[29] A copy of this letter, but dated March 23, 1284, is preserved at The Public Record Office in London and was published by T. Rymer, *Foedera* I, 2, no. 230.

[30] Among those who doubt it, is F.J. Hernández, "Alfonso X y Andalucía," *HID*, 22 (1995), p. 300; and among those who accept it is J.F. O'Callaghan, *The Learned King*, p. 319.

moment was Sancho, or the king of France, as he had arranged in his second will.

Knowing the partisanship of the author of the *CAX*, we must admit the possibility that the chronicler invented not only the story of the pardon, but also the deathbed scene between don Juan and Alfonso for the purpose of legitimating don Sancho's rights to each and every part of the kingdom. Yet it is also possible that there was a true reconciliation, and that it may have taken place between the date of the second will (January 21) and the death of the king (April 4). In that case, such reconciliation or pardon would indeed have been reflected in the letter to Pope Martin IV and in the quoted passage from the *CAX*. In fact, it is precisely the *CAX* that speaks of an intervention by doña Beatriz and doña María de Molina to reconcile father and son, and while it does not tell us when it took place, it is possible that these two noble ladies persisted in their efforts until the final days before Alfonso's death. In any event, at the end of February 1282, Sancho returned to Salamanca from his trip to the south. Alfonso remained in Seville until he died. There is no evidence that they met or saw each other ever again.

None of the known documentation, with the exception of the letter to the pope and the cited passage of the *CAX* confirms that Alfonso forgave his son.[31] But knowing his affectionate temperament and his inability to hold a grudge (recall his grief when he found out about Sancho's death), we must admit that Alfonso indeed forgave him.[32] In any event, however, if there was such a pardon, Sancho never learned of it, either through his father's letter to the pope, or through one that Alfonso would also have written to him, according to the *CAX*. From the deathbed conversation that Sancho held with his cousin, don Juan Manuel, who at the time was a twelve year-old boy, it is not entirely clear that he learned of his father's pardon. He affirmed explicitly that he was unable to give his blessing to Juan Manuel because he himself had not received it (see above chap. 14, p. 487). Don Sancho

---

[31] Cf. *MHE*, II, no. 229, pp. 122–134; Daumet "Testaments," pp. 87–89; Procter, *Curia and Cortes*, p. 182.

[32] This is also Dr. Torres's opinion: "Briefly before dying—with that terrifyingly lucid death of heart patients—he did what he, deep down, indeed desired: to forgive his rebellious son, attributing his betrayal to lack of reflection typical of young men...Some historians have cast doubt on this pardon, but it seems to be more and more accepted as a fact. Resentment was not part of Alfonso's psychology." ("Rasgos médico-psicológicos," p. 137)

died without knowing that his father had, in the Christian spirit, forgiven him.

The anonymous chronicler concludes the story of the subject of his biography by narrating the final moment in these terms:

> After King Alfonso had finished and stated all this [the letters of forgiveness], he received very devoutly the Body of Christ, and after part of an hour he gave his soul to God. Prince Don Juan and all the nobles, the Queen of Portugal, his daughter, and the other princes, his sons, wept greatly for King Alfonso; and afterward they buried him in Saint Mary's of Seville, close to King Don Fernando, his father, and his mother, Queen Doña Beatriz. (*CAX*, chap. 77, p. 258)[33]

It was April 4, 1284, Holy Tuesday. Don Alfonso X of Castile and León was 63 years and 5 months old. As he had ordered in his last will, his body was buried in the cathedral of Seville, at the foot of the grave of his parents, Fernando III *the Holy* and Beatriz of Swabia. But his heart is not there.

5. *Alfonso's Portraits*

Alfonso X was probably the most frequently depicted king of the entire Middle Ages. His figure appears in many illustrations of the *Cantigas*, the *Lapidario*, the *Libro de Axedrez dados e tablas*, at the front of the most important manuscript that contains the *Estoria de España*, and in some of the manuscripts of the *General Estoria* and the *Partidas*.[34]

---

[33] Most probably, Alfonso, did not die of the skin carcinoma, but rather of a heart ailment he had suffered from at least from the time of his journey to Beaucaire. News about his father's death surprised Sancho in Ávila. The next day, wearing mourning clothes, he attended a solemn funeral celebration in honor of the soul of the deceased at the cathedral (*Crónica de Sancho IV*, p. 69a–b).

[34] R. Cómez Ramos, "El retrato de Alfonso X, el Sabio en la primera Cantiga de Santa María," in *Studies on the Cantigas de Santa Maria: Art, Music, and Poetry. Proceedings of the International Symposium on the Cantigas de Santa María of Alfonso X, el Sabio (1221–1284) in Commemoration of its 700th Anniversary Year-1984 (New York, November 19–21)*, eds. I.J. Katz and J.E. Keller, Madison: Seminary of Medieval Studies, 1987, pp. 35–52; and "Esbozo de la personalidad de Alfonso X el Sabio como poeta y mecenas," *AH*, 62, núm. 191 (1979), pp. 105–128; A. Domínguez Rodríguez, "El libro de los juegos y la miniatura alfonsí," in his *Libros del ajedrez, dados y tablas*, facsimile ed., Madrid – Valencia, 1987, pp. 30–123; J. Filgueira Valverde, "Pedro de Lorenzo, Pintor de Alfonso X," *El Museo de Pontevedra*, XXXII (1979); C. Scarborough, "A Summary of the Research on the Miniatures of the *Cantigas de Santa María*," *BC*, 1 (1987), pp. 41–50. A reproduction of the most representative images and portraits of Alfonso X can be seen in the Spanish version of this work.

Scholars of Alfonsine iconography divide his portraits into two main categories: images of dedication or presentation and images of the king as troubadour.[35] The first category includes all those images in which a notary, a translator, a collaborator, or an illustration artist, generally kneeling, presents the king with the manuscript that contains the completed work. A variant of this presentation image appears in those miniatures in which the prologue or the entire book is attributed to the king. In this case, the miniature depicts Alfonso seated on a stool and pointing with his index finger to scribes seated Turkish-style on the floor, taking dictation.[36]

Despite what has been said about Alfonso's monumental ego in wanting to leave his mark on everything he did, the presentation images are never original or unique, but rather, as some scholars think, "heirs of Carolingian and Ottonian works, which probably follow late Roman and Byzantine models and often show the emperor in majestic representations, surrounded by many of the attributes of power."[37] This fits in perfectly with the political moment in Alfonso's life when he was struggling to obtain the imperial crown. Therefore, because of their content and the location in which they are placed, they are a clear sign of a specific objective. Alfonso would have had himself depicted with all the insignia and pomp of royalty—the crown, rich regalia, surrounded by elegant courtiers, scribes, musicians, and singers—as can be clearly gleaned from the most representative miniatures (such as the one in Ms.T.I.1, fol. 5—illustration 1—and the one in Ms. b-l-2, fol. 29 in El Escorial—illustration 3). The purpose would have been, first, to exalt and make known the splendor of his enlightened court, and at the same time to advance his qualifications to assume the imperial crown, both as descendant of the Staufens, and ultimately, of Charlemagne; and, second, to show the role that he, as

---

[35] Cf. A. Domínguez, "La miniatura del 'scriptorium' alfonsí," *Estudios Alfonsíes*, Granada, 1985, pp. 127–161; "Imágenes de Presentación de la miniatura alfonsí," *Goya*, 131 (1976), pp. 287–291; and "Imágenes de un rey trovador de Santa María (Alfonso X en las cantigas)," in *Il Medio Oriente e l'Occidente dell'Arte del XIII secolo*, Bologna: Hans Belting, 1982, pp. 229–239; J.J. Rey, "El trovador don Alfonso X," *RO*, 43 (1984), pp. 166–183.

[36] Examples of these two types of images of presentation are the translations of the *Libro de la Escala* and of the *Libro de las Formas y Imágenes*. Cf. A. Domínguez, "La miniatura del 'scriptorium' alfonsí", pp. 7–8.

[37] A. Domínguez, "Imágenes de un rey trovador," p. 229.

a man of letters, had had in the composition of the work or prologue in question.[38]

The presentation portraits are not many, compared with those in the second category, those of the troubadour king. However, if we consider that Alfonso was "the only European monarch of his century who opens almost all of his manuscripts with his image as sovereign in a presentation scene,"[39] we will have to conclude that, in this aspect of his culture too, he was a continuator of the Carolingian tradition that in a way connected him with the Roman Empire, to whose title he was aspiring. On the other hand, this also shows him as a true precursor of humanism, as a patron of artists to whom they present their works.

The portraits of the king as "troubadour of Holy Mary," are much more numerous. There are many of these images in the so-called *Codice rico* of the *Cantigas*, just as in the Florentine codex. In fact, all the *"loor" cantigas*, which coincide with the ones numbered in tens, are preceded by an image of the troubadour king. The only exception is the first *cantiga* that opens the collection in the *Códice rico*, in which the Joys of Mary are narrated in eight vignettes. But starting with *Cantiga* X, Alfonso as troubadour appears in every tenth *cantiga*. The Learned King, who was very familiar with Provençal courtly poetry, appears here as the loving servant of Mary, portrayed in a variety of poses—standing, kneeling, in frontal and profile views, frequently pointing with the index finger to an image of the Virgin, or in a gesture of instructing or admonishing those present who, judging by the elegance of their dress, are always courtiers.

The participants in the recitation of the *cantigas de loor*, as mentioned, were always courtiers or figures from his *scriptorium*. Rustic or poor characters are never present. This indeed had something to do with the difficulty of the topic of the *cantiga*, which was not accessible to the general public, unlike the narratives and *milagros* (miracles), which everyone could easily understand and spiritually benefit from.

---

[38] Cf. Ib., p. 230; G. Menéndez Pidal, "Los manuscritos de las Cantigas," *BRAH*, CL (1962), pp. 25–51.

[39] A. Domínguez, "Imágenes de un rey trovador," p. 230. Among the various images of presentation, a typical one appears in fol. 1v of the manuscript of the *Primera Partida* housed in the British Library (Ms. Add. 20.787), also containing two more. It is a perfect portrait of Alfonso seated on a stool and with a raised index finger, dictating the prologue to a scribe who appears seated Turkish-style in the middle of two courtiers. The king is clearly the protagonist: "For this reason, we […] made these laws which are written in this book […]"

Poor and needy people are also the object of attention in the *Cantigas*, but only in *Cantigas* 20 and 170, vignette 2, where the illustration shows how Mary intercedes and protects them too.

One of the most interesting aspects of the intellectual profile and personality of the Learned King, as depicted in this group of the *cantigas de loor* and some of the narrative and miracle *cantigas*, is that Alfonso presents himself as the intermediary between the Virgin and the faithful. In fact, the King seems to be performing before an audience, reciting the poems, sometimes singing them, and at others, obviously explaining them.[40] It is in these *cantigas*, as mentioned in chap. 8, where Alfonso assumes the function of intermediary between the Virgin and the audience attending a recitation that, in the Church's ordinary practice, he was not authorized to hold. But, as we have been saying, this is the tone and the direction of his lay vision of Marian spirituality, even in the religious acts traditionally presided over by a priest.

The concept of intermediary, which says much about his personality, is masterfully expressed in the two-tier illustrations. In these, on the upper level we see Christ on a throne among angels, and the Virgin by his side, and in the lower level, the earth where the troubadour-king, standing or kneeling, is pointing with his finger to the sky and leading the gaze of those present in that direction (*Cantiga* 70, vignettes 1 and 3—illustration 9). This concept of intermediary, in its most daring theological form, is found in *Cantiga* 190, where we see the troubadour king kneeling at the foot of the cross pointing to the figure of Christ on the cross and the Virgin, who is also at the foot of the cross. The composition is a copy of the traditional image of the crucifixion with the Virgin and St. John to the right and left, but in which Alfonso has taken St. John's place.[41] Vignette 2 in *Cantiga* 70 is not less daring, where Alfonso is clearly leading the prayer in the

---

[40] A. Domínguez writes about these *cantigas de loor*: "They are very original, and I believe I can affirm that they are unique in medieval art: the presence of a king in images that depict him reciting of explaining his poems to the Virgin in front of a group of courtiers and even performing them, as in a kind of authentic religious or liturgical theater in the palace" ("Iconografía evangélica en las Cantigas de Santa María," *Reales Sitios*, 80, 1984, pp. 37–44).

[41] Cf. E. Mâle, *L'art religieux du XIIIᵉ siècle en France*, 2 vols., Paris, 1958, II, p. 106; L. Réau, *Iconografía del arte cristiano. Iconografía de la Biblia. Nuevo Testamento*, trad. cast., Barcelona, 1996, pp. 494–523; G. Schiller, *Ikonographie der Christlichen Kunst*, 1966, Engl. trans., *Iconography of Christian Art*, 2 vols., London, 1972, II: *The Passion of Jesus Christ*, pp. 88–164 and plates 321–539.

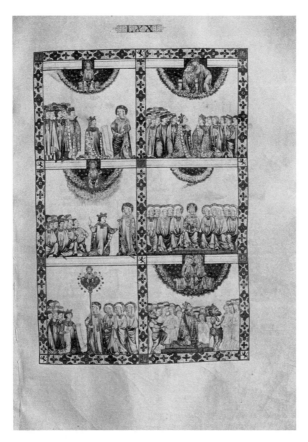

9. Vignettes 1 and 3, Alfonso leads the faithful to Mary; in vignette 2 Alfonso
is clearly leading the prayer in the middle of a congregation, while in the upper
level Christ is rising from his throne to elevate his Mother, who intercedes for
sinners. Códice Rico, Bibl. Escorial, Ms. T.I.1, fol. 104r, Cantiga 70.

middle of a congregation, while he observes the scene in the upper
level, where Christ is rising from his throne to raise up his prostrate
Mother, who intercedes for sinners (illustration 9).

In his function as intermediary, the King frequently appears on the
same level, under the same arch next to the Virgin, touches her, and,
in his persistence, also tugs at her mantle in order to obtain what he's
asking for. In another image (*Cantiga* 50, third vignette), Alfonso falls
on his knees and cries when he contemplates the scene of the flagellation, as if it were taking place in his own palace, like a drama performance (illustration 5). In fact, this vignette is the one that offers us the
most convincing argument for the hypothetical dramatic performances

10. Dramatic performance of the Cantigas: King Alfonso together with a group of musicians and singers sings a Cantiga to Virgin Mary represented by a living actress. Códice Rico, Bibl. De El Escorial, Ms. T.I.1, Cantiga 120, fol. 170v, vignette 1.

at the Alfonsine court, about which we also have direct testimony in the *Partidas*. The composition of the scene, of course, could not be explained otherwise. Inside a Gothic interior we see Christ standing and embracing a column, without ropes or any kind of strapping. The flagellation is being performed not by a Jew or a Roman, but by a character who curiously occupies the central arch of the composition, and who, judging from his dress and the fact that his face is not rendered as caricature, appears to be an Alfonsine courtier. The king, dressed in rich regalia, separated from the main scene by a column, appears in the same setting, kneeling and covering his eyes with a handkerchief to hide his tears. Behind him, four courtiers are seen observing the scene. In its simplicity and schematic design, which do not attempt to reproduce the historical setting of the events, it is clearly an artistic recreation that the miniature artist has masterfully rendered. The same argument of a dramatic performance could be made of the Cantiga 120, vignette 1 (illustration 10).

In all of these *cantigas* it is unquestionable that the center of attention is Alfonso and his conscious projection as intermediary between Mary and his courtiers. The topic of Mary as mediator of all graces, and Alfonso as *her* intermediary, is presented in an extraordinary, almost glorified fashion in the first illustration of the Florence Codex where, surprisingly, there is no presentation image, but rather one of the troubadour-king, perhaps, as we have suggested, because it was not thought of as an independent volume but rather as the second part of the *Códice rico* in El Escorial. In a wide rectangle occupying the upper part of the folio, Alfonso is depicted standing and pointing to an image of the Virgin among angels, which is on the other side of an arcade (illustration 4). The king is presenting Mary as the mediator between men (represented by a group of courtiers) and Christ, who appears on the throne, in the upper part of the scene over a sky covered with stars. It is a way of adding another rung (Alfonso>Mary>the Son>the Father) to the *scala salutis* ("ladder of salvation") discussed in chapter 8.

It is indeed in this type of image of the troubadour king in which the artist seems to have gone to great pains to leave his physical and intellectual portrait. What historical and physiognomic value can be attributed to these portraits of the Learned King? In principle, knowing the intensity with which Alfonso worked on the compilation of the songs to Mary and the personal dedication to illustrate it profusely, portraying himself in every tenth *cantiga*, it seems logical to think that there was not only an explicit will on the king's part to portray himself, but also on the artist's part to do so as faithfully as possible.[42] To this effect, I find validity in the argument based on the state in which many of the Florence codex miniatures were left, this being the last manuscript that was copied and where we can find evidence of the process of its production. Many of the figures, especially Alfonso's, are lacking

---

[42] These, according to Gallienne Francastel, are the two features that define the portrait (*Le droit au trone. Un problème de prééminence dans l'art chrétienne d'occident du IV au XII siècles*, Paris, 1973, p. 9 and ff.), quoted by A. Domínguez, "Imágenes de un rey trovador," p. 234.

a finished head, which shows that the portrait of the king was probably entrusted to a specific artist, either because he was particularly skilled at portraiture and did it directly from life, or because he was very familiar with the features of the subject and was trusted completely by the sovereign.[43] Obviously, this artist, for unknown reasons, was unable to complete his work.

We do not mean by this that Alfonso looked exactly as he is portrayed in the *Cantigas*. The concept of the portrait in the 13th century was not the same as the one we have today. As the great specialist in Alfonsine miniature, Ana Domínguez, writes: "The artist, or rather artists, of the *Cantigas* did not possess an adequate formal language to individualize features, nor was this language otherwise pursued in a period when drawing was ruled by geometrical patterns [...] But in the *Cantigas* as in other codices, we can perfectly distinguish king Alfonso as much through his garments and kingly attributes, as partly through his physical features. What I mean to say by this is that he is presented throughout the *Cantigas* with a youthful appearance, which distinguishes him clearly from, for instance, king Jaime of Aragón, who in *cantiga* CLXIX (third vignette) receives a group of Moors kneeling before him and is distinguished by his robe decorated with the coat of arms of Aragón and a gray beard and gray hair."[44]

For my part, after analyzing and comparing the miniatures in question, I believe that these portraits go further than the garments and royal attributes, attempting, within the restrictions of the techniques at that time, to portray the subject as close to physical reality as possible. The *Cantigas*, and to a lesser extent other works, while not giving us a faithful image of Alfonso's physical appearance, do maintain a great consistency in certain bodily features (aquiline nose, fair skin, blonde hair, and blue eyes) which allows us to think that Alfonso truly looked like that. The forensic medical exam discussed above generally also confirms these features.[45]

---

[43] Cf. G. Menéndez Pidal, "Los manuscritos de las Cantigas," *BRAH*, CL (1962), p. 25–51; R. Cómez Ramos, "El retrato de Alfonso X, el Sabio en la primera Cantiga de Santa María," in *Studies in the Cantigas de Santa María...*, Katz and Keller..., pp. 35–52.

[44] "Imágenes de un rey trovador," pp. 234–235.

[45] Some of the characteristics of Alfonso's bodily features can be gleaned from the forensic medical exams of his remains (in 1579 and 1948). According to Dr. Delgado's calculations, Alfonso was 5'9," "of superior height without being overly tall" (*qtd. art.*, p. 141). Regarding the face, one of the structural peculiarities was its elongation and

On the other hand, regardless of the efforts the artist made to recreate a physical similarity of the subject of his painting, we must take into account the conventions that ruled all portraits of the period. Especially when the subject of the portrait was the patron, royal dignity and the perfect appearance of its bearer do not permit the artist to portray him in negative or disrespectful manner. This convention imposed severe restrictions and explains why none of the extant portraits depict Alfonso as an old or deformed man (which was not the case with don Jaime, for instance). Although in several miniatures Alfonso appears ill in bed, he preserves his royal dignity and an impeccable physical appearance. He was never portrayed as old or deformed, not even in a work such as *Libro de los juegos* [Book of Games], which was begun one year before his death, when we know his physical appearance was not very comely: he had a weak heart; had lost his left eye, and perhaps the right as well, due to the carcinoma in the left maxillary antrum, he had lost all his teeth; his legs were swollen and full of infected pustules; and had lost all the nails of his fingers and toes. Physically, at the time he was working on the *Libro de los juegos*, Alfonso was not presentable in public. However, in the lavish miniatures where he appears among players and rowdy people, the artist continues to depict him as a young and robust man, wearing flashy and fashionable garments. Therefore, although there is a similarity between some of his physical features and several portraits in the *Cantigas*, in general we agree with the opinion of the scholar Ana Domínguez, who writes: "In my view, these are not physiognomic or individualized portraits, but rather idealized portraits that attempt, above all, to depict the social hierarchy through age, general features, and, above all, royal garments and attributes, in this case. I do not believe that it is possible to know the features of the person through them, but rather only to discern his will to fulfill certain roles in the images of his manuscripts."[46]

Despite art historians' opinions to the contrary, there are many scholars who hold that the *Cantigas*, especially the Florence codex, faithfully depict in the miniatures, not only life at the court, but also

---

narrowness. "Another feature worthy of note," the report reads, "was the length of the nose, its posterior overlapping and the obtuse, yet somewhat closed angle it forms with the forehead. This makes us think that king Alfonso had a long, overlapping and narrow nose" ("Examen médico legal," 150). For the 1579 exam, cf. José Alonso de Morgado, *Historia de Sevilla. Libro Quarto*, Sevilla, 1587, esp. p. 108.

[46] "La iconografía evangélica," p. 43, note 5.

the most intimate aspects of the Learned King's personality. Through the miniatures, some undoubtedly painted from life, the king's evolution and changes in physical appearance can be noted. In the first 100 *cantigas*, he is depicted as a young, attractive, and robust man, with an elegant appearance, a round, clean, beardless face, an aquiline nose, and two large, blue, sparkling, intelligent eyes.[47] In the last portraits, however, he is seen as physically debilitated by his age and illnesses.[48]

Based on existing documents, on his political and government activity, or on the abundant written work by the Learned King, it is difficult to describe his psychological profile, to which many of his modern biographers have resorted in order to explain some of his apparently erratic and heartless actions and behavior. In chap. 8, when dealing with his illnesses, we attempted a psychological diagnosis, making use of the study of a psychiatrist, Dr. Torres, who has recently dealt with this subject. I would like to return briefly to some of these observations to better depict Alfonso X's complex personality.

According to Dr. Torres, Alfonso was an "introverted" and "immature" individual. Both are terms from modern psychology, which, based on certain physical characteristics described by Dr. Delgado in his forensic medical report, he attempts to apply to Alfonso X.[49] Introverted individuals, he says, may give the impression of being cold and lacking in emotion. This is not the case. What happens is that they do not externalize their emotions. They feel a certain embarrassment. We recall that Alfonso, upon hearing of the death of don Sancho, despite his rebelliousness and having promoted his deposition, locks himself up in a room and cries in secret, away from his courtiers (*CAX*, p. 257). But we must not forget, putting the psychiatrist's opinion in

---

[47] The features also coincide with the statue in the Burgos cathedral with the brief description of a qualified witness who knew him for a long time: "...beautiful in form and with a graceful appearance" (Jofré de Loaysa, *Crónica*, p. 15); or in the words of his modern biographer: "His clean-shaven face, as he is presented in many of the authentic portraits of the *Cantigas*, is a perfect oval where his bright, sweet eyes gleam. His mouth with fine corners, aquiline nose, and upright pose, youthful and majestic at the same time, are represented in the magnificent state of his time in the cloister of the Burgos cathedral" (Ballesteros, *Alfonso X*, p. 58).

[48] The Florence codex of the *Cantigas* is, according to some scholars, particularly instructive to this effect; it shows the figure of Alfonso progressively from his accession to the throne to his last years. Cf. A. García Cuadrado, *Las Cantigas, el códice de Florencia*, Murcia: Universidad de Murcia, 1993.

[49] Besides Dr. Delgado's report, he also uses the *CAX* and, like the majority of modern researchers, the *Cantigas*: "These *Cantigas*, of a charming naïveté, are a very personal work of the king and therefore have been very useful in researching his psychology" (pp. 115–116).

perspective, that Alfonso was also able to directly confront situations, the way he did at the Seville Cortes when his son Sancho shamelessly lashed out against him, or in Burgos against the rebellious nobility. Introverted individuals, according to Dr. Torres, are deeply sensitive, but in the face of adversity, they withdraw into private suffering. When Alfonso describes the rebellion of don Sancho and the behavior of the nobles who deposed him, he writes in his last will: "There was very much that we hid and suffered in silence" (in García Solalinde, *Antología*, p. 226).

But such a sketch of an introvert is incomplete. "Sometimes introverted individuals have outbursts. They cannot always carry inner feelings under a mask of unperturbed calm, especially when it comes to irritability or aggressiveness. We recall how the king lost his patience—and he was a patient king—when faced with the arrogance of the nobles. This is recorded by the *CAX*: 'And when the king heard these words he was filled with rage'" (p. 112). Despite these outbursts, Alfonso was a kind man who held no grudges. He knew how to forgive. On the other hand, "these unpredictable outbursts make close interaction with introverted individuals difficult: marriage, for instance [...] On the other hand, they are pleasant, agreeable people with strangers, because in those situations they reinforce their self-control" (p. 112). In his analysis of the behavior of the Learned King, Dr. Torres notes: "Despite sporadic outbursts of impatience, Alfonso was a kind man who held no grudges" (p. 112). He also often felt remorse, and he explains why: "Guilt is felt frequently by introverted individuals. They direct towards themselves repressed aggressive impulses" (pp. 112–113).

Regarding adaptability to the environment and the world around him, Dr. Torres holds that, "Introverts tend to avoid reality, which they handle poorly despite their good intentions...Alfonso took the job of king very seriously...Yet he preferred, in critical moments, to pay attention to his cultural projects" (p. 113). This aspect of the Learned King's life is what has most drawn the attention of his critics, because they assume it was the cause of his poor administration. However, we believe it is where he was least understood. Of course, Alfonso, as the introverted type Dr. Torres speaks of, was better at abstract thinking than at solving concrete problems, yet the fact that he had his mind on cultural enterprises, which he was truly passionate about, does not mean he abandoned the administration of his kingdom. His legislation and initiatives are sufficient proof of this. Alfonso probably did lack practical sense, and immersed in his own world, perhaps he did not perceive many of the changes in the world around him. His interests, as a ruler, we could say in today's terminology, were macro-management, rather than in the daily bureaucratic operations, or micro-management. For these latter tasks he had courtiers and aides, some quite good, whom he had handpicked. But in this aspect of bureaucracy he also drafted very detailed norms that surprise us seven hundred years later. And, of course, he had great attention to detail in the drafting and correction of his works, something he did personally. Despite these objections to Dr. Torres's opinions, I believe the following expert opinion of his very adequately fits Alfonso's introverted personality: "Because just as extroverts seem to have a primarily analytical intelligence (which allows them to understand the details of life easily and, therefore, to navigate reality easily), introverts such as Alfonso, have a synthetic kind of intelligence, which allows them to see the big picture, being able at times to harmonize apparently contradictory elements. In this way, for example, in his prologue to the *Lapidario*, Alfonso harmonized the influence of the stars with personal freedom" (p. 115).

If generosity and the romantic, chivalric spirit, as Dr. Torres argues, are features of the introvert, we must acknowledge that Alfonso excelled at these. In a passage of a letter to his son don Fernando, he writes about the rebellion of the nobles, whom he calls "unfortunate traitors," that he would have rather "died a thousand deaths" than not keep his word (Solalinde, *Antología*, p. 221). This generosity and innocence, at times even childish, in a primitive society and with a rapacious nobility, caused him many psychological problems, since, as Dr. Torres notes, when the introvert descends into reality, he or she suffers greatly from anxiety. It would be enough to remember the dream or nightmare he had, when he was staying at the Monasterio de Silos, at a time when he was desperately looking for a solution to the problem of the nobility. During the night, Saint Dominic appeared to him, and showing him an iron rod, he told him how he had to use it with the nobility. It is the best example of the anxiety and uneasiness he had to suffer at many points in his life, we could say without irony, as a punishment for his kindness. But not to exaggerate too much, we should also say that Alfonso also learned how to say no, and even take his word back, when this attitude seemed to him politically expedient. The cases may be uncountable, but the most well-known, which had terrible consequences, was the pact with the king of Granada to return the *arraeces* to him, as Alfonso categorically refused to do for two reasons: to take revenge on the Moorish king, who had stirred up the southern territories, and to keep him constantly on tenterhooks, so that he would never dare betray him again.

According to Dr. Torres, besides an introverted personality, Alfonso "displayed, in effect, a strikingly immature personality." He argues: "We all know that there is a long period of maturation, of psychological transformation, from childhood to adulthood. This process, however, may be left unfinished, and we thus speak of immature adults: people of great intelligence, perhaps, but who approach life in a somewhat childish way. They are insecure, dependent, and have unstable feelings. Alfonso was that way" (p. 119). In chapter 8 I have already expressed my disagreement with some of Dr. Torres's psychiatric pronouncements about Alfonso's "immaturity". However, I think that overall, the diagnosis fits in very well with the very affective profile of Alfonso, who, "as [with] all immature people, had unstable feelings and emotions. Immature people, in effect, suffer from very strong but fleeting impressions. Therefore, their anger lasts for a short time, and they forget offences easily. They don't hold grudges. In this sense, they have hearts of gold" (p. 125). The following statements appear to me particularly valid: "Immature people seem to be as trusting as children. And Alfonso was so. Such a candid nature caused serious political conflicts" (p. 124). The story of many of the events we have narrated fully confirms this diagnosis. As Ballesteros had already written, "The distinctive feature of his personality was an unlimited vanity and the simplicity of a child's heart, almost unbelievably trusting and candid" (*Alfonso X*, p. 258). This peculiarity of his personality would explain why Alfonso, a trusting man with no malice, never understood the reasons for his betrayal by the king of Granada, whom he considered a faithful vassal, or the rebellion of the nobles, whom he had showered with benefits, and even less the violent reaction of his son, the abandonment by his wife, and the insubordination of his subjects. All these adversities for someone with a trusting and kind disposition must have been an incomprehensible mystery. This is clearly seen in the bitterness if not irritation or vengefulness that permeates his letters and even his last will. Dr. Torres concludes: "And thus was the end of this king who devoted himself to books and studied stars without learning about the world of betrayal that was brewing next to him. Introverted. Candid, vain, and kind, as a child. Wise but a poor politician. With great state projects but mediocre determinations. He knew all kinds of misfortune and disloyalty, always a surprise to his trusting spirit. He wanted to be an exemplary Christian, but only partially managed to be so" (p. 137). "An intellectual much ahead of his time, an outstanding genius of conceptual abstraction, who had the bad luck of becoming a king" (p. 137).

The physical and psychological profile of the Learned King we have presented is only part of his complex personality and character, which can be better understood through his works, in which he left unmistakable autobiographical details. It is in his works that we can perhaps contemplate the best spiritual portrait of the Learned King, drafted by himself, both in his legislative works, especially the *Espéculo* and the *Partidas*, as in his historical works, particularly the *General Estoria*. It is in these works, perhaps even more clearly than in the *Cantigas*, that we find the autobiographical details of his moral and spiritual personality, as for instance when he describes the figure of the model king (*Partida* II, 1–5), or when he presents the ideals and aspirations of countless historical and mythological characters (Jupiter, Nimrod), in which he sees himself mirrored and who, clearly, are a projection of himself.

The personal testimony of his contemporaries is also a component of the moral and intellectual profile that must be taken into account. We have clear and direct testimonies of those who knew him well. The Castilian historian, Jofré de Loaysa, for example, tells us: "From childhood he was very liberal and a lover of justice, which he exercised diligently."[50] His first biographer, and one of the most learned men of the court, Fr. Gil de Zamora, who indeed knew him personally and interacted with him for many years, has left us the following moral portrait:

> After a sweet childhood, as befits the children of kings, he displayed, for his teen-age years, a sharp intelligence. He was diligent in his studies, had a brilliant memory, and in exterior appearance, he was eloquent, a leader in elegance, modest in his laughter, honest in his gaze, serene when he walked, sober when he ate. There was no one as liberal as he, to the point that his liberality was almost prodigality.[51]

Another one of his contemporaries, Fr. Pero Marín, prior of Silos, who also knew him personally, has left us his impression of an unexpected

---

[50] *Crónica*, quoted ed., p. 15.
[51] In F. Fita, "Biografías de San Fernando y de Alfonso el Sabio por Gil de Zamora," *BRAH*, 5, 1885, p. 319.

feature: his sense of humor. The prior of Silos tells us that when he was still a prince, on April 6, 1246 (Alfonso was then 25), he arrived at the monastery bringing with him a prisoner who was one of his squires, a native of Palencia, who had raped a woman. For this crime, he was to be executed the next day. During the night, thanks to Saint Dominic's intervention, the prisoner was liberated from prison, and in the morning he appeared in front of the Saint's tomb with his chains.

> The abbot and the other monks went seeking for the prince [don Alfonso], and when they arrived before him, the prince asked, "Why have you come?" The abbot said, "Sir, I believe we have a debt with you." The prince said, "How can that be? Sir, the squire who was jailed was released by Saint Dominic and he is now before the altar and your followers want to expel him from the church, and Saint Dominic up till now has always been exempt [from justice] but you should order now what you think is best. The prince said, "It seems to me that Saint Dominic gets involved in this matter because that squire you have seen forced this woman and I had decided to kill him, and it would seem that Saint Dominic did not want us to forbid evil; but since he was the one who released him from prison, it would be a serious mistake if I went against that deed. I order that the squire be left to go in his good luck and I absolve him, but from now on, let him be warned and not get into trouble again, because he shouldn't think that Saint Dominic is going to protect him forever.[52]

On another occasion (Monday, November 5, 1255), when he was already king, during another visit to the monastery, the abbot and the monks requested that he grant them the tribute paid on the day of St. Martin that Alfonso was entitled to in the city. Alfonso was already on his horse at the steps of San Lorenzo, ready to leave for the city, when the abbot arrived with the monks and they gave him the petition: the king read it and began to laugh, saying to the abbot, "You don't want me to own anything in this town? So I will give you and the convent what you are asking me by right of inheritance for ever; come with me and I will have the privilege delivered to you."[53]

In both cases, it was a very peculiar kind of humor, which bordered on irony and sarcasm, but perhaps not "black humor," typical

---

[52] *Los "Miraculos romanzados" de Pero Marín*, critical ed., introduction, and indexes by Karl-Heinz Anton, Studia Silensia, XIV, Abadia de Silos, Studia, 1988, p. 42.
[53] *Miráculos romançados*, p. 45.

of the introverted-immature personality, according to Dr. Torres.[54] In these cases, as in the irony used in the letter to his son Fernando, when speaking of his enemies, ridiculing their alleged prudence, what Alfonso was doing was decreasing the drama from the events. Of course Saint Dominic did not want to protect women rapists, but this does not mean that he would not liberate one on order that he repent and behave well from then on. And Alfonso in an ironic and skeptical tone, accepts the miracle, but tells the abbot: "it would seem that Saint Dominic did not want us to forbid evil; but since he was the one who released him from prison, it would be a serious mistake if I went against that deed."

The collaborators of the Learned King, for their part, in the portrait they paint of him as a consummate man of letters, when he was still a prince, write in the prologue of Las tablas alfonsíes [The Alfonsine Tables], that Alfonso exceeded in wisdom, intelligence, understanding, law, kindness, piety, and nobility all other wise kings.[55] And toward the end of his days, when many of his works, especially the scientific ones, were finished, other collaborators who had lived for a long time next to him and had benefited from his wisdom and gifts, described him in the various prologues of his works as the new Messiah of the arts and sciences, which he adorned with new garments, the Castilian language:

May we praise and thank God [...] who in our time granted us a lord on this earth [...] a scrutinizer of sciences, examiner of doctrines and teachings; he loves and surrounds himself with learned men whom he employs in the arts and compensates them with his favors because each one of them strives to present the sciences he is expert in and disseminates them in the Castilian language for the praise and glory of God [...] His name is king don Alfonso [...] who from the day he arrived on this earth loved and associated himself with the sciences

---

[54] Introverted types also have a sense of humor at times, but it's a black kind of humor (art. cit. p. 118).

[55] See the complete text at the beginning of our Introduction (in G. Solalinde, Antología, p. 193); and cf. "El libro de las taulas alfonsíes," chap. 1, in Los libros del saber de astronomía del rey don Alfonso X de Castilla, ed. M. Rico y Sinobas, 5 vols., Madrid: Aguado, 1863–1867, IV, p. 119; and Las tablas de los movimientos de los cuerpos celestiales del ilustrísimo rey Don Alonso de Castilla, ed. J. Martínez Gázquez, Murcia, Academia Alfonso X el Sabio, 1989.

and with those who cultivate them, and enlightened and completed the great lack thereof that there was among the speakers of Spanish.[56]

One generation later, don Juan Manuel, nephew of Alfonso X and a great admirer of his work, when all around him were anti-Alfonsine, wove the most complete known eulogy of him: Among the many qualities and good things that God Bestowed as ornaments on king don Alfonso, he instilled in him the desire to increase knowledge to the best of his ability, and he did much in this respect, so that, from king Ptolemy on, no other king did as much as he did."[57]

Regardless of how exaggerated some of the eulogies by his collaborators and by those who knew him may seem, scholars in our days cannot resist the temptation of agreeing with his modern biographer:

> His oval-shaped, somewhat inexpressive face however clearly showed the kindness of a temperament inclined towards clemency, generous to the point of prodigality, and weak in his excessive tolerance. His intelligence was plunged into the most abstract calculations of astronomical sciences, and into the most abstruse legal disquisitions, also reaching lyrical heights with the delicate vibrations of his poetic fever, reflecting a unique and sensitive soul. As a rare contrast, as a fervent Catholic, with a pure piety tested a thousand times, through his vanity he paid homage to the moral freedom of an age of corrupt customs. But the peculiar mark of his personality was his boundless vanity and the simplicity of a childlike heart, unbelievably candid and trusting.[58]

Naturally, the detractors of the Learned King, starting with the anonymous author of the *Crónica de Alfonso X*, all the way up to Juan de Mariana, did not think the same.[59] The fact that he ended his reign weakened and deposed needed an explanation, and those who did not share his cultural project, such as his son Sancho and his advisors and supporters, could find no better explanation than to emphasize his failures as a statesman and minimize his successes as a learned man. As Mariana would say, "because he contemplated the sky and

---

[56] Texts gathered by G. Menéndez Pidal, "Cómo trabajaron las escuelas alfonsíes," *NRFH*, V (1951), p. 365. A traditional eulogy can be consulted, such as the one by H. Quiñones, *Elogio de Alfonso X, rey de Castilla y León, llamado el Sabio*, Madrid: P. Barco López, 1786.

[57] *Libro de la caza*, in *Obras*, I, p. 519.

[58] Ballesteros, *Alfonso X*, p. 258.

[59] Robert A. MacDonald has studied the various attitudes of the historians towards Alfonso X, from his contemporary Jofré de Loaysa, to his modern biographer, A. Ballesteros, in "The Varying Historical Perspective of Alfonso X of Castile" (cited by J.F. O'Callaghan, in *Emperor of Culture*, p. 216 note 2).

the stars, he lost his land and his kingdom," followed by a modern historian as respectable as R.B. Merriman, who said, "[h]e aspired to be emperor, though he was not even able to play the king."[60] Ignoring the fact that between 1252 and 1284 it was more difficult to be king of Castile and León than emperor of the Holy Roman Empire, these positions today have been practically abandoned by the great majority of scholars. After a careful scrutiny of his cultural legacy and in view of the positive and undeniable value of his prodigious poetic, scientific, legislative, and historiographical oeuvre, we can affirm today that it was the initiatives and the efforts of the Learned King that set in motion the Castilian cultural renaissance of the 13th century.[61]

---

[60] J. de Mariana, *Historia de rebus Hispaniae*, Madrid: P. Rodríguez, 1592, p. 649, ed. *Historia de España*, ed. F. Pi y Margall, in *Obras del Padre Juan de Mariana*, 2 vols., *BAE*, XXX–XXXI, Madrid: Real Academia Española, 1854, chap.XIII.XX; repr. Madrid: Atlas, 1950, I, pp. 1–530. R.B. Merriman, *The Rise of the Spanish Empire in the Old World and the New*, 4 vols., New York: Macmillan, 1918–1934; I, p. 112.

[61] Among the most recent works on the Alfonsine cultural legacy already cited, see: R.I. Burns, "*Stupor mundi*: Alfonso X of Castile, the Learned," in R.I. Burns, ed.: *Emperor of Culture*, pp. 1–13. Cf. A.J. Cárdenas, "Alfonso's Scriptorium and Chancery: Role of the Prologue in Bonding the *Translatio Studii* to the *Translatio Potestatis*," in R.I. Burns, ed. *Emperor of Culture*, p. 90; C.J. Socarrás, *Alfonso X of Castile*, p. 11; J.F. O'Callaghan, *The Learned King*, pp. 272–282.

IN PRAISE OF KNOWLEDGE

...et eritis sicut dii (*Genesis* 3:5)

The serpent said: "Of course you will not die...as soon as you eat it, your eyes will be opened and *you will be like gods* knowing both good and evil."

The invitation the serpent made to our forefathers in the Garden of Eden to eat the forbidden fruit from the tree of knowledge which would make them *like gods*, that is, capable of distinguishing between good and evil and free to choose between the two, is apparently the same one Alfonso would insistently make to his subjects and readers throughout his thirty-two years of government: knowledge will make you wise and free, *like gods*.

Conclusions and epilogues usually contain the balance of the events of someone's life presented in his or her biography. The balance of Alfonso's life and his activities as king and man of letters has been done so many times, that it seems superfluous to repeat things that are well-known: a wise man, a patron of law, history, and astronomy, but a poor ruler. That, with rare exceptions, has been the verdict. The preceding pages are witness to the fact that he was not such a poor ruler, but he neglected public relations because he thought that his generosity exempted him from them. He unfortunately ended his days in misfortune, and after his death, a long anti-Alfonsine period followed, in which his life and works were derided ("a foolish king who devoted himself to astrology and magic, rather than to ruling") a judgment that has not yet been overcome.

In the narrative of his life, his actions and the creation of his most important works, this biography has also touched upon numerous topics that unmistakably identify Alfonso's reign with the beginning of many novelties that would gradually become part of European culture. In general terms it must be acknowledged that Alfonso's reign was, from the beginning, extraordinarily innovative thanks to the fact that the king reached the throne as a mature man with a level of experience in government that was rare among medieval kings. Thus, from the start, he had a political program thought out, which he would go on to execute as opportunities allowed.

One such opportunity presented itself at the 1252 Seville Cortes. The kingdom was in a precarious economic state as a consequence of the uninterrupted war his father had had to maintain in the last years. Alfonso adopted extraordinary economic measures in order to control inflation and moderate prices, salaries, and excessive luxury expenses. The following year, he restructured the offices in his court, appointing new figures of his generation to key positions. Regarding the perpetually problematic territorial administration, he substituted the old *merinos* by *adelantados* who were in charge of the new districts into which the newly conquered lands were divided.

Alfonso's reform program, geared towards modernizing the kingdom, is seen more clearly in his intense legislative activity launched in 1254. Based on an absolutist conception of royal power, Alfonso claimed for himself a monopoly on legislation. This was what led him to the promulgation of his three great legal codes: the *Fuero real* (1254–55), the *Espéculo* (interrupted in 1256), and the *Partidas*, whose writing began in 1256 and went on until 1265. In all works, the true obsession of the Learned King was the renewal of some of the law codes by instituting Roman law in order to unify the norms of interaction between all the kingdoms. His legislative work, setting aside the failure of its application during Alfonso's lifetime, should be considered the most important legal monument of the Middle Ages, truly *aere perennius* (more long-lasting than bronze). Whether he suspended drafting the *Espéculo* in order to devote himself more fully to the *Partidas* as a result of his imperial aspirations is a subject of endless debate. The foresight of such a vast compilation could clearly have included the very legitimate desire to extend such legislation not only to his Peninsular subjects, but also to his European supporters, who legitimately elected him King of the Romans. There is no proof, however, that that was his intention.

The cultural projects of the Learned King in all fields of knowledge were countless, both as creator of new cultural horizons as well as disseminator of the natural sciences, philosophy, astronomy, and even board games, in an extensive program of translation from Arabic, Hebrew, and Latin. But I will leave aside for now his innovations in the field of institutional reforms, law, history, the sciences, and poetry, which have been aptly discussed by other biographers, in order to emphasize in particular two aspects of his cultural legacy that have seldom been discussed and must be counted among the most long-lasting contributions in the field of Spanish and European cultural history.

Alfonso X has been termed the *Learned* and the *Stupor mundi* ("the wonder of the world"), not only because of the impressive number of works credited to him that he has left us, but also and primarily because of the passion for learning that accompanied him his entire life.[1] From his desire to "resuscitate branches of knowledge that were lost" stemmed his practical ambition to make them available to his lay subjects, that is, those who spoke the Castilian romance language through the dissemination of a culture written in the vernacular and through schools that would turn them into learned and good people. Alfonso was very aware at all moments that he was creating (or "giving life to") a new language whose roots were found in Latin, hence the need to know it.[2] It was precisely his linguistic and literary/scientific knowledge and the contact with great masters that allowed him to gather around himself a team of writers, poets, legal scholars, musicians, painters, scientists, and historians who would collaborate with him in the creation of a corpus of literature and knowledge unmatched anywhere in Europe in the 13th century.[3]

No testimony compares with that of his nephew, don Juan Manuel, Alfonso's a great admirer and imitator, who describes to us the intellectual environment of the court and the world that surrounded the King. Given the caliber of the witness, he is particularly eloquent regarding the cultural aspirations of his uncle, when he writes that they were realities already:

> And this for many reasons: first, because of the great intelligence that God gave him; second, because of the great willingness he had to do noble and useful things; third, because at his court he had many masters of the sciences and knowledge, whom he generously compensated to advance knowledge and ennoble his kingdoms, because we find that in all the sciences he created many books and all very good. Also, because he devoted much time to studying the subjects about which he wanted to compose his books, for which purpose he spent a year or two in some

---

[1] R.I. Burns, "Stupor mundi": Alfonso X of Castile, the Learned," in R.I. Burns, ed., *Emperor of Culture. Alfonso X the Learned of Castile and his Thirteenth-Century Renaissance*, Philadelphia: University of Pennsylvania Press, 1990, pp. 1–13.

[2] Cf. H.A. Van Scoy, "Alfonso X as a Lexicographer," *HR*, VIII (1940), pp. 277–284; and *A Dictionary of Old Spanish Terms Defined in the Works of Alfonso X*, ed. I.A. Corfis, Madison: Hispanic Seminary of Medieval Studies, 1986; D.W. Lomax, "La lengua oficial de Castilla," *Actas del XII Congreso de Lingüística y Filología Románicas*, 2 vols., Bucarest: Academiei Republicii Socialiste România, 1970, II, pp. 411–417.

[3] J. O'Callaghan, *The Learned King*, p. 169; and R.I. Burns, "Stupor mundi," pp. 1–13.

places and sometimes more, and according to those who lived from his favor, whoever wanted could speak with him, whenever they wanted and whenever he wanted, and in such a way he had time to study what he wanted on his own and even to supervise and finish the works of knowledge he commissioned from learned men and teachers he had at his court for this purpose.[4]

Don Juan Manuel paints a picture of Alfonso as someone completely devoted to the search for knowledge and who employed much of his time studying the matters about which he or his collaborators were writing books. Don Juan Manuel's words, written during an anti-Alfonsine period, are also the most direct and impartial testimony (Juan Manuel disagreed with his uncle about many things, including the elimination of the nobility's privileges) we have of Alfonso's personal participation in all phases of the composition of his works. This total dedication to study, in a period in which some kings could not even read or write, was what earned him the reputation of "learned," which in the 13th century was associated mainly with scientific knowledge in general, and with astronomy and other natural sciences in particular (hence the fact that frequently "wise man" was a synonym of "wizard"); but this also earned him a reputation as a poor administrator of the kingdom.

When trying to understand what led Alfonso to work so tirelessly in all areas of knowledge and obtain such unthinkable results in the midst of a difficult and intense political and military life, scholars have often sought a driving idea, a seminal concept that serves as the key to the great Alfonsine mystery. Half a century ago García Solalinde gave us a clue:

> Alfonso X oriented his cultural activity in a precise direction: determining the behavior of human beings, that is, to find out what human beings did in the past in order to point out the quality and nature of their actions when they are subjected to invisible powers—astral or divine influence—and to set civic duties. This moralist aim can clearly be deduced from his historical works, astronomical, astrological, or miracle books and his masterful legislative production. The other sciences—mathematics, geography, zoology, alchemy, medicine, and grammar—were not the subject of specific treatises, because he only saw them as ancillary to the former (*GE*, I, p. IX).

---

[4] *Crónica abreviada*, Prólogo, ed. Grismer, p. 38, 26–39.

In other words, if Alfonso X as a prince of letters and scientific knowledge had the great ambition of collecting encyclopedic knowledge to make it available to his subjects in the vernacular, it is clear that the sheer volume of his achievement in all fields and the most diverse disciplines, does not explain all this royal activity, especially if we consider that the material work was commissioned from experts in such areas and technical writers working in the *scriptorium*. We need to postulate that above and beyond the immense production, there is a driving idea, a plan of action or program that connects them all. This plan, which was like the axis around which his entire political and cultural program revolved, was his great ideal to perfect man in his double spiritual and earthly nature, qualities which distinguish all authentic humanists.

The first one of these contributions to 13th-century culture was a new conception of knowledge and science in general, and the ability of knowing to raise the human spirit and stimulate social progress in direct proportion to the level of knowledge and the education of the individual and society as a whole.

One of the first works whose translation Alfonso commissioned opens with the following words that became like a life motto for his collaborators:

> Just as Ptolemy stated in the *Almagest*, he who keeps alive science and knowledge shall not die, nor whoever devotes himself to the understanding of things...Therefore, our lord, the very noble king don Alfonso, king of Spain, son of the very noble king don Fernando, and the very noble queen doña Beatriz, to whom God granted good judgment, and intelligence, and knowledge above all other princes of his time, reading the various books of the learned men, through the enlightenment he received from God, from whom stem all good things, always made an effort to illuminate and revive the branches of knowledge that had been abandoned when God sent him to rule on earth...[5]

This intellectual profile of the Learned King is completed in the prologue to the translation of Ali Iben Abi-l-Rijal's astrological work *Libro conplido en los iudizios de las estrellas* [The Complete Book on the Judgment of the Stars], where he is described in these terms:

> [he was] an expert in all laws and all good things, a lover of truth, an examiner of the sciences, an enquirer of doctrines and teachings, who,

---

[5] *El libro de las cruzes*, ed. Ll.A. Kasten and L.B. Kiddle, Madrid: CSIC, 1961, p. 1.

from the moment he came into this world, loved and attracted to his
court learned men and those who devote themselves to knowledge, and
granted them his gifts and favors...and he illuminated and filled the
vacuum that existed in the vernacular for lack of books by good and
proven philosophers.[6]

From these texts and many others that could be quoted, it can be clearly
gleaned that Alfonso's main preoccupation (even more than becoming
emperor) was the acquisition of knowledge and the education of his
subjects. So much so, that this could be called the cornerstone of his
cultural, political, and social program. In the prologue to the *Tablas
alfonsíes* he is described as one who "loved knowledge and valued it."[7]
Following this, Alfonso was a true researcher in the widest and most
complete sense of the word, as stated in the same work: "from the time
he came to this world, he attracted the sciences to his court and the
learned men who devoted themselves to them."

Alfonso's historical works, in particular the *General Estoria*, are full
of quotes and observations about the priceless value of knowledge
which delights our spirit, brings us earthly happiness, gives us permanent fame, and leads us to God. In the comment to the *Bucolics*,
which could be part of any anthology of medieval humanism, Alfonso
displays his artistic sensibility, not so much to Virgil's metaphor of the
seven liberal arts, but to the beauty of the *Bucolics*:

> ...the learned men among the Gentiles called the branches of knowledge
> golden apples because they are something appreciated and delightful to
> men like gorgeous and good fruit. And that is how Virgil considered the
> branches of knowledge in the epistles he wrote in his famous book called
> the *Bucolics*, which also means the labors of the countryside, because in
> it he speaks about the branches of knowledge as being similar to apples.
> Therefore he said in this Latin verse "Aurea mala decem misi; cras altera
> mittam," which means, "Today I sent you these ten golden apples, tomor-
> row I will send you ten more." And he called those letters golden apples
> because of the good things he said in them. (*GE*, II, 2, p. 30b)

The passion for knowledge is a constant that fills many pages in his
Estorias. Alfonso never fails to point out, when describing a historical or mythological character, his or her attitude towards knowledge
and ability in the arts. The simple reason was that for him knowledge
was life and ignorance, death. When telling us, for instance, the origin

---

[6] Aly Aben Ragel (Abenragel), *El libro conplido*, ed. G. Hilty, Madrid, 1954, p. 3.
[7] In A. García Solalinde, *Antología*, p. 191.

of the name of Athens, formerly Eleusina, he writes, "...and because later all future kings grew up there and there gathered teachers of all branches of knowledge, and the princes gave them big salaries, and there they made them teach and apprentice everyone who came to learn, the name Eleusis was changed and it became Athens" (*GE*, I, p. 192a).

The arrival of kings, a symbol of power, and of teachers, a symbol of knowledge, under the aegis of Jupiter, was what made Athens immortal, something the name reflects (*a-thanatos*, without death). Alfonso explains that when it was time to rename Athens with a name that would reflect its new mission as center of knowledge, Jupiter "chose twelve of those he deemed the most learned and more honest than the rest, and there gathered these twelve wise men of the Gentiles" (*GE*, I, p. 197b); and after consulting their idols, they answered that it should be called Athens:

> And that is why Ovid in his Great Book says that Athens means place without death, because, as we said, that is where all the arts and branches of knowledge were taught. They are things that do not die, but rather live forever, and they give life to whomever knows them, and whoever doesn't know them or knows little about them, is like a dead person; and for this reason learned men call knowledge life, and lack of knowledge death. (*GE*, I, p. 197b)

It is quite symptomatic that, in order to illustrate this concept that knowledge is life and ignorance, death, Alfonso does not turn to the Bible, where it already appeared prominently (*Ecclesiastes* 7:13), but rather to a secular work, such as the *Metamorphosis* ("Great Book") by his favorite poet, Ovid: "And in such a way the ancients appreciated knowledge, that they termed whomever possessed it alive, and whomever didn't, dead" (*GE*, I, p. 198b). What the twelve sages and the powerful inhabitants of Olympus did to answer Jupiter's request changing the name of Eleusina to Athens was indeed a metaphor for Alfonso's project, that he, like Jupiter, had set out to accomplish by gathering learned men and scholars in all areas of knowledge to remedy the "lack of books by good and proven philosophers."[8]

---

[8] The topic of the books that were lost and thanks to his intervention and action were recovered permeates all of his works. In the prologue to the Sixth Part of the *GE* he writes: "I, don Alfonso, by the grace of God [...] ordered the composition of this book after gathering all the ancient books and chronicles and all the histories in Latin,

But it was not merely knowledge of the classics and the liberal arts what kept Alfonso awake at night. Swept away by the great influence that Aristotelian philosophy was having in his day, when the humanistic knowledge of the past was crumbling under the pressure of logic, on the one hand and the *libri naturales*, on the other, Alfonso conceived of the seven liberal arts as golden boughs, apples, fruit, and leaves that grow in the garden of philosophy, arguing that philosophy was the supreme science that comprises all others. In the end, it is the effort of a humanist who attempts to pour traditional knowledge into the new molds of Aristotelian/Averroan philosophical thought, adapting it to the new intellectual demands and unprecedented scientific paradigms in order to save it. Unlike the first intellectuals of the School of Chartres, the Learned King lived in the days when the scientific works of Aristotle were already being disseminated. This is also the culminating moment of the schools of the "Victorines" and the last days of the School of Chartres, for whom the scientific ideal was grounded on observation, analysis, and causal explanation of data drawn from direct experience, and not an allegory of the great book of nature written by the Creator, as a previous generation had believed.

The Learned King, in his most significant works, advocates not only for the importance of knowledge, but traces as well the itinerary that the aspiring scholar should follow to achieve his goal, insisting, like any humanist king, on the extraordinary importance of the seven liberal arts in the educational process. The Alfonsine itinerary which, at the level of society as a whole may be defined as the educational program for his kingdom, included in the first place, the education of the kings that would inherit the throne, so that "they know how to keep, through knowledge, the peoples they are to govern." Alfonso insists on the fact that the king, given the social rank he occupies, must be the model in the search for knowledge, behaving in such a way that, "knowledge may lead him to know things according to the way they are, firstly God, then himself, and finally, all that he must say or do." The same educational program and methodology laid out for the kings should also be followed by the subjects. Such a process, "to know things according to the way they are," and the order of knowledge,

---

in Hebrew, and in Arabic that had been lost or had fallen into oblivion, as was said at the beginning of the other ages" (ed. CD-ROM, Medieval Studies, Wisconsin, p. 2).

first God, then oneself, and finally everything else, permeates Alfonso's entire life and work.

As mentioned, the instruments to attain knowledge are the liberal arts, or *saberes*, whose end is to educate man and make him "learned". But, surprisingly, Alfonso also affirms as necessary, besides the seven arts, the study of the natural sciences, which at his time, thanks to the influence of Aristotle's *libri naturales*, had acquired particular significance in the philosophical process man should follow to achieve the goal of being learned and, more importantly, to achieve the rational knowledge of the existence of God: "Hence, through these branches of knowledge, which are known as arts, men learned to know God and all the things He made, what they are in themselves, and how they operate; and also through them they knew the seven heavens in which dwell the seven stars that are known as planets, and the names of each one of them" (*Set.*, p. 39). In the *Libro de las estrellas de la ochava esfera* (Book of the Stars of the Eighth Sphere), Alfonso speaks of this double function of the creatures that God has made available to man so that he may profit from their knowledge and they may lead him to the knowledge, love, and fear of God.[9]

Ultimately, knowledge is valid as a way to reach God because, in some way, it stems from him and participates of his own nature, and through it we may ascend to His Divine nature:

> And for these reasons, it is clearly known that all branches of knowledge [liberal arts] come from God and not from any other, and they are known through him, and he is known through them. And the components of this currency of exchange are the arts and skills that men seek in order to understand what is wisdom and how to profit from it. For this reason the ancients called the liberal arts the currency of God [...] (*Set.*, p. 42).

Although Alfonso identifies the learned man with the philosopher, in these texts he insists that the complete education that leads to true wisdom is the one that, based on the curriculum of the seven liberal arts, is complemented by the three other sciences: "And the three arts of the *trivium*, as we said, teach men to reason properly, and the four of the *quadrivium* turn him into a wise man, and these three other arts (metaphysics, physics, and ethics), together with the former, make him

---

[9] In *Libros del saber de Astronomía*, ed. Rico y Sinobas, II, p. 76.

complete and accomplished in kindness and take him to that state of
blessedness beyond which there is no other" (GE, I, p. 197a).[10]

On the other hand, we must not forget that for Alfonso, the seven
arts or *saberes*, already had, before the dissemination of Aristotelian metaphysics, a much wider sphere of influence than the strictly
humanistic study of rhetoric and the classics. In fact, in the *Setenario* they also had a scientific dimension. This not because he wanted
to oppose the sciences to the humanities, but because those were an
integral part of the same knowledge that all men need in order to live
as rational beings and arrive at that "that state of blessedness beyond
which there is no other," namely, the knowledge of God:

> Hence, through these branches of knowledge, which are known as arts,
> men learned to know God and all the things He made, what they are in
> themselves, and how they operate; and also through them they knew the
> seven heavens in which dwell the seven stars that are known as planets,
> and the names of each one of them. And from these they took the names
> of the week and to each they gave the name of a planet. And they divided
> day and night into hours, degrees and points [minutes and seconds] and
> into other divisions so small that they can only be understood using the
> mind rather than the eyesight. And they learned also to divide the weeks
> into months, the months into years, the years into times [centuries],
> and the times into ages. And according to these arts they divided the
> sphere of the sky into seven parts. And likewise they divided the earth
> into seven parts, both the inhabited and the uninhabited part, which the
> Greeks called the *klimas*, which means the specific places where each one
> of the planets exerts its dominion and virtue. (*Set.*, pp. 39–40)

It seems clear to me that in the first three lines of the quote, the Learned
King alludes to the fact that the knowledge of things leads to the rational knowledge of God, which is their cause. But such knowledge implies
the study of both metaphysics ("what they are in themselves"), as well
as physics or mechanics ("and how they operate"), where physics as a
science of nature would encompass all natural knowledge, including
astronomy, whose object is also discussed in detail in the quote.[11]

---

[10] Cf. H.S. Martínez, "*Paideia* y *filantropía*. Sentido y alcance del humanismo
alfonsí," in *Clarines de pluma. Homenaje a Antonio Regalado*, ed. V. Martin, Madrid:
Editorial Síntesis, Letras Universitarias, 2004, pp. 75–96.

[11] Regarding the origin of astronomy and how the science of the stars was the
means to know all other sciences, there's an interesting passage in the GE where an
old woman, descendant of Nimrod and the giants, reveals to Asclepius the secrets of
the book of Hermes that he had found but could not decipher: "Likewise, she told him
that through what is above in the heavens and sheds light down here on us, that they

The profound, essentially philosophic-scientific reason why Alfonso devoted himself to the study of astronomy and its practical application in astrology is not in any way foolish or worthless. On the contrary, according to his collaborators in the prologue to the *Libro de las cruzes*, considered the first astrological treatise in Castilian, this was, as always, the result of studying and reading: "And because he read—and all wise men confirm this—the words of Aristotle that say that the bodies down below, which are the earthly ones, are sustained and are governed by the movements of the bodies above, which are the heavenly ones, it was God's will that it be understood and known that the science and knowledge of the meanings of the heavenly bodies over the earthly ones was very necessary for man" (*quoted* ed., p. 1).

The subject of "the branches of knowledge which are part of the treasure of God" is a motif that recurs often in Alfonsine works and is associated with that of power, whose origin is also divine. Power and knowledge, along with will, are also human attributes that reflect the essence of divinity itself, and according to Alfonso's humanistic vision of history are intimately associated with and have a temporal dimension in society, manifesting themselves in two fundamental concepts of medieval political and educational philosophy: *Imperium* and *Studium*, with which he attempted to express the origin and transmission of power and knowledge.[12] Alfonso's idea of history as a science that deals with the past of nations as well as individuals is structured around these two concepts. Hence, the king, in imitation of God and similar to him, is powerful if above all he is wise:

> This is how God, at the beginning of his works, wanted to show above all that he was God and he displayed this in three things that make him God and not any other. And if he failed in any of these three things, he

---

identified and composed those twenty-four signs which are the branches of knowledge through which man can understand and know what is to come and what has already happened" (II, 1, 39b). It's worth recalling that this old woman named Goghgobon was the niece of Nimrod (II, 1, p. 36a), the first king of the world whom Alfonso considered his ancestor.

[12] If we want to delve further into the "medium," that is the "saberes" (branches of knowledge), and find out in what way they proceed from God and lead us to God, we find that for Alfonso, knowledge stems from God not only in the theological sense that everything stems from God, who is the "Father of all light," as the Apostle writes, but also in a real sense, physical and historical. The search of this history of knowledge takes Alfonso in the *General Estoria* along a tortuous road that goes "from the beginning [of the world] to our times" (I, p. 3). This issue is also related to the contemporary idea of *translatio studii*.

could not be God. These are the three things: to want, to know, and to be able to; because if he wanted to, but didn't know or wasn't able, he could not be God; and if he was able to, but didn't want to or didn't know, man could hardly believe that he was God. But like he who completely is God, he had to want to, know, and be able to. And without a fault he proved it so then, and continues to show it in the marvels he created. (*GE*, Sixth Part, ed. CD-ROM, p. 2)

Clearly, Alfonso here is speaking of the Christian God, but the principle is equally valid for pagan divinities. In fact, he illustrates Christian doctrine with examples from mythology. Speaking of Jupiter, whom Alfonso admired profoundly because he represented the sum of these two qualities, knowledge and power, he says: "...and king Jupiter at the time ruled in Crete and in may other kingdoms where he was obeyed and he had dominion, and likewise he was the most powerful and wise king in the world at the time among the Gentiles...and he accomplished in the world all the things he set his mind to thanks to his wisdom" (*GE*, 2, 1, pág. 53a). In another passage of the *GE*, commenting on Boethius, he writes, "Boethius, who was a very wise gentleman, said that it does not befit any other man better than a king to learn the good knowledge [...] Thus, the king who despises to acquire knowledge despises God from whom all knowledge comes" (*GE*, II, 1, V, 16). Knowledge and power, along with will, are qualities that should adorn the king and therefore all human beings.

According to Alfonso, man occupies a special place among creatures. The level of perfection of each human being depends on the level on which each individual finds himself in the scale of knowledge in relation to his peers. In the same way that the angel is higher than man thanks to his knowledge, the highest among men is he who has received the most understanding from God (*Libro de las Cruzes*, p. 1). Therefore, he concludes: "The wise men among the Gentiles say that the more knowledge a person has and acquires through study, the more he learns, and grows, and gets closer to God, just as the mountain that rises to the heights of the heavens" (*GE*, II, 2, 31b). In other words, knowledge, which comes from God and through creatures and education, leads us to God, makes us participate in divine nature. This is how, paradoxically, the promise of the serpent ("*et eritis sicut dii*"; "and you shall be as gods"), becomes through knowledge and virtue a reality. The fundamental difference, therefore, between the invitation of the serpent mentioned at the beginning and the one Alfonso made to his subjects is the fact that, while the serpent instigated humans to the acquisition of knowledge as a way to acquire independence, thus distancing the creature from the creator, Alfonso saw the acquisition of knowledge as a way for creatures to approach and "reach" God, making them participate in divine knowledge and nature.

Perhaps forcing the similarity a bit, it could be said that, for Alfonso, knowledge is like sanctifying grace: just as grace makes those who possess it participate in divine nature, and in that sense they are like God, knowledge too, which is by nature goodness, kindness, and virtue, makes the wise similar to God, who is infinite knowledge and kindness. In the *General Estoria*, commenting on the significance of the name Perseus, he writes: "And we find that some explain the name Perseus through the term *pertheo* which means "like god," because every man who is full of virtues and knowledge resembles God, because he comes from Him; and the more each person has of this, the more he resembles God and the more he is closer to His nature" (II, 1, p. 290a).

I do not know to what extent Alfonso as a Christian thinker wanted to introduce Aristotelian philosophy into theology, as was being done by the Scholastics of his time, by establishing a relation between knowledge and sanctifying grace, but in the *General Estoria*, the two concepts appear frequently. However, from the perspective of Christian theology, the force of the comparison is reduced considerably when the proof of the authority of Aristotle is adduced, since Aristotle, clearly, did not think in Christian terms. Still, Alfonso attempts to profit from some of Aristotle's expressions in the *Metaphysics*. Speaking of the wisdom of Abraham in the *General Estoria*, he writes:

> ...[A]nd Abraham was very wise regarding this [he refers to arithmetic and geometry], and regarding other branches of knowledge much more than the other masters there were among the Chaldeans; and through these branches of knowledge he came to know what God was and to do what pleased Him, because no one can know God unless he is wise or he strives to be so. About this the very wise Aristotle says that to resemble God is nothing other than to know things completely and to behave well, and in this way man comes to be with God and to participate with Him of His glory which has no end. (I, p. 107b)

The first part of the quote, where resembling God is identified with scientific knowledge and with righteous behavior, fits in well with Aristotelian philosophy. However, the second part, where technical theological vocabulary such as "to participate with Him of His glory" (that is, "participes divinae naturae" in patristic-scholastic theology) is used, seems to exceed the hermeneutic possibilities of Alfonso's favorite philosopher. That was the risk Alfonso ran in his attempt to innovate.[13]

In any event, it is clear that Alfonso intimately links knowledge, on the one hand, with virtue, and on the other, with an approximation to God: "[...] and therefore they said about Atlas that he had been transformed into a mountain, and that he grew every day because of the great knowledge he possessed; and that each day that he studied, he knew more. And they also say of any person that, the more knowledge he has and the more he gets closer to it through studying, the more he learns and grows, and therefore the closer he gets to God, like the mountain that rises towards the heights of the heavens" (II, 2, p. 31b). Alfonso's metaphor, according to which the wise man is like a high mountain, is taken from *Calila e Dimna* [*The Tales of Kalila and Dimna*], the book of Eastern wisdom whose translation he commissioned when he was still a prince, as Alfonso himself explains in a summary of the same that appears in Chapter 31 of the First Part of the *General Estoria*, in a section regarding how books should be understood. The Indian sage tells Berzeuay, messenger of the king of Persia who was seeking wisdom: "Books should be understood in the following way: mountains should be interpreted as wise men, because just as mountains are higher than other places, likewise are wise men higher than all other men with respect to knowledge. And what he says about India [Alfonso's note] should be understood as the time in which we live and that in this land we seek knowledge much more than in any other" (I, p. 198a).

The text and context of the Alfonsine commentary are of extraordinary value in terms of how works should be read, that is, according to their allegorical, hidden meaning. It also illustrates the literary technique used in Alfonsine hermenutics for the interpretation of pagan myths. But perhaps the most significant aspect of the passage is the last phrase, spoken by the Indian sage to the messenger of the Persian king, which does not seem to make much sense in the context of the narrative. I therefore think that Alfonso, as in many other occasions, inserts here a personal observation in order to reflect what was really to be sought "in this land," that is, in his "more than in any other."

---

[13] That is not how St. Thomas Aquinas understood Aristotle in his *Commentary on the Metaphysics* (I, lect.III, 64), if it is the case that Alfonso is commenting on a passage of the *Metaphysics* (*Met.*, A, 2, 983), as Francisco Rico suggests, *Alfonso X y la General Estoria*, p. 131.

Alfonso was very proud of what was being accomplished in his court and his kingdom. He was not being boastful here, but truthful. Alfonso did not achieve the title of Emperor of the Holy Roman Empire, but as the historian R.I. Burns says, he was the "Emperor of Culture" in Europe and his enlightened court was the vehicle of transmission of ancient and medieval culture to Christian Europe.

Finally, knowledge should be the goal of all rational beings regardless of their religious orientation, even if only because it achieves immortality for man.

The second great contribution of Alfonsine culture to the development of 13th-century humanism we'd like to point out is its secular nature.[14] As we pointed out at length when discussing the *Memoriale secretum* (Chapter 13) and speaking of Alfonso's function as the "troubadour of Mary" in the "*cantigas* of praise" tracing his intellectual profile (Chapter 15), the Learned King, although not breaking entirely with the Church of Rome, did have serious differences with the Peninsular hierarchy for political, religious, jurisdictional, and fiscal reasons. At the root of the conflict was Alfonso's absolutist conception of power, shared by most medieval European kings. The king is in his kingdom as the emperor in the empire, namely, he only answers to God:

> Kings, each one in his kingdom, are the vicars of God, appointed over people to maintain them in justice and in truth in temporal matters, just as an emperor does in his empire [...] And naturally the wise men declared that the king is the head of the kingdom, for, as from the head originate the feelings by which all the members of the body are controlled; so also by the commands which originate from the king, who is the lord and head of all the people of his kingdom, they should be directed and guided, and act in harmony with him, to obey him, and support, and protect, and aggrandize the kingdom, of which he is the soul and head, and they are the members. (*Partida* II, Tit. I, Law V, *Las Siete Partidas*, ed. Robert I. Burns, trans. By Samuel Parsons Scott, pp. 270–271)[15]

---

[14] Although not referring specifically to Alfonso X, the following work is worth keeping in mind: G. Lagarde, *La naissance de l'esprit laique au déclin du Moyen Age*, Paris-Louvain, 1956.

[15] For the concept of king in *Partida* II as a true mirror for princes and vassals, see G. Martin, "La concepción del rey en la Segunda Partida," in Seminario del CSIC, *El señorío del Rey (De la Castilla Condal a la Baja Edad Media)*, Madrid, 1997; and Francesco C. Cesareo, "The Centrality of the King in the Thought of Alfonso of

Although Alfonso never thought of the creation of a "national Spanish Church," as some critics argue, he did believe that the ecclesiastical structures of the kingdom should be at the service of the crown, that the bishops and the clergy were his subjects, as were the rest of his vassals, and should therefore, respect him as a representative of God in the kingdom and stand up in his presence and kiss his hand, not vice versa. Only the pope was exempt from this act of respect (although not from the act of standing up). But I believe this was not due to the fact that the pope is the successor of St. Peter and the Vicar of Christ on earth, but because he was the temporary lord of the Pontifical States, which were free and sovereign, like the king of France or England.

I do not know what Alfonso might have told his father-in-law, Jaime I of Aragón, during the Christmas days of 1269 they spent together, that caused Jaime advised him "above all, don't mess with the Church." I suspect that Alfonso must have presented to his father-in-law the essential elements of his government plan and his legislative projects, which aimed at making all subjects equal before the law. In the *Memoriale secretum*, he is accused of abusing his jurisdiction in violating Church exemptions. Alfonso, who, as we saw, legislated all, created in the *Partidas* norms of behavior that also affected high Church officials such as bishops. As king and legislator, he was concerned with the physical and spiritual well-being of all his subjects, recommending to the prelates:

> Moreover, eating too much is forbidden to every man, and especially to the prelate, because chastity cannot be easily preserved where there is inordinate indulgence in food, and great excesses prevail. For this reason the saints declared that it is not proper that those whose duty it is to preach poverty, and the hardships which our Lord Jesus Christ suffered for us in this world, should do so with faces that are red from eating and drinking to excess. And, leaving this out of consideration, serious illnesses naturally result from immoderate eating, in consequence of which men die before their time, or perish from the result of some injury. (Partida, I, Tit. V, ley 36 *Las Siete Partidas*, ed. Robert I. Burns, trans. by Samuel Parsons Scott, p. 65)

The somewhat comical detail of the "faces that are red" is quite indicative of Alfonso's very skeptical attitude regarding the perfection of the

León–Castile," in *Kings and Kingship*, Binghamton: State University of New York, 1976, pp. 121–131.

official representatives of the Church, who at the time were not very different from the nobles and the "ricoshombres" (rich gentlemen).

Much more serious were his interventions in other areas. As lord and owner of all his subjects he believed he had the right to retain at the service of the court and the *Scriptorium* the most enlightened minds for his cultural projects, assigning certain bishops and abbots to advising and diplomatic missions. Herman the German was promoted to the bishopric of Astorga in 1266, but only after he had worked tirelessly for Alfonso as translator in Toledo. Fernando Martínez of Zamora, a great legal scholar, author of the *Summa aurea de ordine iudiciario*, was elected to the diocese of Oviedo in 1275, but he died as bishop-elect without ever taking office. Fernando together with Gonzalo Pérez Gudiel, later bishop of Toledo, was part of the extraordinary group of legal scholars that he surrounded himself with in Toledo, Seville, and Murcia. Something similar happened with another court scholar, Suero Pérez of Zamora, Alfonso's notary for the kingdom of León and later bishop of Zamora, whose consecration Alfonso had postponed for a year simply because he needed him. Sometimes he had bishops consecrated, but he retained them at his court, as was the case of Agustín of Osma and Pedro Lorenzo of Cuenca in 1262, justifying his decision by simply saying he needed them. It is obvious that Alfonso, abusing his powers, retained in his service the subjects who were ecclesiastically, intellectually, and spiritually better prepared, and he sent the mediocre and less capable ones to the dioceses.[16]

A similar thing happened also with the members of the mendicant orders. Apparently, Alfonso was more interested in the pens of the friars than in their sermons. He preferred to employ them in his diplomatic teams and as translators and specialists in the *scriptorium* and chancellery, although he also chose among them chaplains and confessors for the court. Pedro Gallego, the king's confessor and later bishop, was also a translator much appreciated by the king. Among other works, Alfonso commissioned him to translate an Arabic treatise on teenage sexuality.[17] Gil de Zamora, a Franciscan we discussed in several chapters, was also a great collaborator in several cultural projects. Later Alfonso would name him Sancho IV's tutor. Naturally,

---

[16] Cf. P. Linehan, *The Spanish Church and the Papacy in the 13th Century*, *passim*; and his *History and the Historians*, pp. 510, 511, 520, 521 and corresponding notes; and O'Callaghan, "Alfonso X and Castilian Church," pp. 417–419.

[17] Cf. Linehan, *History and the Historians*, p. 524, note 60.

Alfonso held these men who were his close collaborators in great esteem, and given his proverbial generosity, he personally bestowed many gifts on them, and later on their dioceses. In the case of Suero Pérez of Zamora, Alfonso would make him his chaplain, which meant oversight of the king's spiritual health, a function that in the *Partidas* comes before that of the chancellor himself.

This administrative policy, however, had serious repercussions for the life of the Church. According to many scholars, during Alfonso's reign the Peninsular church lost much of its power and, with the exception of a few bishoprics (Toledo, Burgos, and Seville), became poorer. The poverty of the rural clergy worsened in particular. So much so that in the border territories and areas recently conquered, mounting poverty, the dues paid to their local churches, excessive taxes, and "services," the situation eventually became unbearable and led to popular unrest.

Even more serious with respect to the discipline of the clergy was Alfonso's decision to legitimate the illegitimate children that priests had with their concubines, approving, or at least condoning, concubinage.[18] Deep down, the Learned King wanted to appear humane and palliate the economic and social inequality suffered by the lower clergy, who lived in utterly degrading conditions. But this new decision only aggravated the situation of that sector of the clergy vis-à-vis the Church authorities, because such priests were practically no different from the peasants, resembling all the inhabitants of the countryside and villages on the border.

These royal decrees were unacceptable to the hierarchy of the Peninsula and to Rome. It was therefore understandable that the bishops denounced him to the pope. In the last section of the *Memoriale secretum*, the pope launched an unexpected and unusual accusation against the Learned King, namely, that he had established a "novum

---

[18] On June 19, 1262 Alfonso granted a royal privilege to the priests in the bishopric of Salamanca so that they could name their children and grandchildren as heirs. It was not an isolated case, because he granted a similar privilege to the priests of Almazán. Cf. Ballesteros, *Alfonso X*, p. 346; P. Linehan, *History and the Historians*, pp. 510 and 511, 521. According to this scholar, in order to appease this sector of the clergy and the people in general, Alfonso asked Fr. Rodrigo de Cerrato in 1276 to compose the *Vitae Sanctorum* (*ib.*, p. 522), a work that was very successful and popular. We know that no one was more qualified to know the needs of the poor, whether religious or lay, than the members of the mendicant orders, who traveled constantly preaching in the rural areas and living among their inhabitants, which was the case of Fr. Rodrigo de Cerrato.

ordinem seu religionem" ("new order or religion"). As we mentioned in Chapter 12, the new order referred to an entire new way of conceiving of the social structure in terms of the relationship between Monarchy and Church, and of the culture, vernacular and secular, that such decrees were part of.

All these displays of secularism had a lot to do with the discipline of the clergy, a matter in which Alfonso took a particular interest, if for no other reason because they were subjects of the crown, entrusted with the education of his subjects. His external displays of secular attitudes, however, did not affect the integrity of his Catholic faith as others attitudes of the king would, in which the heterodox side of his secular spirit was more evident.

In the first part of this Conclusion we saw how easily the Learned King made use of secular texts, including mythological ones, even if they were written by the Church's favorite philosopher, in order to prove or illustrate certain theological doctrines or matters of faith, instead of availing himself of Scripture or Patristic literature. This peculiar aspect of Alfonsine culture has not been studied at length, but the influence of Averroes's philosophy may not be dismissed, since it introduced reason as an element in the proof of revealed truth and it was able to penetrate the intellectual world of European universities. On the other hand, we also saw how in the work that most faithfully portrays Alfonso's religiosity, the *Songs of Holy Mary*, Alfonso eliminates, both in the poems and in the miniatures, all allusions to Church authorities as mediators of grace between God and people, frequently putting himself in their place.

If from the theological point of view this attitude was outright unorthodox, Alfonso would go even further in his scientific works, especially in his astrological texts and in the *Lapidaries*. (One of the longest chapters of the *Libro de las cruces* deals with the most auspicious moment, according to the constellations, to depose a prelate or a court official.) Alfonso was very aware of his stances in relation to the traditional doctrine of the Church. He therefore often placed notes and disclaimers at the beginning of his scientific works warning about the content and how the works were to be read and interpreted. Despite all those caveats (such as the one we quoted in Chapter 12 taken from the *Libro de Astromagia*), many of the Peninsular church authorities who were familiar with such works still thought they had an Oriental magus as their king, and that would also be the image held by many others, in various European courts and in Rome.

This very lay ideology is the reason for his desire to unhinge knowledge from its ties to the Church and Latin, to open it instead to the new scientific currents transmitted by Muslim and ancient Greek scholars. His preference for certain philosophers and poets such as Lucan and especially Ovid also must have been deemed suspect. In his historical works, especially in the *General Estoria*, Alfonso was particularly careful to observe the positive aspects of the lay, earthly, and material culture that was far from God. The words of the serpent quoted at the beginning of this Conclusion must have exerted an irresistible charm over a man as thirsty for knowledge as Alfonso was: "Of course you will not die. God knows that as soon as you eat it [the forbidden fruit of knowledge], your eyes will be opened and you will be like gods knowing both good and evil" (*Gen.* 3:4–5). There is, to be sure, a fair degree of Manicheism in his historiography, especially in the *GE*, where he seems to identify evil with natural wit, beauty, and physical strength. Nimrod was a tyrant and oppressor, but at the same time he was a wise astronomer, a builder of towers that touched the skies, the architect of magnificent cities that were the model and envy of antiquity. The wives of Cain were very beautiful and irresistible, and they seduced the tribe of Seth and would even "ride on top of them" [a sexual innuendo] (*GE*, I, p. 25b). There remnants of biblical influence in this Alfonsine attitude that presents evil as more attractive than good. This is the topic of the "sons of God" and the "daughters of men" (*Genesis* 6:4), whose union resulted in the giants, who were strong, wise, and inventive, creators of superior civilizations and cultures.

Despite his obsession with biblical and pagan mythology and the classics, Alfonso must not have made those responsible for orthodoxy in his days nor subsequent critics doubt his truly Christian vision of life. The Learned King was perfectly aware where his intellectual roots lay. In a key passage of the *Setenario* where he discusses several basic topics of dogmatic and moral theology, he holds, as a leitmotif of the entire work, that the religions and myths of paganism were but a prophecy of Christianity and the Christian mysteries (p. 65).

The text of the *Setenario* entails a number of problems typical of 13th-century philosophy and about which Alfonso adopts a clear position: God created the world out of nothing, not because he needed it, but freely and to show his power. The created world is the clue that leads to knowledge of its creator, whose existence and the truthfulness of its doctrine Alfonso attempts to prove not only through the

Bible, but also through Aristotelian-Averroist proofs, which make use of scientific arguments, "according to the nature of the heavens and of other spiritual things." This profession by a Christian apologist who defends faith with the latest arguments from the sciences was perhaps what diminished the prejudice of the popes against him on account of his relation to the "cursed race" of the Hohenstaufens. Of the ten popes who occupied the throne of St. Peter during his reign,[19] none ever dared to sanction him with canonical punishments, as they did with Frederick II and later with his son Sancho IV. The treatment of all these topics and the philosophical-positivistic method of argumentation are typical of the works composed toward the end of the Learned King's life, which would support the theory that the *Setenario* was composed late, as some scholars argue, rather than being an early work.

As a true Christian humanist, Alfonso planned his ouvre around the proposition: "The branches of knowledge [arts] come directly from God; and whoever rejects them, also rejects God" (*Set.*, p. 44). What follows in the rest of this work is an admirable literary construction previously attempted by the Fathers of the Church in order to rescue Christendom from the world of pagan letters and myths by building around them an allegorical interpretation. The foundations of this literary edifice are to be found in Biblical exegesis, mystical theology, and contemporary medieval letters, which describe visible reality as a reflection of God and his attributes. But Alfonso's secular humanism goes beyond this exercise in the hermeneutics of the symbol. It extends to the traditional technique of the "figure" of the Old Testament (which is manifested in the "reality" of the New); to the secular literature, pagan myths, and all worldly realities, including human language, that is, words and their lexical and semantic correspondences in Castilian; to even the *Setenario* and its structure itself. As Lapesa puts it: "All the similarities, parallels, and prefigurations that are woven into the *Setenario* revolve around the axis of the idea that the being and becoming of the entire universe are symbolic" (*Set.* p. XIV).

---

[19] Innocent IV (1243–1254), Alexander IV (1254–1261), Urban IV (1261–1264), Clement IV (1265–1268), Gregory X (1271–1276), Innocent V (1276, five months), Adrian V (1276, one month), John XXI (1276–1277, eight months), Nicholas III (1277–1280), and Martin IV (1281–1285). Alfonso only met one of them personally, Gregory X.

When speaking of Alfonsine humanism, we are not referring to, or even less comparing it with, the Latin humanism of the Italian Renaissance launched by a handful of men in 15th-century Florence who formed an exclusive intellectual elite whose obsession was to restore classical letters.[20] Western culture owes much to these men, but their limitations must also be recognized, because in its greatness, the exclusive study and imitation of the classics prevented the men of their time from having contact with other forms of ancient culture. Alfonsine humanism, on the other hand, with all the limitations of the medieval world in which it was born and developed, had a much wider scope, going from the earth sciences to the complexities of astronomy, passing through classical letters, Greek-Muslim philosophy, and Scholastic theology. According to Américo Castro: "Alfonso the Learned in his time fulfilled the imperative of affirmation demanded by the organic development of the Neo-Latin world; without this 13th-century humanism, the humanism of the 15th century would have been impossible, with its different preoccupations, mainly to theorize and justify the value of the human—more felt than reasoned—as a valuable and independent quality. It is in such a context that one must judge the colossal impetus of the Alfonsine project."[21]

An essential component of Alfonsine humanism in its secular form was to dissociate the human knowledge of the Latin world, which from this moment on would also be transmitted through other languages such as Arabic, Hebrew and especially Castilian. The Alfonsine cultural concept was born accompanied by or derived from the concept of vernacular humanism, without which its inherent didacticism would not be understood. A logical corollary of this didactic aim was the invention of the linguistic vehicle that would allow Alfonso to reach the minds of his subjects; hence the promotion of the vernacular, in which he reached unprecedented levels of perfection and which was disseminated to all territories of the Crown of Castile. Therefore, when in the middle of the following century don Juan Manuel composed his literary oeuvre, vernacular writing already had the force that drove

---

[20] See Southern, *Medieval Humanism*, pp. 29–60, where the author explains what should be understood by medieval humanism and identifies the typical themes of the intellectual work of a humanist in the Middle Ages. For Alfonso's "protohumanism," see A. Domínguez, "Imágenes de un rey trovador," p. 231, note 1; and the quoted essay by H.S. Martínez, "*Paideia y filantropía*. Sentido y alcance del humanismo alfonsí," in *Clarines de pluma*, pp. 75–96.

[21] *Glosarios latino-españoles de la Edad Media*, Madrid, 1936, p. LXV.

him also to write so that all lay people could understand him. The didacticism that was an essential component of the Alfonsine cultural concept and the supreme mission of his reign was unconditionally embraced by don Juan Manuel and an entire new generation of "lay" erudite writers.

Only a king who had the economic resources and the prestige of a man of letters could carry out such a cultural revolution. For the erudite men of Christian Europe it was unthinkable that in the 13th century someone could imagine that philosophy, the sciences, and particularly the works of antiquity could be transmitted in any language other than Latin. That was only possible in Spain where a very peculiar sociolinguistic environment existed as a result of the interaction of three cultures whose common language was Castilian.[22]

It was precisely this multicultural environment that awakened in a man like Alfonso, who admired Greek-Arabic natural philosophy, an interest in the traditions of Biblical wisdom and Jewish hermeneutics, Roman jurisprudence and the Scholasticism of the clergy of his era, together with the traditions of popular vernacular poetry, which led him to promote a secular and vernacular culture. Alfonso was well aware that he lived in a pluralistic society, and despite the fact that he lived in era of Christian reconquest, his reign was marked by an almost total lack of compulsory conversion to the Christian religion and submission to Church authorities.

All of this is also part of his cultural milieu, reflecting some aspects of a humanism whose objective was the human being in his totality, as an entity composed of nature and spirit. This dual nature identifies him and differentiates him as a unique being in the universe and in his relations to the surrounding world. It is therefore a humanism that preoccupies itself with man from the perspective of his individuality as a being in creation, and even more, inasmuch as he represents the synthesis of other creatures (a microcosm).[23] Hence Alfonso's interest in the sciences of man, both in their physical and natural dimensions

---

[22] See the important essay by F. Díaz Esteban, "La convivencia lingüística del árabe, el hebreo y el romance reflejadas en un documento del siglo XIV," *I Congreso Internacional "Encuentro de las tres culturas,"* Toledo, 1983, pp. 195–205. More on the specific "vernacularization" of history in the 13th century in Spain and France in K. Uitti, "Note on Historiographical Vernacularization in 13th-Century," *Homenanje a A. Galmés de Fuentes,* Madrid: Gredos, 1985, I, pp. 573–592.

[23] Cf. *GE,* I, pp. 572b–573a and also the theory of the five senses in Partida, II, XIII.

(*Lapidario, Libros del saber de astrología*) as well as others that deal
with man as a social and moral entity, with certain rights and duties
(*Setenario, Partidas*). His humanism also includes those aspects which
deal with the needs that derive from spirituality and sociability of the
human being, such as games, leisure, and recreation, dealt with in the
Libros de ajedrez dados e tablas (*Book of Chess, Dice and Backgam-
mon*) and the *Libro de la caza* (*Book of Hunting*). Alfonso even became
interested in the bylaws governing gambling excesses in the *Libro de
las tahurerias* (*Book on Gambling*).²⁴ Still within this same concept of
man as a social animal that interacts and communicates with others,
Alfonso dealt with music (*GE*, I, p. 195), poetry, entertainment, and
the pleasure of beautiful things that soothe the soul wearied by worries and work:

> There are other pleasures, in addition to those we mentioned in the pre-
> ceding laws, which have been devised in order that a man may take
> comfort when oppressed with care and affliction. These are listening to
> songs and musical instruments, and playing chess, draughts, or other
> similar games. We also include histories, romances, and other books,
> which treat of those matters from which men derive joy and pleasure.
> (*Partida*, II, Tit. V, Law 21, *Las Siete Partidas*, ed. Robert I. Burns, trans.
> By Samuel Parsons Scott, p. 297)

Alfonso surrounded himself with poets and artists from all places.
At his court there was room both for Spanish Hebrew poets, such
as Todros Abulafia, as well as for Galician-Portuguese poets, and the
latest fashion, Provençal troubadours, whom the poet king greatly
admired. We have no information about his attitude toward Muslim
erotic poetry, which he undoubtedly knew judging from some of the
details in his profane *cantigas*, but we must postulate that, guided by
the way he dealt with erotic legends in classical mythology in his historical works, he did not consider it compatible with the exemplary
and educational mission of the king. His great poetic love, especially
in his last years, was Marian poetry and its related themes, a topic to

---

²⁴ About these last works, see P. García Morencos, *Libro de ajedrez, dados y tablas
de Alfonso X el Sabio*, Madrid: Editorial Patrimonio Nacional, 1977; R.A. MacDonald,
ed., *Libro de las Tahurerias. A Special Code of Law, Concerning Gambling, Drawn Up
by Maestro Roldán at the Command of Alfonso X of Castile*, Madison, WI: Hispanic
Seminary of Medieval Studies, 1995. Cf. M. Isabal, "Ordenamiento de las tahurerías,"
in *Enciclopedia jurídica española*, XXIV, 17–18; and J. Lalinde Abadía, "Ordenamiento
de las tahurerías," in *Nueva enciclopedia jurídica*, XVIII, 1986, pp. 523–525.

which he devoted his most extensive poetic work, the *Songs of Holy Mary*.

When in the spring of 1284, Alfonso died in Seville, he had been abandoned by all, except his beloved daughter, Beatriz, born from a youthful love. In that moment of desolation it seems as if his own body had abandoned him: almost blind, with a cancer in the left maxillary antrum that made his eye pop out of its orbit, with legs swollen from dropsy and having lost all teeth, he must have been the image of that mythical "honest Silenus," old, ugly, and repugnant on the outside, but full of wisdom and beauty on the inside. He could not expect more from this life, and still he continued fighting, polishing his works and working on other new projects where he dealt with board games and pastimes that make man's life more pleasant, convinced that "the branches of knowledge are a part of God's treasure that never die and never abandon those who know, and never let them die a permanent death, for the wise men in these arts, although they die in the flesh, they live for ever in [people's] memory" (*GE*, I, p. 198b). Truly admirable until the end.

Goodbye, Alfonso! I have spent too much time in your company. I know that you have taken revenge on me for having disturbed your eternal sleep, digging into certain matters you considered "ugly." Before you end up killing me, I will let you rest in peace with your fame and your pipe dreams.

BIBLIOGRAPHY

1. Alfonso X's Works Available in English

Cantigas de Santa María, Songs of Holy Mary of Alfonso X, the Wise: A Translation of the Cantigas de Santa María, by K. Kulp-Hill, Tempe, AZ: Arizona Center for Medieval Studies, 2000.

Las Siete Partidas del rey don Alfonso el Sabio cotejadas con varios códices Antiguos por la Real Academia de la Historia, 3 vols., Madrid: Imprenta Real, 1807, English translation by S.P. Scott, ed. R.I. Burns, 5 vols., Philadelphia: University of Pennsylvania Press, 2001.

2. Bibliography on Alfonso X and his Time

Alfonso X of Castile, the Learned King (1221–1284): An International Symposium, ed. F. Márquez Villanueva and C.A. Vega, Cambridge, Mass., Harvard Studies in Romance Languages 43, 1990.

Allen, H.D.: "Christian Doctrine in the *General Estoria* of Alfonso X," Madison: University of Wisconsin, Doctoral diss., 1960.

Andrachuk, G.P.: "Alfonso X. Courtier and Legislator," *Revista Canadiense de Estudios Hispánicos*, 9 (1985), 439–450.

Armistead, S.G.: "New Perspectives in Alfonsine Historiography," *Romance Philology*, XX (1966), 204–217.

Barton, B.: *The Aristocracy of Twelfth-Century León and Castile*, Cambridge: Cambridge University Press, 1997.

Blake, M.E.: "Alfonso X and the Birth of Spanish Literature," *Catholic World*, LVI (1982–1983),

Bloom, L.: *Emergence of an Intellectual and Social Ideals in Selected Writings of Alfonso X and Juan Manuel*, Ph.D. Diss., University of Pittsburgh, 1967.

Buck, D.C.: "Alfonso X as Role Model for the Eighteenth-Century *Ilustrados*," *Romance Quarterly*, 33 (1986), 263–268.

Burke, J.F.: "Alfonso X and the Structuring of Spanish History," *Revista Canadiense de Estudios Hispánicos*, 9 (1985), 464–471.

Burns, R.I.: "*Stupor mundi*: Alfonso X of Castile, the Learned," en R.I. Burns, ed., *Emperor of Culture. Alfonso X the Learned of Castile and his Thirteenth-Century Renaissance*, Philadelphia: University of Pennsylvania Press, 1990, 1–13.

——: ed., The Worlds of Alfonso the Learned and James the Conqueror. Intellect and Force in the Middle Ages, Princeton, NJ: Princeton University Press, 1985.

Chronicle of Alfonso X, translated by Shelby Thacker and José Escobar with an Introduction by Joseph F. O'Callahan, Lexington: The University Press of Kentucky, 2002.

Dinneen, F.P.: "The Linguistic Conceptions of Alfonso X, King of Spain," *Historiographia Linguistica*, 6 (1979), 87–102.

Fraker, Ch.: *The Scope of History: Studies in the Historiography of Alfonso el Sabio*, Ann Arbor, MI: University of Michigan Press, 1996.

Franssen, M.: "Did King Alfonso of Castile Really Want to Advise God Against the Ptolemaic System?," *Studies in History and Philosophy of Science* 24 (1993), 313–325.

García Ballester, L.: "Medical Science in Thirteenth-Century Castile: Problems and Prospects," *Bulletin of the History of Medicine*, 61 (1987), 183–202

Gelsinger, B.: "A Thirteenth-Century Norwegian-Castilian Alliance," *Medievalia et Humanistica*, New Series 10 (1981), 55–80.

González-Casanovas, R.J.: *Imperial Histories from Alfonso X to Inca Garcilaso. Revisionist Myths of Reconquest and Conquest*, Potomac, MD: Scripta Humanística, 1997.

——: "Fernando III as Enlightened Ruler in Alfonso's *Setenario*: A Historicist Critique of the Discourse of Power," *Romance Languages Annual*, 9 (1996), 495–502.

Goodman, A.: Alfonso X and the English Crown," in *Alfonso el Sabio. Vida, obra y época*, I, Madrid, 1989, 39–54.

Greenia, G.D.: "The Court of Alfonso X in Words and Pictures: The *Cantigas*," Courtly Literature. Culture and Context, eds. K. Busby and E. Kooper, Amsterdam / Philadelphia: John Benjamins, 1990, 227–237.

——: "The Politic of Piety: Manuscript Illumination and Narration in the *Cantigas de Santa Maria*," *Hispanic Review*, 61 (1993), 325–344.

Harvey, L.P.: "The Alphonsine School of Translators: Translation from Arabic into Castilian Produced Under the Patronage of Alfonso the Wise of Castile," *Journal of the Royal Society* (1977), 109–117.

——: *Islamic Spain, 1250 to 1500*, Chicago and London, 1990.

Haskins, Ch.H.: *The Renaissance of the Twelfth Century*, Cambridge: Harvard University Press, 1927.

——: "Translators from the Arabic in Spain," *Studies in the History of Medieval Science*, Cambridge: Harvard University Press, 1924.

Hatton, V. y Mackay, A.: "Anti-Semitism in the *Cantigas de Santa María*," *Bulletin of Hispanic Studies*, 60 (1983), 189–199.

Hernández, F. and Linehan, P.A.: *The Mozarabic Cardinal. The Life and Times of Gonzalo Pérez Gudiel*, Firenze: SISMEL / Edicioni del Galluzzo, 2004.

Hillgarth, J.: *The Spanish Kingdoms, 1250–1516*, 2 vols., Oxford: Clarendon Press, 1976–1978.

Historical Literature in Medival Iberia, ed. A. Deyermond, London: London: Papers of the Medieval Hispanic Research Seminar, Queen Mary and Westfield College, 1996.

Holliday, F.R.: "The Relations Between Alfonso X and Pero da Ponte," *Revista da Faculdade de Letras*, 3a serie, Lisboa, IV (1960).

Holloway, J.B.: "The Road through Roncesvalles: Alfonsine Formation of Brunetto Latini and Dante-Diplomacy and Literature," en R.I. Burns, *Emperor of Culture*, 109–123.

——: "Alfonso el Sabio, Brunetto Latini and Dante Alighieri," *Thought*, 60 (1985), 468–483.

Holmes, U.T.: *Medieval Man: His Understanding of Himself and the World*, Chapel Hill, N.C.: North Carolina Studies in Romance Languages and Literatures, 1980.

Jayne, C.: "The Virgin's Cures for Lust," in *Estudios Alfonsinos y otros escritos*, New York: National Hispanic Foundation for the Humanities, 1990.

Jonxis-Henkemans, W.L.: "The Last Days of Alexander in *General Estoria IV*," in *Alexander the Great in the Middle Ages*, ed. W.J. Aerts et al., Nimega, 1978, 142–169.

——: "The Dating of the Parts of the *General Estoria* of Alfonso el Sabio," *La Corónica*, XIV (1985–1986), 272–273.

Kagay, D.J. and Snow, J.: *Medieval Iberia: Essays on the History and Literature of Medieval Spain*, New York: Peter Lang, 1997.

Kahane, H. y Pietrangeli, A.: "Hermetism in the Alfonsine Tradition," *Mélanges offerts à Rita Lejeune*, 2 vols., Gembloux: Editions Duculot, 1969, I, 443–457.

Kasten, L.: "Alfonso el Sabio and the Thirteenth Century Spanish Language," in R.I. Burns, *Emperor of Culture*, 33–45.

——: "The Utilization of the *Historia Regum Britanniae* by Alfonso X," *HR*, 38.5 (special issue, Nov. 1970), 97–114.

——: "*Poridat de las Poridades*: A Spanish Form of the Western Text of the *Secretum secretorum*," *RPh*, 5 (1951–1952), 180–190.

——: y Nitti, J.: *Concordances and Texts of the Royal Scriptorium Manuscripts of Alfonso X, el Sabio*, 2 vols., Madison: Hispanic Seminary, 1978.

Keller, J.E.: *Alfonso X, el Sabio*, New York: Twayne, 1967.

——: "Daily Living as Revealed in King Alfonso's 'Cantigas'," *Kentucky Foreign Languages Quarterly*, VII (1960), 45–63.

——: "King Alfonso's Virgin of Villa-Sirga, Rival of St. James of Compostela," in *Middle Ages-Reformation-Volkskunde: Festschriften for John Kunstman*, ed. V.R. Bernhardt, Chapel Hill: University of North Carolina Press, 1959, 95–102.

——: "More on the Rivalry between Santa María and Santiago," *Crítica Hispánica*, 1 (1979), 37–43.

——: "The Lapidary of the Learned King," in *Gems and Gemology*, IX, no. 4 (1957–1958), 105–110; 118–121.

——: "Depiction of Exotic Animals in 'Cantiga' XXIX of the Cantigas de Santa María," in *Studies in Honor of Tatiana Fotitch*, Washington: Catholic University Press, 1972, 247–252.

——: "An Unknown Castilian Lyric Poem: The Alfonsine Translation of 'Cantiga' X of the *Cantigas de Santa María*," *HR*, XLV (1975), 43–47.

——: "Iconography and Literature: Alfonso Himself in *Cantiga* 209," *Hispania.*, 66 (1983), 348–352.

——: "The Art of Illumination in the Books of Alfonso X (Primarily in the *Canticles of Holy Mary*)," *Thought*, 60 (1985), 388–406.

——: and Grant Cash, A.: *Daily life depicted in the Cantigas de Santa María*, Lexington, Ky.: University Press of Kentucky, 1998.

——: and Kinkade, R.P.: *Iconography in Medieval Spanish Literature*, Lexington: University of Kentucky Press, 1983.

Kiddle, L.B.: "The Prose *Thèbes* and the *General Estoria*: An Illustration of the Alphonsine Method of Using Source Material," *Hispanic Review*, VI (1938), 120–132.

——: *La Estoria de Tebas: The Version of the Siege and Destruction of Thebes Contained in the General Estoria of Alfonso X*, Madison, 1935.

——: "A Source of the *General Estoria*: The French Prose Redaction of the *Roman de Thèbes*," *Hispanic Review*, IV (1936), 264–271.

Kinkade, R.P.: "Alfonso X, *Cantiga* 235, and the Events of 1269–1278," *Speculum*, 67 (1992), 284–323.

——: "A Royal Schandal and the Rebellion of 1255," in F.M. Toscano (ed.), *Homage to Bruno Damiani from his loving Students and various friends a Festschrift*, Boston, 1994, 185–198.

——: "Violante of Aragón (1236–1300): An Historical Overview," *Exemplaria Hispanica*, 2 (1992–1993), 36–54.

Kruger Born, L.: "The Perfect Prince: A Study in Thirteenth and Fourteenth Century Ideals," *Speculum*, 3 (1928), 470–504.

Kulp-Hill, K.: "Sidelights on Daily Life of the Iberian Peninsula in the Thirteenth Century as seen in the *Cantigas de Santa María*," Paper Presented at the Kentucky Foreign Language Conference, Lexington, April, 1985.

——: "Clothing in the *Cantigas de Santa María*," Paper Presented at the American Associations of Teachers of Spanish and Portuguese, San Francisco, August, 1997.

——: "Captions and Miniatures in the *Codice Rico* of the *Cantigas de Santa María*: A Translation," *Boletín of the Cantigueiros*, 6 spring (1995), 3–62.

Lasley, M.M.: "Secularization of the creation story in the *General Estoria*," *Revista Hispánica Moderna*, 34 (1968), 330–337.

Linehan, P.: *The Spanish Church and the Papacy in the Thirteenth Century*, Cambridge: Cambridge University Press, 1971.

——: *History and the Historians of Medieval Spain*, Oxford: Clarendon Press, 1993.

——: "The Accession of Alfonso X (1252) and the Origins of the War of the Spanish Succession," in D.W. Lomax y D. Mackenzie, *God and Man in Medieval Spain*, Warminster, 1989, 59–79

London, G.H.: "A Note on Alphonsine Transcription of Arabic," *Studies in Honor of Lloyd A. Kasten*, Medison: Hispanic Seminary of Medieval Studies, 1975, 129–134.

Macdonald, R.A.: "Alfonso the Learned and Succession: A Father's Dilemma," *Speculum*, XL (1965), 647–653.

——: "Law and Politics: Alfonso's Program of Political Reform," in R.I. Burns, *The Worlds of Alfonso the Learned and James the Conqueror*, 150–202.

——: "Alfonsine Law, the *Cantigas* and Justice," in *Studies on the Cantigas de Santa María*, 313–327.

——: "Kingship in Medieval Spain: Alfonso X of Castile," Madison: University of Wisconsin, 1957. Doctoral diss.

Mann, V.B.: *Convivencia: Jews, Muslims, and Christians in Medieval Spain*, New York: George Braziller Publishers, 1992.

Marchand, J.W. y Baldwin, S.: "Singers of the Virgin in Thirteenth-century Spain," *Bulletin of Hispanisc Studies*, LXXI (1994), 169–184.

Martínez, H.S.: *Alfonso X, el Sabio. Una biografía*, Madrid: Ediciones Polifemo, Crónicas y Memorias, 2003.

——: *La convivencia en la España del siglo XIII. Perspectivas alfonsíes*, Madrid: Ediciones Polifemo, 2006.

——: "*Paideia* y filantropía. Sentido y alcance del humanismo alfonsí," in *Clarines de pluma. Homenaje a Antonio Regalado*, ed. V. Martin, Madrid: Editorial Síntesis, Letras Universitarias, 2004, 75–96.

Medieval Translators and the Transmission of Culture, 13th–15th Centuries, eds. J. Beer and K. Lloyd-Jones, Kalamazoo: Western Michigan University, 1995.

Menocal, M.R.: *The Ornament of the World: how Muslims, Jews, and Christians Created a Culture of Tolerance in Medieval Spain*, Boston: Little, Brown & Company, 2002.

——: *The Arabic Role in Medieval Literary History: A Forgotten Heritage*, Philadelphia: University of Pennsylvania Press, 1987.

——: Scheindlin, R.P., y Sells, M., eds.: *The Literature of Al-Andalus*, New York: Cambridge University Press, 2000.

Montero, A.M.: "A Possible Connection between the Philosophy of the Castilian King Alfonso X and the *Risalat Hayy ibn Yaqzan* by Ibn Tufayl," *Al-Massaq*, 18,1 (2006), 1–26.

Nelson, Ch.L.: "Art and Visualization in the *Cantigas de Santa Maria*: How the Artists Worked," in *Studies on the Cantigas*, 111–134.

Neuman, A.A.: *The Jews in Spain and their Social, Political and Cultural Life During the Middle Ages*, 2 vols., Philadelphia: The Jewish Publication Society of America, 1942.

O'Callaghan, J.F.: *The Learned King. The Reign of Alfonso X of Castile*, Philadelphia: University of Pennsylvania Press, 1993.

——: *Alfonso X and the Cantigas de Santa María: A Poetic Biography*, Brill: The Medieval Mediterranean Series, 16, Leiden–Boston–Cologne, 1998.

——: "Alfonso X and the Castilian Church," *Thought*, 60 (1985), 417–429.

——: "The Ideology of Government in the Reign of Alfonso X of Castile," *Exemplaria Hispanica*, 1 (1991–1992), 1–17.

——: "Paths to Ruin: The Economic and Financial Policies of Alfonso the Learned," in R.I. Burns, *The Worlds*, 41–67.

——: *A History of Medieval Spain*, Ithaca: Cornell University Press, 1979.

Parkinson, S.: "The First Reorganization of the *Cantigas de Santa María*," *The Bulletin of the Cantigueiros de Santa Maria*, 1, no. 2 spring (1988), 83–97.

Pattison, D.G.: *From Legend to Chronicle. The Treatment of Epic Material in Alphonsine Historiography*, Oxford: The Society for the Study of Mediaeval Languages and Literature, 1983.

Pedersen, O.: *The First Universities. Studium Generale and the Origins of University Education in Europe*, Aarhus University, Denmark, 1998.

Peters, F.E.: *Aristotle and the Arabs*, New York – London, 1968.

Pingree, D.: "The Diffusion of Arabic Magical Texts in Western Europe," in *Convegno Internazionale, 9–15 Aprile 1969. Tema: Oriente e Occidente nel Medioevo: Filosofia e Scienze*, Roma: Accademia Nazionale dei Lincei, 1971, 57–102.

——: "Learned Magic in the Time of Frederick II," *Micrologus: Natura, Scienze e Societa medievali. Nature, Sciences and Medieval Societies*, 2 (1994), 39–56.

Powicke, F.M.: *The Thirteenth Century, 1216–1307*, 2ª ed., Oxford: Oxford University Press, 1991.

Post, G.: "Blessed Lady Spain. Vincentius Hispanus and Spanish National Imperialism in the Thirteenth Century," *Speculum*, XXIX (1954).

Powers, J.: *A Society Organized for War: The Iberian Municipal Militias in the Central Middle Ages*, Berkeley: University of California Press, 1988.

Presilla, M.: "The Image of Death and Political Ideology in the *Cantigas de Santa María*," en *Studies on the Cantigas de Santa Maria: Art, Music and Poetry*, ed. I.J. Katz, J.E. Keller, et al., Madison: Wis., 1987, 403–459.

——: "Conflicts Between Ecclesiastical and Popular Culture in the Cantigas de Santa Maria," *RQ*, 33 (1986), 331–342.

Procter, E.S.: *Alfonso X of Castile: Patron of Literature and Learning*, Oxford: Clarendon Press, 1951.

——: "The Scientific Works of the Court of Alfonso X of Castile: the King and His Collaborators," *The Modern Language Review*, XL (1945), 12–29.

——: "Materials for the Reign of Alfonso X of Castile, 1252–1284," *Transactions of the Royal Historical Society*, 4th series, XIV (1931), 39–63.

Ramos, G.: "The Portrait of Alfonso X in the first Cantiga," *Symposium sobre las Cantigas de Santa Maria en su 700 aniversario*, New York, 1981.

Rand, E.K.: *Founders of the Middle Ages*, London, 1928.

Reilly, B.F.: *The Medieval Spains*, Cambridge: Cambridge University Press, 1993.

Rodgers, P.K.: "Alfonso X Writes to His Son: Reflections on the *Crónica de Alfonso X* (together with a commentary on and critical text of the unique Alfonsine letter that it preserves)," *Exemplaria Hispanica*, 1 (1991–1992), 58–79.

Roth, N.: "Jewish Collaborators in Alfonso's Scientific Work," in R.I. Burns, *Emperor of Culture*, 59–71.

——: "Jewish Translators at the Court of Alfonso X." *Thought*, 60 (1985), 443–455.

——: "Two Jewish courtiers of Alfonso X colled Zag (Isaac)," *Sefarad*, XLIII, 1 (1983), 75–85.

Rubio, D.: *Classical Scholarship in Spain*, Washington, D.C., 1934.

Ruiz, T.: "Unsacred Monarchy: The Kings of Castile in the Late Middle Ages," in *Rites of Power*, ed. Sean R. Wilartz, Philadelphia: University of Pennsylvania Press, 1985, 109–144.

Samsó Moya, J.: "Alfonso X and Arabic Astronomy," in *De Astronomia Alphonsi Regis. Actas del Simposio sobre Astronomía Alfonsí celebrado en Berkeley (Agosto 1985) y otros trabajos sobre el mismo tema*, Comps. M. Comes, R. Puig y J. Samsó, Barcelona: Universidad, 1987, 23–38.

———: *Islamic Astronomy and Medieval Spain*, Aldershot, United Kingdom & Brook-field, Vermont: Variorum, 1994.

———: and Comes, M.: "Al-Sufí and Alfonso X," *Archives Internationales d'Histoire des Sciences*, 38 (1988), 67–76.

Scarborough, C.: "Alfonso X: A Monarch in Search of a Miracle," *Romance Quarterly*, 33 (1986), 349–354.

———: *Women in Thirteenth-Century Spain as Portrayed by Alfonso X's Cantigas de Santa María*, Lewiston, N.Y.: Edwin Mellen, 1993.

Schaffer, M.: "Epigraphs as a clue to the Conceptualization and Organization of the Cantigas de Santa María," *La Corónica*, 19 (Spring 1991), 57–88.

Scholberg, H.: *Spanish Life in the Late Middle Ages*, University of North Carolina Studies in the Romance Languages and Literatures, no. 57, Chapel Hill, 1965.

Seniff, D.P.: "*Muchos libros buenos*. The New MSS of Alfonso XI's *Libro de la montería* and Moamyn / Alfonso X's *Libro de las animalias que caçan*," *Studia Neophilologica*, 60 (1988), 251–262.

———: "Falconry, Venery, and Fishing in the *Cantigas de Santa María*," in *Noble Persuits: Literature and the Hunt*. ed. D.M. Wright and C.L. Scarborough, Newark, Del.: Juan de la Cuesta, 1992.

———: "Introduction of Natural Law in Scientific and Legal Treatises in Spain and Portugal," in Harold J. Johnson, ed., *Medieval Tradition of Natural Law*, Kalamazoo: Western Michigan University, Studies in Medieval Culture, 1987.

Shoemaker, Th.H.: "Alfonso X as Historian," Madison: University of Wisconsin, 1941. Doctoral diss.

Snow, J.T.: "The Central Role of the Troubadour Persona of Alfonso X in the *Cantigas de Santa María*," *Bulletin of Hispanic Studies*, LVI (1979), 305–316.

———: "Poetic Self-Awareness in Alfonso's *Cantiga 110*," *Kentucky Romance Quarterly*, 26 (1979), 421–432.

———: "A Chapter in Alfonso X's Personal Narrative: the Puerto de Santa María Poems in the *Cantigas de Santa María*," *La Corónica*, VIII (1979), 10–21.

———: "Self-conscious Reference and the Organic Narrative Pattern of the *Cantigas de Santa María* of Alfonso X," *Medieval, Renaissance and Folklore Studies in Honor of John Esten Keller*, Newark, 1980, 53–66.

———: "Alfonso as Troubadour: The Fact and the Fiction," in R.I. Burns, *Emperor of Culture*, 124–140.

———: "Trends in Scholarship on Alfonsine Poetry," *La Corónica*, XI, 2 (1983), 248–257.

———: "Current Status of *Cantigas* Studies." en *Studies on the Cantigas de Santa María*, 475–486.

———: "An Overview of Recent Studies Devoted to the *CSM*," BC, 1 (1987–1988), 5–10.

———: "The Satirical Poetry of Alfonso X: A Look at Its Relationship to the *Cantigas de Santa María*," in *Alfonso X of Castile the Learned King (1221–1284). An International Symposium, Harvard University, 17 November 1984*, eds. F. Márquez Villanueva y C.A. Vega, Cambridge, Mass.: Harvard University, 1990, 110–131.

Socarrás, C.J.: *Alfonso X of Castile: A Study on Imperialistic Frustration*, Barcelona: Ediciones Hispam, 1984.

Sontag, S.: *Illness as Metaphor*, New York: Farrar, Straus and Giroux, 1988.

Southern, R.: *Western Views of Islam in the West in the Middle Ages*, Cambridge, Mass., 1962.

Studies on the Cantigas de Santa María: Art, Music, and Poetry. Proceedings of the International Symposium on the Cantigas de Santa María of Alfonso X, el Sabio (1221–1284) in Commemoration of its 700th Anniversary Year-1981 (New York, November 19–21), eds. I.J. Katz and J.E. Keller, Madison: Seminary of Medieval Studies, 1987.

Sturm, S.: "The Presentations of the Virgin in the *Cantigas de Santa María*," *Philological Quarterly*, 49 (1970), 1–7.

The Worlds of Alfonso the Learned and James the Conqueror. Intelect and Force in the Middle Ages, R.I. Burns, S.J., ed., Princeton, NJ, 1985.

Thorndike, L.: *A History of Magic and Experimental Science*, 6 vols., New York: Macmillan, 1923–1951.

Todesca, J.: "The Monetary History of Castile-León (ca. 1100–1300) in Light of the Bourgey Hoard," *American Numismatic Society Museum Notes*, 33 (1988), 129–203.

Trend, J.B.: "Alfonso el Sabio and the Game of Chess," *Revue Hispanique*, 81 (1933), 393–403.

Van Kleffens, N.E.: *Hispanic Law until the End of the Middle Ages*, Edinburgh: Edinburgh University, 1968.

Van Scoy, H.A.: "Alfonso X as a Lexicographer," *Hispanic Review*, VIII (1940), 277–284.

——: *A Dictionary of Old Spanish Terms Defined in the Works of Alfonso X*, ed. I.A. Corfis, Madison: Hispanic Seminary of Medieval Studies, 1986.

Walsh, J.J.: *The Thirteenth. Greatest of Centuries*, New York: Catholic Summer School Press, 1924.

Watt, W.M.: *History of Muslim Spain*, Edinburgh: Edinburgh University Press, 1965.

Waverly Consort, *Las Cantigas de Santa María: Medieval Music and Verse in the Court of Alfonso X, el Sabio*, Vangard Recording Society, 1972.

Wright, D.: "Folk-Motifs in the Prose Miracles of the *Cantigas de Santa María*," BC, 1 no. 2 spring (1988), 99–109.

INDEX OF NAMES

Studies in the History
of Christian Traditions

(formerly Studies in the History of Christian Thought)

Edited by Robert J. Bast

Recent volumes in the series

116. Stroll, M. *Calixtus II (1119-1124)*. A Pope Born to Rule. 2004.
117. Roest, B. *Franciscan Literature of Religious Instruction before the Council of Trent*. 2004.
118. Wannenmacher, J. E. *Hermeneutik der Heilsgeschichte. De septem sigillis* und die sieben Siegel im Werk Joachims von Fiore. 2004.
119. Thompson, N. *Eucharistic Sacrifice and Patristic Tradition in the Theology of Martin Bucer, 1534-1546*. 2005.
120. Van der Kool, C. *As in a Mirror. John Calvin and Karl Barth on Knowing God*. A Diptych. 2005.
121. Steiger, J. A. *Medizinische Theologie*. Christus medicus und theologia medicinalis bei Martin Luther und im Luthertum der Barockzeit. 2005.
122. Giakalis, A. *Images of the Divine*. The Theology of Icons at the Seventh Ecumenical Council – Revised Edition. With a Foreword by Henry Chadwick. 2005.
123. Heffernan, T. J. and Burman, T. E. (eds.). *Scripture and Pluralism*. Reading the Bible in the Religiously Plural Worlds of the Middle Ages and Renaissance. Papers Presented at the First Annual Symposium of the Marco Institute for Medieval and Renaissance Studies at the University of Tennessee, Knoxville, February 21-22, 2002. 2005.
124. Litz, G., Munzert, H. and Liebenberg, R. (eds.). *Frömmigkeit – Theologie – Frömmigkeitstheologie – Contributions to European Church History*.
125. Ferreiro, A. *Simon Magus in Patristic, Medieval and Early Modern Traditions*. 2005.
126. Goodwin, D. L. *"Take Hold of the Robe of a Jew"*. Herbert of Bosham's Christian Hebraism. 2006.
127. Holder, R. W. *John Calvin and the Grounding of Interpretation*. Calvin's First Commentaries. 2006.
128. Reilly, D. J. *The Art of Reform in Eleventh-Century Flanders*. Gerard of Cambrai, Richard of Saint-Vanne and the Saint-Vaast Bible. 2006.
129. Frassetto, M. (ed.). *Heresy and the Persecuting Society in the Middle Ages*. Essays on the Work of R.I. Moore. 2006.
130. Walters Adams, G. *Visions in Late Medieval England*. Lay Spirituality and Sacred Glimpses of the Hidden Worlds of Faith. 2007.
131. Kirby, T. *The Zurich Connection and Tudor Political Theology*. 2007.
132. Mackay, C.S. *Narrative of the Anabaptist Madness*. The Overthrow of Münster, the Famous Metropolis of Westphalia (2 vols.). 2007.
133. Leroux, N.R. *Martin Luther as Comforter*. Writings on Death. 2007.
134. Tavuzzi, M. *Renaissance Inquisitors*. Dominican Inquisitors and Inquisitorial Districts in Northern Italy, 1474-1527. 2007.
135. Baschera, L. and C. Moser (eds.). *Girolamo Zanchi*, De religione christiana fides – Confession of Christian Religion (2 vols.). 2007.
136. Hurth, E. *Between Faith and Unbelief*. American Transcendentalists and the Challenge of Atheism. 2007.
137. Wilkinson R.J. *Orientalism, Aramaic and Kabbalah in the Catholic Reformation*. The First Printing of the Syriac New Testament. 2007.
138. Wilkinson R.J. *The Kabbalistic Scholars of the Antwerp Polyglot Bible*. 2007.
139. Boreczky E. *John Wyclif's Discourse On Dominion in Community*. 2007.
140. Dowd C. *Rome in Australia: The Papacy and Conflict in the Australian Catholic Missions, 1834-1884* (2 vols.). 2008.
141. Perrone S.T. *Charles V and the Castilian Assembly of the Clergy*. Negotiations for the Ecclesiastical Subsidy. 2008.
142. Smith, K.A. and S. Wells (eds.). *Negotiating Community and Difference in Medieval Europe*. Gender, Power, Patronage and the Authority of Religion in Latin Christendom. 2009
143. Mixson, J.D. *Poverty's Proprietors*. Ownership and Mortal Sin at the Origins of the Observant Movement. 2009
144. Moser, C. and P. Opitz (eds.). *Bewegung und Beharrung*. Aspekte des reformierten Protestantismus, 1520-1650. 2009
145. Henriksen, E. *Milton and the Reformation Aesthetics of the Passion*. 2010
146. Martínez, H.S. *Alfonso X, the Learned*. Translated by O. Cisneros. 2010